Foundation Flash CS4 for Designers

Tom Green and David Stiller

friends of

DESIGNER TO DESIGNER™

an Apress company

Foundation Flash CS4 for Designers

Credits

Lead Editor
Ben Renow-Clarke

Production Editor
Laura Cheu

Technical Reviewer
Tiago Dias

Compositor
Lynn L'Heureux

Editorial Board
Clay Andres, Steve Anglin, Mark Beckner,
Ewan Buckingham, Tony Campbell, Gary Cornell,
Jonathan Gennick, Michelle Lowman,
Matthew Moodie, Jeffrey Pepper,
Frank Pohlmann, Ben Renow-Clarke,
Dominic Shakeshaft,
Matt Wade, Tom Welsh

Proofreader
Liz Welch

Indexer
Carol Burbo

Artist
Kinetic Publishing Services, LLC

Project Manager
Beth Christmas

Cover Image Designer
Corné van Dooren

Copy Editor
Marilyn Smith

Interior and Cover Designer
Kurt Krames

Associate Production Director
Kari Brooks-Copony

Manufacturing Director
Tom Debolski

*To Brian and Carl in British Columbia because
I have run out of people.*

—Tom Green

*To Lotte Reiniger, creator of the oldest surviving animated
feature film (Die Abenteuer des Prinzen Achmed, 1926),
whose work hinges on the principles described in Chapter 8.*

—David Stiller

CONTENTS AT A GLANCE

CONTENTS

Chapter 2   **CREATING ARTWORK IN FLASH**. **55**

Chapter 10 **VIDEO**. **441**

Chapter 11 **BUILDING INTERFACES WITH THE UI COMPONENTS** **493**

ABOUT THE AUTHORS

Tom Green is currently Professor of Interactive Media in the School of Media Studies at the Humber Institute of Technology and Advanced Learning in Toronto, Canada. He has written eight previous books on Adobe technologies and many articles for numerous magazines and websites, including *Layers* magazine, Community MX, *Digital Web Magazine*, and Computer Arts. He has spoken at more than 20 conferences internationally, including Adobe MAX, National Association of Broadcasters (NAB), FITC, MX North, Digital Design World, TODCon, and SparkEurope. You can contact Tom at tom@tomontheweb.ca.

David Stiller is an independent contractor whose portfolio includes multimedia programming and design for the US National Aeronautics and Space Administration (NASA), US Department of Transportation (DOT), Nickelodeon, MTV, Wendy's, Adobe, and dozens of clients across the United States and Canada. David gets a kick out of sharing "aha!" moments with others through consultation and mentoring, as well as regular contributions to the Adobe Flash and ActionScript forums; his blog (http://quip.net/blog/); and articles for Community MX, *Layers* magazine,

and other outlets. You can contact David using the form on his website (http://quip.net/contact.php). In off hours, his interests include unicycling, anaglyph 3D photography, finely crafted wooden game boards, Library of Congress field recordings, and Turkish coffee. David lives in Virginia with his amazing wife, Dawn, and his beguiling daughter, Meridian.

ABOUT THE TECHNICAL REVIEWER

Tiago Dias started to get into Flash around the time of Flash 3, after seeing a Flash site for the first time. He started off by doing freelance work on the side from his day job as a network/systems engineer. On the motion graphics side of things, he got a lot of After Effects and Premiere experience at multimedia school in Zurich. From those humble beginnings, he now works as a video producer and Flash developer at a corporate television and news production company based in London with subsidiaries around the world. This is Tiago's ideal job, as it combines two of his favorite technologies! In his free time, he writes tutorials on Flash and After Effects for various communities, tries to go snowboarding every time the sun is shining in the Swiss Alps, or hops on a plane to visit new countries. He currently lives and works in Zurich, Switzerland.

ABOUT THE COVER IMAGE DESIGNER

Corné van Dooren designed the front cover image for this book. After taking a brief from friends of ED to create a new design for the *Foundation* series, he worked at combining technological and organic forms, with the results now appearing on this and other books' covers.

Corné spent his childhood drawing on everything at hand, and then began exploring the infinite world of multimedia—and his journey of discovery hasn't stopped since. His mantra has always been "The only limit to multimedia is the imagination," a saying that keeps him moving forward constantly.

Corné works for many international clients, writes features for multimedia magazines, reviews and tests software, authors multimedia studies, and works on many other friends of ED books. You can see more of his work at and contact him through his website, http://www.cornevandooren.com.

If you like Corné's work, be sure to check out his chapter in *New Masters of Photoshop: Volume 2* (friends of ED, 2004).

ACKNOWLEDGMENTS

As I said in the CS3 version of this book, "Working with a coauthor can be a tricky business. In fact, it is a lot like a marriage. Everything is wonderful when things are going well, but you never really discover the strength of the relationship until you get deep into it." When David and I started working together on this volume's predecessor, I don't think either of us expected it to become the deep friendship and close professional relationship that has developed over the past couple of years. It truly is an incredible experience to write a book with a coauthor when you can't tell who wrote what in the book.

What makes this partnership work is that we both are passionate about what we do and are unwilling to settle for the path of least resistance. Many are the times Dave yanked me off that path, gave me a good shake, and shoved me forward.

We also didn't merrily go our separate ways when the CS3 book was released. Both of us started listening in on conversations going on at Amazon, talked to teachers around the world who were using the book, and even corralled a few readers at conferences and other industry gatherings to ask a simple question: what can we improve? This book is the result of those conversations, and to all of you who told us, in no uncertain terms, where things needed to change, we offer you our thanks.

As we dug into this book, we realized that we could tell you what to do, but the "names" in this business could reinforce, from personal experience, the concepts. We deeply appreciate the help we got from Jennifer Shiman, Kristen Henry, Chris Georgenes, John Kricfalusi, and David Schroeder for sharing their experiences and insights with you.

Next up is our editor, Ben Renow-Clarke. This is the first book I have written with him, and I'm thrilled that we also connected at a personal and professional level. Ben stayed out of the way, but was always there when we got stuck and needed a kick in the pants or a "have you thought of this . . . ?" idea.

Finally, writing a book means I hole myself up in my office and become generally moody and difficult to be around as I mull over a technique or try to identify why something isn't quite working. It takes a very unique individual to live with that, let alone understand why—and my wife, best friend, and life partner over the past 30 years, Keltie, has somehow put up with it.

Tom Green

When Tom invited me to jam on the *Foundation Flash* riff a second time, there was no question I'd oblige. It has been ridiculously cool to hear feedback on forums, in e-mail, and at conferences, and to see firsthand the creative outlet people get from Flash. I really do appreciate the way these books keep me in touch with friends and acquaintances in the Flash community. (Never mind that it's a hoot eating crocodile tail with Tom Green. Conferences aren't *just* for tech talk!)

I tend to think of this second edition in terms of jazz: all the great standards have a recognizable tune (of course!). In that sense, this is "the same book" as the first edition. But like any jazz performance, you're getting a new interpretation of the standard. In this case, the performance is more nuanced than the first one, with new melodies and a better sense of cohesion overall. You're also getting a considerably bigger page count with this book, because Flash CS4 gives you so much more to do! The improvements, revisions, and new material in this edition are largely the result of input from readers, students, colleagues, and friends.

Over the years, I've learned quite a bit about programming and life in general from a dear friend who both exists and does not, and who goes by the name Uncle Chutney. "Big things are made up of lots of little things," he keeps telling me, and he's right. That proverb has gotten me out of many a tight squeeze.

Numerous people helped us write this book, from engineers at Adobe and partners at Community MX to IM buddies at the ready to test this-and-that, lend a pair of ears, or simply laugh (or not) at a pun. For me, that list includes Marisa Bozza, Noah DiCenso, Jen deHaan, Greg Dove, Tink (Stephen Downs), Chris Georgenes, Branden Hall, Bruce Hartman, Ted Johns, Keenan Keeling, San Khong, John Mayhew, Trevor McCauley, Colin Moock, Amy Niebel, Robert Penner, Nivesh Rajbhandari, Robert Reinhardt, Steve Schelter, Rich Shupe, and dozens more.

While writing this book, I took an exciting journey through the first seven of L. Frank Baum's *Oz* books with my daughter. At the same time, my wife introduced me to the magic of Georges Méliès. These books and films were a remarkable encouragement to me, made all the more enchanting by the family who enjoyed them with me. *Danke, für deine Phantasie*, Meridian; thanks, Dawn, as always, for being my best friend.

David Stiller

INTRODUCTION

I can remember the day as clear as if it were just yesterday. I was walking by my boss's office late one winter afternoon at the college where I teach, and he called me into his office. Sitting on his desk was a thin, white box with some sort of weird swirl on it. He slid the box across to me and asked, "You know anything about Flash?"

To be honest, as a Director user, what I knew about Flash was filtered through the eyes of a Director guy, which meant I didn't know much, and what I did know convinced me it was a windup toy compared to Director. I replied, "A bit." The boss leaned back in his chair and said, "Well learn a lot more because you are teaching it in four weeks." This was the start of one of the longest, strangest, and most exhilarating trips I have ever been on. The version was Flash 3, and I have been using and teaching Flash ever since.

Flash CS4 will most likely be regarded by the industry as one of the most significant in the history of the product. Flash CS4 has evolved into a serious design tool, able to handle everything from simple motion graphics to broadcast-quality animations. It also marks the point where Flash is fully integrated into the Adobe product lineup. The new Motion Editor, a rejigged Media Encoder, and a fistful of sophisticated animation tools are evidence of that.

This book is also a bit different from any Flash book you may have read or considered purchasing. From the very start of the process, Dave and I put ourselves in your shoes and asked a simple question: what do you need to know and why? This question led us into territory that we didn't quite expect. As we were grappling with that question early in the process, we kept bothering our network of Flash friends to be sure we were on the right track. At some point, both of us simultaneously came to this conclusion: why not just let them explain it in their own words? This is why, as you journey through this book, you will encounter various experts in the field telling you why they do things and offering you insights into what they have learned. The encouraging thing is that at some point in their careers, they were no different from you.

One other aspect of this book is that we had a lot of fun developing the examples and exercises. The fun aspect is important, because if learning is fun, what you learn will be retained. Anyone can show you how to apply a Glow filter to a line on the Flash stage. It is more effective when you do exactly the same thing to a guy wearing a Tron costume. Anyone can dryly explain 9-slice scaling, but it becomes less techie when you apply it to a guy dressed as Peter Pan. Nested movieclips are a "yawner" at best, but when they are related to a Hostess Twinkie, the concept becomes understandable. Shared libraries are an important subject. Instead of filling a library with circles and text, the concept becomes relevant when the library is populated with "bunny bits." Need to experience how to mix high-definition video with regular FLV video? Why not mix up a cutting-edge Chinese motion graphics piece by a student in Beijing with a beatbox flautist in New York?

As you may have guessed, we continue to exhibit a sense of joy and wonder with Flash, and we hope a little of our enthusiasm rubs off on you as well.

Book structure and flow

To start, this is not a typical Foundation book. There is no common project that runs throughout the book. Instead, each chapter contains a number of exercises to help you develop some "Flash chops," and then we turn you loose in the "Your turn" section.

We start by dropping you right into the application and creating a small Flash movie we call "Moonrise Over Lake Nanagook" (told you we were having fun). This chapter familiarizes you with the Flash workspace and the fundamentals of using Flash Professional CS4. Chapter 2 introduces you to working with the graphic tools and graphics files, and finishes with the exploration of a Monty Python–style banner ad.

Chapter 3 introduces you to symbols and libraries in Flash CS4. In this chapter, you learn how to create and use symbols, and we even let Peter Pan explain how 9-slice scaling works. With those fundamentals under your belt, we show you how to share symbols and libraries between movies, and how to manipulate symbols with filters and blend effects. Along the way, you travel from a riot in Paris to Times Square, discovering how to create some rather powerful effects in your Flash movies. The chapter finishes by showing you how to use masks to your advantage in Flash.

After Chapter 3, you have pretty well mastered the fundamentals. The rest of the book builds upon what you have learned. Chapter 4 picks you up and throws you into the ActionScript 3.0 pool. Don't worry if you're not a programmer! Chapter 5 starts by explaining how to use audio in Flash and finishes with constructing the beginnings of an MP3 player. Chapter 6 reinforces the message that text isn't the gray stuff that surrounds your animations. We show you how it is both serious and fun by stepping through how to create scrolling text and how to blow up your name.

Chapter 7 is one of the more important chapters in the book because Flash began as an animation application. You learn the full arsenal of basics here, but don't expect to be shoving boxes and circles around. You will be banging hammers, eating apples, dropping parrots, lighting up a Tron suit, and setting a butterfly in motion. Did we mention we believe in having fun? Chapter 8 continues the animation theme by getting you deep into the new Motion Editor and inverse kinematics (IK) tools. Chapter 9 walks you through the 3D tools introduced in Flash CS4.

From animation, we move to video in Flash. In Chapter 10, we show the entire process, from encoding to upload. In fact, the chapter finishes with a "Your turn" in which you add captions and a full-screen capability to a Superman movie. Along the way, you will visit heaven and also meet a rather neurotic cartoon character.

Chapters 11, 12, and 13 give you the chance to play with all of the Flash user interface components, actually style a Flash movie using Cascading Style Sheets (CSS), and explore how XML gives you a huge amount of flexibility when it comes to adding dynamic data to your movie.

Chapter 14 is where you get to pull it all together and build everything from a simple preloader to a completed version of the MP3 player you started in Chapter 5. Along the way, you also create a custom slide show and code up a custom video player that weighs in at under 10KB.

The final chapter focuses on the end game of the design process. It shows you a number of the important techniques you need to know that will keep your movies small and efficient. You also learn how to create the SWF that will be embedded into a web page, and how to keep that process as smooth as possible.

Finally, David and I are no different from you. We are learning about this application—what it can and cannot do—at the same time as you are learning about it. Though we may be coming at it from a slightly more advanced level, there is a lot about this application we're still discovering. If there is something we have missed or something you don't quite understand, by all means, contact us. We'll be sure to add it to the book's site. And here are our final words of advice for you:

The amount of fun you can have with this application should be illegal. We'll see you in jail!

Layout conventions

To keep this book as clear and easy to follow as possible, the following text conventions are used throughout.

- Important words or concepts are normally highlighted on the first appearance in *italics*.

- Code is presented in `fixed-width` font.

- New or changed code is normally presented in **`bold fixed-width font`**.

- Pseudo-code and variable input are written in *`italic fixed-width font`*.

- Menu commands are written in the form Menu ➤ Submenu ➤ Submenu.

- Where I want to draw your attention to something, I've highlighted it like this:

  Ahem, don't say we didn't warn you.

- Sometimes code won't fit on a single line in a book. Where this happens, I use an arrow like this: ➡

  ```
  This is a very, very long section of code that should be written all
  ➡ on the same line without a break.
  ```

Tom Green

Chapter 1

LEARNING THE FLASH CS4 PROFESSIONAL INTERFACE

Welcome to Flash CS4 Professional. We suspect you are here because you have seen a lot of the great stuff Flash can do, and it is now time for you to get into the game. Flash can be one great big, scary application to those unfamiliar with it. Or you may be here because, as a Flash user, you have found that CS4 is suddenly a lot different from Flash 8 or Flash CS3, and you need to get up to speed with this new stuff in relatively short order. In either case, both of the authors have been in your shoes at some point in our careers, which means we understand what you are feeling. So instead of jumping right into the application, let's go for a stroll.

Here's what we'll cover in this chapter:

- Exploring the Flash interface
- Using the stage
- Working with panels
- Understanding the difference between a frame and a keyframe
- Using frames to arrange content on the stage
- Using layers to manage content on the stage
- Adding objects to the library
- Testing your movie

The following files are used in this chapter (located in Chapter01/ExerciseFiles_Ch01/Exercise/):

- Magnify.fla
- Ball.fla
- Properties.fla
- MotionPath.fla

- Layers.fla
- MoonOverLakeNanagook.fla
- Nanagook.mp3

The source files are available online from either of the following sites:

- http://www.FoundationFlashCS4.com
- http://www.friendsofED.com/download.html?isbn=15905910931

In this chapter, we'll take a walk through the authoring environment, called the Flash interface, pointing out the sights and giving you an opportunity to play with the features. By the end of the stroll, you should be fairly comfortable with this toolbox called Flash, and have a good idea of what tools you can use and how to use them as you start creating a Flash movie.

As we go for our walk, we will also be having a conversation that will help you to understand the fundamentals behind the creation of a Flash movie. Having this knowledge right at the start of the process gives you the confidence to build upon what you have learned. So let's start right at the beginning of the process, at the Welcome screen.

Getting started

The first thing you see when you launch Flash is the Welcome screen shown in Figure 1-1. This interface, common to all of the Adobe CS4 applications, is divided into three areas:

Figure 1-1. The Welcome screen appears when you launch Flash CS4.

- Open a Recent Item: The area on the left side shows a list of documents you have previously opened. Click one of them, and that document—provided it hasn't been deleted or moved to another location on your computer—will open. The Open link at the bottom of the list lets you navigate to a document that isn't on the list.

- Create New: The middle area of the page is where you can choose to create a variety of new Flash documents. Your choices include a blank Flash file (called a FLA, pronounced "flah") for web content; an Adobe Integrated Runtime (AIR) file for desktop applications; a mobile document, aimed at cell phones or PDAs; a series of code-based files; and a Flash project for organizing multiple files in a given project. A published Flash movie—not available from this menu—is called a SWF (pronounced "swiff").

> *You can select a new document based on the version of ActionScript that will be used in the document. The current version of ActionScript is 3.0, which was introduced in Flash CS3. The previous version of this language, used in Flash 8 and Flash MX 2004, was ActionScript 2.0. As you can see, it's still available in Flash CS4, but we won't be covering it in this book. We will be digging into ActionScript 3.0 in greater depth in Chapter 4. Unless otherwise stated, you will be selecting the* Flash File (ActionScript 3.0) *option when creating new documents throughout this book.*

- Create from Template: The right area of the page is reserved for a variety of templates you can use. Clicking one of the folders opens the New from Template dialog box, as shown in Figure 1-2. The Extend area at the bottom of this column of the Welcome screen contains a link to the Flash Exchange, an Adobe website where you can download a variety of tools and projects that are available for free or a nominal cost.

Figure 1-2. Flash contains a variety of templates designed to help you become more productive.

Creating a new Flash document

Let's create a new document. To accomplish this, simply click Flash File (ActionScript 3.0) in the Create New area of the Welcome screen to open the Flash interface, as shown in Figure 1-3. This feature-rich authoring environment is the heart and soul of Flash. If you are already a Flash user, the first thing that will catch your attention is that the interface is radically different from previous versions of the application.

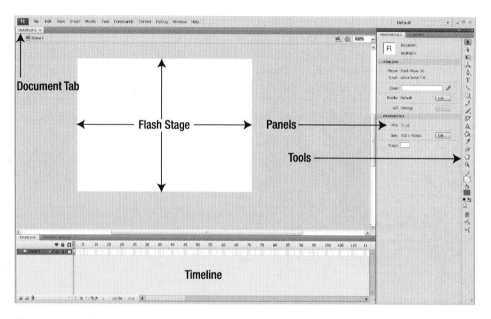

Figure 1-3. The Flash authoring environment

Flash CS4 marks the introduction of the Object Windows Library (OWL) interface, shown in Figure 1-3, which is common to all of the applications in the CS4 lineup from Adobe. If you are a Mac user, depending on your "rabidity" of all things Mac, you are either going to love this interface or hate it. Adobe has dispensed with the floating panels that tended to drive Flash developers and designers who worked cross-platform up a wall, across the ceiling, and down the other wall.

The *stage*—the large white area in the center of the screen—is where the action happens. A good way of regarding the stage in relation to Flash is this: if it isn't on the stage, the user isn't going to see it. Although this is not *always* true, as you'll learn later in this book, it's definitely a rule of thumb.

On the far right side of the screen is a set of tools that will allow you to draw, color, and otherwise manipulate objects on the stage. Just left of that is the Properties panel, called the Property inspector, which longtime Flash users will remember used to appear along the bottom of the screen.

In Flash CS4, the bottom of the interface is populated by the Timeline panel (officially called the *timeline*). As you can see, the timeline is broken into a series of boxes called *frames*. The best way of regarding frames is as individual frames of a film. When you put something on the stage, it will appear in a frame. If you want it to move from here to there, it will start in one frame and end in another a little further along the timeline. The box with the vertical stem draped over frame 1—this is red in Flash—is called the *playhead*. Its purpose is to show you the current frame being displayed. When a Flash movie is playing through a browser, the playhead is in motion, and the user is seeing the frame where the playhead is located. This is how things appear to move in Flash. Another thing you can do with the playhead is drag it across the timeline while you are creating the Flash movie. This technique is known as *scrubbing* the timeline, and has its roots in film editing.

The right side of the interface is where panels appear by default. Panels are used to modify and manipulate whatever object you may have selected on the stage or to add objects to the stage. These objects can be text, photographs, line art, short animations, video, or even interface elements (check boxes, radio buttons, and so on) called *components*. You can use the panels and the menus to change not only the characteristics of the objects, but also how the objects behave on the stage. Panels can be connected to each other (docked) or can float freely in the interface (floating), and can be positioned practically anywhere you like. To move a panel, simply click the panel's tab and drag it to a new location. If you see a temporary blue line or bar, the panel will dock to that location.

From our perspective, one of the most indispensable panels is the Property inspector. As you become more comfortable with the application, this panel will become a very important place for you. We'll talk more about the Property inspector later in the chapter, in the "Exploring panels in the Flash interface" section.

> *For those of you who have used Flash in the past, we are willing to bet you had a "Holy smokes!" reaction when you first fired up the application. If you are still in a bit of shock, take a deep breath. Not everything has changed. Mostly, things have just been moved around. If you find this disturbing, then be our guest and move everything back to where it "should be." To do this, select* Window ➤ Workspace ➤ Classic *or select* Window ➤ Workspace ➤ Essentials *to revert to the default workspace for Flash CS4.*

Managing your workspace

As you may have surmised, the Flash authoring environment is one busy place, and if you talk to an experienced Flash developer or designer, you'll hear it can become one crowded place as well, as it fills up with floating panels and other elements. This has all changed in Flash CS4.

As you start creating Flash projects, you will discover that real estate on your screen is a valuable commodity. Here's how you can manage the panels:

- **Collapse panels**: At the top of the Tools panel and the other panels area on the right side of the workspace is an icon that looks like a double-headed arrow (see Figure 1-4). Click this icon, and the panels will collapse and become icons with text. (Actually, the Tools panel collapses to just an icon by default.) This process is called *panel collapse*, and is designed to free up screen space in Flash. In fact, Adobe is so thrilled with this feature that you can expect to see it added to all of the applications in the Creative Suite over the next couple of years.

Figure 1-4. Panels can be collapsed to give you more screen space.

- **Show collapsed panels as icons only**: With the panel collapsed, place the cursor to the left of the icons in the panel strip. When the cursor changes to a double-headed arrow, drag the panel strip to the left or to the right. As you drag to the left, the panel icons will expand and show the name of the panel. As you drag to the right, the names will disappear and only the icon will be visible.

- **See tooltips for panel icons**: Place the cursor over any icon on a panel strip that has been reduced to icons only. The icon will change from gray to color, and a tooltip will appear, telling you what the item is.

- **Open and close drawers**: With the panel collapsed, click an icon in the strip, and the contents of that panel will fly out, as shown in Figure 1-5. Click it again, and the contents of the panel will slide back. These panels that fly out and slide in are called *drawers*.

- **Minimize panels**: Another method of saving some screen real estate is to collapse a panel vertically by minimizing it. Double-click the panel's name, and it will collapse upward. Double-click it again, and the panel will grow to its original dimensions. This is especially helpful with free-floating panels.

- **Close panels**: Right-click (Ctrl-click) a panel and select Close, and the panel will be removed from the group. If you do remove a panel, all is not lost. Open the Window menu and click the name of the panel you closed to restore it.

- **Add panels to sets**: Drag one of the panel icons onto another panel. When you release the mouse, the panel will expand to include the new panel. This is called a *panel set*. To remove a panel from a set, just drag the panel icon to the bottom of the stack.

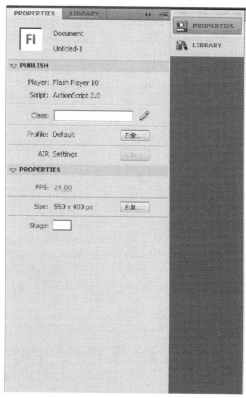

Figure 1-5. Click a panel icon, and the contents slide out. Click the icon again, and they slide in.

> *Though not a technique, this tip falls squarely into the "well, it's about time" category of neat stuff. If you drag a floating panel over another interface element, the floating panel temporarily becomes partially transparent so you can see what is under the panel. This was new with Flash CS3.*

To save your customizations, select Window ➤ Workspace ➤ New Workspace, enter a name for your custom workspace into the dialog box, and then click the OK button. Create as many of these as you like. To delete a custom workspace, select Window ➤ Workspace ➤ Manage Workspaces.

Now that you have learned to become the master of the work environment, let's take a look at how you can also become the master of your Flash document.

Setting document preferences and properties

Managing the workspace is a fundamental skill, but the most important decision you will make concerns the size of the Flash stage and the space it will take up in the browser. That decision is based upon a number of factors, including the type of content to be displayed and the items that will appear in the HTML document in addition to the Flash movie. These decisions affect the stage size and, in many respects, the way that the document is handled by Flash. These two factors are managed by the Preferences and Document Properties dialog boxes.

Document preferences

To access preferences, select Edit ➤ Preferences (Flash Professional ➤ Preferences). This will open the Flash Preferences dialog box. There's a lot to this dialog box, and we'll explore it further at various points throughout this book. For now, we are concerned with the general preferences in the Category area of the window. Click General, and the dialog box will change to show you the general preferences for Flash, as shown in Figure 1-6.

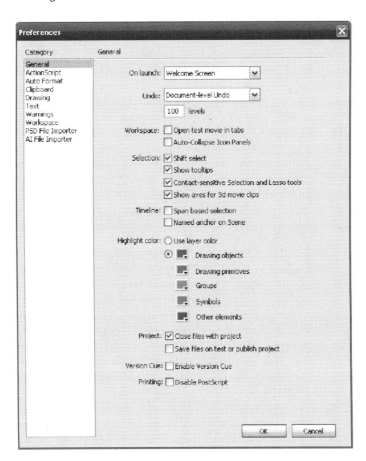

Figure 1-6. The General preferences can be used to manage not only the workspace, but also items on the stage.

If you examine the selections, you will realize they are fairly intuitive. You can choose to see the Welcome screen when the application starts, to see tooltips when the cursor is over a tool or object, and to have a test movie appear in a tabbed window or float. You can also specify how items are selected on the stage and the timeline, and even the colors that will be used to indicate which type of object has been selected on the stage.

> *If you have been using Flash for a few years, you'll find the expansion of the Highlight color list to include a variety of objects a welcome addition.*

Now that you know how to set your preferences, let's look at managing the document properties. Click the Cancel button in the Preferences dialog box to close the window and return to the Flash interface.

Document properties

To access the Document Properties dialog box, use one of the following methods:

- With the stage selected, click the Edit button in the Properties (not Publish) area of the Property inspector.
- Select Modify ➤ Document.
- Press Ctrl+J (Cmd+J).
- Right-click (Ctrl-click) on the stage and select Document Properties from the context menu.

> *As you have just seen, there are a number of methods you can use in Flash to obtain the same result. In this case, it is opening the Document Properties dialog box. Which one is best? The answer is simple: whichever one you choose.*

The Document Properties dialog box is shown in Figure 1-7. The Dimensions input area is where you can change the size of the stage. Enter the new dimensions, press the Enter (Return) key or click the OK button, and the stage will update. The Match area is commonly used to shrink the stage to the size of the content on the stage when you select Contents (which happens to be grayed out in Figure 1-7 because there is currently nothing on the stage). You can also change the stage (background) color, how fast the movie plays, and the units for the ruler.

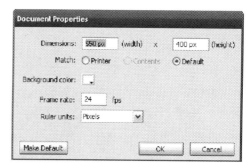

Figure 1-7. Set the stage size through the Document Properties dialog box.

> *If you have been using Flash prior to this release, did you catch the change in the Document Properties dialog box? The default Flash frame rate has increased from 12 to 24 frames per second.*

For example, if you change the Dimensions setting to a width of 400 and height of 300, set Background color to #000066, and click OK, the stage will shrink to the new dimensions and change color to a dark blue. These changes will also be shown in the Property inspector, as shown in Figure 1-8.

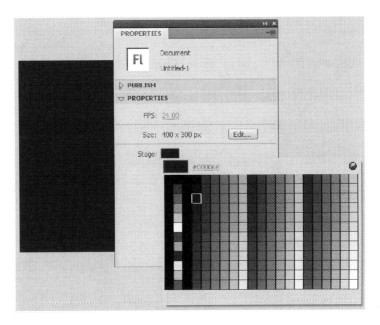

Figure 1-8. Changes made to the document properties are shown in the Property inspector.

Zooming the stage

You may discover that the stage is a pretty crowded place. In these situations, you'll want to be sure that each item on the stage is in its correct position and is properly sized. Depending on the size of the stage, this could be difficult because the stage may fill the screen area. Fortunately, Flash allows you to reduce or increase the magnification of the stage through a technique called *zooming*. (Zooming the stage has no effect on the actual stage size.)

To zoom the stage, click the Magnification drop-down menu near the upper-right corner of the screen. As shown in Figure 1-9, this menu contains a variety of sizes, ranging from Fit in Window to 800% magnification. For example, click the 400% option, and the stage will likely fill or overflow the screen, as shown in Figure 1-10. Click the Show Frame option, and the stage will be visible in its entirety.

If you want more zoom, you can get a lot closer than 800%. Select View ➤ Zoom In or View ➤ Zoom Out to increase the zoom level to 2000%. If you want a real god's-eye view of the stage, Zoom Out allows you to reduce the magnification level to 8%. For you keyboard junkies, Zoom In is Ctrl+= and Zoom Out is Ctrl+-. On the Mac, use the Apple key instead of the Ctrl key.

Figure 1-9.
Select a zoom level using the Magnification drop-down menu.

Figure 1-10. Selecting a 400% zoom level brings you close to the action.

If you want a side-by-side comparison in which one image is at 100% and the other is at some other percentage, follow these steps:

1. Open the Magnify.fla file in the Chapter 1 Exercise folder.

2. Select Window ➤ Duplicate Window. The current document will appear in a separate tab.

3. Set the new window's magnification level to 800%.

4. Undock the new window and let it float, as shown in Figure 1-11.

5. Click the Selection tool (the solid arrow) at the top of the toolbar.

6. Click and drag the image in the new floating window around the stage. You will see that the version in the docked window also moves. This is a really handy feature if precise positioning of elements on the stage is critical.

7. Click each window's close button to close it. Don't save the changes.

Figure 1-11. Duplicating a window gives you a bird's-eye view and a detailed view of your work simultaneously.

Exploring panels in the Flash interface

At this point in our stroll through the Flash interface, you have had the chance to play with a few of the panels. We also suspect that by now you have discovered that the Flash interface is modular. By that, we mean it's composed of a series of panels that contain the tools and features you will use on a regular basis, rather than an interface that's locked in place and fills the screen. You have also discovered that these panels can be moved around and opened or closed depending on your workflow needs.

In this section, we are going to take a closer look at the more important panels that you will use every day. They include the following:

- The Timeline panel
- The Property inspector
- The Tools panel
- The Library panel
- The Motion Editor panel
- The Help menu (not actually a panel, but very useful)

The Timeline panel

There is a fundamental truth to becoming a proficient designer with Flash: master the timeline and you will master Flash.

When someone visits your site and an animation plays, Flash treats that animation as a series of still images. In many respects, those images are comparable to the images in a roll of film or one of those flip books you may have played with when you were younger. The ordering of those images on the film or in the book is determined by their placement on the film or in the book. In Flash, the order of images in an animation is determined by the timeline. The timeline controls what users see, and more important, when they see it.

Animation and the timeline

At its most basic, all animation is movement over time, and all animation has a start point and an end point. The length of your timeline will determine when animations start and end, and the number of frames between those two points will determine the length of the animation. As the multimedia author, you control those factors.

Figure 1-12 shows a simple animation. A ball is placed at the left and right edges of the stage. In between, the ball is at the top of the stage. From this, you can gather that the ball will move upward when the sequence starts and will continue to its finish position at the right edge of the stage after it has reached the middle of the sequence.

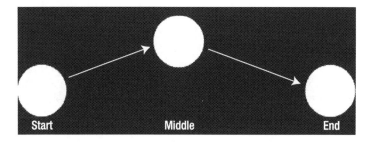

Figure 1-12. A simple animation sequence

Obviously, just having three images won't result in a ball moving. Between the start point and the middle point, and the middle point and the end point, there needs to be a series of ball images. These will give the user the illusion of a ball moving up and then down again to its finish position. These images will represent the various locations of the ball as it moves through time, as shown in Figure 1-13.

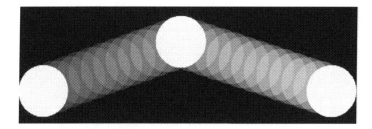

Figure 1-13. Animation is a series of frames on the timeline.

So where does time come into play? It is the number of frames (discussed in the next section) between the start and middle, and middle and end points in the animation. The default timing in a Flash CS4 movie—called the *frame rate*—is 24 frames per second (fps). In the animation shown previously, the duration of the animation is 24 frames, which means it will play for 1 second. You can deduce from this that the ball's middle location is the twelfth frame of the timeline. If, for example, you wanted to speed up the animation, you could reduce the length of the timeline to 12 frames or increase the frame rate to, say, 48 fps; if you wanted to slow it down, you could increase the number of frames to 48 or decrease the frame rate.

Let's wander over to the timeline and look at a frame.

Understanding frames

If you unroll a spool of movie film, you will see that it is composed of a series of individual still images. Each image is called a *frame*, and this analogy applies to Flash as well.

When you open Flash, your timeline will be empty, but you will see a series of rectangles—these are the frames. You may also notice that these frames are divided into groups. Most frames are white and every fifth frame is gray (see Figure 1-14), just to help you keep your place. Flash movies can range in length from 1 to 16,000 frames, although a Flash movie that is 16,000 frames in length is highly unusual.

Figure 1-14. The timeline is nothing more than a series of frames.

A frame shows you the content that is on the stage at any point in time. The content in a frame can range from one object to hundreds of objects, and a frame can include audio, video, programming, images, text, and drawings, either singly or in combination with each other.

When you first open a new Flash document, you will notice that frame 1 contains a hollow circle. This visual clue tells you that frame 1 is waiting for you to add something to it. Let's look at a movie that actually has something in the frames and examine some of the features of frames.

Open the Ball.fla file located in the Chapter 1 Exercise folder. You will see a yellow ball, in frame 1, sitting on the stage. You should also note the solid dot in the Ball layer (layers are discussed later in this chapter). This indicates there is content in the frame. The Empty layer above it has a hollow dot, which indicates there is no content in that frame. This is also shown in Figure 1-14.

Place the cursor on any frame of the timeline and right-click (Ctrl-click) to open the context menu that applies to frames, as shown in Figure 1-15. As you can see, quite a few options are available, ranging from adding a frame to the timeline to adding actions (code blocks) that control the objects in the frame. We aren't going to dig into what each menu item does just yet, but rest assured, by the time you finish this book, you will have used each one.

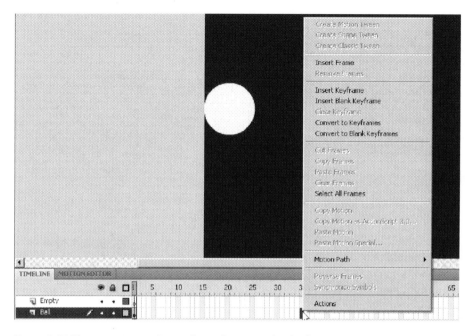

Figure 1-15. The context menu that applies to frames on the timeline

Place the cursor at frame 12 of the Ball layer, open the context menu, and select Insert Keyframe. Repeat this step at frame 24 as well. You will see that the timeline changes to the series of extended gray rectangles and three black dots, as shown in Figure 1-16. These gray rectangles represent spans of frames, separated by keyframes.

> *If you prefer to use the keyboard, place the cursor at frame 24 and press F5. With that frame selected, press F6. The F5 command adds a frame (which creates a span of frames), and pressing F6 converts the selected frame to a keyframe. If you prefer to do that all in one move, just select frame 24 and press F6.*

Figure 1-16. The timeline contains three keyframes.

An obvious question at this point is, "So, guys, what's a keyframe?" Remember when we talked earlier about animations and how they have a start point and an end point? In Flash, those two points are called *keyframes*. Any movement or changes are thanks to keyframes. In Flash, there are two types of keyframes: those with stuff in them (indicated by the solid dot shown in frame 1 of Figure 1-16) and those with nothing in them. Blank keyframes are shown as frames with a hollow dot. The first frame in any layer, until you add something to that frame, is always indicated by a blank keyframe.

To navigate to specific frames in the timeline, you use the playhead. It is the red rectangle with the line coming out of it. Drag the playhead to frame 12 and click the ball on the stage. Move the ball to the top center of the stage. Drag the playhead to frame 24 and move the ball to the right edge of the stage.

As you moved the ball in frame 12, you may have noticed there was a ghosted version of the ball's previous position until you released the mouse. This feature is new to Flash CS4. It gives you a reference to the starting position of the motion.

> As mentioned earlier in the chapter, the technique of dragging the playhead across the timeline is called scrubbing. As you scrub across the timeline, you will see the values in the Current Frame and Elapsed Time areas at the bottom of the timeline change as well. This is quite useful in locating a precise frame number or time in the animation.

Scrub the playhead across the timeline. The ball snaps to a new position as the playhead encounters each keyframe. But this movement isn't smooth! To fix that, right-click (Ctrl-click) anywhere inside the gray span of frames between each pair of keyframes and select Create Classic Tween from the context menu. Scrub again, and the ball will move smoothly across the stage. Those arrows that appeared indicate a classic motion tween.

> Yes, classic tweens are new! To Flash old-timers, this is what used to simply be motion tweens. Flash CS4 introduces a completely new—and mind-blowingly cool—timeline tweening model, which is touched on later in this chapter and discussed in detail in Chapter 8.

A *classic tween* is one of the ways simple animations are created in Flash. Flash looks at the locations of the objects between two keyframes, creates virtual copies of those objects, and puts them in their positions in the frame. If you scrub through your timeline, you will see that Flash has placed copies of the ball in frames 2 through 11 and 13 through 23, and put them in their final positions to give the illusion that the ball is moving up and down.

That was interesting, but we suspect you may be wondering, "OK, guys, do tweens work only for stuff that moves?" Nope, you can also use tweens to change the shapes of objects, their color, their opacity, and a number of other properties. We'll get to those uses later in the book.

Drag the playhead to frame 12 and click the ball on the stage. Drag the ball to the bottom of the stage. If you scrub through the timeline again, you will see the ball move in the opposite direction. This tells you that you can change an animation by simply changing the location of an object in a keyframe. Close the file without saving it.

The Property inspector

Another key concept to grasp, especially if you are new to Flash, is that everything on the stage has properties that can be changed or otherwise manipulated. To understand this concept, let's step away from Flash and consider the authors.

At our most basic, we are two humans on the planet Earth. In Flash terms, we are two objects on the stage. The things that describe us are our properties. For example, our height, weight, hair color, and location on the planet are properties that describe visual facets of who we are. If we were somehow able to be placed on the Flash stage, those descriptive properties of us would appear in the Property inspector when the mouse selects us. The neat thing is that the Property inspector lets you do more than just review those properties: it also lets you change them.

The Property inspector, shown in Figure 1-17, is designed to make your life easy. As you become more proficient and comfortable with Flash, this panel will become an indispensable aid to your workflow.

> Why is it called an inspector, even though it behaves like a panel? And why does it say Properties, when it's called the Property inspector? Ah, there are mysteries in life, and we make no honest claim to fathom them all.

The panel is positioned, by default, to the right of the workspace. You can move it elsewhere on the screen by simply dragging it into position and releasing the mouse. There are locations on the workspace where you will see a shadow or darkening of the location when the panel is over it. This color change indicates that the panel can be docked into that location. Otherwise, the panel will "float" above the screen.

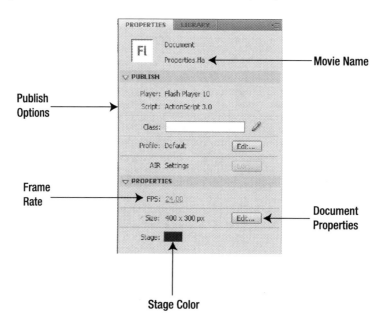

Figure 1-17. The Property inspector

When an object is placed on the stage and selected (or even when the stage itself is selected), the Property inspector will change to reflect the properties of that object that can be manipulated. For example, in Figure 1-18, a box has been drawn on the stage. The Property inspector shows the type of object that has been selected (Shape), and tells you the stroke and the fill color of the object can be changed. In addition, you can change how scaling will be applied to the object and the treatment of the red stroke around the box.

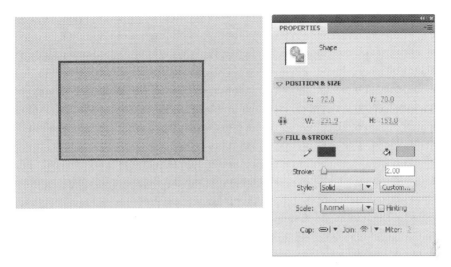

Figure 1-18. The Property inspector changes to show you the properties that can be manipulated regarding a selected object on the stage (in this case, the stroke and fill properties of the box on the stage).

Let's experiment with a Flash file:

1. Open the file named Properties.fla in the Exercise folder. You will see an image of kayaks over a black background and the words Ocean Kayaks at the bottom of the stage.

2. In the Tools panel, click the Selection tool, which is the solid black arrow at the top of the Tools panel (see Figure 1-19).

> *Clicking tools is one way of selecting them. Another way is to use the keyboard. When you roll the cursor over a tool, you will see a tooltip containing the name of the tool and a letter. For example, the letter beside the Selection tool is V. Press the V key, and the Selection tool will be highlighted in the Tools panel.*

Figure 1-19. Click a tool
or use the keyboard to select it.

3. Using the Selection tool, click the text. The Property inspector will change to show all the properties you can change for text, as shown in Figure 1-20.

4. In the Property inspector, click the Fill Color rectangle—called a *color chip*—to open the Color Picker. Click the white color, and the text will turn white. You have just changed the color property of the selected text.

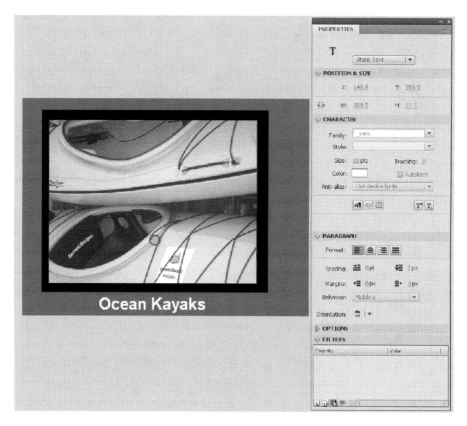

Figure 1-20. Text properties in the Property inspector

5. Click the gray area of the stage. The Property inspector will change to show the stage properties. Change the stage color to a dark gray: #666666. When you select the color, the stage will change color, and the color selected will appear in the Property inspector.

6. Click the black box surrounding the image. The Property inspector will change to show that you have selected a shape and that the fill color for this shape is black. It also lets you know that there is no stroke around the shape. In the Position & Size area, four numbers tell you the width, height, and x and y coordinates of the shape on the stage. Select the width (W) value and change it from 428.9 to 435. Change the height (H) number from 333 to 335, as shown in Figure 1-21. Each time you make a change, the selected object will get wider or higher.

> If you are an After Effects user, seeing properties as links is not new. It is seriously new if you have been using Flash prior to this release. If you want to quickly change any value, simply click and drag that value to the left or right (the technique is called scrubbing). As you drag, the numbers will change, and the selected object on the stage will reflect these new values. Hold Shift while dragging, and the range of values changes to a less finely grained degree. Adobe calls these links hot text.

Figure 1-21. The width, height, stage location, fill, and stroke are properties of objects on the stage.

The Tools panel

The Tools panel, shown in Figure 1-22, is divided into four major areas:

- **Tools**: These allow you create, select, and manipulate text and graphics placed on the stage.
- **View**: These tools allow you to pan across the stage or to zoom in on specific areas of the stage.
- **Colors**: These tools allow you to select and change fill, stroke, and gradient colors.
- **Options**: This is a context-sensitive area of the panel. In many ways, it is not unlike the Property inspector. It changes depending on what you have selected.

If there is a small down arrow in the bottom-right corner of a tool, this indicates additional tool options. Click and hold that arrow, and the options will appear in a drop-down menu, as shown in Figure 1-23.

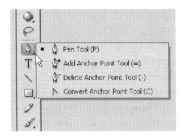

Figure 1-23. Some tools contain extra tools, which are shown in a drop-down list.

Figure 1-22. The Tools panel

21

The Library panel

The Library panel (officially called the *library*) is one of those features of the application that is so indispensable to Flash developers and designers that we simply can't think of anyone who doesn't use it religiously.

In very simple terms, the library is the place where content used in the movie is stored for reuse later in the movie. It is also the place where symbols and copies of components are automatically placed when the symbols are created or the components are added to the stage.

Let's take a look at the library. Assuming your Library panel is collapsed, click the Library icon on the right side of the screen. The Library panel will fly out, as shown in Figure 1-24. Inside the library, you will see that the image of the kayaks is actually a library asset. Drag a copy of the kayaks image from the library to the stage. Leave it selected and press the Delete key. Notice that the image on the stage disappears, but the library asset is retained.

To collapse the Library panel, click the stage. Panels are configured by default to collapse automatically. You can change this preference under Edit ➤ Preferences (Flash Professional ➤ Preferences) ➤ General ➤ Auto-Collapse Icon Panels. Another way of opening and closing the library is to press Ctrl+L (Cmd+L).

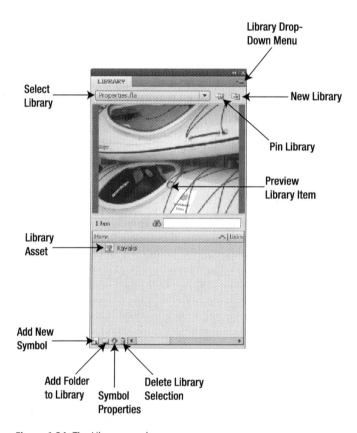

Figure 1-24. The Library panel

The Motion Editor panel

In previous versions of Flash, the Property inspector could be used to change the properties of an animation. This would include techniques such as ramping the speed of an animation, called *easing*, or even changing how an animation occurs, such as adding or removing rotation. This is still true for shape tweens and classic tweens, but the new home for this sort of configuration—for motion tweens—is the Motion Editor panel.

Though we are going to get deeper into using this new panel in Chapter 8, now would be a good time to stroll over and take a peek at it. Open the MotionPath.fla file in the Chapter 1 Exercise folder. The first thing you will notice is a different icon beside the layer name. This "zooming square" icon indicates the layer is a *tween layer* (more on those in Chapter 8). The other thing you may have noticed, especially if you've used Flash before, is the absence of an arrow between the two keyframes. The tween span is indicated in blue, and because of the icon, the use of the arrow is not necessary. The dotted line on the stage, visible when you select the tween layer, indicates a tween path.

> *If you are an After Effects user, you may be looking at that tween path and thinking, "Nah . . . it can't be!" Yes, it is a motion path and, just like an After Effects motion path, you can adjust that path by clicking and dragging one of the dots. Each dot represents a frame of the animation.*

Drag the playhead across the timeline in the Timeline panel, and you will see that the object fades in, tumbles, and grows as you move the playhead from left to right. Click anywhere in the span of tweened frames and select the Motion Editor panel, as shown in Figure 1-25.

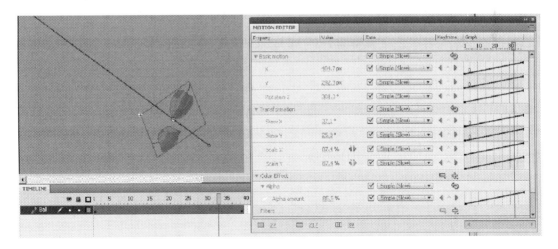

Figure 1-25. A tween layer, tween path, and the Motion Editor panel

One of the really interesting aspects of the Motion Editor panel is that it gives you more control over how things move than at any point in the history of Flash. When Adobe acquired Macromedia a few years back, there was a lot of speculation in the Flash design community about whether Flash would start to inherit some of the powerful features of After Effects. We didn't have to wait very long to find

23

out. The process started in Flash CS3 with how After Effects creates an FLV video file used by Flash. This version of Flash essentially "seals the deal" and sends a very strong message to both the video and Flash communities that these two applications were made for each other.

The Motion Editor panel can trace its roots in a straight line back to After Effects (Adobe's powerhouse video postproduction software). In that application, objects put in motion or otherwise manipulated over time have a full set of properties and guides for each layer of content in an After Effects project. The major property is motion. Flash users who use After Effects to create motion graphics for their Flash projects find the "After Effects way of doing things" to be relatively compact and simple. The result over the years has been Flash designers wondering why Flash didn't have this feature. Obviously, enough of you have asked the question, because it is now an integral feature of Flash CS4.

> *Back in the year 2000, one of the authors attended the first ever Flash Conference—Flashforward—and Adobe introduced a Flash competitor called LiveMotion. LiveMotion used the same timeline as the Motion Editor. At the time, the author (and practically everyone at the conference) thought the LiveMotion version was one "sweet" piece of work, and wondered if Macromedia would ever change the timeline.*

If you have never used After Effects, now would be a good time to start easing you into the application. We'll start with terminology. See those triangles beside the property names in Figure 1-25? If you click one, it rotates down and the area is revealed. After Effects users call those triangles *twirlies*, and the term for clicking one of them to reveal the contents of its area is *twirl down*. We will be using these terms quite extensively when we talk about the Motion Editor panel.

The Motion Editor panel is divided into five distinct areas:

- Basic motion: If you twirl down Basic motion, you will see that it controls movement of the object on the x and y axes, and rotation on the z axis.
- Transformation: Think of this panel as a "by-the-numbers" version of the Free Transform tool, which allows you to resize (scale), slant (skew), and rotate objects.
- Color Effect: This panel allows you to manipulate alpha (transparency), color, brightness, and tint.
- Filters: This is where you apply one of the filters—Drop Shadow, Blur, Glow, Bevel, Gradient Glow, Gradient Bevel, or Adjust Color—to the object on the stage.
- Eases: This area is where you affect the ramping up or down of an animation's motion, transformation, color, or filter changes.

When you twirl down an area of the panel, all of the properties it can affect are revealed.

At the bottom of the panel are three icons with a blue number beside each one, as shown in Figure 1-26. These allow you to control how the graph and frames appear in the panel.

Place the cursor over one of the numbers, and notice how the cursor changes to a pointer finger with a double arrow. This tells you the number can be changed, because it's hot text. One way to change the value is to double-click the number and type a new value. Another

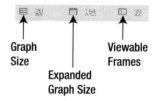

Figure 1-26. You can manage the look of the Motion Editor panel.

way is to click and drag across the number; as you do so, the value changes. This click-and-drag method is called *scrubbing*. Yup, it's just like scrubbing the timeline. Hold Shift while you scrub to change the rate at which your values change. Scrubbing here works as follows:

- Scrub across the Graph Size value, and the height of every graph in the panel gets larger or smaller.

- Scrub across the Expanded Graph Size value, and the expanded size of the selected graph gets larger or smaller. You'll need to actually click one of the properties first to see this. For example, in the Basic motion area, click the X property anywhere that isn't a check box, drop-down menu, or some other widget. When you do, the property expands to a full grid, and now you can adjust its expanded size.

- Scrub across the Viewable Frames value, and you will see the frames in the graph get larger or smaller. The maximum value for this feature is the current number of frames in the selected tween span, not the Flash movie. Notice how you can't get a number larger than the 39 frames in this particular because the selected tween span has only 39 frames.

Twirl down the Basic motion section. Scrub across any of the values, and the object in that particular frame will change.

> Be careful with that "U-turn" back arrow on the layer strip. This is the Reset Values *button, but it does more than simply reset the values to their original values. Click it, and the whole tween is removed!*

Click the drop-down list in the Eases area, and you see that you can remove any eases or apply a Simple (Slow) ease to the entire area or to individual properties. We aren't going to explain a Simple (Slow) ease yet, because you have strolled over here for a peek, rather than a lesson. We'll cover this in greater depth in Chapters 7 and 8.

You will notice that you have a timeline in this panel's grids. Obviously, if you have a timeline, you should be able to add a keyframe. Drag the playhead to frame 15 of the timeline in this panel. In the keyframe area are two arrows on either side of a diamond. Click the diamond. This adds a keyframe to the animation. The keyframe is visible as a dot on the graph and, if you look back to the Timeline panel, you'll see a keyframe has also been added in frame 15 of the main timeline, as shown in Figure 1-27. The diamond also turns golden. If you move the playhead to another position, the keyframe changes back to gray. This should tell you that a golden diamond means there is a keyframe in the frame. If you click the arrows on either side of the diamond, you will jump to the previous or next keyframe. When one of those arrows is grayed out, you are essentially being told there are no further keyframes beyond the current position of the playhead.

> Technically speaking, keyframes added with the Motion Editor panel's diamonds are called property keyframes. *You'll learn all the nitty-gritty on this new panel in Chapter 8.*

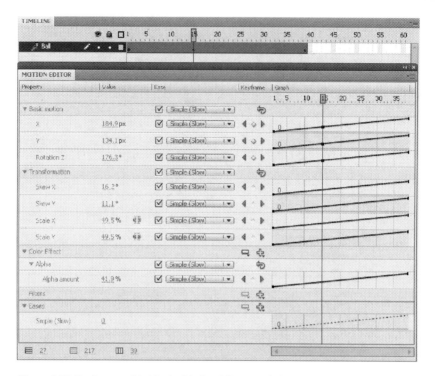

Figure 1-27. Keyframes added in the Motion Editor panel also appear on the main timeline.

The Color Effect, Filters, and Eases strips are treated a bit differently. Instead of a curved arrow, they have plus and minus signs. Click the + in the Filters area. A drop-down menu containing a list of the available filters appears, as shown in Figure 1-28. To remove a filter, click and hold on the –. A drop-down list of the filters applied to that object will appear. Click a filter in that list, and it will be removed.

Figure 1-28. Filters can also be added and tweened.

The Help menu

In the early days of desktop computing, software was a major purchase, and nothing made you feel more comfortable than the manuals that were tucked into the box. If you had a problem, you opened the manual and searched for the solution. Those days have long passed. Software is more complex, and printing large manuals would be costly. Today, such manuals are supplied on discs or are web-based. In this version of Flash, the user manuals are found in the Help menu, which opens these documents in your default web browser.

To access Help, select Help ➤ Flash Help or press the F1 key. The content that opens (see Figure 1-29) is one of the most comprehensive sources of Flash knowledge on the planet (other than this book, of course) and, best of all, it's free.

The documentation is divided into a series of books, listed on the left side. They cover a variety of subjects, ranging from the use of Flash CS4 Professional to the coding languages used to program content for mobile devices. The right side is where the information you are looking for is displayed.

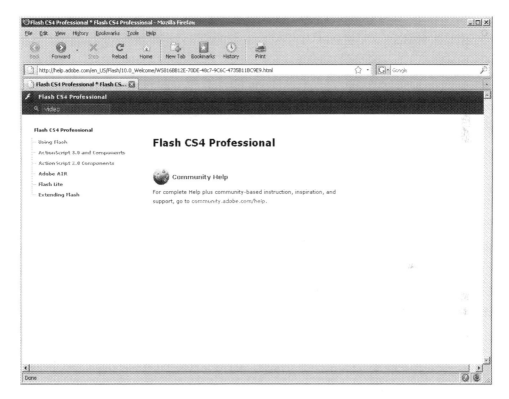

Figure 1-29. The Flash documentation is extensive.

Click the Using Flash book to open it, and then click Adobe Flash CS4 Professional. As you can see, the books are actually collections of individual documents designed to help you learn what you need to know, along with practical examples of specific techniques.

To go to a specific topic, just continue to click hyperlinks on the left to drill down to the subject of interest. For example, click the + next to Working with video to open that book. Notice the documents About digital video and Flash, Importing and playing Flash video files, and so on.

Alternatively, you can use the Search field to look for answers both in the documentation and among tutorials, articles, and blogs on various Adobe and third-party websites. For example, search for the phrase Video class and note that results include free training videos from Lee Brimelow's lauded gotoAndLearn.com website and the flash.media.Video entry of the ActionScript 3.0 Language and Components Reference, as shown in Figure 1-30. Use the drop-down filter to the right of the Search field to sort by product (in this case, Flash, obviously).

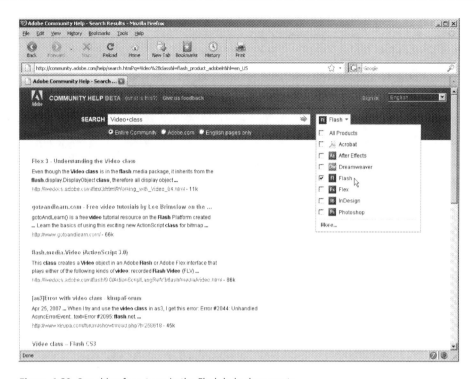

Figure 1-30. Searching for a term in the Flash help documents

> *So, why search for* Video *class, rather than just* video*? What does* class *mean? Does it mean lessons? Not in this context. You don't have to use the term, but if you're looking for ActionScript-specific results, the word* class *refers to a concept or an object's type—the sort of thing it is. For code-oriented searches, try* MovieClip *class when you're looking up movieclips,* TextField *class when you're looking up text fields, and so on. More on this in Chapter 4.*

Using layers

The final stop on our walkabout is back at the bottom of the interface: the layers facet of the timeline. Let's begin with a few things you need to know regarding layers:

- You can have up to 16,000 layers in a Flash movie. They have no effect on the file size.

- Use layers to manage your movie. Flash movies are composed of objects, media, and code, and it is a standard industry practice to give everything its own meaningfully named layer. This way, you can easily find content on a crowded stage. In fact, most kinds of tweens require that the objects involved be on their own layers. (That said—not to get too ahead of ourselves—the new tweening model does allow multiple objects on a single layer, as you will learn in Chapter 8.)

- Layers can be grouped. Layers can be placed in a layer folder, which means you can, for example, build a complex animation and have all of the objects in the animation contained in their own layers inside a folder.

- Layers stack on top of each other. For example, you can have a layer with a box in it and another with a ball in it. If the ball layer is above the box layer, the ball will appear to be above the box. You can easily change this stacking order.

- Name your layers. Yes, we mentioned this already, but it bears repeating. This is another standard industry practice that makes finding content in the movie much easier than a jumble of the default layer names: Layer 1, Layer 2, Layer 3, and so on.

> *Want to collapse the layers to buy yourself some screen real estate? Double-click the* Timeline *tab. This will reduce the height of the* Timeline *panel. Double-click again to bring it back.*

Layer modes

Layers can be switched among very specific modes, which change the behavioral characteristics of the layer. We will be using this feature quite extensively in Chapter 3 (which covers symbols) and Chapters 7 and 8 (on animation).

To configure modes, right-click (Ctrl-click) a layer's name and choose Properties. The modes are as follows:

- **Normal layer**: This is what you've seen so far. When you tween an object using the Flash CS4 version of a motion tween—as opposed to a shape tween or classic tween—your normal layer enters a special submode in which tween properties on the layer are no longer controlled by the Property inspector, but rather through the new Motion Editor panel. The icon for a normal layer is a folded-up sheet of paper.

- **Masking layer**: The shape of an object on a masking layer is used to hide anything outside that shape, and reveals only whatever is under the object. For example, place an image on the stage and add a box in the layer above it. If that layer is a masking layer, only the pixels of the part of the image directly under the box will be seen. The icon for a masking layer is a square with an oval in the middle of it.

- **Masked layer**: It takes two to tango, and the same goes for masking. Assuming a masking layer is already in place, layers immediately beneath it can be made masked layers of the masker. The icon for a masked layer is a folded-up sheet of paper, facing the opposite direction as the icon for a normal layer. We'll get into masks in much more detail in Chapter 3.

- **Folder layer**: You won't necessarily think of this as a layer—it really is a folder that *contains* layers—but Flash CS4 lets you save FLAs as CS3 files (meaning that they can be opened with Flash CS3). In turn, Flash CS3 can save FLAs as Flash 8 files, and so on. You'll lose new features as you travel back in time, but eventually, folder layers become regular layers, so at least they're not lost. Since you'll be using Flash CS4, it really makes no difference. Think of folder layers as timeline folders. The icon for a folder layer is an open file folder.

- **Guide layer**: A guide layer contains shapes, symbols, images, and so on that you can use to align elements on other layers in a movie. These things are really handy if you have a complex design and want a standard reference for the entire movie. What makes guide layers so important is that they aren't rendered when you publish the SWF. This means, for example, that you could create a comprehensive design, or *comp*, of the Flash stage in Fireworks CS4 or Photoshop CS4, place that image in a guide layer, and not have to worry about the comp adding file size to the published SWF. With classic tweens, guides can also provide paths on which to animate symbols. The icon for a guide layer is a T-square.

> *Flash CS4 Professional allows you to optionally omit layers that are hidden when you publish the SWF. As with guide layers, this means that hidden layers can be configured to not add weight to published content. This feature was introduced in Flash CS3.*

Creating layers

Let's start using layers. First, we'll create some new layers.

1. Open the Layers.fla document in the Chapter 1 Exercise folder. You will see two colored shapes on the stage, as shown in Figure 1-31. These shapes are sitting in one layer.

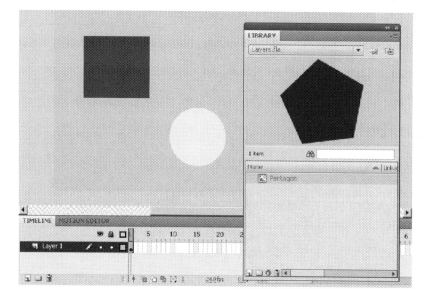

Figure 1-31. We start with two objects on the stage and one in the library.

2. Open the library. You will notice that there is an object named Pentagon contained in the library. That object is a movieclip. We'll get into movieclips in a big way in Chapter 3.

3. Each object should be placed on its own layer. Click the New Layer button—it looks like a page with a turned-up corner—directly under the Layer 1 strip. A new layer, named Layer 2, is added to the timeline. Flash keeps track of your timelines on a per-FLA basis, so you might see other numbers besides 2, 3, and so on. The point is that new layers are sequential.

4. Select Layer 1 and add a new layer. Notice how the new layer is placed between Layer 1 and Layer 2. This should tell you that all new layers added to the timeline are added directly above the currently selected layer. Obviously, Layer 3 is out of position. Let's fix that.

5. Drag Layer 3 above Layer 2 and release the mouse. Now you know how to reorder layers and move them around in the timeline. Layers can be dragged above or below each other.

6. Add a new layer. Hold on—we have four layers and three objects. The math doesn't work. That new layer has to go.

7. Select Layer 4 and click the Trash Can icon under the Layer 1 strip. Layer 4 is deleted, and now you know how to get rid of an extra layer.

8. Double-click the Layer 1 layer name to select it. Rename the layer Box. Now that you know how to rename a layer, rename the remaining two layers Ball and Pentagon.

Adding content to layers

Content can be added to layers in one of two ways:

- Directly to the layer by moving an object from the library to the layer
- From one layer to another layer

Let's put some content in our layers:

1. Select the Pentagon layer and drag the movieclip from the library to the stage. The hollow dot in the layer will change to a solid dot to indicate that there is content in the frame. When moving objects from the library to the stage, be sure to select the layer, sometimes called a *target layer*, before you drag and drop. This way, you can prevent the content from going in the wrong layer.

2. Click the ball on the stage. Notice how the layer is also selected? This is a handy way of determining the layer where an object is located.

3. Select Edit ➤ Cut, or press Ctrl+X (Cmd+X).

4. Click the Ball layer and select Edit ➤ Paste in Place, as shown in Figure 1-32. When you release the mouse, a copy of the ball will appear in the precise location at which you cut it.

Whatever happened to a simple paste command in the Edit *menu? The* Paste in Center *command replaces it. It has always been a fact of Flash life that any content on the clipboard is pasted into the center of the stage. The change in name simply acknowledges this. The other paste command—Paste Special—opens a dialog box that asks you if you want the contents of the clipboard as text. This is a handy way of adding a block of text from a word processor into Flash.*

Figure 1-32. Paste in Place pastes objects in the precise location of the original object that was either cut or copied to the clipboard.

Showing/hiding and locking layers

You may have noticed three icons—an eyeball, a lock, and a hollow square—above the layers, as shown in Figure 1-33. Let's see what they do.

Figure 1-33. The Show/Hide All Layers, Lock/Unlock All Layers, and Show All Layers as Outlines icons. Note the pencil icon in the Ball layer, which tells you that you can add content to that layer.

31

Click the eyeball icon. Notice that everything on the stage disappears and the dots under the eyeball in each layer change to a red *x*. This eyeball is the Show/Hide All Layers button, and clicking it turns off the visibility of all of the content in the layers. Click the icon again, and everything reappears. Using this feature lets you temporarily hide all existing content while you add something new. Or you can hide everything, and then unhide the one layer of interest.

> *In previous versions of Flash, a layer's visibility did not carry into the SWF file itself. This was merely a feature to be used for convenience during authoring. In Flash CS4, invisible layers may optionally be omitted from the published SWF. Select* File ➤ Publish Settings *and select the* Flash *tab. The preference is listed as a check box labeled* Export hidden layers.

Next, select the Pentagon layer, and click the dot under the eyeball. Just the pentagon disappears. This tells you that you can turn off the visibility for a specific layer by clicking the dot in the visibility column.

When you click a layer, you may notice that a pencil icon appears on the layer strip. This tells you that you can add content to the layer. Click the Ball layer, and you'll see the pencil icon. Now click the dot under the lock in the Ball layer. The lock icon will replace the dot. When you lock a layer, you can't draw on it or add content to it. You can see this because the pencil has a stroke through it. If you try to drag the pentagon symbol from the library to the Ball layer, you will also see that the layer has been locked—the cursor changes from a tan arrow to a circle with a line through it. Also, if you try to click the ball on the stage, you won't be able to select it. Locking a layer is handy in situations where precision is paramount and you don't want to accidentally move something or delete something from the stage.

> *Actually we sort of "fibbed" by telling you that you can't put anything on a locked layer. The only thing that can be added to a locked layer is ActionScript. In fact, it is a common practice to create an ActionScript-only layer and then lock that layer. This prevents anything other than code from being added to that layer.*

The final icon is the Show All Layers as Outlines button. Click it, and the content on the stage turns into outlines. This is somewhat akin to the wireframe display mode available in many 3D modeling applications. In Flash, it can be useful in cases where dozens of objects overlap, and you simply want a quick "X-ray view" of how your content is arranged. With animation in particular, it can be helpful to evaluate the motion of objects without needing to consider the distraction of color and shading. Like visibility and locking, the outlines icon is also available on a per-layer basis.

> *You can change the color used for the outline in a layer by double-clicking the color chip in the layer strip. This will open the* Layer Properties *dialog box. Double-click the color chip in the dialog box to open the Color Picker and click a color, and that color will be used.*

Grouping layers

You can also group layers using folders. Here's how:

1. Click the folder icon in the Timeline panel. A new unnamed folder—Folder 1—will appear on the timeline. You can rename a folder by double-clicking its name and entering a new name.

2. Drag the three layers into the folder. As each one is placed in the folder, notice how the name indents. This tells you that the layer is in a folder.

3. Next, remove the layers from the folder. To do so, simply drag the layer above the folder on the timeline. You can also drag it to the left to unindent it.

4. To delete the folder, select it and click the Trash Can icon.

> *Make sure that the folder is empty before you click the* Trash Can *icon to delete it. If you delete a folder that contains layers, those layers will also be deleted. If this happens to you, Adobe has sent a life raft in your direction: an alert box telling you that you will also be deleting the layers in the folder. Click* Cancel *instead of* OK *if you've changed your mind.*

Now that you have had a chance to wander through the interface and try out a few things, let's put what you have learned to practical use. Moving squares and circles around the stage isn't exactly why you are here, so let's take what you have learned and hike over to Lake Nanagook.

Your turn: build a Flash movie

We have shown you where many of the interface features can be found and how they can be used. Now we are going to give you the opportunity to see how all of these features combine to create a Flash movie.

You will be undertaking tasks such as the following:

- Using the Property inspector to precisely position and resize objects on the stage
- Creating layers and adding content from the library to the layers
- Using the drawing tools to create a shape
- Creating a simple animation through the use of a tween
- Saving a Flash movie
- Testing a Flash movie

By the end of this exercise, you will have a fairly good understanding of how a Flash movie is assembled and the workflow involved in the process.

Preparing the stage

The specifications for the project dictate the stage is to be 400 pixels wide by 300 pixels high. It also calls for a dark-blue stage color to give the illusion of night. Follow these steps to set up the stage:

1. Open the MoonOverLakeNanagook.fla file in the Chapter 1 Exercise folder.

2. Show the Library panel, if it isn't already in view, by selecting Window ➤ Library or pressing Ctrl+L (Cmd+L). As you can see in Figure 1-34, you are starting with a blank stage, a few movieclips, an audio file, and a graphic symbol.

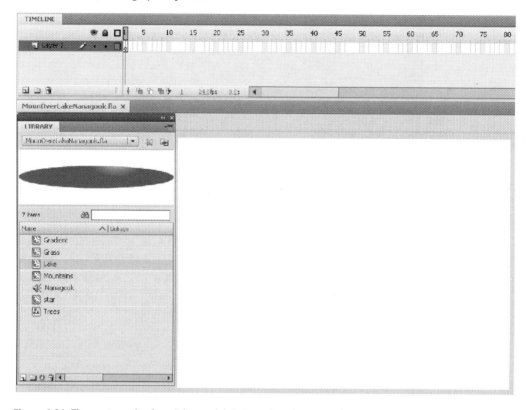

Figure 1-34. The assets are in place. It is your job to turn them into a movie.

3. Click the stage, and then click the Edit button in the Properties area of the Property inspector to open the Document Properties dialog box.

4. Change the width value to 400 and the height value to 300. Click the Background color chip to open the Color Picker. Select the color text and change it from #FFFFFF to #000066 (dark blue). Click OK to accept the changes and close the dialog box. The stage will shrink to its new size and be colored a dark blue. The new size and color will now appear in the Property inspector, as shown in Figure 1-35.

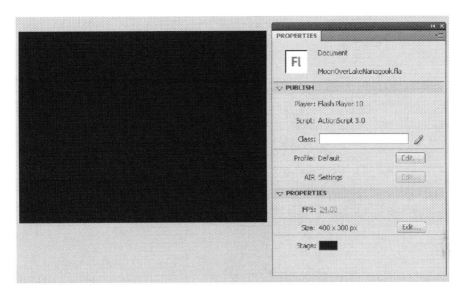

Figure 1-35. The stage is set.

Adding the sky

Next, use the Gradient movieclip for the sky. Although using your eyes for object placement on the stage is a great way to get stuff into position, your eyes aren't as precise as Flash. The gradient needs to completely cover the stage and not hang out on the pasteboard (the nonstage work area) by even one pixel. Why? So that the gradient covers the whole "sky" area. Here's how you do that:

1. Rename Layer 1 to Gradient by double-clicking the layer name and entering that text.

2. Drag the Gradient movieclip from the library to the stage.

3. Click the gradient on the stage to select it. In the Property inspector, set its X and Y values to 0. The object will align itself with the upper-left corner of the stage.

4. Click frame 60 of the Gradient layer and press the F5 key. This adds 59 new frames to the timeline; you can tell this because the layer expands to the sixtieth frame and a rectangle (indicating the new span of frames) is shown at the end of the layer. This gradient is going to be animated later in the exercise.

When Flash measures the location of an object on the stage, it uses the upper-left corner of the stage as its 0,0 point. The actual position of the object is based on something called its *registration point*. In the case of this gradient, the registration point of the symbol also happens to be its own upper-left corner, which is why x and y values of 0 cause it to fit neatly on the stage. If the registration point of the gradient were changed to 200,150—that is, down and in from its own upper-left corner—the gradient would end up being positioned partly on the pasteboard and partly on the stage, as shown in Figure 1-36. The symbol's registration point is indicated by the + sign you see inside the symbol (near the small circle) in Figure 1-36. In the sample file, you'll see the + sign is in the symbol's upper-left corner instead. In Chapter 3, you'll learn how to change a symbol's registration point however you see fit.

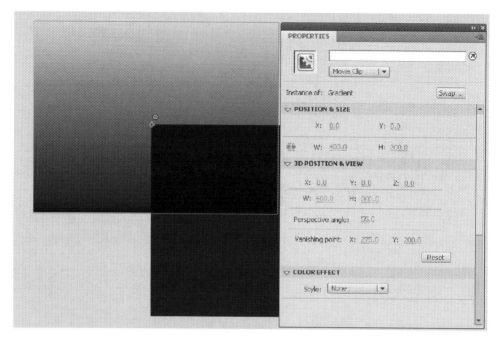

Figure 1-36. The stage and the object's registration point determine position on the stage when using the Property inspector.

5. Lock the layer by clicking the black dot under the Lock icon on the timeline. This is a good habit to develop. Flash projects, including this one, can get fairly complex in a relatively short time. By locking the layer, you are ensuring that you don't accidentally move the background later while you're working on the project.

One of the really great things about Flash is that it gives us designers the chance to practice the art of illusion. If you look at the gradient on the stage, you will notice that the sky is a dark blue that gradually changes to black as it approaches the bottom of the stage. This gives the illusion of a night sky. Let's look at how this was accomplished.

6. Double-click the Gradient symbol in the library to open the Symbol Editor. This is also known as entering a symbol's timeline.

The Symbol Editor looks suspiciously like the main timeline. In fact, symbols have their own timelines that can function independently of the main timeline. You'll see what we mean by this in a couple of minutes. For now, let's just get you oriented. Beside the Scene 1 link on the top-left corner of the stage, you see a movieclip icon and the name Gradient. This tells you that you are in the Symbol Editor, editing the Gradient symbol. Clicking the Scene 1 link returns you to the main timeline. But for now, get yourself back to the Symbol Editor.

7. Once in the gradient's timeline, click the gradient. The first thing you should notice is that the gradient becomes pixelated. This is a visual clue that you have selected a vector shape. Colors and gradients can be associated with shapes by way of the Paint Bucket and Ink Bottle tools.

8. Select Window ➤ Color to open the Color panel. Click the Fill color button (a paint bucket) to activate the fill color chip. You will see that the gradient is a linear gradient that runs from black to black. The default colors for any gradient you create are black and white, but these can be changed at any time with the little arrows under the gradient strip, which are called *crayons*.

9. Click the left black crayon, and you will see the color appear in hexadecimal format: #000000. Note that the Alpha value is 100%. *Alpha* is Flash's term for opacity, and 100% means that the color is fully opaque; in other words, it cannot be seen through at all. Click the right black crayon. This time, the Alpha value is 0% (as shown in Figure 1-37).

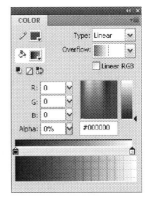

Figure 1-37. You use the Color panel to fill shapes with gradients.

The color in the gradient actually fades in from transparent black to opaque black. As the color moves from the top to the bottom, the pixels become visible, hiding the blue. As they increase in number, the black takes over and the blue looks like it is transforming to black. Now you know how the illusion of a night sky was created.

10. Click Scene 1 or select Edit ➤ Edit Document to exit the Symbol Editor.

Adding the mountains and playing with color

With the stage prepared and the sky in place, you can now turn your attention to adding the assets to the movie. The scene involves mountains, trees, grass, a lake, a twinkling star, and the moon. What this tells you is that the objects furthest away need to be placed near the bottom of the layering order. This means that the mountains are the next piece of content to be added.

1. Add a new layer to the main timeline and name it Mountains.

2. With the new layer selected, open the library and drag the Mountains movieclip onto the stage.

3. With the mountains selected on the stage, in the Property inspector, set the X value to -34 and the Y value to 203. The mountain range will sit at the bottom of the stage and hang off both sides of the stage. There is, of course, one great big problem: the mountains are black and they have been placed against a black background. Let's fix that.

4. Select the mountains on the stage and, in the Color Effect area of the Property inspector, select Tint from the Style drop-down menu. The Property inspector will change to show you a color chip, a tint percentage, and the RGB color of the selected object.

> *Remember that everything on the stage, including the stage itself, has unique properties, including its color. Changing the tint of a selected object allows you to manipulate the color property of that object. The original library asset's color is not affected.*

5. Click the color chip, and when the Color Picker opens, select the dark-gray color directly under the black chip on the left side of the picker (#333333). The mountains become a lot more distinct; in fact, they are now too obvious if your Tint value is applied at 100%.

6. With the mountains still selected, move the Tint slider until the value is 70%. Now move it to 50% (as shown in Figure 1-38). What you have discovered is that the strength of a tint color is another tool in the color arsenal for you to deploy as needed. If you are a power user, feel free to set the Tint value to 50 by typing it manually.

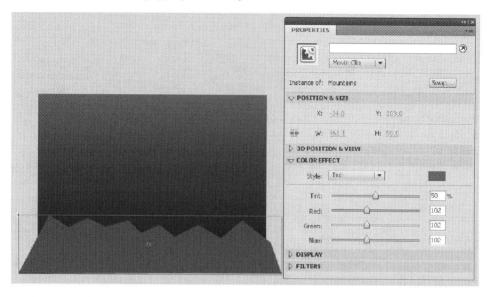

Figure 1-38. Objects can have their color properties manipulated.

7. Now would be a good time to save your work. Select File ➤ Save As, and when the Save As dialog box opens, navigate to the Exercise folder for this chapter and rename the project. Click OK to close the dialog box.

> *If you have been using Flash for a while, we are willing to bet you missed something rather significant when you added the new layer. Did you happen to catch that the frame span of the new layer matched that of the Gradient layer? In the past, any new layer started off as a single frame, and you pressed the F5 key to add a frame to create the span.*

Using trees to create the illusion of depth

The mountains are in place and are faintly visible against the night sky. Let's add some depth to the scene by adding a couple of trees.

1. Create two new layers, named Tree1 and Tree2.

2. Drag one copy of the Trees symbol to the stage while each tree layer is selected. This puts each tree on its own layer. You may notice that the icon for the Trees symbol is different from the other symbols in the library. This icon indicates that the tree is a *graphic symbol*. Graphic symbols can be created with the various drawing tools in Flash—which is the case with this tree—and also make good containers for imported photographs.

Graphic symbols' timelines are locked in step with the timeline they're in, unlike movieclip symbols, whose timelines run independently. This explains why graphics are the de facto symbol for JibJab-style animation (http:// www.jibjab.com). Complex nested symbols can be scrubbed in this way for testing in the timeline, whereas movieclips only show nested animation when published. A symbol placed on the stage is called an instance. We will cover symbols in Chapter 3, and animation in Chapters 7 and 8.

3. Select the tree on the lower of the two tree layers. Use these values to precisely place the selected tree on the stage, resize it, and darken it:

- X: 49
- Y: 178.5
- W: 65
- H: 105
- Color Effect: Tint
- Tint Color: #000000 (black)
- Tint Amount: 48%

The tree gets smaller, moves to the left side of the stage, and darkens. Resizing the image and darkening it give the illusion of depth in this scene.

4. Select the remaining tree and use these values in the Property inspector:

- X: 76.2
- Y: 160.6
- W: 68
- H: 123
- Color Effect: Tint
- Tint Color: #000000 (black)
- Tint Amount: 26%

The tree gets a bit smaller, moves to the left side of the stage, and, due to the low tint amount, becomes a bit brighter than the tree behind it, as shown in Figure 1-39. The reason for this is that it will be lit by the moon, which you will create in a couple of minutes.

If you have used Flash prior to this version, setting the location and size properties of a selected object using the Property inspector will, as one of the authors discovered, take a bit of "brain rewiring." In previous versions, the first properties you changed, due to their location in the Property inspector, were width and height; then you set the x and y coordinates. These have been reversed in the Position & Size area in Flash CS4.

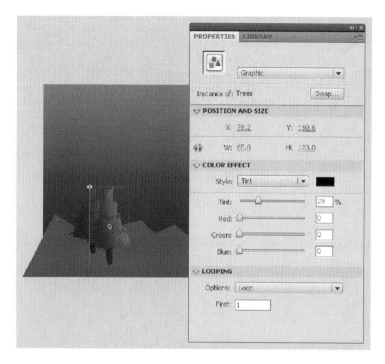

Figure 1-39. Location and size are other properties that can be manipulated using the Property inspector.

Let's finish off the scene by adding the grass and the lake.

5. Add a new layer named Grass. With this new layer selected, drag the Grass movieclip from the library to the stage. Set its X and Y values in the Property inspector to -277.6 and 268.9, respectively.

> *What's with the decimals? This is deliberate. You need to know how to input values as well as scrub the values. You may have noticed that when you scrub values, the numbers don't have decimals. If precise placement of objects on the stage is "mission-critical," you need to know that typing the numbers by hand accomplishes this task. But isn't a decimal value smaller than a pixel? You bet it is, but we're dealing with vector graphics here, and vectors don't need to sit exactly on a pixel.*

6. Add a new layer named Lake. With this new layer selected, drag the Lake movieclip from the library to the stage. Set its X and Y values in the Property inspector to -252 and 274, respectively.

So far, so good. It is starting to look like Lake Nanagook (see Figure 1-40), but we need to add two more elements to make it a bit more realistic: the moon and a twinkling star. We obviously need the moon because it is reflected in the lake, and a twinkling star is a subtle bit of eye candy that will make the scene that much more interesting and catch the viewer's attention. Let's start with the star.

Figure 1-40. The project is starting to come together.

Using a motion tween to create a twinkling star

One of the steady messages running throughout this chapter is that we, as Flash designers, are illusionists. In this exercise, you will discover how to create the illusion of a star twinkling in the night sky.

1. Open the library and double-click the star movieclip to open it in the Symbol Editor. When the movieclip opens, you will see that it is composed of a layer named diamond. The shape on the stage was created using the Rectangle Primitive tool, making the sides concave and filling the shape with #FFCC00, which is a gold color.

> If the shape is too small, select the Zoom tool (with the magnifying glass icon) on the Tools panel, and click and drag it across the star. This is how you can precisely zoom in on an object on the stage.

2. Add a new layer named diamond2. Click the star in the diamond layer and copy it to the clipboard.

3. Select the first frame of the diamond2 layer and select Edit ➤ Paste in Place.

4. Move the playhead back to frame 1 and click the star. This will select the star in the diamond2 layer.

5. In the Property inspector, change the star's Fill Color, in the Fill & Stroke area, to #FFFF99, which is a faint-yellow color.

6. With the star in the diamond2 layer selected, right-click (Ctrl-click) the star to open its context menu. Select Convert to Symbol. In the New Symbol dialog box, name the symbol star2 and select Movie Clip from the Type drop-down list. Click OK to accept the change.

You need to convert the rectangle primitive to a symbol in order to apply the sort of tween you're about to do. Note that converting a symbol from a shape or primitive already in place keeps everything positioned where it was.

If you are an After Effects user, you are about to discover the Motion Editor panel is a very familiar place. If you are new to Flash or have never used After Effects, you are about discover that creating motion in Flash has moved, in one leap, from a general tool to a finely tuned precision instrument. We will be getting deeper into this panel in Chapter 8, which means the intent of this exercise is to give you an opportunity to take the Motion Editor panel for a short spin around the block. In this exercise, you are going to do nothing more than have the star rotate 360 degrees in a clockwise direction, and best of all, it requires only a couple of mouse clicks.

7. Right-click (Ctrl-click) on any frame in the diamond2 layer to open the context menu. When the menu opens, select Create Motion Tween. The span will turn blue. Open the Motion Editor panel and move the playhead to frame 60 of the timeline.

8. In the Basic motion area, set the Rotation Z value to 360. When you finish, you will see that a motion tween has been added to the timeline, as shown in Figure 1-41. Positive values will rotate an object in a clockwise direction; negative values will rotate the object in a counter-clockwise direction.

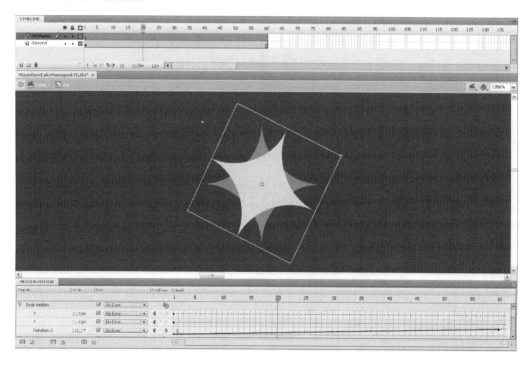

Figure 1-41. Putting a star in motion

9. Scrub across the frames to see the rotation.

10. Zoom the stage to the 100% view, and click the Scene 1 link on the top left of the stage to return to the main timeline.

11. Save the project.

Adding a moon over Lake Nanagook

To this point, we have essentially handed you the assets and let you put them in place and otherwise manipulate them. It is now your turn to go solo and create the moon that rises over Lake Nanagook, complete with shadow.

1. Select Insert ➤ New Symbol. This will open the New Symbol dialog box. Name the symbol Moon and select Movie Clip as its Type. Click OK. The dialog box will close, and the Symbol Editor will open.

> *So far, we have used the term* movieclip *and not put a space between the two words. The use of the single word has developed into a standard when writing about Flash. The* New Symbol *dialog box is actually one of the very few places that Adobe uses the two-word form.*

2. Rename Layer 1 to bg. Add a new layer named shadow. The shadow layer should be above the bg layer.

3. In the Tools panel, click and hold the Rectangle tool, and when the tool drop-down list appears, select the Oval tool. In the options area of the Tools panel, hover until you find the Object Drawing button (a tooltip will tell you when you've hit it; this is the button adjacent to the horseshoe magnet). Make sure the Object Drawing button is *not* selected before completing the next few steps.

4. Click the Stroke Color chip in the Property inspector to open the Color Picker. Select the red on the left as the stroke color (#FF0000). Click the Fill color and select a light blue. While you're there, give the Stroke a value of 3 to help it show up better.

5. Select the first frame of the bg layer and, with the Oval tool selected, click the stage and drag out a circle. Switch to the Selection tool and double-click the circle to select both the fill and the stroke. In the Property inspector, change the circle's width and height values to 120, making a perfect circle, and set the X and Y values to 0. This is your moon (well, the beginnings of it).

6. With the moon still selected—again, you've selected both the stroke and the fill—copy it to the clipboard.

7. Select the first frame in the shadow layer and paste the shape from the clipboard into this layer.

8. With the newly pasted shape still selected, move it upward and to the left, so that it overlaps the bottom layer, but both circles show. These shapes should look something like what you see in the movies when a character looks through binoculars.

9. Click the Show All Layers as Outlines button to temporarily display both circles as outlines. The intersection between the two shapes should look like football or rugby ball. Click the Show All Layers as Outlines button again to exit outlines mode.

10. Click the red stroke on the shape in the shadow layer to select it. Press the Delete key to remove it. You now have a solid blue circle over another circle that has a red stroke, as shown in Figure 1-42.

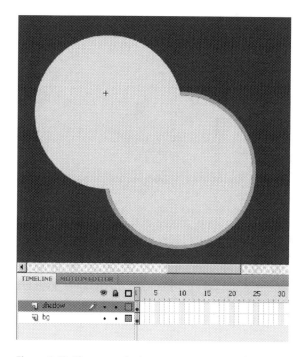

Figure 1-42. The moon shadow starts out as a couple of circles.

11. Select the red stroke around the circle in the bg layer and cut it to the clipboard. Select the shadow layer and select Edit ➤ Paste in Place.

What has happened here is that the stroke you just pasted into the shadow layer has actually cut the football shape for you. The reason this is possible is because you turned off Object Drawing mode in step 3. You'll learn more about this mode in Chapter 2.

12. In the shadow layer, click the portion of the blue circle that is outside the stroke. Press the Delete key. Now select and delete the stroke itself. If you turn off the visibility of the bg layer, you will see that you have created the shadow shape. Let's make it a true shadow.

13. Click the football shape to select it, and then open the Color panel by selecting Window ➤ Color.

14. Set the fill color to #000066 and reduce the alpha value to 36%. Turn on the visibility of the bg layer, and you will see that you indeed have a shadow, as shown in Figure 1-43.

The final task in the process of creating the moon is to add a gradient fill in order to give it a bit of a glow.

15. Select the circle in the bg layer and open the Color panel.

16. Select Radial from the Type drop-down list. The moon turns into a black-and-white radial gradient. Click the black crayon to select it. Change the hex color under the Color Picker to #C4DDEE. Click the white crayon and change its color to #93BDE0. The moon takes on a faint glow, thanks to the similar colors in the gradient, as shown in Figure 1-44.

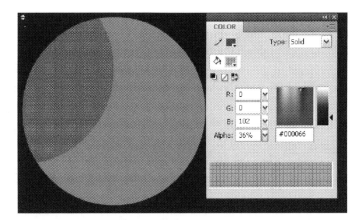

Figure 1-43. The shadow is created by using the Color panel.

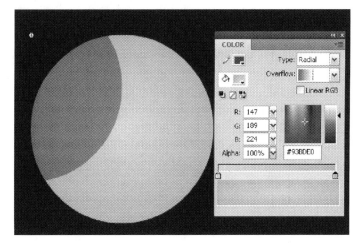

Figure 1-44. Add a radial gradient through the Color panel.

17. Click the Scene 1 link to return to the main timeline.

18. Add a layer named Star and another named Moon. These layers should appear above the others.

19. Add the star symbol to the Star layer, and set its X and Y values to 219 and 42, respectively.

20. Add the moon symbol to the Moon layer, and set its X and Y values to 241 and 43, respectively.

Making some moonshine

Next, let's really make the moon and the star shine in the sky over Lake Nanagook. Let's add a glow effect to both of them. Here's how:

1. Select the star on the stage and click the Filters twirlie on the Property inspector to open the Filters area.

2. Click the leftmost icon at the bottom of the Filters area to open the Add Filter menu list of the filters. Select the Glow filter.

3. Use these settings in the Glow filter:

   - Blur X: 14
   - Blur Y: 14
   - Strength: 418%
   - Quality: High
   - Color: #93BDE0

The star looks like it is about to go into supernova. Let's make it a bit smaller.

4. With the star selected on the stage, set its width and height values in the Property inspector to 13.

5. Select the moon on the stage and apply the following Glow filter values:

   - Blur X: 26
   - Blur Y: 26
   - Strength: 70%
   - Quality: High
   - Color: #93BDE0

6. The moon and the star now look like they belong together in the sky, as shown in Figure 1-45. Save the project.

> *Filters can be added only to movieclips, text fields, and buttons.*

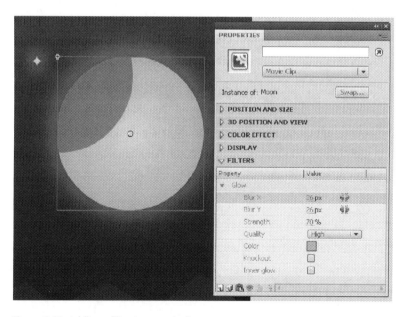

Figure 1-45. Adding a filter to a movieclip

Breaking the stillness of the night at Lake Nanagook

If we are going to have an outdoor scene, it only makes sense to add a bit of outdoor sound to the mix. Fortunately, adding audio to a Flash file is not terribly complicated.

1. Add a new layer and name it Audio.

2. Open the library and locate the imported Nanagook.mp3 audio file. Double-click it to open the Sound Properties dialog box.

3. Click the Advanced button to reveal all of the features of this dialog box, as shown in Figure 1-46. Click the Test button to preview the audio file. Ah, the sounds of crickets and wolves howling in the night. Click OK to close the dialog box.

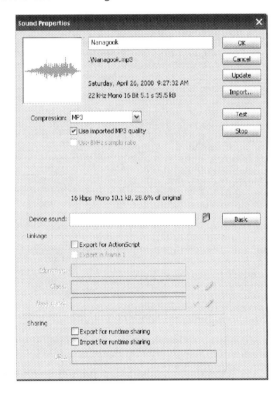

Figure 1-46. Preview sound in Flash by clicking the Test button.

4. With the Audio layer selected, drag the sound file from the library onto the stage. When you release the mouse, the audio waveform appears in the layer.

> *Dragging a sound file from the library to the stage isn't the only way to get an audio file to the timeline. In many respects, what we've shown is not exactly regarded as a best practice because audio can be big, and when it is in the library, it can increase the SWF size. We have a whole chapter, Chapter 5, devoted to audio best practice, so for now, let's content ourselves with getting sound into the presentation and getting it to play.*

5. Click anywhere on the sound's waveform in the Audio layer, and you will see the Property inspector change to show the sound properties (open the Sound twirlie, if you necessary).

6. Click the Sync drop-down menu and select Stream, as shown in Figure 1-47.

7. Scrub across the timeline, and you will hear the audio file. This is possible because of the Sync change you made in step 6. Drag the playback head to frame 1 and press the Return (Enter) key. The sound will start playing, but it abruptly ends at frame 50. This is because the audio was originally recorded for a slower movie frame rate.

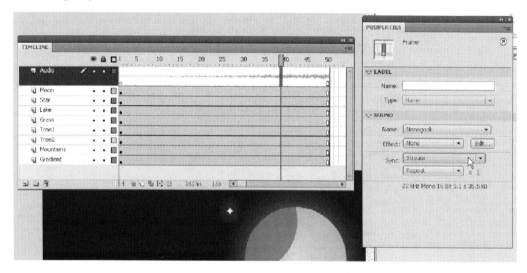

Figure 1-47. Audio on the timeline, and the sound properties in the Property inspector

8. Scroll the timeline so you can see frame 130. Click into the Audio layer at frame 130 and drag downward without lifting the mouse—until you hit the Gradient layer. This selects the last frame of all your layers. Press the F5 key. This adds enough frames to every layer so that the sound has enough room to play out completely.

9. Save the file.

> Picking up a pattern here? Get into the habit of saving the file every time you do something major to your movie. This way, if the computer crashes, you won't have a lot of extra work in front of you trying to reconstruct the movie up to the point of the crash.

You may have looked at Figure 1-47 and thought, "Hey, my Audio layer doesn't look like yours." Good eye. Layers can also be made larger. To do this, right-click (Ctrl-click) on a layer's name to open the context menu. Select Properties to open the Layer Properties dialog box, as shown in Figure 1-48. Select 200% in the Layer height drop-down list, or enter your own value. Click OK to accept the change.

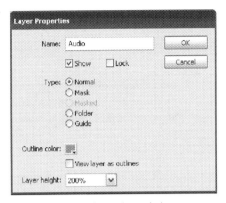

Figure 1-48. Even layers have their own properties.

Testing your movie

You have created the animation and scrubbed through the timeline, and everything looks like it is in order. Now would be a good time to test your movie in Flash Player. We can't overstate the importance of this step in your workflow. The procedure, as one of the authors is fond of telling his students, is, "Do a bit. Test it. Do a bit more. Test it." Flash movies can be quite complex. Each element you add to your movie adds to the complexity of the movie. Developing the habit of regularly testing your work, regardless of how simple it may be, will point out mistakes, errors, or problems in the work that you've just completed. What it comes down to is this: do you really want to burrow through a complex movie, and even more complex code, searching for an issue, or do you want to catch it early?

Figure 1-49. Testing a movie in Flash Player

To test your Flash movie, press Ctrl+Enter (Cmd+Return). If you prefer to use a menu, select Control ➤ Test Movie. You will see an alert box telling you that the movie is being exported, and the movie will open in Flash Player, as shown in Figure 1-49. You should see the star twinkling in the sky and that all of the stuff that is outside the boundaries of the stage has been trimmed off.

If you open the folder where you saved the FLA file, you will see that a SWF file has also been added to the folder.

Making the moon rise over Lake Nanagook

We've been gently reminding you that Flash involves the art of illusion. The other thing you need to know is that Flash developers are fanatics about detail. They pay close attention to their environment, and then try and mimic it in their projects.

In this final piece of this exercise, we are going to get you up close and personal with that last statement. The plan is to have the moon rise into the night sky. On the surface, that sounds like a no-brainer: tween the motion of the moon between its start position and its finish position. But that's not quite how it works.

This is a night scene, and if there is no moon, things are quite dark. They only light up when the moon is in the sky. If you look at Lake Nanagook, you can see there is a problem. The lake already contains the reflection of the moon. The lake should be dark and only start to light up as the moon rises in the sky. The other issue is the trees. They, too, are lit by the moon. but they should be dark and start to light up as the moon rises.

Although fixing the movie may sound rather complex, it can all be handled by the Property inspector and Motion Editor panel. Follow these steps to start yourself on the path to becoming a fanatic about detail:

1. The first issue is the moon itself. It is in a higher layer. This means that if you animate the moon in its current position, it will appear to rise in front of Lake Nanagook. Drag the Moon layer down to just above the Gradient layer. Now the moon will rise behind the mountains.

2. Turn off the visibility of the Lake layer. You will need to see what you are doing, and the lake will hide the start point of the moon rise.

3. Right-click (Ctrl-click) the Moon layer and select Create Motion Tween. This layer can now be used with the Motion Editor panel.

4. Select the Moon layer and open the Motion Editor panel.

5. Drag the playhead to frame 1 and, using the Position & Size area of the Property inspector, set the moon's position to 230 on the x axis and 305 on the y axis.

6. Drag the playhead to frame 50 and make sure the Basic motion twirlie is open. Add keyframes to the X and Y rows by clicking the Add or Remove Keyframe button (the diamond) for either one of them.

7. Move the playhead to frame 100 and set the X and Y values to 241,43 (the original position of the moon). If you scrub across the timeline—either in the Timeline panel or the Motion Editor panel—the moon rises from behind the mountains.

Want to earn some "bonus marks"? How about we have the moon travel through an arc to its final position?

8. Lock the Mountains layer. You are going to manipulate the motion path—the series of dots—to create the arc, and you don't want to move the mountains by accident.

9. Click one of the dots where the path crosses the edge of the mountain range and drag it to the left. A couple of things happened:

   ■ When you rolled the cursor over the path, an arc appeared under the arrow. This tells you the path can be changed.

   ■ When you dragged the path, it changed to a solid line, which bent in the direction you were dragging, and the graph in the Motion Editor panel also bent. This tells you motion paths can be thought of as vectors.

10. When you release the path, it becomes a dotted line again, as shown in Figure 1-50. Scrub the playhead across the animation, and the moon follows a gentle arc as it moves into the night sky.

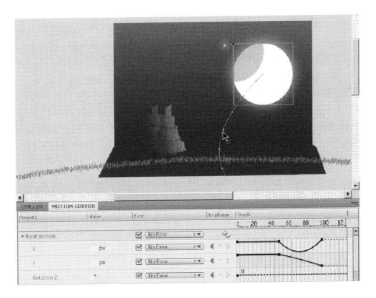

Figure 1-50. Manipulating a motion path

If you are an experienced Flash user, you'll notice the ability to directly edit a motion path on the stage has replaced the Add Motion Guide *button used in previous versions of the application. Old-style motion guides are still available with classic tweens (see Chapter 7 for details).*

Lighting up Lake Nanagook

Obviously, if the moon is behind the mountains when the movie starts, the lake and trees shouldn't be lit up. Let's have them become distinct as the moon rises.

1. Unhide the Lake layer on the Timeline panel and right-click (Ctrl-click) to select Create Motion Tween. Drag the playhead to frame 1.

2. With the Lake layer selected, open the Motion Editor panel and click the + sign in the Color Effect area.

3. Select Brightness. Reduce the Brightness value to -100. This will turn the lake black because you have essentially removed all of the color from the lake.

4. Drag the playhead to frame 50 and click the Brightness diamond to add a keyframe. Do this again at frame 100 and increase the Brightness value to 0%. The lake returns to its original color state. Scrub across the timeline, and the reflection of the moon in the lake becomes brighter as the moon moves across the night sky.

5. Return to the Timeline panel and perform the next few steps with each tree layer in turn:

- Right-click (Ctrl-click) at frame 50 and select Insert Keyframe. This adds a classic keyframe to the layer at that position. Do the same at frame 100.

- Right-click (Ctrl-click) anywhere in the layer between frames 50 and 100 and select Create Classic Tween.

- Drag the playhead to frame 50. Click the tree in the current layer and use the Color Effect area of the Property inspector to change the tree's Tint value to 100%, which completely darkens that tree, as shown in Figure 1-51. (The keyframe at frame 100 still holds the tree's original Tint value.)

- Drag the playhead to frame 1 and change the tree's Tint value to 100% there as well.

6. Save and test the movie. Your movie should look a lot more realistic. This tells you that the new motion tween model and classic tweens can be combined.

You have concluded your introductory walk through Flash CS4 Professional.

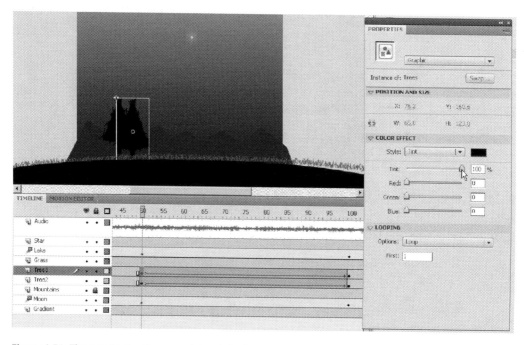

Figure 1-51. The new Motion Tween model and classic tweens can be combined.

What you have learned

In this chapter, you learned the following:

- How to customize your Flash workspace
- A number of methods for manipulating objects on the Flash stage
- How to dock, undock, collapse, and minimize panels
- The importance of the Property inspector in your daily workflow
- The difference between a frame and a keyframe
- The process involved in using frames to arrange and animate content and the properties of content on the stage using the Timeline and Motion Editor panels
- How to add, delete, nest, and rearrange layers
- How to test a Flash movie

In the next chapter, you'll learn how to use the tools to create content in your movies, and how Fireworks CS4, Photoshop CS4, and Illustrator CS4 are important elements in your workflow.

Chapter 2

CREATING ARTWORK IN FLASH

In the previous chapter, we handed you a bunch of movieclips and graphics and essentially said, "Here, you toss them on the stage." In this chapter, we start digging into how those objects were created. In fact, you are going to be drawing trees, creating venetian blinds, and playing with Chinese dancers and T-shirts, among other things. We will be looking at the Illustrator and Photoshop File Importers, and also playing with JPG and GIF images.

Here's what we'll cover in this chapter:

- Understanding Flash graphic fundamentals
- Using the drawing tools
- Working with fills, strokes, and gradients
- Managing and working with color
- Working with bitmap images
- Importing images into Flash, including Fireworks, Illustrator, and Photoshop documents

The following files are used in this chapter (located in Chapter02/ExerciseFiles_Ch02/Exercise/):

- Deco.fla
- SprayBrush.fla
- GradientLock.fla
- ImageFill.fla
- Stools.jpg
- Dancer.jpg
- Trace.fla
- JPGCompression.fla
- JPGCompression.swf
- GIF.fla
- Counterforce.gif

- Fireworks.fla
- Clouds.png
- x-factor.ai
- banner.psd
- wheat_grass_01.psd
- wheat_grass_02
- wheat_grass_03
- text_fields_01.psd
- text_fields_02.psd
- banner.swf
- banner.fla

The source files are available online from either of the following sites:

- http://www.FoundationFlashCS4.com
- http://www.friendsofED.com/download.html

Let's start with the basics of Flash artwork.

Flash's two kinds of artwork

Artwork in Flash comes in two flavors: vector and bitmap. *Vector images* are created in a drawing application such as Illustrator CS4 or Fireworks CS4. When you draw an object on the Flash stage, you are using the drawing tools to create a vector image directly in Flash. *Bitmap images* are created in graphics applications such as Photoshop CS4 and Fireworks CS4, and imported into Flash (they actually can be created in Flash, but only with the use of advanced ActionScript).

At its heart, Flash is a vector-drawing and animation tool. The great thing about vectors is their relatively small file size compared to their bitmap cousins. Flash's roots began as a vector-animation tool (FutureSplash Animator) for the Web. When it was introduced, broadband was just getting established, and the ubiquitous 56K modem was how many people connected to the Internet. In those days, size was paramount. Vectors, being extremely small, load very quickly.

What makes vectors so appealing is that they generally require very little information and computing power to draw. In very simplistic terms, a circle of 100 pixels in diameter can be described by five points—four on the circle (north, east, south, and west) and one in the center—and those points are used in a mathematical calculation that results in the diameter of that shape. The computer might also need to know whether there is a stroke around the circle and whether the circle is being filled with a solid color, a gradient, or nothing. If you assume the circle is yellow and the stroke is black and 1 point in width, the description of this circle needs only a handful of data: the five points, fill color, stroke width, and stroke color.

Its bitmap counterpart is treated a lot differently. Instead of requiring a limited amount of information to draw the circle, each pixel's location in the circle is charted and remembered. Not only that, but each pixel requires three units of color information to produce the red, green, and blue values for that pixel. Additionally, the computer also needs to map and draw each pixel in the background on which the circle is sitting. This means that producing the yellow circle requires thousands of pieces of information, which explains why bitmap images usually add a lot of weight to a SWF's file size.

> *Every rose has its thorn, and you will encounter vector art that is mind-bogglingly complex—with anchor points in the hundreds of thousands, and even millions—so let your conscience (and a bit of testing) be your guide. Create a test SWF with the artwork in its original vector format—just the artwork in question, and nothing else. Then create a test SWF with the artwork converted to JPG, TIF, or the like. Use the format that adds the least weight to the SWF.*

Vectors are also device-independent. This means they can be scaled to 200% and still maintain their crisp edges. Scale a bitmap by that percentage, and the pixels become twice their original size. The image degrades because the pixels are tied to the device displaying them, which, in this case, is a computer monitor. If you've ever printed a photograph and seen a series of blocks in it, as if a mesh had been laid over the image, you've experienced what can happen when a device-dependent format is handled by another device.

What types of graphic objects does Flash support? Flash supports four types of graphic objects:

- **Shapes**: These are vector drawings, usually created with the Flash drawing tools or files imported into Flash from Illustrator CS4 or Fireworks CS4.
- **Drawing objects**: These are an alternate sort of vector shape you can draw with the Flash drawing tools. They behave differently from the shapes described in the first item, when combined in the same layer, thanks to something called Object Drawing mode, which you'll learn about in this chapter.
- **Primitives**: These are created with the Rectangle Primitive and Oval Primitive tools in the Tools panel. They're vector shapes yet again, but with a difference: they can be modified in nondestructive ways even after they're drawn.
- **Bitmaps**: These are raster images created in something like Photoshop CS4 and Fireworks CS4, and then imported into Flash.

So much for the raw material. Now let's look at the drawing tools in Flash.

> *There are a few additions to the drawing tools in Flash CS4: the 3D Translation and 3D Rotation tools, and the Bone and Bind tools. These are major upgrades to the lineup, and simply skimming over them in this chapter won't be doing you any favors. The 3D tools are covered in Chapter 9, and the Bone and Bind tools are covered in Chapter 8.*

The Tools panel

The Tools panel, shown in Figure 2-1, is where all of your drawing tools are located. Used along with Flash's Property inspector, effects, blends, and panels such as Color and Transform, Flash's drawing tools put a powerful, high-end graphics package at your disposal.

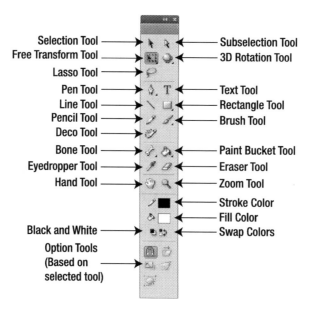

Selection Tool — Subselection Tool
Free Transform Tool — 3D Rotation Tool
Lasso Tool
Pen Tool — Text Tool
Line Tool — Rectangle Tool
Pencil Tool — Brush Tool
Deco Tool
Bone Tool — Paint Bucket Tool
Eyedropper Tool — Eraser Tool
Hand Tool — Zoom Tool
Stroke Color
Fill Color
Black and White — Swap Colors
Option Tools
(Based on
selected tool)

Figure 2-1. The Flash Tools panel

The tools can roughly be grouped into six distinct categories (they are not always logical groupings), as follows:

- **Selection**: The first two tools and the Lasso tool allow you select objects, select points within objects, and even select a piece of an object. Thematically, the Free Transform tool and 3D Rotation tool fit better in the modification category.

- **Drawing**: The seven tools in this section—Pen tool through Deco tool—can be used to draw images, create graphics and text elements, and draw shapes and lines.

- **Modification**: The tools in this group—the Bone tool through the Eraser tool, plus the Free Transform and 3D Rotation tools—allow you manipulate the shape and angle of existing objects, apply color changes to objects, and even remove a color or portions of an object. For example, you use the Paint Bucket tool to fill a shape or change its color. Color-related tools are typically used in conjunction with the color modification category.

- **Viewing**: The Hand tool and Zoom tool allow you to organize and magnify the stage while you work.

- **Color modification**: The four tools in this area—Stroke Color through Swap Colors—allow you to directly change colors of selected shapes or set the colors used by certain modification tools.

- **Options**: The options in this area change according to the tool you have selected. For example, select the Brush tool, and the options at the bottom will change to allow you to choose the size of the brush, the type of brush, and so on, as shown in Figure 2-2.

> *If you have used previous versions of Flash, you may notice that the tools have not only been regrouped, but also the names for the grouping sections have been removed. Certain tools—Free Transform, 3D Rotation, Pen, Rectangle, Brush, and Paint Bucket—have a small triangle at the bottom right. Clicking these tools and holding for a few seconds opens a drop-down menu that offers you a subselection of related tool choices. Color chips open the Color Picker.*

Figure 2-2. Select the Brush tool, and the tool options change.

Selecting and transforming objects

The odds are almost 100% that Selection and Subselection are the tools you will use most frequently in your everyday workflow. You'll also find the Free Transform tool indispensable, and its variant, Gradient Transform, very handy.

The Selection and Subselection tools

In the previous chapter, you used the Selection tool to move objects around the stage. It does a lot more than that. Let's experiment.

1. Click the Rectangle tool and make sure the Object Drawing button (in the Options section) is deselected. Draw a rectangle on the stage. Don't worry about colors for this exercise.

2. Switch to the Selection tool by either clicking it or pressing the V key. When you roll the tool over the square, a cross with arrows appears under the cursor. This means you are hovering over an object that can be moved by clicking and dragging.

> *Remember, all tools can be selected using the keyboard. If you roll the cursor over a tool, a tooltip will appear, and the letter between the parentheses is the key that can be pressed to select the tool.*

3. Click the rectangle and drag to the right. Holy smokes, you just pulled the fill out of the rectangle (see Figure 2-3)! Press Ctrl+Z (Cmd+Z) to undo that last action.

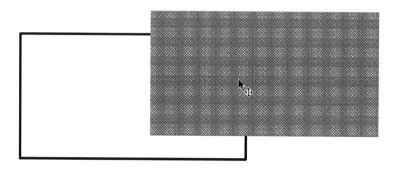

Figure 2-3. Selections in Flash aren't always what they seem.

You have just discovered that Flash regards all objects you draw as being composed of two components: a stroke and a fill. If you are an Illustrator, Photoshop, or Fireworks user, this may strike you as being a bit odd, because in a vector universe, separating stroke from fill is not a common behavior. Give us a minute, and we'll ease you back into more familiar territory. We have a rectangle to move.

4. To select the entire rectangle, you have two choices. The first is to double-click the item. The second is to "marquee" the stroke and the fill by drawing a selection box around the object. To draw your selection box, click outside the rectangle near one of its corners, and then drag toward the opposite corner. Go ahead and try both methods of selection, and then drag the rectangle. You'll see the whole thing move this time. You can also draw a selection with the Lasso tool.

5. Actually, there is a third approach to selecting and moving the stroke and fill as a unit. Marquee the object and select Modify ➤ Group. Now, when you click the object, it is regarded as a single entity and can be dragged at will.

The Selection tool can be used for more than simply dragging objects around the stage. You can also use it to modify the shape of an object. The stroke and fill of the rectangle on the stage, as you now know, are both vector objects. This means they can be resized or reshaped and still retain their crisp strokes and fills. Let's see how that works.

6. Select your object on the stage and select Modify ➤ Ungroup. Place the tip of the cursor on one of the strokes around the square. Do you see the little quarter circle below the arrow (see Figure 2-4)? That symbol indicates that you can reshape the stroke.

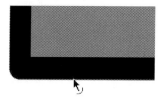

Figure 2-4. The shape under the cursor means the stroke can be reshaped.

7. Click and drag the stroke. When you drag the stroke, it actually bends. This tells you that the stroke is anchored, and, as in Illustrator CS4 or Fireworks CS4, if you drag a point on a line between two anchor points, the line changes its shape. The stroke uses the location where you released the mouse as the apex of its new curve, as shown in Figure 2-5. And did you notice that the fill also updates to reflect the new shape?

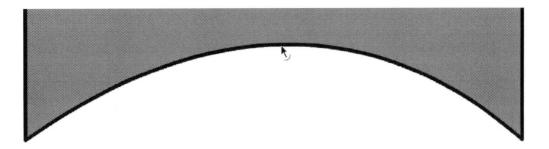

Figure 2-5. Both the stroke and the fill will change to reflect the new shape.

8. Select the Subselection tool or press the A key to switch to this tool. Double-click one of the corner points for the curve you have just created. The points and the handles become visible. You can further adjust the curve by moving either the handles or the points. These handles are only available on curves.

Another tool that allows you to manipulate objects on the stage is the Free Transform tool, which we'll look at next.

The Free Transform tool

If there is such a thing as an indispensable drawing tool in Flash, the Free Transform tool may just be it. This tool scales, skews, and rotates objects on the stage. Here's how to use it:

1. Select the object on the Flash stage and select the Free Transform tool by either clicking it or pressing the Q key. The selected object sprouts a bounding box with eight handles and a white dot in the center.

2. Roll the cursor over each of the corner handles. Notice how the cursor develops a rotate icon, as shown in Figure 2-6. This tells you that if you click and drag a corner, you can rotate the object. Try it out. You should also see a ghosted representation of the original rotation, which is a handy feature to ensure your transformation is correct.

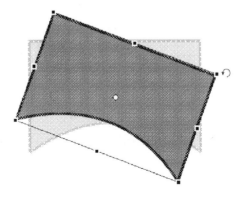

Figure 2-6. Rotating an object using the Free Transform tool

3. Place the cursor on the bounding box. The cursor changes to split arrows. This tells you that clicking and dragging will skew (or slant) the object in the direction in which you drag. Go ahead and give it a try.

4. Place the cursor directly over one of the handles. It changes to a double-headed arrow, meaning you can scale the object from that point.

The key to the Free Transform tool is mastering that white dot. It is the transformation point of the object. Rotations use that dot as a pivot, and any of the other transformations applied using this tool are based on the location of that dot when you hold down the Alt key.

5. Click the white dot and drag it over the upper-left corner handle. Rotate the object using the handle in the lower-right corner. The rotation occurs around that white dot. Undo the change, and this time scale the object using the bottom-right corner. Again, the upper-left corner is used as the anchor for the transformation, as shown in Figure 2-7.

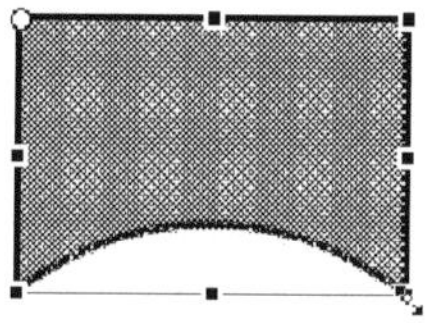

Figure 2-7. Scaling an object using the Free Transform tool

6. Now try another skew. With the white dot close to one of the corners, but not actually in a corner, place the cursor on the bounding box to see the split-arrows icon. Click and drag, and then hold down the Alt key and drag again. See the difference? Do the same with a scale transform.

To constrain the proportions of an object when using the mouse to scale the object, hold down the Shift key before you drag the handle. You can use Shift at the same time as the Alt key, as described previously, to both constrain and use the white dot as a pivot.

> *Have you applied a couple of transformations and now decided that you don't want to use them? To remove transformations, select* Modify ➤ Transform ➤ Remove Transform *or press Ctrl+Shift+Z (Cmd+Shift+Z). All transform actions applied to the object will be removed.*

The Gradient Transform tool

To the novice, gradients in Flash can be a little tricky. Moving the colors in the gradient around and changing their direction is not done at the time the gradient is created; this manipulation is done using a separate tool.

Let's try a couple different techniques with gradients:

1. Select the Oval tool, deselect the stroke, and draw a circle on the stage. (To deselect the stroke, choose the Stroke color swatch with a red slash through it.)

2. With your circle drawn and selected, change the width and height values of the circle to 120 and 120 in the Property inspector.

3. Click the Fill color chip to open the Color Picker and select the predefined blue gradient at the bottom of the panel, as shown in Figure 2-8.

There are a couple of ways to change this gradient in order to position the centered highlight elsewhere in the graphic. One method is to use the Paint Bucket tool. This tool simply fills a selected shape with the color in the Fill color chip, but it does something really interesting when the color is a gradient.

4. Choose the gradient and click the Paint Bucket tool to select it (or press the K key to switch to this tool).

5. Click in the upper-left corner of the circle. The center of the gradient moves to the point where you clicked the mouse, as shown in Figure 2-9. This happens because the "paint" pouring out of the tool's icon is the hotspot for the tool. The center of the gradient will be the point where the "pour" is located.

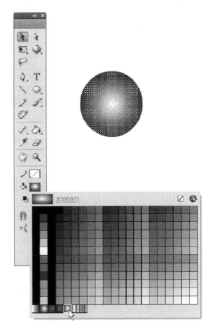

Figure 2-9. The tip, or "pour" point, of the Paint Bucket's icon is its hotspot.

6. Click again somewhere else on the shape to reposition the center point of the gradient.

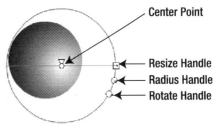

Figure 2-8. Selecting a preset gradient using the Fill color in the Tools panel

The other technique for changing the gradient is to use the Gradient Transform tool, which is more precise than using the Paint Bucket.

7. Click and hold on the Free Transform tool to open the drop-down menu and select the Gradient Transform. Alternatively, press the F key to switch from the current tool to the Gradient Transform tool.

8. Click the object on the stage. When you do, it will be surrounded by a circle, a line will bisect the selection, and three handles will appear, as shown in Figure 2-10. The circle represents the area of the gradient fill. Let's look at each of these controls:

Figure 2-10. The Gradient Transform tool allows you to precisely control a gradient.

- **Center point**: This is actually composed of two features. The white dot is the center point of the gradient and can be moved around in the usual manner. The triangle, which moves only along the line, determines the focus of that center point. Dragging the triangle to the edges can make the center point look a bit like a comet.

- **Resize handle**: Dragging this handle resizes and distorts the gradient without affecting the size of the filled object.

- **Radius handle**: Moving this handle inward or outward resizes the gradient proportionately.

- **Rotate handle**: Drag this handle, and the gradient rotates around the center point. The effect can be quite subtle with a radial gradient, but you'll see a difference if you first squeeze the gradient into a lozenge shape with the resize handle.

63

Now that you know how to use the tool on a radial gradient, give it a try on a linear gradient.

9. Select one of the linear gradients from the Fill color chip in the Tools panel.

10. Select the Rectangle tool and draw a square. Click the square with the Gradient Transform tool.

11. As you can see in Figure 2-11, most of the same gradient controls are in place. This time, two lines appear. These lines indicate the range of the gradient. If you click the resize handle and drag it downward toward the top of the box, the colors in the gradient become more compressed. The rotate and center point handles work the same as with radial gradients.

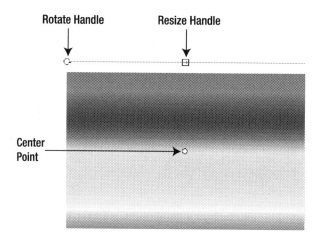

Figure 2-11. The Gradient Transform tool can be used on linear gradients as well.

Object Drawing mode

Introduced in Flash 8, the Object Drawing mode was greeted with wild cheering and dancing in the streets. Well, it didn't exactly happen that way, but a lot of designers became seriously happy campers when they discovered this feature.

Prior to the release of Flash 8, shapes that overlapped each other on the stage were, for many, a frustrating experience. If one shape was over another—in the same layer—and you selected and moved it, it would cut a chunk out of the shape below it. This is not to say it was a flaw in the application. In Flash, once you understand the "one piece eats the other" phenomenon, it becomes a great construction tool. It can be much simpler to throw down a base shape and take bites out of it to achieve a complex figure than to draw the same figure from scratch. Object Drawing mode uses the opposite concept. You get the best of both worlds, and the choice is yours.

When you select a drawing tool, the Object Drawing icon appears in the Tools panel, as shown in Figure 2-12. Click it, and the oval you are about to draw will be created as a separate object on the stage. It will not automatically merge with any object under it, even on the same layer. Let's see how it works.

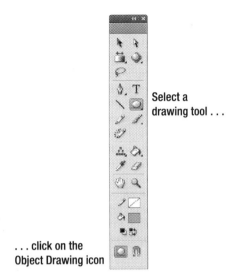

Select a
drawing tool . . .

. . . click on the
Object Drawing icon

Figure 2-12. Select Object Drawing mode
to turn on this feature.

1. Select the Oval tool, turn off the stroke in the Tools panel, and draw a circle over the shape on the stage.

2. Select the circle and drag it off the shape. When you release the mouse, you will see that your circle has bitten off a chunk of the shape.

3. Select the Oval tool, click the Object Drawing icon in the Tools panel, and draw another circle over the shape.

4. Drag the new circle away, and nothing happens, as shown in Figure 2-13. Hooray for Object Drawing mode!

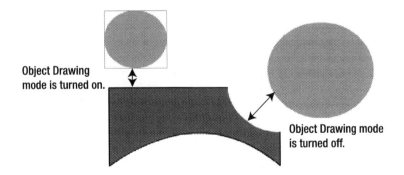

Object Drawing
mode is turned on.

Object Drawing mode
is turned off.

Figure 2-13. The effects of having Object Drawing mode turned on and turned off

When you drew that second circle, Flash offered you a visual clue that you were in Object Drawing mode: when you selected the shape, it was surrounded by a bounding box.

There's a little trick you can use to edit a single object in Object Drawing mode. Double-click the second circle you just drew. Everything but the object clicked fades, and the words Drawing Object *appear beside the* Scene 1 *link. This allows you to edit the object in place without disturbing anything else on the stage. To return to the stage, click the* Scene 1 *link or double-click outside the shape to go back a level.*

Drawing in Flash CS4

In this section, we will review the four main drawing tools:

- Pencil: This tool is used to draw free-form lines and shapes. It draws strokes.
- Brush: This tool paints fills. A new variant in Flash CS4 is the Spray Brush tool.
- Eraser: This tool is quite similar to the Brush tool, but it erases rather than paints.
- Pen: This tool draws Bezier curves.

The Pencil tool

When you select the Pencil tool, the Property inspector changes to allow you to set properties for the lines you will draw such as line thickness, style, and color. Also, when you select this tool, you can choose to use the Object Drawing mode. The Pencil tool has a modifier that appears under its lower-right corner. Click it to see a drop-down menu with three choices (see Figure 2-14), which control how the line behaves when you draw:

- **Straighten**: Use this mode if you want curves to flatten.
- **Smooth**: Use this mode to round out kinks or otherwise smooth awkward curves.
- **Ink**: This is the mode that gives you exactly what you draw. If you use this mode, make sure that Stroke Hinting is selected in the Property inspector. This will ensure crisp, nonblurry lines.

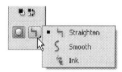

Figure 2-14. The Pencil tool has three modes.

To start, you'll get in touch with your inner child—you'll do some scribbling.

1. Open a new Flash document.
2. Select the Pencil tool or press the Y key.
3. Using the Pencil tool, draw three squiggly lines. Use one of the three modes (Straighten, Smooth, and Ink) for each line. The results will be slightly different for each, as shown in Figure 2-15.
4. Click the top line. Notice how you selected just a piece of it. The lines you draw with the Pencil tool are vectors.

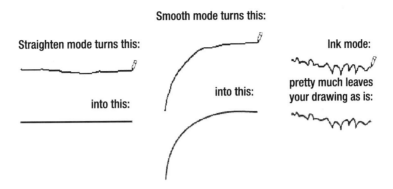

Figure 2-15. Use the Smooth and Straighten buttons to remove awkward angles.

5. Deselect the line segment, and then roll the mouse over the line. When you see a small curve appear under the mouse, click and drag. This tells you that you can change the shape of the lines you draw by simply moving their segments.

6. Double-click one of the lines and change the thickness and line style using the drop-down menu in the Property inspector. You'll see choices for solid, dashed, dotted, ragged, and so on.

7. Draw a circle using the Pencil tool in Smooth mode. Select the shape, and in the Tools panel's options area, click the Smooth button. Notice how the awkward edges of your circle become rounded. Now click the adjacent Straighten button a couple of times. Your awkward circle actually becomes a round circle. Double-click one of your lines, and click the Smooth and Straighten buttons to see how they work on nonclosed shapes. These buttons work independently of the Straighten and Smooth options available on the Pencil tool's drop-down menu.

> *Flash has preferences that will help you with your drawing chores. Select* Edit
> ➤ Preferences *(Flash* ➤ Preferences*) to open the* Preferences *panel. Click the* Drawing *category, and the panel will change to show how Flash handles the drawing tools, lines, and shapes. The* Recognize shapes *drop-down list can be set to take your hand-drawn approximations of circles, squares, triangles, and the like and replace them with truer shapes, as if drawn by the* Oval *or* Rectangle *tools.*

The Brush tool

You have discovered that all objects drawn on the stage are separated into strokes and fills. The Pencil and the Brush tools follow that separation. The Brush tool feels quite similar to the Pencil tool in how it is used. The difference between the two is subtle but also quite profound.

When you select the Brush tool or press the B key to select the tool, a number of options will appear at the bottom of the Tools panel (see Figure 2-16):

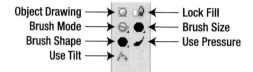

Figure 2-16. The Brush tool options

- Object Drawing: You saw this with other shape tools. It's the button that toggles Object Drawing mode. Piece of cake.

- Lock Fill: Select this to fill multiple objects with a single gradient or some other fill. This can be useful in cases where the gradient implies a highlight, as the "lighting" will be shared evenly across all selected objects.

- Brush Mode: This controls how the strokes are painted, and the drop-down menu contains the following five modifiers:

  - Paint Normal: Paints over any existing strokes or fills, provided they're on the same layer and not in Object Drawing mode. These caveats apply to the other mode options as well. If your content is a drawing object, use Modify ➤ Break Apart to turn it into a shape. When you finish, you can put it back together by selecting Modify ➤ Combine Objects.

  - Paint Fills: Paints the fill and leaves the stroke alone.

  - Paint Behind: Paints on only the empty areas of the layer.

  - Paint Selection: Paints on only the selected areas of the object.

  - Paint Inside: Paints only inside the area surrounded by a stroke. This mode works only if the Brush tool starts inside the stroke; otherwise, it acts like Paint Behind.

- Brush Size: Use this to change the width and spread of the brush strokes.

- Brush Shape: This drop-down menu offers a number of brush shapes, ranging from round to square to angled calligraphy nibs.

- Use Tilt and Use Pressure: These two options allow you to use the tilt and pressure sensors of a graphics tablet (a piece of hardware with a special drawing surface and "pen" that translates your actual hand motions into drawings on the screen).

The final control is the Smoothing option in the Property inspector. This option determines the amount of smoothing and sharpness applied to an object drawn with the Brush tool. In many respects, it is the same as the Smooth mode for the Pencil tool. Try it out:

1. Select the Brush tool and select a fill color.

2. Turn off Object Drawing mode and make sure the Brush mode is set to Paint Normal.

3. In the Property inspector, set the Smooth value to 0 and draw a squiggle on the screen.

4. Set the Smooth value to 50 and draw another squiggle on the screen. Repeat this step with a value of 100. As you can see in Figure 2-17, the edges move from rough to smooth flowing. Just be aware that high values tend to remove the curves from your drawings.

If these brush strokes don't look especially dissimilar to you, take a gander at the difference in the number of points required to display each one. By selecting each scribble with the Subselection tool, you can see the vertexes that make up each distinct line or curve in the whole shape, as shown in Figure 2-18.

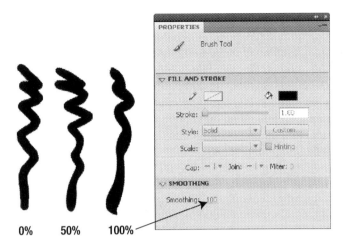

0%   50%   100%

Figure 2-17. Smoothing brush strokes

Figure 2-18. A haze of points on the left decreases to a countable number toward the right.

The Deco tool

The Deco tool seems to be something of an oddball, until you look past its surface. At first glance, all it seems to do is, well, draw vines—that's right, Tarzan's favorite mode of travel. If you think we're kidding, give it a try for yourself:

1. Open the Deco.fla file in the Exercise folder for this chapter.
2. Select the Deco tool, and then click somewhere near the upper-left corner of the stage to see Flash draw a series of pretty vines, as shown in Figure 2-19.

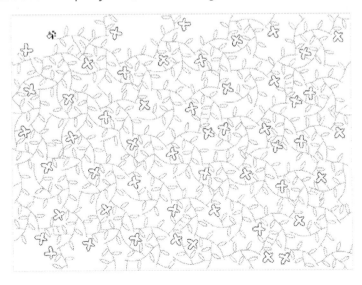

Figure 2-19. The Deco tool's default values result in a series of vines.

While this foliage is interesting, we suspect that few of you will actually want to use these vines in many of your projects (sure, maybe once, but after that?). The value of this tool isn't in its default settings, but rather in how the tool works. The Deco tool, as well as the Spray Brush tool introduced in the next section, is part of a new infrastructure in Flash CS4 called *procedural modeling*, which is just a fancy term for generating drawings with programming. In this case, Flash does all the programming.

So how can you make the Deco tool more useful? Keep reading.

3. Double-click the Eraser tool to clear the stage.

4. Reselect the Deco tool and take a look at the Drawing Effect area in the Property inspector. You'll see a drop-down menu. That's your ticket. Change that drop-down from Vine Fill to Grid Fill.

At this point, you can use the Deco tool as is, but it's more interesting if you give the tool an existing piece of artwork to play with.

5. Click the Edit button in the Drawing Effect area of the Property inspector. This opens a dialog box that lets you select a symbol named square from the library. Select square by clicking it, and then click the OK button to close the dialog box.

6. In the Advanced Options area of the Property inspector, change the Horizontal spacing and Vertical spacing values to 0. This will tighten up the spacing between the repeated square symbols you're about to see. Make sure to experiment with these values later as you try this tool on your own.

7. Click near the upper-left corner of the stage, and you'll get something like the image shown in Figure 2-20. Note that the resultant grid is grouped together as a single entity, which means you can use the Selection tool to move it around as a whole.

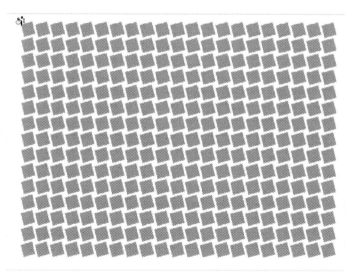

Figure 2-20. By using the Deco tool's Grid Fill option, you can quickly create grids.

Use this technique to create interesting backgrounds, flags, quilts, or whatever else makes sense for a grid layout. Using the Deco tool is considerably less work than positioning those elements by hand!

Remember that you can change the spacing between the symbol tiles, and you can select whatever library symbol artwork you want by clicking the Edit button before clicking the tool on the stage.

Ready for a truly versatile Deco tool option?

8. Double-click the Eraser tool again to clear the stage.

9. Click the Deco tool and select Symmetry Brush from the drop-down list in the Drawing Effect area of the Property inspector.

10. Using the Edit button, verify that square is still your selected library symbol.

11. In the Advanced Settings area of the Property inspector, select Reflect Across Line in the drop-down list.

12. Start clicking the stage with the Deco tool. Take care not to immediately release the mouse. Instead, click and hold, and then drag around a bit to see how that affects the symbol that is dropped onto the stage. Because you're in Reflect Across Line mode, you'll see a mirror image of your clicking on the opposite side of a pivoting handle (see Figure 2-21).

Figure 2-21. The Reflect Across Line option lets you create mirrored artwork.

13. After clicking a few times, hover over the top of the pivoting handle (the end with the curved double-headed arrow). Click that end of the handle and drag along a curve to rotate your mirrored artwork. Click and drag the opposite end of the handle to reposition the whole shebang.

14. In the Property inspector, change Reflect Across Line to Reflect Across Point. You'll see the draggable handle turn into a draggable circle, and one of the "arms" of your mirrored artwork is flipped (the mirroring is now up and down, as well as left and right).

15. Change Reflect Across Point to Rotate Around. This time, the mirroring increases many times. In fact, the result looks something like a kaleidoscope (Figure 2-22).

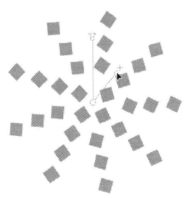

Figure 2-22. The Rotate Around option lets you create kaleidoscopic artwork.

16. As before, the curved double-headed arrow lets you rotate the artwork, and the opposite circle lets you drag it around the stage. A new handle—a shorter one, with a + on the end—lets you change the number of "arms" of your starfish. Click and drag the + circle clockwise or counterclockwise to make the change.

17. Let's try one last tool option. Double-click the Eraser tool, and then reselect the Deco tool. Choose Grid Translation from the Advanced Options area of the Property inspector. While you're in the Property inspector, put a check mark in the Default shape option in the Drawing Effect area. You'll use the default shape, rather than the square symbol from the library, which will give you a clearer view of the handles provided by this option.

18. Click the stage to paint a series of square dots, which is the default shape you just selected, as shown in Figure 2-23.

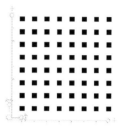

Figure 2-23. The Grid Translation option gives you dynamically modifiable grids.

Remember that you could have chosen a symbol from the library, just as you did to create the grid in step 5. In fact, the Grid Translation option is a lot like the Grid Fill option you saw earlier in this exercise. The difference is that with Grid Translation, you can actually modify the grid's characteristics dynamically.

Notice that the draggable handles are reversed from their previous configuration. This time, the curved double-headed arrow is the shorter handle, while the + handle is the longer one. In addition, the grid has two such pairs of handles: one for each of the x and y axes.

In Figure 2-23, the bottom-left circle lets you drag around the whole grid. Dragging either + handle away from (or closer to) that circle adds (or removes) dots or symbols for that axis. By dragging the respective double-headed arrow, you change the angle of that axis, which means you can slant (that is, skew) the grid along either axis, and then change your mind and slant it another way.

Experiment with the drag handles, and then take note of the Test collisions check box in the Advanced Options area. Keep that configuration in mind when you're using library symbols instead of dots. With symbols, you'll often find that the grid contains gaps. When that happens, it's because your symbols are overlapping. The Test collisions setting keeps that from happening by removing overlapped symbols. Deselect that option to suppress symbol removal.

> Grid Translation *isn't the only option that features the* Test collisions *setting. You'll see it with other* Deco *tool options, and it does the same thing every time.*

The Spray Brush tool

There is a new brush tool in the CS4 lineup, and it is seriously fun to use. It's called the Spray Brush tool, and like the Deco tool, it's part of the new procedural modeling framework. Here's how to use it:

1. Open the SprayBrush.fla file in the Chapter 2 Exercise folder.

2. Click the drop-down menu for the Brush tool and select the Spray Brush tool. The tool's icon looks like a can of spray paint. This should tell you that you are about to become a graffiti artist.

3. Open the Property inspector to see the tool's properties, as shown in Figure 2-24. Set them as follows:

- **Default shape**: You can spray with a symbol in the library or with a series of dots by selecting Default shape. If a symbol is not selected, you can't deselect Default shape. You get the dots.

- **Color**: Click the color chip under the Edit button to change your paint color. Set the color to #000099 (blue).

- **Scale**: Scrub across this value to make the paint drops wider. Set it to 200%.

- **Random scaling**: This gives you nonuniform paint drops. Select it for this example.

- **Width, Height, and Brush angle**: These configure the basic shape of the brush. Leave these at their default settings for now.

4. Click the mouse a couple times on the stage. Now click and drag the mouse. Having fun? Double-click the Eraser tool to clear the stage.

5. Change the brush's Width value to 20 and the Height value to 100 in the Property inspector. In addition, change the Brush angle setting to 45 CW.

6. Click and drag. As you can see, you can create some pretty interesting effects by changing the properties of the brush. With the current settings, you get a tilted calligraphy brush.

Figure 2-24. Spray Brush tool properties

Where this tool moves from neat to really cool is its ability to spray library items onto the stage. If you open the library, you will see that we have included a graphic symbol called pepper.

7. With the Spray Brush selected, click the Edit button in the Property inspector. This will open the Select Source Symbol dialog box. Click once on the pepper symbol, and then click OK. This updates the available properties for the brush, allowing you to set scaling separately for width and height, as well as choose additional random settings.

8. Use these values in the Property inspector:

- Scale width and Scale height: **20%**

- Random scaling: **Selected**

- Random rotation: **Selected**

- Width and Height: **120**

9. Click the mouse. Holy peppers! Click and drag around. You have just created a whirlwind of tamales, as shown in Figure 2-25.

Given the right library symbols, we're thinking this would make a great tool for snowstorms, starry skies, windblown leaves, and so on.

> *Want to know a neat trick? If you use a movieclip as your source symbol, you can even spray paint artwork that's animated! Graphic symbols will do that, too, but you'll need to add frames in the parent timeline to let the graphic symbol's own timeline play out.*

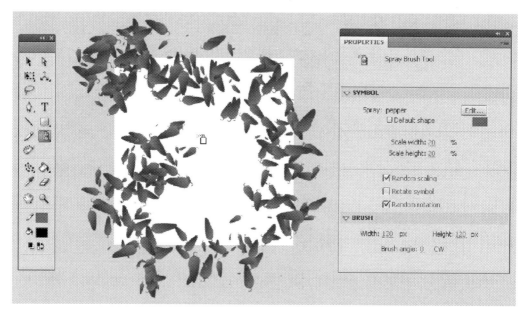

Figure 2-25. Using the Spray Brush with a symbol

The Eraser tool

You can erase only vector artwork that isn't protected inside a group of some kind. In other words, if you try to erase a symbol, a text field, or something drawn in Object Drawing mode, it won't work unless you break apart the grouped objects.

Select the Eraser tool or press the E key, and the following three modifiers appear in the Tools panel, as shown in Figure 2-26:

- Eraser Mode: This drop-down menu offers five choices, matching those for the Brush tool.
- Eraser Shape: The choices in this drop-down menu let you select from a number of shapes for the eraser.
- Faucet: Select this, and you can erase an entire fill or line with one click. The hotspot is the drip on the faucet.

Figure 2-26. The Eraser options

> Here's a quick way to erase the contents of an entire layer: double-click the Eraser tool to clear that layer. As an exception to the rule, this trick even erases grouped content in the relevant layer.

The Pen tool

If you use Illustrator, Fireworks, or Photoshop, you are accustomed to using the Pen tool. The interesting thing about this tool is that its roots aren't found in the graphics industry. It started out as a solution to a tricky problem faced by the auto industry in the 1970s.

Computers were just starting to be used in some areas of car design, and the designers involved faced a rather nasty problem: they could draw lines and simple curves, but squiggles and precise curves were completely out of the question. The solution was to use a calculation developed by the mathematician Pierre Bezier to produce what we now know as *Bezier curves*.

A simple curve is composed of a number of points. A Bezier curve adds two additional pieces of data called *direction* and *speed*.

The Pen tool draws Bezier curves. The two additional data bits are visually represented by the handle that appears when you draw a curve with the Pen tool. Here's how to create a Bezier curve:

1. Select the Pen tool or press the P key. When you place the cursor on the stage, it changes to the pen, and a small x appears next to it.

2. Click and drag. As you drag, you will see three points on the line, as shown in Figure 2-27. The center point, called the *anchor point*, is the start of the curve. The two outer points, called *handles*, indicate the direction and degree of the curve.

Figure 2-27. The start of a Bezier curve

3. Roll the mouse to another position on the screen, and click and drag the mouse. As you drag, the mouse handles and the curve get longer, and the curve follows the direction of the handle, as shown in Figure 2-28.

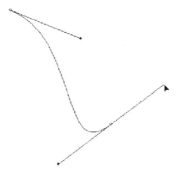

Figure 2-28. The curve shape changes based on the length and direction of the handle.

4. Click and drag a couple of more times to add a few more points to the shape.

5. Roll the mouse over the starting point of the shape. Notice the little o under the Pen tool (see Figure 2-29)? This tells you that you are about to create a closed shape. Click the mouse.

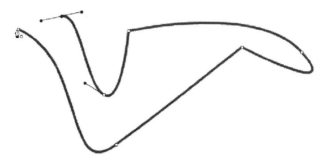

Figure 2-29. The shape is about to be closed.

A few other options available with the Pen tool allow you to edit your curves. If you click and hold the Pen tool in the Tools panel, you will see there are three extra choices:

- Add Anchor Point: Select this tool and click anywhere on the line to add an extra point.

- Delete Anchor Point: Click an anchor point to remove it. The shape will change.

- Convert Anchor Point: Click an anchor point, and the point will be converted to a corner point. Unfortunately, this conversion does not go both ways. To get your curve back, switch to the Selection tool and hover near a line that extends from the corner point. When you see the curve cursor, drag out a bit of curvature yourself, and then switch back to the Pen tool.

Prior to Flash CS3, these alternate Pen tool modes were not available as separate tools. Instead, they were presented as built-in features of an all-in-one Pen tool. The distinct choices were certainly a welcome addition, but the old way ends up providing a decent workflow boost, even though hovering in the right place takes a bit of practice. So take your pick. If you prefer using a single Pen tool, notice how cursor cycles among the following modes:

- **Add an anchor point**: Use the Subselection tool, if necessary, to select an existing pen drawing. Then, using the Pen tool, hover over an existing line. Notice how the normal x under the pen cursor becomes a +. Click to add a new anchor point.

- **Delete an anchor point**: There are two sorts of anchor points: curves and corners. Hover over a corner point, and you'll see the cursor acquire a little -. Click to delete the anchor point. Hover over a curved point, and you'll need to click twice: once to convert the anchor to a corner point, and the second time to delete it.

- **Convert an anchor point**: This converts curved anchors into corner points. In addition, the Alt key temporarily converts the Pen tool into the Convert Anchor Point tool.

Your turn: Trees grow at Lake Nanagook

In this little exercise, you are going to draw the tree that is used in the Lake Nanagook movie from the previous chapter. Along the way, we are going to introduce you to a couple of new tools. Let's get to work.

1. Create a new Flash document.

2. Select Insert ➤ New Symbol. When the New Symbol dialog box opens, name the symbol Trees and select Graphic as its Type. Click OK to accept the changes and to open the Symbol Editor.

Drawing the tree trunk

We'll start with the trunk of the tree.

1. Select the Pencil tool and, in the Smooth mode, draw a stretched oval shape. This will be the tree trunk. Select the shape on the stage and click the Smooth button.

2. Select the Zoom tool, which looks like a magnifying glass, and click and drag over your shape. When you release the mouse, the shape will be larger, so you will be able to manipulate it more easily.

3. Switch to the Subselection tool and click your shape. You will see the vector anchor points and handles. Manipulate the anchor points and handles to change the shape of the trunk. With the Selection tool, refine the shape by rolling the cursor over its edges, and when you see the curved line under the cursor, drag the line segment inward or outward to alter the shape.

4. Double-click the Zoom tool on the Tools panel to zoom out to 100% view.

5. Switch to the Selection tool if necessary, click your shape, and in the Property inspector specify these values:

   - Width: 17
   - Height: 37
   - X: 35
   - Y: 104.5
   - Stroke Color: #480000 (dark brown)

   > *If you really need to see the decimal values while scrubbing, hold down the Ctrl key. This allows you to scrub using decimal values.*

6. In the Tools panel, set the Fill color to #480000 and select the Paint Bucket tool or press the K key. Place the tip of the bucket in the hollow part of the shape and click the mouse. The tree trunk will fill with the dark-brown color, as shown in Figure 2-30. (An alternative would be to select the Brush tool, and, using the Paint Inside mode, paint the fill color into the shape.)

   Figure 2-30.
   The tree trunk is filled using the Paint Bucket tool.

   > *You are probably looking at the hex color value in the panel and thinking, "Hey, it's hot text. I can scrub it to get the color?" Be our guest. Give it a shot. Not easy, is it? When choosing color values, forget about scrubbing and input them directly instead. Why? Because you have more than 16 million colors to scrub through.*

7. Name the layer trunk and lock the layer.

With the trunk in place, next you'll draw the pine tree.

Drawing the pine tree

Think back to your youth and how you drew a pine tree. It was nothing more than a triangle. Here, you'll do the same and fill it with a gradient color.

1. Add a new layer named fir.

2. Select the new layer and select the Line tool in the Tools panel or press N on your keyboard. The Line tool draws straight lines and is great for drawing things like triangles.

3. Click and drag the tool on the stage to draw a line at an angle. Release the mouse, and the line is drawn. Repeat this step two more times to draw the three lines.

4. When you reach the start point of the first line, a circle will appear, indicating you are about to close the path. Click the mouse.

5. Select the Subselection tool and click the triangle. Notice how the stroke disappears and the anchor points become visible. Select an anchor point with the Subselection tool, as shown in Figure 2-31, and using either the mouse or the arrow keys on your keyboard, move the points until the triangle takes on the shape of a pine tree.

6. Switch to the Selection tool and roll the mouse to the bottom line of your triangle. When you see the small curve under the pointer, drag the line slightly downward. Your triangle should now look like a cone.

7. Double-click the shape to select it, and in the Property inspector, set its width to 81 and its height to 114.

8. With the object selected, open the Color panel and select Linear from the Type drop-down menu.

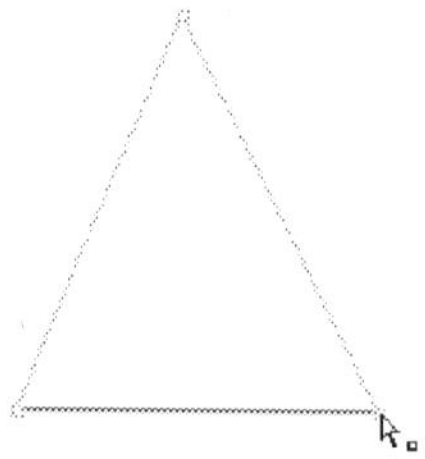

Figure 2-31. Use the Subselection tool to select and move move anchor points.

9. Click the left crayon and set its color value to #002211 (dark green). Set the color value of the right crayon to #004433, which is a lighter green.

10. Select the Paint Bucket tool and fill the triangle. The gradient, shown in Figure 2-32, gives the tree a bit of depth.

11. Switch to the Selection tool, double-click the stroke to select it, and press the Delete key. Move the tree over the trunk and lock the layer.

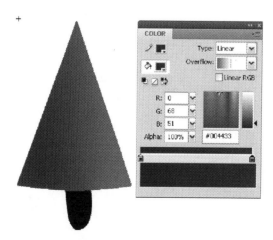

Figure 2-32. Use a gradient to give the tree some depth.

Adding pine needles

The final step in the process is to give your pine tree some needles. The key to this technique is to match the gradient on the tree. It is a lot easier than you may think.

1. Add a new layer named needles.

2. Open the Color panel, select the Stroke color chip, and select Linear from the Type drop-down menu. The gradient you just created is now in the Stroke area of the Tools panel.

3. Select the Pencil tool and set the Stroke Width to 20 pixels in the Property inspector.

4. Click the Custom button in the Property inspector to customize your stroke. In the Stroke Style dialog box, specify the following settings, as shown in Figure 2-33:

   - Type: Hatched
   - Thickness: Medium
   - Space: Very Close
   - Jiggle: Wild
   - Rotate: Medium
   - Curve: Medium Curve
   - Length: Random

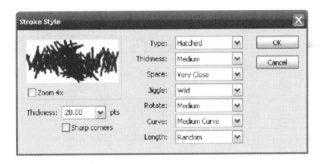

Figure 2-33. You can set the stroke style for the Pencil tool.

5. Use the Zoom tool to zoom in on the tree. Draw four lines across the tree, as shown in Figure 2-34.

This should also help you to understand how we did the grass that runs around Lake Nanagook. We simply applied a smaller stroke width to the oval used for the lake than the one for the pine needles.

> A number of preset strokes are available from the Property inspector's Style drop-down list, to the left of the Custom button.

Figure 2-34. Drawing a styled stroke

Working with color

So far, you have spent some time filling objects or strokes with either a solid or a gradient color.

Here, we will review the Color panel, and then discuss the color models and Color Picker.

The Color panel

As you've seen in the exercises so far, although the Color panel may look complicated, it is quite intuitive. The areas and controls are as follows (see Figure 2-35):

- Type: This drop-down list allows you to create fills using solid colors, gradients, and even photographs.
- Gradient Range: The two pointers, called *crayons*, allow you to condense or expand the colors' range. Additional crayons can be added or removed, as described after this list.
- Gradient Preview: Drag a crayon to the right or the left, and this area will change to show you the result of the movement.
- Alpha: Move this slider up and down to increase or decrease the opacity of the fill or stroke color.
- Swap Colors: Click this, and the fill and the stroke colors are swapped with each other.
- No Fill: Click this icon, and the stroke or the fill color will be turned off. Click it again to restore the stroke or fill.
- Black and White: Click this icon, and the stroke color becomes black and the fill color becomes white. This is basically a reset button.

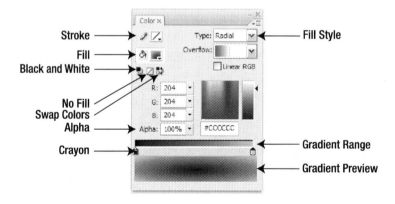

Figure 2-35. The Color panel

Crayons are the workhorses of this panel. These controls, in an area called the *crayon well*, slide along the Gradient Range area and condense or expand the range of the gradient. Swap their positions, and the gradient reverses. If you click anywhere between two crayons, you can add a third crayon (or more), and add new colors to the gradient. To remove a crayon, drag it anywhere outside the crayon well and release the mouse.

Color models

The purpose of this section is to dig a bit deeper into the color models available to you as a Flash designer and to show you a couple of really snazzy color techniques you can use in your day-to-day workflow. What we aren't going to do is get into color theory or take color down to its molecular level. Entire books have been written on those subjects.

In Flash, you have three basic color models available to you: *RGB*, *HSB*, and *Hexadecimal* (the default). Let's briefly look at each one.

The RGB model is the computer color model. Each pixel on your computer monitor is composed of a mixture of red, green, and blue lights. The value for each color is actually based on the old black-and-white model for computers, where there were 256 possible shades of gray, from black to white. The values started at 0 and ended at 255. The best way to imagine this is to think of 0 as being "no light," which means the color is black. Conversely, 255 is pure white. When it comes to the RGB model, each pixel can have a color value that ranges from 0 to 255. If you are looking at a pixel with values of 0 for red, 0 for green, and 255 for blue, you can assume the pixel is pure blue.

The letters in the HSB model represent hue, saturation, and brightness. Hue is the color, saturation is the amount of the color or its purity, and brightness (Flash uses the other term for brightness: luminosity) is the intensity of the color. The ranges for each value differ in this model. Hue goes from 0 to 360; that's one of 360 degrees around an imaginary wheel of color. Red starts at 0 (the same as 360). Green is one third of the way around the wheel, 120. Blue is two thirds around, 240. To see your secondary colors, shift your travel around the wheel by 60 degrees: yellow is 60, cyan is 180, and magenta is 300. Saturation and brightness are percentages. That pure blue value from the RGB model would here be hue: 240, saturation: 100, luminosity: 100.

> *The RGB and HSB color modes may be switched in the top-right corner of the Color panel, just below the x that closes the panel.*

The Hexadecimal model is the one commonly used on the Web. In this model, the red, green, and blue values for a pixel can include letters, which we realize may not make immediate sense. Hexadecimal colors have six characters, which are actually three pairs of values: red, green, and blue. These hexadecimal characters are a bit different from the decimals we're used to seeing. We humans, with ten fingers, count in decimal notation. We start with nothing and keep adding one to the "ones column" until we hit 9—that's a range of ten values, 0 to 9. Add one more, and the ones column can't go any higher, so it resets to 0, while the "tens column" advances by one.

Computers aren't so simple. Sometimes, they have 16 fingers on each hand, so their ones column goes from 0 to 15. Columns can hold only one character at a time, so after 9, the value 10 is represented by a letter—the letter A. 11 is represented by B, and so on, until 15, which is F. Add one more, and the ones column can't go any higher, so it resets to 0, while the tens column—actually, the "sixteens column"—advances by one. If your brain hasn't already turned to jelly, good, because even though this doesn't feel normal to us humans, it's not so hard.

That 1 in the sixteens column and 0 in the ones column look like 10, but in hexadecimal notation, that value is 16; 17 would be 11, 18 would be 12, and so on. A 10 in the ones column, as you now know, would be A. So what we would call 26—that is, a 1 in the sixteens column and a 10 in the ones column—would be 1A. Follow that through, and you'll see that FF refers to what we call 255 (that's 15 in the sixteens column, a total of what we call 240, plus a 15 in the ones column). Therefore, in the case of a completely blue pixel, the hexadecimal value would be #0000FF, which means zero red, zero green, and the full 255 blue. Note the pound sign, #, which tells the computer, "Hey, read this as a hexadecimal—rather than a decimal—number."

So hexadecimal notation is really just another rehashing of the RGB model. It's just a way to represent a range from 0 to 255 in each of the primary colors.

The Color palette and Color Picker

When you click a color chip in Flash, the current Color palette, shown in Figure 2-36, opens. The color swatches are arranged in hexadecimal groupings. As you run your cursor across them, you will see the hex value for the swatch you are currently over. The colors on the left side of the Color palette are referred to as the *basic colors*. These are the grays and solids used most often, although we don't know how often you'll use the bright pink and turquoise at the bottom of the common colors!

> *Actually, there is a reason for the pink and turquoise on the left in the Color palette. The left-hand column in that Color palette goes like this, from top to bottom: six even distributions of gray, from black to white; then the three primaries (red, green, blue); and finally the three secondaries (yellow, cyan, magenta). These colors, by the way, follow this hex pattern: red, #FF0000; green, #00FF00; blue,#0000FF; yellow, #FFFF00; cyan, #00FFFF; magenta, #FF00FF.*

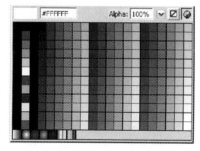

Figure 2-36. The current Color palette

Another really useful feature of the Color palette is the ability to sample color anywhere on the computer screen. When the Color palette opens, your cursor changes to an eyedropper and, if you roll the cursor across the screen, you will see the hex value of the pixels you're over appear in the Hex edit box, and the color will appear in the preview box. This is a relatively dangerous feature, because if you click the mouse over a pixel on your screen, that will be the selected color.

Clicking the color wheel in the upper-right corner opens the Flash Color Picker. Figure 2-37 shows the Windows version. The swatches in the top left are the basic system colors, and you probably noticed the pane on the right with all of that color that sort of looks like the Northern Lights gone haywire. This pane, called the color window, contains all of the color you can use in your movies. Click a color, and you will see its RGB and HSB values as well as a preview of the color chosen. You can adjust that color by moving the Luminance slider up or down.

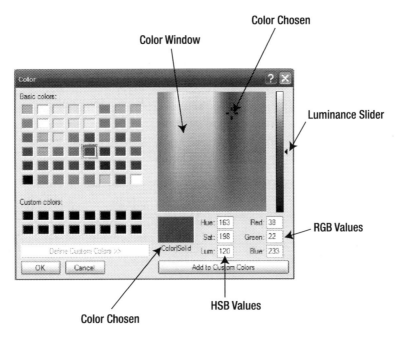

Figure 2-37. The Flash (PC) Color Picker

How many individual colors are available to you in the color window? The answer is over 16 million. One of the authors once answered this question, and the student who asked the question remarked, "Is that all?" The author told him that was one seriously large number of crayons in his box, and the student responded, "What if I want more?" The author thought about that one for a couple of seconds and asked the student to imagine a crayon box with 16 million crayons. "If you have a box of crayons, are they all given a color name on the label?" asked the author. The student replied, "Of course." The author then said, "OK, you have in your hands a box containing 16 million crayons. None are labeled. Start naming them." That ended the discussion.

How do we get 16 million colors? First off, the exact number is 16,777,216. At rock bottom, computers use base 2 notation (a.k.a. binary), and the use of millions of colors is referred to as being *24-bit color*. Three primary colors comprise each pixel, and each color is defined by 8 bits (2 to the eighth power is 256—aha, we've seen that number already). So that's where the 24 comes from: three times 8 bits, which is the same as saying 256 to the third power (256 × 256 × 256)—or 2 to the twenty-fourth power.

Figure 2-38 shows the Mac version of the Color Picker. Although the Color Picker may look different than the Windows version, it works in almost the same manner.

In the Mac-only color wheel, a color is chosen by clicking it in the wheel. If you want to adjust the RGB values, click the Color Sliders button at the top and select RGB Sliders from the drop-down menu. Figure 2-39 shows the Color Picker after making this selection. The Mac color-picking options are actually far superior to those on the PC. What the Mac can't do is create multiple custom colors. You will need to mix those individually.

You don't need to click OK on the Mac to save a color. You can drag and drop a color from the preview area into the Custom Color boxes at the bottom of the dialog box.

Figure 2-38. The Macintosh Color Picker

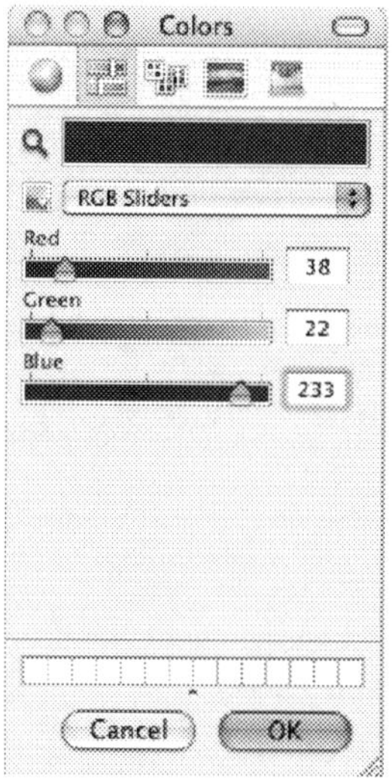

Figure 2-39. Choosing the sliders to change a color value

To add the color to your palette, either click the Add to Custom Colors button (PC) or click OK (Mac). Sadly, things are not always a bowl of cherries for PC users. The custom color you just added appears in the Custom Colors area of the Color Picker. That's the good news. The bad news is that if you add another custom color, Flash will, by default, overwrite your first color. If you are creating a number of custom colors, select the empty box before you pick your color.

Now suppose that you have a created a bunch of custom colors. Are they ready for use in all of your projects? Not quite. They are *not* automatically saved when you close Flash. If you create some custom colors and then close Flash, they will be gone—forever—when you return to Flash. So how do you save your custom colors?

Creating persistent custom colors

Saving custom colors in Flash is not exactly up there in the category of "dead simple." After you have created your custom color, you need to add it to the main Color palette, and then save it as a color set. Here's a quick exercise to demonstrate how to do this:

1. Open the Color panel, select the Fill color, and select Solid as the fill type. Create the color #B74867 (dusty rose), and make sure it is now the Fill color.

2. Click the menu in the upper-right corner of the panel to open the panel's drop-down menu. Select Add Swatch, as shown in Figure 2-40.

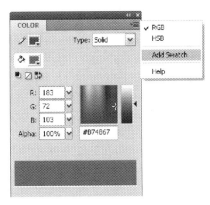

Figure 2-40. You start saving a custom color by selecting Add Swatch from the Color panel menu.

3. Click the Fill drop-down menu to open the current Color palette. Your new swatch will appear in the bottom-left corner of the swatches, as shown in Figure 2-41. You can add as many colors as you wish, but we'll stick with the one we are using here.

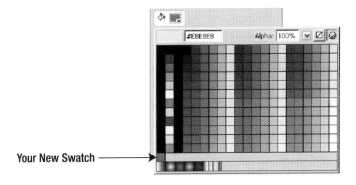

Your New Swatch

Figure 2-41. Your custom color now appears on the current Color palette.

4. Open the Swatches panel by selecting Window ➤ Swatches or pressing Ctrl+F9 (Cmd+F9).

5. When the panel opens, click the panel menu and select Save Colors, as shown in Figure 2-42. The Save As dialog box will open.

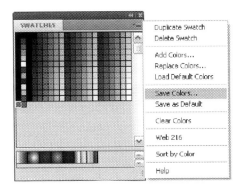

Figure 2-42. Saving a swatch

6. Name your file myFirstSet.clr and, as shown in Figure 2-43, save it to C:\Program Files\ Adobe\Adobe Flash CS4\Common\First Run (PC) or <Hard Drive>/Applications/Flash CS4/ Common/First Run/Color Sets (Mac). The .clr extension means the file is being saved as a Flash Color Set (CLR) file. Click OK to create the file and close the dialog box.

> You don't need to use the Flash application folder for your CLR files. Just put them in a location where they will be handy. Some Flash designers stick them in their My Documents folder, and others put them in the current project folder.

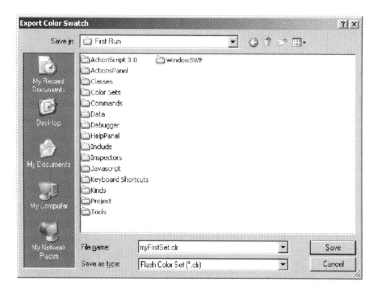

Figure 2-43. Saving a color set

7. To load the color set, open the Swatches panel and select Add Colors from the panel menu. Navigate to the folder containing the set and double-click it to add the set to Flash.

Yes, we agree that is a lot of work. Is there an easier way? In fact, there is. Why not do what the print guys do and attach a color swatch directly to the file? Let's assume you have a client who has six specific corporate colors that must always be used. Create a graphic symbol containing squares filled with those colors, and then simply put that symbol on the pasteboard (the area just outside the stage that doesn't show in the published SWF by default). Anytime you need the color, select the Eyedropper tool and sample it. If you are really lazy, don't add it to the pasteboard and sample the color using the Library Preview pane. If you use the colors in a lot of projects, you might even consider adding it to a shared library along with the client's logos and other common elements used in the client's Flash projects.

The Kuler Color Picker

A couple of years back, Adobe introduced a small web-based color picker named Kuler. The whole premise behind the application was to give the international design community an opportunity to freely share custom color schemes with each other. Needless to say, the application was a hit, and it has been quietly added to practically every Adobe application containing a color palette. Flash is no exception.

To access the Kuler color application, shown in Figure 2-44, select Window ➤ Extensions ➤ Kuler. Scroll through the list in the panel. If you see a combination, called a *theme*, you like, you can add it to your Swatches panel. Just click the arrow to the right of the set's name and select Add to swatches panel. When you open the Swatches panel (Window ➤ Swatches), you will see your selection has been added to the bottom of the color chips.

> *If the Kuler panel shown in Figure 2-44 doesn't appear, the odds are very good that you're looking at a dialog box that says you need to connect to the Internet and that this is accomplished through the Flash preferences. At the time this chapter was being written, there was nothing in the application preferences in regard to online services. Instead, select Window ➤ Extensions ➤ Connections to open the Connections panel. Here, you can enter the same username and password you use when logging in to the Adobe website (or create an Adobe user account), which allows you to access online features in component panels like the Kuler panel.*

You can also edit a swatch in the panel. Click the right arrow and select Edit the Theme. The Create area of the Kuler panel will open, as shown in Figure 2-45. Select a swatch and start making changes. Once you have a color or theme you like, click the Save Theme button to name your theme. If you want to return to the selection panel, click the Browse button.

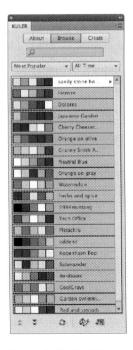
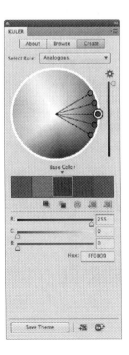

Figure 2-44. The Kuler panel   **Figure 2-45.** Editing a Kuler theme

> For more information about using the Kuler application, click the About button and then click the Kuler link to visit the Kuler site, or visit the Kuler tutorial at http://kuler.adobe.com/links/tutorial/.

Your turn: Play with color

Let's try a few tricks with color. Two involve the standard use of a tool, but the other is right up there in the realm of "That is *waaay* cool."

Creating gradient effects

The first trick involves a gradient. Did you know Flash allows you to create a variety of gradient effects with the click of a mouse? Here's how:

1. Open a new Flash document and create a big rectangle filled using the leftmost gradient in the Color Picker.

2. Switch to the Gradient Transform tool and resize the fill so it is much smaller than the rectangle. When you shorten the gradient, the black areas and the white areas of the gradient become larger. This is because Flash is filling the rectangle with the end colors. This process is called *overflowing*.

3. Open the Color panel and click the Overflow drop-down menu. You will see three choices (see Figure 2-46):

    - Extend: The last two colors in the gradient extend outward to fill the shape. This is the default.

    - Reflect: The overflow area of the rectangle will be filled with repeating versions of the gradient. Every other version is mirrored/reflected. Select this, and the rectangle looks like stacked pipes (see Figure 2-47).

Figure 2-46. The Gradient Overflow options

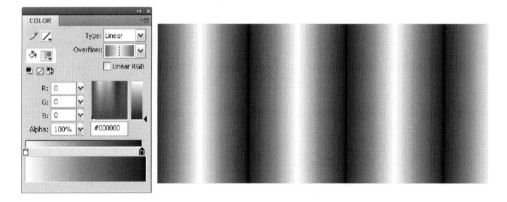

Figure 2-47. The Reflect overflow

- Repeat: The gradients aren't reflected. The result is the "venetian blind" look. as shown in Figure 2-48.

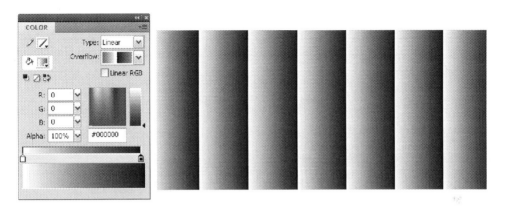

Figure 2-48. The Repeat overflow

If you really want to rock and roll with this technique, change the gradient type to Radial, reduce the size of the gradient with the Gradient Transform tool, and select the Repeat option. As shown in Figure 2-49, the result resembles the background of the Looney Tunes logo.

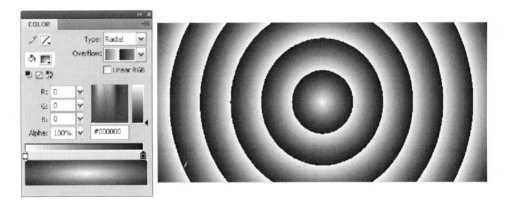

Figure 2-49. That's all folks.

Locking a fill

The next trick involves using a gradient fill to span across multiple unrelated objects. Here's how:

1. Open the GradientLock.fla file in your Chapter 2 Exercise folder. You will see a long rectangle filled with a gradient and a series of shapes under the rectangle.

2. Select the Eyedropper tool and click the gradient. The icon changes to a paint bucket with a lock under it. This is the Lock Fill feature of the Paint Bucket tool.

3. Click once inside a shape, as shown in Figure 2-50. You'll see that the gradient fill in the object exactly matches the portion of the gradient directly above it.

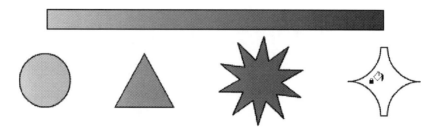

Figure 2-50. Using the Lock Fill feature of the Paint Bucket tool

4. If you want to unlock the fills, click the Lock Fill button on the toolbar. If you click inside a shape, Flash will regard the fill as being a new gradient, not a continuation of the one above it, and the gradient color will change accordingly.

5. When you finish experimenting, close the file without saving the changes.

Using an image as a fill

The final technique is one a lot of Flash designers tend to overlook: using an image, as opposed to a gradient or solid color, to fill an object. There are two methods of accomplishing this, and they each have a different result. Let's try them:

1. Open the ImageFill.fla file in the Chapter 2 Exercise folder and open the Color panel.

2. Select Bitmap as the fill type. In cases where the FLA does not yet contain imported images, an Import to Library dialog box will open at this point. In this sample file, an image already exists in the Library panel, so you'll see the Import button instead.

3. If you would like to import an image of your own, click the Import button. If you go this route, use the Import to Library dialog box to navigate to an image. Select the image and click OK to close the dialog box. Of course, you're welcome to use the already-imported Stools.jpg image. The image will appear in the Fill chip in the Color panel and in the Fill area of the Tools panel.

4. Select the Paint Bucket tool and click inside the object on the stage. It fills with several tiled copies of the image, as shown in Figure 2-51.

5. Select the Gradient Transform tool to adjust the tiled image in various ways. Given the minuscule size of the tiles, you may want to zoom in first.

Now let's see what happens with the second method:

6. Click the photo on the stage and select Modify ➤ Break Apart or press Ctrl+B (Cmd+B). The image looks crosshatched. Why? Because you've essentially converted the photo into a shape and filled it with its own bitmap, all in one go.

7. Select the Eyedropper tool and click once inside the photo. The image will appear in the Fill color chip of the Tools panel.

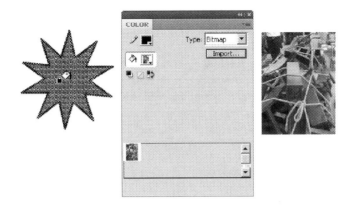

Figure 2-51. Using a bitmap as a fill

8. Select the Paint Bucket tool and click the star shape on the stage. The image, shown in Figure 2-52, now fills the star. Using this technique, the bitmap fill appears at actual size. If you want to tile it, or otherwise manipulate it, use the Gradient Transform tool.

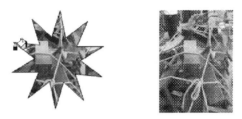

Figure 2-52. Another way of using a bitmap as a fill

Now that you have finally had a chance to use a bitmap, let's take a closer look at how such images are used in Flash.

Using bitmap images in Flash

Up to this point in the book, you have been working with vectors. Though we have been telling you they are the most wonderful things in the Flash universe, we are sure our photographer friends are not exactly happy campers. Let's face it—you are going to be using bitmaps in your workflow. You can't avoid them, and they are just as important as vectors. In fact, Adobe has really improved how Flash manages images and integrates with Photoshop CS4, Illustrator CS4, and Fireworks CS4.

Now we will look at how you can use bitmap images in your workflow. We are going to talk about the image formats you can use; cover how to import images from Photoshop, Illustrator, and Fireworks into Flash; and even show you how to convert a bitmap image to a vector image in Flash. Let's start with the formats that can be imported.

Importing image files into Flash

As an Adobe application, it is not surprising that Flash can import the following formats:

- **AI (Adobe Illustrator)**: This is the native Illustrator file format. This format allows Flash to preserve the layers in your Illustrator document. The good news is that the Illustrator-to-Flash workflow has had its molecules rearranged and turned inside-out—in a good way.

- **GIF (Graphic Interchange Format)**: This is the former standard for imaging on the Web. The upside of this format is the very small file size. The downside is the Color palette is limited to 256 colors. These files come in two flavors: transparent and opaque. The increasing use of Flash banner ads, with their strict file size requirements, has resulted in a resurgence of this format on websites (yes, for use inside SWFs).

- **PNG (Portable Network Graphic)**: This is the native format for Fireworks. Think of PNG files as a combination vector/bitmap file. This format supports variable bit depth (PNG-8 and PNG-24) and compression settings with support for alpha channels. PNG files imported into Flash from Fireworks arrive as editable objects and will preserve vector artwork in the file.

- **JPG or JPEG (Joint Photographic Experts Group)**: This is the current standard for web imaging, and any image arriving in Flash will be converted to this format when the SWF is published.

- **PDF (Portable Document Format)**: PDF is a cross-platform standard used in the publishing industry.

- **EPS (Encapsulated PostScript)**: Think of this as a raw vector file.

- **PSD (Photoshop Drawing)**: This is the native Photoshop file format. A PSD image usually contains multiple layers. Again, the workflow between Flash CS4 and Photoshop CS4 has undergone a profound change for the better.

- **PICT**: This is a Macintosh format comparable to a BMP file on the PC.

- **TIF or TIFF (Tagged Image File Format)**: This is usually a high-resolution CMYK document.

A bitmap, or raster, image is nothing more than a collection of pixels. Bitmap images have taken a bit of a bum rap in the Flash community because image files contain information that maps and remembers the location of each pixel in the image. The result is often a large file size, which tends to go against the grain in a community that chants: "Small is beautiful. Small loads fast."

Use bitmaps when you need photos or lifelike images, when you need a screenshot, or when the raster version of a drawing would actually demand less of the processor than its vector equivalent. Generally speaking, a good rule of thumb is to look at a bitmap image and ask, "Could I draw this in Flash?" If the answer is yes, you might want to consider doing exactly that.

The best advice we can give you about bitmaps is to make them as small as possible—a process called *optimization*—when exporting them from the originating application. That means reducing the Color palette when feasible and scaling the image to the actual dimensions used in Flash, rather than using Flash to resize the imported bitmap. For example, Fireworks CS4 contains an Optimize panel, shown in Figure 2-53, which allows you to compare the effects of various image settings for an image. In Illustrator CS4, see if you can reduce the number of points in your shapes, and make sure you have removed all of the stray points that aren't connected to anything. In Photoshop CS4 and Fireworks CS4, reduce the image size to fit the image size in Flash. These applications were designed to perform these tasks; Flash wasn't.

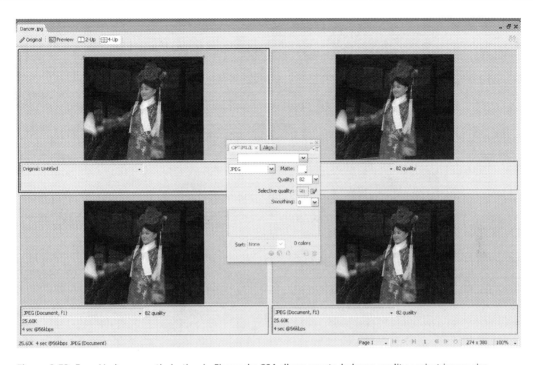

Figure 2-53. Four-Up image optimization in Fireworks CS4 allows you to balance quality against image size.

Editing imported bitmaps

The decision is final. You need to use a bitmap and place it in Flash. Then you discover the color is all wrong or something needs to be cropped out of the image. It needs to be edited. How do you do it? Follow these steps:

1. Open a new Flash document and select File ➤ Import ➤ Import to Stage. When the Import dialog box opens, navigate to the Dancer.jpg file.

2. Select the file and click Open to close the Import dialog box. The image will appear on the stage and in the library, as shown in Figure 2-54.

> *Do not delete the image from the library. This is the original bitmap, and deleting it will ripple through an entire project. If you mess up something on the stage, delete the image on the stage.*

3. Right-click (Ctrl-click) the image in the library to open the context menu.

4. Select Edit With. This will launch the Open dialog box, allowing you to navigate to the application folder containing the application you will be using to edit the image. If you select Photoshop CS4, the image will launch in Photoshop. When you make your changes, select Edit ➤ Save. When you return to Flash, the change made in Photoshop CS4 will be reflected both in the image on the stage and in the library.

Figure 2-54. Images imported to the stage are automatically placed in the library.

Fireworks CS4 has a rather cool feature called *round-tripp*ing. If you launch Fireworks CS4 as your editor, the image will open, and you will see a Done button at the top of the canvas, as well as notification that you are, indeed, "Editing from Flash," as shown in Figure 2-55, Make your changes and click the Done button. Fireworks will close, you will be returned to Flash, and the change will be visible on the stage and in the library.

Figure 2-55. Round-trip editing between Fireworks and Flash

If you're not using an Adobe product to edit your bitmaps, or if you edited them on another computer or at a different time, just right-click (Ctrl-click) the bitmap in the library and select Update.

Tracing bitmaps in Flash

Tracing converts an image to a series of vectors. On the surface, this sounds like a win/win for everyone. But that's not quite the case. Yes, you get a vector image with all the benefits of scalability and so on, but you also inherit a lot of potential problems along the way.

Tracing an image

There are no hard-and-fast rules in this area, so it is best to experiment. Let's fire up the Bunsen burner:

1. Open the Trace.fla file in the Chapter 2 Exercise folder. You will see two images of a T-shirt hanging in front of a street vendor's stall in Beijing, China.

2. Click the image over the text field that says Default Values and select Modify ➤ Bitmap ➤ Trace Bitmap to open the Trace Bitmap dialog box. Specify the values as follows (see Figure 2-56):

Default Values

Figure 2-56. The Trace Bitmap dialog box

- Color threshold: The higher the number, the more colors are considered a match and the fewer the vectors. Set it to 100.

- Minimum area: The number entered here defines the smallest size for a vector shape. If you want a really detailed image, use a low number. Just keep in mind that smaller the number and the more shapes you have, the larger the file size. In fact, extremely complex vectors can, and often do, carry a greater file size penalty than the bitmap images on which they're based. Set this to 8 pixels for this example.

- Curve fit: Think of this as being a smoothing setting. Select Pixels, and you get a very accurate trace. Select Very Smooth, and curves really round out. Again, the fewer the curves, the smaller the file size. This should be set to Normal for this example.

- Corner threshold: This value determines how much a line can bend before Flash breaks it into corners. The fewer the corners, the smaller the file's size. (Picking up a theme here?) This should be set to Normal for this example.

3. Click the Preview button to see the effect of your choices, as shown in Figure 2-57.

Figure 2-57. A traced bitmap is on the left, and the original image is on the right.

> *If you have used previous versions of Flash, you will find the* Preview *button in the* Trace Bitmap *dialog box a welcome addition to Flash CS4.*

4. Click OK to apply the change and close the dialog box.

5. Now let's see what happens when you use even closer tolerances. Select the image on the right of the stage and open the Trace Bitmap dialog box. Specify these values:

- Color threshold: 5

- Minimum area: 2

- Curve fit: Pixels

- Corner threshold: Many corners

6. Click the Preview button. The progress bar will take a bit longer this time, and when the tracing finishes, the difference between the original image and the vector image is not readily evident. Click OK to apply the changes.

You are about to find out that there is indeed a major difference between the original bitmap and the traced image. The difference becomes clear when you optimize the image.

Optimizing the drawing

In Flash, optimizing a drawing means you are reducing the number of corners in a traced image and smoothing out the lines in the traced image to give you a smaller and less-precise image. Though you can optimize any drawing you have in Flash, this technique is best applied to traced bitmaps, because traced bitmaps are usually very complex once they become vectors. Here's how:

1. Change to the Selection tool and marquee the first image you traced.

2. Select Modify ➤ Shape ➤ Optimize to open the Optimize Curves dialog box, as shown in Figure 2-58.

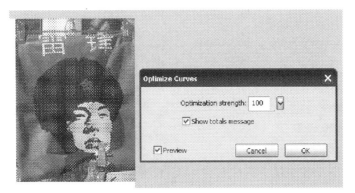

Figure 2-58. The Optimize Curves dialog box lets you reduce the size of a traced image.

3. Drag the Optimization strength slider up to the Maximum value of 100 and click OK. The process starts, and when it finishes, you will be presented with an alert box telling you how many curves have been optimized, as shown in Figure 2-59.

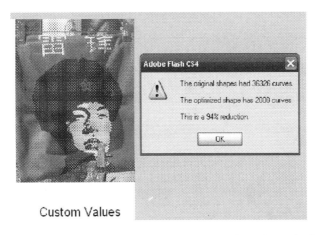

Figure 2-59. A 94% curve reduction means a significantly smaller file size.

The downside is that the image loses a lot of its precision, and some of the curves become spiky because Flash converted all the pixelated smoothness to vectors. If you repeat the process on the second image but move the Optimization strength slider only to the midpoint, the process will take a lot longer than the previous one, and the curve reduction will be minimal. This is because you essentially created a high-resolution vector image, so there are a lot more curves to check out. The bottom line here is that the decision regarding using a bitmap, tracing it, and optimizing the curves is up to you.

Using JPG files in Flash

The JPG (or JPEG) file format is the one used for photos. As mentioned earlier, JPEG stands for Joint Photographic Experts Group and is a method of compressing an image using areas of contiguous color. The file size reductions can be significant, with minimal to moderate image quality loss. This explains why this format has become a de facto imaging format for digital web media. In this section, you are going to learn how to optimize a JPG image in Flash.

Before you do this, it is extremely important to understand that the JPG format is *lossy*. This means each time a JPG image is compressed in the JPG format, the image quality degrades. The point here is that you must make a decision regarding JPG images before they arrive in Flash. Will the compression be done in Photoshop or Fireworks, or will Flash handle the chores? If the answer is Flash, always set the JPG Quality slider in Photoshop or Fireworks to 100% to apply minimal compression. If you don't know where the image came from or what compression was used, don't let Flash handle the compression.

Let's experiment with a JPG:

1. Open the JPGCompression.fla file in your Chapter 2 Exercise folder. Notice that the movie contains nothing more than a single JPG image, and the stage matches the image dimensions. In short, there is no wasted space that can skew the results of this experiment.

2. Minimize Flash and open the Chapter 2 Exercise folder. Inside the folder is a file named JPGCompression.swf. It is the compiled version of the FLA file, and if you check its file size, you will see it comes in at about 44KB. Let's see if we can shed some weight from this file.

3. Return to Flash and save the open Flash file to your Exercise folder by selecting File ➤ Save As and naming the file JPGCompression2.fla.

4. Double-click the image in the library to open the Bitmap Properties dialog box, as shown in Figure 2-60. The image on the left side is the preview image. As you start playing with some of the settings, this image will show the final result of your choices. This is a good thing, because changes you make in this dialog box are visible only when the SWF file is running; they won't be reflected in the image on the stage. The other areas are as follows:

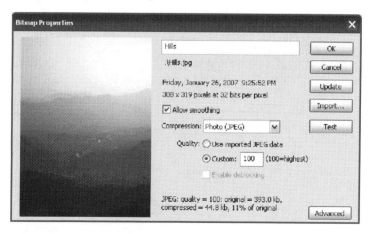

Figure 2-60. The Bitmap Properties dialog box

- **Name**: The name of the file. If you want to rename the file, select it and enter a new name. This changes only the name by which Flash knows the file; it does not reach outside Flash and rename the original image.

- **Path, date, and dimensions**: There will be the odd occasion where this information will not be displayed. This happens when the image was pasted in from the clipboard.

- **Update button**: If you have edited the image without using the Edit with feature, clicking this button will replace the image with the new version. This button will not work if you have saved or moved the original image to a new location on the computer. To reconnect such a broken link, respecify the image file's location with the Import button, as explained next.

- **Import button**: Click this button to open the Import Bitmap dialog box. When using this button, the new file will replace the image in the library, and all instances of that image in your movie will also be updated.

- **Allow smoothing option**: Think of this as anti-aliasing applied to an image. This feature tends to blur an image, so use it judiciously. Where it really shines is when it is applied to low-resolution images, because it reduces the dreaded jaggies.

- **Compression drop-down menu**: This allows you to change the image compression to either Photo (JPEG) or Lossless PNG (PNG/GIF). Use Photo (JPEG) for photographs. Use Lossless PNG (PNG/GIF) for images with simple shapes and few colors, such as line art or logos. To help you wrap your mind around this, the image in the dialog box uses Photo (JPEG) compression, and if you click the Test button, the file size is about 2.4KB. Apply Lossless compression and click the Test button, and the file size rockets up to 142KB.

- **Quality option**: Select the Use Imported JPEG data check box if the image has already been compressed or if you aren't sure whether compression has been applied. Checking this avoids the nasty results of applying double compression to an image. If you deselect the Use Imported JPEG data check box, you can apply your own compression settings. In fact, let's try it.

> *Be aware that any changes made in the* Bitmap Properties *dialog box ripple through the entire movie and will override the defaults used in the* Publish *dialog box.*

5. Make sure your compression setting is Photo (JPEG) and that you have deselected the Use Imported JPEG Data check box. Change the Quality value to 10% and click the Test button. The image in the preview area, shown in Figure 2-61, is just plain awful. The good news is the file size, at the bottom of the dialog box, is 1KB.

6. Change the Quality setting to 50% and click the Test button. Things are a little better, but the sky in the upper-left corner looks pixelated, and the file size has gone up to 2.4KB.

7. Change the Quality value to the normal 80% value used by imaging applications and click the Test button. The sky issue is resolved, but the file size has risen to 6.1KB, as shown in Figure 2-62. As you are seeing, there is an intimate relationship between the Quality setting and file size.

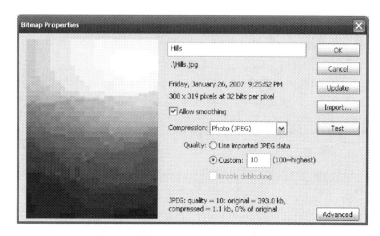

Figure 2-61. At 10% quality, the image is terrible.

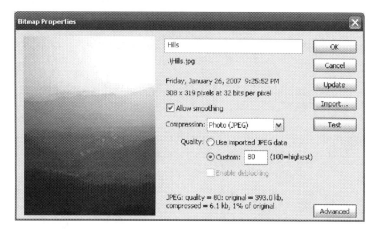

Figure 2-62. At 80% quality, the image is much better.

8. Knowing that the quality between 50% and 80% is a vast improvement, let's see if we can maintain quality but reduce the file size. Set the Quality value to 65% and click the Test button. The difference between 65% and 80% is minimal, but the file size has reduced to 3KB. Click OK to apply this setting and close the dialog box.

9. Save the movie and press Ctrl+Enter (Cmd+Return) to test the movie. This will create the SWF you need.

10. Minimize Flash and the SWF window and navigate to your Exercise folder. The results are, to say the least, dramatic. The file size has reduced to 6KB from 44KB, as shown in Figure 2-63.

Figure 2-63. Applying compression in Flash can result in seriously smaller and more efficient SWF files.

11. Save and close the open movie.

Using GIF files in Flash

There was a point a few years back where many web and Flash designers were preparing to celebrate the death of the GIF image and the GIF animation. The reason was simple: in a universe where bandwidth is plentiful and every computer on the planet is able to display 16-bit color, the limited color range and small file size of a GIF image become irrelevant. GIF images were developed for a time of limited color depth—monitors that could display only 256 colors—and dial-up modems. Then a funny thing happened on the way to the wake: the GIFs arose from their deathbed. The reason was banner advertising.

Ad agencies and their clients were discovering the Web really was a viable advertising medium and that Flash was a great interactive tool for ads. The problem was that standards for banner advertising appeared on the scene, and the agencies discovered they were handed a file size limit of 30KB. This tended to go against the grain, and as they grappled with the requirement for small files, they rediscovered the GIF image and the GIF animation. This isn't to say you should use the GIF format only in banner ads. It can be used in quite a few situations where size is a prime consideration.

Working with GIF images

Here's how to use GIF images in Flash:

1. Open the `GIF.fla` file in your Chapter 2 Exercise folder. When the file opens, open the library. There are two GIF files in the library.

2. Drag the Figurines image from the library to the stage. Notice how you can see the stage color behind the image. This image is a transparent GIF. GIF transparency is an absolute: it is either on or off. There are no shades of opacity with this format. GIFs may contain up to 256 colors, and one of those colors can optionally be transparent.

3. Drag the FigurinesNoTrans image to the stage and place it under the image already there. This is a GIF image with no transparency applied.

4. Select the image you just dragged onto the stage and press Ctrl+B (Cmd+B) to break apart the image (see Figure 2-64). Hold on—that isn't right. Shouldn't the background disappear? Nope, it's still there, because it's a part of the original GIF file. Break apart the Figurines image, and you'll see the same thing. Even the transparent area gets the pixelated look of all selected, ungrouped vector artwork. So in both cases, the GIF's background color is present; it's just that one color is transparent.

Figure 2-64. Transparent and regular GIFs are treated the same, but displayed differently in Flash.

When you break apart an image like this, the image is simply translated into a shape with a bitmap fill. It is the same thing as drawing a shape and filling it with that bitmap. This is why the file size is identical for the white and transparent versions of this image. The GIF is the same in all respects, except that the color slot in one file's color table is white and in the other file's color table is transparent. Both GIFs have the same number of colors and weigh the same.

5. To get rid of the white background, drag in the edges of the shape that contains the white version (just as with the star shape from the earlier bitmap fill example). Use the Selection tool or the Subselection tool. Obviously, this would be nearly impossible by hand with an image of this complexity, but any portion of the bitmap fill can be hidden by changing the shape that contains it.

6. Close the file and don't save the changes.

Working with GIF animations

Animated GIFs are a bit different. They are a collection of static images—think of a flip book—that play, one after the other, at a set rate, all stored inside a single GIF file. These flip book pages can be imported either directly into the main timeline (not a good idea) or into a separate movieclip (good idea, because you can move the image sequence as a single unit). Here's how:

1. Open a new Flash document and create a new movieclip named Counterforce. The Symbol Editor will open.

2. Select File ➤ Import ➤ Import to Stage, and when the Open dialog box appears, locate the Counterforce.gif file, select it, and click the Open button.

3. When the import is finished, you will see that each frame of the animation has its own Flash frame, and each image in the animation has its own image in the library, as shown in Figure 2-65.

Figure 2-65. Importing GIF animations into a movieclip

4. Press the Enter (Return) key to test the animation, or click the Scene 1 link to return to the main timeline, add the movieclip to the stage, and test the movie.

> A good habit to develop is to place your bitmap images in the library into a library folder. This way, your library doesn't end up looking like what mom would call "a pig sty."

Importing Fireworks CS4 documents

When Macromedia was acquired by Adobe in 2006, the betting in the Macromedia community was that Fireworks, Macromedia's web imaging application, would simply not make the cut. The market regarded Fireworks as a competitor to Photoshop—even though it wasn't—and so considered the application doomed to extinction.

What the Macromedia community failed to comprehend was that Adobe, prior to the acquisition, had quietly announced it was no longer supporting ImageReady, which was the web imaging application for Photoshop. When the acquisition was settled, Fireworks did indeed make the cut. In fact, Adobe had decided to reposition Fireworks CS4 as a rapid prototyping application for web designers. Along the way, Adobe improved how Fireworks PNG files integrate with Flash CS4 (as well as Illustrator CS4, Flex Builder 3, and Photoshop CS4) and the movement of files from Photoshop and Illustrator into Fireworks. The end result is that Flash designers now have a tool that will seriously improve their workflow.

In later chapters, we will show you how Fireworks integration can be a huge time-saver. For now, let's concentrate on getting a PNG image—the native file format used by Fireworks—into Flash.

As you can see in Figure 2-66, the Fireworks file we will be working with is composed of one layer, Background, and three sublayers. When you import this PNG image into Flash, you will see these layers move, intact, into the movie.

Figure 2-66. We start with a Fireworks CS4 PNG image.

To import the PNG image, follow these steps:

1. Open the Fireworks.fla file. You will see the stage is blank and is set to the dimensions of the Fireworks image.

2. Select File ➤ Import to Stage and navigate to the Clouds.png image in the Chapter 2 Exercise folder.

3. When you click the Open button, the dialog box will close, and the Import Fireworks Document dialog box will open, as shown in Figure 2-67. Let's review the options:

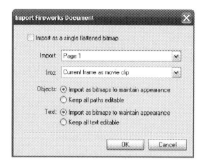

Figure 2-67. The Import Fireworks Document dialog box

- Import as a single flattened bitmap: This option flattens all of the layers into a bitmap.

- Import: The important aspect of this is not the image, but the fact you are being asked to import pages. This feature was first introduced to Flash CS3. Because it is a rapid prototyping application, Fireworks CS4 is able to create multipage documents for websites. If the PNG file contains multiple pages, you can select the page to be imported from the drop-down menu.

- Into: Select Current frame as movie clip so all of the layers in the image are placed into separate layers in the movieclip. When this occurs, Flash creates a new folder in the library named Fireworks Objects and places the movieclip in this folder. The other Into choice allows you to add the selected page as a new layer on the main timeline.

- Objects: The choices are to flatten everything on the Fireworks layer or to keep each object editable.

- Text: The choices are the same as those for objects. We tend to keep text editable just in case there is a typo.

4. Go with the default values for this example. Click OK to import the image into Flash.

5. When the import finishes, you will see the Fireworks Objects folder in the library. Open it, and you will see that Flash has created a folder for the page just imported. If you open that folder, you will see the movieclip and a flattened bitmap of the file.

6. Double-click the movieclip to open it. Compare the Flash file (shown in Figure 2-68) to the Fireworks file (shown in Figure 2-66). You can now either save the file or close it without saving the changes.

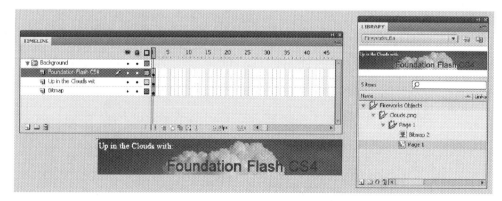

Figure 2-68. The Flash movieclip layers match those in the Fireworks PNG image.

Importing Illustrator CS4 documents

Prior to Flash CS3, the movement of Illustrator documents into Flash was, understandably, difficult. The products came from different companies, and Flash designers, realizing this, took the path of least resistance and simply copied and pasted their Illustrator drawings into Flash movieclips. This has all changed.

Flash lets you import Illustrator AI files directly into Flash, and it generally allows you to edit each piece of the artwork when it is in Flash. The Illustrator File Importer (introduced in Flash CS3) also provides you with a great degree of control in determining how your Illustrator artwork is imported into Flash. For example, you can now specify which layers and paths in the Illustrator document will be imported into Flash, and even have the Illustrator file be converted to a Flash movieclip.

The Illustrator File Importer provides the following key features:

- It preserves editability of the most commonly used Illustrator effects, such as the Flash filters and blend modes that Flash and Illustrator have in common.
- It preserves the fidelity and editability of gradient fills.
- It imports Illustrator symbols as Flash symbols.
- It preserves the number and position of Bezier control points; the fidelity of clip masks, pattern strokes, and fills; and object transparency.
- It provides an improved copy-and-paste workflow between Illustrator and Flash. A copy-and-paste dialog box provides settings to apply to AI files being pasted onto the Flash stage.

To many Flash designers, that list is nirvana, but there are two critical aspects of the Illustrator-to-Flash workflow that must be kept in mind:

- Flash supports only the RGB color space. If the Illustrator image is a CMYK image, do the CMYK-to-RGB conversion in Illustrator before importing the file into Flash.
- To preserve drop shadow, inner glow, outer glow, and Gaussian blur effects in Flash CS4, import the object to which these filters are applied as a Flash movieclip. In Flash, these filters can be applied only to movieclips, buttons, or text, and movieclips usually provide the best mapping between the applications.

Let's import an Illustrator CS4 drawing to see what is causing all of the joy. The file we will be using, x-factor.ai, contains a number of Illustrator layers and paths (see Figure 2-69). One path—in the star layer—contains a drop shadow.

> *The authors would like to thank Bruce Hartman for the use of the x-factor.ai file. His original design, built from this file, won the Best Bowed Kite in the Adult Division at the 35th Annual Smithsonian Kite Festival in 2001 and the Grand Master award at the Old Dominion Sport Kite Championships in the same year. Bruce likes to get his hands dirty in all sorts of artistic endeavors, many of which he recounts on his blog, http://www.BruceHartman.net/.*

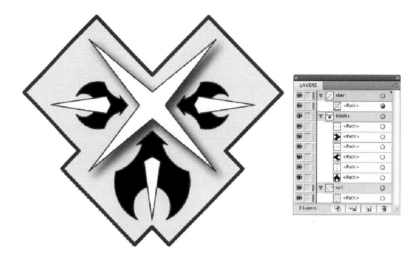

Figure 2-69. The Illustrator CS4 file for this example contains a number of layers and paths.

Importing an AI file

Follow these steps to import an Illustrator CS4 document into Flash CS4:

1. Open a new Flash document and import the x-factor.ai file into the Flash library. The Import dialog box, shown in Figure 2-70, will appear. Keep in mind the star layer contains a drop shadow filter, and as you can see, Flash will import that layer as a movieclip in order to retain the drop shadow.

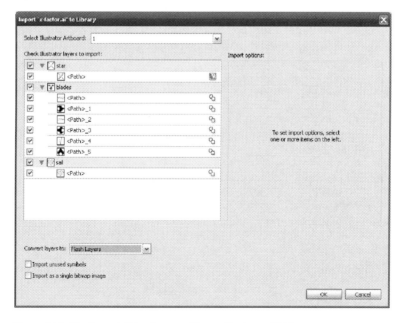

Figure 2-70. The Import dialog box used for an Illustrator CS4 image

2. Select the remaining layers, not the paths, and select Create movie clip, as shown in Figure 2-71. You can leave the Instance name field blank, because you don't need ActionScript interaction here. The Convert layers to drop-down menu allows you to convert your Illustrator layers to Flash layers or to a series of Flash keyframes (this is handy if they'll be animated), or to put the whole image into one Flash layer. You are also given the opportunity to import unused symbols created in Illustrator or to flatten the image and bring it in as a bitmap.

> The Import unused symbols *option may be a bit confusing. Illustrator allows you to create symbols, and these symbols can be imported directly into Flash from Illustrator. We will show how this works in the next chapter.*

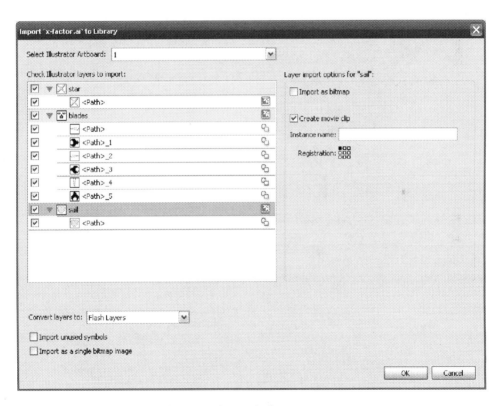

Figure 2-71. Illustrator layers can be coverted to movieclips.

3. Click OK. When the import process finishes, open the library, as shown in Figure 2-72. The image has been brought into Flash as a graphic symbol, but each of the layers has its own folder containing the movieclip you created in the Import dialog box.

107

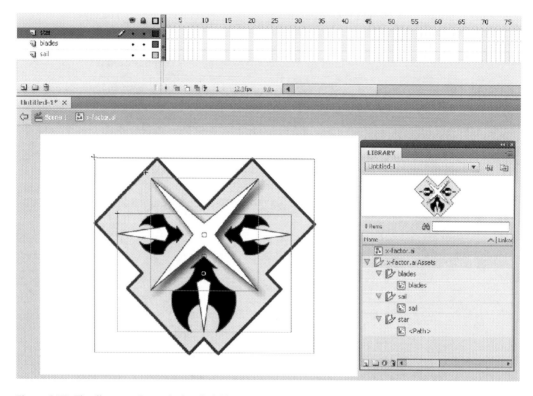

Figure 2-72. The Illustrator image in the Flash library. Note the drop shadow on the star.

Copying and pasting an AI file

At the beginning of this section, we mentioned how developers would simply copy Illustrator documents and paste them into Flash to avoid "issues." This can still be done. When you paste the drawing into Flash CS4, the dialog box shown in Figure 2-73 appears. This dialog box is fairly self-explanatory, though you may be wondering about the AI File Importer preferences choice.

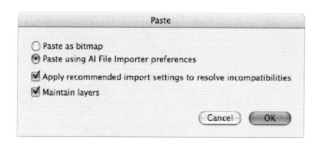

Figure 2-73. Pasting a drawing from Illustrator to Flash will bring up this dialog box.

The preferences can be found in Edit ➤ Preferences (Flash ➤ Preferences). In the Preferences dialog box, click the AI File Importer selection at the bottom of the Category list. This will open the AI File

Importer preferences, as shown in Figure 2-74. As you can see, many of the choices are also available in the Import dialog box.

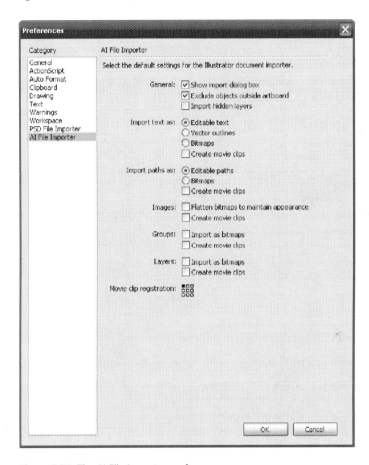

Figure 2-74. The AI File Importer preferences

Putting the AI file on the stage

You are most likely looking at the kite image in the library and thinking, "That's all well and good, but how do I get the dang document onto the Flash stage and play with it?" You simply drag the x-factor.ai library asset from the library on to the stage, and then double-click the image on the stage. You will see the image is actually composed of the movieclips in the Assets folder from the library, and that each movieclip is on a separate, named layer, as shown earlier in Figure 2-72.

Importing Photoshop CS4 documents

As with Illustrator CS4, the process of importing Photoshop CS4 documents into Flash has been streamlined, and you are in for a rather pleasant surprise. Even so, there are some important gotchas you need to be aware of, and we will review them a little later, in the section "Notes from the PSD File Importer front." First, let's look at the import procedure.

Importing a PSD file

Follow these steps to import a Photoshop document into Flash:

1. Open a new Flash document. From the document, select File ➤ Import ➤ Import to Stage and navigate to the banner.psd document. Click Open to launch the PSD File Importer, as shown in Figure 2-75.

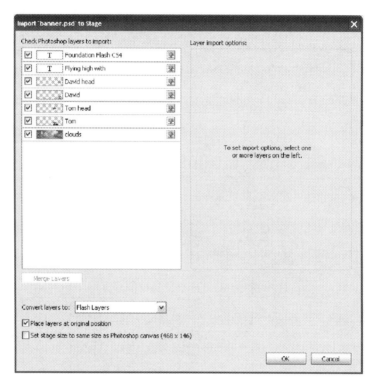

Figure 2-75. The PSD File Importer

2. The dialog box looks similar to its Illustrator counterpart, but with a couple of major differences:

   ● Place layers at original position: Checking this option ensures the contents of the PSD file retain the exact position that they had in Photoshop. For example, if an object was positioned at X = 100, Y = 35 in Photoshop, it will be placed at those coordinates on the Flash stage. If this option is not selected, the imported Photoshop layers are centered on the stage.

   ● Set stage to same size as Photoshop canvas: This check box is a real godsend. In the case of this image, the canvas size is not the default Flash size—550 × 400—but rather 468 × 146. When the file is imported, the Flash stage will be resized to the dimensions of the Photoshop document.

> *The manner in which PSD files are imported into Flash is set in the Flash Preferences dialog box. You can reach them by selecting* Edit ➤ Preferences *(Flash ➤ Preferences) and selecting* PSD File Importer *in the* Category *listing.*

3. Hold down the Shift key and click the first two layers to select them. The Merge Layers button lights up. This means you can combine the selected layers into one layer. This works for selected adjacent layers only. Deselect the layers.

4. Click the check box beside the first layer. This tells Flash to ignore importing that layer. Reselect the check box.

5. Click the name of the first layer. The import options appear on the right side of the dialog box, as shown in Figure 2-76. The first thing you should notice is the Importer has figured out that you clicked a text layer. You have three choices as to how the text will be handled, and if you wish, you can put the selection in its own movieclip. Select the Editable text import option.

> *If the text in the PSD file is PostScript or TrueType, always select* Editable text.
> *If you select either of the other two options, typos get cemented in place once inside Flash.*

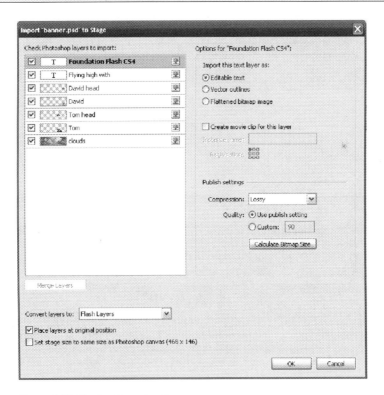

Figure 2-76. The text import options

6. With the layer still selected, click the Create movie clip for this layer check box option and enter Headline as the instance name. Notice the placement of a movieclip icon on the layer strip.

7. Click the David layer. Pay attention to how the import options change to reflect the selection of a bitmap, as shown in Figure 2-77. You can choose to put the layer in a movieclip—Bitmap image with editable layer styles—or import a flattened bitmap image. It makes sense with this image to choose the first option to maintain the layer transparency.

111

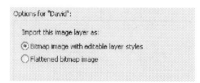

Figure 2-77. The import options for a bitmap image

8. Hold on, does this mean you have to repeat this step with the remaining four layers? No. Shift-click each layer to select all of them and click the first option. A movieclip icon, as shown in Figure 2-78, will appear beside each layer.

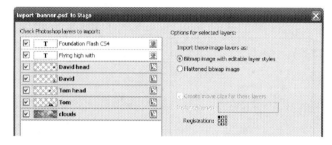

Figure 2-78. How to import a series of bitmap layers as movieclips

9. Click OK to import the image. The layers are placed on the main timeline, and the movieclips requested appear in the library, as shown in Figure 2-79. Save the file as `BannerEx.fla`.

Figure 2-79. The Photoshop file is imported and placed on the Flash stage and in the library.

Notes from the PSD file import front

We took some time to dig into the PSD File Importer feature. The files we used (provided in the Chapter 2 Exercise folder) have the potential to demonstrate some pretty useful gotchas. Here's what happened with the wheat grass files:

- wheat_grass_01.psd: In this file, the navigation buttons, shown in Figure 2-80, are masked vectors of the Photoshop variety with filters applied. The filters make an important difference. As this file stands, you may choose Import this shape layer as and specify either Editable paths and layer styles or Flattened bitmap image. Because of the filters, both choices amount to pretty much the same thing: a bitmap asset in Flash wrapped in an object, wrapped in an enigma. If you clear the filters in Photoshop—not hide, but actually *clear* them—and then reimport the PSD, you'll see an interesting thing. This time, if you choose editable paths, you get a masked bitmap in Flash. This has potentially dangerous consequences, as the bitmap is much larger than it needs to be. It's simply a huge (big as the stage) bitmap, masked to the size of the button. In this case, it happens three times—not the sort of overlap a good designer would do by hand.

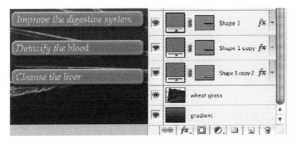

Figure 2-80. The buttons are masked vectors.

- wheat_grass_02.psd: In this file, the navigation buttons have been rasterized in Photoshop, but each is still on its own layer, as shown in Figure 2-81. In this case, you don't get the unnecessarily large bitmap, but this approach still produces three identical button images in the library, when the ideal would be a single, reusable asset. Although it's possible, in theory, for Flash to recognize that each button is identical, that isn't what happens here.

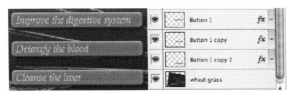

Figure 2-81. The buttons are rasterized and placed on separate layers.

- wheat_grass_03.psd: In this file, the buttons have been merged into a single layer, as shown in Figure 2-82. Be advised that the layer comes in as a single asset. In this case, we believe Flash is doing the only possible thing it can do. There is no way to second-guess the designer's intent: a layer is a layer, and Flash doesn't have the artificial intelligence of, say, C-3PO to make good guesses about how to optimize the designer's assumed intent. Just keep in mind that if one layer in Photoshop contains merely 2 pixels—one on opposite corners—the imported PNG will be as large as the stage itself. Unless separate objects are close together, put them on their own layers in the PSD.

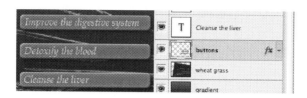

Figure 2-82. The buttons are in a single layer.

Why bring up these points?

While this import feature is amazing and facilitates a significant workflow improvement, it's important you make sure to keep yourself at the helm. You're the Flash designer. Babysit the process, and be prepared to override the results with your own best judgment.

In this example, since the button text can be overlaid in separate text layers, the button image itself needs to be imported only once. The background gradient should by no means be imported: the effect can be reproduced easily with a vector gradient in Flash.

There are a few more noteworthy issues. When importing a layer as a bitmap image with editable layer styles, you'll find that Photoshop filters are imported into Flash whether or not they're visible in the original PSD. So hiding them temporarily isn't enough. If you want them gone, either clear them or import the layer as a flattened bitmap image. None of the filters actually carry over as editable effects. Even though Flash supports many of them, the filters are flattened and imported as PNGs. This differs from filters imported from Illustrator files, which are retained.

Naturally, there are pros and cons to everything. On the plus side, imported PSDs can be published as pre–Flash Player 8 SWFs just fine (because they don't rely on the relatively new Flash filters). On the minus side, any changes to the filters means that the affected PSD must be reimported. Plus, the bitmapped filters are bulkier than their native filter counterparts.

Text with filters in Photoshop may be imported as text fields in Flash, but if that's your choice, filters don't come along for the ride. You'll need to reapply text field filters by hand after the import. Speaking of text fields, check out text_fields_01.psd. This is a mixed bag, but mostly good.

As Figure 2-83 shows, vertical text in Photoshop converts into a proper vertical Flash text field. Horizontal left-aligned, centered, and right-aligned text fields are correctly translated into Flash equivalents. You can verify this by opening text_fields_01.psd directly in Flash and choosing Editable text for each text field. Warped text does not convert, but that's no surprise. Left-aligned, centered, and right-aligned multiline text converts just fine, but left-aligned, centered, and right-justified text fields all become left-justified in Flash. To be fair, the Property inspector features only left justification. Italic and bold convert correctly, but *faux* italic and bold become their non-*faux* cousins (in other words, actual bold and italic variants, if available). This is all good stuff to know.

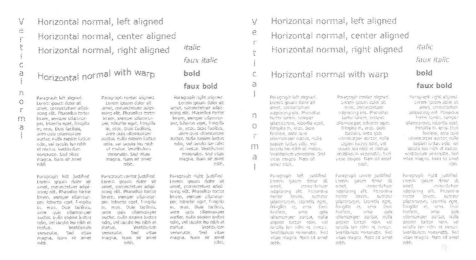

Vertical normal
Horizontal normal, left aligned
Horizontal normal, center aligned
Horizontal normal, right aligned
italic
faux italic
Horizontal normal with warp
bold
faux bold
Vertical normal
Horizontal normal, left aligned
Horizontal normal, center aligned
Horizontal normal, right aligned
italic
faux italic
Horizontal normal with warp
bold
faux bold
Photoshop Original
Flash Conversion

Figure 2-83. Text effects can be problematic.

The `text_fields_02.psd` file demonstrates that a single paragraph with several different fonts, colors, and styles (italic, faux italic, bold, faux bold) comes out more or less as you would expect, as shown in Figure 2-84, following the same caveats as previously discussed. It even accounts for custom leading. This is a good thing.

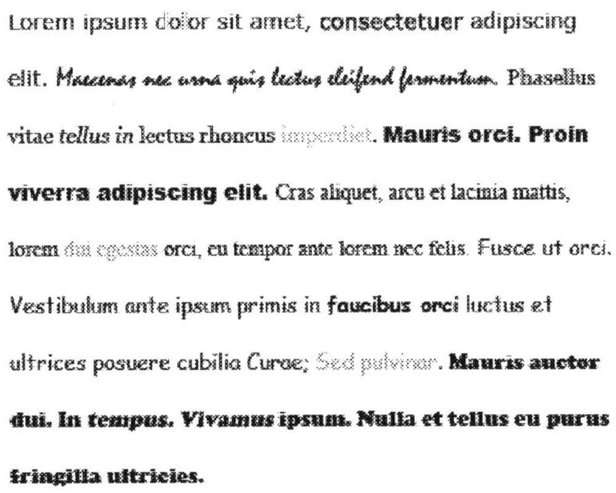

Lorem ipsum dolor sit amet, consectetuer adipiscing
elit. Maecenas nec urna quis lectus eleifend fermentum. Phasellus
vitae tellus in lectus rhoncus imperdiet. Mauris orci. Proin
viverra adipiscing elit. Cras aliquet, arcu et lacinia mattis,
lorem dui egestas orci, eu tempor ante lorem nec felis. Fusce ut orci.
Vestibulum ante ipsum primis in faucibus orci luctus et
ultrices posuere cubilia Curae; Sed pulvinar. Mauris auctor
dui. In tempus. Vivamus ipsum. Nulla et tellus eu purus
fringilla ultricies.

Figure 2-84. Single paragraphs with multiple styles will import into Flash.

Creating a banner ad

This has been a long chapter, and we have covered a lot of topics that have a direct effect upon your future as a Flash designer. At this point, you may be feeling a bit overwhelmed. Recognizing this, we are going to give you a break. Instead of asking you to complete an exercise that pulls together everything we covered in this chapter, we are going to dissect one.

As you may have gathered, Flash designers live in a world of small and fast. They live there because they intimately understand their audience. Think of a site you may have encountered where it took maybe 20 seconds to load. We are willing to bet that after 5 seconds, you were getting impatient, and that 5 seconds later you moved on. In the early days of the Internet, when modems were even slower than the 56K dial-up standard still prevalent today, a site that loaded in 20 seconds was regarded as blazingly fast. In an Internet awash in bandwidth and high-speed access, the situation has changed dramatically.

In this dissection, we are going to look at a banner ad, banner.fla (based on the banner we created in the previous section), and explain how the SWF, banner.swf, comes in under 24KB. We employed a lot of the techniques presented in this chapter to accomplish this feat, because we have learned, in the words of one of the most important Flash designers on the planet, Hillman Curtis, to "keep an eye on the pipe."

Figure 2-85. GIF images are often really small, in terms of file size.

If you double-click the SWF file to run the movie, you will see it uses the same assets and stage size as the Photoshop import exercise. It even includes the kite used in the Illustrator import exercise. The difference is how the images were created. We didn't simply import an entire Photoshop image and put it into motion. Each image in that presentation was individually created and compressed to be the smallest file size possible with the best quality possible. That is a fundamental truth of imaging. Reducing file size reduces quality, so the trade-off is to find the balance between low file size and acceptable image quality. Let's see how we reached that balance.

Open the banner.fla file, and then open the library. When you look at the assets in the library, you will see that the images are, on the whole, GIF images, as shown in Figure 2-85. One of the things you can do with a GIF image is to reduce the number of colors in the Color palette used for the image. This reduces the file size. If you double-click the david.gif file in the library, you will see the original image in the Bitmap Preview dialog box is about 3KB in size. With compression, it reduces to about 1.5KB.

How did we get the file size so small but still retain a quality standard? Each image started out as a 4 × 5 inch high-resolution image. Each one was opened in Photoshop, and the head was tightly cropped and reduced to a physical size of around 50 × 50 pixels. This change in physical size also reduced the file size by a rather massive percentage. The images were then converted to GIF images. The conversion to a GIF image reduced the file size even further, to 3.0KB.

The kite image was treated a bit differently. It was imported into the library at the original size of 381 × 324. We could do this because it is composed of vectors, and as you now know, resizing a vector has no impact on the resolution of the image or upon its file size. By placing the kite into a symbol, we could bring the kite onto the stage and resize it using the Free Transform tool.

The beams that shoot out of our heads, starting in frame 222, are nothing more than a shape drawn into a graphics symbol. Double-click the library symbol and click the edge with the Subselection tool. The shape has no stroke, and if you switch to the Selection tool and click the fill, you will see in the Property inspector that the fill is nothing more than a solid color whose opacity was reduced to 35% in the Color Picker. By drawing the shape using the Flash Tools panel, we knew it would be extremely small and be painted to the screen rather rapidly when the movie played.

From there, the project was simply assembled on the stage, and the tweens added between the key-frames.

Speaking of tweens, in the previous chapter we introduced you to the new Motion Editor panel, which was used again here (see Figure 2-86). In the first edition of this book, there was no such thing, as the feature didn't exist in Flash CS3. For sake of comparison, we've included two sample files of this banner ad, demonstrating each tweening model, so you can study the differences between them. Both models are explained in detail in Chapters 7 and 8.

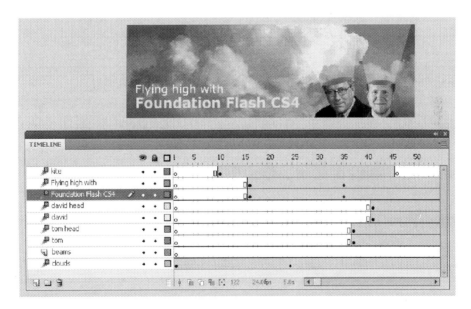

Figure 2-86. Handcrafted optimization produces satisfyingly low-carb SWF files.

We're guessing that a two-model system for shoving stuff around the stage probably has a few of you wondering which method works best. The answer is, honestly, "Who cares?" That may seem a bit glib, but it makes the point that as long as you achieve your goal, no one really cares how you got there. Both tweening models can produce animations compatible with older versions of Flash Player. Notice, for example, that even banner.fla, which uses new-style tweens, is configured for Flash Player 6 and ActionScript 1.0 (see File ➤ Publish Settings ➤ Flash).

What you have learned

In this chapter, you learned the following:

- How to use the drawing tools in the Tools panel
- The process of creating and customizing gradients
- How to create custom strokes and fills
- The various color features in Flash and how to create and save a custom color
- How to trace a bitmap in Flash
- The process of importing and optimizing graphics in Flash
- How to use the Illustrator and Photoshop File Importers in Flash CS4

We aren't going to deny this has been a pretty intense chapter. Even so, all of the topics covered here will ripple through the remainder of this book. Most important of all, you have learned how graphic content is created, added to Flash, and optimized in Flash. The next step is making that content reusable in Flash movies or available to different Flash movies. That is the subject of the next chapter. See you there.

Chapter 3

SYMBOLS AND LIBRARIES

Symbols, the topic of this chapter, are one of the most powerful features of the Flash application. This is because they allow you to create reusable content. You only need one copy of a symbol. Once it is on the stage, that symbol can then be manipulated in any number of ways, without those changes affecting the original piece of content.

Here's what we'll cover in this chapter:

- Creating and using symbols
- Creating, using, and sharing libraries
- Adding filters and blends to symbols
- Grouping and nesting symbols
- Using rulers, stacking, and alignment to manage content on the Flash stage
- Creating masks, including soft masks

The following files are used in this chapter (located in Chapter03/ExerciseFiles_Ch03/Exercise/):

- GraphicSymbol.fla
- ButtonSymbol.fla
- MovieClip.swf
- MovieClip.fla
- SymbolEdit.fla
- 9Slice.fla
- PeterPan.fla
- 9Slice2.swf
- WoodFrameMasked.fla
- WoodFrame.fla
- MoonOverLakeNanagook.fla

- Filter.fla
- Blends.fla
- NuttyProfessor.fla
- Stacks.fla
- AlignPanel.fla
- SimpleMask.fla
- Windows.fla
- Places.fla
- JacobsLadder.jpg
- silk.jpg

The source files are available online from either of the following sites:

- http://www.FoundationFlashCS4.com
- http://www.friendsofED.com/download.html?isbn=9781430210931

Symbols are the building blocks of everything you will do in Flash (other than write ActionScript). You'll create a symbol when you come to the realization that the piece of content you are looking at will be used several times throughout a movie. In fact, the same content may appear in a number of movies, even if it has only a single use, such as a movieclip that plays a particular video or sound. An extremely important aspect of symbols is they keep the file size of a SWF manageable. The end result of a small SWF is a fast load time—and users who aren't drumming their fingers on a desk waiting for your movie to start.

Symbol essentials

Reduced to its basics, a *symbol* is something you can use and reuse. It could be an image, an animation, a button, or even a video used within the main movie. When a symbol is created, it is placed in the library, and any copy of that symbol on the stage at any point in the movie is said to be an *instance* of that symbol.

Creating a symbol

Let's create a symbol and start examining how these things work. Follow these steps:

1. Create a new document in Flash. Select the Rectangle tool and draw a rectangle on the stage.
2. Right-click (Ctrl-click) on the shape and select Convert to Symbol from the context menu, as shown in Figure 3-1. You can also select the object on the stage and press the F8 key, or select the object and choose Modify ➤ Convert to Symbol.

3. In the Convert to Symbol dialog box, name the symbol Box and select Movie Clip as its Type. Figure 3-2 shows the dialog box with the extra options available after you click the Advanced button. Let's look at each element in the dialog box:

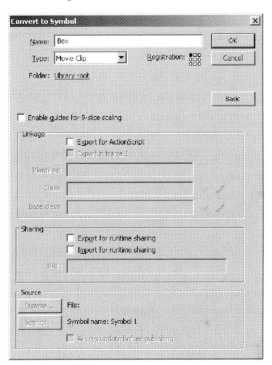

Figure 3-1. Creating a symbol   **Figure 3-2.** The Convert to Symbol dialog box

- Name: The name you enter here will be the name for the symbol as it appears in the library.

- Type: Select the symbol type here. Symbol types are discussed in the next section.

- Registration: Each of the nine dots represents a possible location for the symbol's registration point. The registration point is used for alignment with other objects on the stage and for movement along a motion guide.

- Folder: This is new to Flash CS4. Click the Library root link to open a Move to dialog box, which lets you specify in which library folder to place your new symbol. You can even create and name a new library folder in the same step, if desired—talk about a productivity booster! In the dialog box, select the New folder radio button to create a folder. Select the Existing folder radio button to save the symbol to any existing Library panel folder, including the root (in other words, not in a subfolder).

- Enable guides for 9-slice scaling: Select this, and the guides for this special scaling will appear. We'll describe 9-slice scaling in a separate section coming up shortly.

- Linkage: You can use ActionScript to pull symbols and other assets out of the library and put them on the stage or use them for other purposes, such as playing audio. To do this, you need to associate the symbol with a nominal ActionScript file, called a *linkage class*, so that Flash can find it in the library when the SWF plays. In spite of the term *class*, you don't actually need to write any ActionScript—Flash will write it for you—but you can provide custom programming if desired. You'll see more information on linkage later in this chapter and in Chapters 5, 6, 11, and 12.

- Sharing: This area allows you to share symbols with other Flash movies or to import symbols from other Flash movies into your project. This used to be bundled into the Linkage area, but Adobe, recognizing that symbols are among the cornerstones of Flash, has made this its own little configuration in Flash CS4.

- Source: This area allows you to identify external content in a shared library or elsewhere to be used as a symbol. This comes into play in cases where you've dragged an asset from one FLA into another. For example, a Flash animator might build a character's body parts in one FLA, save it, and then use that external library in a completely different series of movies. If she changes the color of a shirt in the original library from blue to red, the shirt can be configured to change in the current movie as well. Note that you can check Always update before publishing, which implements the change in each FLA to which it is linked, minimizing duplicated effort.

4. Click OK. The dialog box will close and the new symbol will appear in the library. If you look at the box on the stage, you will see it is now surrounded by a thin blue line. This tells you that the object just selected is a symbol. The Property inspector will also change to show that you have, indeed, selected a symbol.

5. Open the library and drag another copy of the symbol to the stage. Click the symbol to select it. Select the Free Transform tool and scale and rotate the object. As you can see, changing one instance of a symbol does not affect any other instance of that same symbol on the stage.

6. Close the movie without saving it.

Understanding symbol types

You can choose from three basic symbol types: graphic, button, and movieclip. Each one has specific capabilities, and the type you choose will be based on the desired goals of what needs to be done. For instance, say you have a logo that will be used in several places throughout a movie. In this case, the graphic symbol would be your choice. If you need a racing car zooming across the screen with the engine sounds blasting out of the user's speakers, the movieclip symbol is your choice. Need a button? Well, that one is pretty obvious. Let's briefly review each symbol type.

Graphic symbols

Graphic symbols are used primarily for static images or content used in a project. They can also be used as the building blocks for complex animations. Although we say they are primarily static, they can be put into motion on the main timeline or the timelines of other symbols.

Graphic symbols, unlike their movieclip cousins, do not play independently of the timeline they're in. For this reason, they need a matching number of frames in the parent timeline in order for each frame in the graphic symbol to display. For example, if a graphic symbol has a length of 80 frames, and you want it to display only half of its frames on the main timeline, you need to allocate 40 frames on the main timeline for this task. That may sound a little convoluted. We agree, and have provided a small movie that shows you what we mean. Let's take a look:

1. Open the GraphicSymbol.fla file in the Chapter 3 Exercise folder. You will see a wizened guru on the stage for a duration of ten frames on the main timeline. Scrub across the timeline, and the guru will move a short distance to the right.

2. Double-click the graphic symbol (guru) in the library. When the Symbol Editor opens, you'll see that the symbol has an internal animation of a length of 85 frames.

3. Click the Scene 1 link to return to the main timeline.

4. Select frame 85 on the main timeline and insert a frame (not a keyframe, just a frame). This increases the span of frames from 1 through 10 to 1 through 85. Scrub across the main time-line. This time, the guru moves all the way across the stage, to match the movement of the symbol's nested animation.

5. Insert a frame in the main timeline at frame 86. Because the guru symbol's internal timeline loops back to the beginning after frame 85, the symbol on the main timeline pops back to the left side of the stage in frame 86 of the main timeline. Add more frames, and the process will eventually loop. This illustrates one potential way to animate a bird, for example. The flapping wings can loop inside the graphic symbol's timeline, while the main timeline handles the motion from one side to another.

6. Select the graphic symbol on the main timeline and look at the Looping area of the Property inspector. A drop-down menu gives you choices for Loop, Play Once, and Single Frame, including a field labeled First that lets you determine which frame of the graphic symbol's timeline to display first. We'll delve into this in greater detail in Chapter 7.

7. Close the file without saving the changes.

Button symbols

Button symbols are rather interesting in that they are able to do a lot more than you may think. Button symbols have a four-frame timeline in which each frame represents a state of the button (Up, Over, Down, and Hit), as shown in Figure 3-3. The button states can be created using graphic symbols, movieclips, imported images, or drawn directly into the frame using the drawing tools.

Figure 3-3. The button symbol timeline

Let's look at a typical button:

1. Open the ButtonSymbol.fla file in your Exercise folder and select Control ➤ Enable Simple Buttons. If you roll over the button and click it, you will see that the button changes in relation to whether it has been clicked or rolled over, and whether the mouse is off the button.

> *If you use the* Control ➤ Enable Simple Buttons *menu item, do your sanity a favor and deselect it after you have tested the button. This menu item puts the button into its "live" state, meaning you can't select the button like a normal authoring asset in order to move it to another location on the stage.*

2. Double-click the button symbol named Button in the library. When the Symbol Editor opens, you will see that each state of the button appears in its own automatically labeled frame. The Hit frame is empty. Let's change that.

3. Select the Hit frame and insert a keyframe.

4. Select the Rectangle tool and draw a large square or rectangle that covers most of the stage. Size doesn't matter because the object in a Hit frame is never visible to the user.

5. Click the Scene 1 link, turn on Enable Simple Buttons, and hover the mouse across the stage. The over state will appear, even though the mouse pointer is not over the visual portion of the button. This is the enlarged hit state coming into play.

The area of the Hit frame determines the active area for a click, rollover, and other mouse-related events. You can, in fact, create a button composed only of a Hit frame—all the other frames empty—and if you do, what you have created is a hotspot, sometimes referred to as an invisible button, on the stage. If you leave the Hit frame empty, Flash uses the other button frames to determine an automatic active area. In fact, this is true of all frames, working from right to left. If you have a button with artwork in the Up frame only, then that's the artwork that will also be visible in the Over and Down frames, and what will determine the Hit frame area.

> Get into the habit of adding a Hit area if the button is composed solely of text. The authors tend to draw rectangles in the Hit area that are a bit larger than the text to ensure the text is clearly "live."

6. Close the movie without saving the changes.

You can add layers to a button symbol. A common use of this feature is adding a sound to a button. For example, you could have something explode when the mouse clicks the button. Drag the BlowUp button to the stage and try it out. The explosion sound is on the Audio layer of the symbol, and it is triggered only when the Down frame is entered.

Movieclip symbols

Movieclip symbols can be thought of as movies within movies. (Indeed, it is a little known fact that the main timeline is a movieclip.) These symbols, unlike their graphic counterparts, actually run independent of the timelines in which they reside. They can contain code, other symbols, and audio tracks. Movieclips can be placed inside other movieclips—the term for this is *nesting*—and they have become so ubiquitous and useful among Flash designers that they are, in many cases, replacing graphic and button symbols on the stage (yes, movieclips can be programmed to respond like buttons).

Because of their timeline independence, movieclips continue to play even if the parent timeline is stopped, which explains why they are often placed in a single frame on the main timeline. In cases where, for example, a movieclip fades in over a period of time, it may extend across a number of frames to accommodate this effect, but technically, movieclips need only a single frame in whatever timeline they appear. The other major feature of movieclips is that they are programmable with ActionScript. We'll get into that in a big way in upcoming chapters. In the meantime, let's see how timeline-independence works:

1. Double-click the MovieClip.swf file in your Exercise folder to launch Flash Player. You will see a sports car come roaring onto the screen and drive off the right edge of the stage. Close the SWF, and let's look at how this was put together.

2. Open the MovieClip.fla file. Look at the timeline, and you will see that the car starts moving in at frame 6 and is off the stage by frame 45.

3. Open the Library panel, and you will see that the car is actually composed of several symbols. The Car graphic symbol doesn't contain a rear wheel. Why is it a graphic symbol? Because it's just a picture. The Rear movieclip contains the wheel, which is rotated over a series of frames. Why is it a movieclip? Because it contains timeline-independent animation.

4. Double-click the Race movieclip in the library to open the Symbol Editor. You will see that the race car is composed of two layers, and each layer contains a symbol. This is what is meant by *nesting*. Movieclips can be placed inside other movieclips. This is also true of graphic symbols, but again, the key difference, in terms of animation, is the fact that movieclip timelines aren't locked in-step with the parent timeline. Notice that each symbol exists in a single frame of its own layer. Even though the Rear movieclip (wheel layer) gets only one frame, it animates fully in the published SWF: the wheel spins.

5. Click the Scene1 link to return to the main timeline. Select the car on the stage. You will see that the Race movieclip is used to house the full animation.

6. Scrub the playhead across the timeline. You'll see that the car gets larger and smaller, thanks to a tween. The key aspect of this is that symbol properties can be changed, and in the case of nested symbols, this change is reflected throughout the structure's hierarchy: as Race gets bigger and moves, so do Car and Rear.

What you *don't* see during scrubbing is the rotating rear wheel—not until you view the SWF. This is why advanced animators often prefer graphic symbols over movieclips for nested animation. In spite of the need for additional frames in the parent timeline, scrubbing does show nested animation for graphic symbols. On the other hand, you can't apply filter effects, such as blur, drop shadow, and the like, to graphic symbols. Everything in life has its trade-offs, and these are some of the pros and cons of two particular Flash symbols.

7. Close the movie without saving the changes.

> Yes, we agree this is not exactly a well-designed piece. In fact, one of the authors saw it and said, "Dude, what's with that?" Sometimes the technique is more important than the actual content. This is an important concept for those of you who are new to Flash: get it to work, understand why it works, and then start playing with it. Everything you will do in Flash starts with a basic concept, and everything else in the movie builds on that concept. For example, Joshua Davis, one of the more influential characters in the Flash community, started one project by simply watching how a series of gray squares rotated on the Flash stage. Once he got the squares to rotate in a manner that worked for him, he simply swapped out the squares for shapes he had drawn in Illustrator.

Editing symbols

There will obviously be occasions where you want to edit a symbol. This is where the Symbol Editor becomes an invaluable tool. Let's take a look at how to open this editor and what it offers:

1. Open the SymbolEdit.fla file in your Exercise folder.

2. Open the library and double-click the Circle movieclip symbol. The Symbol Editor will open. This is also known as *entering the timeline* of a symbol. Click the Scene 1 link to return to the main timeline.

3. Double-click the squashed circle on the stage. This will also open the Symbol Editor, but, as you may have noticed, the other symbol instances on the stage are still visible, yet dimmed. If you try to select the instance of the Box, you will notice you can't. This technique, called *editing in place*, allows you to see how the change to a symbol affects, or works with, the rest of the content on the stage.

The editing-in-place technique often provides a helpful sense of context. The other important thing with this technique is that changes you may have made to the symbol on the main timeline—such as the squashed dimensions of this circle—are reflected in the symbol's timeline, but only because of the edit-in-place context. If you double-click Circle in the library, the squash will go away. That's because the original library asset isn't flattened.

4. In the Symbol Editor, you can make changes to the symbol. Click the circle shape to select it and, in the Tools panel, change the fill color to a different color. When you do this, both instances of the symbol on the stage change color.

5. Close the file without saving the changes.

What you can gather from this brief example is that instances of symbols can be changed without affecting the original symbol in the library. Change the symbol in the Symbol Editor, and that change is applied to every instance of the symbol in the movie.

9-slice scaling

Until the release of Flash 8, Flash designers essentially had to put up with a rather nasty design problem. Scaling objects with rounded or oddly shaped corners was, to put it mildly, driving them crazy. No matter what they tried to do, scaling introduced distortions to the object. The release of Flash 8 and the inclusion of 9-slice scaling solved that problem. To be fair, there are still a few quirks with this feature, but it was so welcome in Flash that it is now appearing in Fireworks and Illustrator. The best part of this addition to the other applications is that symbols created in Fireworks or Illustrator, but destined for Flash, can have 9-slice scaling applied to them that carries over.

As we pointed out earlier in the chapter, 9-slice scaling is applied to movieclips in the Convert to Symbol dialog box. If you create a movieclip and then decide at a later date to apply this special scaling, select the movieclip in the library and right-click (Ctrl-click) to open the context menu. Select Properties, and add 9-slice scaling by selecting this option at the bottom of the Symbol Properties dialog box. Movieclips with 9-slice scaling applied to them will show the grid in the Library panel's preview window.

How 9-slice scaling works

What the heck is 9-slice scaling?

That question is not as dumb as it may sound, because it is a hard subject to understand. With this feature, the symbol in question—in Flash it can only be a movieclip—is overlaid with a 3 × 3 grid. This grid divides the movieclip into nine sections, and allows the clip to be scaled in such a way that the corners, edges, and strokes retain their shape.

Figure 3-4 shows the actual grid that Flash places over the object. The object is broken into the nine areas. The eight areas surrounding the center area—the area with the 5 in the figure—will scale either horizontally or vertically. The area in the middle—area 5—will scale on both axes. The really interesting aspect of this feature is that each section of the grid is scaled independently of the other eight sections.

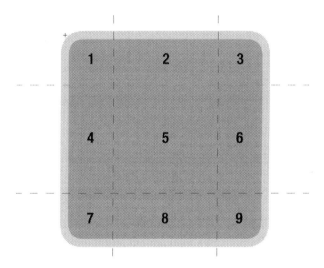

Figure 3-4. The 9-slice scaling grid

The best way of understanding how all of this works is to actually see it in action.

1. Open the 9Slice.fla file in the Chapter 3 Exercise folder. You will see two movieclips on the stage. The upper movieclip doesn't have 9-slice scaling applied; the lower one does (see Figure 3-5). The key to both of these objects is they are the identical size, and the stroke width around both shapes is also identical.

2. Click the upper movieclip, open the Transform panel (Window ➤ Transform), and change the Horizontal scaling value to 300%. When you press the Enter (Return) key, the shape scales along the horizontal axis, but as you can see, the corners flatten out and distort, and the stroke gets fatter.

3. Click the lower movieclip, open the Transform panel, and change the Horizontal scaling value to 300%. When you press the Enter (Return) key, the shape scales along the horizontal axis, and the corners don't distort (see Figure 3-6). You can see why by looking at Figure 3-4. The areas numbered 2, 5, and 8 are scaled horizontally, and the corner areas are unaffected.

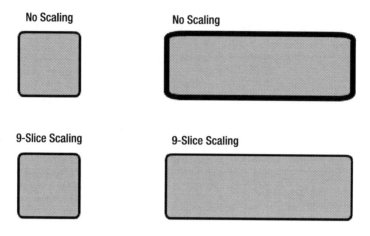

Figure 3-5. You start with two movieclips on the stage. They look the same so far.

Figure 3-6. Both movieclips are scaled at 300% along the horizontal axis; the movieclip without 9-slice scaling is distorted.

Additionally, the guides are adjustable. They can be moved, which allows you to control how the scaling will be applied.

4. Double-click the 9Scale movieclip in the library to open the Symbol Editor. You will see the grid.

5. Roll the cursor over one of the slice guides, and it will change to include a small arrow pointing to the right if you are over a vertical guide, or pointing downward if you are over a horizontal guide (see Figure 3-7).

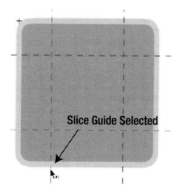

Figure 3-7. The guides can be repositioned.

6. Click and drag the selected guide to its new position. When you release the mouse and return to the main timeline, you will see the change in the Library panel's preview window.

7. Close the file without saving the changes.

So far, so good. You have applied the slice guides to a geometric object. OK, we hear you. You are probably muttering, "Not exactly a real-world project." We thought about that, and agree with you. What about occasions where the corners are irregular? Let's go visit Peter Pan in Never Land to give you some "real-world" experience with that issue.

Your turn: Frames for Peter Pan

When we approached this exercise, the question was, "What could we put in a picture frame that would be memorable?" Flowers and other images are interesting, but really don't make the point. Then one of the authors said, "How about a picture of Peter Pan?" The reply was, "Disney would never go for it." To which the author who made the original suggestion responded, "No, no, no. There is a guy that has a whole site of pictures of himself as Peter Pan. Everyone would recognize him. Maybe we can use those?"

Randy Constan has gained quite a bit of fame by portraying himself as Peter Pan on his website, http://peterpan.pixyland.org. This hasn't gone unnoticed, and he has appeared on TechTV, *Late Night with Conan O'Brien*, *Jimmy Kimmel Live*, and other outlets. We contacted Randy, and the end result was this exercise.

1. Open the PeterPan.fla file in the Exercise folder. You will notice that the images of Peter Pan don't exactly fit their frames (see Figure 3-8). Let's fix that.

Figure 3-8. The picture frames don't fit the images.

2. Select the Frame movieclip in the library and enable 9-slice scaling. Open the movieclip in the Symbol Editor and adjust the guides to match those shown in Figure 3-9. Note that the top guide, in area 1, is positioned low enough to encompass the full extent of the feather.

3. Click the Scene 1 link to return to the main timeline.

4. Select the Free Transform tool and adjust the picture frames to fit the image, as shown in Figure 3-10. Even though each photo has its own width, the same symbol can now be used to neatly frame these different dimensions.

5. Save and close the file.

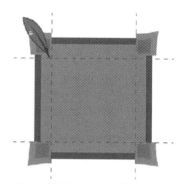

Figure 3-9. Applying 9-slice scaling and adjusting the guides

http://peterpan.pixyland.org

Figure 3-10. 9-Slice scaling allows Peter Pan to fly.

9-slice "gotchas"

In the first edition of this book, *Foundation Flash CS3 for Designers*, we discovered a number of 9-slice "gotchas" that took us by surprise. Most of these have disappeared in Flash CS4, even when publishing to previous versions of Flash Player (keeping in mind that Flash Player 8 is the minimum version to support 9-slide scaling). Some of these issues included the use of rotated graphic symbols in the corners—simply not workable at the time—as well as batty behavior when a 9-slice symbol was edited in place, but pixie dust seems to have truly come to the rescue. 9-slice scaling is a lot more stable in Flash CS4 than it used to be. That said, there are still a few issues you should know about.

The first issue concerns the area in the middle of the 9-slice grid, which scales across both the horizontal and the vertical axes. If you have content in the center area of the grid (area 5), such as a gradient or image, it will distort if the scaling is uneven. Take a look for yourself. Open the 9Slice2.swf file and click the frame to drag out a corner (this is an interactive SWF). Notice how the flower distorts, as shown in Figure 3-11. This happens because the frame and the flower are both in the area 5 slice. Depending on your needs, this makes 9-slice symbols useful only as background borders, layered behind content that simply must not be distorted. In the PeterPan.fla file, the photos are on layers of their own.

Figure 3-11. The center area of a symbol containing 9-slice scaling scales on two axes. The area in the middle will distort.

Another issue involves maintaining the integrity of any drawings or objects used in the corners. Shapes, drawing objects, primitives, graphic symbols, and even imported bitmaps can be used. Movieclips can't be used. You can see what we're talking about in Figures 3-12 and 3-13. We started with nothing more than a rounded rectangle with a square in the upper left. The square is represented by a shape, a drawing object, a primitive, a graphic symbol, a movieclip symbol, and an imported TIFF file.

When the objects are stretched along the horizontal axis using the Free Transform tool, the object in the upper-left corner is fine in all versions except the movieclip, which is distorted (see Figure 3-13).

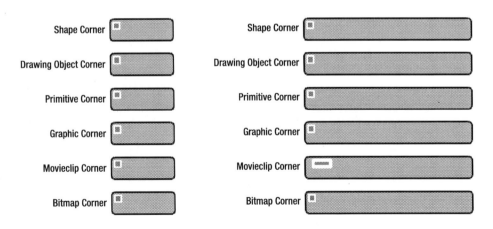

Figure 3-12. We start with a simple object.   Figure 3-13. Note the distortion in the bottom two examples.

It's OK to rotate symbols that are not movieclips in 9-slice corners, but they look right only when your FLA is configured for ActionScript 3.0.

Finally, masking layers inside a 9-slice movieclip will decisively pummel that symbol and kick it to the curb. Masking just can't be combined with this feature, as cool as it would be. Consider the example of a wooden frame, where the intent is to use an actual snapshot of a distressed piece of wood—an imported bitmap—with 9-slice scaling to create a wooden frame that can fit any photograph. In Figure 3-14, an imported JPG is used as a bitmap fill for four rectangles. To angle the corners, masks are applied to the layers named top and bottom.

What's the result? Take a look at WoodFrameMasked.fla in the Chapter 3 Exercise folder, and you'll see the problem right away. The rectangles simply don't resize according to the rules of 9-slice scaling. Fortunately, those angled corners can be made without masking layers. Look at WoodFrame.fla, and you'll see that the Subselection tool was used to bring in the actual corner anchor points directly (Figure 3-15). The result—without the masking—succeeds, as shown in Figure 3-16.

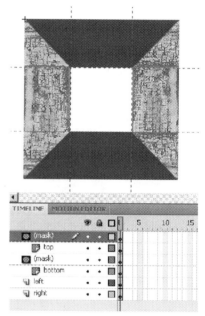

Figure 3-14. Masking will break 9-slice scaling.

Figure 3-15. Rearranging anchor points gets rid of the masking issue.

Figure 3-16. A resizable wood frame using 9-slice scaling and a single JPG for the wood

The bottom line is that you should use 9-slice scaling with care. The idea is a good one, but don't go nuts with it. Keep it simple! Avoid nesting symbols too deeply in the corners and sides. If you insist on using bitmaps, bear in mind that they will sometimes stretch in ways that may not be predictable. We encourage you to experiment on your own, but by all accounts, the simpler, the better.

Sharing assets

One of the really useful features of library assets—symbols or otherwise—is that they can be made available to FLAs other than the current movie. Assets in a Flash library can be shared with other Flash movies in two ways: *author-time shared libraries* and *runtime shared libraries*. This is extremely helpful if you are working on a stockpile of movies and need to use the same assets across numerous Flash documents. Here's a quick look at the difference between the two.

Author-time shared libraries

The term *author-time* refers to production time—the time during which you, the designer (author), actually build your content. Author-time shared libraries, therefore, refer to assets shared among FLA files that haven't yet been converted to SWFs. Animators make extensive use of this feature. An animator will, for example, create a character composed of a number of symbols—eyes, arms, legs, and hands, for instance—that are used to put the character in motion. As the animations are built in a series of movies, the animator will use symbols that were created in a centralized (and separate) character library instead of redrawing them. If a change happens in the centralized author-time shared library, the edit ripples across to all the FLAs that borrow from it. Here's how to use symbols from another FLA:

1. Create a new Flash document and open the new document's library. As you can see, it is empty.

2. Select File ➤ Import ➤ Open External Library, or press Ctrl+Shift+O (Cmd+Shift+O), as shown in Figure 3-17.

Figure 3-17. Importing a library from one Flash document into another

3. In the Open dialog box, navigate to the Chapter 3 Exercise folder and open MoonOverLakeNanagook.fla.

4. The library for the selected movie will open, but there are a couple of things missing from that library: the drop-down menu, the pushpin, and the Open New Library button. In addition, the Library panel itself looks grayed out. All of these are visual clues that the MoonOverLakeNanagook.fla file itself isn't open—only its library is.

5. Drag the Trees symbol from the shared library to the empty library. When you release the mouse, the symbol will appear in the empty library and become available for use in that movie (see Figure 3-18).

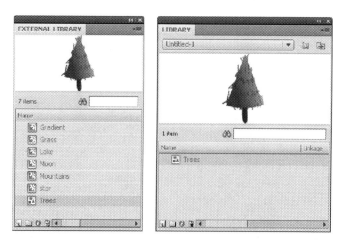

Figure 3-18. Drag a symbol from the imported library to the empty library.

6. Right-click (Ctrl-click) the Trees symbol you just dragged to the empty library and select Properties. Take a look at the Source area of the Symbol Properties dialog box (Figure 3-19).

- Next to the Browse button, it tells you the original FLA of the shared symbol. Clicking the Browse button lets you "unhook" the association from one FLA to another.

- The Symbol button gives you the same concept, but for symbols, once the origination FLA is chosen.

- The Always update before publishing check box is important. It ensures that the current movie, when you publish it, runs through all its associated external FLAs to see if any of their shared assets have been updated. If so, it updates the current movie's version of them before publishing.

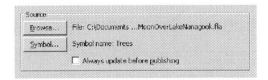

Figure 3-19. The Source area of the Symbol Properties dialog box manages shared assets.

7. Close the file without saving the changes.

You can share any library item between movies as described in the previous steps. That includes fonts, audio files, and bitmaps, not just symbols.

Runtime shared libraries

The concept of author-time shared libraries is useful enough, but it gets better. Since the introduction of Flash 5, Flash designers and developers have had the ability to extend this "interlibrary loan" process to published SWFs, which means the benefits extend past author-time into . . . runtime. Why would you want to create a runtime shared library? Because such a library needs to be downloaded only once, even if several other SWFs access its symbols. To continue with the animator example, you might be creating a character animation that uses the same large background image in ten separate movies. Rather than adding the image to all ten FLAs—not a good idea, because its file size will be added to each final SWF, even with an author-time shared library—you can have that symbol reside in a runtime shared library on the web server. This way, the library SWF is loaded only once, but used by several movies.

The key to runtime sharing is something called a *linkage class*. Select an item in the library, right-click (Ctrl-click), and select Properties. In the Symbol Properties dialog box, you will see a Linkage area (shown in Figure 3-20). If an asset is to be shared at runtime, you must select Export for runtime sharing, and then enter the location of the intended shared library SWF. In the example in Figure 3-20, the URL field indicates that the SWF will be named SharedLibrary.swf and will be located in the same folder as the other SWFs that use it. If the shared library were in a different location, you would enter a full path, such as http://www.MyExcellentSite.com/SharedLibrary.swf.

Clicking Export for runtime sharing automatically selects the Export for ActionScript check box, which in turn enables the Class field. This linkage class provides ActionScript with a unique label for this particular asset. (The field fills automatically, but you can change the class name, if you like.) Does the usage of runtime shared libraries require ActionScript? Oddly, not necessarily. But runtime sharing doesn't work without the linkage class.

Runtime sharing is possible for any asset that supports a linkage class, which includes quite a few assets: fonts, audio files, movieclips, and bitmaps, but not graphic symbols. Items in shared libraries can also be created when a symbol is first created (see Figure 3-21). This works because the Create New Symbol dialog box is essentially the same as the Symbol Properties dialog box.

Figure 3-20. Adding items to a shared library using the Symbol Properties dialog box

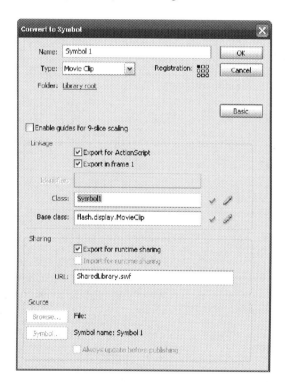

Figure 3-21. Symbols can be added to shared libraries when they are created.

Using a runtime shared library requires, of course, that the shared library be published as a SWF—the file named in the URL field of the Symbol Properties dialog box—and that this SWF be uploaded to the server along with your actual movie SWFs.

To include an asset from a runtime shared library, follow the same steps listed in the previous section for author-time shared libraries. Just open the shared library as an external library and drag over any assets that can be given a linkage class. The difference is that runtime assets don't contribute to the borrowing SWF's file size, even though they appear as library items in the receiving FLA.

Updating shared assets

Obviously, things will rarely remain the same in your workflow. Things change and, more often than not, these changes ripple through a number of movies. As an example, let's assume that you need to add or remove something from the background image used in your runtime shared library. This is quite easily accomplished:

1. Open the originating FLA that contains the image and make your revisions in the Symbol Editor. When you finish, save and publish the document, and close the FLA.

2. Open a Flash document that uses the shared asset and open its library.

3. Select the symbol that was changed, and select Update from the library's drop-down menu or, alternatively, right-click (Ctrl-click) on the desired item and select Update from the context menu. This will open the Update Library Items dialog box (shown in Figure 13-22).

Figure 3-22. Symbols that have changed in a shared library can quickly be updated wherever they are used.

4. In the Update Library Items dialog box, select the check box next to the item's name, and then click the Update button.

As mentioned earlier, you can also use the Symbol Properties dialog box to configure shared items to update automatically.

If you have been carefully going through the chapter to this point, you are probably thinking, "Man, there is a lot of serious stuff that I have to know!" We don't deny that, but once you understand the serious stuff, you can then start having fun with symbols. In fact, let's start.

A word from the bunnies

Jennifer Shiman has created what is arguably one of the funniest sites on the Web (http://www.angryalien.com/). On a regular basis, she releases a Flash movie that uses the following premise: the movie is a 30-second synopsis of a popular film and the actors are bunnies. Drawing and animating each bunny would be a daunting task. Jennifer's solution is the use of a shared library containing all of the "bunny bits" needed to create the animations (see Figure 3-23). This is what Jennifer says about how she does it:

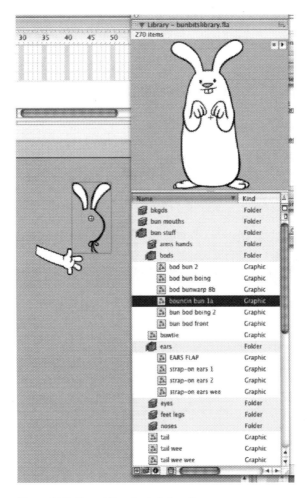

Figure 3-23. Shared libraries help Jennifer manage complex animations.

This is my library of "bunny bits," which I incorporate into each of my 30-Second Bunnies Theatre cartoons. I've compiled a bunch of the symbols I use most commonly in animating the bunnies, and I grouped them into folders. For instance, within the "bun mouths" folder are subfolders of different mouth shapes for lip sync; mouths smiling and frowning; mouths in color and black and white; mouths of differing line thickness. The "bkgds" folder contains background symbols I frequently use, such as standardized clouds, grass, and trees. At the beginning of production, I'll open the bunny bits Library and drag the folders into the Library of my current cartoon file. Then I import the additional artwork specifically pertaining to that cartoon.

During the course of production, if I create new bunny-related artwork I want to use in future files (such as a new version of a bunny mouth shape or a bunny arm position I'll use often), I drag those symbols into the bunny bits Library file. It saves time to have one central location for these types of reusable elements.

Filters and blend modes

The introduction of filters and blend modes in Flash 8 was a direct response to Flash designers asking for more eye candy. These features are just as fulfilling in Flash CS4.

Applying filters

For years, designers have been quite comfortable using Photoshop filters or Fireworks Live Effects. Back in the old days, if an asset with blurs, drop shadows, and glows needed to appear in Flash, it meant leaving Flash and opening an imaging application where such filters could be applied, then exporting as a PNG file and importing that bitmap image into Flash. If the asset needed revision, boom—you had to make the round-trip again. Thankfully, these same filters have become a part of Flash. The ability to use filters directly gives you a quick-and-easy method to create some fascinating visual effects.

The following filters are available in Flash:

- **Drop Shadow**: Places a gray or colored shadow beneath an object, which gives it the appearance of floating over the background.
- **Blur**: Takes the subject out of focus, making it look smudged or out of the depth of field.
- **Glow**: Creates a faint colored outline that glows around an object by following its curves.
- **Bevel**: Gives an object a 3D look by creating shadows and highlights on opposite edges.
- **Gradient Glow**: Nearly the same as the Glow filter, except that the glow follows a gradient of colors from the inside to the outside edges of the object.
- **Gradient Bevel**: Comparable to the Bevel filter, except that a gradient is applied to the shadow and the highlights of the bevel.
- **Adjust Color**: Allows you to adjust the brightness, contrast, hue, and saturation of an object.

> *There are also three filters that can be applied only through the use of ActionScript: Color Matrix, Displacement Map, and Convolution. Check out the ActionScript 3.0 Language and Components Reference for explanations and demonstrations of how to use these filters. Look for the* `ColorMatrixFilter`, `DisplacementMapFilter`, *and* `ConvolutionFilter` *classes. See Chapter 4 for details on using the ActionScript 3.0 Language and Components Reference.*

A filter can't be applied to everything. Filters can be applied only to movieclips, buttons, or text. This makes sense, as far as importing goes, because the bulk of the movieclips that receive filters will either arrive in Flash as exports from Photoshop or Fireworks or as line art from Illustrator. When you import these assets into Flash, you will most likely import them as movieclip symbols. If an imported image has transparent areas, the filter—such as a drop shadow—is applied only to the opaque edges of the symbol that contains the image.

Applying a Drop Shadow filter

In Flash, you can apply filters using a couple of methods. The most common is to select the object on the stage and then twirl down the Filters twirlie on the Property inspector. Filters can also be applied through ActionScript.

As an example, let's see how to get creative with the Drop Shadow filter:

1. Open the Filter.fla file in the Chapter 3 Exercise folder. You will see that a cartoon of one of the authors has been placed over an image of something going on in a street in Paris (see Figure 3-24). The cartoon is a Photoshop image that was imported into the library as a movieclip.

Figure 3-24. We start with a Photoshop image imported into Flash.

The authors would like to thank Chris Flick of Community MX and CSFGraphics (http://www.csf-graphics.blogspot.com/) for allowing us to use this caricature of Tom. Chris is a colleague at Community MX, where he produces the weekly strip CMX Suite every Tuesday at http://www.communitymx.com/.

2. Select the character on the stage and turn your attention to the Filters area in the Property inspector.

3. Click the Add Filter button in the bottom left to open the drop-down menu. Select Drop Shadow. The Property inspector will change to show the various options for this filter and the selection on the stage will also develop a drop shadow using the current default values for the Drop Shadow filter.

4. Change the Blur X and Blur Y values to 8 to make the shadow a little bigger. Also change the Quality setting to High and the Distance value to 10. The shadow should now look a lot better (see Figure 3-25).

Figure 3-25. The filter is applied to the selection.

The lock joining the Blur X and Blur Y values ensures that the two values remain equal. Click the lock if you want the Blur X and Blur Y values to be different.

The first rule of "Flash physics" states, "For every action, there is an equally opposite and ugly implication." Selecting High quality results in a great-looking shadow. The ugly implication is that this setting requires more processing power to apply. This is not a terrible thing if the image is static. For objects in motion, however, keep the setting at Low.

Our result is not bad, but we can do a lot better than that. The problem is the real-life shadows in the photo. Notice how they are at a different angle from the one used for the character? Let's fix that.

Adding perspective

We are going to make this effect look a little more realistic. Applying the Drop Shadow filter in the previous steps resulted in a character that looks flat. In this exercise, you are going to add perspective. Follow these steps:

1. Select the object on the stage and click the Trash Can icon at the bottom of the Property inspector to remove the Drop Shadow filter. With the object selected on the stage, copy it to the clipboard.

2. Add a new layer, give it a name, and with the new layer selected, select Edit ➤ Paste in Place. A copy of the character is pasted into the new layer. Turn off the layer's visibility.

> You also have the ability to copy the contents of a particular frame in the time-line. Right-click (Ctrl-click) the frame or sequence of frames and select Copy Frames from the context menu. Select the frame where the content on the clipboard is to be placed, open the context menu again, and select Paste Frames.

143

3. Select the character—the one that's visible—on the stage and apply a Drop Shadow filter. Use these settings:

- Blur X: 6
- Blur Y: 5
- Strength: 40% (this is an opacity value)
- Quality: High
- Hide Object: Selected

What you should see is nothing more than a somewhat transparent shadow on the sidewalk, due to selecting Hide Object (see Figure 3-26). This opens up some rather creative applications. For example, just a shadow appearing over something adds a bit of a sinister feeling to a scene.

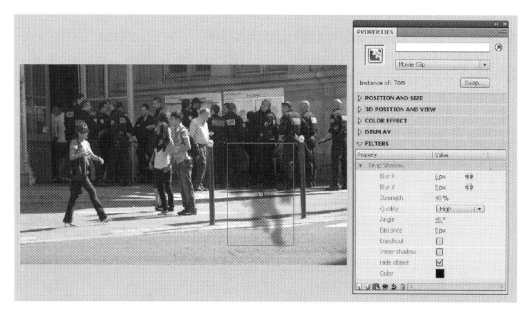

Figure 3-26. Hiding the object allows you to show only the shadow.

4. To add the perspective, select the object with the Free Transform tool and scale, rotate, and skew the selection.

5. Turn on the visibility of the hidden layer. Select the shadow on the stage and, using the arrow keys, move the shadow to align with the foot that is on the ground.

6. Select the copy without a shadow on the stage and apply the Drop Shadow filter affect again. This time, leave the values alone, but select High as the Quality setting, and select Inner shadow. The character takes on a bit of a 3D look to go with the shadow he is casting, as shown in Figure 3-27.

7. Close the file without saving the changes.

Figure 3-27. Apply an inner shadow to add some depth.

Some filter facts

Before we move on to applying a blend, here are a few things you should know about adding and using filters:

- You can apply multiple filters to an object. For example, the character in the previous exercises could have the Drop Shadow, Glow, and Bevel filters applied to it all at once. If you need to remove one, select that filter's name and click the Trash Can icon in the Filters area.

- You cannot apply multiple instances of a filter to an object. You saw that in the previous exercise. Each movieclip has a single Drop Shadow filter applied to it.

- Filters do result in a hit on the user's processor. Use them judiciously.

- Filters applied to layers in Photoshop will be visible in Flash, but will not be editable in Flash when the image is imported into the Flash library or to the stage.

- Alpha channel video in a movieclip can have filters applied to it.

Playing with blends

The blend modes operate quite differently from the filters. If you are a Fireworks or Photoshop user, you may already be familiar with the concept. In applications like those two, such modes are commonly used to manipulate the colors of pixels to create new colors based on combinations with underlying pixels.

The blend modes in Flash are as follows:

- Normal
- Layer
- Darken
- Multiply
- Lighten
- Screen
- Overlay
- Hard Light
- Add
- Subtract
- Difference
- Invert
- Alpha
- Erase

Blend modes work like this: the pixel colors values are considered from two separate layers of an image and mathematically manipulated by the mode to create the effect. An excellent example of this manipulation is the Multiply mode. This mode will multiply the color values of a pixel in the source layer with the color values of the pixel directly below it in the destination layer. The result is divided by 256, and is always a darker shade of the color. In Flash, these calculations are performed on overlapping movieclips or buttons on the stage.

When applying a blend mode in Flash, keep in mind that it is not the same task as it is in Photoshop or Fireworks. Flash lets you place multiple objects in a layer or layers. When a blend mode is applied to a movieclip or button in Flash, it is the object directly *under* the movieclip or button—which could be a photo, the color of the Flash stage, or whatever—that supplies the color for the change to the movieclip or button.

Blends are extremely powerful creative tools in the hands of a Flash artist. Although they can only be applied to movieclips and buttons, when applied judiciously, the blend modes can provide some rather stunning visual effects. To apply a blend mode, you simply select the symbol to which it is to be applied— movieclip or button—and then select the mode from the Blend drop-down menu in the Property inspector. Let's look at a few of the blend modes and review some blend fundamentals along the way.

1. Open the Blends.fla file in the Chapter 3 Exercise folder. You will see we have put two movieclips on the stage (see Figure 3-28). The movieclips are also in separate layers named Source and Destination. These layers have been given those names for a reason: *blending modes are applied in a top-down manner*. This means that the effect depends on the source layer's pixels, doing its manipulation based on those, and applying the result to the destination layer. That's right— anything visible under the source (including the stage) will be affected by the transformation.

Figure 3-28. The pixels in the Source layer—the flowers—are used to create the effect with the pixels in the destination layer—the Smurfs.

2. Select the image in the Source layer—the flowers—and click the twirlie in the Display area of the Property inspector. Select Normal from the Blending drop-down menu, as shown in Figure 3-29. The Normal mode does not mix, combine, or otherwise play with the color values.

Figure 3-29. Blend modes are applied through the Property inspector.

3. With the image still selected, select Multiply from the Blending drop-down menu. As you can see in Figure 3-30, the colors have mixed, and the darker colors make the Source image darker. The important thing to notice here is how the medium gray of the stage is also being used where the Source image overlaps only the stage. If you return the mode to Normal, select the image in the Destination layer, and choose the Multiply blend mode, the image will darken due to the color of the stage. Nothing happens to the image in the Source layer.

Figure 3-30. The Multiply mode

4. Set the blend mode of the Destination layer to Normal. Select the image in the Source layer, set its x and y coordinates to 0 in the Property inspector, and select Lighten from the Blending drop-down menu. In this example, the lighter color of both the Source and Destination images is chosen. As you can see in Figure 3-31, the lighter pixels in the Destination image are replacing the darker pixels in the Source image (particularly noticeable with the white hats).

Figure 3-31. The Lighten mode

5. Finally, select the image in the Source layer and select Difference from the Blending drop-down menu. This mode is always a surprise. It works by determining which color is the darkest in the Source and Destination images, and then subtracting the darker of the two from the lighter color. The result, shown in Figure 3-32, is always a vibrant image with saturated colors.

Figure 3-32. The Difference mode

6. Close the file without saving the changes.

Managing content on the stage

Now that you've had some fun, playtime is over. It is now time to get back to the serious issue of managing your work. Though we have talked about using folders in layers and in the library, we really haven't addressed the issue of managing the content on the stage.

As we have been telling and showing you to this point, you can determine the location of objects on the stage by dragging them around. We look upon that practice in many respects as attempting to light your BBQ with an atom bomb. You will light the BBQ, but taking out the neighborhood is a lot less precise than striking a match and lighting a burner. This is why we have been doing it by the numbers. We enter actual values into the Property inspector or use menus to precisely place items on the stage, and resize and otherwise manipulate content.

Grouping content

We'll start by showing you how to group content:

1. Open the NuttyProfessor.fla file in the Chapter 3 Exercise folder. Then open the Professor movieclip from the Library.

2. Click the Professor layer. You will see that the drawing is composed of quite a few bits and pieces (see Figure 3-33). If you wanted to move that drawing over a couple of pixels, you would need to select each element to be moved. There is an easier method.

Figure 3-33. Line art, in many cases, is the sum of its parts.

3. Select Modify ➤ Group or, if you are a keyboard junkie, press Ctrl+G (Cmd+G). The pieces become one unit, as indicated by the square surrounding them.

4. Deselect the group by clicking the stage, and then click the image of the professor on the stage. Again, you will see the box indicating that the selection is grouped, and you will also be given the same information in the Property inspector, as shown in Figure 3-34.

Figure 3-34. A group is indicated both on the stage and in the Property inspector.

5. To ungroup the selection, select Modify ➤ Ungroup, or press Ctrl+Shift+G (Cmd+Shift+G).

6. Close the file without saving the changes.

Aligning objects by snapping

Now that you know how to make your life a little easier by grouping objects, let's turn our attention to how objects can be aligned with each other by snapping. Reopen the NuttyProfessor.fla file and click the Scene 1 link to return to the main timeline. You will see the movieclip and some text on the stage.

Using Snap Align

The first technique is to use Snap Align. You can switch on this very handy feature by selecting View ➤ Snapping ➤ Snap Align, and then select View ➤ Snapping ➤ Snap to Objects. When Snap Align is switched on, the selected snapping type(s) become active. In this case—Snap to Objects—when you drag one object close to another object, Flash will show you a dotted line. This line shows you the alignment of the moving object to the stationary object.

Click the words on the stage and slowly drag them toward the bottom-left corner of the movieclip. You will see the Snap Align indicator line (see Figure 3-35), telling you that the left edge of the text field is aligned with the left edge of the movieclip. By dragging the text up and down the indicator line, you can align objects at a distance. Release the mouse, and the text will snap to that line.

> *The dotted line appears only when* Snap to Objects *is the only snap type under consideration. If other choices are also active—grid, guides, and so on—you may not see the* Snap Align *indicator.*

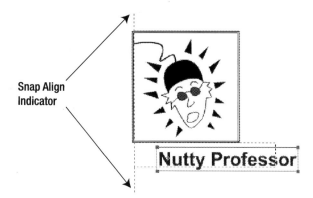

Snap Align
Indicator

Figure 3-35. Using Snap Align

Snapping to the grid

You can also align objects on the stage through the use of a grid. This is a handy way of precisely positioning objects on the stage. Turn on the grid by selecting View ➤ Grid ➤ Show Grid. When you release the mouse, a grid will appear on the stage. This grid is an author-time feature. That means the grid won't appear when you publish the SWF and put it up on a web page.

You can also edit the grid by selecting View ➤ Grid ➤ Edit Grid. The Grid dialog box, shown in Figure 3-36, will appear. Here you can change the color of the grid lines, determine if items snap to the grid, and change the size of the squares in the grid. The Snap accuracy drop-down menu lets you choose how snapping to the grid lines will be managed by Flash.

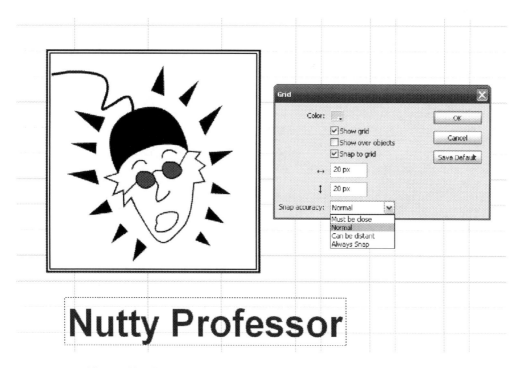

Figure 3-36. Adding a grid and managing it on the stage

> For the first time ever, Flash CS4 allows you to display the grid above objects on the stage, which pleases one of the authors to no end. In previous versions of Flash, one large background image would completely obscure the grid, even though you could still snap to it. The option to always see the grid is super cool.

Aligning with guides

Another method for aligning objects or placing them in precise locations on the stage is to use guides. You can add guides by dragging them off of either a horizontal or a vertical ruler. The ruler isn't shown by default in Flash. To turn it on, select View ➤ Rulers. At 100% view, the rulers are divided into 5-pixel units. If you need even more precise placement, zooming in to 2000% view allows you to work in units of 0.5 pixel.

To add a guide, drag it off of either the horizontal or vertical ruler and, when it is in position, release the mouse. To remove a guide, drag it back onto the ruler.

Once a guide is in place, you can edit it by selecting View ➤ Guides ➤ Edit Guides. This will open the Guides dialog box (see Figure 3-37), which is quite similar to the Grid dialog box. The Snap accuracy drop-down menu allows you to determine how close an object needs to be to a guide before it snaps to the guide. You can also choose to lock the guides in place. Locking guides once they are in position is a good habit to develop. This way, you won't accidentally move them.

Figure 3-37. Rulers, guides, and the Guides dialog box

If you need to turn off the guides, select View ➤ Guide ➤ Show Guides; reselect it to turn them on again. If you no longer need the guides, you can remove them with a single click of the mouse by selecting View ➤ Guides ➤ Clear Guides.

Snapping in a guide layer and to pixels

Finally, you can snap objects to items in a guide layer—not to be confused with the guides we just discussed—and even to pixels.

Snapping to a guide layer object is nothing more than a variation on Snap to Objects, except the layer in question has been converted into a guide layer by right-clicking (Ctrl-clicking) a layer and selecting Guide. What's the difference? Guide layer content isn't included in the SWF.

Snapping to pixels is best suited for ultra-precise positioning, which is sometimes useful with text fields and bitmaps. In fact, you won't even see the pixel grid until you've zoomed in to at least 400%. The pixel grid is not the same as the grid explored earlier.

> For better or worse, the pixel grid still appears only behind stage content. Ah, well, can't win 'em all.

Stacking order and using the Align panel

Layers are effective tools for managing content, but there is another related concept you need to be aware of: *stacking*. When multiple objects are in a layer, the objects also have a front-to-back relationship with each other, appearing to be placed on top of each other, which is called the *stacking order*.

Stacking objects

Symbols, drawing objects, primitives, text fields, and grouped objects can be stacked. Everything else (for example, vector shapes) essentially falls to the bottom of the pile in the layer. To accomplish stacking, each new symbol or group added to a layer is given a position in the stack, which determines how far up from the bottom it will be placed. This position is assigned in the order in which the symbols or objects are added to the stage. This means that each symbol added to the stage sits in front, or above, the symbols or objects already on the stage. Let's see how this works.

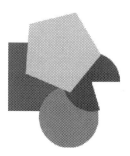

1. Open the Stacks.fla file in the Chapter 3 Exercise folder. You will see four objects on the stage.

2. Drag the objects on top of each other. You will see a stack, as shown in Figure 3-38. The location of each object in this stack is a visual clue to when it was placed on the stage.

Stacking order is not fixed. For example, let's move the circle to the top of the stack and move the yellow pentagon under the Pac-Man shape.

3. Select the circle on the stage and select Modify ➤ Arrange ➤ Bring to Front. The circle moves to the top of the stack. This tells you that the Bring to Front and Send to Back menu items are used to move selected objects to the top or the bottom of a stack.

Figure 3-38. Objects stacked in a layer

4. Select the pentagon and select Modify ➤ Arrange ➤ Send Backward, as shown in Figure 3-39. The pentagon moves under the Pac-Man symbol. This tells you that the Bring Forward or Send Backward menu items can be used to move objects in front of or behind each other.

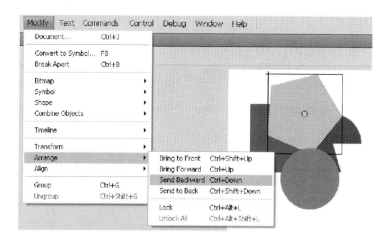

Figure 3-39. Use the menu to change the stacking order of objects.

Distributing to layers

Throughout this book, we have talked about the use of layers to manage content. Obviously, stacking objects on top of each other flies in the face of what we have said. Not so fast. There is an incredibly useful menu item that actually allows you to bring a bit of order to the chaos. Let's try this feature with the Stacks.fla file.

1. Select all the items on the stage.

2. Select Modify ➤ Timeline ➤ Distribute to Layers. When you release the mouse, the order of the objects in relation to each other doesn't change, but each object is now on its own named layer, as shown in Figure 3-40.

3. Close the file without saving the changes.

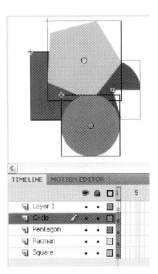

Now that you see what you can do with this powerful menu item, you also need to understand some rules regarding its use:

- Symbols, shapes, drawing objects, primitives, text fields, and grouped objects will be placed on their own individual layers.

- For symbols, the name of the layer is based on either the symbol's library name or its instance name in the Property inspector. If both names are present, instance names take precedence.

- For text fields, the name of the layer is based on the text content—or the text field's instance name in the Property inspector. Again, instance names take precedence.

Figure 3-40. Distribute to Layers places each selected object on its own layer.

Using the Align panel

The Align panel allows you to line up and center objects, and otherwise bring order to chaos with a click or two of the mouse.

You can access the Align panel by either selecting Window ➤ Align or pressing Ctrl+K (Cmd+K). As shown in Figure 3-41, this panel offers a number of alignment possibilities: 17 options and one toggle button labeled To stage. The To stage button lets you align selected objects with each other or align them to the stage.

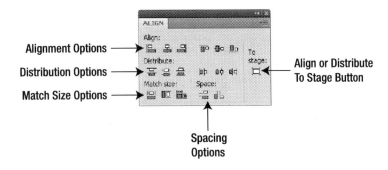

Figure 3-41. The Align panel

Let's see how all of this works.

1. Open the `AlignPanel.fla` file in the `Exercise` folder. As you can see, the file consists of a number of button components scattered across the stage. Open the Align panel.

2. Select all the components, make sure the To stage button is not selected, and then click the Align Left Edge button in the panel (see Figure 3-42). The components all line up along their left edges.

Figure 3-42. Aligning objects vertically using the Align panel

3. Click the Vertical Spacing button in the Space options, and the components will be spaced evenly on the vertical axis. Click the Distribute Top Edge button to even out the spacing.

Now let's use the panel to create a button bar across the top of the stage.

4. Click the To stage button on the Align panel.

5. Select all the buttons and click the Align Top Edge button. The buttons will all pile on top of each other at the top of the stage.

6. With the buttons still selected, click the Distribute Horizontal Center button. The buttons spread out along the top of the stage, as shown in Figure 3-43. Not bad—two clicks, and you have a button bar.

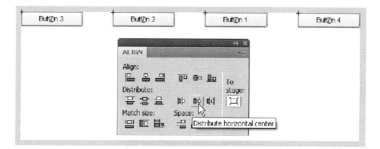

Figure 3-43. Two clicks is all it takes to create a button bar.

7. Close the file without saving the changes.

Masks and masking

Before we turn you loose on a project, the final subject we will be examining is the issue of masking in Flash. As you know, masks are used to selectively show and hide objects on the Flash stage. The value of a mask is, in many respects, not clearly understood by Flash designers. They tend to regard masking as a way to hide stuff. They see it as an overly complicated method of doing something that could be more easily done in an imaging application. This is not exactly incorrect, but what they tend to miss is the fact that masks in Flash can be animated and can even react to events on the stage. For example, one of the authors connects a webcam to his computer, and using Flash, is able to broadcast himself peering out of billboards in Times Square, waving at people walking by in Piccadilly Circus in London, or looking out of the porthole of a sensory deprivation tank. When the camera is not connected, the background images revert to their normal states.

Here, you'll learn how to create a simple mask, create a masked animation, and use text as a mask. Finally, you'll tackle creating a soft mask, an exercise that puts together some of the techniques covered in this chapter.

Creating a simple mask

We'll begin with the basic steps involved in a creating a mask in Flash. Once you have the fundamentals under your belt, you can then apply what you have learned in a rather creative manner.

1. Open the SimpleMask.fla file in the Chapter 3 Exercise folder.

2. Add a new layer named Mask and draw a circle with no stroke on the new layer.

3. Right-click (Ctrl-click) on the Mask layer to open the Layer context menu and select Mask. When you release the mouse, the image of the statue will look like it is circular. You should also notice that the appearance of the layers has changed, and that they are locked (see Figure 3-44). The icon beside the Mask layer name (the rectangle with a cutout) indicates that the layer is a mask, and the indent for the Statue layer name indicates that it is the object being masked.

Figure 3-44. Applying a mask

You see the image showing through the circle in the Mask layer, with the stage color visible. One thing you should know about masks is that you need to be careful dragging other layers under them. Do that, and they also will be masked—depending on how you do the dragging. The following steps explain what we're getting at:

4. Add a new layer above the mask and name it Square. Select the Rectangle tool and draw a rectangle on this new layer.

5. Drag the Square layer under the Statue layer, and slightly to the right. When you release the mouse, the circle and the square are both visible. Click the Lock icon in the Square layer, and the square will disappear because it is under the photograph.

> *The locks turn the masks on and off and allow you to edit or manipulate the content in the layers, including the masks. When you finish making your changes, click the locks to reapply the mask. When all layers are locked (the masked layers and the mask), the mask goes into a preview mode.*

6. Unlock the Square layer and drag it back above the Mask layer. This time, drag the Mask layer above the Square layer (to the left or right—it doesn't matter). When you release the mouse, you will see that both the Mask and Statue layers have moved above the Square layer, and that the shape in the layer is visible, as shown in Figure 3-45.

Figure 3-45. Masking layers can be moved around.

7. Drag the Square layer below the Statue layer again, this time keeping to the left. When you release the mouse, the Square layer is no longer associated with the mask. This is an alternate way to toggle between the Normal and Masked (or Mask) layer options seen when you right-click (Ctrl-click) a layer and select Properties.

8. Close the file without saving the changes.

Now that you understand the fundamentals, let's get a little more complex.

Creating a masked animation

As we've said before, the art of Flash is, in many respects, the art of illusion. In this exercise, you'll create the illusion of a couple of people—the authors—suddenly appearing in the windows of a building. The problem to contend with is the fact the windows are large and each window is broken into eight pieces of glass, each pane separated by a thin wooden frame. How do you get the authors to appear in the window but behind a frame? You think a bit differently.

The effect you want to create is shown in Figure 3-46. Instead of using the windows as the mask, you only need to use the bottom four panes of glass as the mask. The following steps show you how to accomplish this.

1. Open the Windows.fla file in the Exercise folder. All of the items you will need for this exercise are located in the library.

Figure 3-46. The authors under glass

2. Drag the Building graphic symbol to the stage. In the Property inspector, set its x and y coordinates to 0. Name this layer Building and lock the layer.

3. Add a new layer named Mask. Select the Zoom tool and zoom in on the bottom four panes of glass.

4. Select the Rectangle tool and draw a rectangle over each of the four panes. Holding down the Shift key, select each of the rectangles you have just drawn, and convert the entire selection to a single movieclip symbol named Mask.

5. Open the Mask movieclip in the Symbol Editor. Change Layer 1's name to Windows, and add a new layer named Guys to the timeline. Drag the Guys layer under the Windows layer.

6. Select frame 1 of the Guys layer and drag a copy of the Authors graphic symbol to the stage. Place the authors just under the rectangles in the Windows layer, as shown in Figure 3-47.

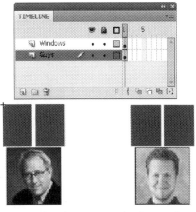

With the assets in place, you can now concentrate on creating the animation. The plan is to have the pictures rise up in the window and then sink back down out of view.

Figure 3-47. The assets are in place, and you can now move on to creating the movie.

7. Select frame 20 of the Windows layer and insert a frame.

8. Select frame 20 of the Guys layer and add a frame. Right-click (Ctrl-click) anywhere between the two frames and select Create Motion Tween from the context menu.

9. Open the Motion Editor panel and twirl down the Basic motion properties. Drag the mouse to frame 10 of the Motion Editor panel and click a diamond to add a key frame. Repeat this at frame 20 as well.

10. Drag the playhead back to frame 10 and set the Y value to 24. The graph will develop the dip shown in Figure 3-48. If you scrub the playhead across the timeline, you will see the authors move upward.

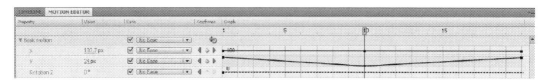

Figure 3-48. The assets are in place, and you can now move on to creating the movie.

11. With the playhead at frame 1 in the Motion Editor panel, click the + sign beside the Color Effect strip and select Alpha. Set the Alpha value to 50%. Add a keyframe at frame 10 and set the Alpha value to 100%. In frame 20, add a keyframe and set the Alpha value to 50%. Scrub across the Motion Editor timeline and you will see the images fade in as they rise and fade back out as they sink.

12. Select the Timeline panel. Select the Windows layer and turn it into a Mask layer. If you scrub across the timeline, you will see the images fade in and back out as they move up and down (see Figure 3-49).

> *Why are the authors' images in a symbol? The primary reason is that the* Motion Editor *can animate only symbols or text fields. Another point to keep in mind is that you can't put both images in motion in the same layer unless they're contained by the same symbol. Each author's image could, of course, be separately animated in its own layer and still be masked by the same mask layer.*

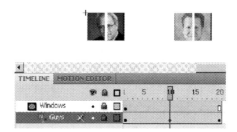

Figure 3-49. The animation and the mask

13. Click the Scene 1 link to return to the main timeline. The Mask movieclip just created is the white dot in the corner of the window.

14. Save the movie and test it.

The point of this exercise was to demonstrate that animations can be masked. We'll cover animation in detail in Chapters 7 and 8.

Using text as a mask

Though we are going to fully explore the use of text in Flash in Chapter 6, we can't overlook the power of using text as a mask. If you are going to be using text for this purpose, pick a font that has a bold version, such as Arial Black, or another font that has the words *Heavy*, *Black*, *Bold*, or *Demi* in its name. These fonts are traditionally used as headline fonts, which makes them ideal for use as a mask.

Let's have some fun with a text mask and create an intro screen for a site named Places.

1. Open the Places.fla file in the Exercise folder. Add a new layer and name it Text.

2. Select the Text layer, and then select the Text tool. Click in the Text layer and enter the word Places. Select the word with the Text tool.

3. In the Property inspector, change the font to a strong sans serif—we chose Arial Black—and set the point size for the text to 140, as shown in Figure 3-50. The font size slider in the Property inspector only goes up to a value of 96, so double-click the value and enter 140 from the keyboard.

Figure 3-50. Use a strong font as the mask.

4. Select the Text layer and turn it into a masking layer. The mountains will appear through the characters in the text.

Now let's add a bit of motion to this movie. To start, turn off the mask in the Text layer and unlock both layers.

5. Select the mountain image on the stage and convert it to a movieclip named Mountains. Add a frame in frame 60 of the Text and Image layers. This spans out the number of frames in both layers.

6. In frame 1, move the mountain upward until the bottom of the image is sitting on the top edge of the text. Add a motion tween to the layer.

7. Click in any frame of the Image layer and select the Motion Editor panel.

8. Drag the playhead to frame 60 of the Motion Editor timeline and twirl down the Basic motion properties. Click the diamond in the Y grid to add a keyframe at frame 60 and scrub the Y hot text to a value of high enough that the mountains move past the bottom of the text. If you now scrub across the Motion Editor timeline, the mountains move down the stage.

9. Select the Timeline panel, lock the two layers to reapply the mask, and scrub across the timeline. The image appears inside the text, as shown in Figure 3-51.

Figure 3-51. The image is animated in the text field mask.

You can also add a bit of graphic interest to the mask by applying a filter to the text. If you intend to go this route, though, keep in mind that filters can't be applied to anything that's being used as a mask. Instead, the filter needs to be applied to a copy of the text in its own layer. You can move the copy layer under the mask to give the illusion that a filter has been applied in the usual way. Let's try that.

10. Add a new layer named Filter to the timeline.

11. Unlock the Text layer, select the text on the stage, and copy the text to the clipboard.

12. Relock the Text layer to apply the mask. Select frame 1 of the Filter layer, and select Edit ➤ Paste in Place to position the text directly over the mask.

13. Select the text in the Filter layer and apply the Gradient Glow filter using the following settings in the Property inspector (see Figure 3-52):

- Blur X: 7
- Blur Y: 7
- Strength: 100%
- Quality: High
- Angle: 295
- Distance: 6
- Knockout: Selected (this turns the text transparent; the glow stays on the edges)
- Type: Outer
- Start Color: #FFFFFF (white)
- End Color: #999900 (olive green)

14. Drag the Filter layer above the Text layer. As you can see in Figure 3-52, the effect gives the mask a bit of a 3D look. Feel free to save the file before moving on.

Figure 3-52. Filters can add a bit of zing to mask effects.

Your turn: Create a soft mask in Flash

You may have gone through the previous sections and thought, "Gosh, the masks all have a hard edge. Is there a way to create a mask that gently fades out an image along the edges of the mask?" Great question. Prior to the release of Flash 8, it could be done, but the process was rather complex and, we might add, time-consuming. With the help of the filters and blend modes, this task has now become quick and painless.

In this exercise, you are going to create a soft mask.

Setting up the stage

To begin, set up your document and objects:

1. Create a new Flash document and save it as SoftMask.fla in your Exercise folder.

2. Select File ➤ Import ➤ Import to Stage, and import the JacobsLadder.jpg image to the stage.

3. Click the pasteboard (the area just outside the photo), and in the Property inspector, click the Edit button to open the Document Properties dialog box. Click the Contents radio button to expand the stage to the size of the image, and then click OK.

4. Create a new layer above the first and name it silk. Import the silk.jpg image to the stage. When the image appears on the stage, select it and convert it to a movieclip named softmask.

> This time, the stage was initially smaller than its content. If you're designing Flash movies and the stage is larger than the stuff on it, get into the habit of reducing the stage size. Wasted space, in the Flash universe, translates into increased download times. Remember that when you think Flash, think small.

5. Add a new layer to the timeline above the other two.

6. Select the Oval tool, turn off the stroke, and pick a fill color in the Tools panel.

7. Make sure you are not in Object Drawing mode, and draw an oval shape on the new layer, large enough to cover a lot of the silk image (see Figure 3-53). This shape will be used to create the mask.

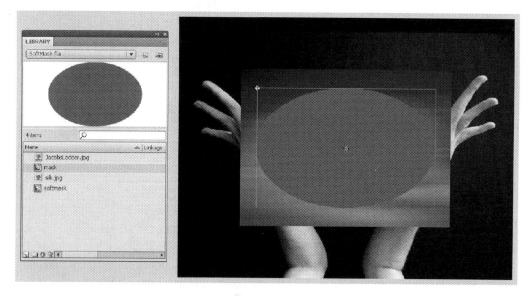

Figure 3-53. The stage is set for a soft mask.

8. Select the oval shape and convert it to a movieclip named mask.

Creating the cutout for the mask

With the objects imported and created, and the mask items converted to movieclips, you can turn your attention to the creation of the effect. First, you need to simulate a mask by manipulating the mask movieclip.

1. Double-click the mask movieclip to open it in the Symbol Editor.

2. Add a new layer below the current layer in the symbol's timeline.

3. Select the Rectangle tool. Making sure you're not in Object Drawing mode, specify a fill color that contrasts with the fill color of the oval—they need to be different colors for what you're about to do. In the new (lower) layer, draw a large rectangle that goes well beyond the edges of the oval.

4. Select the oval, and then select Edit ➤ Cut to move the oval to the clipboard.

5. Select the bottom layer containing the rectangle, and select Edit ➤ Paste in Place to paste the oval into the rectangle. Deselect the oval. You can delete the oval's layer now, because you won't be needing it anymore.

6. Select the oval and press the Delete key to cut a hole in the rectangle (see Figure 3-54). You should see the silk.jpg image showing through the hole.

> *Why not just do the delete thing when the oval is pasted onto the rectangle? When you pasted the oval, it was actually floating over the rectangle. Deselecting the object actually commits it to the rectangle and makes it a part of that shape. Only after you commit to the drop can you cut the oval out of the rectangle.*

Figure 3-54. Poking a hole through an object creates a cutout that can be used as a mask.

A mask without a masking layer

It should be obvious that this effect is going to involve the background image showing through the hole you just created in the rectangle. Through the clever use of filters and blend modes, you are going to remove the solid color around the hole and feather the edges of the oval to create the soft mask effect. Here's how:

1. Click the Scene 1 link to return to the main timeline.

2. Double-click the softmask movieclip—it's in the silk layer—to edit it in place.

3. Create a new layer above the existing layer and drag a copy of the mask movieclip from the library to the stage. Select the mask movieclip and click to open the Filters twirlie of the Property inspector. When the filters appear, click the + sign and select the Blur filter.

4. When the Blur filter properties appear, use these settings:

   - Blur X: 40
   - Blur Y: 15
   - Quality: Low

The outside edges of the rectangle and the inside edges of the cutout will have a blur applied to them, as shown in Figure 3-55.

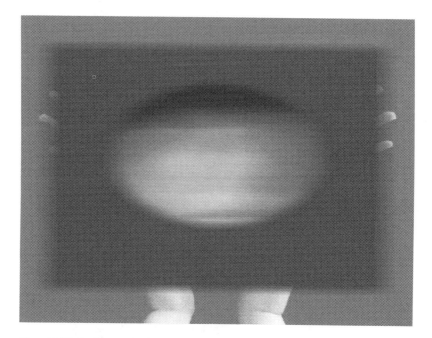

Figure 3-55. Applying a Blur filter to the masking object

5. Select the mask movieclip. In the Display area of the Property inspector, select Erase from the Blending drop-down list. The whole in-progress mask disappears . . . or does it?

The Erase blend mode removes the base color from the pixels of the object to which it is attached. It also removes anything behind it. In this case, the content will show through the hole. Also, as we pointed out in an earlier masking exercise, content on a masking layer can't have a filter applied to it. The blend modes allow filters, which means that the content showing through the hole will gradually fade out.

6. To complete the effect, return to the main timeline by clicking the Scene 1 link. Click the soft-mask movieclip on the stage to select it.

7. With the softmask movieclip selected, apply the Layer blend mode in the Property inspector. The mask effect now becomes apparent, as shown in Figure 3-56.

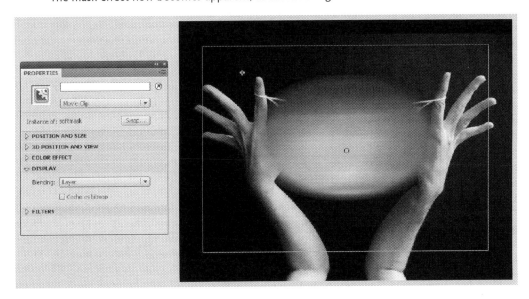

Figure 3-56. Apply the Layer blend mode to the movieclip on the stage to create the effect.

8. Save the movie.

What happened? There are 11 blend modes in Flash, and 2 of them—Alpha and Erase—require that a Layer blend mode be applied to the parent movieclip or object. In this exercise, the softmask movieclip is the parent of the mask movieclip. The parent is required because of the hierarchy that Flash uses for managing content on the stage, which is different from how Photoshop CS4 and Fireworks CS4 work. This is why the Alpha and Erase modes require that an additional movieclip be set to the Layer blend mode.

Flash treats this movieclip as an entirely different canvas. In this specific case, the embedded blending modes are first calculated, and then the parent—softmask—is redrawn using the Normal blend mode. This is needed because you can't have an invisible stage on the main timeline. This is awfully techie, but you now know how to use the Erase and the Layer blend modes to create a soft mask effect.

What you have learned

In this chapter, you learned the following:

- How to create and use symbols in Flash animations and movies
- How to create and share libraries among Flash movies
- The power of filters and blend modes
- A variety of methods for managing onstage content
- How to create and use a mask
- A rather neat technique for creating soft masks

In the next chapter, you will be exposed to ActionScript 3.0, the most up-to-date version of Flash's programming language. Don't worry if you've never thought of yourself as the programmer type. We're not here to make digitheads out of anyone, but we guarantee you'll run into at least a smidgen of coding in your Flash travels. To get a leg up, just turn the page.

Chapter 4

ACTIONSCRIPT BASICS

Programming is a discipline all its own. In fact, Flash has grown so much over the ten years of its existence that people are actually earning fairly decent incomes as ActionScript programmers, or as they are known in the industry, Flash developers. This is not to say our intention is to turn you into a programmer outright, but an understanding of the ActionScript 3.0 language and the fundamentals of its use will make your day-to-day life easier.

Here's what we'll cover in this chapter:

- Using the Actions panel
- Understanding the fundamentals of objects
- Commenting code
- Creating and using variables
- Using data types, operators, and conditionals
- Getting help

The following files are used in the exercises in this chapter (located in Chapter04/ExerciseFiles_Ch04):

- twinkie.fla
- PauseTimeline.fla

Additionally, we've provided completed versions of several exercises for your reference (located in Chapter04/ExerciseFiles_Ch04/Complete/).

The source files are available online from either of the following sites:

- http://www.FoundationFlashCS4.com
- http://www.friendsofED.com/download.html?isbn=9781430210931

Using ActionScript is a lot like owning a car. Our hunch is that most of you own one, or have at least thought about owning one. We also suspect that some of you (including one of the authors) find the mechanics of a car so mystifying that you prefer to let a mechanic handle routine maintenance. Others of you won't be happy unless the hood is up and you're covered in grease up to your elbows. Whichever way you lean, it's hard to argue against acquiring at least the basic skills necessary to change the oil and maybe fix a flat tire. You never know when you'll be stuck on the side of the road without a cell phone!

This chapter gives you an introduction to programming as it relates to Flash CS4. We trust the following information will guide you past the first few mile markers.

> *If you find yourself inspired, we encourage you to pursue ActionScript further with* Foundation ActionScript 3.0 with Flash CS3 and Flex *by Steve Webster, Todd Yard, and Sean McSharry (friends of ED, 2007)—useful from a coding standpoint, even though it was written for Flash CS3—or* Object-Oriented ActionScript 3.0, *by Todd Yard, Peter Elst, and Sas Jacobs (friends of ED, 2007).*

The power of ActionScript

When Flash first appeared on the scene (first as FutureSplash Animator, and then later as Flash), web designers were quite content to populate sites with small movies that moved things from here to there. The result was the rise of bloated Flash movies and, inevitably, the infamous Skip Intro button. But once ActionScript was introduced into the mix, Flash started its march forward.

Today, Flash is a mature application, and Adobe now refers to the use of Flash CS4 as part of the Flash Platform, an umbrella term that includes industrial-strength programming tools like Flex and AIR. This means that SWF files are no longer the exclusive property of the Flash authoring environment. Flex Builder 3 also produces SWFs. They're fundamentally the same as SWFs built in Flash—they all run in the same Flash Player 9 or higher—but Flex is geared toward programmers who normally work in applications like Microsoft Visual Studio or Borland JBuilder—not at all the domain of artsy types! As you have seen in the preceding chapters, Flash can still be used to move things from here to there. On the one hand, you have an animation tool for building scalable, lightweight motion graphics that renders animated GIFs extinct, and many Flash designers are using the application to create broadcast quality cartoons for display on the Web and television.

On the other hand, even without Flex Builder 3, Flash developers have plenty of room to spread their wings. They use the platform for everything from building online banking applications to fully realized clones of Super Mario Brothers. In between is a wealth of content ranging from interactive banner ads to MP3 players, from viral e-cards to video-enhanced corporate multimedia presentations. How far you go, and the directions you take, are up to you—that's an exciting prospect! These are all possible thanks to ActionScript.

Put simply, ActionScript brings your movies to life. No matter how impressive your sense of graphic design, the net result of your artistry gets "baked," as is, into a published SWF. What's done is done—unless you introduce programming to the picture. With ActionScript, your opportunities extend beyond the bounds of the Flash interface. You can program movies to respond to user input in orderly or completely random ways.

ActionScript also has a pragmatic side. You can reduce SWF file size and initial download time by programming movies to load images, audio, and video from external, rather than embedded, files. You can even make things easier for yourself by loading these files based on information stored in XML documents and styled with CSS (these topics are covered in Chapters 12 and 13).

ActionScript 3.0 is the latest and most mature incarnation of the programming language used by Flash. As a point of interest, it was supported a full year before Flash CS3 came to market by two related, but distinct, Adobe products: Flex Builder 2 and Flash Player 9. This was an all-time first in the history of Flash. The decision to do so was a wise one on the part of Adobe. What it meant was that Flash developers had already become familiar with the new features and improvements of ActionScript 3.0 by hearing about it around the watercooler. If you were in an academic or office setting during the release of Flash CS3, chances were good that a kind and wise soul had already forged ahead and cleared the path. With the release of Flash CS4, few are looking back. Numerous tutorials and articles on ActionScript 3.0 are already available online at the Adobe Developer Connection (http://www.adobe.com/devnet/). All of the examples in this book use the ActionScript 3.0 language.

> *Flash CS4 is perfectly capable of using ActionScript 2.0 and even older versions of the language. But do note that ActionScript 1.0, the first iteration, is on its last legs, and ActionScript 2.0 is heading for that status as well. The adoption of ActionScript 3.0 has become more rapid than in the past due to the introduction of Flex and the fact that the Flash developer community was exposed to the language so far in advance of Flash CS3.*

So where did ActionScript come from? Before Macromedia joined the Adobe family, it looked at the programming languages used for web interactivity and realized JavaScript was predominant. Rather than add yet another language, the decision was made in Flash 5 to stay within the parameters of something called the ECMA-262 specification. This makes ActionScript a close cousin of JavaScript, so if you're already comfortable with that, you may find ActionScript encouragingly familiar.

> *Ecma International (formerly the European Computer Manufacturers Association) is an industry standards association that governs a number of specifications for data storage, character sets, and programming languages, including specs for C++ and C#. It's something like the World Wide Web Consortium (W3C), which manages the specifications for HTML, XML, and CSS.*

So much for history. Let's roll up our sleeves and get covered in electrons up to our elbows by getting to know the interface for ActionScript: the Actions panel.

The Actions panel

The Actions panel is your portal into the powerful realm of ActionScript. Other entryways do exist, but they are geared toward hard-core programming, in which ActionScript code is stored in external text files. These entryways include the Script window—a full-screen version of the Actions panel that temporarily locks out access to other panels—and third-party script editors, such as SE|PY (http://www.sephiroth.it/python/sepy.php), PrimalScript (http://www.primalscript.com/), FDT (http://fdt.powerflasher.com/), and Adobe Flex Builder 3 (http://www.adobe.com/products/flex/features/flex_builder/). In advanced scenarios, in which ActionScript does most of the legwork in a published SWF, such alternative coding environments are a good idea. But here, we're more interested in using basic ActionScript to assist with the techniques discussed so far—to boost what's possible with the Flash interface alone.

Of the script editors mentioned, the Actions panel has been around the longest. It has evolved through significant changes since its introduction in Flash 4, and even reveals a handful of new features since Flash 8.

Actions panel components

Let's take a look at what the Actions panel has to offer. Create a new Flash File (ActionScript 3.0) document. When the document appears, select Window ➤ Actions or press F9 (Option+F9) to open the Actions panel. As shown in Figure 4-1, this panel has three distinct zones: the Actions toolbox, the script navigator, and the Script pane.

Actions Toolbox

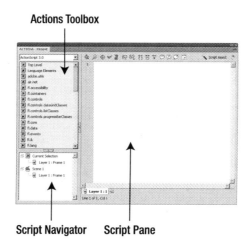

Script Navigator   Script Pane

Figure 4-1. The Actions panel

Actions toolbox

The Actions toolbox provides a kind of "card catalog" for the available scripting functionality in Flash. Clicking one of the little book icons with arrows opens that book to reveal either more books—in an extensive, cascading organization of categories—or a circle icon that lets you add that particular bit of ActionScript to your code. You may do this by double-clicking the desired circle icon or by dragging it to the Script pane at the right. In theory, this gives you a helpful point-and-click mechanism for building complex expressions without having to memorize the whole language. In practice, however, this is like using alphabet magnets to compose sonnets on the refrigerator . . . with a spatula. It's much easier and quicker to simply type the code you need by hand. ActionScript 3.0 is significantly larger in scope than previous versions of the language, and no one has the full application programming interface (API) memorized.

Script navigator

ActionScript may be placed in any frame on any movieclip timeline. The script navigator area shows which frames have scripts, and allows you to quickly jump to the desired code.

Selected scripts may be "pinned" beneath the Script pane. Each pinned script is displayed as a new tab, which provides an alternative navigation method.

Script pane

The Script pane is the high-traffic zone of the panel, because it's where you type your code. Along the top of the pane, you'll find the following buttons for working with your code (see Figure 4-2):

- Add a New Item to the Script: Provides functionally equivalent to the Actions toolbox.

- Find: Lets you find and replace text in your scripts.

- Insert a Target Path: Helps you build dot-notation reference paths to objects.

- Check Syntax: Provides a quick "thumbs up" or "thumbs down" on whether or not your code is well formed.

> *If you relied on the* Check Syntax *feature back in Flash 8, be prepared for a bit of disappointment. This button behaves very differently for ActionScript 3.0 documents, though it still works the same for ActionScript 2.0 documents. For details, see the "Syntax checking" section later in this chapter.*

- Auto Format: Sweeps through your code to correct its posture, based on your own formatting preferences. In a pinch, this can act as a backup Check Syntax button, because it applies formatting only to legal code.

- Show Code Hint: Summons a tooltip that suggests what you might want to type next.

- Debug Options: Lets you set and remove breakpoints, which are used to help debug ActionScript.

- Collapse Between Braces, Collapse Selection, and Expand All: Allow you to "fold up" long stretches of code to reduce clutter, and then open them again.

- Apply Block Comment, Apply Line Comment, and Remove Comment: Allow you to add code comments in two different ways, and then remove them again.

- Show/Hide Toolbox: Opens and closes the books in the Actions toolbox.

- Script Assist: Puts the Actions panel into a special line-by-line mode that provides programming hand-holding.

- Help: Opens the ActionScript section of the Flash documentation.

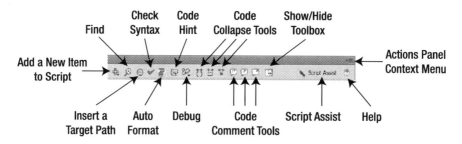

Check Syntax
Find
Code Hint
Code Collapse Tools
Show/Hide Toolbox
Add a New Item to Script
Actions Panel Context Menu

Insert a Target Path
Auto Format
Debug
Code Comment Tools
Script Assist
Help

Figure 4-2. The Script pane buttons

Panel context menu

The Actions panel's context menu, shown in Figure 4-3, resides in the upper-right corner of the panel. Many of its choices repeat functionality already discussed—Pin Script, Auto Format, and Check Syntax—but a good handful of choices show features unavailable anywhere else. These include the ability to import in, export out, and print script from the Actions panel; show and hide hidden characters and line numbers; and wrap text.

A really good habit to develop is to keep Line Numbers *selected in the context menu. Code can get very long, and if there is a mistake, Flash usually tells you the line number where the mistake can be found.*

Figure 4-3. The Actions panel's context menu

The Actions panel vs. the Behaviors panel

If you're not new to Flash, you may be familiar with the Behaviors panel. This panel allows you to select an object with the mouse, such as a button symbol, and apply a prewritten script—a *behavior*—to it. Behaviors include common functionality such as pausing and playing embedded video, sending the playhead to a particular frame, dragging a movieclip, and so on. The Behaviors panel is still available in Flash CS4—under Window ➤ Behaviors—but Behaviors are not compatible with ActionScript 3.0 documents.

That's right. If you're using ActionScript 3.0, you need to write your own code. This is partly because the on() and onClipEvent() functions, which allowed earlier ActionScript to be attached directly to objects, are no longer part of the language. Is this a big loss? Not really. The truth of the matter is that code written through the Behaviors panel is of the canned, one-size-fits-all variety. This means that it is often more complicated than it needs to be, which can make your code harder to maintain or customize. In fact, many Flash developers avoid behaviors because, as they rightly claim, it produces "bloated code." By that, they mean that a behavior may need six lines to accomplish what could otherwise be done using one or two lines.

Are behaviors a bad thing? No, but they frequently give you a false sense of freedom. As soon as you find yourself in a position where you "just need this one part to act a bit differently," you're stuck, because you haven't the foggiest idea where to begin. That isn't the Behaviors panel's job. Its purpose is to write the code for you, not tell you what it is doing.

It is a lot like buying coffee from a vending machine in the office. Coffee from a vending machine might seem convenient at first, but it is never as good as a pot you have attentively brewed on your own. When you finish this chapter, you'll be well equipped to explore ActionScript on your own and use much more of it than the Behaviors panel offers.

Before you start entering code in the Actions panel, let's step back and understand exactly what it is you are working with when you enter code. It is called an *object*.

Everything is an object

Your first step in using ActionScript, and possibly the most important, is to think in terms of objects. This concept is fundamental to ActionScript's object-oriented environment and ties the whole language to an elegant, unifying metaphor. So, what is an object? Well, that's just it: you already know what an object is! An object is a *thing*—something you can look at, pick up, and manipulate with code.

The Flash interface allows you to "physically" manipulate certain objects—movieclips, text fields, and so on—by means of the Free Transform tool, the Property inspector, and other tools and panels. But that's only the tip of the iceberg, and merely one way of looking at the "reality" of the parts of a Flash movie.

In ActionScript, objects aren't physical things, but if you place yourself mentally into Flash territory, you'll find it helpful to imagine them that way. With programming, you're dealing with an abstract world. In this world, objects "live" in the parallel universe determined by the binary information stored in a SWF. That information may be governed by tools and panels or by ActionScript, or both.

Every movieclip in a SWF is an object. So is every text field and button. In fact, every content element, interactive or not, is an object. For visual elements, this is generally an easy concept to grasp—you can see them on the stage—but it goes further. Things you might not think of as objects, such as the characteristics of the Glow effect or changes in font settings, can be described in terms of objects. Even nonvisual notions—such as math functions, today's date, and the formula used to move an object from here to there—are objects. Thinking of these in this way may seem disorienting at first, but the concept should ultimately empower you, because it means you can manipulate everything of functional value in a SWF as if it were a tangible thing. The best part is that all objects are determined by something called a *class*. In many respects, classes provide a kind of owner's manual for any object you encounter, which is a big tip on how to approach the documentation.

Before we move on to the owner's manual, let's look at two objects: David and Tom. The authors of this book, in object terms, are human beings. We'll refine this analogy in just a moment, but for now, let's say our class is Male. You can look at either one of us and say, with certainty, "Yep, those are two guys." But drill deeper, and you'll discover that even though we are of the same class, we are also quite different, which is where the owner's manual comes into play.

Classes

Think of a class as a sort of blueprint or recipe for a given object. If you're a fan of pizza, all you need is a single pizza recipe, and you're good to go. As long as you follow the recipe, every pizza you make will be as good as the one that came before it. Some pizzas will be larger than others, some will be square, some round, and the toppings will certainly change, but there's no mistaking what's on your plate. It's the same with objects.

A movieclip symbol is defined by the MovieClip class. Any given movieclip will have its own width and height, and it might have a longer or shorter individual timeline, but all movieclips *have* dimensions, and all movieclips *have* a timeline. Along the same lines, every type of object in ActionScript has its own unique qualities. These are generally defined by some combination of three facets:

- Characteristics the object has
- Things the object can do
- Things the object can react to

In programming terms, these facets are known respectively as *properties*, *methods*, and *events*. Collectively, these are called *members of a class*. This also explains why even though David and Tom fit into the class Male, we are also different. We feature the same properties across the board—height, fishing license, Moose Lodge membership, and, say, hair—but each has his own unique values for those properties. For example, Tom's Moose Lodge membership expires next year, but David's has only begun. Someday, one of us might have the value bald for his hair property—but not yet. It's the same with methods and events. Both of us can throw a football, and because our married properties are set to true, both of us respond to the wifeIsCalling event.

It's time to refine the analogy in which David and Tom are instances of the Male class. Both of the authors have a daughter, and it's immediately clear these daughters aren't instances of the Male class. So let's reshuffle our thinking a bit.

In a broader sense, the authors are instances of a class that could be called Human. That means our daughters are too, which is immediately more fitting. As it turns out, the Human class, in turn, fits into an even broader category called Mammal, which fits into a broader category still, called Vertebrates, then Animal, and so on. The broader you go, the more these group members have in common. It's when you get more narrow—down the Human branch, for example—that specifics come into play. Mammals, for example, don't lay eggs (with *very few* exceptions!); they feed their young milk, and so forth. This distinguishes mammals from other vertebrates, such as fish or amphibians; and yet, as vertebrates, all backbone animals at least have a spine in common.

It works the same way in ActionScript. Movieclip symbols are defined by the MovieClip class. You learned about movieclips in Chapter 3, but at the time, we didn't clue you in to the fact that movieclips belong to a larger family tree. The reason we withheld this information earlier is because the ancestors of movieclips are available only in ActionScript, not something you can create with drawing tools. Just as Human is a sort of Mammal, MovieClip is a sort of Sprite. Where mammals are a particular sort of vertebrate, the Sprite class is a particular sort of DisplayObjectContainer. The list continues. Further down the family tree, the DisplayObjectContainer class is simply one branch of the InteractiveObject class, which itself is a particular branch of the DisplayObject class.

If your eyes are already starting to glaze over, don't worry. You won't see a quiz on this stuff—not in this book. The important part is that you get a general sense that classes define only the functionality that's specific to the type of object they represent. The Mammal class wouldn't define what a spine is, because all mammals are vertebrates—along with fish and amphibians—so it would be redundant for each group of animal to restate that definition. All of these animals share a spine, and therefore all of their classes rely on the definition of "spine" from the Vertebrate class, from which they all inherit information. Bearing that in mind, let's take a closer look at properties, methods, and events.

> *Do you want to know the name of the absolute rock-bottom object—the class used as the starting point of all classes, inherited by them all? You'll smile when you hear it. The mother of all objects is . . . the* Object *class.*

Properties

Properties might be the easiest class members to conceptualize, because they seem the most concrete. For example, David and Tom both have hair, but the value of our hair property is different. David's is red; Tom's is black. Now wrap your mind around a movieclip on the Flash stage. That movieclip symbol clearly exists at a particular position on the stage. Its position is apparent during authoring because you establish it yourself, perhaps by dragging the movieclip by hand or by setting its coordinates with the Property inspector. To access these same properties with ActionScript, you'll need to be able to call the movieclip by name, so to speak.

Using instance names

As you learned in Chapter 3, you may drag as many instances of a symbol to the stage as you please. So that an instance is set apart from the others—at least in terms of ActionScript—each instance needs a unique instance name. Recall that the two authors are unique instances of the Human class. You tell us apart by giving each of us an *instance name*.

A symbol's library name and its instance name are not the same thing, so they can overlap if you like. But the instance name must be unique from other instance names in the same scope. What's scope? We'll touch on this later in the "Scope" section of this chapter, but think of scope as ActionScript's take on the concept of point of view. David and Tom can both have a dog named Finnegan, and those names do count as unique from the point of view that refers to each dog as "David's dog Finnegan" and "Tom's dog Finnegan." But there's another point of view—in Tom's head, for example—that simply refers to the dog as "Finnegan." From Tom's point of view, he can have only one dog by that name; otherwise, he won't know which of his dogs is which. In the same manner, two movieclips on the main timeline can't share the same instance name.

You name an instance through the appropriately named Instance Name field of the Property inspector. Once a movieclip has an instance name, you can access its MovieClip class members in terms of that particular movieclip instance. Here's how:

1. Create a new Flash document and save it as Box1.fla.
2. Rename Layer 1 to content and add a new layer named scripts.

> *A standard practice in Flash development is to put scripts in a separate layer named* scripts, actions, *or some other meaningful description. This way, all the code is in one place.*

3. Use the Rectangle tool to draw a square approximately 75 × 75 pixels into the content layer.
4. Convert the square to a movieclip symbol. In the Convert to Symbol dialog box, give it the name square so that it appears in the library by that designation.

5. Select the movieclip on the stage and use the Property inspector to give it the instance name box, as shown in Figure 4-4.

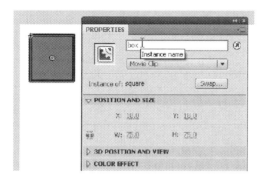

Figure 4-4. Instance names are added in the Property inspector.

6. Use the Selection tool to drag the box instance to the upper-left corner of the stage—not flush with the corner, just in the vicinity. Note its x and y coordinates as indicated by the Property inspector. You're about to see ActionScript tell you these same figures.

7. Open the Actions panel by selecting Window ➤ Actions.

8. Select frame 1 in the scripts layer. This directs the Actions panel to that frame, where your script will be stored.

9. Type the following ActionScript into the Script pane:

```
trace(box.x, box.y);
```

10. Close the Actions panel and test your movie.

After the SWF has been created, locate the Output panel, which will have opened automatically (it should appear in the area where the Timeline and Motion Editor panels are docked, but you can always show and hide it with Window ➤ Output). In the Output panel, you'll see two numbers, as shown in Figure 4-5. These numbers appear as a result of the trace() function you just typed. They are the horizontal and vertical coordinates—the MovieClip.x and MovieClip.y properties—of the box instance of the MovieClip class. In fact, they match the x and y coordinates shown in the Property inspector.

Figure 4-5. The box movieclip on the stage shows its coordinates in the Property inspector. In the SWF, the movieclip's coordinates appear in the Output tab, thanks to the trace() function.

How does this work? The trace() function accepts *parameters*, which affect the way the trace() function acts. The values—called *expressions*—you place between its parentheses, separated by a comma, are displayed in the Output panel. In this case, the two expressions are box.x and box.y. Like methods, functions are coding keywords that do things, but functions aren't associated with a class. We'll show you some additional examples of functions later in the chapter.

> You'll find the trace() *function to be a useful tool in experimenting with ActionScript. Its sole purpose is to display information normally under wraps, such as the value of an object property, an expression, or a variable. In practice, you might use a movieclip's position, or the value of a property of an object, to determine the outcome of some goal. For example, you might want a movieclip to stop being draggable after it has been dragged to a certain location on the stage. You wouldn't need the* trace() *function to accomplish such a task, but it could certainly help you test your code along the way.*

For interest's sake, the x and y properties of this movie clip don't originate with the MovieClip class. This is where the concept of inheritance, touched on earlier, comes into play. Movieclips certainly aren't the only objects that can be positioned on the stage. The same is true of button symbols, text fields, and many other objects. The classes that define these objects, many in their own offshoot branches of the family tree, all inherit x and y properties (and more, besides) from the DisplayObject class. If you look up the MovieClip class entry in the ActionScript 3.0 Language and Components reference, you might not see the x and y properties at first. The documentation features headings for Properties, Methods, and Events, and each heading has a hyperlink that lets you see inherited functionality. We'll talk more about the documentation in the "How to read the ActionScript 3.0 Language and Components Reference" section later in this chapter.

Setting properties via ActionScript

In addition to being retrieved, or read, in this manner, many properties (but not all) can also be set via ActionScript. Here's how:

1. Save your current file as Box2.fla.

2. Select frame 1 of the scripts layer, if it isn't already selected, and return to the Actions panel.

3. Delete the existing line of ActionScript. Enter the following new lines:

```
box.x = 300;
box.y = -50;
```

4. Test your movie.

This time, you'll see the box instance positioned at 300 pixels in from the left and 50 pixels past the top of the stage, just as if you had placed it there yourself. Want to adjust something else? How about width?

5. Save your current file as Box3.fla.

6. Replace the existing ActionScript to make it look like the following code:

```
box.x = 200;
box.y = 100;
box.width = 300;
```

7. Test your movie again.

See what happens? Not only does the movieclip change position—this time to 200 pixels in from the left and 100 pixels down from the top—but it also stretches to a new width of 300 pixels.

> Changing the code and then testing it may seem a bit mundane in these simple examples. There is a very good reason why we are doing this. ActionScript can get pretty complex. Now would be a good time to get into the habit of "Do a bit. Test it." This way, if there is a problem or an unexpected result, you can easily fix it because you know exactly where the change was made.

There are literally dozens of MovieClip properties. Not all of them are settable. One example is the MovieClip.totalFrames property, which indicates the number of frames in a movieclip's timeline. Another is MovieClip.mouseX, which indicates the horizontal position of the mouse in reference to a given movieclip. Some things simply are what they are. The documentation tells you at a glance the full set of an object's properties, and which of those is read-only. Later in the chapter, we'll discuss how to best approach the documentation—in particular, the ActionScript 3.0 Language and Components Reference—but for now, let's keep rolling.

Methods

Methods are the "verbs" of an object—things the object can do. You can spot them right away, because they usually end in parentheses (()), which is the punctuation that actually runs the method or function in question. Staying with the David and Tom metaphor, both of us can walk, but David may decide to take a left turn at the corner, while Tom takes a right. Like functions, methods can accept parameters that alter the way the method is carried out.

As with properties, each unique object type has its own set of methods. The TextField class, for example, provides for the selection of text in various ways. These methods are absent in the MovieClip class, which makes perfect sense, because movieclips do movieclip things and text fields do text field things. The Loader class provides for the loading of files and data from outside a SWF. It makes equally good sense that its methods are unique to instances of Loader, and that neither loader objects nor text fields can send the playhead to a frame of some movieclip's timeline.

> ActionScript 3.0 is much better organized in this regard than previous versions of the language. In ActionScript 1.0 and 2.0, movieclips were optionally responsible for loading external SWFs and images. There was also a class called MovieClipLoader that did the same thing, but in a more useful way. Thanks to the new virtual machine in Flash Player 9 and higher, ActionScript 3.0 slices through that sort of legacy ambiguity.

Let's keep exploring our movieclip instance, because movieclips are arguably the most important object in Flash to learn. Why? Because the main timeline, itself, is a MovieClip instance, which means SWF files are functionally equivalent to movieclip symbols. If you're interested in controlling the main timeline, you'll want to know where to look for the necessary methods, and those are found in the MovieClip class. Some advanced developers will tut-tut this by pointing out that the main timeline can be configured as its immediate ancestor class, Sprite. Technically, they're right, but that's not the sort of hairsplitting we'll get into in this book. You could also say that binoculars are actually a pair of telescopes strapped together. The bottom line is that if you're planning to send the playhead from frame to frame on the main timeline, it means you're *using a timeline*, which means you're using the MovieClip class.

As you learned in previous chapters, timelines have frames. By default, the playhead runs along those frames, displaying whatever visual assets they contain. In other words, the natural tendency of a movieclip is to move, rather than stand still. As you'll see, the MovieClip class provides methods to stop the playhead, send it to a specified frame (skipping frames in between), and stop or play from there, plus plenty more.

1. Save your current file as Box4.fla.

2. Delete the existing three lines of ActionScript and close the Actions panel for now.

3. Click frame 50 of the content layer. Select Insert ➤ Timeline ➤ Frame to add a frame, which spans out the box instance over a series of 50 frames.

4. Right-click (Ctrl-click) anywhere inside the span of frames and select Create Motion Tween.

5. In frame 50, use the Selection tool to reposition the box instance to the right side of the stage and use the Free Transform tool to increase its size.

6. Test your movie. You should see the box instance move from the left side of the stage to the right, increasing in size as it goes. So far, this is nothing new. This is the same sort of tweening done in Chapter 1.

In the previous section, we referred to the box instance to access its MovieClip properties. Here, we could access its methods in essentially the same way—and we will in the next section, "Events"—but for the time being, let's refer to the main timeline instead. Ah, but wait a moment! The main timeline doesn't have an instance name. How is this going to work? The solution depends on a special, flexible keyword: this. The meaning of the this keyword changes depending on context. Since your ActionScript is in a keyframe of the main timeline, it refers, in this context, to the main timeline.

> The this *keyword is one of a small selection of special statements in ActionScript that stands apart from all the classes that make up the language's objects. When you see* this *in code, recognize it as a reference to the timeline or object it's in.*

7. Click in frame 1 of the scripts layer and open the Actions panel.

8. Type the following ActionScript:

```
trace(this);
```

9. Test your movie. The movie will animate as before, but this time you'll see a new message in the Output panel: [object MainTimeline]. Bingo!

As the movie naturally loops, this message will repeat itself whenever the playhead enters frame 1. So, because you know the main timeline is a movieclip, you now have your reference to a MovieClip instance. At this point, you simply follow that reference with a dot and refer to the desired MovieClip method.

10. Replace the existing code with the following ActionScript:

```
this.stop();
```

183

11. Test your movie. This time, the movie stays put at frame 1. Visually, that's pretty boring, but the fact is, you just used ActionScript to direct the course of a SWF! Let's do something a little more interesting.

12. Comment out the existing ActionScript by putting two slashes at the beginning of line 1. You may either type them yourself or use the Actions panel's Apply line comment button. To use this button, either position your cursor at the beginning of the line or highlight the entire line, and then and then click Apply line comment. If code coloring is active, you'll see your ActionScript change color.

```
//this.stop();
```

> *What's code coloring? Certain words, phrases, and other terms that ActionScript recognizes will be colored black, blue, green, or gray. The words* this *and* stop *are reserved for ActionScript and are blue by default, though you can customize these colors by selecting* Edit (Flash) ➤ Preferences ➤ ActionScript. *Gray is the default color for commented code, which is nonfunctional as long as it remains a comment. Keep an eye on the code color. If the word* stop, *for example, is not blue, you may have a problem (maybe a typo). As you can imagine, code coloring is especially helpful with longer words and expressions.*

13. Click frame 50 of the scripts layer and add a blank keyframe (Insert ➤ Timeline ➤ Blank Keyframe). Select this keyframe, and notice that the Actions panel goes blank. That's because no code exists on this frame. You're about to add some.

14. Type the following ActionScript into this frame:

```
this.gotoAndPlay(25);
```

> *The keyword* this *isn't always needed, strictly speaking. If you drop the reference to* this *in these examples, Flash understands that you're referring to the timeline in which the code appears.*

15. Test your movie. You'll see that, because the ActionScript in frame 1 is commented out, it's ignored.

The playhead breezes right on past frame 1. When it reaches frame 50, the MovieClip.gotoAndPlay() method is invoked on the main timeline, and the movie jumps to frame 25, where it eventually continues again to 50. At frame 50, it will again be invoked and send the playhead to frame 25, and the cycle will repeat—sort of like a dog chasing its tail. The only difference between ActionScript and a dog is that a dog will eventually stop. The only way to stop this movie is to quit Flash Player.

What makes the playhead jump to frame 25? That's determined by the number inside the method's parentheses. Like the trace() function we used earlier, some methods accept parameters, and MovieClip.gotoAndPlay() is one of them. If you think about it, the idea is reasonably intuitive. A method like MovieClip.stop() doesn't require further input. Stop just means "stop," but gotoAndPlay() wouldn't be complete without an answer to the question "go where?"

To be fair, it isn't always obvious when parameters are accepted. In fact, in many cases, when they are, they're optional. Some methods accept many parameters; others accept none. What's the best place to find out for sure? The answer, once again, is the documentation. Seriously, it's is your quickest source for definitive answers to questions about class members.

Events

Events are things an object can react to. Yell at David, and he will turn his head in your direction. Push Tom to the right and, if he is walking, he will veer in that direction. It is no different in ActionScript. Events represent an occurrence, triggered either by user input, such as mouse clicks and key presses, or Flash Player itself, such as the playhead entering a frame or the completion of a sound file. Because of this dependence on outside factors, your response to events—called *event handling*—requires an additional object.

It's something like you see in physics: for every action (event), there is a reaction (event handling)—and it only applies if you want Flash to do something when an event occurs. On its own, Flash doesn't actively respond to anything. You have to tell it to respond. At this point, you may want to roll up your pant legs a few twists, because we're going to wade a little deeper here.

Event handling in ActionScript 3.0 requires an instance of the Event class or one of its many derivatives, including MouseEvent, ScrollEvent, TimerEvent, and others listed in the Event class entry of the ActionScript 3.0 Language and Components Reference. The handling itself is managed by a custom function, written to perform the response you want to see when the event occurs. Before this begins to sound too complex, let's return to our movieclip instance.

1. Save your current file as Box5.fla.

2. Double-click the box instance on the stage to open the Symbol Editor.

3. Select frame 2 and select Insert ➤ Timeline ➤ Blank Keyframe to add a blank keyframe.

4. Use the Oval tool to draw a circle that is approximately 75 × 75 pixels in frame 2. If you like, use the Property inspector to adjust these dimensions precisely and to position the shape at coordinates 0,0.

5. Test the movie. You will see the box instance animate from left to right, increasing in size as before. This time, however, that second frame inside box's timeline causes it to naturally loop, fluttering between the square and circle—something like an abstract artist's impression of a butterfly. It's a neat effect, but let's harness that and make it act in response to the mouse instead.

6. Click the Scene 1 link to return to the main timeline.

7. Select frame 1 of the scripts layer and open the Actions panel.

8. After the existing ActionScript, type the following new line:

    box.stop();

9. Test your movie. You will see that the fluttering has stopped, and only the square shape (the first frame of the box instance) is visible on the stage, even though the main timeline continues, which means the box moves to the right and increases in size. This happened because you invoked the MovieClip.stop() method on the box instance, which told *that* movieclip—as opposed to the main timeline—to stop. Now let's use the mouse to manage some events and make this even more interactive.

185

10. Open the Actions panel and click at the end of line 2 of the code. Press the Return (Enter) key and add the following code block:

```
box.addEventListener(MouseEvent.CLICK, clickHandler);
box.addEventListener(MouseEvent.MOUSE_OVER, mouseOverHandler);
box.addEventListener(MouseEvent.MOUSE_OUT, mouseOutHandler);

box.buttonMode = true;

function clickHandler(evt:MouseEvent):void {
  trace("You just clicked me!");
}

function mouseOverHandler(evt:MouseEvent):void {
  box.gotoAndStop(2);
}

function mouseOutHandler(evt:MouseEvent):void {
  box.gotoAndStop(1);
}
```

That may seem like an awful lot of complicated code, but it really isn't. We'll go over it in a moment.

11. Test the movie. You'll see that the cursor now controls the action. In fact, just place the cursor in the path of the box moving across the stage and watch what happens.

> If you get errors or the code doesn't work, don't worry. You can use the Box5.fla file we've provided in the Chapter 4 Complete folder. We'll talk about checking for coding mistakes a little later in the chapter.

In the code, you are essentially telling Flash to listen for a series of mouse events (the three addEvent Listener() lines) and do something in response to them (the three blocks of code beginning with the word function). The events happen, regardless. It's your call when you want to handle an event. The first three lines do just that. Let's dissect the first line, which will illuminate the other two.

In plain English, the line first tells the box to listen up (box.addEventListener()), and then says, "When the mouse clicks (MouseEvent.CLICK) over the object on the stage with the instance name box, perform the action called clickHandler()."

It's a lot like visiting the local fire station. Let's assume you're in a fire station for the first time. Suddenly, there is a bell sound and the firefighters slide down a pole, jump into their suits, and pile onto the truck. The truck, with the firefighters aboard, goes roaring out of the front door of the station. This is all new to you, so you just stand there and watch. The firefighters, trained to react to the bell (addEvent Listener()), did something completely opposite from what you did. The difference is that the firefighters knew what to do when the bell rang. You did not. The firefighters knew what to listen for—a bell, and not the phone or an ice cream truck driving past (either one of which could be considered an event)—and what to do when that event occurred (execute an event handler). What you are doing with this movie is telling Flash how to behave when the bell rings (MouseEvent.CLICK), when the phone rings (MouseEvent.MOUSE_OVER), or when the ice cream truck arrives (MouseEvent.MOUSE_OUT).

You might be curious why the function references—clickHandler, mouseOverHandler, and mouse-OutHandler—don't end in parentheses in the first three lines. They're functions, right? Functions and methods are supposed to end in parentheses. Well, this is the exception. It's the parentheses that kick a function or method into gear, and you don't want the functions to actually do anything quite yet. In those three lines, you're simply referencing them. You want them to *act* when the event transpires, and addEventListener() does that for you. (Incidentally, the addEventListener() method *does* feature parentheses in those lines precisely because that method *is being asked* to perform immediately: it's being asked to associate a function reference to a specific event.)

The fourth line essentially tells Flash to treat the box like a button:

```
box.buttonMode = true;
```

This means the user is given a visual clue—the cursor changes to the pointing finger shown in Figure 4-6—that the box on the stage can be clicked.

Figure 4-6. The mouseOverHandler() function is the event handler that changes the box into the circle.

The remaining functions tell Flash to put some text in the Output panel if the box is clicked, to go to frame 2 of that movieclip (showing the circle) when the mouse moves over the box, and to go to frame 1 of that movieclip (showing the square) when the mouse moves off it.

So what about the parameters inside the event handler functions? What's the :void for, and what's evt:MouseEvent? We'll get into :void in the "Data types" section later in this chapter, but it basically means these functions don't return a value; they simply do something without reporting back. In contrast, the Math.round() method, for example, does return a value; if you feed in 4.2 as a parameter, you get back 4.

The expression evt:MouseEvent represents the mouse event itself—literally, an instance of the MouseEvent class—that gets fed to the event handler automatically. It isn't being used in the functions as shown, but it must be present or the compiler complains (you'll see error messages if you leave the parentheses blank). Using the mouse event is pretty easy. The MouseEvent entry of the ActionScript 3.0 Language and Components reference lists a number of properties for this class. One is called shift-Key, which lets you know if the Shift key was pressed while the mouse event was dispatched. To see this in action, revise the clickHandler() function so that it looks like this:

```
function clickHandler(evt:MouseEvent):void {
  trace("You just clicked me!");
  if (evt.shiftKey == true) {
    trace("The Shift key was pressed while that happened.");
  }
}
```

As you can see, the MouseEvent instance is referenced by the arbitrarily named evt parameter. This object features a number of properties, which can be accessed by referencing the object first (evt), followed by a dot (.), and then naming the desired property (shiftKey). If the value is true—because the user is holding down Shift while clicking—then a second trace() statement is sent to the Output panel. Test the movie again and see for yourself. Pretty neat!

Coding fundamentals

Now that you understand the idea of objects and what can be done with them, let's look at how to write ActionScript code. We'll begin with the most basic language rules.

Syntax

Just like English, ActionScript has a set of grammatical rules that governs its use. In English, for example, sentences begin with a capital letter and end with a period, exclamation point, or question mark. Of course, it gets much more complicated than that, but we assume you know most of the important stuff, even if you don't have an English degree. ActionScript's grammar is called *syntax*, and it's easier than you might think. In fact, there are only three major rules when working with ActionScript.

Capitalization matters

ActionScript 3.0 is a case-sensitive language. If you want to know which frame a movieclip is currently on, you must reference its MovieClip.currentFrame property, spelled just like that—not currentframe or any other combination of uppercase and lowercase letters.

If the thought of memorizing arbitrary capitalization has you worried, have no fear. ActionScript follows a manageably small set of conventions. As a general rule of thumb, just imagine a camel. Those humps will remind you of something called *camel case*, a practice in which spaces are removed from a group of words, and each letter that begins a new word (other than the first word) is capitalized. So "current frame" becomes currentFrame, "track as menu" becomes trackAsMenu, and so on.

Add to this the observation that class names begin with a capital letter. The class that defines text fields is TextField, the class that defines movieclips is MovieClip, and the class that defines the stage display state is StageDisplayState. Still camel case, but with an initial cap.

An exception to this rule is *constants*, which always appear in full uppercase, with underscores where the spaces should be. For example, in the StageDisplayState class just mentioned, the constant that refers to "full screen" is FULL_SCREEN, and the constant that refers to "normal" is NORMAL. You've already seen a few constants in the "Events" section, such as MouseEvent.CLICK.

Semicolons mark the end of a line

As you've already seen, every line of ActionScript code terminates with a semicolon (;). Adding semicolons is optional, but if you omit them, Flash will make the decision on your behalf as to when a given statement has ended. It's better to place them yourself.

Mind your keywords

Certain words belong to you, and certain words belong to ActionScript. The ones that aren't yours are called *keywords* or *reserved words*. You've run into some of these already. For example, function is a keyword that means something to Flash (it declares a function); the term true is a Boolean value that tells you if something is true; the term this gives you a reference to the current scope. These words aren't part of the class structure that defines ActionScript's objects, but they're essential to the language, so you can't commandeer them for your own uses. For example, you can't create a custom function named new(), because new is used to create instances of a class (as in, var mc:MovieClip = new MovieClip();). Search the phrase "keywords and reserved words" in the Programming ActionScript 3.0 book in the documentation to find a full list, as shown in Figure 4-7.

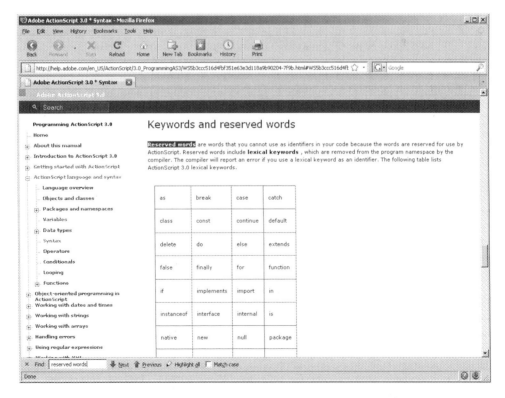

Figure 4-7. The documentation spells out all of ActionScript's keywords and reserved words.

What, only three rules of syntax? Truthfully, no. But these three rules will help you ward off some of the most common beginner errors. Offshoots of the syntax concept are discussed in the following sections.

Additionally, the Actions panel provides help in the form of code coloring. Correctly typed ActionScript is displayed in color, as opposed to plain old black and white. In fact, different categories of ActionScript are colored in different ways. You may configure these colors as you please, or turn them off completely, under the ActionScript user preferences (select Edit (Flash) ➤ Preferences ➤ ActionScript or the Preferences choice under the Actions panel's context menu).

You also might have noticed the Check Syntax button of the Actions panel's toolbar. We'll talk about that after we cover some other coding essentials.

Commenting code

Now that you are aware of the three major grammar rules, you should also be aware of a coding best practice: *commenting*.

In the previous exercise, we asked you to enter a lot of code. We are willing to bet that when you first looked at it on the page, your first reaction was, "What the heck does this stuff do?" A major use of commenting is to answer that question. Flash developers often comment their code to let others know what their code does, to point out bugs or hacks, and to leave notes for further reading (such as a URL to a blog entry that explains the technique in use).

A single-line comment always starts with a double slash (//), which tells the Flash compiler to ignore everything that follows in the same line. If we had added comments to the earlier code, you might not have wondered what was going on. For example, doesn't this make your life easier?

```
// Tell the box movieclip what events to listen for and
// what to do when an event is detected
box.addEventListener(MouseEvent.CLICK, clickHandler);
box.addEventListener(MouseEvent.MOUSE_OVER, mouseOverHandler);
box.addEventListener(MouseEvent.MOUSE_OUT, mouseOutHandler);

// Treat the box like a button to let the user know it's clickable
box.buttonMode = true;

// Put a message in the Output panel when the box is clicked
function clickHandler(evt:Object):void {
  trace("You just clicked me!");
}

// Show the circle shape (frame 2) when the mouse is over the box
function mouseOverHandler(evt:Object):void {
  box.gotoAndStop(2);
}

// Show the rectangle shape (frame 1) when the mouse
// leaves the box
function mouseOutHandler(evt:Object):void {
  box.gotoAndStop(1);
}
```

You can even put the two slashes at the end of line, if you like.

```
someObject.someProperty = 400; // The words here will be ignored by Flash
```

You may also use a comment to temporarily "undo" or "hold back" a line of ActionScript. For example, you might want to experiment with a variety of possible values for a property. Single-line comments make it easy to switch back and forth. Just copy and paste your test values, commenting each one, and remove the slashes for the desired value of the moment.

```
//someObject.someProperty = 400;
someObject.someProperty = 800;
//someObject.someProperty = 1600;
```

You can comment whole blocks of ActionScript by using a block comment. Rather than two slashes, sandwich the desired code or personal notes between the special combination of /* and */ characters.

```
/*someObject.someProperty = 400;
someObject.someProperty = 800;
someObject.someProperty = 1600;*/
```

Here's another example, with the block quote characters on their own lines:

```
/*
The following code uses the NumberFormatter class from
Adobe's corelib project on Google Code
http://code.google.com/p/as3corelib/
*/
```

Dot notation

Objects can be placed inside other objects, just like those Russian stacking dolls, *matryoshki*. Actually, that analogy gives the impression that each object can hold only one other object, which isn't true. A better comparison might be folders on your hard drive, any of which might hold countless files and even other folders. On Windows and Macintosh systems, folders are usually distinguished from one another by slashes. In ActionScript, object hierarchies are distinguished by *dots*. As you have already seen, class members can be referenced by a parent object followed by a dot, followed by the desired member.

plasticWrapper.yellowPastry.creamyFilling

Figure 4-8. Real-world dot notation

Nested movieclips can be referenced in the same way, because after all, movieclips are just objects. All you need is a movieclip with an instance name.

Junk food is a great example of this concept. Imagine a nested set of movieclips in the main timeline that, combined, represent the Hostess Twinkie in Figure 4-8. The outermost movieclip is made to look like the plastic wrapper. Inside that is another movieclip that looks like the yellow pastry. Finally, the innermost movieclip represents the creamy filling.

If each movie clip is given an instance name that describes what it looks like, the innermost clip would be accessed like this from a keyframe of the main timeline:

```
plasticWrapper.yellowPastry.creamyFilling
```

Note the camel case. Because creamyFilling is a MovieClip instance, it contains all the functionality defined by the MovieClip class. If the innermost movieclip had a number of frames in its own timeline and you wanted to send the playhead to frame 5 of that timeline, you would simply reference the whole path, include another dot, and then reference a relevant MovieClip method, like this:

```
plasticWrapper.yellowPastry.creamyFilling.gotoAndPlay(5);
```

This linked series of objects is known as a *path*. The extent of a path depends on the "point of view" (scope) of the ActionScript that refers to it. In Flash, this point of view depends on where the ActionScript itself is written. In this case, it's written inside a keyframe of the main timeline, and you're aiming for the innermost object; therefore, the full path is required. If ActionScript were written inside a keyframe of the innermost movieclip's timeline, the this keyword would suffice. The creamyFilling instance would simply be referring to itself.

```
this.gotoAndPlay(5);
```

It wouldn't make sense to mention yellowPastry or plasticWrapper in this case, unless you needed something from those movieclips. From the point of view of creamyFilling, you could reference yellowPastry via the Movieclip.parent property, like this:

```
this.parent;
```

But bear in mind that it's usually best to keep your point of view in the main timeline. Why? Well, when all of your code is on one place—in the same layer or even in the same frame—it's much easier to find six months from now, when the boss is breathing down your neck for changes.

That said, the most important thing to realize is that you're the one in control of what you build. If it's easier for you to drop a quick MovieClip.stop() method into some keyframe of a deeply nested movieclip—as opposed to "drilling down" to it with a lengthy dot-notated path—then do that. Just keep in mind that paths are fundamentally important, because they serve as the connection between objects.

If you want to actually see how movieclips are nested using dot notation, open the twinkie.fla file in this chapter's Exercise folder. We have constructed the image on the stage as a series of movieclips from the library. The scripts layer has this code:

```
trace(plasticWrapper.yellowPastry.creamyFilling);
```

This essentially asks, "What is the object at the end of this path?" If you test the movie, the Output panel will tell you the object is a MovieClip.

If you consult the MovieClip *class entry in the ActionScript 3.0 Language and Components Reference, you'll find the built-in class members that ship with Flash. Obviously, it won't list whatever instance names you might assign on your own. This example works because the* MovieClip *class is a dynamic class, which means you can add members to it right in timeline code. Not all classes are dynamic; in fact, most are not.*

Scope

Movieclips aren't the only objects that can be nested. And just as plasticWrapper, yellowPastry, and creamyFilling in the previous example each has its own point of view, so do all objects. These points of view can be thought of as special compartments that manage the availability of variables, class members, and other information to the code currently being executed.

If you trace x, for example, from the scope of creamyFilling—that is, if you put code inside a keyframe of the creamyFilling timeline that says trace(x);—you'll get the horizontal position of that movieclip in relation to its parent, yellowPastry. You won't get the position of any other movieclip, and that makes sense. creamyFilling's scope reports its own x value when asked because that scope looks into its own private world first. When it sees that it has such a property, it says so. If creamyFilling didn't have an x value, its scope would look "up the chain" to yellowPastry and try to find an x value there. This tells you that outer scopes are visible to inner scopes, but it doesn't go the other way around.

Here's a quick hands-on example:

1. Create a new Flash document and rename Layer 1 to scripts.

2. In frame 1, open the Actions panel and type the following ActionScript:

```
var loneliestNumber:int = 1;
trace(loneliestNumber);
```

3. Test the movie. You'll see 1 in the Output panel. You've created a numeric variable named loneliestNumber, set it to 1, and traced its value. Close the SWF.

4. Beneath the existing ActionScript, add the following new code:

```
function quickTest():void {
  trace(loneliestNumber);
}
quickTest();
```

5. Test the movie again. You'll see 1 in the Output panel twice: once from the original trace and once from the trace inside the custom quickTest() function. Close the SWF.

The idea is a bit harder to grasp, but try to wrap your head around the notion that quickTest() is an instance of the Function class. Remember that everything is an object! Just like creamyFilling is a MovieClip instance nested inside yellowPastry, this is a Function instance nested inside the main timeline. Because quickTest() doesn't have its own loneliestNumber value, it looks outside its own scope to find that value in the scope of its parent.

6. Replace the existing ActionScript altogether with this variation:

```
trace(loneliestNumber);

function quickTest():void {
  var loneliestNumber:int = 1;
  trace(loneliestNumber);
}
quickTest();
```

7. Test this movie one last time. You'll see an error in the Compiler Errors panel: 1120: Access of undefined property loneliestNumber. Close the SWF.

This time, the variable is declared inside the function. The function's scope can see it, but the main timeline's no longer can. Why? Outer scopes can't look in; the process only moves from inside out. You got an error because, when the main timeline looks into its own private world, it doesn't see anything named loneliestNumber. There's nothing above it that has that value either, so it gives up.

You've seen that scope has the potential to trip you up with variables. Now let's dig deeper into variables.

Variables

Variables are often described as buckets. It's not a bad analogy. Like buckets, variables are containers that temporarily hold things. Like buckets, variables come in specific shapes and sizes, and these configurations determine what sorts of things, and how many of them, a given variable can hold. In fact, variables are practically the same as properties.

A great way of understanding the concept of a variable is to consider a trip to the supermarket. You pay for a bunch of tomatoes, a can of soup, a box of Twinkies, a head of lettuce, and a package of paper towels. The clerk puts them in a bag, you pay for them, pick up the bag, and walk out of the store. If someone were to ask you what you carrying, the answer would be "groceries." The word describes all of the objects you have purchased, but it doesn't describe any item in particular, and the contents of your bag certainly might change. The word *groceries* is a suitable placeholder.

Essentially, variables are properties that aren't associated with a particular class, which means you can create a variable in any timeline and access it from that timeline without needing to refer to an object first. The formal term for creating a variable is *declaring* a variable. This is done with the var keyword, like this:

```
var theGreatStoneFace:String = "Buster Keaton";
```

or this:

```
var groceries:Array = new Array("tomatoes", "soup", "Twinkies",
➥"lettuce", "toweling");
```

From that point forward, the variable theGreatStoneFace is a stand-in, or placeholder, for the phrase "Buster Keaton," referring to the deadpan comedian of early silent films. If you type trace(theGreatStoneFace); after the variable declaration, you'll see Buster Keaton in the Output panel. The variable groceries is a placeholder for an instance of the Array class, which lets you store lists of things.

To summarize, the var keyword dictates, "All right folks, time for a variable." theGreatStoneFace and groceries are arbitrary names provided by you, used to set and retrieve the contents of the variable. The :String or :Array part is interesting. While not strictly necessary, its presence declares the variable as efficiently as possible, as explained in the next section. Finally, the equality operator (=) sets the value of the variable. In the first example, its value is set to a string, delimited by quotation marks. In the second, the variable value is an array, with its elements in quotation marks, separated by commas, and enclosed in parentheses.

> One of the authors, in order to get his students to understand variable naming, tells them they can use any name they wish, and then he creates a variable named scumSuckingPig. A few years back, Macromedia asked for a video tape of one of his lessons, and not even thinking while the camera was rolling, he wrote "scumSuckingPig" on the white board, pointed to it, and asked the class, "What is this?" Thirty voices answered, "a variable." To this day, those Macromedia people who saw the tape never forget to mention this to him.

You pick the names for your variables, but remember the third grammar rule: you can't name your own variable after an existing keyword in ActionScript. That makes sense—how is Flash supposed to know the difference between a variable named trace and the trace() function? As noted earlier, search the phrase "keywords and reserved words" in the documentation, and you'll find the full list. Also, your variable names can contain only letters, numbers, dollar signs ($), and underscores (_). If you decide to use numbers, you can't use a number as the first character.

Data types

Arguably, data types are just another way to describe classes. When used with variable declarations, however, they provide a useful service. Specifying a variable's data type not only helps you avoid code errors, but in ActionScript 3.0, it can also reduce memory usage, which is always a good thing. Many of the people who have been test-driving ActionScript 3.0 have discovered that this also is a factor in the speed of playback in Flash Player 9 and 10. Adobe is not shy about claiming speed boosts of an order of magnitude, and we aren't disputing that claim.

Thanks to the way Flash Player 10 is built, strongly typed variables in ActionScript 3.0 can reduce memory usage because they allow variables to be only as big as they need to be. When it creates a variable, what's actually going on is that Flash Player asks the computer to set aside a certain amount of memory (RAM) to hold whatever information needs to be stored in the variable. Some data types require more memory than others, and when ActionScript knows what type you intend to use, it requests the minimum amount necessary.

Another important result of using data types is that you avoid coding errors. The more Flash knows about your intentions, the better it's able to hold you accountable for them. If a variable is supposed to hold a number and you accidentally set it to a bit of text, Flash will let you know about it. Mistakes like that happen more often than you might think, and to be honest, it will happen to you. Let's make a mistake and see how Flash reacts.

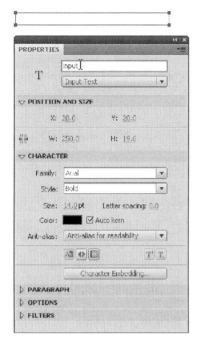

Figure 4-9. Configuring a text field to receive user input

1. Start a new Flash document and save it as `DatatypeError.fla`. Rename Layer 1 to text field.

2. Use the Text tool to draw a text field somewhere on the stage. Select the text field and use the Property inspector to configure it as Input Text, as shown in Figure 4-9. Give it the instance name input.

3. Create a new layer and name it scripts.

4. Select frame 1 and open the Actions panel. Type the following ActionScript:

```
var num:Number = 0;
num = input.text;
```

> *An alternate way of writing the first line would be like this:* var num:Number = new Number(0);. *The* new *keyword is normally used when creating new instances of complex data types, such as a* Sound *object or a* NetStream *object used to play a video. Less complex data types, including simple stuff like numbers and strings, really don't require the* new *keyword for them to be instantiated.*

5. Test the SWF and keep your eye on the Compiler Errors panel. You'll see a helpful error warning that lets you know the num variable, a Number data type, doesn't like the idea of being fed a `String`, which is what the `TextField.text` property provides. In all its nerdy glory, it goes like this: 1067: Implicit coercion of a value of type String to an unrelated type Number (see Figure 4-10). And now you know what that means.

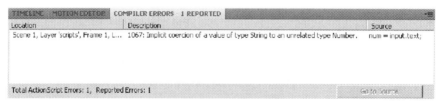

Figure 4-10. Trying to set a numeric variable to a string results in an error, thanks to data typing.

> *You can double-click the error in the* Compiler Errors *tab, and it takes you to the exact line in the* Actions *panel that contains the error. This helpful feature was introduced in Flash CS3.*

6. For extra credit, use Number() to convert the input string to a number. This lets the compiler know that you understand what you're asking for, and that it should trust you on this one. When you finish, close the file and don't save the changes.

```
var num:Number = 0;
num = Number(input.text);
```

Besides indicating the sort of variable something is, data typing can also specify the return value of functions and methods. If a function returns a string, for example, it can (and should) be typed like this:

```
function showMeTheMoney():String {
  return "$$$";
}
trace(showMeTheMoney());
```

Many functions don't return anything, which means they get :void tacked on the end.

```
function manipulateAMovieclipSomewhere():void {
  // movieclip manipulation code here
  // notice the function doesn't return anything
}
manipulateAMovieclipSomewhere();
```

For further details on available data types, search the topic "Data type descriptions" in the Programming ActionScript 3.0 book of the documentation.

Operators

"Hello, operator? Connect me with Grand Central, will ya?" Actually, that's not the sort of operator we're talking about here. Whether you are a casual ActionScript programmer making things move from here to there or a hard-core coder, you will use operators—they can't be avoided.

In ActionScript, *operators* are special characters—usually punctuation, but sometimes words—that evaluate or change the value of an expression. Some of those most commonly used look and act just like mathematical symbols. For example, the addition operator, +, adds numbers together; the subtraction operator, -, subtracts them. The multiplication and division operators, * and /, multiply and divide numbers, respectively. These are appropriately called *arithmetic operators*. Let's use our old friend trace() to see these in action.

Type the following ActionScript into a keyframe and test your movie to see the results of these simple math problems:

```
trace(5 + 5);
trace(7 - 2);
trace(5 * 5);
trace(7 / 2);
```

The Output panel shows 10, 5, 25, and 3.5, as you would expect. The thing about operators is they deal with complexity in a very different manner than they deal with simplicity. For example, consider this:

```
trace(5 + 5 / 2 * 3 - 1);
```

Now, what number would that expression produce? If you answered 14, you are wrong. The answer is 11.5, and it is vitally important to your sanity that you understand how Flash arrives at this answer. The result depends on something called *operator precedence*. Generally speaking, expressions are evaluated

197

from left to right. However, certain calculations take priority over others. This is the concept of precedence. The rule is simple: *multiplication and division take priority over addition and subtraction*. A good way to remember this is to think of how multiplication and division problems quickly reach higher (or lower) numbers than addition and subtraction do. Let's slowly walk through that calculation to help you grasp the precedence concept.

In the preceding expression, various pairings are considered in the order in which they appear, and operator precedence determines which pairings are evaluated in which order. For example, the first pairing is 5 + 5, and, sliding over one "slot," the next pairing is 5 / 2. Between those first two pairings, the division operation wins. Under the hood, the division is done before the addition, and the "new" expression reads as follows:

    5 + **2.5** * 3 - 1

Now the process starts again. The first two pairings at this point are 5 + 2.5 and 2.5 * 3. Of those, which one wins? Multiplication. The process continues, with the "newest" expression now reading as follows:

    5 + **7.5** - 1

Here, the pairings have been simplified to 5 + 7.5 and 7.5 - 1. Neither trumps the other in this case, so the 5 is added to 7.5, making 12.5; and 12.5 has 1 removed, which leaves 11.5.

    5 + **7.5** - 1
    12.5 - 1
    11.5

As you can see, precedence can get pretty complex. Thankfully, there happens to be a way to override the natural precedence of operators. Unless you aim to specialize in operators (and there's nothing wrong with that), we recommend that you use parentheses to group expressions. For example, 3 + 5 * 4 is 23, because 5 * 4 takes priority and evaluates to 20, and then 3 plus 20 is 23. However, (3 + 5) * 4 is 32, because (3 + 5) now takes priority and evaluates to 8, and then 8 times 4 is 32.

> *Here's another way of wrapping your mind around precedence. It's one of those tricks you learn in high school, and the good ones stick. Although the word doesn't mean anything on its own, the acronym PEDMAS (Please Excuse My Dear Aunt Sally) is easy to remember. It spells out the order of operations:*
>
> *P: Parentheses*
>
> *E: Exponents*
>
> *D: Division*
>
> *M: Multiplication (D and M in the order they appear)*
>
> *A: Addition*
>
> *S: Subtraction (A and S in the order they appear)*
>
> *Thanks to Adam Thomas for the tip!*

The addition operator also works for text, in which case it does what's called *concatenation*, which is a fancy word for joining things. For example, the concatenation of the strings "Twin" and "kie" is the complete word Twinkie, as illustrated here:

```
trace("Twin" + "kie");
// Outputs the value Twinkie, which is a string
```

Numbers concatenated with text become text, so be careful of your data types!

```
trace(5 + 5); // Outputs the value 10, which is a number
trace(5 + "5"); // Outputs the value 55, which is a string
```

Even though the 55 in the output generated by that second line looks like a number, it's actually stored by Flash as a string of two characters that, by coincidence, happen to be numerals.

Another operator you'll see frequently is the assignment operator (=), which we've already used several times in this chapter. The assignment operator assigns a value to a variable or property. It is an active thing because it changes the value. In the following lines, the value of the looseChange variable is updated repeatedly.

```
var looseChange:Number = 5;
looseChange = 15;
looseChange = 99;
```

Here, it happens with a string:

```
var author:String = "David";
author = "Tom";
author = "Tiago";
```

In plain English, the assignment operator could be described as "equals," as in "looseChange now equals 99" (hey, that's almost a dollar!) or "author now equals Tom Clancy."

Contrast this with the equality operator (==), which is used for checking the value of a variable. Don't confuse the two! When you see something like this:

```
if (looseChange = 67) {
  // buy a Twinkie
}
```

you're actually changing the value of that variable, looseChange, to 67. When you want to *see if it equals 67*, use this:

```
if (looseChange == 67)
```

If you want to check for any number but 67, use the inequality operator (!=, think of it as "not equal to"), like this:

```
if (looseChange != 67) {
  // buy something else
}
```

These are examples of a group called *comparison operators* (as well as conditional statements, which are discussed in the next section). These particular comparison operators are narrow, though. The equality operator seeks a very specify value, not a range. The inequality operator seeks a very specific value too, just from the opposite angle.

What if you don't know the exact value you're looking for? As often as not, you'll find yourself in a position to make decisions on whole sets of numbers. Think of it in terms of those restriction signs at the theme park: "You must be at least 42 inches tall to ride this roller coaster." They're not looking for people exactly 3.5 feet tall; they're looking for people greater than or equal to that number. ActionScript offers quite a few ways to compare values in this manner, including the following:

- < (less than)
- > (greater than)
- <= (less than or equal to)
- >= (greater than or equal to)

In the next section, you'll see some of these in action. But be aware there are plenty more operators than we've touched on here. To see the full list, search the term "Operators" in the documentation.

Conditional statements

One of the cornerstones of programming is the ability to have your code make decisions. Think about it. You make decisions every day. For example, if you want to visit the authors of this book, you have a decision to make: do I go to Canada to visit Tom, to Switzerland to visit Tiago, or do I go to the United States to visit David?

ActionScript provides a handful of ways to make this determination, and the most basic is the if statement. An if statement is structured like this:

```
if (condition is true) {
  do something
}
```

Thus, in ActionScript terms, the decision to visit an author might look somewhat like this (remember, == checks for equality):

```
if (visitTom == true) {
  bookflightToCanada();
}
```

The condition between the parentheses can be relatively simple, like this:

```
if (fruit == "apple")
```

This might mean something like "if the fruit is an apple" (hand it over to Snow White). On the other hand, it might be a little more complex, such as the following:

```
if (beverage == "coffee" && dairy == "milk" || dairy == "cream")
```

This may seem to mean "if the beverage is coffee and the dairy is either milk or cream," but actually means something quite different. In the preceding expression, two new operators, && and ||, represent "and" and "or," respectively. Because of the way precedence works, the expression hinges on the ||. We're checking if the beverage is coffee and the dairy is milk (both must be true) **or** simply if the dairy is cream. As stated, the full expression doesn't actually care what the beverage is (if there even is a beverage). Contrast that with this:

```
if (beverage == "coffee" && (dairy == "milk" || dairy == "cream"))
```

In the revision, the nested parentheses group the || elements together, and the full expression now requires that beverage not only be present, but be coffee, and that dairy be present and be either milk or cream.

As you may have guessed by now, the only decision an if statement ever makes is whether something is true or false. Let's just jump in and take a look at this concept.

In the following example, you're going to make a draggable star that dims when it's moved too close to the moon. The determination will be made by an if statement.

1. Create a new Flash document. Rename Layer 1 to sky stuff.

2. Select the Polystar tool—it's under the same button as the Rectangle and Oval tools—to draw a polygon or star.

3. Click the Options button in the Property inspector to open the Tool Settings dialog box. In the Style drop-down list, select star, as shown in Figure 4-11, and then click OK.

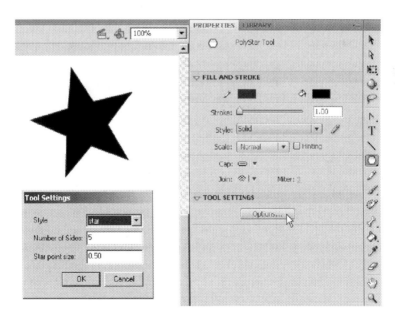

Figure 4-11. Click the Options button in the Property inspector to draw a star.

4. Click and drag to create a star shape. Convert this shape into a movieclip and give it the instance name star. Position it on the left side of the stage.

5. Use the Oval tool to draw a circle. Convert it into a movieclip and, in the Property inspector, give it the instance name moon. Position it on the right side of the stage.

6. Create a new layer and name it scripts. In frame 1, open the Actions panel and type the following ActionScript (which we'll explain after the exercise):

```
star.addEventListener(MouseEvent.MOUSE_DOWN, mouseDownHandler);
star.addEventListener(MouseEvent.MOUSE_UP, mouseUpHandler);

star.buttonMode = true;

function mouseDownHandler(evt:MouseEvent):void {
  star.startDrag();
  star.addEventListener(MouseEvent.MOUSE_MOVE, mouseMoveHandler);
}

function mouseUpHandler(evt:MouseEvent):void {
  star.stopDrag();
  star.removeEventListener(MouseEvent.MOUSE_MOVE, mouseMoveHandler);
}

function mouseMoveHandler(evt:MouseEvent):void {
  if (star.x > moon.x) {
    star.alpha = 0.4;
  }
}
```

7. Test your movie. When the SWF opens, drag the star around and see it turn semitransparent when you drag it to the right of the moon, as shown in Figure 4-12. Leave the SWF open for now.

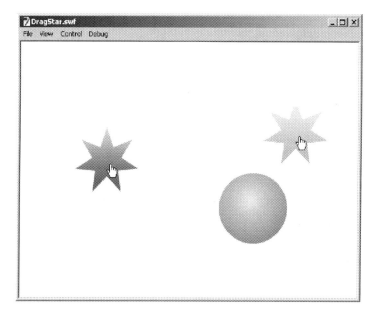

Figure 4-12. An opaque star turns semitransparent when dragged to the right of the moon.

We've used what may look like a lot of code, but there really isn't a whole lot that's new. Just as you saw earlier in the "Events" section, you're calling the star instance by name and assigning a couple event listeners: one for when the mouse is down (the user presses the mouse button) and one for when the mouse is up (the user releases the mouse button). Once again, the buttonMode property supplies the visual clue that star is clickable.

The function that handles the MouseEvent.MOUSE_DOWN event does an interesting thing. First, it invokes the MovieClip.startDrag() method on the star instance. This causes the movieclip to follow the mouse. (If you poke around the documentation, you'll find that the startDrag() method is inherited from the Sprite class. This inheritance business happens all over the place.) Second, it adds a new event listener to the star instance—this time for an event that occurs while the mouse is moving. Just like the other event handlers, this one has its own function, and that's where the if statement appears. The event handler assigned to MouseEvent.MOUSE_UP stops the dragging and tells star to stop listening for the MouseEvent.MOUSE_MOVE event. So, pressing down starts the dragging and letting go stops it. That's pretty straightforward.

The third event handler is where the decision making occurs. An if statement evaluates the expression star.x > moon.x by asking if star's horizontal position is greater than moon's horizontal position. The answer, as you know, can only be true or false. This question is asked every time you move the mouse inside the SWF. When the star instance moves beyond the right side of the moon instance, as determined by the registration point of each movieclip, the comparison expression evaluates to true. In this case, the MovieClip.alpha property (or transparency) of the star instance is set to 0.4 (40%), which makes it partially see-through.

Now, try one more thing with your open SWF file, While the SWF is open, drag the star back to the left side of the moon. It's still semitransparent! With the current if statement, the opacity of star is reduced the first time its path crosses that of moon, but once dimmed, it will never go back. Depending on your goals, that might suit you just fine, but if you want the star to repeatedly change between both transparencies, you need to add an else clause to your if statement. An else clause essentially says, "Do this other thing if the condition is *not* met." Close the SWF and update your mouseMoveHandler() function to look like this:

```
function mouseMoveHandler(evt:MouseEvent):void {
  if (star.x > moon.x) {
    star.alpha = 0.4;
  } else {
    star.alpha = 1;
  }
}
```

Now, when the expression inside the if statement evaluates to false—that is, when star's x property is no longer greater than moon's x property—star's alpha property is set back to 1 (100%).

In cases where you want to test several conditions in a row, you may want to consider a switch statement. From a practical standpoint, switch and if do the same thing, so it's really up to you which you use. Compare the two to settle on which looks cleaner or more compact to you. Here's an example that demonstrates the use of both (note that else and if can be combined in the same line):

```
var favoriteColor:String = "deep purple";
if (favoriteColor == "red") {
  // do something reddish
```

```
    } else if (favoriteColor == "blue") {
      // do something blueish
    } else if (favoriteColor == "green") {
      // do something greenish
    } else {
      // do something else, because no one guessed
    }

    var favoriteColor:String = "deep purple";
    switch(favoriteColor) {
      case "red":
        // do something reddish
        break;
      case "blue":
        // do something blueish
        break;
      case "green":
        // do something greenish
        break;
      default:
        // do something else, because no one guessed
    }
```

What are all those break statements? In the context of switch statements, break tells ActionScript to ignore the rest of the list as soon as it matches one of the case values.

Class files and the document class

With all of this talk of objects and classes, you may be wondering if it's possible to create classes of your own. The answer is yes and is squarely in the realm of "advanced ActionScript not covered in this book." Still, be aware that ActionScript allows you to come up with completely new objects of your own design.

In Flash, classes are stored in external text files and imported as needed during the compile process. There are many benefits to writing code in this way, not the least of which is that classes allow you to separate your visual design from your programming design. An experienced programmer might, for example, program a game in a series of classes—a SpaceShip class, a LaserBeam class, and so on—which would allow new laser beam objects to be created as needed, regardless of which library assets might be used to visually portray those lasers. Artwork could be given to a designer and later "married" with the code with relative ease, because external class files aren't spread among dozens of keyframes.

It is, in fact, entirely possible to produce a heavily coded SWF without any ActionScript touching the FLA at all. This is accomplished via something called the *document class*.

Figure 4-13. Document class files are accessed through the Property inspector.

Click somewhere on the stage or work area to put the Property inspector into stage mode. You'll see a Class field in the Publish area of the Property inspector, as shown in Figure 4-13. This field allows you to associate a class file with the Flash document itself. Technically, it's how you can redefine the main timeline, making it more than just a movieclip (or configuring it to be a Sprite, and then optionally making it more than just a sprite).

Think of a document class as the main script that creates all the other ActionScript objects necessary to do the developer's bidding. Prior to Flash CS3, and even in Flash CS4 in anything other than ActionScript 3.0, this sort of association wasn't possible. Developers could get close, by typing a line or two of ActionScript into frame 1 and importing the main class there, but ActionScript 3.0's document class concept allows a fully programmed FLA file to literally be code-free in the FLA itself.

On migrating to ActionScript 3.0: the pain and the joy

Kristin Henry is president and lead developer at GalaxyGoo (http://www.galaxygoo.org/), a non-profit organization dedicated to increasing science literacy. She specializes in developing educational applications and interactive visualizations of scientific data using Flash. She has also contributed to Flash books and has presented at both industry and academic conferences including Flashforward and the Gordon Research Conference on Visualization in Science and Education. To the authors of this book, it was a no-brainer to ask such an accomplished developer for an "in the trenches" glimpse at what it's like to migrate from ActionScript 2.0 to 3.0. We're grateful to Kristin for sharing a few of her impressions. Here is what she had to say:

> Learning AS3, after years of working with Flash, was both exciting and frustrating for me. At first, I was going back and forth between the versions. That didn't work well for me. So I jumped in with both feet and started coding everything in AS3. Once I'd gone through deep immersion in the new language, it was easier for me to go back and forth to earlier versions when needed.

> The syntax is very similar to previous versions of ActionScript, but subtle differences took some getting used to. For a while, my fingers twitched into habitually typing an underscore for properties like this._x. In AS3, most of these properties have lost the underscore and are now this.x.

> In my projects, I use XML to format external data all the time. The way AS3 handles XML is fantastic! It's so much simpler to work with, and it's wonderful for searching and moving through an XML structure. [Note: This is covered in Chapter 13 of this book.]

> One of my favorite things about AS3 is the display list concept. Instead of attaching a movieclip to the stage and then building up its content, you can now prepare your movieclip first, building up any content and computational graphics, assign property values, and then add it to the display list, by way of the addChild() method, when you're ready. [Note: This is true not only of movieclips, but also of any class that extends the DisplayObjectContainer class, including dynamic text fields. You can see an example in Chapter 6.]

> I'm a bit of a foodie, and to me this is a lot like preparing mise en place before firing up the pots and pans. Get everything ready first, then add it. It can be much more elegant and clean to code in that style. After coding with AS3 for a while now, I'm not sure how I got by without it for so long.

Syntax checking

In Flash 8, and even earlier, the Check Syntax button of the Actions panel's toolbar was a little more reliable than it is today. Even in Flash CS4, if you set the document's publish settings to ActionScript 2.0 (File ➤ Publish Settings ➤ Flash), you can get a taste of the "good old days." But ActionScript 3.0 documents represent a new era, where all is not as it seems, and the Actions panel hasn't entirely caught up yet. Here's a look at what we mean.

1. Create a new Flash File (ActionScript 2.0) document—that's right, 2.0; we're going retro—and save it as AS2Syntax.fla in the Exercise folder for this chapter. Rename Layer 1 to scripts.

2. Open the Actions panel and type the following ActionScript into frame 1:

   var str:String = 5;

   Can you spot the error?

3. Click the Check Syntax button at the top of the Script pane. Boom! Flash sends you an alert box, as shown in Figure 4-14. It tells you to check the Compiler Errors panel, which in turn tells you about a "type mismatch" error: Flash was looking for a string value in that str variable, but you gave it a number instead.

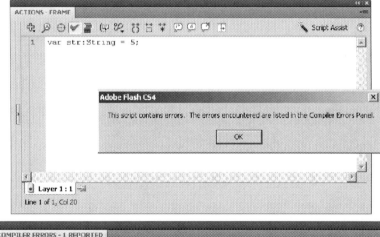

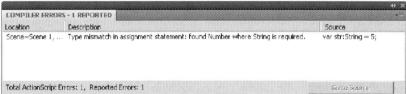

Figure 4-14. In ActionScript 2.0 documents, the Check Syntax button helpfully provides even the most basic syntax checking.

4. Click OK, and then save and close the document.

5. Create a new Flash File (ActionScript 3.0) document—yes, this time 3.0—and save it as AS3Syntax.fla in the Exercise folder for this chapter. You're about to perform the same experiment, so rename Layer 1 to scripts.

6. Open the Actions panel and type the following identical ActionScript into frame 1:

```
var str:String = 5;
```

> *Syntax doesn't necessarily carry over so easily from one version of the language to another, but in this case, the variable declaration in question is indeed the same in both ActionScript 2.0 and 3.0.*

7. Click the Check Syntax button. You'll see an alert box as before, but this time it tells a fib, as shown in Figure 4-15.

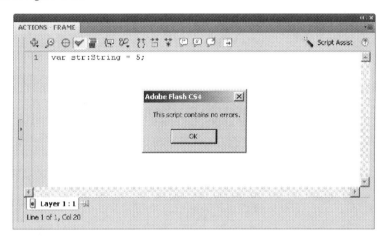

Figure 4-15. In ActionScript 3.0 documents, the Check Syntax button doesn't always tell the truth.

8. As you saw in the "Data types" section, Flash does check syntax during a compile, but you must go as far as creating the SWF before you see the error. To prove it here, click OK, and then select Control ► Test Movie. Keep an eye on the Compiler Errors panel. Sure enough, you get the expected "type mismatch" error (see Figure 4-16). It's worded a bit differently, but the gist is the same.

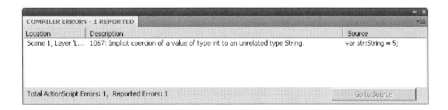

Figure 4-16. Thankfully, syntax is checked when a movie is tested.

The trouble with testing a movie in order to "proof" your syntax becomes clear as soon as your movie takes on any complexity. There will be times you simply want to "check your bearings" in place, without having to go to the trouble of generating a SWF file. Does this mean the Check Syntax button is useless in ActionScript 3.0 documents? Well, the word *useless* might be a little harsh. To be fair, the Check Syntax button does report on certain kinds of errors; it's just that you won't find them nearly as often.

You have two documents handy, so let's tag-team between them and look at a few more examples. We recommend you keep both AS2Syntax.fla and AS3Syntax.fla open, and flip back and forth as you test the following code.

9. Delete the existing code in your ActionScript 3.0 document and type the following into the Actions panel in frame 1:

```
var d:Date = new Date();
d.setMillennium(3);
```

As you do, you'll see some code hinting when you get to line 2. Thanks to the strongly typed variable d in line 1 (the strong typing is provided by the :Date suffix), Flash knows that d is an instance of the Date class. As a courtesy, the Actions panel gives you a context-sensitive drop-down menu as soon as you type the dot after the variable. The drop-down menu suggests Date class members (see Figure 4-17).

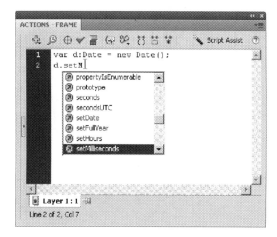

Figure 4-17. Using strongly typed variables gives you useful code hinting.

10. Type s, and the drop-down menu jumps to class members that start with that letter, such as setDate(), setFullYear(), and so on.

11. Type as far as setM, and you'll see setMilliseconds(). At this point, you're going to be a rebel. Rather than go with any of the suggestions, type setMillennium(3); to complete line 2 of the code shown previously. As you can see from the drop-down menu, the Date class features no such method. Does Check Syntax agree?

12. Click the Check Syntax button to find out. In the ActionScript 3.0 document, the alert box will put on a shady poker face: This script contains no errors. Shucks, we know better than that ourselves! Click OK to close the alert box.

13. Repeat the same steps in the ActionScript 2.0 document. Once you've replaced the existing code with the two-line Date-related ActionScript—complete with the made-up setMillennium() method—click the Check Syntax button. Here, the alert sends you to the Compiler Errors panel, which slams you with the hard truth: There is no method with the name 'setMillennium'. Hey, even if the truth hurts, it's good to know.

14. Return one last time to the ActionScript 3.0 document. Delete the last two characters in your code, so that it looks like this:

```
var d:Date = new Date();
d.setMillennium(2000
```

15. Click the Check Syntax button. Are you holding your breath? Go ahead and exhale. Ahhh, finally, we get a useful error message! The alert box leads us to the Compiler Errors panel, which reads: 1084: Syntax error: expecting rightparen before end of program. Sure, it sounds a little stilted. You can imagine it intoned by the colossal WOPR computer from the 1980s nerd classic *WarGames*, just before it asks Professor Falken about a nice game of chess. But it's an error message, and that's a good thing. Click OK to close the alert box.

16. For good measure, make a final visit to the ActionScript 2.0 document and remove the closing); characters there, too. Click the Check Syntax button. What do you get? You get an alert box that tells you to check out the error message in the Compiler Errors panel: ')' or ',' expected. It's more or less the same message, just stated more succinctly. Honestly, the ActionScript 3.0 version is a bit more helpful. Click OK to close the alert box.

What can you learn from this? In ActionScript 3.0 documents, the Actions panel's Check Syntax button reports on gross structural problems. If you have a missing parenthesis or bracket, such as in this expression:

```
if ((2 + 2) == 4) {
  trace("Yes, 2 + 2 is 4.");
} else
  trace("Oddly, it isn't.");
}
```

you'll be warned about it. In the preceding code, the else clause is missing a bracket ({) to its right. This sort of error reporting, even if it's all you get, is a positive asset. In the words of our mothers, "Be thankful for what you have." To that, we add this: if you need a bit of something to lean on in your programming, use the resources at hand. They include the ActionScript 3.0 Language and Components Reference and code hinting, at the very least.

Even the Script Assist feature of the Actions panel, which will step you through code writing line by line, only catches the sort of errors found by the Check Syntax button in ActionScript 3.0 documents. So, tuck your feet, pretzel-like, beneath you, and then up again over your legs. This is the lotus position. It encourages breathing and good posture, and is said to facilitate meditation. Don't lose heart! The very best syntax checker is sitting closer than you think—it's right there between your shoulders.

How to read the ActionScript 3.0 Language and Components Reference

Have you ever had to give a presentation in front of a room full of people? If you're not used to that, it can be pretty nerve-wracking. In spite of hours of preparation, presenters have been known to draw a complete blank. The authors have seen many newcomers to Flash react in the same way to the Help menu, especially when faced with the ActionScript 3.0 Language and Components Reference. You may have been following along just fine in this chapter—nodding your head, because things seem to make sense—but then, when you find yourself sitting in front of an empty Flash document . . . gosh, where to begin?

In Flash CS4, the Help menu launches your default browser, which then displays the full complement of Adobe-authored Flash documentation. This includes "books" on everything from using Flash for design and/or programming—that is, essay-style manuals as well as dictionary-style references—to altering the authoring environment itself in order to better suit your workflow needs. It doesn't take long before you feel a sense of the old "dictionary catch-22": how are you supposed to look up a word to find out how it's spelled if you don't know how it's spelled?

Let's get you past Help menu stage fright.

Getting help

There are several places where you can access the Help files. If you are working in the Flash interface, select Help ➤ Flash Help. If you have the Actions panel open and want to quickly jump to code-specific documentation, select Help from the panel's upper-right menu (see Figure 4-18), or click the Help button in the Actions panel toolbar. If you really need help in a hurry, press the F1 key or use the search field in the upper-right corner of the authoring environment (see Figure 4-19).

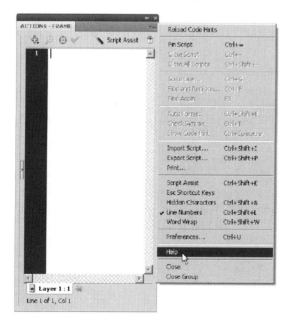

Figure 4-18. Help can be accessed from the Actions panel's context menu.

If you want quick help regarding a specific term in the code, highlight that term in the Actions *panel's* Script *pane—in other words, select a keyword in your actual code—and then press the F1 key, click the* Actions *panel's* Help *button, or select* Help *from the panel's menu. Flash automatically detects which version of ActionScript you're using and opens the documentation to the keyword you highlighted. Be aware that if you go this route, results can sometimes go astray. For example, the* TextField *class and the* Label *class (a component) both feature an* htmlText *property. In one particular test, one of the authors highlighted the* htmlText *property of a* TextField *instance and pressed F1. The documentation jumped to the* Label.htmlText *entry.*

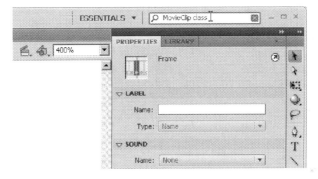

Figure 4-19. A search field in the upper-right corner provides quick access to the documentation.

Search tactics

Browsing the ActionScript 3.0 Language and Components Reference is a good thing. We heartily encourage the practice. Flip open a section, even at random, and dig in; there's always plenty to learn, even for the expert. That said, busy schedules often mean that spare moments come at a premium. Flash's search field can be a speedy assistant when your manager is breathing down your neck.

At the time this chapter was being written, the Flash CS4 documentation was not yet complete. For this reason, you'll have to take our next few suggestions as principles. The commercial release of Flash CS4 may or may not have certain search filters. If present, they might be implemented as buttons, drop-downs lists, radio buttons, or other widgets.

Your number one strategy at all times is to reduce the number of places you need to look. If the a book filter is available, use it to filter the books in which you're interested. If you're not looking for ActionScript-related information, select a choice that doesn't include ActionScript in the title. If you're tracking down programming information, select ActionScript 3.0. If a product filter is available, make sure to filter results for Flash only, as opposed to Flash and Flex Builder. This prevents Flash from looking at books you don't need, which means you won't need to wade through unnecessary search results, including results that might steer you down a very wrong path. For example, remember that if your movie's publish settings are configured for ActionScript 3.0, you can't put code from any other version of ActionScript into the mix.

> For the last several versions of Flash, advanced developers have had access to something called the Flash JavaScript API, also known as JSFL. This special language is different from ActionScript altogether, because it allows the Flash interface itself to be manipulated programmatically. For example, you can automate repetitive tasks with JSFL or even build new drawing tools from scratch. But this language can be used only with the authoring environment and Flash documents, not SWF files. The last thing you want to do is search and discover some exciting "new feature" in JSFL and spend hours trying to figure out why it doesn't work in your movie.

Take the time to learn two important descriptive ActionScript terms. Write them on a sticky note, if you like, and keep it taped to your monitor. Why? Because a number of ActionScript keywords match common English words used in everyday language. You won't get anywhere searching the word "if," for example, because although if is an important ActionScript statement, it's also used all over the place in help documents that have nothing do with programming. If you want to see the entry on if, if..else, and the like, look up the *sort* of ActionScript an if statement is: a *conditional*. Here's that helpful two-item cheat sheet:

- Conditionals, which include if, if..else, switch, and so on
- Operators, which include <, >, +, -, and tons more practically impossible to find otherwise

Perhaps the biggest tip we can give you is this: think in terms of objects. Sounds familiar, right? We hit that topic pretty hard early in the chapter, so why is it coming up again here? Well, remember that objects are defined by classes, and class entry gives you all the owner's manuals you'll need. If you're dealing with a movieclip instance, think to yourself, "Which class would define this object?" Nine times out of ten, the answer is a class of the same name. Search "MovieClip" or "MovieClip class," and you're ushered pretty quickly to the MovieClip class entry.

A class entry will show you the properties, methods, and events relevant to any instance of that class. No more hunting and pecking! If you're dealing with a text field and stumble across a question, search "TextField." If you're having trouble with audio, look up the Sound class. If your problem involves any of the user interface components—such as CheckBox, ColorPicker, or ComboBox—look up the class for that component. The only common object whose class name doesn't match the item it represents is the class that defines button symbols. In ActionScript 3.0, button symbols are instances of the SimpleButton class. (There's always an exception, right?)

Once you get to a class entry, use the hyperlinks in the upper-right corner to quickly jump to class member category you need. Remember that properties are an object's characteristics; methods are things the object can do; events are things it can react to. When you get to the desired category, make sure to show the inherited members in that category.

Edgar Allen Poe once mentioned something about a "dream within a dream." It was actually a pretty tormented poem about not being able to hold onto life, or perhaps time. Fortunately for you, it's not so bad with Flash. Because the documentation appears in your favorite browser, you have all your browser's usual tools at your disposal, including in-page searching and bookmarks.

Using ActionScript

You are going to be using ActionScript throughout the rest of the book. If you have made it to this point of the chapter, you should feel pretty confident about facing it. In fact, once you have coded a few projects, you will actually be able to read code. Once you arrive at that point, you are on your way to mastering the application.

Flash has come a long way from its vector animation roots and has improved significantly with ActionScript 3.0. It's a more powerful language than ever. The really neat thing about ActionScript is that it's relatively accessible for navigational programming of the sort used in presentations, banner ads, and other interactive projects you may undertake.

Here's a recap of our recommendations:

- Get into the habit of creating a scripts or actions layer in the main timeline and movieclip timelines, if you choose to add code to nested symbols. When everything has its place, it's easier to find, which means it's easier to update. Lock your script layers, to keep from accidentally adding graphics to them.

- Take a pragmatic approach. Hard-core programmers may insist that you put all your code in a single frame, or better, in external files. In complex situations, that may be the best way to go. When you're ready to undertake complex coding and the circumstances require it, go for it. In the meantime, don't lose any sleep over doing this the old-fashioned way in Flash, which amounts to little snippets of code among many keyframes. Remember that *no one cares how it was done; they only care that it works.*

- Strongly type your variables.

- Use comments to leave footnotes through your code. Even if you are the only one working on your files, you'll appreciate your efforts later, when the client asks for a change. Comments help you get your bearings quickly.

- Use the trace( ) function to help yourself see what your programming is doing in a compiled SWF.

> *ActionScript has matured to the point where there are a lot of people making a very good living from writing ActionScript code. If code isn't your thing, learn it anyway. Take a stab at it. The odds are almost 100% you will eventually work with an ActionScript programmer, and being able to speak the language will make your design efforts even smoother.*

With the advice out of the way, let's look at two practical uses for ActionScript by applying it to two very popular requests on the Adobe support forums.

Your turn: Pause and loop with ActionScript

People often want to know how to pause the main timeline for a certain amount of time before moving on, and they often want to know how to loop a movie a certain number of times before stopping at the end. Let's wire up these features.

Pausing a timeline

Here's an example of how a small bit of ActionScript can really make your life easier. Let's say you're building a presentation in which numerous photos advance from one to the next. You have 20 of these on the main timeline, and have added visual interest by tweening the symbols' alpha property to make each photo fade in and out. Your instructions are these: after an image fades in, make it hold for 5 seconds before moving on. Assuming your movie frame rate is the default 24 fps, you'll need 120 frames for each hold. Considering the 20 photos, that's a lot of frames! And what are you going to do when the boss says, "Ehh, you know what? Change the pause to 10 seconds"? That's a lot of manual keyframe wrangling. As soon as you redo those tweens, just watch . . . your boss will come back with, "Sorry, make it 3 seconds." (We guarantee something like this will happen to you in a real-life office setting.)

The key to a quick solution is understanding Flash's wristwatch. If you have an analog wristwatch, the minutes are marked around the dial, and the second hand ticks around the face. Flash doesn't have a second hand; it has a millisecond hand. And the watch face is not divided into minutes or seconds; it sports 1,000 little division marks. This gives you quite a bit of control, which is a good thing.

You've already seen how Flash can pay attention to mouse-related events. You've seen event handlers for mouse clicks, rollovers, and the like. Now, you're going to see an event handler for a timer-related event. In this exercise, you are simply going to tell Flash, "When you hit this point on the timeline, hang around for 5 seconds (actually, 5,000 milliseconds) before moving on."

1. Open the PauseTimeline.fla file in the Exercise folder for this chapter. If you scrub the playhead across the timeline, you'll see a number of illustrations fade in and out, thanks to a handful of motion tweens.

2. In the scripts layer, select frame 1 and open the Actions panel. Enter the following code into the Script pane:

```
var timelinePause:Timer = new Timer(5000, 1);
timelinePause.addEventListener(TimerEvent.TIMER, timerHandler);
```

This is new stuff, but the gist should start to look familiar. In the first line, you're declaring a variable, timelinePause, which points to an instance of the Timer class. Think of timer objects as triggers. They nudge other functions into action at a given (and adjustable) interval. The constructor for the Timer class—that is, the mechanism that actually creates the object, new Timer()—accepts two parameters. The first tells timelinePause how long its interval is. In other words, it tells timelinePause to consider itself a 5,000-millisecond timer. The second parameter tells the timer to trigger its associated function once, and then quit. If you define the second parameter as 0, the timer will trigger its function on an endless loop, once every interval. If you define the second parameter as 3 (or 10, or 300), the timer will trigger its function that many times, and then quit.

In this case, the associated function is determined in line 2, thanks to addEventListener(). You've seen this method before. Here, it instructs timelinePause to listen for a TimerEvent.TIMER event, and then perform the timerHandler() function when it encounters that event. You haven't written timerHandler() yet, but you will in just a few milliseconds.

> *In ActionScript 3.0, nearly every object you'll use can be created with a constructor (new SomeClassName()), but a few objects can alternatively be created with the drawing tools, such as movieclips, buttons, and text fields. When such objects are created by hand, ActionScript has no reference to them, which explains the need for instance names. Instance names are nearly interchangeable with the variables, in that both give you a reference to a class instance.*

3. Add the following new ActionScript after the existing code:

```
function timerHandler(evt:TimerEvent):void {
  play();
}
```

This function is written like any other event handler you've seen in this chapter. In this case, the function simply invokes the MovieClip.play() method on the timeline in which this code appears. As mentioned earlier in the chapter, you could precede the play() method with the this keyword (this.play()), but even in its absence, Flash understands that you're referring to the main timeline. The scope of this function tells Flash to look in the current object (the main timeline) and see if it has a play() method—and it does. Obviously, this is the part that restarts the timeline after it's been halted. To complete the equation, you'll need to hit the proverbial pause button a few times.

4. In the scripts layer, add keyrames to frames 5, 14, and 23. These are the frames in which each symbol's alpha property is fully opaque (the image is fully visible). Type the following ActionScript into each of those keyframes (see Figure 4-20):

```
stop();
timelinePause.start();
```

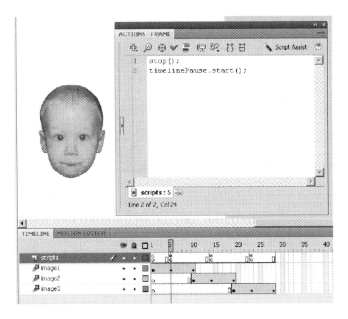

Figure 4-20. Later frames refer back to objects defined in frame 1.

So here's the breakdown. When you test this movie, the playhead begins in frame 1. When it encounters the ActionScript there, it takes note of its instructions, sets up a timer named `timelinePause`, and commits a `timerHandler()` function to memory. Then it notices a graphic symbol with an alpha set to 0 and renders that. Since nothing tells the playhead to stop, it continues to frame 2, and so on. Until it hits frame 5, the playhead doesn't see anything new, code-wise, so it continues updating the alpha of the symbol in each frame.

In frame 5, it sees the `MovieClip.stop()` method. "Sure thing," says Flash, and stops the main timeline. It also sees `timelinePause.start()`, which tells Flash to invoke the `Timer.start()` method on the `timelinePause` instance declared in frame 1. Five seconds later, the timer dispatches its event, which is handled by the `timerHandler()` function, and the playhead restarts. It doesn't matter that the timer and the event handler were declared in frame 1: they're still available afterward to any frame of this timeline.

5. Test your movie to verify that each image pauses for 5 seconds. After frame 28, the timeline naturally loops and the process repeats.

Has the boss told you yet to change the timer interval? You have two ways to do it. Either revise the 5000 parameter in frame 1 to some other number—10 seconds would be 10000, 2.5 seconds would be 2500—or set the `Timer.delay` property of the `timelinePause` instance in later frames. The first approach updates the interval across the board. The latter approach lets you tweak each frame's pause individually. For example, to make frame 5 pause for 5 seconds, leave it as is. To make frame 14 pause for only 1 second, and then frame 23 for 5 seconds again, change the code in frame 14 to this:

```
stop();
timelinePause.delay = 1000;
timelinePause.start();
```

and change the code in frame 23 to this:

```
stop();
timelinePause.delay = 5000;
timelinePause.start();
```

Any way you slice it, using ActionScript has considerably reduced the horizontal expanse of your timeline, and timing changes are easy to make.

Looping a timeline

We've all seen banner ads that play two or three times and then stop. As you witnessed in the previous section, timelines loop on their own without any help. The trouble is that they do it forever. It's easy enough to add a quick `stop()` method to the very last frame of the scripts layer. That would keep the timeline from looping at all. But what if you want to control the looping?

To loop a timeline three times (a popular number for banner ads, but it could be any number), declare a counting variable in frame 1 (call it `loop` if you like), and initialize it to 0. Then increment that value in the last frame, and use an `if` statement to decide when to quit. Here's how:

1. Save your PauseTimeline.fla file from the previous exercise as LoopTimeline.fla.

2. Select frame 1 of the scripts layer and open the Actions panel. You'll see the Timer code already in place. Add the following new variable declaration after the existing ActionScript:

```
var loop:int = 0;
```

This just introduces a variable, loop, whose data type is int (integer) and whose value is currently 0.

3. In the scripts layer, add a keyframe at frame 28. Select that frame and enter the following new code. Then save and test the movie.

```
loop++;
if (loop < 3) {
  gotoAndPlay(2);
} else {
  stop();
}
```

In the first line, the loop variable is incremented by one. That's what the increment operator (++) does. If you prefer, you can swap the expression loop++ with its longhand equivalent—long = long + 1—but that's the nice thing about operators: ActionScript has tons of them, and they make light work of your efforts.

Next is an if statement that checks if the value of loop is less than 3. Naturally, this is true during the first pass (you declared loop as 0 in step 3). It was just incremented, so at this point, its value is 1, but that's still less than 3. Therefore, Flash sends the playhead back to frame 2, where it plays through the tweened animation (complete with scripted pauses) until it hits frame 28 again.

Why go back to frame 2 instead of 1? Frame 1 declares the value of loop as 0, so if the playhead enters frame 1 again, you negate the increment gained at frame 28. Going back to frame 2 leaves the value of loop as is. On the playhead's second visit to frame 28, the value of loop increments again. Now its value is 2. That's still less than 3, so it loops for a third pass. This time, when it increments, its value climbs to 3. At that point, the if statement's condition no longer evaluates as true (3 is not less than 3), which means the else clause tells the playhead to stop.

What you have learned

In this chapter, you learned the following:

- The basics of ActionScript
- The anatomy of the Actions panel
- Why objects are so important, and what a class is
- The roles of properties, methods, and events
- Why instance names are needed to reference objects on the stage
- Some syntax rules of thumb

- How to comment your code
- How dot notation and scope help you locate objects
- How to strongly type your variables
- How precedence affects operators
- How to use conditional statements
- How to check syntax
- Tips on using the ActionScript 3.0 Language and Components Reference

A lot of ground has been covered in this chapter. We hope that you are eager to start learning how to use ActionScript in your everyday workflow.

In fact, every chapter from here on out will use it, so feel free to keep returning here to refresh your knowledge. Also, we recommend that you continue to learn about ActionScript in other reference books. As noted at the beginning of the chapter, two helpful books are *Foundation ActionScript 3.0 with Flash CS3 and Flex* and *Object-Oriented ActionScript 3.0* (both published by friends of ED).

In Chapter 1, we told you we would get you deep into using audio in Flash. With the basics of ActionScript under your wing, let's see what we can do with audio in Flash and how ActionScript and audio make an ideal pairing.

Chapter 5

AUDIO

If you're one of those who treat audio in Flash as an afterthought, think again. In many respects, audio is a major medium for communicating your message. In this chapter, we dig into audio in Flash: where it comes from, what formats are supported, and how to use it in Flash. Regardless whether you're new to Flash or an old hand, you are about discover that ActionScript 3.0 has changed the rules for audio in Flash . . . for the better.

Here's what we'll cover in this chapter:

- Selecting an audio file format
- Adding and previewing audio in Flash
- Playing audio from the library
- Playing remote audio files
- Using ActionScript 3.0 to control audio
- Playing and controlling multiple audio files

The following files are used in this chapter (located in Chapter05/ExerciseFiles_Ch05/Exercise/):

- SeeYouInTheSpringtime.aif
- Frog.fla

- Frog.mp3
- FrogLoop.fla
- FrogPan.fla
- PreachersAndThieves.mp3
- TayIntro.fla
- RemoteSound.fla
- RemoteSound2.fla
- RemoteSound3.fla
- TinBangs.fla
- WhiteLies(Timekiller).mp3
- YoungLions.mp3
- YourSkyIsFalling.mp3

The source files are available online from either of the following sites:

- http://www.FoundationFlashCS4.com
- http://www.friendsofED.com/download.html?isbn=15905910931

The authors would like to express their deep appreciation and thanks to a number of recording artists for supplying us with audio tracks and permission to use them in this chapter. Specifically, we doff our hats—and hold up our lighters—to:

- Tay Zonday (http://www.tayzonday.com/) for a great intro
- Billy Donato (http://www.billydonato.com/) for "See You in the Springtime"
- Molly McGinn (http://www.myspace.com/mollymcginn and http://www.amiestreet.com/mollymcginn) for "Preachers and Thieves"
- Dave Schroeder of Pilotvibe (http://www.pilotvibe.com/) for his words of wisdom and for the collection of Pilotvibe audio clips (found in the Pilotvibe folder)
- Benjamin Tayler, Bryan Dunlay, Philip Darling, and Robbie Butcher, of Tin Bangs (http://www.tinbangs.com/) for "White Lies (Timekiller)," "Your Sky Is Falling," and "Young Lions"

Flash and audio formats

When it comes to sound, Flash is a robust application in that it can handle many of the major audio formats out there, including the more common formats listed here:

- **MP3 (Moving Pictures Expert Group Level-2 Layer-3 Audio)**: This cross-platform format is a standard for web and portable audio files. In many respects, the growth of this format is tied to the popularity of iPods and audio players on cell phones. Though you can output these files in a stereo format, you'll want to pay close attention to bandwidth settings for your MP3s.

- **WAV**: If you use a PC to record a voice-over or other sound, you are familiar with the WAV format. WAV files have sample rates ranging from 8 kHz (the quality of your phone) up to 48 kHz (DAT tapes) and beyond. These files are also available with bit depths ranging from 8 bits right up to 32 bits. Just keep in mind that a file with a sample rate of 48 kHz and a 32 bit depth will result in a massive file size that simply shouldn't be used with Flash.

- **QuickTime**: These files have a .qt or .mov extension, and can contain audio in many formats. If you do create a QuickTime audio file, you need to make the QT or MOV self-contained in QuickTime Pro.

- **AIFF (Audio Interchange File Format)**: AIFF is the standard for the Macintosh and offers the same sample rates and bit depths as a WAV file. Many purists will argue that the AIFF format is better than the WAV format. This may indeed be true, but to the average person, the difference between this format and WAV is almost inaudible.

- **AAC (Advanced Audio Coding)**: AAC is the new "audio kid on the block" when it comes to working with audio in Flash. It is another lossy codec, but it is regarded as being far superior to its MP3 cousin. In fact, AAC was developed as the successor to the MP3 standard. Though you may not be familiar with the format, if you have ever downloaded a song from iTunes or used the Sony Playstation, the Nintendo Wii, or even an iPhone, you have heard an AAC-encoded audio file.

> *Take this obscure fact to a trivia contest, and you will clean up. AIFF also has a sample rate of 22,254.54 kHz. Why the odd sample rate? This was the original Macintosh sample rate and was based on the horizontal scan rate of the monitor in a 128KB Mac.*

Bit depth and sample rates

We traditionally visualize sound as a sine wave—when the wave rises above the vertical and then runs below it, that shape defines numbers that encode the sound. These waves, shown in Figure 5-1, are called the *waveform*. The horizontal line is silence, and the audio is measured from the top of one blip to the top of the next one along the waveform. These blips are called *peaks*, and the sampling is done from peak to peak.

For any sound to be digitized, in the same way as a color image in Fireworks or Photoshop, the wave needs to be sampled. A *sample* is nothing more than a snapshot of a waveform between peaks at any given time. This snapshot is a digital number representing where on the waveform this snapshot was taken. How often the waveform is sampled is called the *sample rate*.

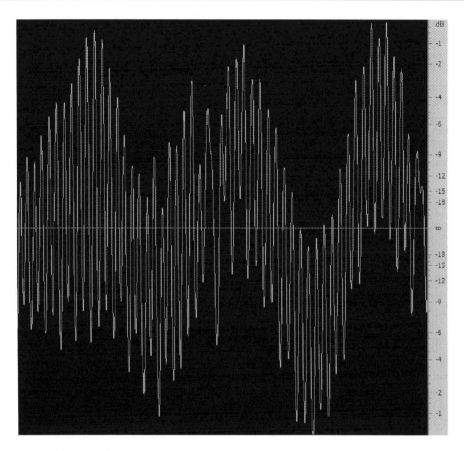

Figure 5-1. A typical waveform

Bit depth is the resolution of the sample. A bit depth of 8 bits means that the snapshot is represented as a number ranging from –128 to 127. A bit depth of 16 bits means that the number is between –32,768 to 32,767. If you do the math, you see that an 8-bit snapshot has 256 potential samples between each peak, whereas its 16-bit counterpart has just over 65,000 potential samples between the peaks. The greater the number of potential samples of a wave, the more accurate the sound. The downside to this, of course, is the more samples on the wave, the larger the file size. These numbers represent where each sample is located on the waveform. When the numbers are played back in the order in which they were sampled and at the frequency they were sampled, they represent a sound's waveform. Obviously, a larger bit depth and higher sample rate mean that the waveform is played back with greater accuracy—more snapshots taken of the waveform result in a more accurate representation of the waveform. This explains why the songs from an album have such massive file sizes. They are sampled at the highest possible bit depth.

One wave cycle in 1 second is known as a *hertz*, which can't be heard by the human ear, except possibly as a series of clicks. Audible sound uses thousands of these waves, and they are crammed into a 1-second time span and measured in that span. A thousand waveform cycles in 1 second is called a *kilohertz* (kHz), and if you listen to an audio CD, the audio rate is sampled at the frequency of 44.1

thousand waves per second, which is traditionally identified as 44.1 kHz. These waves are also commonly referred to as the sample rate.

The inference you can draw from this is the more samples per wave and the more accurate the samples, the larger the file size. Toss a stereo sound into the mix, and you have essentially doubled the file size. Obviously, the potential for huge sound files is there, which is not a good situation when dealing with Flash. Large files take an awfully long time to load into a browser, which means your user is in for a painful experience. One way of dealing with this is to reduce the sample rate or number of waves per second.

The three most common sample rates used are 11.025 kHz, 22.05 kHz, and 44.1 kHz. If you reduce the sample rate from 44.1 kHz to 22.05 kHz, you achieve a significant reduction, roughly 50%, in file size. You obtain an even more significant reduction, another 50%, if the rate is reduced to 11.025 kHz. The problem is reducing the sample rate reduces audio quality. Listening to your Beethoven's *Ninth Symphony* at 11.025 kHz results in the music sounding as if it were playing from the inside of a tin can.

As a Flash designer or developer, your prime objective is to obtain the best quality sound at the smallest file size. Though many Flash developers tell you that 16-bit, 44.1 kHz stereo is the way to go, you'll quickly realize this is not necessarily true. For example, a 16-bit, 44.1 kHz stereo sound of a mouse click or a sound lasting less than a couple of seconds—such as a whoosh as an object zips across the screen—is a waste of bandwidth. The duration is so short that average users won't realize it if you've made your click an 8-bit, 22.05 kHz mono sound. They hear the click and move on. The same holds true for music files. The average user is most likely listening through the cheap speakers that were tossed in when they bought their PC. In this case, a 16-bit, 22.05 kHz soundtrack will sound as good as its CD-quality rich cousin.

Flash and MP3

The two most common sound formats used in Flash are WAV and AIFF. Both formats share a common starting point—they are both based on the Interchange File Format proposal written in 1985 by Electronic Arts to help standardize transfer issues on the Commodore Amiga. Like video, sound contains a huge amount of data and must be compressed before it is used. This is the purpose of a *codec*. Codec is an acronym for enCODer/DECoder, and the format used by Flash to output audio is the MP3 format, although you can import both AIFF and WAV files (and others) into Flash.

From your perspective, the need to compress audio for web delivery makes the use of AIFF or WAV files redundant. The MP3 format is the standard, which explains why WAV and AIFF files are converted to MP3 files on playback. If you are working with an audio-production facility, you will often be handed an AIFF or a WAV file. Even if you have the option of receiving an MP3, you are better off with the AIFF or WAV file, for the same reason that you wouldn't want to recompress a JPG file: because they are both lossy compression schemes.

Why are MP3 files so small but still sound so good? The answer lies in the fact that the MP3 standard uses perceptual encoding. All Internet audio formats toss a ton of audio information into the trash. When information gets tossed, there is a corresponding decrease in file size. The information tossed when an MP3 file is created includes sound frequencies your dog may be able to hear, but you can't. In short, you hear only the sound a human can perceive (and this sort of explains why animals aren't huge fans of iPods).

All perceptual encoders allow you to choose how much audio is unimportant. Most encoders produce excellent quality files using no more than 16 Kbps to create voice recordings. When you create an MP3, you need to pay attention to the bandwidth. The format is fine, but if the bandwidth is not optimized for its intended use, your results will be unacceptable, which is why applications that create MP3 files ask you to set the bandwidth along with the sample rate.

So much for theory; let's get practical.

Adding audio to Flash

Knowing that you can bring all of these formats into Flash and that MP3 is the output format for Flash is all well and good. But how do they get into Flash, and, more important, how does an AIFF or WAV file get converted to an MP3 file when it plays in Flash? Let's explore that right now, starting with an import.

Importing an audio file

To see what happens when you import an audio file, open a new Flash document and import SeeYouInTheSpringtime.aif (in the Exercise folder for this chapter) to the library. Due to the unique manner in which sound files are added to a Flash movie, they simply cannot be imported to the stage.

> *If you select* Import to Stage *when importing an audio file, it won't be placed on the stage. Instead, it will be placed directly into the library.*

When you open the library and select the file, you will see the file's waveform in the preview area, as shown in Figure 5-2. You can click the Play button located above the waveform in the preview area to test the sound file.

Figure 5-2. Select an audio file in the library, and its waveform appears in the preview area.

Setting sound properties

To set the sound properties for an audio file, double-click the speaker icon next to the audio file's name in the library. Figure 5-3 shows the Sound Properties dialog box for SeeYouInTheSpringtime.aif.

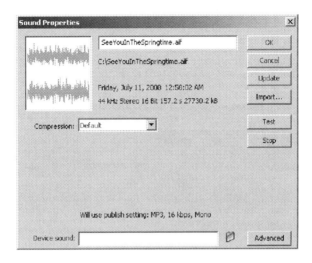

Figure 5-3. The Sound Properties dialog box is opened when you double-click an audio file in the library.

This dialog box is a really useful tool. You can use it to preview and stop an audio file: click the Test button to preview the sound file, and then click the Stop button to stop the sound playback. The Update button is also handy. If an audio file has been edited after being placed into Flash, you can click the Update button to replace the imported copy with the edited version—as long as its original location on your hard drive hasn't changed since the file was imported. If the file has moved, use the Import button to find it again, or replace this library asset with a new file.

> *Speaking of editing an audio file, if you right-click (Ctrl-click) on the file in the library, the context menu that opens allows you to edit the file directly in Soundbooth. Though Soundbooth is positioned as an entry-level audio editor, it is widely regarded as the audio editor for Flash. Once you make your edits in Soundbooth, simply save the file, and the changes will be reflected in Flash.*

Notice the audio information under the path and date. This file—at over 2.6 minutes in duration (157.2 seconds) and more than 27MB (27,730.2KB)—is massive.

Don't worry about the Device sound input field at the bottom. Device sounds are used in PDAs and other devices that employ Flash Lite.

From our perspective, the Compression drop-down list is of major importance. In this drop-down, you are asked to pick a codec. In Flash, the default is to export all sound in the MP3 format. Still, the ability to individually compress each sound in the library is an option that shouldn't be disregarded. Your choices are as follows:

- ADPCM: This type of sound file is best suited for very short clips and looped sound. This format was the original sound output format in older versions of Flash. If, for example, you are outputting for use in Flash Player 2 or 3, ADPCM is required.

- MP3: Use this for Flash Player versions 4 or higher. This format is not compatible with Flash Player 4 for Pocket PC. It is, however, compatible with the Flash Lite player, which is used in devices such as cell phones and PDAs. MP3s are also not suitable for looping sounds, because the end of a file is often padded with nonaudio information. This adds gaps to the loop.

- Raw: No compression is applied, and it is somewhat useless if sound is being delivered over the Web. If you are creating audio for use on a DVD or CD, or developing a Flash movie for incorporation into a video, this format is acceptable.

- Speech: Introduced in Flash MX, this codec (originally licensed by Macromedia from Nellymoser) is ideal for voice-over narrations.

Once you select a codec, additional compression settings will appear. For our example, select MP3 from the Compression drop-down menu, and the settings change as shown in Figure 5-4. Click the Test button and listen to the sound. You may notice how flat the audio is compared to the original version. If you take a look at the Bit rate and Quality settings, you will see why. That 27MB file is now sitting at about 1% of its original size, or 314KB.

Figure 5-4. Setting MP3 compression

Change the bit rate to 48 kbps and select Best in the Quality drop-down menu. Also make sure that Convert stereo to mono is checked. Click the Test button again, and you will hear a marked improvement in the audio quality. And, of course, correspondingly, there will be a significant increase in file size (to around 943KB).

> *Unless your audio includes specialized panning or there is some other compelling reason for using stereo, feel free to convert the stereo sound to mono. The user won't miss it, and the audio file size will plummet. Flash even allows mono sounds to be panned in the authoring environment or ActionScript.*

Asking you to compare the audio quality to the original is a bit disingenuous on our part. Our intention was to let you "hear" the quality differences, not compare them with the original audio. In the final analysis, comparing compressed audio against the original version is a fool's game. The users never hear the original file, so what do they have as a basis for comparison? When listening to the compressed version, listen to it in its own right, and ask yourself whether it meets your quality standard.

> *No, you can't "super size" an audio file. If an MP3 being used has bit rate of 48 Kbps in the original file imported into Flash, you can never increase the bit rate above that level in Flash. "Up-sampling" recordings actually decreases the audio quality, as often as not.*

One other place where the sound output format can be set is through the Publish Settings panel. To access these settings, select File ➤ Publish Settings and click the Flash tab in the panel. Near the top of this panel, are preferences for Images and Sounds, which include Audio stream and Audio event settings, as shown in Figure 5-5. We'll get into these two settings in the next section, but the important thing to note for now is the Override sound settings check box. If you select this check box, the audio settings shown for the Audio stream and Audio event areas will override any settings applied in the Sound Properties dialog box. Think of this as the ability to apply a global setting to every sound in your movie. Unless there is a compelling reason to select this choice, we suggest you avoid it. It's better to give each file individual attention, configuring lower fidelity for minor user interface sounds (button clicks and the like) and greater fidelity to meaningful content, such as narration. If you do have a compelling reason to use these audio settings, click the relevant Set button, and you will be presented with the same options as are available in the Sound Properties dialog box.

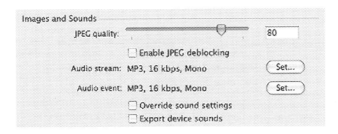

Figure 5-5. The audio publish settings

Next, we'll move on to how to use your sound file after you have it in Flash. If you have been following along, close any open dialog boxes, and close the movie without saving the changes.

Using audio in Flash

In Chapter 1, you enhanced the ambiance of your Lake Nanagook movie by adding an audio file containing crickets and howling wolves. We asked you to do a couple of things in that chapter, but we didn't tell why you were doing them. The purpose was to get you hooked on Flash, and it obviously worked, because you are now at this point of the book. The time has arrived to give you the answers to those "Why?" questions.

Choosing a sound type: event or streaming

Flash has two types of sound: event and streaming. *Event sound* tells Flash to load a sound completely into memory—as soon as the playhead encounters the frame with this audio—before playing it. Once loaded, the sound continues to play, even if the movie's playhead stops, which means event sounds are not locked to the timeline. (Audio can be forced to stop, but that takes specific action on your part.)

In a 24 fps Flash movie, a file like SeeYouInTheSpringtime.aif from the previous section takes about 3,720 frames to play out completely. If you're hoping to synchronize that with animation in the same timeline, think again. If the resultant SWF is played back on a slower machine than yours, it's almost certain the audio will not conclude on the frame you expect. Also, a movie would take a long time to start playing, because Flash must load the sound fully before playback can begin.

Event sound is ideal for pops, clicks, and other very short sounds or in situations where the audio will be played more than once or looped. If you want to synchronize extended audio with timeline animation, use streaming sound.

Streaming sound is a sound that can begin playing before it has fully loaded into memory. The trade-off is that it must be reloaded every time you want to play it. This sound type is ideal for longer background soundtracks that play only once. Because it is locked in step with the timeline, streaming sound is the only realistic option for cartoon lip-synching, or any scenario that requires tight integration between audio and visuals.

Now that you know what to expect, let's work with both types.

1. Open the Frog.fla file. You will see we have included a Frog.mp3 audio file in the library.

2. Rename the layer in the timeline to audio, and drag the Frog.mp3 file from the library onto the stage. Audio files can be added to the timeline by dropping them on the stage, where they seemingly vanish—but not by dragging them to the timeline. When you release the mouse, you may see a line running through the middle of frame 1 in the timeline. This line is the start of the waveform.

3. Insert a frame at frame 15 of the timeline. You can now see the entire waveform.

4. Right-click (Ctrl-click) on the layer name and select Properties from the context menu. In the Layer Properties dialog box, select 300% from the Layer height drop-down menu, as shown in Figure 5-6, and then click OK. When you release the mouse, the layer view is three times larger, and you can see the waveform in greater detail.

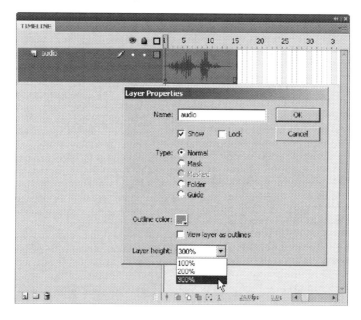

Figure 5-6. Use the layer properties to "zoom in" on the timeline.

Being able to see the waveform on the timeline is a huge advantage, because you can now use the waveform's peaks or valleys to time animation or other events to the audio file in stream mode.

5. Click in the waveform on the timeline anywhere but frame 1. In the Sync area of the Property inspector, select Event from the drop-down menu and press Enter (Return). The playhead moves, but the sound doesn't play. Drag the playhead to frame 1 and press Enter (Return) again.

What you have just heard is a fundamental truth of an event sound: you can preview event sounds only by playing them in their entirety, and only from the keyframe in which they appear.

> *Being the nice guys we are, you can thank us for using a short audio file in this exercise. If you had set SeeYouInTheSpringtime.aif as an event sound, you would be sitting there listening to the full 2.5 minutes of the file. Event sounds play for their entire duration, and you can't stop playback by pressing Enter (Return). All that does is to start playing another copy of the sound over the one that is currently playing. To stop an event sound in the authoring environment, press the Esc key.*

6. Change the Sync setting to Stream, as shown in Figure 5-7. This time, drag the playhead across the timeline. Notice you can hear the sound as you scrub across it. Drag the playhead to frame 2 and press Enter (Return). The sound plays from that point forward and, for longer audio files, playback does stop when you press Enter (Return) again.

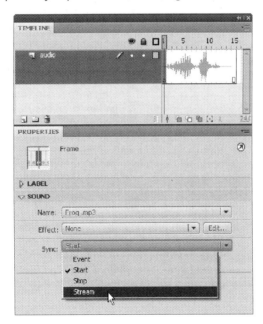

Figure 5-7. Choosing stream mode for sound in the Property inspector

The downside is that the streaming playback lasts for only the frame span on the timeline. For example, the SeeYouInTheSpringtime.aif file would require nearly 4,000 frames on the timeline to play the entire track. If the span were only 50 frames, you would be able to play about 2 seconds of the file, assuming your frame rate is set to the default 24 fps.

Did you notice the Start and Stop choices in the Sync drop-down? They're similar to the Event option, with the addition that they keep sounds from overlapping. Let's try them.

7. Add a new timeline layer and name it audio2. Add a keyframe to frame 8 of the new layer, select that frame, and drag Frog.mp3 from the library to the stage. Now you have two layers associated with the frog sound.

8. In the audio2 layer, set the Sync property to Event for the audio in frame 8. Drag the playhead to frame 1 and press Enter (Return). You'll hear two frogs.

9. Change the Sync property in frame 8 to Stop. Press Enter (Return) again from frame 1, and you'll hear only single frog. Not only that, but its ribbit gets cut off halfway through. That's the playhead encountering the Stop keyframe. It's important to understand that a Stop keyframe doesn't halt all sounds. The halted sound must be specified.

10. Select frame 8 and choose None from the Property inspector's Name drop-down list. Now you merely have a keyframe set to Stop, but without an associated sound. Press Enter (Return) from frame 1, and you'll hear the full ribbit.

11. Reselect Frog.mp3 from the Name drop-down list.

12. Select frame 8 one last time and change the Sync property to Start. Press Enter (Return) from frame 1, and you might be surprised to hear only one frog. Didn't you just tell two of the sounds to play (one as Event and one as Start)? You did, but the Start option waits until the specified sound has finished before it starts another copy of it.

13. Drag the keyframe at frame 8 until you move it past the waveform in the audio layer—frame 16 should do it. Now that the Start keyframe has moved beyond the previous sound, you should hear two frogs again when you press Enter (Return) from frame 1. Users on a slower computer might hear only one frog, because the first sound may not have finished by the time the play-head hits frame 16. Like the Stop option, Start relies on an explicit sound file reference in the Name drop-down list.

Before finishing up with the Frog.fla, let's get an interesting quirk out of the way.

Removing an audio file from the timeline

Audio files can't be deleted from the timeline. Try it:

1. Hold down the Shift key and select frames 1 and 15 in the audio layer to select the audio file. Press the Delete key. Nothing happens.

2. To remove an audio file from the timeline, select a frame in the audio waveform and, in the Property inspector, select None from the Name drop-down menu, just as you did in step 10. The sound is removed.

3. To put the Frog.mp3 audio file back on the timeline, reselect that file in the Name drop-down menu. If you have a number of audio files in your library, you'll see them all listed there, and you could choose a different file to place on the timeline.

4. Close Frog.fla without saving your changes.

Getting loopy

If you want to loop your audio, the Property inspector puts a couple choices at your disposal. Here's how to set up looping:

1. Open FrogLoop.fla in the Exercise folder for this chapter, and take a gander at the audio layer. This is the same ribbit as before, and the waveform shows that the croaking only happens once, even though the timeline spans 60 frames. Surely, the frog has more to say than that. Let's give it something to really sing about.

2. Select anywhere inside the waveform and change the 1 next to the Repeat drop-down list to 4, as shown in Figure 5-8. Notice that the waveform now repeats four times.

Figure 5-8. Use the Sync area's Repeat drop-down list to configure looping.

3. Scrub the timeline to verify that, as an event sound, the audio does not preview until you press Enter (Return) from frame 1.

4. Change the Sync property to Stream and scrub again. As expected, you can now hear the audio as you drag the playhead. This tells you that streaming sound can be looped just like event sound.

5. Change the Repeat property value to Loop. The x 4 value next to the drop-down list disappears, and the waveform changes visually to what looks like a single play-through. In spite of its looks, this sound will repeat forever unless you stop it with a Stop keyframe later in the timeline— or until your user closes Flash Player out of desperation. The Loop setting repeats a sound indefinitely.

6. Close the file without saving the changes.

> Be very careful with the Loop setting! If a sound is set to Event and Loop, you can accidentally cause instant psychosis if the timeline has more than one frame. Timelines naturally loop when they hit the end of their frame span. If the timeline cycles back to frame 1 while the audio is still playing, you can quickly produce an unwanted echo torture chamber.

Adjusting volume and pan

Flash lets you adjust the volume of audio files even after they've been imported to the library. Because of the way Flash outputs its internal audio mix, this also means you can pan your sounds by adjusting each speaker's volume separately. In effect, you can bounce audio back and forth between the two speakers, even if those audio files were recorded in mono.

> Ideally, you'll want to set a file's overall volume with audio editing software, such as Adobe Audition or Soundbooth. Flash can't magnify a file's volume; it can only reduce the volume. So the volume of your file as recorded is the volume it plays back in Flash when the settings are turned all the way up.

You'll be surprised how easy it is to slowly pan our frog serenade from left to right in the timeline. Here's how:

1. Open the FrogPan.fla file in the Chapter 5 Exercise folder. Click into frame 1 of the audio layer and verify that the Sync property is set to Event and Repeat x 4.

2. Select Fade to right in the Effect drop-down list in the Property inspector, as shown in Figure 5-9. Test the SWF so far.

Figure 5-9. The Effect drop-down list lets you change volume and panning.

You'll hear that the effect works, but the panning moves to the right almost immediately, rather than spread over the four ribbits. This happens because Flash evaluates the actual length of an audio file when assigning one of its effects presets. It's easy enough to tweak.

3. Click the Edit button next to the Effect drop-down list. This opens the Edit Envelope dialog box, as shown in Figure 5-10.

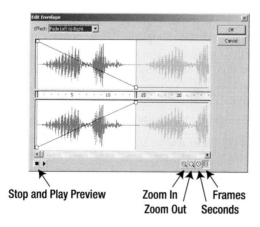

Stop and Play Preview   Zoom In / \ Frames
                         Zoom Out   Seconds

Figure 5-10. The Edit Envelope dialog box lets you apply volume changes to audio files.

In the Edit Envelope dialog box, the diagonal lines represent a change in volume in the left (top) and right (bottom) speakers. The volume steadily decreases on the left (moves down) while increasing on the right (moves up), which gives the illusion that the croaking sweeps across the screen. Note that the effect applies to only the first occurrence of the waveform.

Notice the series of buttons along the bottom of the dialog box. You can preview your effect settings by clicking the Play and Stop buttons on the left. On the right, you can zoom in and out to show less or more of the waveform span. The Seconds and Frames buttons affect how the horizontal number line in the middle looks: seconds or timeline frames.

4. Click the Zoom Out button until all repeats of the waveform are visible. Drag one of the right-side squares on the diagonal lines toward the end of the fourth repeat, as shown in Figure 5-11. It doesn't matter if you drag in the top or bottom—both will move. The Effect field in this dialog box changes to show Custom, because you've altered one of the presets.

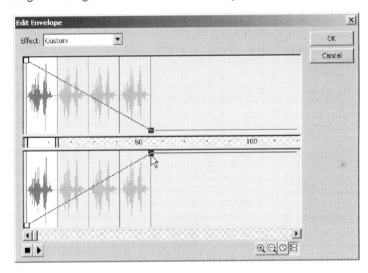

Figure 5-11. The Edit Envelope dialog box lets you apply custom audio effects.

5. Click the Play button to preview the updated effect. Now the panning happens more slowly, arriving fully in the right speaker only after the fourth ribbit ends.

6. Experiment with other Effect drop-down presets. Play around with altering them. Here's a hint: you can add new draggable white squares by clicking anywhere along one of the diagonal lines. Remove white squares by dragging them off the dialog box.

7. Click OK and save your movie.

A note from a master

Dave Schroeder is regarded by many in this industry as being a master when it comes to the use of audio in Flash. He has spoken at a number of very important industry conferences and his company, Pilotvibe (http://www.pilotvibe.com/), has developed a solid international reputation for supplying the industry with high-quality sound loops and effects for use in Flash. In fact, Dave's home page, shown in Figure 5-12, can be regarded as a master class in the effective use in audio to set the "mood" in a Flash movie.

Figure 5-12. The Pilotvibe home page is a master class in the effective use of sound in Flash.

Who better to talk to you about the use of audio in Flash than the guy who is setting the standard? Here's what he had to say:

Once you start to play around with adding sound to Flash files, you'll probably realize that it can add an incredible dimension to your project. Sound can really tie an experience together. It can bring an animation to life. It can create a mood, or suggest characteristics that reinforce your message. It can be entertaining, or informative, or both.

If sound is an option for your project, start with some simple planning. First determine why adding sound makes sense. What purpose does it serve? Does voice-over communicate a story? Do button sounds make the site easier to navigate? Do sound effects make a game more fun, or easier to play? Does music give it a cool character? Use answers to these questions to generate a short "sonic mission statement" that outlines why and how you plan to use sound. Do this early in project planning, not after the Flash work is done.

Sourcing sounds is easier and cheaper than ever before, thanks to the Internet. There are many web sites that will allow you to search and download files for reasonable fees. Once you've found sounds, use audio editing software to adjust them to have similar sonic qualities. You want them to sound like they're in the same room, or in the same canyon, or the same secret underground lair, and so on. Adjust their volumes and equalization (EQ) to achieve this. Use your ears, listen; you'll do fine. Do they sound close or far, light or heavy, fast or slow? Also, trim the heads and tails of the sound files to be as short as possible without cutting the sound off. The shorter the file, the better it syncs, and the smaller the file size.

When you're picking music, try to find a piece that fits the mood or reinforces the story. Don't just use death metal because you like death metal, or techno for techno's sake. Music has emotional power that transcends genre, and you want to leverage it to make your project as engaging as possible. If you're working with loops, try to use as long a loop as possible given your file size considerations. Anything under 10 seconds gets old pretty fast unless it's something minimal like a drumbeat. Look into layering loops to create the illusion of a longer track with more variation.

A sound on/off button is a courtesy I always recommend. [You'll see how to allow users to mute the sound in the "Adjusting volume with code" section later in the chapter.] Compress your sounds so they sound good. A little bit bigger file is worth it if it means people will listen to it. A tiny file that sounds lousy is worse than no sound. Also, compress each sound so it sounds good by itself, and in relation to the other sounds. A combination of hi-fi and lo-fi sounds wrecks the illusion of the sounds existing together.

Thanks Dave, and also thank you for supplying our readers with the Pilotvibe clips in this chapter's Pilotvibe folder.

Your turn: Add sound to a button

Now you'll put what you have learned to practical use. It has been decided that the frog sound should play when a button is clicked on the stage. Follow these steps to accomplish this task:

1. Open a new Flash document and import the Frog.mp3 sound into the library.
2. Select Window ➤ Common Libraries ➤ Buttons to open a collection of button symbols that are included when you installed Flash CS4.
3. Scroll down to the playback flat folder in the Buttons library, open it, and drag a copy of the flat blue play button to the stage.
4. Double-click the button on the stage to open it in the Symbol Editor.
5. Add a new layer named audio and add a keyframe to the Down area of the audio layer.
6. With the keyframe selected, drag a copy of the Frog.mp3 audio file to the stage. Your timeline should now resemble that shown in Figure 5-13.

Figure 5-13. You can add sound to buttons.

7. Click in the waveform, and in the Property inspector, select Event from the Sync drop-down menu. Why Event? Because you want the sound to play on only the Down frame, which means you can only use one frame. If you had chosen Stream, the audio would not have been able to play out.

> This may seem like an odd instruction because all sounds added to the stage are event sounds by default. We have been around this silly business long enough to embrace the wisdom of the following rule: trust no one and nothing, especially yourself. Get into the habit of double-checking everything and never assuming everything is correct.

8. Click the Scene 1 link to return to the main timeline.
9. Select Control ➤ Enable Simple Buttons. Click the button on the stage, and you will hear the frog croak.

So far, so good. If you stopped here, you would have a competent Flash movie—basically a C on your report card—which isn't bad. If you want the A, though, you'll refine this button just a tad, based on what you've already learned in this chapter.

So, what's wrong with it? Click the button in rapid succession, like a double-click. Heck, click it five times in a row (you'll be surprised at what users do when playing with your content). What do you hear? Because of the numerous triggering of that Event keyframe, you end up with a whole chorus of frogs. This may not be what you want. Fortunately, the remedy is simple.

10. Deselect Enable Simple Buttons.

11. Double-click the button symbol to open it again in the Symbol Editor. Change the audio keyframe's Sync property from Event to Start.

12. Reselect Enable Simple Buttons.

13. Return to the main timeline and test the button with repeated clicks.

14. Save the file as SimpleButton.fla and publish the SWF file. Just as in testing mode, the croaks don't overlap when you click the button.

Be careful with this technique, because when you create a SWF file that contains audio, the audio files in the library are embedded into the SWF file. The result, depending upon the audio files and their length, could be an extremely large SWF file that will take a long time to load.

Now that you understand how audio files can be used in Flash, let's take that knowledge to the next level and actually control sound using ActionScript. This is where the full power of audio in Flash is handed to you.

Controlling audio with ActionScript 3.0

In this section, we'll cover the basics of controlling audio with code:

- Playing a sound in the library without adding it to the timeline
- Using movieclips and buttons to load sound dynamically—from your HTTP server—into your Flash movie
- Turning audio on and off with code

Be aware that any sound played through ActionScript is treated as a streaming sound, but is not synchronized with the timeline.

> If you're familiar with controlling sound through ActionScript 2.0, you need to know there have been some important renovations in ActionScript 3.0. For example, the Sound.attachSound() method is no longer around, and even familiar things like creating linkage identifiers have fundamentally changed.

Playing a sound from the library

Playing audio from the library is ideal for short sounds that need to play in the background. In order to play audio files contained in the library and control them through ActionScript, you must first give them a special designation to let ActionScript find them in the library. You can do this through the Linkage area of the Sound Properties dialog box.

Let's try having a sound play, as background audio, when the movie starts.

1. Open a new Flash document and import the PreachersAndThieves.mp3 file into the library. (True, this sound isn't a short one, but this is a demonstration.)

2. Select the PreachersAndThieves.mp3 file in the library. Right-click (Ctrl-click) the audio file and select Properties from the context menu.

3. In the Sound Properties dialog box, click the Advanced button to see the Linkage area, as shown in Figure 5-14.

> In ActionScript 2.0, linkage was accomplished with a linkage identifier. In fact, you'll see a disabled Identifier field in the dialog box. What gives? In ActionScript 3.0, the rules are different. You need to create a custom class that extends the native Sound class. Fortunately, Flash handles the entire process for you. However, advanced developers may prefer to write the actual external text file normally needed.

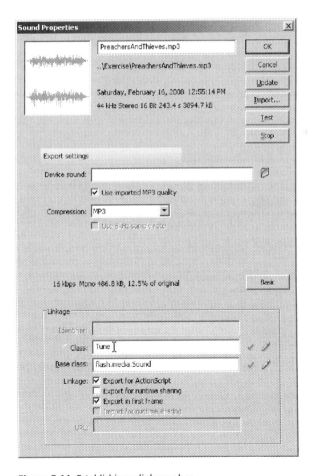

Figure 5-14. Establishing a linkage class

4. Select Export for ActionScript and enter the text Tune into the Class text field. Click OK to close the dialog box.

5. You will get a warning dialog box telling you there is no such thing as a Tune class. Click OK to close it. By clicking OK, you are telling Flash to go ahead and create this class on your behalf. (The name Tune is arbitrary, but as our audio file is a song, Tune makes good sense.)

6. Rename Layer 1 to scripts. select the first frame in the layer, and open the Actions panel. Enter the following code:

```
var audio:Tune = new Tune();
audio.play();
```

The first line of the code creates a variable named audio and uses the Tune class—from the Linkage Properties dialog box—as its data type. In Chapter 4, you learned about classes and inheritance, and this custom Tune class inherits all its functionality from the Sound class. This means it is a bona fide Sound instance, but a very specific kind. The second line simply uses the Sound class's play() method to play the audio file.

7. Save the file as AttachSound.fla, and then test the movie by pressing Ctrl+Enter (Cmd+Return). When the SWF opens in Flash Player, the sound will play. To stop the audio, close Flash Player.

> If you are used to using the attachSound() method from ActionScript 2.0, understand that it doesn't apply in ActionScript 3.0. All you need to do now is to specify a subclass—Tune (or whatever name suits your fancy)—that extends the Sound class.

Using a button to play a sound

In an earlier example, you added the frog sound directly to the timeline of the button symbol. This time, you are going to use a button—though you can just as easily use a movieclip—and, instead of embedding a sound in the button, you will have the sound play from the library. Follow these steps:

1. Open the TayIntro.fla file in this chapter's Exercise folder. In the library, you will see a button added from the Buttons library (Window ➤ Common Libraries ➤ Buttons) and an audio file, TayZonday_FFCS4.mp3.

2. Select the TayZonday_FFCS4.mp3 audio file in the library. Use the advanced Sound Properties dialog box, as in the previous exercise, to give this audio file a linkage class named Tay.

3. Click the button symbol on the stage and give it the instance name of btnPlay. (Remember that symbols controlled by ActionScript need an instance name.)

4. Add a new layer named scripts to the timeline, select the first frame, and open the Actions panel. Enter the following code:

```
var audio:Tay = new Tay();

btnPlay.addEventListener(MouseEvent.CLICK, clickHandler);
function clickHandler(evt:MouseEvent):void {
  audio.play();
};
```

The first line creates an instance of the Tay class—actually a Sound instance that has been extended by an automatically generated custom class—and stores a reference to that instance in a variable named audio. After that, an event handler function, mouseUpHandler(), is associated with the MouseEvent. CLICK event for the btnPlay button.

The event handler works the same as you've seen in Chapter 4, even though the object in question—an instance of the Tay (Sound) class—is different from movieclips and buttons. In ActionScript 3.0, event handling is consistent across the board (with very few exceptions, and you'll see those in the chapter on video). When the MouseEvent.CLICK event occurs, the clickHandler() function is triggered. In turn, the clickHandler() function makes a reference to the Tay instance, by way of the audio variable, and invokes the Sound.play() method on it. The result is that you hear Tay introduce us and the book when you click the button.

5. Save the file and test the movie. When you click the button on the stage, Tay Zonday introduces us.

> For those of you wondering who Tay Zonday is, he became an Internet sensation thanks to a video—Chocolate Rain (see Figure 5-15)—he posted on YouTube in April 2007. This resulted in an avalanche of publicity and stardom, including an appearance on South Park and a Dr. Pepper commercial. If you have never seen the video, point your browser to http://www.youtube.com/watch?v=EwTZ2xpQwpA. To find out more about this baritone crooner, head over to http://www.t ayzonday.com/.

"Chocolate Rain" Original Song by Tay Zonday

Figure 5-15. Thanks, Tay . . . you rawk!!!

Playing a sound from outside Flash

You know that embedding sound into a SWF file adds to its file size. Is there a way to play a sound that isn't inside the SWF file? The answer is absolutely.

1. Open the RemoteSound.fla file in this chapter's Exercise folder. You will see that we have placed a button symbol on the stage and given it the instance name of btnPlay.

2. Select the first frame in the scripts layer, open the Actions panel, and enter the following code (we'll review it after you test the movie):

```
var audio:Sound = new Sound();
var req:URLRequest = new URLRequest("PreachersAndThieves.mp3");
audio.load(req);

btnPlay.addEventListener(MouseEvent.CLICK, clickHandler);
function clickHandler(evt:MouseEvent):void {
  audio.play();
};
```

3. Test the movie to create your SWF. When you click the button, the sound plays.

The second and third lines of the ActionScript you entered handle the external sound. In ActionScript 3.0, you can't simply tell Flash, "There's an audio file in this folder that you need to play." Instead, you need to use an instance of the URLRequest class to specify the file's location. That object, referenced by a variable named req, gets passed as a parameter to the load() method of the Sound instance created in the first line of the code.

In ActionScript 3.0, most things brought into a Flash movie—audio, images, and even SWF files—need to be "called in" through a URLRequest instance (one notable exception is video, which is covered in Chapter 10).

If the MP3 is in the same folder as the HTML document that contains the SWF, you can simply name the MP3 without a file path. Of course, you can just as easily use an absolute path to a folder on your server. In that case, the syntax would be something like this:

```
var req:URLRequest = new URLRequest("http://www.domain.com/audio/
➥PreachersAndThieves.mp3");
audio.load(req);
```

Turning an external sound on and off

In this exercise, you will wire up two buttons: one button will play the sound, and the other will turn it off.

1. Open the RemoteSound2.fla file in this chapter's Exercise folder. Again, we have provided you with the raw material, as shown in Figure 5-16. The Play button with the instance name btnPlay will be used to turn the sound on. The Stop button, btnStop, will be used to turn the sound off.

> The choice of instance names is deliberate. Many Flash designers and developers try to use names that tell the coder what type of object is being used. Here, btnPlay could also be written as Play_btn. The key is the btn part, which indicates it is a button symbol. Ultimately, though, name it what you like.

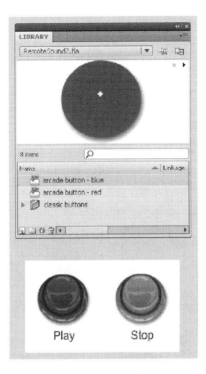

Figure 5-16. Two button symbols are used to turn a sound on and off.

2. Click the first frame in the scripts layer and open the Actions panel. Enter the following code:

```
var audio:Sound = new Sound();
var req:URLRequest = new URLRequest("PreachersAndThieves.mp3");
audio.load(req);

var channel:SoundChannel = new SoundChannel();

btnPlay.addEventListener(MouseEvent.CLICK, playSound);
function playSound(evt:MouseEvent):void {
  channel = audio.play();
};

btnStop.addEventListener(MouseEvent.CLICK, stopSound);
function stopSound(evt:MouseEvent):void {
  channel.stop();
};
```

3. Save and test the movie.

The only major difference between this code and that used in the previous example is the addition of a SoundChannel object. The SoundChannel class controls sound in an application. Each sound playing in a Flash movie now has its own sound channel, and you can have up to 32 concurrent sound channels playing different audio files. Flash mixes them down to a two-channel stereo mix (or a mono mix) for you. The SoundChannel class features a stop() method for turning sound off, but you need to assign the sound to a SoundChannel instance first.

In this case, the Play button does just that. When clicked, its event handler associates the remote sound represented by the audio object (a Sound instance) with the SoundChannel instance named channel. The Stop button, when clicked, uses the stop() method to stop playing the sound in that channel.

Adjusting volume with code

What if you don't want to stop the audio, but simply allow the user to temporarily mute it? Providing your users with this option is a courteous thing to do. Fortunately, it's not very hard to do.

To see how muting is accomplished, open the RemoteSound3.fla file in this chapter's Exercise folder. By this point, you should be feeling a sense of *déjà vu*. The file looks nearly the same as in the previous exercise, but the instance names have changed. The buttons now have instance names btnMute and btnUnmute. The code has also changed, but not by much. Click into frame 1 of the scripts layer and take a look in the Actions panel. You'll see the following code:

```
var audio:Sound = new Sound();
var req:URLRequest = new URLRequest("PreachersAndThieves.mp3");
audio.load(req);

var channel:SoundChannel = audio.play();
var xform:SoundTransform = new SoundTransform();

btnMute.addEventListener(MouseEvent.CLICK, muteSound);
function muteSound(evt:MouseEvent):void {
  xform.volume = 0;
  channel.soundTransform = xform;
};

btnUnmute.addEventListener(MouseEvent.CLICK, unmuteSound);
function unmuteSound(evt:MouseEvent):void {
  xform.volume = 1;
  channel.soundTransform = xform;
};
```

This time, the channel instance is associated with the audio instance right away in line 4. No button click is needed to play this song; it just plays. Just as before, the Sound.play() method, as invoked on audio, lets channel know which sound it controls.

The new part is an instance of the SoundTransform class, stored in a variable named xform. Check out the muteSound() function, which acts as the event handler for the btnMute button's MouseEvent. CLICK event. The SoundTransform class features a volume property, and this property is referenced in terms of the xform instance. It is given a value of 0 (silence). In the next line, the xform instance is assigned to the SoundChannel.soundTransform property of the channel instance. That's all there is to it.

In the unmuteSound() function, the same process takes place, except that the volume property is set to 1 (full volume). Want to turn down the volume, instead of muting it? That's easy.

Inside the muteSound() function, change the 0 to 0.5. Your code should now look like this:

```
btnMute.addEventListener(MouseEvent.CLICK, muteSound);
function muteSound(evt:MouseEvent):void {
  xform.volume = 0.5;
  channel.soundTransform = xform;
};
```

Test the movie and click the buttons. Then close the SWF. Change the 0.5 back to a 0 and test again. Neat stuff!

For those of you wondering why we stop with this exercise and don't get into using a slider to adjust the volume, the reason is simple: you need a bit more ActionScript experience before you tackle that. You will add such a slider to a full-bore MP3 player in Chapter 14. You'll start working on that MP3 player in the next section.

Your turn: Let users select from multiple audio files

Up to this point, you have been working with individual audio files. But in many cases, more than one audio file will be involved. We conclude this chapter by showing you how to choose from among a number of audio files and to play your selection. To accomplish this task, we are going to start the construction of an MP3 player for a band: the Tin Bangs.

This portion of the project will simply add the ability to choose one of three songs and to turn a sound on and off. You will be reintroduced to this project in Chapter 14 to round out the functionality. By the time you reach that chapter, you should be quite familiar with ActionScript, which will make it easier for you to complete such tasks as creating an audio volume controller, Next and Previous buttons, and use ActionScript to access and display the metadata found in an MP3 file. Of course, nothing is stopping you from flipping right to Chapter 14 after you complete this exercise.

This exercise uses the ComboBox component, which can be regarded as a form of "drop-down" menu. We will cover this component in greater depth in Chapter 11.

So much for the chatter. Let's get busy,

Begin by opening the TinBangs.fla file found in your Chapter 5 Exercise folder. You will see that we have constructed the interface, as shown in Figure 5-17. If you open the library, you will also discover that the controller you will be "wiring up" was actually drawn in Illustrator CS4 and imported into Flash.

Double-click the Play movieclip symbol inside the AudioPlayer.ai Assets ➤ Play folder in the library, and you'll see how it's set up. It has two frames, each with its own artwork, and corresponding frame labels in a labels layer.

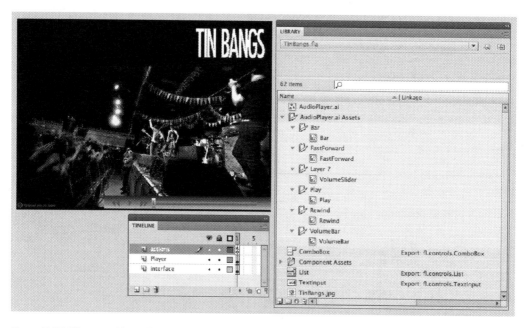

Figure 5-17. We start with an Illustrator controller and a partially assembled project.

Setting up the component

First, you need to add some code to handle the ComboBox. Select the first frame of the scripts layer, open the Actions panel, and enter the following code block into the Script pane:

```
import fl.controls.ComboBox;
import fl.data.DataProvider;

var song:Sound;
var channel:SoundChannel;
var req:URLRequest;
var pos:Number;

var songList:Array = new Array(
  {label:"Select a song", data:""},
  {label:"White Lies (Timekiller)", data:"WhiteLies(Timekiller).mp3"},
  {label:"Young Lions", data:"YoungLions.mp3"},
  {label:"Your Sky is Falling", data:"YourSkyIsFalling.mp3"}
);
```

When you work with components, you have two options: real and virtual. By that, we mean you can drag a component to the stage, in a real-world sense, and manipulate it like any other symbol, text field, or image. In a "virtual" sense, you can also pull a component from the library at runtime, adding it to the stage when the SWF plays. In the case of this ComboBox, you'll be operating in a virtual world, which means you need to import its class. To understand where this comes from, take a look at the ComboBox component in the library. Notice the Linkage column? (You might need to scroll horizontally in the library to see it.) That class lets the compiler know exactly which object you mean when you tell Flash to create a new ComboBox instance.

Think of import statements as calling cards for the classes they introduce. They tell the compiler where to find the class definition it needs when it attempts to compile an instance of the class(es) in question. So, why do some classes need this calling card, while others don't? The answer lies in how the class is organized. Classes are arranged in logical groupings called packages. The most commonly used classes—think MovieClip, TextField, Sound, and so on—are organized in the flash package. Components and other advanced classes, such as ComboBox and DataProvider, are organized elsewhere (in this case, fl.controls and fl.data, respectively). In frame scripts, any class outside the flash package must be imported.

The next import statement is there because, to put it gently, the ComboBox is "stone cold stupid." You need something to tell it, "Dude, here's the song list to show the user and the files to play." That, in very simplistic terms, is the purpose of the DataProvider class, which formats the data in a way conducive for use with user interface components.

The next chunk establishes the variables used throughout this exercise. They are fairly self-explanatory. Well, the pos variable will be used to do something seriously cool, but telling you what that is at this point would ruin the surprise.

The final code block creates a list (an Array instance). The list contains several generic objects—instances of the Object class, and indicated by the curly braces ({})—each of which features two properties: label and data. The label property will be used to add text to the ComboBox, and the data property, as you may have surmised, associates each label with its MP3 file. This array will be set as the data provider for the ComboBox component.

With the housekeeping out of the way, let's turn our attention to getting the component onto the stage.

Press the Return (Enter) key twice and add the following code:

```
var songsCB:ComboBox = new ComboBox();
songsCB.dropdownWidth = 200;
songsCB.width = 200;
songsCB.height = 24;
songsCB.x = 26;
songsCB.y = 68;
songsCB.dataProvider = new DataProvider(songList);
addChild(songsCB);
```

We start by simply creating an instance of the ComboBox class, which is stored in a variable named songsCB. The rest of the code block follows a common workflow when a component is on the stage. You decide how wide it will be, how high it will be, and its x and y locations on the stage. In a made-by-hand "real" scenario, you would be setting all these properties with the Property inspector. In this case, though, because the component is "virtual" and isn't on the stage, you need to set these values with code.

The final line—addChild(songsCB)—adds the ComboBox to the display list of the stage, which makes it visible. This is a bit like when Pinocchio is turned into a real boy. Now that the user can see the song list, let's turn our attention to making the ComboBox functional.

Press the Return (Enter) key twice and add the following code:

```
songsCB.addEventListener(Event.CHANGE, changeHandler);

function changeHandler(evt:Event):void {
  if (songsCB.selectedItem.data != "") {
    req = new URLRequest(songsCB.selectedItem.data);
    if (channel != null) {
      channel.stop();
    }
    song = new Sound(req);
    channel = song.play();
    btnPlay.gotoAndStop("pause");
  }
}
```

A lot of this may be new to you, so let's take this code block "low and slow."

As you can see in Figure 5-18, the ComboBox is a sort of drop-down menu. Selections are highlighted when the mouse is over them, and the selection is made when the mouse is clicked. Instead of listening for a number of specific events—MOUSE_OVER, CLICK, and so on—which can complicate matters, we're simply going to listen for a single Event.CHANGE event and react to any selection change based on that. Thanks to the first line (addEventListener()), this event will trigger the changeHandler() function.

Figure 5-18. The ComboBox can react to an Event.CHANGE event. Here, when Young Lions is clicked, that song starts playing.

The first line of the function tells the ComboBox what to do if there is no data associated with the selection—selectedItem.data !=""—which is to do nothing. The actual code line tells the ComboBox to proceed only if the data property of its selectedItem property is not equal to an empty string (the inequality operator, !=, is the opposite of the equality operator, ==):

```
if (songsCB.selectedItem.data != "")
```

In plain English, this line says, "Do the rest of the code block only if there is data associated with this selection."

Assuming all is well, and that the user has chosen a selection with data, Flash follows through with the req variable you declared by setting it to an instance of the URLRequest class and feeding it the MP3 specified by the current selection. A second if statement again uses the inequality operator to ensure that the channel instance has a value (channel != null), which is only true after a song has been chosen. If a song happens to be playing, the SoundChannel.stop() method halts channel's playback.

After that, the song variable, also declared earlier, is set to an instance of the Sound class; channel is associated with its playing; and the Play button movieclip is sent to frame 2 of its own timeline, which displays the double bars that represent "pause."

> *Notice the absence of the Sound.load() method, as shown earlier in the chapter. ActionScript gives you the option of bypassing this method by feeding your URLRequest instance directly to the Sound constructor. We're just showing you the alternatives at your disposal.*

Wiring up the Play button

Now that you have the component functioning, let's turn our attention to the Play button on the controller bar.

Press the Return (Enter) key twice and enter the code that "wires up" the Play button:

```
btnPlay.stop();
btnPlay.buttonMode = true;

btnPlay.addEventListener(MouseEvent.CLICK, clickHandler);

function clickHandler(evt:MouseEvent):void {
  if (channel != null) {
    if (btnPlay.currentLabel == "play") {
      channel = song.play(pos);
      btnPlay.gotoAndStop("pause");
    } else {
      pos = channel.position;
      channel.stop();
      btnPlay.gotoAndStop("play");
    }
  }
}
```

There really isn't much new here. In the first two lines, the Play button movieclip is referenced by way of its instance name, btnPlay, and instructed to stop in its tracks (which displays an arrow shape that represents "play") and to respond visually to a mouseover (the cursor becomes a pointer finger thanks to buttonMode = true).

Remember how we said that we had a rather cool thing to tell you about the pos variable? Here it is.

Don't you just hate it when you pause a song, and then when you resume it, the silly thing starts playing right from the start again? The position property of the SoundChannel class makes this irritation a thing of the past. It notes exactly where, in milliseconds, you paused the song, and when you click the Play button again, provides the information necessary to resume from that precise location. How does it do that?

Because of how we're using frame labels inside the Play movieclip, it's possible to tell immediately whether audio is playing. After the first if statement ensures that channel has a value, a second if statement checks the MovieClip.currentLabel property of the btnPlay instance. If we're currently on the "play" label, it means the audio has been paused; therefore, channel is reassociated with the playing of the song instance, and btnPlay is sent to its "pause" label. On the other hand, if we're currently on "pause", the value of channel.position is stored in the pos variable, channel is stopped, and btnPlay is sent to its "play" label.

Notice, a few lines earlier, that song.play() receives pos as a parameter? That's the key. The Sound.play() method optionally accepts a parameter, which tells it how many milliseconds into the audio to start playing (if absent, playback starts from the beginning). We told you this was cool!

Testing the movie

Carefully review your code, save the movie and test it. It should look like Figure 5-19.

Figure 5-19. Bring on the Young Lions!

You have completed the first part of a rather slick MP3 player. You'll wire up the other buttons, the slider, and more in Chapter 14.

What you have learned

In this chapter, you learned the following:

- How to add audio to Flash
- The difference between an event sound and a streaming sound
- How to set the preferences for sound output in Flash CS4
- Various approaches to playing a sound in the Flash library and one located outside Flash
- The various classes, properties, and methods ActionScript 3.0 uses to control and manage sound in Flash
- How to use a ComboBox component to select from among multiple audio files

As you have discovered, there is a lot more to audio in Flash than simply tossing in some sort of electronica beat and becoming a "cool kid." Audio is a powerful communications tool, and savvy Flash designers and developers who realize this are leveraging audio in Flash to its full potential.

Speaking of communication tools, text is no longer that gray stuff that goes around your animations. To find out more, turn the page, because text is the focus of the next chapter.

Chapter 6

TEXT

Letterforms that honor and elucidate what humans see and say deserve to be honored in their turn. Well-chosen words deserve well-chosen letters; these in their turn deserve to be set with affection, intelligence, knowledge and skill. Typography is a link, and it ought, as a matter of honor, courtesy and pure delight, to be as strong as the others in the chain.

Robert Bringhurst

This quote from Bringhurst's master work, *The Elements of Typographic Style, Second Edition* (Hartley & Marks Publishers, 2002), sums up the essence of type in Flash. The words we put on the stage and subsequently put into motion are usually well chosen. They have to be, because they are the communication messengers, providing the user with access to understanding the message you are trying to relay. In this chapter, we focus on using type to communicate the message your client is delivering.

The introduction of the Adobe CS4 product line puts some powerful typographic tools in your hands—notably, a new rendering technology called CoolType—and with applications like After Effects nudging closer to a confluence point with Flash, the field of motion graphics on the Web is about to move into territory that has yet to be explored. To start that exploration, you need to understand what type is in Flash and what you can do with it to honor the communication messengers of your content.

Here's what we'll cover in this chapter:

- Understanding the basics of type
- Using static, dynamic, and input text fields
- Putting type in motion
- Creating, formatting, and using dynamic text
- Using ActionScript to create, format, and present text
- HTML formatting with ActionScript
- Creating hyperlinks
- Using the spell checker

The following files are used in this chapter (located in Chapter06/ExerciseFiles_Ch06/Exercise/):

- Static1.fla
- Static2.fla
- Static3.fla
- HTML.fla
- StaticTriggerAS.fla
- DynamicTriggerAS.fla
- EmbedButton.fla
- EmbedFontSymbol.fla
- SpellItOut.txt
- ScrollComponent.fla
- scrollingAS.fla

The source files are available online from either of the following sites:

- http://www.FoundationFlashCS4.com
- http://www.friendsofED.com/download.html?isbn=15905910931

Type basics

Let's begin by getting really clear on one point: type is not that gray stuff that fits around your "whizzy" Flash animations. It is your primary communications tool.

Reading is hard-wired into us. If it were not, you wouldn't be looking at this sentence and assimilating it in your brain. You have a need for information, and the printed word is how you get it. Realize that the choice of font and how you present the text not only affects the message, but it also affects the information. You can see this in Figure 6-1. The phrase "Flash rocks" takes on a different meaning in each instance. Although we use the same Times New Roman typeface, the message changes depending on the style applied (the bold and italic variants).

You can take this to the next level and see that not only variants, but the typeface itself has an effect on the message. Figure 6-2 shows five examples of the same information presented using different typefaces. You can see how the message changes even more dramatically.

Flash rocks

Flash rocks

Flash rocks

Flash rocks

Times .... Flash Rocks

Futura Book .... Flash Rocks

Party .... Flash Rocks

Brush Script .... Flash Rocks

Rockwell .... Flash Rocks

Figure 6-1. It is all about the message.

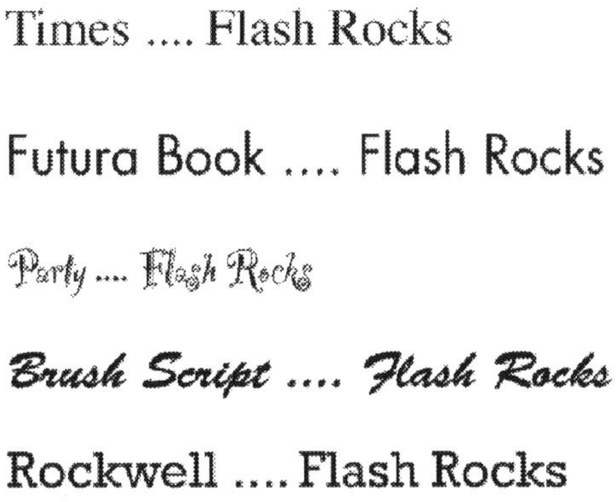

Figure 6-2. It is all about the message and the typeface chosen.

When choosing your fonts, you also must be aware of their impact upon readability and legibility. This requires an acute awareness of the qualities and attributes that make type readable: typeface, size, color, and so on.

To illustrate this point, take a look at a small exercise one of the authors uses in his classes. What word is shown in Figure 6-3? Don't be too hasty to say "legibility." What are the sixth, seventh, eighth, and ninth characters? What letters are the first and second letters? Suddenly things become a bit disorienting.

ı८gıυıιιιty

Figure 6-3. What word is this?

This disorientation is important for you to understand. Our visual clue to legibility and readability is the flow along the tops of the letters, as shown in Figure 6-4. This is why text that consists of all capital letters is so hard to read.

legibility

Figure 6-4. We get our clues to letterforms from the tops of the letters.

We include this exercise because there is a huge temptation on the part of people new to Flash to prove they're one of the "cool kids" and use font and color combinations that make otherwise legible text impossible to read. A good example of this is Figure 6-5. The word is set in a medium-gray color on a dark-gray background, and the size of the text is 10 pixels. The text is very difficult to read, and yet somehow the "cool kids" think this is some sweet action. Wrong! They just destroyed all access to the information contained in the text. The text in the next figure, Figure 6-6, goes in the opposite direction. There, type is used as a clear communications vehicle for the message.

Figure 6-5. It is all about the message and the font chosen.

Figure 6-6. The message—"Opel drives on natural gas"—comes through loud and clear.

Even though paying attention to design is critical, from a type perspective, font-rendering technology in Flash was still a huge issue until the introduction of CoolType into Flash CS4.

Adobe CoolType

Flash CS4 contains a rather major change "under the hood," and we suspect that not a lot of people will pay much attention to it. That change is the inclusion of CoolType technology.

Designers are an odd bunch. They can pick out something that doesn't "look quite right" with what seems to be a cursory glance at the page or the screen. For years, designers have noted that type in Flash just didn't "look right" and, as strange as this may seem, they were correct. This was an odd situation, because Adobe has always been in the lead with font technologies, yet one of its flagship applications seemed to be lagging in this important area. So, font rendering and management in Flash have always been a sore point with designers. Flash CS4 may have just put that one to rest with the inclusion of CoolType.

A little screen type history

To understand how big a deal CoolType is, you have to go back into the gray mists of time to around 1984 and the introduction of the Macintosh. For many of you, 1984 is a murky year in your childhood. For some of us, especially one of the authors, it was the year that graphic layout started its move from art boards, waxers, and X-Acto knives to the computer screen. Two companies—Apple and Adobe—made this possible. Apple supplied the computer and the LaserWriter printer, while Adobe supplied PostScript.

Up to that point, layout on a computer was interesting, but the problem was that stuff called "type." A letter would show up on the computer screen, but it would be blocky. There was essentially no way to differentiate a capital letter *A* set in Garamond from its Times counterpart. This was due to the way computers rendered on-screen type. Essentially, the letters were constructed in a grid of pixels, which gave them the rather blocky, pixelated look we have come to call "the jaggies." PostScript, developed by Adobe, somewhat solved this problem by creating a language—PostScript—that, in very simple terms, drew the letter over the pixels and gave designers what they wanted: Garamond *A* characters that actually *looked like Garamond As* on the screen. The fact that they looked even crisper when run through the LaserWriter was also a huge factor in moving the graphics industry to computers.

Still, designers spent a lot of time whining about on-screen resolution and font crispness. As the Web took hold and Flash took off, designers continued to notice the fonts they used didn't look quite right. Pixels were still being lit up to create letters, so they were subject to the lingering problems inherent in on-screen text.

As we have stated, the relatively poor readability of on-screen text compared to its paper counterpart has been a significant sticking point with designers almost from the word "Go." The source of the problem is low-resolution computer screens. While the resolution of the typical printer is often 600 dots per inch (dpi) or more, the resolution of the average laptop, PDA device, or desktop screen is only 72 (Macintosh) or 96 (PC) dpi. This means that type that looks crisp and smooth on paper appears coarse and jagged on the screen.

To combat the jaggies, traditional grayscale font anti-aliasing (also called *font smoothing*) buffs out the corners in text by filling in the edges of bitmapped characters with various shades of gray pixels. This can make text appear blurry at small point sizes. Also, a lot of the designers' work was in color, and adding fuzzy gray pixels around colorful letters wasn't a great solution. Macromedia attempted to address this issue when it introduced a number of anti-aliasing features into Flash in 2004. Though these features provided a huge improvement, Flash designers were not satisfied, because their text still didn't look "quite right." They looked at the introduction of CoolType in Acrobat in 2000 and asked, "Uh, what about us?"

CoolType to the rescue

What CoolType does is to create clearer, crisper type using a font-rendering technique Adobe calls *color anti-aliasing*. This works on digital liquid crystal display (LCD) screens such as those in laptops, handheld devices, and flat-panel desktop monitors. Unlike conventional anti-aliasing, which manipulates only whole pixels, CoolType controls the individual red, green, and blue subpixels on a digital

LCD screen. The key word here is *subpixels*. The hundreds of thousands of squares on the screen, which are the pixels, are actually further subdivided into even more squares. These are the subpixels, which are something like quarks in the realm of the formerly indivisible atom.

According to Adobe, by adjusting the intensity of the subpixels independently, the strokes of a character can be aligned on any subpixel boundary, thus achieving sharper, more precise smoothing along the edges of characters. Using this subpixel technique, CoolType can dramatically increase horizontal resolution for improved readability. The key word in that last sentence is *horizontal*. We read text across the page, which means the characters are even sharper, which, in turn, makes them even more legible and readable. Figure 6-7, taken from the Adobe CoolType web page, shows how subpixels reinterpret character display.

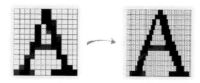

Figure 6-7. On the left is regular pixelated type; on the right is the same character using subpixels.

Typefaces and fonts

What is a typeface, and what is a font? Technically speaking, a *typeface* is an organized collection of glyphs (usually letters, numbers, and punctuation) that shares stylistic consistency. A *font* is one particular size or variety of a typeface. So Arial 10 and Arial 12 represent two distinct fonts but belong to the same typeface. The same goes for Arial and Arial Bold or the Times variations used in Figure 6-1 (Times, Times Italic, Times Bold, and Times Bold Italic): they are separate fonts that belong to the same font family. In everyday language, for better or worse, most people simply use the word *font* for all of the preceding.

Flash offers an interesting advantage when it comes to typography: while HTML is capable of displaying only fonts that are installed on the viewer's computer, Flash can display whatever font you like. Want to use some zany dingbat characters or an extravagant cursive font you designed yourself? Have at it. Even input text fields—the sort typed into by the user—can be displayed in whatever font suits your fancy. Flash text fields even support the effects filters discussed in Chapter 3.

Does this sound too good to be true? Well, everything has a price. Fonts can add to a SWF's file size— the more ornate, the greater the penalty. Take a moment to consider what fonts are, and you'll see that this makes sense. Most fonts store a mathematical description of the lines and curves that define each glyph. Simple shapes require less description than complex shapes.

> *Does that sound oddly familiar? It should, because most fonts today are drawn in a PostScript drawing application. In fact, Illustrator CS4 is rapidly becoming the tool of choice among the type design community.*

Flash CS4 supports the following font formats: TrueType, OpenType, PostScript Type 1, bit (Macintosh), and device fonts.

Staying with PostScript, you know that the more complex the shapes—that is, shapes with a lot of points—the larger the file size. Let's try an experiment to prove this:

1. Head over to http://www.lipsum.org, a terrific site for generating placeholder text, and copy a paragraph of "Lorem ipsum" (we'll call it *lipsum*, for fun) to the clipboard.

2. Select the Text tool. In the Property inspector, choose a simple sans serif font, like Arial, and confirm that the type of text is Static Text. Click in the upper-left corner of the stage, and, with the mouse still down, drag to the other side of the stage and release.

3. Paste the lipsum text into this text field.

4. Test your movie and select View ➤ Bandwidth Profiler to see file size information. Your SWF should be in the neighborhood of 4KB to 8KB.

5. Close the SWF and change your text field's font to something more elaborate, such as Blackadder ITC, Brush Script, or whatever decorative typeface catches your fancy. Test the movie again and compare file sizes. Your mileage will vary, of course, but experiment a bit and see how different fonts carry different weights.

> *Where did Lorem Ipsum originate? Being a wealth of absolutely useless information, we are glad to oblige you with an answer. The earliest known example of its use is from an unidentified type specimen produced in the 1500s. A printer jumbled up the text from Cicero's* de Finibus Bonorum et Malorum, Liber Primus, *sections 1.10.32 and 1.10.33, and used it to show off his typefaces. It stuck and has been used ever since.*

By the end of this chapter, you'll know what your options are and will be equipped to make informed choices. For starters, let's look at how to dial back to zero the weight that a font adds to a SWF.

Working with device fonts

If you want, you certainly can go with fonts that are installed on the user's machine, just as HTML does. The benefit is that your SWF's weight will be completely unaffected by text content. The drawback is that you must count on your audience having the same font(s) installed as you do (not a good idea) or choose among three very generic font categories: _sans (sans serif), _serif, and _typewriter (monospace). These are the device fonts, and they are ideal for use on mobile devices.

In the Property inspector, take another look at your font choices in the font drop-down list. The top three, shown in Figure 6-8, are preceded by an underscore. That's the tip-off. If you select one of these fonts, Flash will choose on your behalf whatever it thinks is the closest fit on the viewer's computer. _sans will probably be Arial or Helvetica, _serif will probably be Times New Roman or Times, and _typewriter will probably be Courier New or Courier—but who knows for sure?

If you have used Flash prior to this release, you may have had the same reaction we did when we saw the font menu: "Whoa!!!" This reorganized font menu was added along with the inclusion of CoolType.

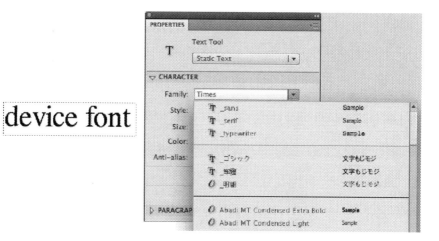

Figure 6-8. The device fonts work everywhere but have limitations.

Another place where you can use device fonts is in situations where you choose a font, say Helvetica, and you aren't sure whether the user has the font. As shown in Figure 6-9, you can select Use device fonts in the Anti-alias drop-down menu, and the fonts will be substituted at runtime.

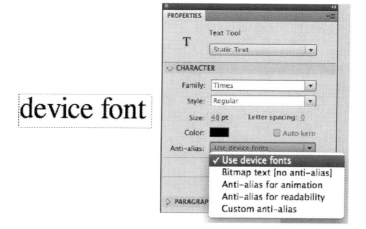

Figure 6-9. Device fonts can be used to override the fonts in the movie at runtime.

Currently, Flash can't treat device fonts as graphics. Tweening stuff containing a device font is going to be unpredictable.

> *Future versions of Flash Player 10 may, in fact, be able to display device fonts as if they were embedded. Adobe Senior Product Manager Justin Everett-Church demonstrates some pretty amazing Flash Player 10 text features in a video, which you can see at* `http://labs.adobe.com/technologies/flashplayer10/demos/videos/text.html`.

Also realize that device font is a "weasel" term for the phrase *pick the closest approximation*. This means you lose all control over the spacing and length of the text on the screen at runtime. Depending on the font chosen by the user's machine, you may wind up having the user view your work through a font that has a bigger x-height than your font. If you need an exact match, device fonts aren't the way to go.

> *X-height? What's that? It is the height of the lowercase letter x in the font. This proportional characteristic can vary widely in different typefaces of the same size. Tall x-heights are two-thirds the height of a capital letter. Short x-heights are one half the height of a capital letter. Staying with our useless information theme, the trend to the larger x-height in the sans category was sparked by Adrian Frutiger in the last century, when he released Univers 55.*

Types of text fields

The Property inspector indicates three ways to classify text on the stage: Static Text, Dynamic Text, and Input Text (set in the drop-down list at the top of the panel). This determines whether the selected text field is static, dynamic, or input.

In a sense, dynamic and input are actually the same thing, but that only matters in terms of ActionScript. In relation to the Property inspector, static text fields contain text that won't be edited after the SWF is published, dynamic text fields contain text that will (or can) be edited, and input text fields contain text that is entered by the user. Each classification carries its own characteristics, but many are shared among all three. Let's get to our penmanship!

Static text properties

Static text is the least powerful sort of text in Flash, but don't let its humble nature fool you. If you're into racing, it's also true that horses run slower than cheetahs, but why split hairs?

As with most other tools in the Tools panel, the Property inspector controls the properties of fields created by the Text tool in a big way. As shown in Figure 6-10, text property categories include Position and Size, Character, Paragraph, and Options. Let's take a look at each configurable item, outside the already familiar Position and Size category.

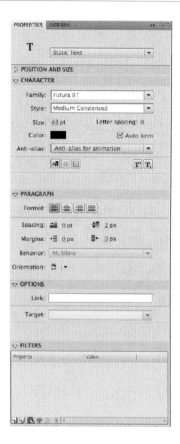

Figure 6-10. The Property inspector and static text

Character properties

The following properties are in the Character category:

- Family: This lets you select from the list of fonts installed on your computer. With static text, in most cases, font outlines are included with the SWF. For that reason, it doesn't matter whether or not your audience has the same font installed. The only exception is when you use the first three device fonts (the ones with the underscores). This setting marks the first of many that may be applied more than once, and in various ways, in the same text field.

- Style: Most typefaces contain Regular, Bold, Italic, and other variants. To apply a style to the whole text field, choose the Selection tool, click the text field, and then make your selection. To apply a style to individual words or characters, use the Text tool to select the text field, high-light the desired glyphs, and then select the desired variant. Bold and italic versions of the chosen font must exist on your computer for this styling to occur.

> *The* Style *drop-down menu replaces the* B *and* I *buttons previously used to specify bold or italic variants. It also groups the font families. Prior to this release, each font was its own entry in the* Font *drop-down list. If you are a font junkie, this resulted in a font list that seemed to stretch for meters. Now the variations of the font, such as the* Medium Condensed *shown in Figure 6-10, are in one neat, tidy package.*

- **Size:** This sets the selected font's size, in points. Multiple font sizes are allowed within the same text field. The scrubber ranges from 8 points to 96 points, but you may type in other values directly, anywhere from 0 (invisible) to 2,500 (jaw-droppingly way huge). This includes noninteger values, such as 12.75. In cases between 1,800 points and 2,000 points, the glyphs of most fonts "jump outside" the bounding box of their text fields, but this doesn't seem to affect text rendering; it merely makes the text field harder to select.

- **Letter Spacing:** This determines the uniform distribution of space between glyphs, also known as *tracking*. The higher the number, the wider apart the characters, and vice versa. If you want, you can even squish letters together by using a negative number. Typographers have a term for this: *crashing text*. Multiple Letter Spacing settings may be applied to the same text field.

- **Color:** Want fuchsia text? Here's where to make that statement. Multiple colors are allowed within the same text field.

- **Auto kern:** This check box toggles auto-kerning. What is *kerning*? This is in the same ballpark as letter spacing, except kerning refers to individualized spacing between pairs of glyphs. Consider the capital letters *A* and *V*: the bottom of the *A*'s right side extends out, which fits neatly under the "pulled-in" bottom of the *V*. Kerning reduces the space between these and other glyphs that "fit together" in this way, which tends to provide greater visual balance.

- **Anti-Alias:** Flash Player 8 introduced a number of new visual effects, and one of those was improved text rendering. This enhancement lives on in Flash Player 10, the Player that corresponds to the default publish settings for Flash CS4. You have five choices for font rendering:

  - **Use device fonts:** This relies on the user having your chosen font installed. Unlike the three device fonts mentioned earlier (_sans, _serif, and _typewriter), this setting uses exactly the font you specify—provided it is available on the computer playing the SWF file. If not, Flash makes the choice.

  - **Bitmap text:** This provides no anti-aliasing, which means characters will have jagged edges.

  - **Anti-alias for animation:** This provides normal text anti-aliasing. Glyphs appear smooth (no jaggies) and may be applied to text fields in older versions of Flash Player.

  - **Anti-alias for reading:** New since Flash 8, this format improves readability of small- and regular-sized fonts. Text animates smoothly because alignment and anti-aliasing are not applied while the text animates (it is reapplied when animation stops). This advanced anti-aliasing is not supported in Flash Player 7 or earlier SWFs, in skewed or flipped text (rotated is okay), in printed text, or text exported as PNG. Under these circumstances, the normal anti-aliasing (Anti-alias for animation) is applied.

  - **Custom anti-alias:** Also considered advanced anti-aliasing, this choice brings up a Custom Anti-Aliasing dialog box, which allows you to specify your own Thickness and Sharpness settings.

- **Selectable:** Determines whether the text is selectable with the mouse in the published SWF. Even rotated, flipped, and skewed text may be set as selectable.

- **Render Text as HTML:** Not available for static text. Note that hyperlinking is still supported (see the "Options properties" section).

- **Show Border Around Text:** Not available for static text.

- **Superscript and Subscript:** Want to put something in superscript or subscript? Here's the place. This can be applied to text fields as a whole, or to individual glyphs.

To see a static text field in action, start a new Flash document, select the Text tool, and click somewhere on the stage. Type your name. Select the second letter of your name by dragging the mouse from one side of the letter to the other. Change the font. Select the third letter, and change the font again.

Notice that the text field automatically widens as you type. The indicator for this is the little white circle in the upper-right corner of the text field, as you can see in Figure 6-11. If you keep typing, the text field will eventually extend past the stage and off into the wild blue yonder. To set a specific width, which causes text to wrap, hover over that white circle until you see the double-headed arrow cursor. Click and drag to the desired width. The white circle turns into a square. To switch back to auto-widen mode, double-click that square.

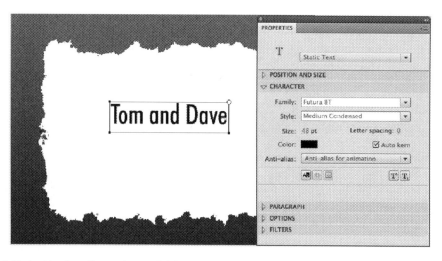

Figure 6-11. A white dot tells you the text field will widen as you type.

Note that the height property is disabled, because the height of static text fields is always determined by the amount of text they contain; that is, when width is taken out of its default auto-widen mode. Setting width in the Property inspector is equivalent to dragging the white circle.

Paragraph properties

The following properties are in the Paragraph category:

- Format: This sets the alignment, and makes practical sense only when applied to fixed-width text fields. In cases where your words wrap, this determines how they do it. Different alignments may be applied to each line of text in a text field. The four buttons work as follows:

  - Align Left means the left edge of your lines of text will be even.

  - Align Center means your lines will be centered inside the text field.

  - Align Right means the right edge will be even.

  - Align Justify means both the left and right edges will be even.

- Spacing: Scrub across the indent value, and you can add space at the start of a line of text within the text box. Scrub across the horizontal space values, and the lines of text will spread out. This is how you can apply leading (the space between lines) to text blocks.

- Margins: Scrub across these values, and you can add space to the right and the left of a text block.

- Behavior (Line Type): Not available for static text. Text fields automatically widen as you type, or you can set a text field's width by dragging the white circle in its upper-right corner, as you saw in the previous section. Doing so causes text to wrap, period. Other types of text fields may be set to single-line or multiline text, but static text fields essentially take care of themselves.

- Orientation: The three choices in this drop-down menu allow you to flip text.

Options properties

In the Options section, the Link and Target settings allow you to create hyperlinks inside text fields. Either select the whole text or use the mouse to select individual glyphs or words, and then type a URL into the Link field (such as http://www.VisitMe.com/). Entering anything at all into the Link field activates the Target field below it, which gives you the same four choices available to HTML anchor tags (<a>):

- _blank: Opens the URL in a new browser window.

- _parent: Opens the URL in the parent frameset of an HTML frameset (this assumes the SWF is embedded in an HTML page that appears in multiple framesets).

- _self: Opens the URL in the same window or frame as the current HTML document that holds this SWF. This is the default behavior.

- _top: Opens the URL in the topmost window of a frameset, replacing the frameset with the new URL.

Hyperlinks in the Link field do not change the appearance of the text in any way, even though a dashed line appears under hyperlinked text during authoring. This differs from HTML hyperlinks, which are traditionally differentiated by an underline and a change in color. Although the Property inspector supports bold and italic, there is no way to add underlines to text without ActionScript (see the section "HTML formatting" later in this chapter). Flash hyperlinks are primarily meant for loading HTML documents, which may or may not contain additional Flash content. As a general rule, this is not the place to load external SWFs into the current movie, though it is possible to trigger ActionScript with the Link field. More on that in the section "Hyperlinks and Flash text" later on in the chapter.

Now that you know what all of that stuff in the Property inspector does, let's take that knowledge for a test drive.

Your turn: Play with static text

There is a ton of stuff you can do with static text on the page, and the three exercises in this section will give you an idea of the creative possibilities open to you.

Applying a filter to text

In this first exercise, you will discover how to apply a filter to text and how to tween text to which a filter has been applied.

1. Open the Static1.fla file in the Chapter 6 Exercise folder. Select the Text tool or press the T key, select the Text layer, click the stage, and enter your name. Use a bold sans serif font and a size ranging from 30 to 48 points depending on the typeface chosen.

> Points? Pixels? Which to choose? They are both the same, so the terms are interchangeable. Here's how that came about. Traditionally, 72-point type was actually 72.27 points, which is a hair over 1 inch. When computers took over print production and typesetting in the 1980s, purists using Apple computers who pointed out this discrepancy to Apple were essentially told, "Our screen resolution is 72 pixels per inch. We don't do 0.27 pixels." Thus a standard was born, and over 300 years of typesetting standards were changed.

2. Switch over to the Selection tool or press the V key, and select the text block.

3. Twirl down the Filters strip, click the Add Filter button, and select Drop Shadow from the Filter list. When the Drop Shadow filter panel appears, specify these settings:

   - Blur X: 14
   - Blur Y: 14
   - Strength: 100%
   - Quality: High

As you can see in Figure 6-12, you can apply a filter to text.

Figure 6-12. Text, buttons, and movieclips are the only Flash objects to which filters can be applied.

4. Add a frame in frame 30 of the Text layer.

5. Right-click (Ctrl-click) anywhere in the Text layer's span of frames and select Create Motion Tween from the context menu. The strip turns blue to indicate a motion tween.

In Chapter 3, you learned that filters can be applied to both text and movieclips. If you need to tween a filter effect, you can do it in the Motion Editor panel.

6. Open the Motion Editor panel and twirl down the Filters strip.

7. Move the playhead to frame 15 in the Motion Editor panel and add keyframes by clicking the diamond in the Bur X or Blur Y and Strength properties. Repeat this for frame 30 as well.

8. Click the back arrow in any one of the three properties to return the playhead to frame 15. Use these values at frame 15 (see Figure 6-13):

- Blur X: 0
- Blur Y: 0
- Strength: 0

Figure 6-13. A motion tween applied to a Drop Shadow filter

9. Press the Return (Enter) key, and the drop shadow will fade out and in. You can save the file or close it without saving the changes.

Exploding text

In this next exercise, you will "explode" some text. Along the way, you are going to learn how to convert text to letters and then to art. You are also going to learn a handy way of putting the individual pieces of a grouped object into motion.

1. Open the Static2.fla file in your Chapter 6 Exercise folder. In the file, create a new movieclip named myName.

2. When the Symbol Editor opens, add a static text field and enter your name into it. We'll leave the font, style, and size to you. Set the text's X value to 88 and the Y value to 170 in the Property inspector. This odd positioning is chosen because we want the text to go flying out from the middle of the stage.

One of the themes that percolates through this book is this: *let the software do the work.* In this case, you have a number of letters that will need to fly off of the screen. Entering each one manually, and then spending time trying to ensure they are perfectly aligned with each other, is both tedious and a waste of billable hours. There is an easier way.

3. Select the text on the stage and press Ctrl+B (Cmd+B). Each letter is separated into its own piece of text, as shown in Figure 6-14. You could keep pressing those keys until the text looks pixelated. When that happens, the text is changed from text fields to shapes.

The command you just issued by keyboard shortcut—Ctrl+B (Cmd+B)—is Break Apart (Modify ➤ Break Apart), and it is a great way of separating complex artwork into its basic pieces (meaning, you can use it for more than just text). Continually applying this command reduces text to nothing more than PostScript outlines, which makes the glyphs no longer editable as text. If you are an Illustrator CS4 or Fireworks CS4 user, this is quite similar to the Create Outlines command used to convert text to art in those applications.

Figure 6-14. Break text apart if you want to animate or manipulate the individual letters.

Now that the text has been broken apart into individual letters, let's get each letter into a layer so it can be animated.

4. Select all of the text on the stage and choose Modify ➤ Timeline ➤ Distribute to Layers. As soon as you do this, each letter is moved to its own layer, as shown in Figure 6-15, and the letters don't change their position on the stage—another great example of letting the software do the work.

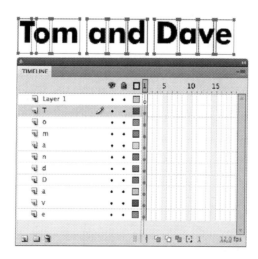

Figure 6-15. Use Distribute to Layers to move multiple selections to individual layers.

5. Delete the empty layer named Layer 1. Click in frame 30 of the top layer, hold down the Shift key, and click in frame 30 of the bottom layer. This selects frame 30 in every layer.

6. With all the layers selected, right-click (Ctrl-click) to open the context menu. Add a frame. Now right-click (Ctrl-click) again—because the layers are still selected—and select Create Motion Tween. You have now prepared each letter to be animated.

7. Select a letter in frame 30, use the Selection tool move the letter to a new location, and use the Rotation Z and the Skew and Scale properties in the Transformation strip to resize, rotate, or otherwise distort the letter. Do this for all of the remaining letters. The changes will be reflected in the graph, and you can scrub the playhead to see the effect, as shown in Figure 6-16.

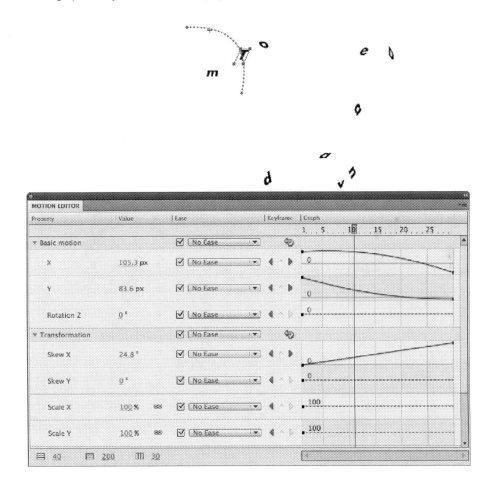

Figure 6-16. Exploding text

8. Click the Scene 1 link to return to the main timeline.

9. Select the Text layer and drag a copy of the myName movieclip to the stage.

10. Select the Actions layer, click the keyframe in frame 1 to select it, and press F9 (Option+F9) to open the Actions panel. Enter the following code:

```
stop();
```

If you didn't add this action, your movie would consist of your name blinking, not exploding, on the stage. The action stops the playhead dead in frame 1 of the main timeline, but allows the movieclip to play. Because your animation is nested inside a movieclip, you can easily reposition the group of exploding letters in one shot.

11. Close the Actions panel, save the movie, and test it. Your name explodes (see Figure 6-17).

Figure 6-17. The movie playing in Flash Player

Applying a Blend mode and color to text

So far, you have discovered that static text can be manipulated and can have filters applied. You have also seen how to turn the text into individual graphics and put them in motion. In this next exercise, you are going to explore how text can be manipulated using a Blend mode and how to change its color. These are useful skills to know if you need to tween color changes or have the text interact with the content under it in the Layers panel.

1. Open the Static3.fla file in this chapter's Exercise folder. You will see that we have added a background image to the stage and supplied you with some text in a movieclip, as shown in Figure 6-18.

2. Click the movieclip on the stage. In the Property inspector, notice that the Color Effect and Blend areas are set to None and Normal, respectively.

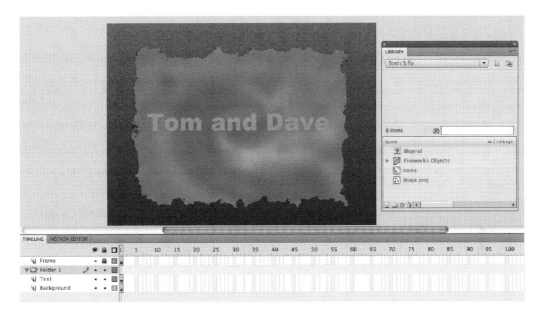

Figure 6-18. We start with text in a movieclip.

3. Click the Style drop-down list and select Advanced. This opens the Advanced Effect dialog box, as shown in Figure 6-19.

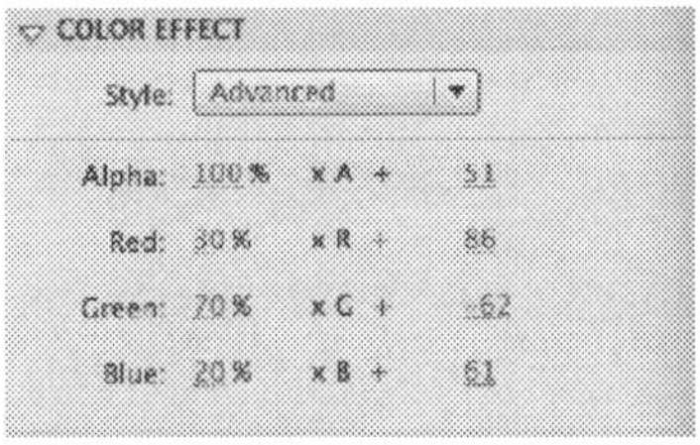

Figure 6-19. The Advanced Effect dialog box can be used to change the colors of selected objects.

This dialog box allows you to adjust both the tint and the alpha values of the selected object. The controls on the left reduce the tint and alpha values for each of the RGB colors. The controls on the right decrease or increase the color and alpha values by a constant amount. When you change a value, the current color values of the selection are multiplied by the numbers on the left, and then added to the values on the right.

4. Use the following settings on the right side of the dialog box:

- Alpha: 100%
- Red: 30%
- Green: 70%
- Blue: 20%

The text changes color from the neutral gray to green, which is understandable, considering green at 70% is now the predominant color.

5. Make the following changes on the right side of the dialog box:

- x A +: 51
- x R +: 86
- x G +: -62
- x B +: 61

The color changes to a purple because you have increased the red and blue values and reduced the green value.

> Remember that even though we are using text in a movieclip, this effect can be applied to any symbol you may make: movieclip, graphic, or button.

Now that you have changed the color, let's make it interact with the color in the image behind it.

6. Select the movieclip and choose Hard Light from the Blending drop-down menu. The text changes color because this effect mimics the shining of a very bright light through the selection.

7. Change the Blending setting to Overlay. This time, the text interacts with all of the colors behind it (see Figure 6-20). Overlay multiplies or screens the colors based on the color of the selected object.

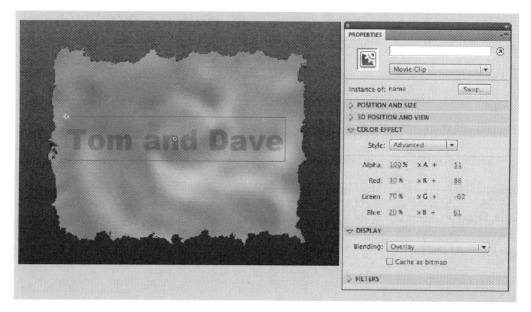

Figure 6-20. Using a Blend mode on text in a movieclip

8. Close the file without saving the changes.

> *Yes, you can apply the Blend modes using ActionScript. It's pretty simple, actually. Just give your movieclip an instance name, and then use that instance name to reference the* MovieClip.blendMode *property. The names of each Blend mode are stored as constants of the* BlendMode *class. For example, for a movieclip with the instance name* mc, *you would set its Blend mode to Multiply like this:*
>
> ```
> mc.blendMode = BlendMode.MULTIPLY;
> ```

Dynamic text

What makes dynamic text fields different from their static counterparts? From the point of view of the Property inspector, not a whole lot. Change the text type setting to Dynamic Text, and you'll see only three new properties. In addition, three previously disabled properties become available, and three previously available properties are dimmed out. The rest is the same. Here's a rundown of the new, enabled, and disabled properties:

- Instance Name: Like an instance name for a movieclip, button, or any other object, a text field's instance name allows it to be "spoken to" by ActionScript. This property appears above the drop-down list that lets you select the text field's type.

- Character Embedding: This button allows you to specify which glyphs are included in the SWF. This happens automatically for static text fields, unless you choose device fonts. With dynamic text, you get more choices.

- Var: This setting, while visible for dynamic text fields, is not supported in ActionScript 3.0, so it's disabled.

> *The* Var *property is a historical throwback to Flash 4, when the way to set the content of a text field was to associate it with a variable. As recently as Flash 8, this approach was still in wide use. In fact, it's still possible in Flash CS4 if you change your publish settings for something earlier than ActionScript 3.0. Generally speaking, though, it's better to separate form from function. Let variables be variables, and use the* TextField. text *property to set the display content of a dynamic text field.*

- Render Text as HTML: This setting is a godsend for quick-and-simple formatting such as bold and italic, and it's the easiest way to underline text in Flash. HTML formatting is covered in detail in its own section later in this chapter.

- Show Border Around Text: This toggles a solid black stroke around the text field. Border color can be changed with ActionScript, as long as the border is showing.

- Behavior (Line Type): You can set the following options for the selected text field:
  - Single line: If you're typing by hand, or cutting and pasting text from another document, this means no line breaks are possible, even if the text field is tall enough to accommodate them.
  - Multiline: In fixed-width text fields, this setting allows text to wrap when it reaches the right side, in addition to breaking along carriage returns.
  - Multiline no wrap: This breaks on carriage returns only.

- Superscript and Subscript: Not available for dynamic or input text fields.

- Orientation: Not available for dynamic or input text fields.

Is there more to it than that? There is, and most of it occurs in ActionScript.

While formatting may be applied partially and more than once in a single static text field, the rules are different for dynamic and input text fields. In nonstatic text fields, when the text properties are set in the Property inspector, it's an "all-or-nothing" proposition. Change the color of one letter, and you've changed the color of the whole text field. The same goes for the font, bold and italic variants, and so on. The only way to apply varied formatting within the same dynamic or input text field is to use ActionScript.

Let's work through some examples. First, we'll start with the basics and add text to an existing dynamic text field. Next, we'll add line breaks and formatting. Finally, we'll explain how to create a text field from scratch.

Adding text to a dynamic text field

Let's start with some poetry.

1. Open a new Flash document. Use the Text tool to draw a text field approximately 300 pixels wide. In the Property inspector, set the text field type to Dynamic Text. Choose whatever font you like, but keep it small, say, 12 points. Set the Line Type to Single line. Select Anti-alias for animation from the Anti-alias drop-down menu and deselect Auto kern, as shown in Figure 6-21.

2. Double-click the text field to enter its bounding box. Type in the following heartrending poem, and press Enter (Return) after each line.

   Roses are red,

   Violets are blue.

   There's more to learn

   Before we're through.

3. Test the movie. You'll see that the whole poem is collapsed into a single line, as shown in Figure 6-22. Why? Because the Line Type option is set to Single line.

Figure 6-21. Applying dynamic text properties

Figure 6-22. This is what happens when you select the Single line type.

4. Change that property to Multiline, and then test the movie again. This time, the poem appears in all its bardic glory.

5. Change the field to Multiline no wrap, and test the movie a third time. No difference, right? That's because none of those lines hits the edge of the text field.

6. Double-click the text field to enter it. Hover over the lower right-edge drag handle until the cursor becomes a double-headed arrow. Drag the right edge toward the left until the text starts to wrap.

7. Still using the Multiline no wrap setting, test the movie again. Each line breaks at the carriage return, but it doesn't wrap.

8. Switch to Multiline, and test the movie to see the effect. Now you understand the Behavior (Line Type) setting.

9. Widen the text field again, and give it the instance name poetry in the Property inspector.

10. Enter the text field, select the existing text, and delete it.

11. Create a new layer in the main timeline and name it scripts. Click in frame 1 of the scripts layer, open the Actions panel, and enter the following:

```
poetry.text = "Roses are red,";
```

Now, remember the discussion of classes from Chapter 4? Dynamic and input text fields are instances of the TextField class, which features a text property. In this line of ActionScript, we're referencing the TextField.text property by way of the poetry instance name. It's a bit like referring to Tom or David, who are instances of Human, by personal name.

12. Test your movie, and you'll see the first line of the poem, including the comma, as shown in Figure 6-23.

But what about line breaks? You'll see how to add them in the next section.

Figure 6-23. ActionScript can be used to add text to a dynamic text field.

Formatting text with ActionScript

ActionScript supports a widespread convention of *escape sequences*, which provide an encoded way to manipulate text or to represent special characters. Escape sequences can also be used to tell ActionScript to accept a character at face value, rather than interpret it as a part of the programming. Here's a practical example.

As you've seen, the TextField.text property accepts a string value. Strings are denoted by a pair of double or single quotes. The quotation mark character (") tells ActionScript when a string begins and when it ends. But what if your string *contains* quotation marks, such as dialogue? You need to either nest your quotes carefully or escape them. This sentence gets it wrong:

```
var shortStory:String = "Mary, said Fred. Mary, I'm pregnant.";
```

Since the preceding is a conversation, Fred's words should actually be in quotes. To accommodate double quotes in this string, you could wrap the whole thing in single quotes, like this:

```
var shortStory:String = '"Mary," said Fred. "Mary, I'm pregnant."';
```

But whoops, there's still a problem. Can you spot it? The contraction *I'm* itself contains a single quote! That means ActionScript considers the string ended immediately after the capital *I*, which makes the "m pregnant" fragment programmatic gibberish. This type of problem is not rare, and it's easy to overlook. To avoid these situations, we prefer to escape quotation marks rather than to nest them. In the following revision, the string is once again denoted by double quotes, and the interior double quotes are escaped:

```
var shortStory:String = "\"Mary,\" said Fred. \"Mary, I'm pregnant.\"";
```

Note that only the double quotes need to be escaped in this example. If the string had been wrapped in single quotes, only the apostrophe in *I'm* would have to be escaped. How? Just put a slash in front of it.

A handful of characters actually perform a task when you escape them, such as \n for a newline and \t for a tab. Let's take a look at both.

To update the ActionScript used in the previous example to add a line break, you could put everything within one line, like this:

```
poetry.text = "Roses are red,\nViolets are blue.";
```

Alternatively, you could break the ActionScript over as many lines in the Actions panel as you like, which is often easier on the eyes. In this case, you will want to use the TextField.appendText() method, which appends text to existing content, rather than replacing it.

```
poetry.text = "Roses are red,\n";
poetry.appendText("Violets are blue.\n");
poetry.appendText("There's more to learn\n");
poetry.appendText("Before we're through.");
```

You may alternately use the addition assignment operator (+=) to build a string first, and then assign it to the text field's text property:

```
var poem:String = "Roses are red,\n";
poem += "Violets are blue.\n";
poem += "There's more to learn\n";
poem += "Before we're through.";
poetry.text = poem;
```

> *Want to be a rebel? Select the poem text field and change its* Line Type *property back to* Single line. *Test your movie. In spite of that "single lines only, please" setting, the* \n *escape sequence succeeds loud and clear.*

What about those tabs we mentioned earlier? The following ActionScript pushes each text field line farther to the right:

```
var poem:String = "Roses are red,\n";
poem += "\tViolets are blue.\n";
poem += "\t\tThere's more to learn\n";
poem += "\t\t\tBefore we're through.";
poetry.text = poem;
```

Note that several tabs can be used in succession, which is also true for new lines.

Is it possible to set tab stops? Sure thing. For this, you'll need an instance of the TextFormat class. Set the TextFormat.tabStops property to an array of pixel values, and then apply the formatting object to your text field.

```
// First, the string
var poem:String = "Roses are red,\n";
poem += "\tViolets are blue.\n";
poem += "\t\tThere's more to learn\n";
poem += "\t\t\tBefore we're through.";

// Then, the formatting
var format:TextFormat = new TextFormat();
format.tabStops = new Array(20, 40, 60, 80);

// Finally, apply the string and the formatting
// to the text field
poetry.text = poem;
poetry.setTextFormat(format);
```

That puts four tab stops at 20-pixel intervals. Try something more extreme to prove that it really works (for example, new Array(100, 200, 300, 400), which might even bump some of the lines out of the text field).

While we're on the subject, the TextFormat class provides a whole lot more. For a full list of functionality, we invite you to consult the TextFormat class entry of the ActionScript 3.0 Language and Components Reference, but here are a few common properties you may want to set:

```
var format:TextFormat = new TextFormat();
format.font = "Verdana";
format.size = "24";
format.color = 0x3355CC;
format.bold = true;
format.italic = true;
existingTextField.text = "Lorem ipsum dolor sit amet.";
existingTextField.setTextFormat(format);
```

The TextField.setTextFormat() method accepts two optional parameters after the first, and those dictate where to start and stop. Let's say you have an overall style in mind for the whole text field. Aside from that, you want to apply special formatting to two words and another set of formatting to a third word. Let's try it:

1. Open a new Flash document and add a new dynamic text field with an instance name of existingTextField to the stage.

2. Add a new layer named Actions, open the Actions panel, and enter the following code:

```
var overallStyle:TextFormat = new TextFormat();
overallStyle.font = "Verdana";
overallStyle.size = 12;

var boldBlue:TextFormat = new TextFormat();
boldBlue.color = 0x0000FF;
boldBlue.bold = true;

var italicRed:TextFormat = new TextFormat();
italicRed.color = 0xFF0000;
italicRed.italic = true;

existingTextField.text = "Lorem ipsum dolor sit amet.";
existingTextField.setTextFormat(overallStyle);
existingTextField.setTextFormat(boldBlue, 0, 5);
existingTextField.setTextFormat(boldBlue, 12, 17);
existingTextField.setTextFormat(italicRed, 22, 26);
```

What's going on here? Think of the styling as a special brush—actually, three brushes. The first brush gives the text field an overall formatting of 12-point Verdana. Next, you switch to a brush that makes things blue and bold, and then finally red and italic. You set your brush down at position 0, where the first letter starts (see Figure 6-24), pull it across the first word, and then lift up at position 5, which is the beginning of the sixth character (the first space).

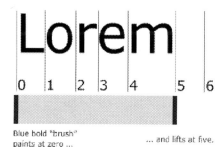

Blue bold "brush"
paints at zero ...   ... and lifts at five.

Figure 6-24. ActionScript can be used to selectively format a dynamic text field.

3. Test the movie. When the SWF opens, you will see the text Lorem and dolor colored blue, and amet colored red.

4. Close the file without saving the changes.

> The TextField *class features a* defaultTextFormat *property that works in a similar way. The difference is that this property sets the default format for a text field, even if there isn't text in it yet. Once that format is set, you can keep replacing the text without needing to reapply formatting. Because* defaultTextFormat *is a property instead of a method, its usage works like this:* existingTextField.setTextFormat = myFormat;.

Creating a text field with ActionScript

Want to create a text field completely with ActionScript? It's pretty straightforward. The TextField class is instantiated like any other class. In this case, the instance name becomes the variable you use to refer to the instance. As always, consult the TextField class entry of the ActionScript 3.0 Language and Components Reference to see the full set of properties. Here are a few in common use:

- autoSize: This property is slightly tricky, because it expects a separate class just to provide its value. The static TextFieldAutoSize.LEFT property instructs the new TextField instance to be left-aligned and widen automatically (toward the right) to accommodate any text it is given. The available TextFieldAutoSize properties are LEFT, RIGHT, CENTER, and NONE. The first three allow the text field to widen as necessary and align the text to the left, right, or centered. The last keeps the text field from widening, in which case a width and height must be specified.

- selectable: This is equivalent to the Property inspector setting by the same name.

- x, y: These are interesting because they may not appear in the properties summary of the TextField class entry for you by default. It's fairly easy to guess what they refer to—the position of the text field on the stage—but where do they come from? This is where our ActionScript basics really come into play. Notice the "Inheritance" heading near the top of the TextField class entry? That tells you this class extends the InteractiveObject class, which in turn extends the DisplayObject class (and it goes further). DisplayObject is the source of the x and y properties. Thanks to the principle of inheritance, it is absolutely correct to say that text fields have their own sense of x and y, it's just that these properties originated elsewhere. To see them in the TextField class entry itself, click the Show Inherited Public Properties hyperlink beneath the Public Properties heading.

- text: Ah, you're already familiar with this one.

Let's try adding a text field with ActionScript:

1. Open a new Flash document and don't add anything to the stage.

2. Add a new layer named Actions, open the Actions panel, and enter the following code:

```
var benFranklinQuote:TextField = new TextField();

benFranklinQuote.autoSize = TextFieldAutoSize.LEFT;
benFranklinQuote.selectable = false;
benFranklinQuote.x = 50;
benFranklinQuote.y = 30;
benFranklinQuote.text = "Energy and persistence conquer all things.";

var format:TextFormat = new TextFormat();
format.font = "Courier";
format.size = 14;

benFranklinQuote.setTextFormat(format);
addChild(benFranklinQuote);
```

What's that addChild() business at the end? Until that final line, the previous ActionScript has gone to the effort of creating a TextField instance—and a TextFormat instance to style it—but hasn't actually displayed anything. ActionScript 3.0 introduces the concept of *display lists*, which gives you much more control over what actually gets displayed to the screen. By adding the benFranklinQuote object (the TextField instance) to the display list, you're effectively "lifting the curtain" to let the show begin.

3. Test the movie. When the SWF opens, you will see the quote, as shown in Figure 6-25.

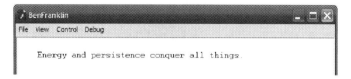

Figure 6-25. A text field added through the use of code

4. Close the document without saving your changes.

Input text

Input and dynamic text fields are practically identical. From the point of view of the Property inspector, only four things change. Three properties go away, and a new one appears:

Figure 6-26. Adding a border to input text

- Selectable: This property becomes disabled, which makes good sense. By definition, input text is something the user types into the field. In order for typing to work, the text field must be selectable—so it is, and you can't make it otherwise.

- Link: This property disappears altogether. You may prepopulate an input text field with text. You can even format it. But you can't give it a hyperlink—without ActionScript. More on this in the section "Hyperlinks and Flash text."

- Target: Without a hyperlink, there's really no use for the Target property.

- Max Chars: This is the new one. It lets you specify the maximum number of characters the user may enter in the text field. Prepopulated text may override this setting, but the user will need to delete what's there in order to add new text—at which point the maximum value holds.

Although not required, it makes good sense to use the Show Border Around Text property, as shown in Figure 6-26, for input text fields, so the user can see where to type. If not, you can certainly position prettier artwork of your own behind the text field. To set the color of this border, use ActionScript, as follows:

```
textFieldInstanceName.borderColor = 0xFFFF00;
```

The TextField.text property works the same way with input text. If you want to know what the user has typed, check the instance name of that text field and look at its text value.

HTML formatting

Although Flash supports only a small subset of the HTML language—and it's a very small subset—the ability to use familiar formatting tags for text is a very cool thing. In addition, most people find it less complicated than the TextFormat class discussed earlier.

HTML formatting is supported only for dynamic and input text fields, and tags must be written and applied with ActionScript. We'll discuss the tags first, and then we'll show you how to use them.

Flash supports the following HTML tags:

- **Anchor tag (<a>)**: If you want to make a hyperlink without using the Property inspector, this is your tag. This tag supports two attributes:

  - href: An absolute or relative URL, up to 128 characters in length. This attribute corresponds to the Link setting of the Property inspector and is required if you want the hyperlink to actually do something. If you're opening a web document, use the http: or https: protocol. If you want to trigger ActionScript instead, use the event: protocol. More on this in the section "Hyperlinks and Flash text."

  - target: One of four values that correspond to the Target setting of the Property inspector: _blank (opens the URL in a new browser window), _parent (opens the URL in the parent frameset of an HTML frameset), _self (opens the URL in the same window or frame as the current HTML document that holds this SWF; this is the default behavior), and _top (opens the URL in the topmost window of a frameset, replacing the frameset with the new URL).

- **Bold tag (<b>)**: Makes text bold, if the current font supports it. Yes, even though HTML jockeys are all using <strong> nowadays, Flash Player doesn't support it. Use the <b> tag.

- **Break tag (<br>)**: Represents a line break.

- **Font tag (<font>)**: Provides three ways to format the styling of text, by way of the following attributes:

  - color: A hex value representing a color.

  - face: The name of a font.

  - size: The size of the font in pixels. You may also use relative sizes, such as +2 or –1.

- **Image tag (<img>)**: Displays a graphic file, movieclip, or SWF inside a text field. Supported graphic formats are JPG, GIF, and PNG. This tag may be configured by way of quite a few attributes:

  - src: This, the only required attribute, specifies the URL of an external image or SWF, or the linkage class for a movieclip symbol in the library (see the "Symbol essentials" and "Sharing assets" sections of Chapter 3). External files do not appear until they are fully loaded, so depending on your needs, you may want to embed content in the SWF itself. To refer to embedded library content, simply use the linkage class as the value for the src attribute—<img src='MyLinkageClass' />—instead of the path to an external file.

  - id: If you want to control the content of your image tag with ActionScript, you'll need to know the instance name of the movieclip that contains that content. This is where you provide that instance name.

- width and height: These specify the width and height of the image, SWF, or movieclip in pixels. If you like, you may scale content along the x axis and y axis by setting these attributes arbitrarily.

- align: This determines how text will flow around the image, SWF, or movieclip. The default value is left, and you may also specify right.

- hspace and vspace: Just as with HTML, these values determine how much "padding" appears around the image, SWF, or movieclip. Horizontal space is controlled by hspace, and vertical space is controlled by vspace. The default is 8 pixels. A value of 0 gets rid of the padding, and negative numbers bring in the edges, pulling in adjacent content with them.

- checkPolicyFile: This instructs Flash Player to check for a cross-domain policy file on the server associated with the image's or SWF's domain.

- **Italic tag (<i>):** Makes text italicized, if the current font supports it. Like our note for the <b> tag, use <i> for italics in text field HTML, as opposed to the <em> tag generally preferred by web developers nowadays.

- **List item tag (<li>):** Indents text and precedes it with a round bullet. In the case of normal HTML, <li> tags may be further managed by parent list tags. The bullets of unordered lists (<ul>), for example, may be specified as circle, disk, or square. The bullets of ordered lists (<ol>) may be specified as numbers, roman numerals, or letters. This is not the case in the microcosm of Flash HTML. Lists require neither a <ul> nor an <ol> tag, are unordered only, and feature only round bullets.

- **Paragraph tag (<p>):** Our good, old-fashioned paragraph tag. Paragraphs come with a built-in line break, and you get two attributes with this tag:

  - align: This affects the text alignment. Valid settings are left, right, center, and justified—the same alignments available in the Property inspector.

  - class: Specifies the name of a CSS class selector, which can be used to stylize content.

- **Span tag (<span>):** This tag doesn't do anything on its own, but it accepts a class attribute that supports CSS, and that attribute is styling.

- **Text format tag (<textformat>):** In many ways, this is the HTML version of the TextFormat class. Use the following parameters to stylize text content:

  - blockindent: Determines block indentation.

  - indent: Determines indentation of the first line only and accepts both positive and negative values.

  - leading: Affects line spacing. It accepts both positive and negative values.

  - leftmargin, rightmargin: Determines the left and right margins of the text.

  - tabstops: Specifies tab stops.

- **Underline tag (<u>):** Makes text underlined. This tag is the easiest way to underline text in Flash (other than through CSS styling).

What? No tables? Yeah, that's been a pretty significant exclusion over the years. Is there a way, then, to easily display tabular data in Flash? There is. It may not seem as straightforward as the more familiar HTML table structure, but it works. In fact, you've already seen an example of it in this chapter. The answer is tab stops. Since we already used the TextFormat class, let's do it again with HTML.

1. Open the HTML.fla file in this chapter's Exercises folder. You will see that we have already added a dynamic text box and given it the instance name of output.

2. Click the first frame of the scripts layer, open the Actions panel, and enter the following code:

```
var htmlContent:String = "";
htmlContent += "<textformat tabstops='50,100,150'><b>One\tTwo
➥\tThree</b></textformat><br>";
htmlContent += "<textformat tabstops='50,100,150'>Eins\tZwei
➥\tDrei</textformat><br>";
htmlContent += "<textformat tabstops='50,100,150'>Un\tDeux
➥\tTrois</textformat><br>";
htmlContent += "<textformat tabstops='50,100,150'>Uno
➥\tDos\tTres</textformat>";

output.htmlText = htmlContent;
```

> It looks a bit awkward to use the \t (tab) escape sequence mixed in with the HTML, but there it is. Note that the quoted tag attributes are denoted by single quotes, since the tag itself is a string denoted by double quotes.

3. Test the movie. The text is all lined up in columns, as shown in Figure 6-27, just like an HTML table.

Figure 6-27. HTML formatting applied to text

For good measure, check out the html-tags.fla file in the Complete folder for this chapter to see most of the tags and their attributes illustrated in one place.

Hyperlinks and Flash text

Every type of text in Flash—static, dynamic, and input—supports hyperlinks. The big difference between static and nonstatic text fields is that, unless ActionScript enters the picture, only static text fields allow for partial hyperlinking (for example, one word linked while the rest of the sentence is unlinked) or for more than one URL to be applied to the same field. All it takes for static text fields is to type in your text, select a few words, and enter the desired URL into the Property inspector, as shown in Figure 6-28. Optionally, you can enter a target as well. If want the whole text field hyperlinked, use the Selection tool to select the text field itself, and then use the Link and Target properties in the same way.

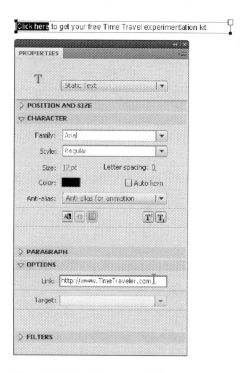

Figure 6-28. Applying a hyperlink to text

As easy as this approach is, a downside is that nothing in the published SWF gives any indication that a hyperlink exists, unless the user just happens to move the mouse over the right spot. Then the cursor changes from the arrow cursor to the finger cursor. But nothing compels the user to put the mouse over a hyperlink in the first place. Pretty odd omission, if you ask us.

To work around it, take advantage of the non-ActionScripted ability of static text fields to display multiple formatting. After you associate a few words with hyperlinks, change the color of those words as well, or make them bold. Give the user a way to distinguish the hyperlinked text from normal content.

Hyperlinks may be absolute, such as http://www.SuperSite.com/thisPageHere.html, or relative, such as ../thisOtherPage.html. For relative paths, it's important to know that the path will be determined not from the point of view of the SWF, but from the HTML file that contains it. For example, you may choose to keep all your HTML files in the root of your website. Because you're an organized developer, you may choose to put all your image files in their own subfolder of the root, and you may just do the same with your Flash content. From a SWF's point of view, the relative path to all HTML files requires stepping back one folder. So, if a SWF links to one of those pages, you might be tempted to precede the destination's file name with ../, but don't! The HTML file that contains the SWF in question is already in the same folder as the destination page, and it's the containing HTML file's point of view that matters.

Using HTML for hyperlinks

The Link setting in the Property inspector works for dynamic text fields, but remember that with non-static text, styling and hyperlinks are one-size-fits-all: either the whole text field links somewhere—even if you only apply the URL to one letter—or it doesn't link somewhere. That is the case unless you use HTML tags, which means unless you use ActionScript.

You've already seen how HTML tags can be applied to dynamic and input text fields. All you need to do is use the anchor tag (<a>) with its href attribute, and you're set.

```
myTextField.htmlText = "<a href='http://www.domain.com/
➥some-page.html'>click me</a>";
```

Note the single quotes around the href attribute's value. The single quotes keep Flash from getting confused regarding where your string starts and stops. This is the same issue we covered earlier in our escape character discussion. If you prefer to use double quotes around your attribute values, you may—but you'll need to escape them.

Ah, but wait! As with static text hyperlinks, the preceding example still doesn't give the user any indication that a portion of the text is clickable. To mimic the traditional underline that appears in HTML hyperlinks, consider using the underline tag (<u>) to set off the link. Here's an example:

```
myTextField.htmlText = "<a href='http://www.domain.com/
➥some-page.html'><u>click me</u></a>";
```

Don't forget the optional target attribute if you want to control the target window of the specified URL. The default value for target is _self, which opens the destination URL in the same window the user is already in. If that window fills the browser window, the new page will also fill the browser window. If that window fills only one frame of an HTML frameset, only that frame will be replaced.

```
myTextField.htmlText = "<a href='http://www.domain.com/
➥some-page.html'target='_self'><u>click me</u></a>";
```

To "break out" of a frameset, use the _top target:

```
myTextField.htmlText = "<a href='http://www.domain.com/
➥some-page.html'target='_top'><u>click me</u></a>";
```

To open a new window altogether, use _blank:

```
myTextField.htmlText = "<a href='http://www.domain.com/
➥some-page.html'target='_blank'><u>click me</u></a>";
```

You may use as many anchor tags in a given text field as you like. Just surround whatever content you like with its own <a> tag, and do your audience a favor by emphasizing the hyperlink with an underline, bold, or italic style.

Using hyperlinks to trigger ActionScript

It's important to realize that hyperlinks are generally used for linking to a new HTML document. This is not the way to load image files or SWFs into the current Flash movie. (Loading is covered in Chapter 14, which touches on optimizing.) Fortunately, it is possible to trigger ActionScript with hyperlinks, so if you want to get fancy, you can use the humble anchor tag to perform whatever programming feat you desire. The trick is knowing how to listen for hyperlink clicks.

In ActionScript 3.0, hyperlinks dispatch a TextEvent.LINK event. (This is different from the ActionScript 2.0 asfunction protocol, which called a custom function directly.) To handle the LINK event in Flash CS4, you need two things. First, get rid of the http: protocol in your href attribute and replace it with event:. This tells ActionScript to forget about the browser and instead trigger a TextEvent.LINK event. Second, write an event handler. The result would look like this:

```
myTextField.htmlText = "<a href='event:'><u>click me</u></a>";
myTextField.addEventListener(TextEvent.LINK, linkHandler);
function linkHandler(evt:TextEvent):void {
    trace("Someone clicked the hyperlink!");
}
```

Pretty neat so far, but not especially useful. You might have any number of hyperlinks in the text field or in other text fields currently showing, so you need a way to tell them apart. Here's how: add an arbitrary value after that event: inside the href attribute. This effectively becomes a parameter passed to the function that handles your event in the addEventHandler() method. Here is an example:

```
myTextField.htmlText = "<a href='event:apples'><u>click me</u></a>";
myTextField.addEventListener(TextEvent.LINK, linkHandler);
function linkHandler(evt:TextEvent):void {
    trace(evt.text);
}
```

The dispatched LINK event object contains a text property specified by you in the text field HTML. The receiving function references that property in its parameter. In the preceding example, we're naming the incoming event object evt, which makes evt.text the property that gives us back the message sent by the hyperlink.

Your turn: A visit to the pond

We've perused quite a bit of theory. Now let's take a few text fields and actually do something with them. We'll look at two ways to use hyperlinks to trigger the ActionScript that will make a frog disappear. Though we are heavily into mystical frogs, you can use what you will learn here to make images, movieclips, and other items on the stage disappear at the click of a mouse.

Using hyperlinks with a static text field

First, let's use a static text field to hide and show the frog.

1. Open the StaticTriggerAS.fla file. You will see the image of a frog on the stage and two empty layers named Text and Actions. If you open the library, you will see the frog is in a movieclip named, well, frog, and if you click the image on the stage, you will see we have given it an instance name as well.

2. Click the Text layer and select the Text tool or press the T key.

3. Click the stage and enter Show the frog, hide the frog. Specify these text settings in the Property inspector:

- Type: Static Text
- Font: Arial
- Size: 14
- Color: #000000 (black)

4. Select the text Show and hide, and in the Property inspector, change their color to #0099FF (bright blue).

5. Using the Text tool, select the text Show and enter event:show into the Link field of the Property inspector, as shown in Figure 6-29. The text you entered is the TextEvent:LINK event you will be using when you write the code.

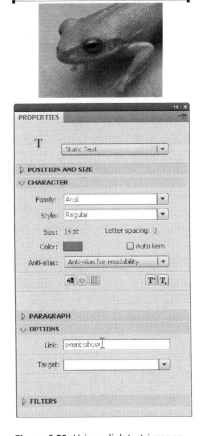

Figure 6-29. Using a link to trigger an ActionScript text event

6. Select the text hide and enter event:hide into the Link field of the Property inspector.

7. Select the first frame in the Actions layer, open the Actions panel, and enter the following ActionScript:

```
addEventListener(TextEvent.LINK, linkHandler);
function linkHandler(evt:TextEvent):void {
  if (evt.text == "show") {
    frog.visible = true;
  } else {
    frog.visible = false;
  }
}
```

The first line of the code creates the listener, and tells Flash what to listen for (textEvent:LINK) and what to do (execute the function named linkHandler()) when it "hears" the event. The function checks to see which of the two hyperlinks was clicked. If it was the word Show and the event's text property is "show", then the frog movieclip has its visible property set to true, which means the frog movieclip appears. The else simply says if it isn't the word Show, then hide the frog movieclip by setting the movieclip's visible property to false.

8. Save and test the movie.

Using hyperlinks with a dynamic text field

Now that you know how to control events using static text, let's try it out using a dynamic text field.

1. Open the DynamicTriggerAS.fla file in this chapter's Exercise folder. It is the same file as the previous exercise, and all we are going to ask you to do is to write the code.

2. Select the first frame in the Actions layer, open the Actions panel, click once in the Script pane, and enter the following:

```
changeTheFrog.htmlText = "<p><font color='#0099FF'>
➥<u><a href='event:show'>Show</a></u></font> the frog,
➥<font color='#0099FF'><u><a href='event:hide'>hide</a>
➥</u></font> the frog.</p>";

changeTheFrog.addEventListener(TextEvent.LINK, linkHandler);

function linkHandler(evt:TextEvent):void {
  if (evt.text == "show") {
    frog.visible = true;
  } else {
    frog.visible = false;
  }
}
```

The first line is the major difference between this and the previous example. The text field on the stage already has an instance name of changeTheFrog. The ActionScript line tells Flash to fill that particular text field with HTML text, and uses HTML tags instead of the Property inspector to add the text and enter the URL link.

3. Save the movie and test it. As you can see in Figure 6-30, the major change is the addition of traditional underlines for the hyperlinks.

Figure 6-30. The links are formatted through the use of HTML tags.

Embedding font outlines

You've learned that static text fields automatically embed font outlines as needed. For this reason, static text can easily be rotated, skewed, and otherwise distorted, as well as set to a semitransparent color. Dynamic and input text fields are different. The moment you do anything to the text that isn't perfectly "square," the text in nonstatic text fields simply vanishes. Rotate it even one degree, and poof!

Why? The reason is simple: unless font outlines are included, Flash relies on fonts that exist on the user's computer. They're not *in* the SWF, so the SWF has no real control over them. But when you embed them in the movie, that's another matter. Keep in mind that adding font information to a movie increases its file size (yet another trade-off to consider).

There are couple ways to embed font outlines. The approach you use will probably depend on the amount of text your movie contains. On the one hand, each individual text field can have its embedding handled separately. Alternatively, you can use font symbols.

Embedding font outlines in individual text fields

If you care to embed font outlines for a few text fields, character embedding might be the quickest approach.

Choosing a character set to embed

Let's see how character embedding works:

1. In a new Flash document, use the Text tool to draw a text field. Make it dynamic and enter a bit of text into it (the standard Lorem ipsum dolor sit amet is fine).

2. With the text field selected, click the Character Embedding button in the Property inspector. The Character Embedding dialog box will open, as shown in Figure 6-31.

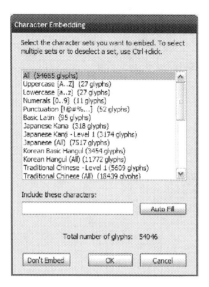

Figure 6-31. Embedding a font into the SWF

The choices are pretty clear-cut. As a general rule thumb, we recommend you embed only the characters you're sure to need. There's no reason to use the All choice, for example, if Basic Latin will do.

> *The Basic Latin character set is generally good for English, but does not include accented characters, so please, no accented résumés.*

3. To see the kind of difference various character sets can make, select All and click OK.

4. Test your movie. In the window that contains the SWF, go to View ➤ Bandwidth Profiler to see how much the SWF weighs.

5. Close that window, choose Basic Latin, and test again. Quite a difference!

If this text field requires only lowercase letters, choose the appropriate selection. To select more than one at the same time, hold down Ctrl (Cmd) while you click.

The Auto Fill button in the Character Embedding dialog box is pretty neat: it includes one of each character currently in the text field, without repeats.

If you change your mind and don't want to embed a character, click the Don't Embed button.

What happens if you fail to embed a character the text field ends up needing? That particular character won't show, even while the others do.

Applying character embedding correctly

Remember the very first topic at the beginning of this chapter, about what actually constitutes a font? Stylistic variations, such as bold and italic, are counted as distinct. Embedding roman (or normal) font outlines for a given character set *does not include* the corresponding bold or italic fonts, even for the exact same characters. To prove this point, let's use another example.

1. Open the EmbedButton.fla in this chapter's Exercise folder and test the movie.

Out of the four existing text fields, only the upper-left field shows any text (see Figure 6-32). Why? Because all four text fields are rotated, but only the upper-left field has its font outlines embedded. Even though the text field below it contains the same letters and features the same font family, the bottom field's particular variant is set to bold, while the upper-left field is set to normal. The fields to the right are interesting, because the one on the bottom is set to italic, so it makes sense that the text in that one doesn't show (no embedded fonts). But the upper-right field is set to normal, so why doesn't its text show? Again, because it doesn't have any embedded fonts. This tells you that it's not enough to have one text field embed font outlines; all text fields that need this feature must be told to use it.

Figure 6-32. Only one of the text blocks uses an embedded font.

2. Select the bottom-left text field and use the Character Embedding button to embed lowercase letters. Now both text fields on the left show.

Here's another interesting point. The upper-left text field is set to embed all lowercase letters. Meanwhile, the upper-right text field, which is composed of lowercase letters—just different ones— still doesn't show. Have lowercase font outlines been embedded, or haven't they? They have, but again, each text field that needs these outlines must make use of them.

3. Test your file and take note of the current SWF file size.

4. Close the SWF window and use the Character Embedding button to embed lowercase font outlines for the upper-right text field.

5. Test again. As expected, the upper-right field now shows, yet the SWF file size does not increase. This is good news: Flash isn't embedding the fonts more than once.

6. Embed lowercase font outlines for the lower-right text field.

7. Test the movie. This time, the SWF's file size will slightly increase again, because glyphs from three distinct fonts—normal, bold, and italic—have been embedded.

> *Here's a neat trick. Change the embedding option from lowercase to a single character in the* Include these characters *field. It can be any character—even a space. Test the movie. You'll see that the upper-right text field still shows! Flash apparently needs to a nudged into "embed mode" for every single text field, but the decision of which characters to embed needs to be made only once.*

Using font symbols

The other way to embed fonts is to use a font symbol. Open EmbedFontSymbol.fla in the Chapter 6 Exercise folder to see what we mean.

At first glance, this file doesn't seem any different from EmbedButton.fla, but there's a key distinction. Take a look in the library. See that capital A? That's a font symbol. That library asset represents the font outlines for the Verdana font. Its presence does an interesting thing to the Family drop-down list in the Property inspector. A new "font" appears, by the name of VerdanaNormal, followed by an asterisk (see Figure 6-33).

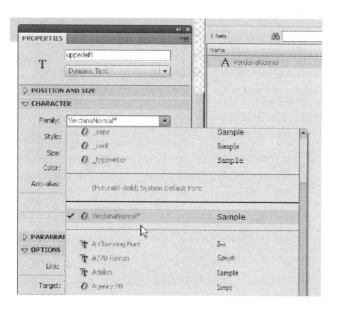

Figure 6-33. A library font symbol adds virtual entries to the Property inspector's Family property.

How did that font symbol get into the library? It's easy enough. Right-click (Ctrl-click) somewhere inside the library that isn't the preview area or an existing asset—or click the upper-right corner under the x—and you'll see a context menu that contains the choice New Font. That's the one you want. It opens the Font Symbol Properties dialog box, which allows you to specify an arbitrary custom name (such as VerdanaNormal), an actual font to embed, optional bold and italic styles, optional bitmap text, and size.

Bitmap text produces text that is not anti-aliased, so it will look jagged. If you choose this option, you must specify the particular font size you're after. If you do not use bitmap text, font size doesn't matter, because the font outlines will be vectors. As explained previously, bold and italic are separate font outlines, so if you want normal text with the occasional italic words for emphasis, you'll need to include two font symbols.

The final step is to export your font symbol for ActionScript. Right-click (Ctrl-click) the font symbol in the library and choose Properties. If the Font Symbol Properties dialog box doesn't show a Linkage area, click the Advanced button. Put a check mark in the Export for ActionScript and Export in First Frame boxes, and you're set. The Class field is automatically filled in for you, based on the font symbol's library name. Its class name might be slightly changed if the library name contains illegal characters, such as spaces or certain punctuation. The base class must be flash.text.Font, which makes sense.

As with EmbedButton.fla, this FLA features four text fields. However, this time, none of them shows text in the authoring tool. If you check the Character Embedding button, you'll see why (no embedding). Interestingly, if you test the SWF, you'll see text in the upper two fields. Have we entered the Twilight Zone yet?

Check the upper two text fields and verify in the Property inspector that they're both set to the VerdanaNormal* "font" (actually a virtual font—the library font symbol). The embedding is happening with ActionScript, by way of the TextField.embedFonts property for each text field instance. As you click each dynamic text field, note that each has an instance name (upperleft, lowerleft, upperright, and lowerright). Open the Actions panel and look at the code in frame 1 of the scripts layer:

```
upperleft.embedFonts = true;
upperright.embedFonts = true;
lowerleft.embedFonts = true;
upperright.embedFonts = true;
```

The lower-left and lower-right text fields do not show in the published SWF, because neither bold nor italic variants have been brought as font symbols into the library.

To prove that VerdanaNormal* really is a virtual font, right-click (Cmd-click) the font symbol and choose Properties. Change the Font entry to a visually different font, such as Courier. Test your movie. Even with a name like VerdanaNormal*, the font outlines look like the replacement font.

Checking spelling

Let's admit it: If we enter text, we will inevitably use the wrong spelling for a word or two. Flash CS4 contains a tool that checks the spelling of all of the text in a document. You don't have heartless editors peering over your shoulders as we do, so spell checking your work before sending it to the Web is a really good idea. It should therefore not come as too much of a surprise to discover that the spell-checking feature of Flash is quite robust. It allows you to check not only the spelling of the text in your text fields, but also the spelling in your layer names.

If you have never used the spelling features of Flash CS4, you need to set up the spelling checker before you undertake your first spell check. Open a new Flash document and select Text ➤ Spelling Setup to open the Spelling Setup dialog box, as shown in Figure 6-34. The Document options area sets up what spelling is to be checked, including any strings you may use in ActionScript. You can choose from a number of dictionaries, and even create your own for commonly used words not found in a dictionary. The Checking options area permits you to decide which words or groups of words will be included or omitted from any spell checks.

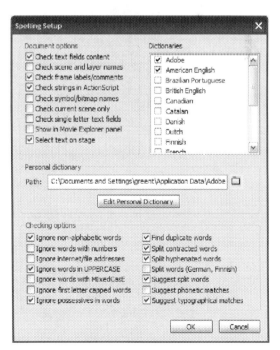

Figure 6-34. The Spelling Setup dialog box

293

It is heartening for one of the authors to see a Canadian dictionary and a British English dictionary. Canadian and British English are understandably similar, but writing for publishers based in the United States can be a bit disorienting. For example, the word color, *which is used extensively throughout this book, is not correct in the United Kingdom or Canada, where it is spelled* colour. *Another word used in the American English dictionary is the word* check. *This important method of payment is spelled* cheque *in the Queen's English.*

Let's bring in some text—with typos—and check the spelling.

1. Open the SpellItOut.txt document in this chapter's Exercise folder in a word processor, select the text, and copy it to the clipboard. Large amounts of text are pasted into Flash. For better or worse, there is no ability in the application to import text into the library. Close the word processor.

2. Return to Flash, select the Text tool, and click the stage. Select Edit ➤ Paste to add the text to the stage.

3. Select Text ➤ Check Spelling. The Check Spelling dialog box will appear, as shown in Figure 6-35. If the word is not recognized, the checker will provide you with a suggestion, which you can choose to either change or ignore.

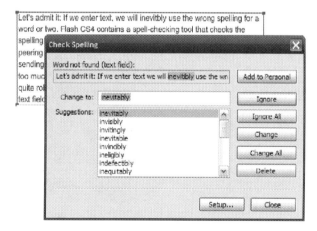

Figure 6-35. Using the Check Spelling dialog box

4. When you complete your spell check, click the Close button.

Although there is no language known as "Adobe," the Flash dictionary is full of terms exclusively used by the Adobe products. A great example of an "Adobian" word is ActionScript. *It wouldn't be flagged by the Adobe spelling checker, but will be considered an error by other spelling checkers.*

Your turn: Scrollable text

The final two exercises in the chapter deal with one of the more frequently asked questions regarding text: "How do I scroll a large amount of text?" In fact, there are several ways of approaching this one. We'll look at two. The first is to use the UIScrollBar component, which, to quote a friend of ours, is "easy peasy." The second is to "roll your own" scroller using ActionScript.

Before you start, let's get clear on the fact that the text field must be dynamic, and Flash needs to know it is scrollable. This is done in one of three ways:

- Hold down the Shift key and double-click the circular handle of the text block. The circle will turn into a black square, as shown in Figure 6-36.

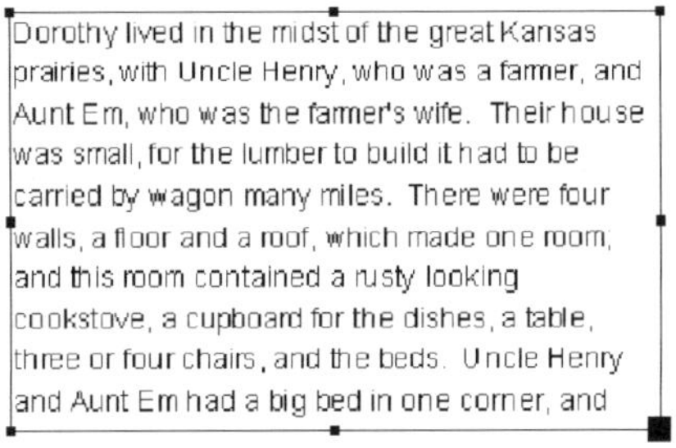

Figure 6-36. Your visual clue that a text field is scrollable

- Using the Selection tool, click the text block and select Text ➤ Scrollable.
- With the text block selected, right-click (Ctrl-click) the text box and select Scrollable from the context menu.

Using the UIScrollBar component

Let's start with the "easy peasy" method: using the UIScrollBar component. We will talk about components in great depth in Chapter 11. For now, just work with us. In this particular case, no ActionScript is involved, which is why we're showing you the UIScrollBar component early. Components usually require a bit of programming.

1. Open the ScrollComponent.fla file in the Chapter 6 Exercise folder. You will see we have put some text on the stage in a dynamic text box.

2. Switch to the Selection tool, click the text field, and select Text ➤ Scrollable. The hollow circle turns to a black box. Drag the bottom of the field to a point between the second and third paragraphs.

3. Select Window ➤ Components. From the Components panel, open the User Interface components and select the UIScrollBar component, as shown in Figure 6-37. Drag a copy of it onto the text.

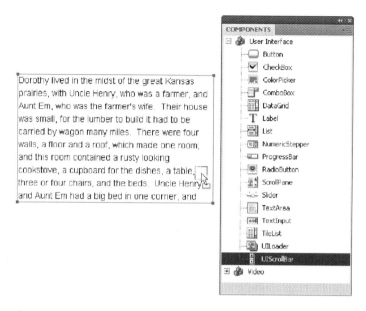

Figure 6-37. The UIScrollBar component is found in the User Interface components.

4. Depending on which side of the text field you chose, the component will spring to the closest side of the text field. Switch to the Selection tool and move it to the opposite side of the field. Now move it back to the right side of the field and release the mouse.

5. Save and test the movie. You will see that can scroll the text up and down, as shown in Figure 6-38.

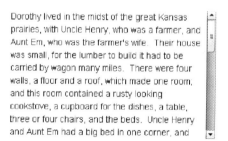

Figure 6-38. The UIScrollBar component in action

Rolling your own scroller

In this final exercise of the chapter, we are going to let you wire up a scroller using ActionScript. Just keep in mind there are several hundred ways of doing this, and the method we are using is a very basic example of creating scroll buttons. In this example, we use two very simple button symbols as the scrollers, whereas others may use movieclips. We use opacity to indicate when the scroll button is no longer active. Others may use different colors or even different shapes to indicate the state of the scroll button. This example moves the text up or down a short distance (one line) with each mouse press. Others may have the text move up or down until the mouse is released. Regardless, the text is scrolling, which is the point of this exercise. Let's get busy:

1. Open the scrollingAS.fla file in this chapter's Exercise folder. You will see that we have added the text field and the buttons to the stage. The text field has been given the instance name of output, and the buttons have the instance names of btnScrollUp and btnScroll-Down.

2. Select the first frame of the Actions layer, open the Actions panel, and you will see we have provided you with the text.

3. Click in line 4 of the Script pane and enter the following code:

```
btnScrollUp.addEventListener(MouseEvent.MOUSE_UP, scrollUp);
function scrollUp():void {
  output.scrollV--;
  updateButtons();
}

btnScrollDown.addEventListener(MouseEvent.MOUSE_UP, scrollDown);
function scrollDown():void {
  output.scrollV++;
  updateButtons();
}
```

These two functions are how the text moves. The TextField.scrollV property moves the text up one line—scrollV— —or down one line — scrollV++ — depending on which button is clicked. The next step in the process is to add the opacity change when a button is clicked and to make sure the finger cursor no longer shows when the start or the end of the text block is reached. That is the purpose of the updateButtons() function.

> This may seem like a lot of effort—and programming often is—but in this case, you're lucky. Text automatically stops scrolling up when the scrollV property is at 1 (the same goes for the bottom end and scrolling down), so you don't actually need to program the text field to stop scrolling when an end is encountered. Flash takes care of that for you. But it is a courtesy to hide the finger cursor by temporarily disabling the relevant button as necessary.

4. Press Enter (Return) twice and enter the following code:

```
function updateButtons():void {
  if (output.scrollV == 1) {
    btnScrollUp.alpha = 0.5;
    btnScrollUp.enabled = false;
  } else {
    btnScrollUp.alpha = 1;
    btnScrollUp.enabled = true;
  }
```

```
    if (output.scrollV == output.maxScrollV) {
      btnScrollDown.alpha = 0.5;
      btnScrollDown.enabled = false;
    } else {
      btnScrollDown.alpha = 1;
      btnScrollDown.enabled = true;
    }
  }

  updateButtons();
```

As step 4 shows, the btnScrollUp and btnScrollDown buttons additionally call this custom function, updateButtons(). This function examines the current value of scrollV against a couple numbers to determine how to manipulate the btnScrollUp and btnScrollDown buttons. When the text is fully scrolled up, its scrollV value is 1. In that case, alpha is reduced to half and enabled is set to false; otherwise, alpha is set to 1 (in ActionScript, alpha values are a number between 0 and 1) and enabled to true. When text is fully scrolled down, scrollV will be the same value as that text field's maxScrollV value. In that case, the same basic procedure is practiced again.

The last line, updateButtons();, actually executes this function immediately after its declaration, in order to update the buttons before they're even pressed.

5. Close the Actions panel and test the movie. The up button is grayed out (actually, its opacity is 50%), as shown in Figure 6-39. This is because it is at the top of the text block and the scrollV value is equal to 1. Notice how it turns dark when the down button is clicked. This is because the scrollV value is now greater than 1.

Lorem ipsum dolor sit amet, consectetuer adipiscing elit. Mauris tempus dignissim risus. Morbi viverra adipiscing dui. Nullam lacinia turpis at tortor. Nunc eleifend. Aliquam tortor tellus, luctus in, venenatis vel, accumsan id, enim. Nunc sit amet velit. Cras tincidunt arcu eget nibh. Etiam et risus. Proin a turpis eu massa aliquet sagittis. Donec massa enim, molestie ac, fringilla aliquam, interdum in, tellus. Donec justo purus, accumsan sed, tincidunt at, fermentum sit amet, erat. Ut ornare quam eu sapien. Pellentesque varius velit eu nunc. Curabitur enim libero, commodo pellentesque, blandit elementum, ornare eget, leo. Nunc semper eros fermentum enim.
Nunc bibendum malesuada urna. Vestibulum mattis sollicitudin pede. Cum sociis natoque penatibus et magnis dis parturient montes, nascetur ridiculus mus. Sed eget orci sed sem dapibus gravida. Vivamus tempus dignissim purus. In ac velit. Pellentesque ultricies mauris sit amet sapien. Sed lectus. Lorem ipsum dolor sit amet, consectetuer adipiscing elit. Cum sociis natoque penatibus et magnis dis parturient montes, nascetur ridiculus mus. Etiam ut augue ut nisl euismod gravida. Morbi eu lacus eget odio pharetra mattis.

Figure 6-39. A custom scrollbar

What you have learned

In this chapter, you learned the following:

- How to add text to Flash
- The various text-formatting features available to you in Flash CS4
- How to choose and work with static, dynamic, and input text fields
- How to put text in motion and manipulate many of its properties
- The ActionScript necessary to create, format, and provide interactivity through the use of text
- When to embed font outlines into a SWF and how to accomplish that task
- How to create scrolling text in Flash

We suspect you are more than a little confounded at the possibilities open to you when it comes to using text in Flash. If you are one of those who saw text as the gray stuff hovering around your animations, we hope you have seen the error of your ways. And, if you are one of those who want to get going and turn out really cool motion graphics pieces, we hope you paid close attention to what Bringhurst was saying in the quote that opened this chapter. Regardless of which camp you fall into, we know that you are now aware that adding text to a Flash CS4 animation doesn't stop with a click of the Text tool and the tapping of a few keys on the keyboard.

Now that you know how to work with text and put it in motion, the time has arrived to put objects in motion. Animation in Flash is covered in the next two chapters, and to find out more, turn the page.

Chapter 7

ANIMATION

Ah, animation! Where would we be without the likes of Disney, Warner Bros., Walter Lanz, Hanna-Barbera, and dozens more like them? For many people, animation is *the reason* to get involved with Flash as a creative outlet. This makes perfect sense, because Flash began life more than a decade ago as an animation tool. Supplemental features like ActionScript, XML parsing, and video integration—every one of which is a tremendous addition—all followed. What hasn't changed in all these years is Flash's increasingly productive ability to help you create high-quality, scalable animation for the Web, and even for television and film.

You caught the faintest whiff of tweening in Chapters 1, 2, and 3. It gets considerably more complex—read *considerably more fun!*—because, for the first time, Flash CS4 gives you a double-dose of animation apparatus. You now have two independent tweening models to work with, the newer of which will make users of Adobe After Effects feel right at home. Each of these tweening models gets its own chapter in this book.

The original Flash approach, now called *classic tweening*, is covered here in Chapter 7. Chapter 8 delves into the new stuff. To get the most out of animation in Flash, you should read both chapters, starting with this one. As you'll discover, you can use both models in the same movie. You'll learn enough in these chapters to help you comfortably choose which approach, or combination of approaches, works best for your particular needs.

Here's what we'll cover in this chapter:

- Shape tweening
- Shape hinting
- Classic motion tweening
- Easing

- Using the Custom Ease In/Ease Out editor
- Animating symbols
- Combining timelines
- Applying motion tween effects

The following files are used in this chapter (located in Chapter07/ExerciseFiles_Ch07/Exercise/):

- PepperShape.fla
- StarStar.fla
- StarCircle.fla
- Ant.fla
- LogoMorphNoHints.fla
- FlowerWeed.fla
- GradientTween1.fla
- GradientTween2.fla
- BitmapFillTween.fla
- PepperSymbol.fla
- MalletNoEasing.fla
- MalletCustomEasing.fla
- CustomEasingComparison.fla
- CustomEasingMultiple.fla
- YawningParrot.fla

- SyncPropertyGraphic.fla
- EditMultipleFrames.fla
- TimelineCombine.fla
- Grotto.fla
- tronguy.png
- TronGuyGlow.fla
- MotionGuide.fla
- TweenMask.fla
- TweenMaskMotionGuide.fla
- AnimatedButton.fla
- Circuit.mov
- Zap.mp3
- CreateMotionAS3.fla
- BadHairDay.fla

The source files are available online from either of the following sites:

- http://www.FoundationFlashCS4.com
- http://www.friendsofED.com/download.html?isbn=9781430210931

Because this chapter has a lot of moving parts, let's cut straight to the "without further ado" and jump directly into the fray!

Shape tweening

As useful as symbols are, both in organizing artwork and reducing SWF file size, they shouldn't over-shadow the importance of shapes. After all, unless a symbol is the result of text or an imported image file, chances are good it was constructed from one or more of Flash's most basic of visual entities: the shape.

Shapes differ significantly from symbols, although many of their features overlap. Like symbols, shapes are tweened on keyframes. Tweening may be finessed by something called *easing*, and can affect things like position, scale, distortion, color, and transparency. The difference comes in how these changes are achieved. In addition, shapes can do something symbols can't: they can actually morph from one set of contours to another!

Scaling and stretching

Let's start with the basics:

1. Open the PepperShape.fla file in the Chapter 7 Exercise folder. You'll notice that there is nothing in the library. This is because the hot pepper on the stage is composed entirely of shapes.

2. Select Insert ➤ Timeline ➤ Keyframe to insert a keyframe at frame 10. This effectively produces a copy of the artwork from frame 1 in frame 10, and makes the copy available for manipulation. Any changes you make to frame 10 will not affect the shapes in frame 1, so you can always remove that second keyframe (Modify ➤ Timeline ➤ Clear Keyframe) and start again from scratch if you desire.

> *If you prefer, you can insert a blank keyframe at frame 10 (Insert ➤ Timeline ➤ Blank Keyframe), and then copy and paste the artwork from frame 1. It makes no practical difference, but clearly the approach in step 2 requires less effort. You may even draw completely new shapes into frame 10, and Flash will do its best to accommodate—but that's skipping ahead. More on that in the "Altering shapes" section.*
>
> *All of these menu choices have right-click (Ctrl-click) equivalents, available from the context menu of any timeline frame.*

3. With frame 10 selected, choose the Free Transform tool and drag the right side of the pepper's bounding box to the right. As you do this, you'll see a live preview of the shapes in their new stretched size, as shown in Figure 7-1.

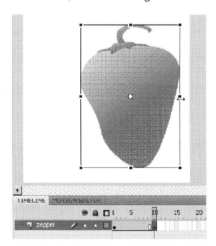

Figure 7-1. Changing a shape's shape in preparation for a shape tween

> *You might find that you have accidentally selected either only the pepper or only its cap. The Free Transform tool's bounding box will let you know at a glance which shape(s) you have selected, because it will either encompass the full surface area of the artwork or it won't. To ensure you've grabbed all the shapes, use the Selection tool to first draw a marquee (that is, a selection) around the whole pepper. An even simpler technique is to click the keyframe at frame 10, which selects everything on that layer in that keyframe.*

4. Select Edit ➤ Undo Scale to undo. (You might need to undo twice: once to reselect and once to remove the widen transform.)

5. Reapply the transform and hold down the Alt (Option) key while dragging to the right. Notice how the artwork now scales out from the center.

This feature often comes in handy, but it's important to understand what's really going on. When the Alt (Option) key is used, it's not the center of the artwork that becomes the pivot, but rather the *transformation point*, as indicated by a small white circle. You can drag this circle where you like, even outside the confines of the shape's bounding box. With or without the Alt (Option) key, the transformation point acts as the fulcrum of your modifications, but using the key changes how the fulcrum is applied.

Because you're dealing with shapes, you can even use the Free Transform tool's Envelope and Distort options (shown in Figure 7-2), which aren't available for symbols. If you do, just be aware that things can quickly fall apart with such transformations unless you use shape hints, which are covered later in the chapter.

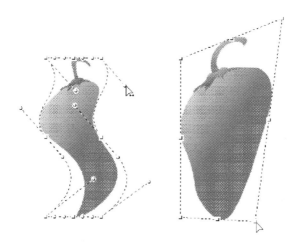

Figure 7-2. Shape transformations include Envelope (left) and Distort (right).

6. Now that you have two keyframes prepared, it's time for the magic. Make sure the pepper is changed in frame 10 (for example, the widening applied in step 5). Right-click (Ctrl-click) anywhere in the span of frames between both keyframes and select Create Shape Tween from the context menu (see Figure 7-3). Two things will happen:

- The span of frames will turn green, which indicates a shape tween. They will also gain an arrow pointing to the right, which tells you the tween was successful.

- The pepper will update to reflect a visual state between the artwork in either keyframe, depending on where the playhead is positioned.

7. Drag the playhead back and forth to watch the pepper seem to breathe.

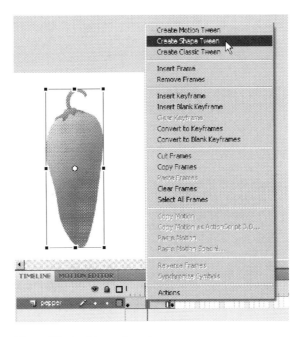

Figure 7-3. Applying a shape tween

If your tweened frames fail to turn green, don't worry. By default, they should, but crazier things have been known to happen. Click in the Timeline panel's upper-right corner to open its context menu and make sure Tinted Frames is selected, as shown in Figure 7-4. (All the hotrods have 'em.)

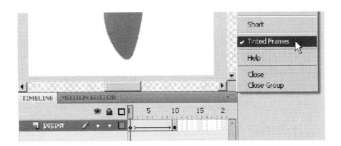

Figure 7-4. The Tinted Frames option helps you recognize tweened frames.

> *If you applied the tween while in frame 1—a perfectly legal choice, by the way—you wouldn't immediately see the pepper change. Why? Because the tweening is applied between the two keyframes, and frame 1 still represents the artwork as it was before tweening changed it. Drag the playhead back and forth, and you'll see the tween.*

8. Right-click (Ctrl-click) anywhere between the two keyframes and choose Remove Tween. The tween goes away.

9. Let's try another tween. Right-click (Ctrl-click) your frame span and choose Create Motion Tween. Motion tweening is not supported for shapes, and Flash gives you an unmistakable sign that you've gone wrong. You'll see an alert box that offers to convert your shape into a symbol, as shown in Figure 7-5. Choose OK, and you'll see most of your frame span turn blue, along with the appearance of a new movieclip in the library.

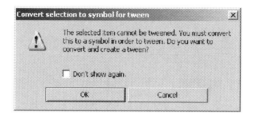

Figure 7-5. Tweens other than the shape variety require symbols.

It's nice that Flash does this for you, but generally speaking, you'll want to decide on your own what sort of symbol to create: movieclip, graphic, or button. Unfortunately, this automated process does the choosing for you.

Motion tweens are part of the new After-Effects–like tweening model you'll learn about in Chapter 8. Motion tweens are nothing like shape tweens; they are an altogether different concept.

10. Select Edit ➤ Undo Create Motion Tween to step back. That sets the frames back and removes the library's movieclip.

11. Time for another mistake. Right-click (Ctrl-click) your frame span and choose Create Classic Tween.

Instead of green, the span of frames will become purple, and you'll see *two* new symbols in the library (this time, graphic symbols)—without even a warning! Purple frames indicate a classic tween, which you'll learn about later in this chapter. These, too, are nothing like shape tweens.

12. Perform an undo, and the frames will revert to a non-tweened state. You'll need to delete the graphic symbols by hand, though. Go ahead and do that.

13. Reapply a shape tween and scrub to frame 10.

14. Select the Free Transform tool and drag around one of the bounding box corners to change both the horizontal and vertical scale. If you like, hold down Shift to constrain the aspect ratio, and Alt (Option) to apply changes from the center of the transformation point. Make the pepper a good bit bigger than the original size. This shows that it's possible to adjust keyframes even after they're already part of a tween.

> *Another way to apply shape tweens is to click between two keyframes and select* Insert ➤ Shape Tween. *To remove a shape tween, select* Insert ➤ Remove Tween. *You'll see that you can do the same with motion and classic tweens.*

Modifying shape tweens

There are a couple ways to refine a shape tween once it's applied. These are shown in the Property inspector when you click in a tweened span of frames: Ease and Blend.

Easing tends to make tweens look more lifelike because it gradually varies the amount of distance traveled between each frame. If an astronaut throws a golf ball in outer space, the ball flies at a constant rate until . . . well, until it hits something. That's not how it works on a planet with gravity. The ball flies faster at first, and then gradually slows down. This deceleration is called *easing out*. A ball dropped from a tall building begins its descent slowly, and then gradually increases speed. This acceleration is called *easing in*.

Adjust the Ease slider in the Property inspector to see how easing affects the shape tween applied to the pepper in the previous exercise. Supported values range from 100 (strong ease out), through 0 (no easing), to –100 (strong ease in). As shown in Figure 7-6, easing can have a profound effect upon an object in motion. We'll cover easing in greater detail in the "Classic tweening" section.

> If you don't see much of a difference after experimenting with easing, try lengthening the duration of your shape tween. To do so, click somewhere in the tween span between the two keyframes, and then press the F5 key several times to insert new frames.

Figure 7-6. Examples of easing, from top to bottom

Blend is a much subtler matter. There are two Blend settings: Distributive (the default) and Angular. According to Adobe, Distributive "creates an animation in which the intermediate shapes are smoother and more irregular," and Angular "creates an animation that preserves apparent corners and straight lines in the intermediate shapes." In actual practice, the authors find this distinction negligible at best. In short, don't worry yourself over this setting. Feel free to use the one with which you are most comfortable. We're willing to bet our hats you won't be able to tell one from the other.

OK, so far, so good. These tweens have been pretty straightforward. In fact, as you'll find later in the chapter, everything you've seen to this point can be accomplished just as easily with classic tweens. This raises a good question: what makes shape tweens so special? Why not just use classic tweens or the motion tweens you'll learn about in Chapter 8?

The answer comes in two parts: gradients and shape. Let's tackle shape first, because it has the potential to set your teeth on edge if you aren't prepared for it.

Altering shapes

The compelling reason to use shape tweens is their ability to manipulate the actual form of the artwork itself, beyond scaling and stretching. Let's keep playing:

1. Continuing with PepperShape.fla, use the Free Transform tool at frame 10 to rotate the pepper about 90 degrees in either direction.

2. You should still have a shape tween applied (if not, add one). Drag the playhead back and forth to see a result that may surprise you. Rather than rotating, the pepper temporarily deforms itself as it changes from one keyframe to another (see Figure 7-7).

What on earth is going on here? Though it may look like an absolute mess, what you are seeing is the key distinction between shape tweening and the other kinds of tweening. Believe it or not, this behavior can be a very useful thing. You'll see an example in just a moment. First, let's take a quick field trip to frame 10 in order to illustrate a point.

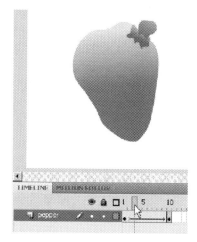

Figure 7-7. Sometimes shape tweens perform unexpected transformations.

> In case you're worried, we'll put your mind at ease without further ado: it is entirely possible to rotate artwork with tweens in Flash. In fact, it's easy. In contrast to shape tweens, classic and motion tweens maintain a strict marriage between the vector anchor points of one keyframe and the next. We'll show you why later in this chapter and in Chapter 8. When you understand what each approach does best, you'll know which one to use for the task at hand.

3. Choose the Subselection tool and click in frame 10. You'll see dozens of tiny squares that act as anchor points among the various lines and curves that make up the pepper's shape. All those points exist in frame 1 as well, of course, but they're in different positions relative to one another.

With shape tweens, Flash does not think of artwork in terms of a whole; instead, it manipulates each anchor point separately. What seems like a rotation to you is, to a shape tween, nothing more than a rearrangement of anchor points—sometimes a chaotic one, at that!

Think of it like a square dance. If a particular point happens to be in the upper-left corner on frame 1, it has no idea that its corresponding point may be in the upper-right corner on frame 10. It simply changes a partner—do-si-do!—and moves to a new spot during the tween. Like square dancing, there are sophisticated rules at play, and movement across the dance floor may appear unpredictable. It's possible, for example, that two keyframes may even present a completely different number of anchor points. Let's look at that next.

Examining anchor points

Open the StarStar.fla file in this chapter's Exercise folder, and examine the 22-point star in frame 1. Use the Subselection tool, if you like, to see the individual anchor points (there are 44). Click in frame 20 to see a seven-point star (14 anchor points). Note that a shape tween has already been applied between these two keyframes. Drag the playhead back and forth to watch the promenade (shown in Figure 7-8). Flash handles the reduction in anchor points in a neat, organized way. In this case, by the way, the star in the second keyframe was drawn as new artwork into frame 20.

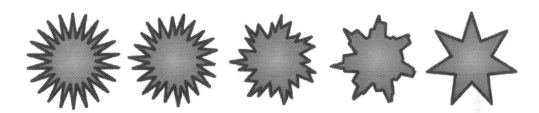

Figure 7-8. The 44 anchor points artfully become 14.

Now open the StarCircle.fla file in this chapter's Exercise folder and run through the same steps to see a 22-point star become an 8-point circle. These are some nifty transformations that are simply not possible with classic tweens.

> In Chapter 2, we described a vector circle as having five points: four on the perimeter and one in the center. So why does the circle in this exercise have eight perimeter points? Frankly, because the Flash engineers know more about vectors than we do. Our discussion in Chapter 2 was for illustrative purposes.

This opens up a whole avenue of vector-morphing possibilities, from sunshine gleams to water ripples to waving hair and twitching insect antennae (see Figure 7-9).

Shape changing

For anything where you need the actual *shape* of an item to change—where anchor points themselves need to be rearranged—shape tweens are the way to go. Keep in mind that tweens happen on a keyframe basis, and timeline layers are distinct. If you have a complex set of shapes, and you wish to tween only some of them, move those shapes to a separate layer. In fact, you may want to put every to-be-tweened shape on its own layer, because that reduces the number of anchor points under consideration for each keyframe. Let's try it by setting some antennae in motion:

1. Open the Ant.fla file in this chapter's Exercise folder and insert a keyframe in frames 15 and 30 of the antenna1 layer.

2. Select the Subselection tool and change the shape of the antenna in frame 30.

3. Add a shape tween between the keyframes and scrub through the timeline. The antennae move around (see Figure 7-9).

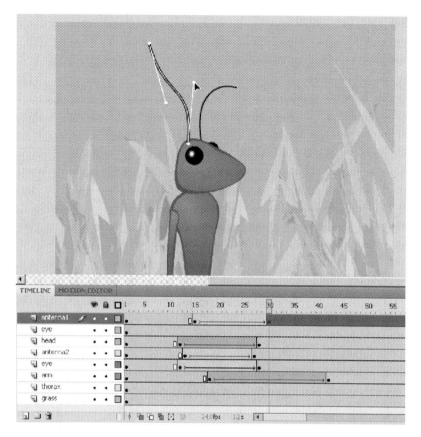

Figure 7-9. Need to change the shape of those antennae? Shape tweens to the rescue!

As you've seen, Flash can make some fairly stylish choices of its own in regard to the repositioning of anchor points. Well, that's true most of the time. The earlier pepper rotation demonstrates that Flash's choices aren't always what you might expect. Fortunately, Flash provides a way to let you take control of shape tweens gone awry. The solution is something called shape hints.

Shape hints

What are shape hints? Often overlooked or misunderstood, these useful contraptions allow you to specify a partnership between a vector region of your choosing from one keyframe to the next. They are a means by which you can guide an anchor point, curve, or line toward the destination you've determined is the correct one. Let's take a look.

1. Open the LogoMorphNoHints.fla file in this chapter's Exercise folder. Take a look at frame 1 to see a lowercase *i* that has been broken apart from a text field into two shapes. In frame 55, you'll see an abstract shape that represents a hypothetical logo.

2. The aim here is to morph between the shapes in an appealing way, but something has gone horribly wrong (see Figure 7-10). Drag the playhead along the timeline and note the atrocities committed between frames 20 and 35.

Figure 7-10. Something has gone horribly wrong.

This looks as bad as (if not worse than) the hot pepper rotation, but why? On the face of it, this should be a basic shape tween. Seemingly, the letter and logo shapes aren't especially intricate, and yet, the timeline doesn't lie.

> *At this point, the authors look deftly side to side, and with a sly, "Hey, pssst," invite you to step with them into a small, dimly lit alley. (Don't worry, we're here to help.) "The thing is," begins the first, "honestly, there's often a bit of voodoo involved with shape tweens, and that's the truth." "That's right," chimes in the other, lowering his voice. "To be frank, if I may"—you nod—"we don't know why these anchor points sometimes go kablooey. It's just a thing, and you have to roll with it." There is a slight pause, and suddenly a cappuccino machine splooshes in the distance. The first author draws a finger across his nose. "Keep that in mind as we continue," he says. Another pause. "You wanna see the shape hints?" You nod again.*

3. Click in frame 20, and select Modify ➤ Shape ➤ Add Shape Hint (see Figure 7-11). This puts a small red circle with the letter a in the center of your artwork. Meet your first shape hint.

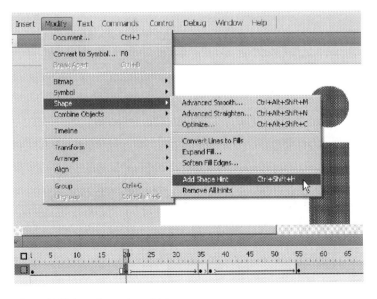

Figure 7-11. Inserting a shape hint

4. Make sure object snapping is on, either by selecting Snap to Objects in the Tools panel or ensuring that a check mark is present under View ➤ Snapping ➤ Snap to Objects. Snapping helps the placement of shape hints significantly.

5. Drag and snap the a circle to the lower-left corner of the letter's upper serif, as shown in Figure 7-12. If you are a stickler for detail, feel free to zoom the stage before you try snapping the circle.

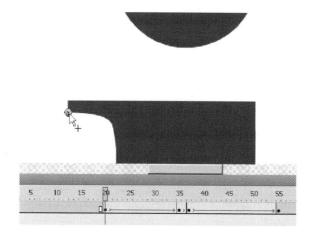

Figure 7-12. Positioning a shape hint

This next point is important: what you've done is placed *one half* of a shape hint *pair*. The other half—the partner—is on the next keyframe, frame 35.

6. Drag the playhead to frame 35 and position the second a circle on the corresponding serif on this keyframe's shape, as shown in Figure 7-13.

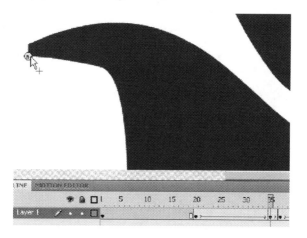

Figure 7-13. Positioning the shape hint's partner

7. When this partner snaps into place, it will turn green. Return to frame 20 and notice that the original shape hint has turned yellow.

It may be that shape hints have a thing for stoplights (not that there's anything wrong with that), but the point is that the color change indicates something. It tells you that this shape hint pair has entered into a relationship. You have now indicated to Flash your intentions that these paired regions now correspond to each other.

8. Slide the playhead along the timeline again, and you'll see a remarkable improvement (as shown in Figure 7-14).

The improvement is so remarkable, in fact, that the authors look deftly side to side, wink, and silently mouth the word "voodoo." To be frank, if we may, the placement of shape hints often makes a noticeable difference, but the decision on placement is something of a dark art. We encourage you to reposition your first shape hint pair at other corners to see how the remaining trouble spots ripple to other areas.

You should get the idea by now that shape hints are a bit like cloves (you know, the star-shaped things you poke into your ham during the holidays)—a little goes a long way. Let's add a few more, but do so sparingly.

Figure 7-14. A dramatic improvement, but there are still a few trouble spots.

9. To get rid of the kink in the upper curve, add a new shape hint to the upper-right corner of the *i* on frame 20. This time, you'll see a small b in a red circle. Snap its b partner to the upper-right corner of the logo at frame 35, and drag the playhead again to see your progress.

10. Add shape hints c and d to the lower-left and right corners, and you should see a very smooth morph along this span of frames.

11. The only problem remaining, if you're a perfectionist, is a slight wrinkle along the bottom of the "egg" between keyframes 37 and 55. Remedy this by adding a new shape at frame 37. It will start again at a, because this is a new pair of keyframes, and snap in place to the corresponding curve at frame 55.

Compare your work with the LogoMorph.fla file in this chapter's Complete folder, if you like. When you open a file that already contains shape hints, you'll need to take one small step to make them show, as they like to hide by default. To toggle shapes hints on and off, select View ➤ Show Shape Hints.

Even with the benefit of shape hints, we caution you to keep simplicity in mind. Certain collections of shapes are simply too intricate to handle gracefully. Remember that not every website visitor will have as powerful a computer as yours. It is entirely possible to choke the Flash Player through the use of an overwhelming number of anchor points. To see what we mean, open the FlowerWeed.fla file in this chapter's Exercise folder, and drag the playhead along the timeline. The morph isn't especially polished (see Figure 7-15), but it certainly doesn't count as a complete eyesore. Test the SWF (Control ➤ Test Movie), and—depending on the power of your computer—you may see that playback slows or skips during the most complex portions of the tween. If that doesn't happen for you, count yourself lucky! But generally speaking, try to avoid asking this much of your users.

Figure 7-15. Moderation in all things! While this transformation doesn't look awful, it nearly chokes Flash Player.

Altering gradients

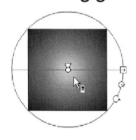

Figure 7-16. Gradients, like anything else, can be edited on keyframes, and those keyframes are tweenable.

If you want to animate gradients, shape tweens are the only way to do it. You may not immediately think of gradients as shapes, but when you select the Gradient Transform tool and click into a gradient, what do you see? You see the handles and points shown in Figure 7-16.

That center point, to Flash, is not much different from an anchor point. The resize, radius, and rotate handles are not much different from Bezier control point handles. In effect, you are manipulating a shape—just a special kind. When animating a gradient, you simply change these gradient-specific features from keyframe to keyframe, rather than a shape's corners, lines, and curves.

Open the GradientTween1.fla file in this chapter's Exercise folder and drag the playhead along the timeline to see an example in action. Frame 1 contains a solid red fill. Frame 10 contains the built-in rainbow gradient, which is rotated 90 degrees in frame 20. Frames 20 through 30 provide a bit of interest because they demonstrate a limitation of gradient shape tweens: it is not possible to tween one type of gradient to another. Well, we take that back. You certainly can, but the results are unpredictable. Flash tries its best to convert a linear gradient into a radial one, but between frames 29 and 30, the gradient pops from one type to the other.

Next, open the GradientTween2.fla file in this chapter's Exercise folder. This example shows a combination of a gradient and a shape change at the same time. Not only does the gradient fill transform, but anchor points move, and even stroke color (and thickness!) changes from keyframe to keyframe. Experiment with solid colors as well as the Color panel's Alpha property. When you finish, close the file without saving the changes.

Even bitmap fills are tweenable, which makes for some interesting visual possibilities, as shown in Figure 7-17. Open the BitmapFillTween.fla file in this chapter's Exercise folder and press the Enter (Return) key to see some roller-coaster camera work. As with other types of gradients, use the Gradient Transform tool to manipulate gradient control handles at each keyframe, and then let the shape tween handle the rest. Easing works the same way.

Figure 7-17. Shape tween your bitmap fill transformations for some real zing!

Classic tweening

When we left that hapless hot pepper hanging, it had been hoping to rotate. It didn't, and instead found its molecules tumbling in a frenzied jumble. We told you there was a much easier way to handle that rotation, and classing tweening is one of them. Shape tweens are for rearranging anchor points and animating gradients. Classic tweens and motion tweens are for everything else, from enlivening text and imported photos to animating vector artwork drawn directly in Flash or imported from another application like Illustrator CS4 or Fireworks CS4. As we've said, we'll cover motion tweening in Chapter 8. Here, we'll continue with classic tweens only, but keep in mind that you'll have additional choices.

In contrast to shape tweens, classic tweens require self-contained entities. These include symbols, primitives, drawing objects, and grouped elements, which many designers find easier to work with than raw shapes. Open PepperSymbol.fla in this chapter's Exercise folder, for example, and you'll see that it's easier to select the whole pepper without accidentally omitting the cap.

> *Be aware that primitives and drawing objects blur the lines somewhat between what constitutes a shape and what constitutes a symbol. It is possible to apply both shape tweens and motion tweens to primitives and drawing objects. However, many properties, such as color, alpha, and the like—and in primitives, shape—are properly animated only with shape tweens. These "gotchas" tend to steer the authors toward a path of least resistance: use shapes for shape tweens and symbols for classic tweens. Within those symbols, use whatever elements you like.*
>
> *One fundamental point: when it comes to classic tweens, always put each tweened symbol on its own layer. If you apply a classic tween to keyframes that contain more than one symbol, Flash will try to oblige—but will fail. It's a simple rule, so abide by it, and you'll be happy.*

Rotation

Let's pick up with that rotation, shall we?

1. Open the PepperSymbol.fla file in this chapter's Exercise folder. You'll see a pepper symbol in the library (the shapes from the earlier PepperShape.fla example have been placed inside a graphic symbol).

2. Add a keyframe in frame 10. Then select the Free Transform tool and rotate the artwork 90 degrees in either direction on that second keyframe. Sounds familiar, right? Here comes the difference.

3. Right-click (Ctrl-click) and select Create Classic Tween from the context menu. There it is!

4. Drag the playhead back and forth to see a nice, clean rotation of the pepper. As you saw with shape tweens, the span of frames between the two keyframes changes color (to purple this time), and a solid arrow appears within the span to indicate a successful tween, as shown in Figure 7-18.

Figure 7-18. Classic tweens, indicated by purple and an arrow between the keyframes, make rotations a snap.

Now, let's think about *real* rotation: topsy-turvy—a full 360-degree spin. How would you do it? (Hint: This is something of a trick question.) In a full spin, the pepper ends up in the same position at frame 10 as it starts with in frame 1, so there's not really a transformation to tween, is there?

Rotation is set through the Rotate drop-down menu in the Tweening area of the Property inspector. Notice that the Rotate drop-down is currently set to Auto, as shown in Figure 7-19. This is because you have already rotated the pepper somewhat by hand. The choices are CW (clockwise) and CCW (counterclockwise). The hot text immediately to the right of the drop-down menu specifies how many times to perform the rotation.

Figure 7-19. The Rotate property makes quick work of rotations.

5. Click the pepper in frame 10 and select Modify ➤ Transform ➤ Remove Transform to reset the symbol's rotation.

6. Click once in frame 1. In the Rotate drop-down menu, change the setting to CW (clockwise), and drag the playhead back and forth. Pretty neat!

Classic tween properties

While we're looking at the Tweening area of the Property inspector, let's go through the other settings. Here's a quick overview of classic tween properties:

- Ease and Edit: These settings apply a range of easing to the tween. The Edit button (a pencil icon) allows for advanced, custom easing. More on this in the "Easing" section of this chapter.

- Rotate and X [number]: These settings control the type of rotation and the number of times the rotation occurs. Only CW and CCW support the X [number] setting.

- Snap: This Snap check box helps position a symbol along its motion guide (discussed in the "Motion guides" section later in this chapter).

- Orient to path: This check box applies only to tweens along a motion guide. It determines whether a symbol points toward the direction in which it moves.

- Scale: If a check mark is present, tweening for the current span of frames will include a transformation in scale (size), *if such a transformation exists*. If you haven't scaled anything, it doesn't matter what state the check mark is in. If scaling and other transformations are combined in a given classic tween, only the other transformations will show if the check mark is deselected.

- Sync: In our experience, most people don't even realize this property exists, but it can be a real time-saver when you're dealing with graphic symbols. Unlike movieclips, which have their own independent timelines, graphic symbols are synchronized with the timeline in which they reside. Even so, there is a bit of flexibility: graphics can be looped, played through once, or instructed to rest on a specified frame of their own timeline. If a particular graphic symbol has been tweened numerous times in a layer, the presence of the Sync check mark means you can update these timeline options for all keyframes in that layer simply by making changes to the first graphic symbol in the sequence. In addition, Sync allows you to swap one graphic symbol for another and have that change ripple through all the synched keyframes in that layer. More on this feature in the "Editing multiple frames" section of this chapter.

Scaling, stretching, and deforming

We visited this topic in the "Shape tweening" section, and honestly, there's not a whole lot different for classic tweens. The key thing to realize is that scaling, stretching, and deforming a symbol is like doing the same to a T-shirt with artwork printed on it. Even if the artwork looks different after all the tugging and twisting, it hasn't actually changed. Shake it out, and it's still the same picture. Shape tweening, in contrast, is like rearranging the tiles in a mosaic. For this reason, the Free Transform tool disables the Distort and Envelope options for symbols. These transformations can't be performed on symbols and therefore can't be classic tweened.

> *Symbol distortion can be performed with the 3D tools (Chapter 9), and can even be animated, but the animation requires motion tweens (Chapter 8), not classic tweens.*

Let's take a quick look at the other transform options:

1. Return to the PepperSymbol.fla file, select frame 1, and set the Rotation setting for the tween to None.

2. Use the Free Transform tool to perform a shear transformation at frame 10.

Shear? What's that? Something you do with sheep, right? Well, yes, but in Flash, shearing is also called *skewing*, which can be described as tilting.

3. With the Free Transform tool active, click the Rotate and Skew option at the bottom of the Tools panel, and then hover over one of the side transform handles (not the corners) until the cursor becomes an opposing double-arrow icon. Click and drag to transform the pepper (see Figure 7-20).

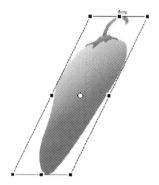

The live preview gives you an idea what the symbol will look like before you let go of the mouse. Note that the skew occurs in relation to the transformation point, indicated by the small white circle.

4. Drag the white circle around inside or even outside the bounding box of the pepper, and then skew the pepper again to see how its placement affects the transformation. Hold down Alt (Option) while skewing to temporarily ignore the transformation point and skew in relation to the symbol's opposite edge.

Figure 7-20. Classic tweening a symbol transformation

We've been using the Free Transform tool quite a bit, so let's try something different.

5. Open the Transform panel (Window ➤ Transform) and note its current settings. You'll see the skew summarized near the bottom and, interestingly, the change in scale summarized near the top (see Figure 7-21). From this, it becomes clear that skewing affects scale when applied with the Free Transform tool.

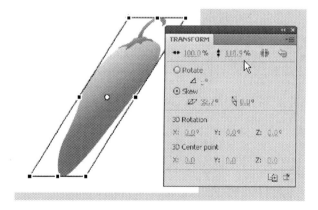

Figure 7-21. The Transform panel provides access to precision measurements.

6. To see the difference, select Modify ➤ Transform ➤ Remove Transform to reset the symbol. The scale area of the Transform panel returns to 100% horizontal and 100% vertical.

7. Click the Skew radio button and scrub the hot text of either skew value to 38. Notice that the scaling stays at 100%, which subtly changes how the skew looks.

8. Enter 200 into the scale input fields at the top. (The Constrain check mark means you need to enter this number into only one of them.) Slide the playhead back and forth to see two transformations tweened at once.

Easing

Here's where classic tweening begins to pull ahead of shape tweening. Easing is much more powerful for classic tweens, thanks to the Custom Ease In/Ease Out editor. Before we delve into that, though, let's look at a sample use of the standard easing controls for a classic tween, so you can see how much easier things are with the custom variety.

1. Open the MalletNoEasing.fla file in this chapter's Exercise folder. You'll see a hammer graphic symbol in the library and an instance of that symbol on the stage. Select the hammer and note that the transformation point—the white dot in the handle—is located in the center of the symbol.

2. We're going to make this hammer swing to the left, so select the Free Transform tool. Selecting this tool makes the transformation point selectable. Click and drag that point to the bottom center of the mallet (see Figure 7-22).

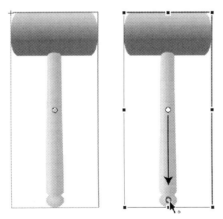

Figure 7-22. You'll need to move that transformation point to make the movement realistic.

3. Insert a keyframe at frame 10 (Insert ➤ Timeline ➤ Keyframe), and rotate the mallet at frame 10 to the left by 90 degrees.

4. Apply a classic tween to the span of frames between 1 and 10, and scrub the timeline to see the effect. Not bad, but not especially realistic. How about some easing and bounce-back?

5. In the Tweening area of the Property inspector, scrub the Ease hot text all the way to the left to specify a full ease in (–100) to the tween. This causes the hammer to fall slowly as it begins to tip and increase speed as it continues to fall (see Figure 7-23).

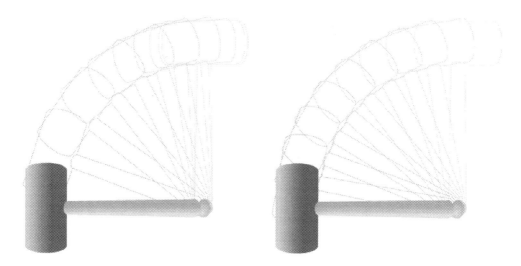

Figure 7-23. Ease in (left) vs. no easing (right). On the left, the hammer falls in a more natural manner.

This is a good start. To push the realism further, let's embellish the animation. We're going to provide some tweening that makes the hammer rebound on impact and bounce a few times.

6. Add new keyframes at frames 15, 20, 23, and 25. At frame 15, use the Free Transform tool or the Transform panel to rotate the hammer to approximately northwest; in the Transform panel, this could be something like –55 in the Rotate area. At frame 23, set the rotation to roughly west-northwest (something like –80 in the Rotation area). A storyboard version of the sequence might look like Figure 7-24.

Figure 7-24. Using several keyframes to make the hammer bounce

> The fading image trails—visual echoes of the mallet—are the result of something called onion skinning—very helpful in animation work. It's used here for illustrative purposes and is covered later in the chapter.

7. Now that the mallet has been positioned, it just needs to be tweened and eased. You can either click separately into each span of frames and apply a classic tween, or click and drag across as many spans as you need (as shown in Figure 7-25). That way, you can apply the tweens all in one swoop.

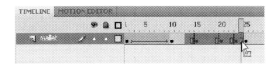

Figure 7-25. Tweens can be applied to more than one frame span at a time.

8. Click into each span of frames to apply easing, for the final touch. Remember that span 1 through 10 already has −100. Apply the following easing to the remaining spans:

- Span 10 to 15: 100 (full ease out)
- Span 15 to 20: −100 (full ease in)
- Span 20 to 23: 100
- Span 23 to 25: −100

9. Drag the playhead back and forth to preview the action, and then test the movie to see the final presentation. If you like, compare your work with MalletNormalEase.fla in the Complete folder.

This exercise wasn't especially arduous, but wouldn't it be even cooler if you could perform all of the preceding steps with a single classic tween?

Custom easing

Introduced in Flash 8, the Custom Ease In/Ease Out dialog box unleashes considerably more power than traditional easing. Not only does it provide a combined ease in/out—where animation gradually speeds up *and* gradually slows down, or vice versa—but it also supports multiple varied settings for various kinds of easing, all within the same classic tween. Let's take a look.

To perform custom easing, select a span of motion-tweened frames, and then click the Edit button (a pencil icon) in the Tweening area of the Property inspector. You'll see the Custom Ease In/Ease Out dialog box, as shown in Figure 7-26. This dialog box contains a graph with time along the horizontal axis, represented in frames, and percentage of change along the vertical axis.

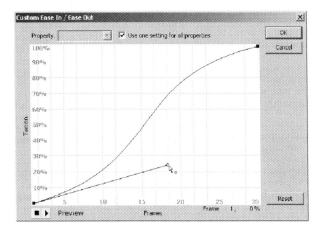

Figure 7-26. The Custom Ease In/Ease Out dialog box

Here's a quick rundown of the various areas of the dialog box:

- **Property**: By default, this is disabled until you deselect the check mark next to it. If the check mark is present, custom easing—as specified by you on the grid—applies to all aspects of the tween symbol. If the check mark is absent, this drop-down menu lets you distinguish among Position, Rotation, Scale, Color, and Filters.

- **Use one setting for all properties**: When checked, this allows multiple properties to be eased individually.

- **Grid**: The Bezier curves on this grid determine the visual result of the custom easing applied.

- **Preview**: Click the two buttons in this area to play and stop a preview of the custom easing.

- **Ok, Cancel, and Reset**: The OK and Cancel buttons apply and discard any custom easing. Reset reverts the Bezier curves to a straight line (no easing) between the grid's opposite corners.

So, how does the grid work? Let's look at a traditional ease in to see how the Custom Ease In/Ease Out dialog box interprets it.

1. Open the CustomEasingComparison.fla file in the Chapter 7 Exercise folder and set the Ease property to –100 (a normal full ease in) for the tween in the top layer.

2. Scrub the timeline to confirm that the upper symbol starts its tween more slowly than the lower one, but speeds up near the end. The lower symbol, in contrast, should advance the same distance each frame (see Figure 7-27).

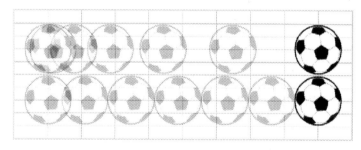

Figure 7-27. An ease in causes the upper symbol to start slower and speed up (artwork by Steve Napiersk).

3. Click the Edit button in the Tweening area of the Property inspector to see what an ease out looks like on the grid. The curve climbs the vertical axis (percentage of change) rather slowly, and then speeds its ascent near the end of the horizontal axis (time in frames). Hey, that makes sense!

4. Click Cancel, apply a full ease out (100), and then click the Edit button to check the grid again. Bingo—the opposite curve.

It follows that a combination of these would produce either a custom ease in/out (slow, fast, slow) or a custom ease out/in (fast, slow, fast). Let's do the first of those two.

5. Click the upper-right black square in the grid to make its control handle appear. Drag it up to the top of the grid and about two-thirds across to the left, as shown in Figure 7-28.

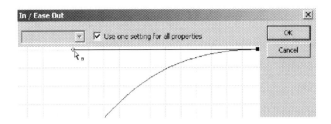

Figure 7-28. Dragging a control handle to create a custom ease

6. Click the bottom-left black square and drag its control handle two-thirds across to the right. The resulting curve—vaguely an S shape—effectively combines the curves you saw for ease in and ease out (see Figure 7-29).

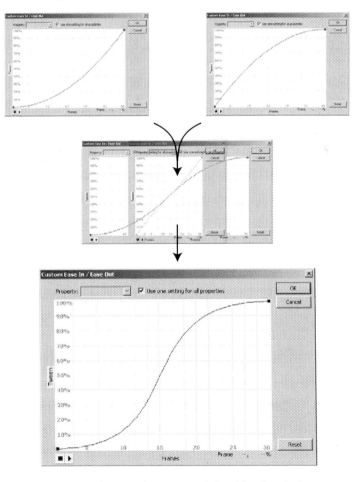

Figure 7-29. An S shape produces an ease in/out (slow-fast-slow) tween.

7. Click OK to accept this setting, and scrub the timeline or test the movie to see the results.

8. Let's inverse this easing for the lower symbol. Select the lower span of frames and click the Edit button. This time, drag the lower-left control handle two-thirds up the left side. Drag the upper-right control handle two-thirds down the right side to create the inverted S curve shown in Figure 7-30. Click OK and compare the two tweens.

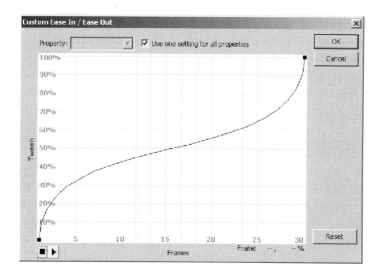

Figure 7-30. An inverted S shape produces an ease out/in (fast-slow-fast) tween.

Think this is cool? We're just getting started!

Adding anchor points

By clicking anywhere along the Bezier curve, you can add new anchor points. This is where you can actually save yourself a bit of work.

1. Open the MalletNoEasing.fla file in this chapter's Exercise folder again. If you saved your work earlier, remove the tween and delete all frames except for frame 1. To do this, click and drag from frame 2 to the right until you've selected all of the frames, and then use Edit ➤ Timeline ➤ Remove Frames.

2. Confirm that the mallet's transformation point is positioned at the bottom center of its wooden handle. Now add a new keyframe at frame 25 and apply a classic tween to the span of frames between 1 and 25.

3. Using the Free Transform tool at frame 25, rotate the mallet 90 degrees to the left. Because a tween is already applied, you can preview the falling mallet by scrubbing the timeline.

This may seem like déjà vu, but things are about to change. You're going to emulate the same bounce-back tween you did earlier, but this time, you'll do it all in one custom ease.

4. Click in frame 1—or anywhere inside the tween span—and click the Edit button in the Tweening area of the Property inspector.

5. In the Custom Ease In/Ease Out dialog box, click the Bezier curve near the middle, and you'll see a new anchor point with control handles. Hold down Shift and click that new anchor point—it disappears. Add it again and straighten the control handles so that they're horizontal, as shown in Figure 7-31.

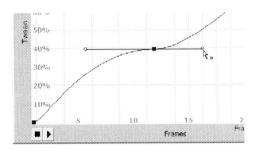

Figure 7-31. Starting a more complex custom ease

6. Repeat this process three more times, up the hill, as shown in Figure 7-32. This prepares the way for the sawtooth shape you'll create in the next step.

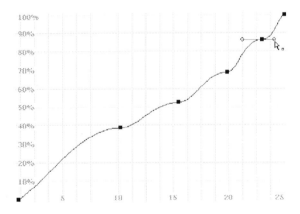

Figure 7-32. Continuing to add anchor points for a sawtooth curve

7. Leave the corner anchor points where they are. Position the four new anchor points as follows:

- 100%, 10
- 60%, 15
- 100%, 20
- 85%, 23

You'll notice that the anchor points gently snap to the grid while you drag. To temporarily suppress this snapping, hold down the X key.

8. You've probably heard of certain procedures described as more of an art than a science. Well, we've come to that point in this step. Here's the basic idea, but it's up to you to tweak these settings until they feel right to you. To achieve the sawtooth curve we're after—it looks very much like the series of shark fins shown in Figure 7-33—click each anchor point in turn and perform the following adjustment:

- If it has a left control handle, drag that handle in toward the anchor point.
- If it has a right control handle, drag that handle out a couple of squares to the right.

You should get something like the shape shown in Figure 7-33.

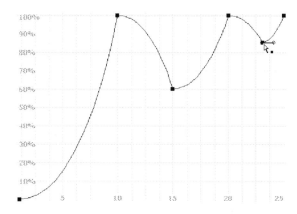

Figure 7-33. Shark fins produce a bounce-back effect.

9. Click the Preview play button to test your custom ease. It should look similar to the original series of mallet bounce-back tweens, but this time you saved yourself a handful of keyframes.

How does this work? As depicted in the grid, and following the horizontal axis, you have an ease-in curve from frames 0 to 10, an ease-out curve from 10 to 15, an ease-in curve from 15 to 20, and so on—just like your series of keyframes from earlier in the chapter. The mallet moves from its upright position to its leaned-over position in the very first curve. From frames 10 to 15, the vertical axis goes from 100% down to 60%, which means that the mallet actually rotates clockwise again toward its original orientation, but not all the way. With each new curve, the hammer falls again to the left, and then raises again, but never as high. Compare your work with MalletCustomEasing.fla in this chapter's Complete folder.

Easing multiple properties

On the final leg of our custom easing expedition, let's pull out all the stops and examine a tween that updates multiple symbol properties at once. You'll be familiar with most of what you're about to see, and the new parts will be easy to pick up.

1. Open the CustomEasingMultiple.fla file in this chapter's Exercise folder. Select frame 1 and note that a movieclip symbol appears in the upper-left corner of the stage. It is solid green. Select frame 55 and note the changes.

At this point, the apple is positioned in the center of the stage, much larger, more naturally colored, and has a drop shadow (see Figure 7-34). From this, we can surmise that color and filters are tweenable—that's the new part.

2. In frame 1, select the apple symbol itself to see that a Tint has been applied in the Property inspector, which is replaced by None in the other keyframe. Next, select the Filters tab at frame 55 and click the apple to see that a drop shadow has been applied that is not present in frame 1. The Filters properties are no different from Position and Scale as far as tweens are concerned.

3. Click into the span of tweened frames and note that a CW (clockwise) rotation has been specified for Rotation. The Tween type is Motion, and Scale is enabled (without it, the apple wouldn't gradually increase in size). The Ease property reads ---, which means custom easing has been applied. That's what we're after. Click the Edit button.

Figure 7-34. You are about to discover that it isn't only rotation that can be tweened.

4. Thanks to the empty Use one setting for all properties check box, the Property drop-down menu is now available. Use the drop-down menu to look at the grid curve for each of five properties, all of which are depicted in the tween: Position, Rotation, Scale, Color, and Filters. Each property has its own distinct curve, which translates into five individual custom ease settings for their respective properties (see Figure 7-35).

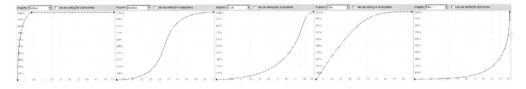

Figure 7-35. The Custom Ease In/Ease Out dialog box lets you specify distinct easing for five different tweenable properties.

5. Click the Use one setting for all properties check box to disable the drop-down menu.

Ack! Have you lost your custom settings? Thankfully, no. Flash remembers them for you, even though they're hiding.

6. Click the Preview play button to preview the tween with no easing (the default lower-left to upper-right curve).

7. Click the check box again to see that the custom ease settings are still intact. Preview the tween again, if you like.

327

Using animation

So far, we've shown you a hefty animation toolbox. We've opened it up and pulled out a number of powerful tools to show you how they work. In doing so, we've covered quite a bit of ground, but there are still a handful of useful animation features and general workflow practices to help bring it all together. Let's roll up our sleeves, then, shall we?

A closer look at the Timeline panel

Whether you use shape, classic, or motion tweens, the Timeline panel gives you a pint-sized but important dashboard (see Figure 7-36). Don't let its small size fool you. This strip along the bottom of the timeline helps you quickly find your bearings, gives you at-a-glance detail on where you are, and even lets you time travel into both the past and the future, to see where you've been and where you're going.

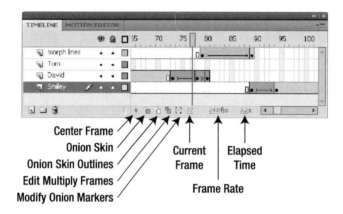

Figure 7-36. The bottom edge of the timeline provides a collection of useful tools.

Let's take an inventory of this useful, if small, real estate.

- **Center Frame**: In timelines that are long enough to scroll, this button centers the timeline on the playhead.

- **Onion Skin and Onion Skin Outlines**: These buttons toggle two different kinds of onion skinning, which give you a view of your work as a series of stills.

- **Edit Multiple Frames**: This button allows you to select more than one keyframe at the same time, in order to edit many frames in one swoop.

- **Modify Onion Markers**: Click this button to see a drop-down menu that controls the functionality of the onion skin buttons.

- **Current frame**: This indicates the current location of the playhead. Scrub or enter a value to move the playhead to that frame.

- **Frame rate**: This indicates the movie's frame rate. Scrub or enter a value to change it.

- **Elapsed time**: Given the current frame and the movie's frame rate, this indicates the duration in seconds of the playhead's position. For example, in a movie with a frame rate of 24 fps, this area will say 1.0s at frame 24. Scrub or enter a value to move the playhead to the frame that closely matches your specified elapsed time.

Onion skinning

Traditional animators—the people who brought us the Mickey Mouse and Bugs Bunny cartoons—often drew their artwork on very thin paper over illuminated surfaces called lightboxes. This "onion skin" paper allowed them to see through the current drawing to what had gone on in the previous frames. In this way, they could make more informed choices about how far to move someone's head, or the anvil about to fall on it.

Flash offers you the same benefit, but with much more flexibility. In Flash, you can choose to see through as many frames as you like—backward and even forward—in solids or in outlines. Let's see how it works.

1. Open the YawningParrot.fla file in this chapter's Exercise folder. Note that the movie's frame rate is 30 fps.

2. Drag the playhead to frame 15, just as the bird begins to lower its head, and confirm that the elapsed time indicator at the bottom of the timeline reads 0.5s (see Figure 7-37). This makes sense: 15 divided by 30 is 0.5.

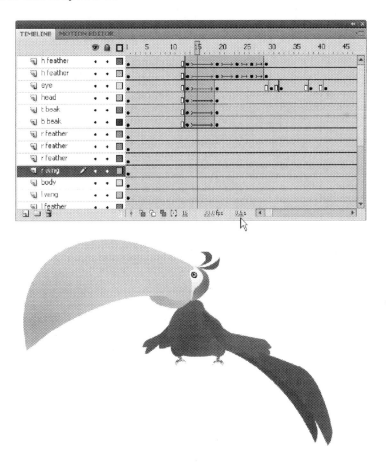

Figure 7-37. Another really good reason this is called the timeline

329

3. Scrub the frame rate hot text at the bottom of the timeline to change the movie's frame rate to 60fps (hold Shift while you scrub to count by tens). Note that the elapsed time is 0.2 seconds (still good: 15 divided by 60 is 0.2—if you don't round up).

4. Change the frame rate to 15 fps and check the elapsed time indicator. You were probably expecting 1.0s, but the elapsed time is a very close 0.9s. Why the discrepancy? We aren't sure, but it is close enough to the original value to satisfy us. Change back to the original 30fps.

5. Drag the playhead to the right far enough that the timeline starts to scroll a bit, and then leave the playhead where it is. Use the timeline's scrollbar to scroll back to the left, which hides the playhead. To quickly bring it back, click the Center Frame button—the leftmost button labeled in Figure 7-36—which centers the timeline on the current frame. This is a good "you are here" panic button that's useful for especially long timelines.

6. Position the playhead at frame 125 and click the Modify Onion Markers button. Choose Onion 5 from the drop-down menu. This positions two new markers on either side of the playhead, as shown in Figure 7-38. If you aren't seeing the markers, return to the drop-down menu and select Always Show Markers.

Figure 7-38. Onion skinning adds two markers on either side of the playhead.

These markers extend five frames back from and ahead of the current position, which explains the name of the Onion 5 setting. What they show are semitransparent views of those frames fading as they get farther from the playhead—just like artwork on thin paper! Not only do they let you see back in time at previous frames, but they also show artwork on future frames, which provides practical sequential context for any moment in time.

7. To actually see these onion skins, click the Onion Skin button. In this case, you're seeing 11 "sheets," including the one under the playhead (which is the darkest), and then five ahead and behind.

8. Click Modify Onion Markers again and choose Onion 2, as shown in Figure 7-39. This reduces your view to five "sheets," as opposed to the previous 11. Drag the playhead slowly to frame 170 and back. Notice that the onion markers move with you.

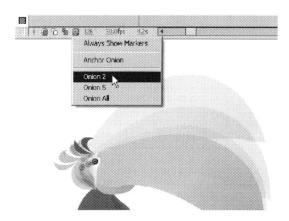

Figure 7-39. Various onion skin settings

What are the other choices on this drop-down menu? Always Show Markers keeps the onion markers visible, even if you toggle the Onion Skin button off. Anchor Onion keeps the onion markers from following the playhead. Onion All spreads the onion markers along the whole timeline. You can try it with this file. The result is overwhelming (and also makes it hard to drag the playhead around), but with timelines of little movement, it probably has its place. If you do select Onion All, be aware that the selected frames—the "all" part of Onion All—will move along with the playhead unless you select Anchor Onion in the Modify Onion Markers menu. If you want some setting besides 2, 5, or All, drag the markers along the timeline yourself. If you like, you can look eight frames back and two frames forward, or any combination that suits your animation.

9. Choose Onion 5 and drag the playhead to frame 15. Click the Onion Skin Outlines button. Note that the same sort of onion skinning occurs, but that the tweened areas are shown in wireframe format (see Figure 7-40). This makes it even clearer to see what's moving and what isn't.

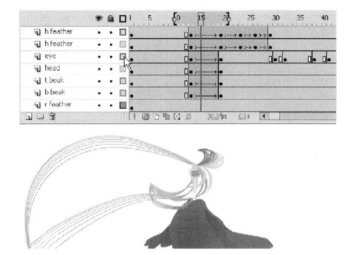

Figure 7-40. Onion skin outlines show tweened artwork in a wireframe format.

Onion skinning is just as relevant to shape and motion tweens as it is to classic tweens. Use it to help you whenever you get the notion.

Modifying multiple frames

Timeline animation can be painstaking work, no doubt about it. Even if you're using onion skinning, chances are good that you're focused on only a handful of frames at a time. There's nothing wrong with that, just as long as you remember to keep your eye on the big picture, too. Sooner or later, it happens to everyone: artwork is replaced, your manager changes her mind, or you find that you've simply painted yourself into a corner and need to revise multiple keyframes—maybe hundreds—in as few moves as possible.

Fortunately, the timeline has a button called Edit Multiple Frames, which allows you to do just what it describes. That's the obvious answer, of course, and we'll cover that in just a moment, but it's worth noting that the concept of mass editing in Flash extends into other avenues.

Due to the nature of symbols, for example, you can edit a library asset and benefit from an immediate change throughout the movie, even if individual instances of that symbol have been stretched, scaled, rotated, and manipulated in other ways. For example, if an imported graphic file, such as a BMP, has been revised outside Flash, just right-click (Ctrl-click) the asset in the library, select either Update (if the location of the external image hasn't changed) or Properties, and then click the Import button to reimport the image or import another one.

Sometimes it's not that easy. Sometimes you will have finished three days of meticulous classic tween keyframing only to learn that the symbol you've tweened isn't supposed to be *that* symbol at all. Time to throw in the towel? Well, maybe time to roll the towel into a whip. But even here, there's hope . . . if you're using graphic symbols.

Swapping graphic symbols

It's easy enough to swap out symbols of any type for any other type at a given keyframe, but the swap applies only to the frames leading up to the next keyframe. With graphic symbols, it's possible to apply a swap across keyframes, but you need to know the secret handshake. Let's try it.

1. Open the SyncPropertyGraphic.fla in this chapter's Exercise folder. Note that a cube has been motion-tweened for you along a clockwise rectangular path.

Use your imagination to picture the rectangular path as something more spectacular. Now, revel in that moment, because in this hypothetical world, you did that—and it's really cool. Here comes the drama: the boss sidles into your cubical, apologetic at first, but steadily annoyed at having to elbow past your high-fiving buddies. "Something is wrong," says the boss. "Something is dreadfully wrong. The client wanted the pyramid, not the cube."

2. Select the cube at frame 1 and click the Swap button. (Remember that the boss is watching.) Select the pyramid symbol and click OK (see Figure 7-41). Scrub the playhead a bit to confirm that the tween movement has picked up the new symbol. Smile as the boss leaves.

3. Now scrub to frame 80 and beyond. Look quickly over your shoulder. Good, the boss is still walking away. Why didn't the swap take?

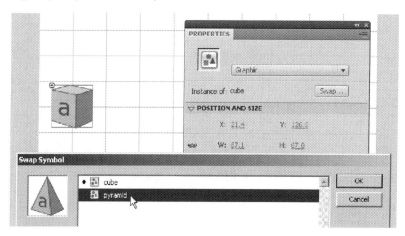

Figure 7-41. Swapping symbols can sometimes produce unexpected results.

The answer rests on a tween property called Sync, which you can see in the Property inspector when you click anywhere in the span of frames that represents a classic tween. The Sync property sets up a relationship between keyframes that locks their symbol in an unbreakable chain (well, unbreakable until you choose to remove the check mark from the Sync setting).

4. Click any frame between each pair of keyframes to select the tween span, and then click Sync to enable that option (see Figure 7-42). As you do this, note that the small vertical line to the left of each keyframe disappears. This indicates the synchronized relationship. Note also that the pyramid swap occurs along all keyframes.

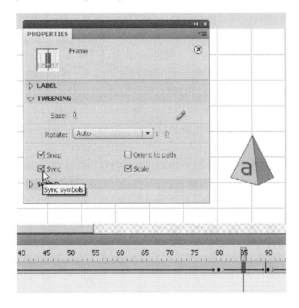

Figure 7-42. Tweens that are absent of Sync are "segregated" by a vertical line to the left of each keyframe in the timeline.

5. Now that all of the keyframes are synchronized, select any keyframe after frame 1 and use the Swap button to change the symbol back to the cube. You'll find that you can't. The Sync option prevents changes to any keyframe but the first link in the chain, so to speak.

6. Select the first keyframe and use the Swap button to change the symbol back to the cube. Scrub the timeline and verify that the swap has occurred across the board.

So much for updating content by swapping out symbols. You may be perfectly happy with the artwork as is. It may be only the *placement* of content that's out of whack. This is where the Edit Multiple Frames button makes its entrance.

Editing multiple frames

Using the Edit Multiple Frames button requires a bit of prep work, so let's step through that:

1. First, you need to decide on a range of possibly editable frames. This range extends both horizontally and vertically. Do you want to edit one layer only, multiple layers, or all layers? The easiest way to keep from editing the wrong layer is to temporarily lock it. Open the EditMultipleFrames.fla file in this chapter's Exercise folder and click the Lock icon in the Pyramid layer. This makes the Cube layer the exclusive focus of your attention.

2. Next, make your horizontal decision. The extent of your onion skin markers determines the lateral range. Use the Modify Onion Markers drop-down menu to select Onion All.

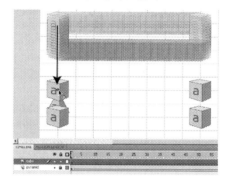

3. Click the Edit Multiple Frames button. At this point, you've chosen a valid range of editable frames and have activated the possibility to select them.

4. Now you can do your editing. Select Edit ➤ Select All and drag the upper-left cube down so that it rests on the pyramid's peak, as shown in Figure 7-43.

Thanks to the Edit Multiple Frames button, all four keyframes of this animation are moved at the same time in relation to each other. The four keyframes are shown as a live preview in their new positions. That haze along the top shows the original positions of the box along every frame in its classic-tweened frame span.

Figure 7-43. The Edit Multiple Frames button lets you adjust many keyframes at the same time.

5. Test your movie to confirm that the cube now rests on the pyramid for the full duration of the animation.

By following this procedure, you can edit not only the position, but also the scale, rotation, and any other property available to the element at hand, whether shape or symbol.

> In complex movies, you may find it tedious to temporarily lock a great number of layers. Instead of using Select All, you can simply select the desired layer by single-clicking its name. Hold Shift while clicking to select multiple adjacent layers and Ctrl (Cmd) while clicking to select multiple nonadjacent layers.

Combining timelines

Pat your head. Good! Now rub your tummy. Excellent. Now do those both at the same time. Until the undertaking snaps into place, it might seem an impossible feat, but once you manage to pull it off, you know you've done something pretty snazzy. Flash animations get interesting in the same way when you combine techniques and timelines. This is where the distinction between graphic symbols and movieclip symbols really comes into play. Both types of symbols have timelines, but each behaves in a different way. Understanding this paves the way toward good decision-making in your animations.

Movieclip timelines vs. graphic symbol timelines

Movieclips operate independently of the timelines they occupy. You can create a 500-frame animation on the main timeline, and then transfer all those frames into a movieclip symbol, and everything will run the same, even if that movieclip occupies only a single frame on the main timeline. This is not so with graphic symbols. Graphic symbols are synchronized with the timelines that contain them. So if you transfer all those frames into a graphic symbol, that symbol will need to span a length of 500 frames in the main timeline in order for its own timeline to play fully.

While movieclips can be instructed by ActionScript to stop, play, and jump to various frames, graphics can only be told to hold their current position, play through once, or loop. This instruction comes not from ActionScript, but by Property inspector settings. ActionScript within the timelines of graphic symbols is not performed by a containing timeline. Sound in graphic symbols is also ignored by parent timelines. Let's see this in action.

1. Open the TimelineCombine.fla file in this chapter's Exercise folder and select the symbol at frame 1.

2. Look in the Property inspector's Looping area, and you'll see that the Options drop-down menu is set to Single Frame. Below it, the First field is set to 1, which refers to the timeline of this graphic symbol. Change this number to 5 and press Enter (Return). Doing so changes the graphic's text content: its lowercase *a* becomes a lowercase *b*, as shown in Figure 7-44.

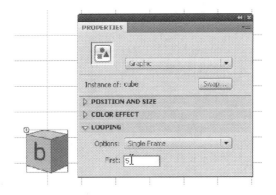

Figure 7-44. Changing the displayed frame of a graphic symbol

3. Double-click the cube symbol in the library, and you'll see why this change occurs. Both cube and pyramid have a timeline, and the text layer in each changes every five frames.

4. Select the symbol again in the main timeline. Change the Single Frame setting to Play Once, and change the First input field to 10. This updates the displayed letter to *c* and instructs the graphic symbol to play through the end of its timeline a single time.

5. Drag the playhead slowly to the right to see the letters *d*, *e*, and so on, displayed through *j* while the symbol moves across the stage. At *j*, the symbol continues to move, but no longer updates its text. The reason for this is that the symbol's timeline has reached its end, but does not repeat.

6. Change the Play Once setting to Loop, and change First to 1. Scrub again, and you'll see the letters start from a and repeat again from a after j is reached.

The Sync property discussed in the previous section applies here, too. When Sync is selected for the various spans in a multiple-keyframe classic tween, Looping properties are applied to all spans. When Sync is deselected, Looping properties apply to only the current span.

Nesting symbols

Designer and animator Chris Georgenes (http://www.mudbubble.com/) has lent his talents to numerous cartoons on television and the Web, including *Dr. Katz, Professional Therapist*, Adult Swim's *Home Movies*, and, well, more online animation than either of us could shake a stick at. One of the giants in the field, Chris uses combined timelines to great effect in practically all of this Flash work. From walk cycles to lip-synching, Chris builds up elaborate animated sequences by organizing relatively simple movement into symbols nested within symbols. The orchestrated result often leaves viewers thinking, "Wow! How did he do that?" Luckily for us, Chris was kind enough to share one of his character sketches, which provides a simplified example.

Open the Grotto.fla file from the Example folder for this chapter. Note that the main timeline has only one frame and only one symbol in that frame (see Figure 7-45). This base symbol is a movieclip, because Chris wanted a slight drop shadow effect on the friendly monster, and graphic symbols don't support filters.

Figure 7-45. Nested symbols allow you to take the most useful features of each symbol type.

Double-click this movieclip to enter its timeline. Even with a basic example like this one, you may be surprised by the number of layers inside. Try not to feel overwhelmed! The layers are neatly labeled, as shown in Figure 7-46. (Now that you see how a pro does it, start labeling your layers as well.) Also, although there are many of them, they all have a purpose. If you like, temporarily hide a number of layers to see how each layer adds to the complete picture. What we're interested in is the mouth.

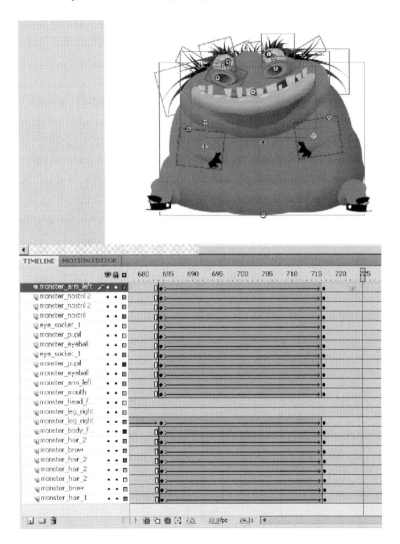

Figure 7-46. Complex images and animations are built up from simple pieces.

Double-click the mouth symbol to enter its timeline. Here, too, there is a handful of layers, comprising the lips, teeth, and a few shadows on this monster. There are 115 frames of animation here—mostly classic tweens, but also a shape tween at the bottom. If you scrub the timeline, you'll see the mouth gently move up and down. This is Grotto breathing (see Figure 7-47). Because the mouth itself is a graphic symbol, its movement can be made to scrub along with the timeline of its parent.

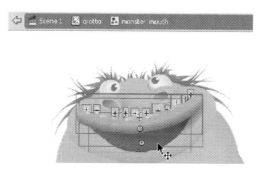

Figure 7-47. Nesting timelines is a way to compartmentalize complexity.

Return to the grotto timeline by clicking the grotto movieclip icon in the breadcrumbs area at the bottom of the Timeline panel (shown above the monster in Figure 7-47). Drag the playhead to a keyframe, such as 11, and click the mouth symbol. Note that it's set to Loop in the Property inspector and starts at frame 11. Because the mouth symbol loops, the mouth itself can be tweened to various locations and rotations during the course of the grotto symbol's timeline. The complexity of the mouth's inner movement is neatly tucked away into the mouth symbol.

At any point, you can pause this breathing movement by adding a keyframe in the grotto symbol's timeline and changing the mouth symbol's behavior setting from Loop to Single Frame.

The phenomenon you've just seen can be nested as deeply as you like. Even limited nesting, like that in Grotto.fla, can, for example, be used to animate a bicycle—the wheels rotate in their own timeline while traveling along the parent timeline—or twinkling stars. Just keep in mind that if a given graphic symbol's timeline is, say, 100 frames long, and you want *all* of those frames to show, the symbol will need to span that many frames in the timeline that contains it. Of course, you may purposely want to show only a few frames.

Graphic symbols as mini-libraries

Let's look at that parrot again for an example of another way to make use of a graphic symbol's timeline.

Open the YawningParrot.fla file in this chapter's Exercise folder. Drag the playhead slowly back and forth between frames 60 and 65. As the head turns, the beak moves from left to right. A bit of classic tweening squashes the beak as it nears the crossover, and the shape changes completely in the middle at frame 62.

Select the upper beak at frame 61. Open the Transform panel (Window ➤ Transform) and note that the width of this symbol has been reduced to half. In the Property inspector, note that this symbol is an instance of the beak top asset in the library. It is set to Single Frame at frame 1.

Select the upper beak at frame 62. This symbol is still the beak top asset and is still set to Single Frame, but this time its First property is set to 2 (see Figure 7-48). All it takes is one quick frame to complete the illusion of a head turn!

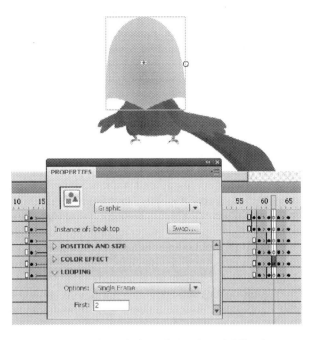

Figure 7-48. Graphic symbols can be used as mini-libraries to keep the real library from overcrowding.

This is a perfect example of how a graphic symbol's timeline can be used to reduce clutter in the library. It's not hard to imagine how handy this would be for swapping out mouth shapes in the case of an animated character that speaks (see Figure 7-49). Sure, you can use the Swap button to replace any symbol with another at any keyframe, but it is much less hassle to update the First field in the Property inspector for graphic symbols. This technique is one of those hidden gems that becomes a favorite once you realize it, and we thank Chris Georgenes for sharing such a useful trick.

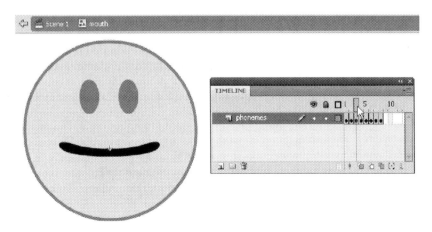

Figure 7-49. Graphic symbol timelines are great for updating characters' mouth shapes.

For more information about character design, advanced tweening, and lip-synching techniques, search "Chris Georgenes" on the Adobe website (http://www.adobe.com/). You'll find a number of Chris's articles and Macrochats (Flash-based recordings of live tutorial presentations).

Classic tween effects

A common question on the Adobe support forums is how to fade in an imported photo, and then fade it out again. People are comfortable enough importing a BMP or PNG, but when they drag it to the stage, there doesn't seem to be a way to adjust its transparency at all, much less over time. The trick here is to convert the photo into a symbol. The type of symbol depends on which effects you want to apply. Both graphics and movieclips support color effects such as Brightness, Tint, Alpha, and Advanced. But if you want to use filters, you'll need a movieclip, because symbols do not support filters.

Applying tween effects to an image converted to a symbol

Let's convert an imported photo to a symbol, and then try some tween effects:

1. Create a new Flash document and save it as TronGuy.fla. Using the Property inspector, make sure the document's dimensions are set to 550 × 400 and its background color to #000000 (black).

2. Select File ➤ Import to Stage to import the tronguy.png graphic file from the Exercises folder for this chapter. Use the Align panel (Window ➤ Align) to center the image horizontally on the stage and align it to the bottom of the stage.

Who is this debonair, futuristic fellow? Ladies and gentleman, we present to you Jay Maynard, better known on the Internet as Tron Guy (http://www.tronguy.net/). Jay, in his homemade costume inspired by the 1982 Disney film Tron, has made numerous appearances on Jimmy Kimmel Live and been featured in a Wired magazine article (http://www.wired.com/entertainment/theweb/magazine/16-07/mf_roflcon/). He was good enough to let us use his likeness for this book.

There is doubtless no better way to demonstrate a tweened Glow filter than to apply it to Tron Guy, but first, let's tween an alpha transition.

3. Select the imported PNG on the stage and note the absence of color styling properties in the Property inspector. With the PNG selected, select Modify ➤ Convert to Symbol and choose Graphic. Name the symbol tron guy, as shown in Figure 7-50, and then click OK.

4. Select the symbol and note that the Property inspector updates to include a Color Effect area, which contains a Style drop-down. You're about to use that.

5. Insert a keyframe at frame 20. Now scrub to frame 1, click the symbol, and choose Alpha from the Style drop-down menu in the Property inspector. A slider will appear. Drag this down to 0.

6. Apply a classic tween between the two keyframes. Suddenly, Tron Guy's entrance is visually more interesting.

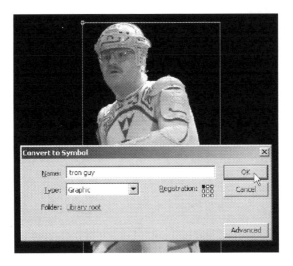

Figure 7-50. Converting an imported image to a symbol

7. To make it even more dramatic, reselect the symbol in frame 1 and choose the Advanced option from the Style drop-down menu. Note the arrival of several new hot text values (Alpha, Red, Green, Blue, and more).

8. Scrub the left-hand Alpha value—the one that shows the % symbol—back up to 100%.

9. Scrub the right-hand Red and Green values down to –225 (see Figure 7-51). This dims out color values in the red and green channels for the image, which takes on a decidedly blue cast.

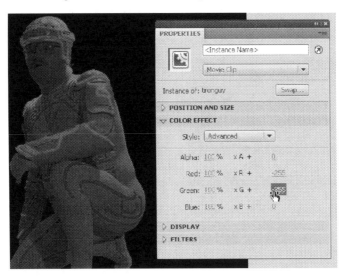

Figure 7-51. After converting an imported image to a symbol, you can apply color and alpha tweens.

10. Scrub the Blue value down to –255 as well, which removes all color.

11. Select the symbol at frame 20 and choose Advanced from the Style drop-down menu. Scrub the right-hand Red and Green hot text—but not the Blue hot text—down to –225.

12. Use the playhead to scrub the timeline to see the results. In place of the previous alpha tween, you now have a striking color tween.

Applying a filter to a tween

For the final touch, let's add some glow to Tron Guy's costume.

1. Open the TronGuyGlow.fla file from the Exercise folder. Here, we've outlined some of his circuits for you.

2. Select the tronguy symbol at frame 20 and take a gander at the Filters area of the Property inspector. (The reason filters are available here is because tronguy is a movieclip in this FLA, rather than a graphic symbol.) Add a Glow filter with the following settings:

   - Color: #0099FF
   - Blur X: 8
   - Blur Y: 8
   - Strength: 330%

3. Unlock the circuits layer, which was locked previously to help you select tronguy. Add a keyframe to frame 40 in the circuits layer.

This particular symbol doesn't have much surface area, because it's filled with only a handful of thin lines. You're about to add another Glow filter, but you'll need to update the Property inspector first to show its Filters twirlie.

4. Select the symbol by clicking its rotation point—the small circle shown in Figure 7-52.

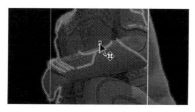

Figure 7-52. Select symbols with little or no artwork in frame 1 by clicking the symbol's rotation point.

5. Now you can add a Glow filter. Use the same settings as in step 2, but this time make the color #FFFFFF (white).

6. Apply a classic tween between the keyframes in the circuits layer. A single line of ActionScript in the scripts layer—gotoAndPlay(20);—loops the movie between frames 20 and 40.

7. Test the movie to see your handiwork (see Figure 7-53).

> The costume *layer's glow follows the contours of the costume because this image is a PNG with a transparent background. If the photo had a solid background, the glow would outline a rectangle around the photo itself.*

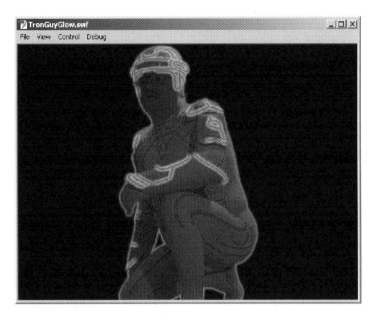

Figure 7-53. Say, that looks just like the movie!

Alpha tweening

If you apply a classic tween to the Alpha property of nested vector art, you may be in for a surprise. Semitransparent graphic and movieclip symbols that are made up of other symbols don't fade out cleanly as a whole. Instead, each piece fades individually, as shown in Figure 7-54.

Figure 7-54. Unintentional X-ray effect caused by alpha reduction to nested symbol

There are two ways to avoid this phenomenon:

- On solid backgrounds, replace the alpha tween with a tint tween (use the Style drop-down menu again) in which the tint's color is set to the same color as the background.
- In the case of movieclips, you may leave the alpha tween as is, but set the Blend mode to Layer.

These solutions are demonstrated in the FadingParrot.fla file in the Chapter 7 Complete folder.

Motion guides

Tweening in a straight line is effortless, and we've shown how easing can make such movement more realistic. But what if you want to tween along a curve? Wouldn't it be great if we could tell you that it's only marginally more difficult? Well, we can, and we'll even show you. The trick is to use something called a *motion guide*, which requires its own layer. When you get to Chapter 8, you'll see an even easier way to do this for motion tweens, but for classic tweens, motion guides are the way to go.

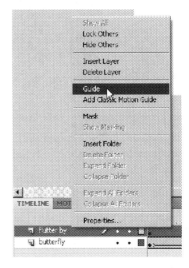

1. Open the MotionGuide.fla file in this chapter's Exercise folder. You'll see a butterfly graphic symbol in one layer and a curvy squiggle in another. If you scrub the timeline at this point, you'll see the butterfly tween in a straight line with a slight rotation between frames 240 and 275. Butterflies don't really fly like that, so let's fix the flight pattern.

2. Right-click (Ctrl-click) the flutter by layer and choose Guide from the context menu, as shown in Figure 7-55. Its icon turns from a folded page to a T-square.

You've changed the flutter by layer into a guide layer, which means anything you put into it can be used as a visual reference to help position objects in other layers. Depending on your snap settings (View ➤ Snapping), you can even snap objects to drawings in a guide layer. Artwork in guide layers is not included in the published SWF and does not add to the SWF's file size. In this exercise, the squiggle is your guide—but setting its layer as a guide layer isn't enough. It must become a motion guide. Let's make that happen.

Figure 7-55. Changing a normal layer into a guide layer

3. Gently drag the butterfly layer *slightly up* and then to the right, as shown in Figure 7-56. Drag too high, and you simply swap layer positions. Do it right, and the T-square icon changes into a shooting comet.

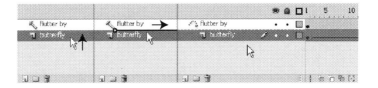

Figure 7-56. Changing a guide layer into a motion guide layer

To undo this association, simply drag the butterfly layer slightly down and to the left again. Practice this a few times, and when you're finished, make sure the butterfly layer is reassociated (the T-square has turned into the comet).

> *Motion guides must have a clear beginning and end point, as does the squiggle shown. Guides that cross over each other may cause unexpected results, so take care not to confuse Flash. Also, make sure your motion guide line extends the full length between two keyframes, including the keyframe at either end.*

4. Thanks to the Snap setting in the tweened frames (see the Property inspector while clicking anywhere inside the tween), the butterfly should already be snapped to the closer end point at the last keyframe. Scrub to make sure. The butterfly should follow the squiggle along its tween (as shown in Figure 7-57). If it doesn't, make sure to snap the butterfly symbol to the squiggle's left end in frame 1 and snap it again to the right end in frame 240.

Figure 7-57. A motion guide affects the tweened path of a symbol.

5. Click anywhere inside the tween and put a check mark in the Orient to Path check box in the Tweening area of the Property inspector. Scrub the timeline to see how this affects the butterfly's movement. The butterfly now points in the direction described by the squiggle.

For more realism, let's add some complexity, as described earlier in the "Combining timelines" section.

6. Double-click the butterfly asset in the library to enter its timeline. Add a keyframe to the upper wings and lower wings layers in frames 10 and 20.

7. In the body layer, click in frame 20 and extend the frames to that point (Insert ➤ Timeline ➤ Frame).

8. Select both wings symbols at frame 10, and use the Free Transform tool to reduce their width by about two-thirds. Use the Alt (Option) key to keep the transformation centered.

9. Add classic tweens to the upper wings and lower wings layers, as shown in Figure 7-58. Make sure to add your tweens between keyframes 1 and 10 and also between keyframes 10 and 20.

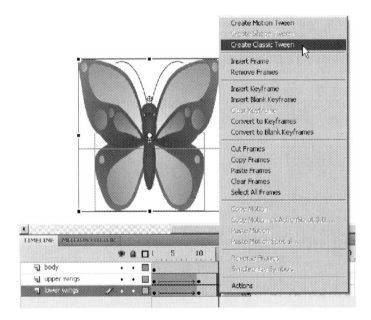

Figure 7-58. Tweening a timeline inside the butterfly graphic symbol

10. Test your movie to see the combined effect.

> *Did you notice an alternate way to create a motion guide in Figure 7-55? The context menu features a selection called* Add Classic Motion Guide *just beneath the* Guide *selection discussed in step 2. If you choose that instead, Flash handles the gentle dragging described in step 3 for you.*

Tweening a mask

Animating masks is no more difficult than animating normal shapes or symbols. In fact, the only difference is the status of the layer that contains the mask itself.

Animating a mask

In Chapter 3, you used text to create a mask. In this exercise, you'll use a shape for a mask, and you'll apply a shape tween to it to produce an iris-wipe transition, like in the old movies.

1. Open the TweenMask.fla file in this chapter's Exercise folder. You'll see three layers: a photo of one of the authors as a young boy, a text layer to provide some background texture, and a small yellow dot.

2. Insert a keyframe at frame 30 in the dot layer. Use the Transform panel (Window ➤ Transform) to increase the size of the dot in frame 30 to 800%. This makes the dot much easier to manipulate.

3. Use the Free Transform tool to increase the size of the dot yet further, so that it matches the width and height of the photo.

4. Because the dot is a shape, apply a shape tween between the keyframes in the dot layer.

5. Right-click (Ctrl-click) and select Mask to convert the dot layer to a mask layer.

6. Scrub the timeline to see the result, as shown in Figure 7-59. Easy as pie!

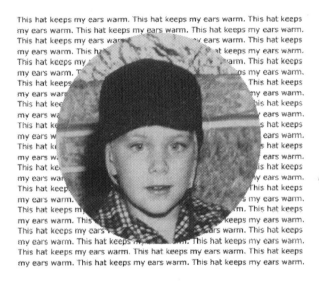

Figure 7-59. Masks can be tweened just as easily as regular shapes or symbols.

Using motion guides with masks

Often, once new designers get comfortable with motion guides and masks, they come to the realization that a layer can either be converted to a guide or mask layer, but not both. Naturally, the question arises, "Is it possible to tween a mask along a motion guide?" The answer is yes, and yet again, combined timelines come to the rescue. Let's see how it's done.

1. Open the TweenMaskMotionGuide.fla file in this chapter's Exercise folder. The setup here is very similar to the TweenMask.fla file, except that the dot layer is now named guide mask.

2. Double-click the guide mask symbol to enter its timeline. Confirm that a dot symbol is classic tweened in association with a motion guide. Return to the main timeline.

3. Right-click (Ctrl-click) the guide mask layer and select Mask from the context menu. This nested combination gives you a motion-guided mask!

Your turn: Make an animated button

So far, we've covered many animation techniques and demonstrated them with a lot of examples. Now you can use some of these techniques to animate a button.

Adding some animated glint

By now, you should get the idea that combined timelines are useful things. Here's a quick look at a very popular effect for the over state of a button symbol. Even a little bit of motion can add just the right touch to liven up an otherwise simple button.

1. Open the AnimatedButton.fla file in the Exercise folder for this chapter. Test the movie to see how the buttons currently work. It's certainly not bad looking, but plain vanilla nonetheless. We're going to add some animated glint to the Over frame.

2. Double-click the glint asset in the library to enter its timeline. There are three things to notice here:

    - A scripts layer tells the timeline to play only once (stop() in frame 5).
    - A mask layer constrains the animation to the shape of the button only.
    - A shape-tweened layer, named glint, moves a rounded rectangle from above to below the mask.

3. Double-click the button symbol in the library to enter its timeline. Add a new layer above the bg (background) layer. Name the new layer glint. Insert a keyframe in the glint layer at the Over frame.

4. Drag the glint movieclip to the stage in the Over keyframe. Use the Property inspector to position the glint symbol at X: 0 and Y: –30.

5. Insert a blank keyframe (Insert ➤ Timeline ➤ Blank Keyframe) in the Down frame of the glint layer. This keeps the animation from occurring while the mouse clicks the button. It will show only when the mouse hovers over the button and when the mouse releases from a clicked state, both of which lead to an over state.

6. Test your movie to see the results.

An even cooler animated button

The next technique you'll try goes right back to the roots of Flash and the first efforts aimed at getting video to play in Flash. You will be dealing with video in greater depth in Chapter 10, but here is a rather interesting technique that doesn't put objects in motion, but instead treats motion as a sort of flip book.

Inside the Circuit folder within this chapter's Exercise folder, you'll find a QuickTime movie named Circuits and a folder named Images, which contains 50 sequentially numbered JPG images. These images were created by opening the MOV file in QuickTime Pro (you can do this with any video editor that has QuickTime output capability) and exporting the movie as an image sequence (as shown in Figure 7-60). This technique, called *rotoscoping*, breaks a video into a series of images (which in this case, we then saved to the Images folder).

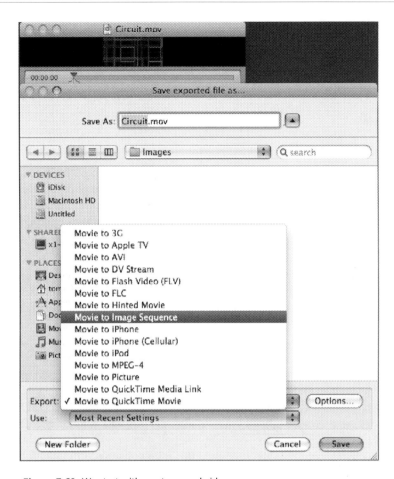

Figure 7-60. We start with a rotoscoped video.

1. Create a new Flash document and change the stage dimensions to 94 pixels wide by 44 pixels high. Name the Flash file Circuit.fla and save it to the Circuit folder in your Exercise folder.

2. Create a movieclip named Circuit, and when you enter the empty symbol's timeline, select File ➤ Import ➤ Import to Stage.

3. When the Import dialog box opens, navigate to the Images folder. Select the first image in the sequence (Image01) and click Open.

4. Flash will grab the image, notice that there is a number after it, and think, "Hmmm, this seems to be part of a sequence." This is why Flash asks you if you want to import the entire sequence, as shown in Figure 7-61. Click Yes. You will see a progress bar appear; when it is finished, each image will appear in the timeline. The neat thing about this is that all the images are in exactly the same position in each frame, and they are also placed in the library.

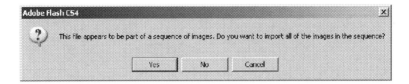

Figure 7-61. Flash, seeing a sequence of images, asks if it can import the entire sequence.

5. Import the Zap.mp3 file into the library.

6. Create a new button symbol named btnCircuit. Drag the Image01 file from the library to the stage and, using the Property inspector, set its X and Y values 0.

7. Add a blank keyframe to the Over frame of the button symbol, and drag the Circuit movieclip to the stage. Set its x and y position to (0,0) using the Property inspector.

8. Insert a frame (Insert ➤ Timeline ➤ Frame) in the symbol's Hit frame.

This provides content for both the Down and Hit frames (the same content as in the Over frame). Hit frames are used by Flash to determine the hotspot for a button, so its content is invisible, but determines the clickable area of the button.

9. Add a new layer named audio to the button timeline, and insert a keyframe in the Over frame of the audio layer.

10. Drag the Zap.mp3 file from the library to the stage. Click the sound in the Over frame and set its Sync property to Start (see Figure 7-62).

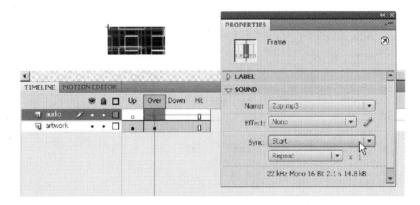

Figure 7-62. Couple audio with rotoscoping to add a bit of zing to an animated button.

This prevents the audio from looping if the user repeatedly mashes the button. When the button is rolled over, sound in the Over frame will play, and the sequence of images in the movieclip will also start to play.

11. Click the Scene 1 link to return to the main timeline, and add the button to the stage.

12. Test the file and click the button.

Copying motion as ActionScript

You may have noticed a distinct lack of ActionScript in this chapter. The reason is that the subject of programmatic motion simply can't be covered with any degree of thoroughness in one chapter. If you are really interested in the subject, buy yourself a copy of *Foundation ActionScript 3.0 Animation: Making Things Move!* by Keith Peters (friends of ED, 2007). It will keep you giddily busy for weeks. One of the authors, in fact, can't help but giggle—like his four-year-old daughter—every time he opens Keith's book. Still, we would like to mention a really neat option, introduced in Flash CS3, that fits this chapter like a glove. The option is called Copy Motion as ActionScript 3.0. Here's how it works:

1. Open the CreateMotionAS3.fla file in the Chapter 7 Exercise folder. You will see that we have added an animated ball and a parrot to the stage, as well as an actions layer (see Figure 7-63).

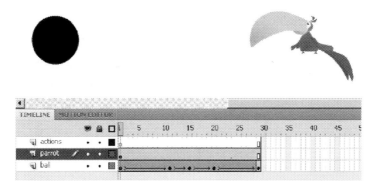

Figure 7-63. We start with a ball and one slightly worried parrot on the stage.

2. Scrub the playhead across the timeline. You will see the ball fall to the bottom of the stage, squash, stretch, and bounce back up to the top of the stage. Let's apply that animation to the slightly worried parrot.

3. Select the parrot on the stage and, in the Property inspector, give it the instance name of Parrot.

4. Select the first frame of the ball layer, press the Shift key, and then select frame 28. This selects all but the last frame of that layer. Why all but the last? Because only the first 28 frames will contain a classic tween.

5. With the frames selected, either select Edit ➤ Timeline ➤ Copy Motion as ActionScript 3.0, as shown in Figure 7-64, or right-click (Ctrl-click) and select Copy Motion as ActionScript 3.0 from the context menu.

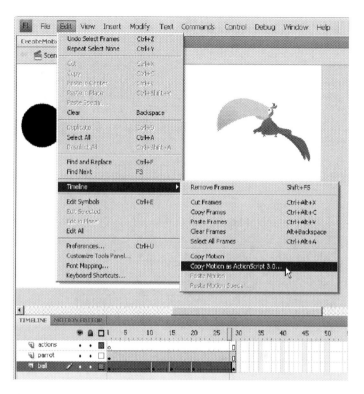

Figure 7-64. You can access the command through the Edit menu item or the context menu.

6. When you select that menu item, a dialog box will open asking you for the name of the symbol to which the motion will be applied (see Figure 7-65). Enter Parrot and click OK.

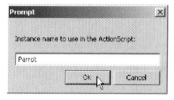

Figure 7-65. You must identify the instance to which the Action-Script will be applied.

What you have done is ask Flash to translate the motion of the ball into ActionScript and apply that same motion to the parrot. This all happens in the background, and when the motion is translated into ActionScript, the code is placed on the clipboard.

> *Be careful not to paste anything to the clipboard at this point! You'll erase the ActionScript that was copied there in step 6.*

7. Select the first frame of the actions layer and open the Actions panel. Click in the Script pane and select Edit ➤ Paste. The code—a lot of it!—will be pasted into the Script pane.

8. Save and test the movie. The parrot takes on the animation and distortion of the ball in the SWF (see Figure 7-66). This happens because of the instance name you entered into the dialog box (Parrot), which matches the instance name you gave the parrot in step 3.

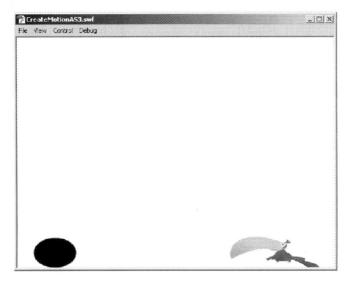

Figure 7-66. Being squashed sort of explains why the parrot looks worried.

> *Did you notice that we named the scripts layer* actions *this time around? Remember that the actual name of the layer doesn't matter, as long as it helps you remember the purpose of that layer. Call it* scripts, actions, code . . . *whatever suits your fancy.*

Now that you know how this works, there are obviously some rules:

- The motion must be a classic or motion tween using a symbol (any symbol will do; the ball happens to be a button).
- The code can be applied only to a movieclip, because you'll need to supply an instance name, and graphic symbols don't allow for that.

The great thing about this feature is that the tween can contain the following properties and features (many of which we've talked about in this chapter):

- Position
- Scale
- Skew
- Rotation
- Transformation point
- Color
- Blend modes

- Orient to path
- Cache as bitmap
- Frame labels
- Motion guides
- Custom easing
- Filters

The bottom line is that you can create, transfer, and reuse some pretty amazing scripted animation effects without writing a single line of ActionScript.

Noggin nuggets of gold from a visionary rascal

Back in high school, one of the authors fancied himself a poet. As often happens in those formative years, the subject was introduced in terms of rhyme schemes. To be sure, there's nothing essentially wrong with that. The usual Romantic role models—Byron, Wordsworth, Keats, Longfellow, Emerson, and so on—wallowed in rhyme. It's a long-standing custom in many artistic disciplines to "study the masters" first, and for good reason. The masters figured out where all the pebbles were, which toughened their feet. Walk in their shoes, and you benefit in the same way.

Of course, once traditions are in place, the path is cleared for visionaries: inventive weirdos who see things differently, who dash off into the brush and break the rules. People who find new pebbles. Think e e cummings. What we've shown you in this chapter are a number of well-worn trails. Shape tweening and shape hints, classic tweening and easing . . . these are familiar corridors for many a Flash master. We encourage you to tramp along these paths until your shoes are good and comfortable, and then be at the ready to kick off your shoes and sprint with the visionaries.

If you can keep up with him, you'll want to chase the flapping longfellows of John Kricfalusi (http://johnkstuff.blogspot.com/), creator of the The Ren & Stimpy Show and pioneer of Flash-animated cartoon series. A full decade ago, John broke new ground with the "The Goddamn George Liquor Program," which had cartoon fans laughing until . . . well, until milk gushed from their noses. For Flash cartooning, that was an Internet first. What's John's rhyme scheme? Enjoy Flash for the useful tool it is, but pile up most of your eggs in that basket called your brain. Here's what he had to say:

> David asked me to write up some tips about how to creatively use Flash. I guess my best advice is to lean on it as little as possible, to not use it as a creative crutch. Flash isn't inherently a creative tool. It's not like a pencil or a brush or talent.

> I use it mainly as an exposure sheet to quickly test my drawings and animation to see if they work. Your best Flash tool is your drawing skill. You will always creatively be limited by your ability to make interesting drawings and movement. I see many animators using Flash mainly for its in-betweens, or "tweens" as they are now called. This little tool makes every movement look smooth. But if you want to compete against the best animators, whether in Flash or in traditional animation, you will be competing with drawings, acting, and real motion [see the following illustration]. Real motion has nonmathematical in-betweening. Every in-between looks different and conveys information that mere tweening can't. Tweening just moves the same drawing from one place to another, and it's completely obvious when you watch most Flash cartoons that you are watching tricks, not animation.

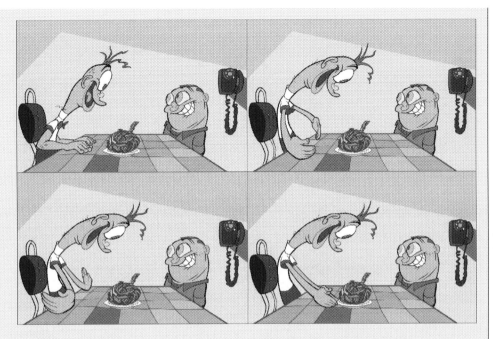

No amount of tweening can accomplish such joyous hand clapping: those are frame-by-frame drawings.

Since I started using Flash back in caveman times, I've been trying to find ways to make it not look like Flash, to try to undermine all its computery tricks. I've tried different approaches. It's hard for me to draw my key poses directly on the computer, so I usually draw them in pencil and scan them in. Once they are in, I time them in the timeline to musical beats. When I'm satisfied with the rough timing, I then draw breakdown poses directly on a Cintiq [http://www.wacom.com/cintiq/] in the timeline. I constantly roll across the animation to see if the motion is smooth. If I'm animating to a dialogue track, I draw the mouth positions in Flash and, again, roll back and forth to see if the animation is working.

I am always trying new ways to beat Flash's limitations and don't have a perfect solution. The best thing about Flash, to me, is that you can instantly see if your animation works, because you can play it back right after you do it. But Flash isn't doing the creative part. The drawings are. My best advice for how to be good at Flash is to learn as much about drawing and traditional animation as you can. That'll put you ahead of every Flash animator who just drags around some simple primitive pictures. More and more real animators are starting to use Flash, so the competition is going to get tougher for those who are lacking in drawing skills.

Your turn: Complete an animated scene

Now that you've been through a ton of theory, we expect you're ready to try your hand at an actual animated scene. This will give you something concrete to play with before exploring how your options expand with the new animation features, which are discussed in the next chapter. Heck, you don't even need to stretch first: you're already prepped! This final exercise lets you add the finishing touches to a humorous scenario in which one of the authors experiences, to put it lightly, a bad hair day.

1. Open the BadHairDay.fla file in the Exercise folder for this chapter. Take a quick look in the file's library, and you'll see an Audio set folder, which holds the audio files used in this FLA. Another library folder, Raster set, holds the imported images.

The images are PNGs because most of them rely on the smooth-edged alpha transparency provided by that image format. You'll also see a number of symbols in the library's root. A few are movie clips, because they make use of filter affects. The rest are graphic symbols, which means that they can take advantage of a technique shown in the "Combining timelines" section earlier in the chapter. In fact, let's take a look at one of them.

2. Still in the library, double-click the head graphic to open it in the Symbol Editor. Scrub the timeline, and you'll see seven different expressions, each in its own keyframe, as shown in Figure 7-67. By keeping all of these expressions in a single graphic symbol, you have quicker access to them from the main timeline (illustrated in just a moment), and your library is less cluttered.

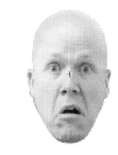

3. Select Edit ➤ Edit Document to return to the main timeline. It takes quite a few timeline layers to pull off this animation, but believe it or not, this particular example isn't especially complex. Notice a layer for ActionScript (scripts), two audio layers (audio a and audio b), and numerous layers for various body parts and props. The layer you're interested in is labeled hand left, and it's approximately halfway down the full height of the timeline.

Figure 7-67. To keep the library less cluttered, numerous expressions are stored in the same graphic symbol.

4. Scrub the timeline slowly to the right. When you get near frame 50, you'll notice that the character's hand swings toward his head. This coincides with a a short bit of sound in the audio a layer at frame 50 (Figure 7-68).

That audio—a squeaky sound—is supposed to correspond to a visual of the character scratching his bald head. Fortunately, that hand symbol is organized just like the head symbol: its timeline contains several photos of various hand positions, so this first task is easy to accomplish.

5. Insert a keyframe (Insert ➤ Timeline ➤ Keyframe) at frame 50 of the hand left layer. Now insert another keyframe in the same layer at frames 52, 54, 56, 58, 60, and 62.

6. Select the hand symbol at frame 50, and then turn your attention to the Looping area of the Property inspector. Change the First value to 2, as shown in Figure 7-69. Doing so causes the hand symbol to display the second frame of its own timeline, which changes the symbol's appearance on the main timeline (the fingers stretch a bit more toward the bald head). Make sure the Options drop-down is set to Single Frame, which holds the symbol steady on its own frame 2.

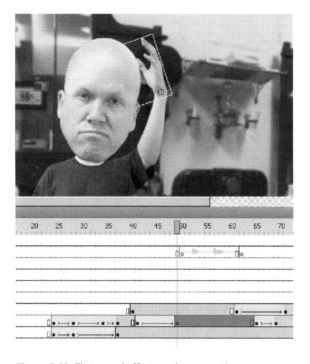

Figure 7-68. That sound effect needs some action.

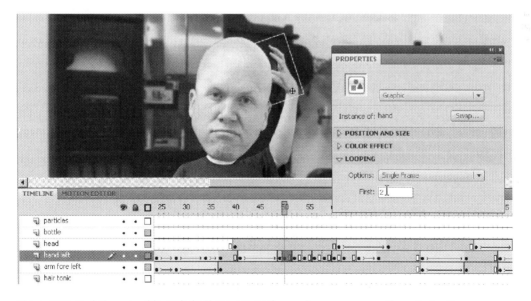

Figure 7-69. Updating a graphic symbol's First property changes its appearance on the main timeline.

7. Perform the same procedure at frame 52, but set the First value to 3 (for frame 3). Do the same for the remaining keyframes you created in step 5. Set the hand symbol's First property to the following values for each keyframe:

- 54: First = 2
- 56: First = 3
- 58: First = 2
- 60: First = 3
- 62: First = 2

8. Scrub the main timeline to review your work so far. With that extra movement, it's starting to look better already. You didn't even need to use tweening for this one! You just witnessed an example of frame-by-frame animation.

As it turns out, the bald guy scratches his head a second time, so you'll have to repeat what you've learned in another span of frames.

9. Scrub the playhead to frame 100. Note the introduction of another sound in the audio a layer. Add keyframes to the hand left layer at frames 100, 102, 104, 106, 108, 110, 112, 114, 116, 118, and 120.

10. Using the Property inspector, set the hand symbol's First property to the following alternating values for each of these new keyframes:

- 100: First = 3
- 102: First = 2
- 104: First = 3
- 106: First = 2
- 108: First = 3
- 110: First = 2
- 112: First = 3
- 114: First = 2
- 116: First = 3
- 118: First = 2
- 120: First = 3

The reason this character is scratching his head—besides the neat sound it makes—is that he is about to get an idea. That idea is to pour several glops of Cycore Hair Tonic on his head. The result of his decision isn't fully visible until you test the SWF, because it makes use of a few lines of ActionScript that can't be previewed in the timeline. We think it's pretty funny, but let's hold off until you animate the hair tonic.

11. Drag the playhead until you get to the neighborhood of frame 300. Scrub between frames 300 and 350 to preview the bottle-shaking hand motions. There are three shakes, and the first one hits its peak at frame 296.

12. Scroll the timeline down a bit and locate the hair tonic layer (two layers below the hand left layer). Insert a keyframe in the hair tonic layer at frame 296.

13. Click your new keyframe to select it. With the Brush tool, and a fill color of 80% alpha #99CCFF (light blue), paint a hearty splatter of hair tonic on the bald head, something like the glop shown in Figure 7-70 (that black dot is the Brush tool).

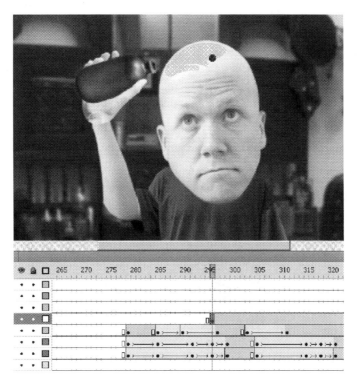

Figure 7-70. You can combine shape tweens and classic tweens on different layers of the same timeline.

To give the hair tonic freedom of movement, we'll leave it as a shape, rather than convert it to a symbol. Remember, shape tweens allow the shape's anchor points to be rearranged. That will help you animate a dripping mess.

14. Insert a keyframe in the hair tonic layer at frame 304. Select the hair tonic shape at that frame and use the Selection or Subselection tools to reshape the splatter. If you like, you can use the Brush tool to make it bigger, or even delete the shape outright and draw it again. For example, you might add a few drips or make it spread away from the bottle, as in Figure 7-71.

Figure 7-71. A shape tween will make this splatter appear to grow.

15. Still in frame 304, change the shape's fill color alpha from 80% to 0%. You can do this with the Fill color chip in the Property inspector, the Tools panel, or the Color panel. When you've changed the alpha, right-click (Ctrl-click) the hair tonic layer between frames 296 and 204, and then select Create Shape Tween from the context menu.

16. Select frame 305 in the hair tonic layer and insert a blank keyframe. That takes care of the first bottle shake. At this point, repeat steps 13 through 15 in the hair tonic layer for the span of frames 318 to 325.

17. Insert a blank keyframe at frame 326. Then repeat steps 13 through 15 again for the span of frames 341 to 350, inserting a final blank keyframe at frame 351.

When you're finished, continue scrubbing the playhead toward the right. After three shakes of the hair tonic bottle, the character gets happy for a few seconds, but finally ends up grumpy. Why? The answer to that question lies in the (very large) hair symbol shown selected on the stage in the particles layer in Figure 7-72.

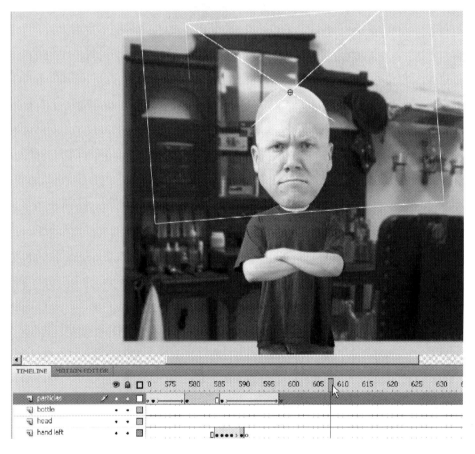

Figure 7-72. The selected movieclip symbol contains a video that shows the punchline.

That hair symbol is a movieclip that contains something called a *video object*, which is covered in Chapter 10. For now, just be aware that the video object is capable of playing FLV (Flash video) files, thanks to the ActionScript in frame 431 of the scripts layer. The video object is wrapped inside a movieclip so that it can be given the same soft-mask treatment demonstrated in Chapter 3.

> *What's inside that video file? We gave you a hint earlier, hidden in the name of the hair tonic. The video file that enhances this animation is a particle system exported from After Effects as* SparksAlpha.flv. *The particles are generated by a set of plug-ins bundled with After Effects, called CycoreFX, by Cycore Systems* (http://www.cycoresystems.com/). *This FLV is included in the* Exercise *and* Complete *folders for this chapter.*

18. Save your FLA, and then select Control ➤ Test Movie to test the SWF.

What you have learned

In this chapter, you have learned the following:

- The difference between a shape tween and a classic tween
- Various methods of using easing to add reality to your animations
- How to use the timeline and the Property inspector to manage animations
- The creation and use of motion guides in animation
- How to animate a mask
- How to translate an animation into ActionScript

This has been a busy chapter, and we've covered one side of the Flash animation coin. The path so far has led from tweening shapes to turning animations into ActionScript. In many respects, this is an important chapter, because whether or not you care to admit it, Flash is quite widely regarded as an animation program first—all that other cool stuff it does is secondary. Many of the techniques and principles presented in this chapter are the fundamentals of animation in Flash. If there is one message you should get from this chapter, it is pay attention to how things move.

Thanks to the new motion tweening model in Flash CS4, that concept—how things move—has been flipped on its head, just like a coin, in a really cool way. The new approach doesn't negate any of the techniques you've seen here. It's just that your kitchen has gotten bigger, and there are a lot of new gadgets! Whenever you're ready to continue cooking, just turn the page.

Chapter 8

ANIMATION, PART 2

What you saw in the last chapter was a compendium of traditional animation techniques—traditional not in the Flash animation pioneer John Kricfalusi sense, but in the sense that they represent the basic tools Flash animators have used since time out of mind. Some tools don't change simply because they don't have to; *they're that useful*. The exciting part is that Flash CS4 introduces a new set of tools in addition to the time-tested tools. This double-whammy puts you in charge of the workflow that makes the most sense to you. Use one set or the other, or combine them—the choice is yours. The best part is that because this is animation, you pretty much have to drink a broth of lukewarm poisonwood oils to not have fun while you're working.

Here's what we'll cover in this chapter:

- Motion tweening, using both the Motion Editor panel and the Timeline panel
- Advanced easing with the Motion Editor panel's graphs
- Manipulating motion paths
- Using motion presets, and copying motion from one symbol to another
- Applying inverse kinematics (IK), including the Bone and Bind tools
- IK tweening

The following files are used in this chapter (located in Chapter08/ExerciseFiles_Ch08/Exercise/) :

- Lunatic.fla
- LunaticEasing.fla
- LunaticCustomEasing.fla
- LunaticMultipleEasing.fla
- ManagingKeyframes.fla
- ChangingDuration.fla
- MotionGuideSimple.fla
- MotionGuideComplex.fla
- LunaticBigCheese.fla
- Bones.fla
- SteamEngine.fla
- BonesRigged.fla
- Bind.fla
- WaveCanadian.fla
- WaveAmerican.fla
- Richard.fla
- jumping.jpg

The source files are available online from either of the following sites:

- http://www.FoundationFlashCS4.com
- http://www.friendsofED.com/download.html?isbn=9781430210931

Animating with the Motion Editor panel

Before there were websites like Digg and Delicious, and before the term *viral marketing* became a cliché, people actually e-mailed hyperlinks to each other. Some of the earliest must-share Flash animations include JoeCartoon.com's "Frog in a Blender" (http://www.joecartoon.com/cartoons/67-frog_in_a_blender/) and Alex Secui's "Nosepilot" (http://animation.nosepilot.com/), shown in Figure 8-1. These are classics that still entertain after nearly a decade, and they were created with shape tweens and what are now called classic tweens, along with a good dose of elbow grease.

Clearly, the existing animation tool set—the Timeline panel and its trusty sidekicks, the Free Transform tool, the Transform panel, and a handful of others—are perfectly adequate to get the job done. But just as it can be good in a relationship to agree on acceptable word pronunciations *(toe-may-toe* and *toe-mah-toe* come to mind), it will be good for your relationship with Flash to consider other ways to animate content. You're about to start flirting with the Motion Editor panel.

Figure 8-1. A scene from Alex Secui's "Nosepilot," representing animation done in the time-honored Flash manner

New to Flash CS4, the Motion Editor panel provides a second non-ActionScript paradigm for moving things from here to there. It's an alternate mechanism to the classic tweens and shape tweens that are carried out in the Timeline panel. In Chapter 1, we gave you a drive-by Motion Editor overview, and you've seen glimpses of it in a handful of other chapters. Now that you have read Chapter 7 and have experimented with the various details and nuances of the traditional tweening model, the differences between the old and the new will become abundantly clear.

The authors suspect there will be a surge of interest in the new-style motion tweens—and there's good reason for that, as you'll see. People will begin to ask, "Which approach is better?" We'll be compelled to reply with the only legitimate answer there is: the best approach depends entirely on whatever works best for the project at hand.

Think of it like this: you've been using a conventional oven for years, when suddenly a newfangled microwave shows up on your doorstep. It's small and sleek, and even has a rotating platter. Grinning, you carry it into the kitchen, plug it in, and slide in some of the goulash leftovers from last night. Two minutes and 20 seconds later—*ding!*—you have an instant lunch. "Let's try that again," you think, and put in a glass of milk with Hershey's syrup—45 seconds later, instant hot chocolate. Does it get any better? From this day forward, it takes you only 3 minutes to get fresh popcorn. In many ways, life has gotten easier, but you can bet your bottom BBQ that the conventional oven isn't leaving its venerable perch. There's no way the microwave bakes a loaf of homemade bread, for example. As for the wasabi lime salmon we talk about in Chapter 12, well, somehow it ends up tasting better broiled than microwaved.

Clearly, you'll want the best of both worlds. And your kitchen is big enough for it.

Getting acquainted: scaling and moving

Let's take a comprehensive tour of the Motion Editor panel, covering all the basics. Portions of this will feel like a review after Chapter 7, but it's important to understand how the mechanics of motion, scaling, and distortion are distinct from the machinery of classic tweens. You won't be seeing any shapes, by the way, until much later in the chapter. The Motion Editor panel deals exclusively in symbols and text fields, just as is the case with classic tweens.

In this case, you'll be creating *motion tweens*, which look and behave like their classic cousins. The differences comes in how they're made and how you can edit them, as you'll see in the following steps.

1. Open the Lunatic.fla file found in the Chapter 8 Exercise folder. You'll notice a lunatic graphic symbol in the library ("lunatic" is sort of a pun) that has already been dragged to the stage and centered.

2. Select the lunatic symbol by clicking it. Now open the Motion Editor panel by clicking its tab or selecting Window ➤ Motion Editor.

What you see is an inactive panel, as shown in Figure 8-2, which tells you a fundamental principle of motion tweens: they must exist on a *tween layer*, which is a particular mode of a normal layer, as opposed to a mask or guide layer.

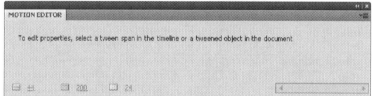

Figure 8-2. The lunatic seems a bit upset, because the Motion Editor panel is useless without a tween layer.

3. Open the Timeline panel. Then right-click (Ctrl-click) frame 1 and select Create Motion Tween from the context menu. This converts the layer into a tween layer and makes it available to the Motion Editor panel. (Alternatively, you can click frame 1 and select Insert ➤ Motion Tween.)

When you apply the motion tween, several things happen at once: the single frame stretches out to a 24-frame span, the span turns light blue, and the Motion Editor panel becomes active.

4. Open the Motion Editor panel again. This time—provided you haven't deselected the tween layer—you'll see the various grids and input controls shown in Figure 8-3. If you see the same message displayed in Figure 8-2, it means you've somehow clicked away from the layer. Either click the layer in the Timeline panel to reselect it or click the symbol itself.

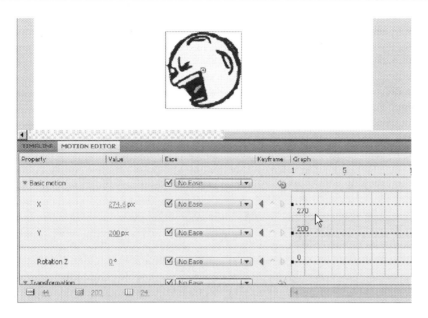

Figure 8-3. Applying a motion tween activates the Motion Editor panel for that layer.

5. Removing a motion tween is as easy as applying one. Switch back to the Timeline panel and right-click (Ctrl-click) the tween layer. Select Remove Tween, and the layer turns gray again.

You might have wondered why the motion tween extended the layer by 24 frames (we certainly wondered that, the first time we saw it). The answer depends on the movie's frame rate. Flash CS4 defaults to 24 fps, and motion tweens give you the courtesy of one second's worth of free real estate to get started. It's kind of neat to see.

6. Use the Properties area of the Property inspector to change the movie's frame rate to 60. In the Timeline panel, select frame 2 by clicking it. Hold down the Shift key and click into frame 24. This selects every frame in the layer but frame 1. Right-click (Ctrl-click) and select Remove Frames or press Shift+F5. The selected frames disappear.

7. Reapply the motion tween and note that it now expands to 60 frames, because the movie's frame rate is 60 fps.

It's time to take a look at the some of the differences between motion tweens and classic tweens. The key is to be aware that the Timeline and Motion Editor panels are fond of each other. You might even say they're connected at the hip. When you apply changes to a tween layer in one panel, you'll see those changes reflected in the other.

8. In the Timeline panel, drag the playhead to frame 20. Use the Free Transform tool or the Transform panel to make the symbol much wider than it should be.

When you widen the symbol, you'll see a black diamond appear under the playhead in frame 20, as shown in Figure 8-4. Notice the diamond is a tad smaller than the dot that represents the default keyframe in frame 1. The difference in shape and size tells you this is a *property keyframe*, which is just tween-layer–speak for a keyframe.

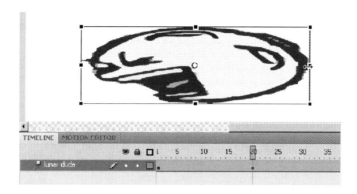

Figure 8-4. Tween layer changes are stored in property keyframes.

9. Open the Motion Editor panel. Scroll vertically until you find the Scale X grid, as shown in Figure 8-5, and then scroll horizontally until you find the property keyframe that was automatically added when you changed the symbol's width in the Timeline panel.

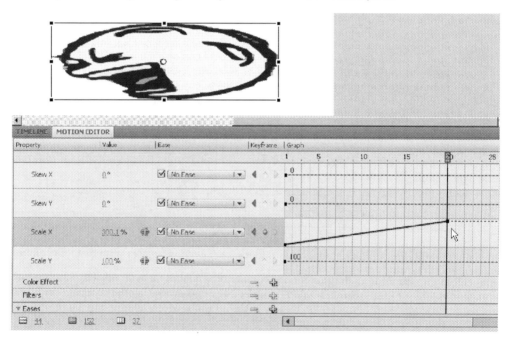

Figure 8-5. The Motion Editor panel shows property changes in detailed, collapsible graphs.

10. Click the left side of the Scale X grid—somewhere that isn't a word, check box, drop-down list, or other input widget. For example, click between the Scale X label and the percentage hot text. You'll see the grid snap open to reveal the taller view shown in Figure 8-6.

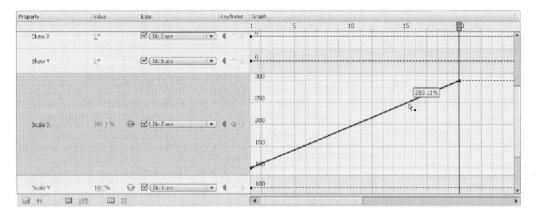

Figure 8-6. Expanded graphs in the Motion Editor panel can make data easier to see.

The particular graph depicted shows a change in x-axis scale; that is—assuming the symbol isn't rotated—the width. The numbers along the left side, stacked vertically, show values that pertain to this property, which are percentages of scale. The numbers along the top show frames, which equate to change over time.

11. Follow the slanted line in the graph from bottom left up toward the upper right. It shows that the selected symbol began at a 100% width—the 100 is partially obscured by the slanted line's left point—and was stretched to 300% over a span of 20 frames. Hover over the line at any point, and a tooltip tells you the value of the percentage at that moment in time, as shown in Figure 8-6.

This is considerably more detail than you get with classic tweens. We'll come back to this graph concept in just a moment. First, back to the kissin' cousin.

12. Open the Timeline panel and, with the playhead still in frame 20, drag the lunatic symbol to the upper-right corner of the stage, as shown in Figure 8-7. At this point, you've tweened three distinct properties: Scale X, X, and Y.

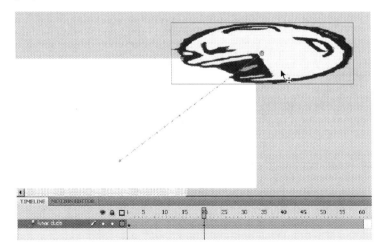

Figure 8-7. Multiple properties aren't shown in the Timeline panel, but do update the graphs in the Motion Editor panel.

Note that the property keyframe, from this view, is still just a small diamond at frame 20 in the time-line. All you can tell at a glance is that at least one property has changed. But even if there's less detail here, the two panels are in agreement, and the Timeline panel does give you a summary. Later in this chapter, in the "Changing duration nonproportionally" section, you'll see how the Timeline panel's abridged view actually makes it easier to update numerous property keyframes at once.

Naturally, you can *see* the changed properties directly on the stage, not only because the symbol itself is stretched and moved, but also because of a dotted line that connects the current position of the symbol (specifically, its transformation point) to the position it held in frame 1. If you count them carefully, you'll see 20 dots along the line, which represent the 20 frames in this tween span. The dots are all evenly spaced apart, which tells you the tween has no easing applied. Let's check back with the Motion Editor panel again before we apply easing.

13. Open the Motion Editor panel. You'll see the Scale X graph as it was before, but in addition, you'll also see the new changes reflected in the X and Y graphs, as shown in Figure 8-8.

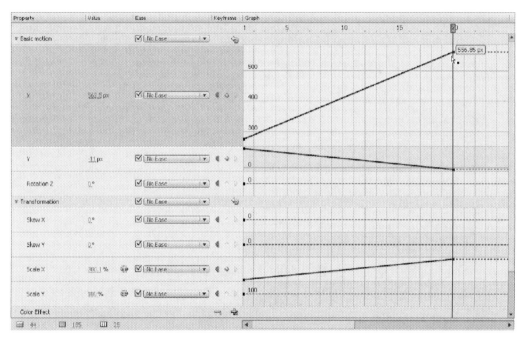

Figure 8-8. In the Motion Editor panel, multiple tweened properties can be viewed at once.

The vertical values in these graphs, along with the tooltips, change depending on the property represented. For example, the X graph starts at just below 300 on the left side (not 100, like the Scale X graph), because the symbol is positioned at 274.6 pixels on the x axis in frame 1. On the right side of the slanted line, the tooltip reads 556.85 px, because that's where the symbol is positioned on the x axis in frame 20. The point to take away from this is that these graphs are adaptable, and they change to suit the values of the property at hand. The X graph shows pixels; Scale X shows percentages; Rotation Z and Skew X show degrees; and so on.

> *If any of these graphs feel cramped to you, use the three hot text areas at the bottom left of the panel to fine-tune your view. From left to right, they adjust the vertical height of collapsed graphs (Graph Size), the vertical height of expanded graphs (Expanded Graph Size), and the horizontal width of the graphs themselves (Viewable Frames). These values apply across all graphs in the Motion Editor panel.*

14. Open the Timeline panel and select the tween layer at frame 40.

15. In the Property inspector, twirl down the Ease twirlie, if necessary, and scrub the hot text value—0, by default—slowly toward the left. Scrub it to approximately -10, and then let go. Scrub again to -20 or so, and then let go. Scrub again to -30, -40, and so on until -100, which is a full ease in.

As you scrub and release in small increments, you'll see that the dots, which were evenly distributed after step 12, begin to cluster toward the lower left, as shown in Figure 8-9, which represents the beginning of the tween. You just applied an ease in, so it makes sense that the dots are packed more closely at the beginning of the tween. Not only do the dots compress, but you'll also see a slightly larger dot partway between the symbol and the dot that represents frame 1. That middle dot represents the property keyframe at frame 20, which used to be right on the symbol and is now offset by the ease.

> *In classic tweens, easing takes effect only between keyframes. In motion tweens, easing is distributed over the frame span of the whole tween, independent of property keyframes. This is a significant departure from the classic model.*

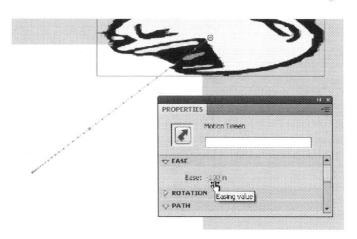

Figure 8-9. Tween layer changes are stored in property keyframes.

16. Close your file without saving it.

Easing applied to a motion tween with the Property inspector is the same sort of easing applied to classic tweens, excluding the special-case Custom Ease In/Ease Out dialog box, discussed in Chapter 7. To get to the exciting stuff, you'll need the Motion Editor panel, and advanced easing merits its own section.

Easing with graphs

When it comes to the Motion Editor panel, the concept of easing ascends to a whole new level. For classic tweens, the Custom Ease In/Ease Out dialog box is the only thing that came close to sharing similar functionality, yet it provides little more than an introduction. The Custom Ease In/Ease Out dialog box associated with a classic tween, while it does get you wet, is an inflatable kiddie pool. It has nothing on the robust flexibility and depth of the Motion Editor panel's graphs. In contrast, those are the marked lanes of a regulation Olympic pool.

A powerful feature of the Motion Editor panel is that it overcomes a subtle, but significant, limitation of the Custom Ease In/Ease Out dialog box: classic easing, for whatever property is under consideration, begins at a starting point of 0% and ends at a destination point of 100%. If you're moving a symbol from left to right—for example, from 25 pixels to 75 pixels—a classic tween begins at its starting point of 25 pixels (0% of the destination) and ends at 75 pixels (100% of its destination). Normal easing lets you adjust the acceleration and deceleration between those two immutable points. The Custom Ease In/Ease Out dialog box lets you adjust the velocity with greater control, thanks to Bezier curve handles. In fact, by adding anchor points, you can even opt to arrive at the destination point early, then head back out again and return later, as demonstrated in Chapter 7 with the bouncing mallet exercise. But in the end, there must always be a final anchor point. With classic easing, the final anchor point is always tethered to the 100% mark (see Figure 8-10).

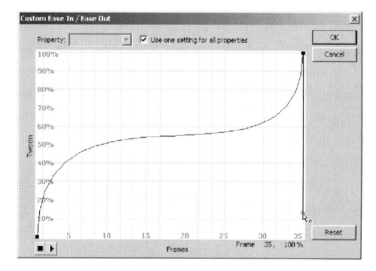

Figure 8-10. With classic tweens, the final easing anchor point (in the upper right here) always ends at 100%.

Unimpeded in this regard, the graphs of the Motion Editor panel can end up where you like. As shown in Figure 8-11, a custom ease can start at its beginning point of 0%, travel three quarters of the way to its destination, dance around a bit, and then return all the way to the beginning.

This freedom within the property graphs is a powerful tool, which is generally a good thing. But as anyone into Spider-Man will tell you, "With great power comes great responsibility." Everything comes at a cost, and the price here is that the banished 100% restriction can occasionally be disorienting, especially when eases continue past the last property keyframe in a tween span. Let's take a look.

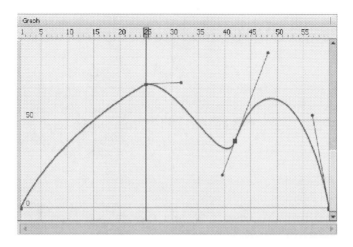

Figure 8-11. With motion tweens, the final easing anchor point (in the lower right) can end anywere between 0% and 100%.

Built-in eases

If you'll pardon the pun, we're going to *ease* into this. Let's start with the built-in eases:

1. Open the LunaticEasing.fla file in the Exercise folder for this chapter. Our crazy moon is back, and this time the symbol has been given a 60-frame motion tween that moves it from the left side of the stage (frame 1) to the right side (frame 30), and then lets it sit in place until frame 60.

2. Select the tween layer or the symbol by clicking it, and then open the Motion Editor panel. Find the X graph and notice the straight line from the beginning point (bottom left) to the destination point (upper right), as shown in Figure 8-12. Because no other X changes occur after frame 30, there are only two property keyframes in the graph.

Figure 8-12. Without easing, the graph shows a straight line.

3. Notice the setting on the left side of the graph that currently says No Ease. Let's change that. Click the drop-down list and select Simple (Slow), which is your only choice.

At this point, you've applied an ease, and the check mark next to the drop-down means the ease is active. (You can select and deselect this check mark to toggle the ease on or off.)

4. Press Enter (Return) and watch the lunatic move from left to right.

If that doesn't look like easing to you, you're right. Selecting Simple (Slow) isn't enough. You need to choose a percentage for that ease, which affects its strength. Think of it as a faucet—applying the ease means you've paid the water bill, but you won't see water until you turn on the faucet.

5. Scroll down to the bottom of the Motion Editor panel, and you'll see an Eases twirlie. Twirl that down, if necessary, and you'll see the reason why Simple (Slow) appeared in the X graph's easing drop-down list.

6. Scrub the hot text as far right as it will go, changing the default 0 to 100. As you scrub, you'll see a dashed line, representing the ease, begin to curve in the graph, as shown in Figure 8-13.

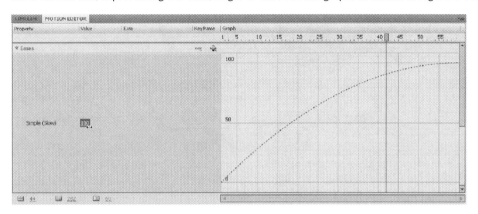

Figure 8-13. Change the default from 0 to 100, and the curve appears.

This particular graph changes the Simple (Slow) ease itself, which is comparable to changing a symbol inside the library. As you learned in Chapter 3, changing a library symbol means that every instance of it is changed on the stage. The same goes for these eases.

7. Scroll back up to the X graph, and you'll see that the ease is now superimposed over the line that represents the symbol's x-axis movement. To get a better view, click the left side of the X graph and scrub the Viewable Frames hot text until all 60 frames are displayed in the graph, as shown in Figure 8-14.

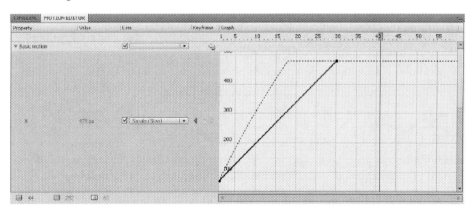

Figure 8-14. With easing, the graph shows actual movement and easing movement.

8. Press Enter (Return) again to preview the movement, but prepare yourself for disappointment: it still doesn't look like much of an ease.

The reason for this is that motion tween eases are applied to the full span of the tween. In this case, the full span is 60 frames, while the only visible change occurs between frames 1 and 30.

9. Click the upper-right property keyframe and, holding down the Shift key, drag the keyframe to the right until you hit frame 60. Doing so brings the solid line and the dashed line into agreement, as shown in Figure 8-15. The tooltip lets you know which frame you're on, and the Shift key constrains your movement.

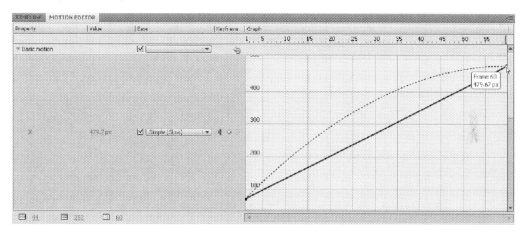

Figure 8-15. Keyframes can be moved from inside a graph.

If you don't use the Shift key while you drag, it's easy to slide the keyframe up and down, even if you intend to move only to the right, which increases the duration between this keyframe and the one before it. Why is it a bad thing to slide up and down? Actually, it isn't. Sometimes, you might *want* to do that, and it's good to know you have the option. Sliding up and down changes the property's destination point. In this case, because you're dealing with x-axis movement, it means that even from this graph, you could push the symbol farther to the right on the stage (slide the keyframe higher) or back toward the left (slide the keyframe lower).

> *The visual result of a property's destination point depends entirely on what the property represents. In the* Y *graph, the destination point affects the symbol's vertical position. In the* Rotation Z *graph, it affects the symbol's rotation. If you add a color effect or filter, the destination point determines how much of that effect is applied.*

10. Press Enter (Return) again. Because the solid and dashed lines' final anchor points meet, you'll see the full Simple (Slow) ease.

11. Using the Shift key again, drag the right-hand property keyframe back to frame 30.

12. Scroll down to the Eases area in the Motion Editor panel and click the + button. This opens a context menu offering more than a dozen built-in eases. Choose Bounce, as shown in Figure 8-16.

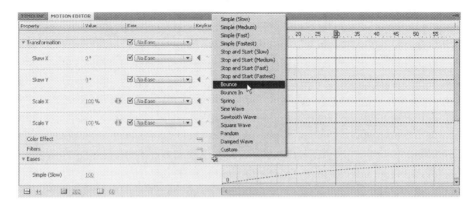

Figure 8-16. Use the + button to add new built-in eases.

13. Scroll down a bit to see the new ease beneath the graph for Simple (Slow). By default, the Bounce ease's hot text is set to 4, which makes the four bounces depicted in its graph. Change the hot text to 3 to reduce the number of bounces to three.

Adding an ease to the Eases area makes that ease available to all of the property graphs in the Motion Editor panel. Eases can be applied and changed for each property individually by using that property's drop-down menu and/or check mark. Eases can be applied and changed for whole groups of properties by using the drop-down menus in the Basic motion and Transformation twirlies. Add as many eases as you like, including multiple custom eases.

As you may have guessed, you can use the − button at any time in the Eases area to remove an ease from consideration for all drop-downs.

14. Scroll back up to the X graph and use the drop-down list to change the easing from Simple (Slow) to Bounce.

Two interesting things happen when you make this change, First, because you moved the property keyframe back to frame 30, part of the Bounce ease is clipped, as you can see in the flattened hump of the first bounce—between frames 6 and 27—in Figure 8-17. The second interesting thing becomes apparent when you preview the ease.

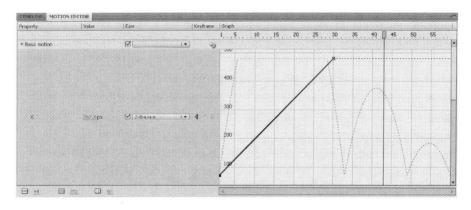

Figure 8-17. Eases can clip when the last property keyframe isn't the last frame in the span.

15. Press Enter (Return) and watch the lunatic slam to the right side, pause for a moment (that's the clipped first bounce), then resume its rebounding course, and finally end up back on the left side of the stage!

With motion tweens, easing can completely override the actual property represented by the solid line in the graph. Without the ease, this is a simple left-to-right movement. With easing, this *could be that*, but as you've seen, it can just as easily change the destination point to one quite outside of Kansas.

> *We chose physical movement to illustrate the mechanics of motion tween easing, because a change in position correlates well with the lines and curves on the graph. Be aware that this concept applies in exactly the same way to rotation, scaling, skewing, color effects like alpha and tint, and filters like Drop Shadow and Blur.*

16. Shift-drag the right-hand property keyframe back to frame 60. Verify that all three bounces are now visible in the X graph.

17. Press Enter (Return) to view the full, smooth three-bounce easing of the lunatic.

Creating custom eases

Even after seeing more than a dozen built-in eases, you might be wondering if you can create your own. The answer is yes, and it's pretty easy. Best of all, custom eases are saved with the FLA, which means you don't need to commit all your easing finagling to memory. Your custom eases will be there when you reopen your files in the morning, and even better, once they are added to the Eases area, you can apply (and reapply) custom eases to any property, just like built-in eases. Here's how:

1. Open LunaticCustomEasing.fla in this chapter's Exercise folder. Again, we start you with a basic left-to-right motion tween, this time over a full 60 fames.

2. Click the tween layer or the symbol, and then open the Motion Editor panel. Scroll down to the Eases area, click the + button, and select Custom from the context menu. This creates a Custom graph for you, so scroll down to take a look.

What you see is a line with run-of-the-mill Bezier curve handles. The anchor points and handles operate very much like those for normal drawings with the Pen tool, and we encourage you to experiment.

> *At the time this chapter was written, Flash CS4 was not yet commercially available, and the authors were unable to drag any Bezier curves higher than the 100% line or lower than the 0% line. Even within those limitations, though, you have plenty of wiggle room.*

3. Create a custom ease. Use the Ctrl (Cmd) key while clicking to add an anchor point along the line or curve. The same procedure removes any anchor point but the first and last (there must always be a beginning and destination point). Use the Alt (Option) key while clicking to convert a curve anchor point to a corner anchor point, and vice versa.

4. When you finish, scroll to the X graph and select your custom ease from the X property's drop-down menu. Press Enter (Return) to preview the effect.

5. Close your file without saving the changes.

Applying multiple eases

It may not immediately sound ambiguous, but the phrase "applying multiple eases" can actually be interpreted in a variety of ways. To be sure, you can apply numerous eases to a given motion tween—one separate ease for each tweenable property is perfectly acceptable. Give your X a bounce, your Y a Simple (Slow), your Rotation Z a custom ease, and so on, down the line. What you can't do is apply more than one ease between property keyframes. If you've used previous versions of Flash, this may take some getting used to, which is why we've stressed that motion tween easing applies to the full tween span, not to the span between property keyframes.

To follow one sort of easing with another sort within the same tween layer, you'll need to use more than one tween span. Here's how:

1. Open LunaticMultipleEasing.fla in this chapter's Exercise folder. This time, to mix it up, we prepared a vertical motion tween for you.

2. Click the tween layer or the symbol, and then open the Motion Editor panel. Scroll down to the Eases area, click the + button, and select Stop and Start (Medium). When its graph appears, scroll down and scrub its hot text to the right until it says 100.

3. Scroll up to the Y graph and select Stop and Start (Medium) in the easing drop-down menu. Press Enter (Return) to preview the ease, which makes the lunatic look as if it were being dragged upward with two heaves of a rope.

4. Select the Timeline layer. Right-click (Ctrl-click) the tween span and select Copy Frames from the context menu. Now right-click (Ctrl-click) frame 31 and select Paste Frames. Just like that, you've created a twin of the original animation, complete with its easing.

5. Right-click (Ctrl-click) the second tween span and select Reverse Keyframes. Preview the animation again, and this time, the lunatic gets heaved up and then heaved down again. Even though the motion is reversed, the tween is still the same for both tween spans.

6. Head back to the Motion Editor panel and use the Eases area's + button to add a Spring ease. Scroll up to the Y graph and change the second span's Y easing from Stop and Start (Medium) to Spring. Preview the animation, and you'll see the lunatic getting heaved up, and then suddenly fall and "sproing" to a halt.

Same tween layer, two tween spans—that's how you get two or more types of easing in the same layer. As an aside, notice that the lunatic doesn't come to a rest at the bottom of the stage. That's because the Spring ease is one of those whose destination point doesn't stop at 100%.

Managing property keyframes

Property keyframes—those diamonds in the timeline—can be managed by either the Timeline panel or the Motion Editor panel, and each has its own way of handling the details. When it comes to the new tweening model's keyframes, the Motion Editor panel should definitely be your tool of choice, but there are a few circumstances when the Timeline panel is more convenient, and we'll cover those after taking a quick look at a diamond. Let's jump in:

1. Open ManagingKeyframes.fla from the Exercise folder for this chapter. Scrub the timeline to see a 60-frame motion tween of our friend, the lunatic. In the property keyframe at frame 30, the lunatic not only moves right and up, but it also increases in size and rotates clockwise.

2. While you're in the Timeline panel, the only way you have to move from keyframe to keyframe is to scrub the playhead. Go ahead and scrub to frame 45.

3. Click the tween layer to select it, and then right-click (Ctrl-click) and select Insert Keyframe ➤ Position from the context menu, as shown in Figure 8-18. A property keyframe (small diamond) will appear at frame 45.

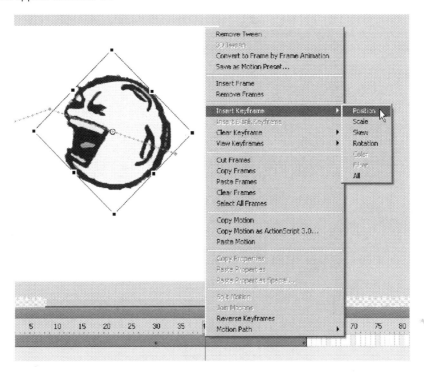

Figure 8-18. Property keyframes can be added with the Timeline panel.

4. Switch to the Motion Editor panel and notice that one keyframe apiece has appeared in the X and Y graphs, which makes sense.

5. Select the lunatic symbol and move it downward. As you saw earlier in the chapter, property keyframes are created for you automatically in the current frame when you change a symbol's position, scale, rotation, or the like. What you learned from step 3 is that it's still perfectly okay to create your keyframe first.

6. Switch back to the Timeline panel and right-click (Ctrl-click) again on frame 45. Note that you have options for clearing keyframes and also determining which property keyframes to display in the Timeline panel.

Don't be fooled by the Clear Keyframe *choice!* You would think, because Insert Keyframe inserts the desired keyframe(s) in the current frame, that Clear Keyframe would follow suit and remove only keyframes in the current frame. This is not so. By choosing Clear Keyframe, you're removing *all property keyframes* in the current tween span. If you select Clear Keyframe ➤ Rotation, for example, you remove all property keyframes in the Motion Editor panel's Rotation Z graph, regardless of in which frame they appear.

Once you see these features and understand them for what they are, you'll surely find them useful, but the Motion Editor panel does more.

7. Open the Motion Editor panel and scrub the playhead of along the Motion Editor's timeline. You get the same sort of preview as the Timeline panel. The difference is that the Motion Editor panel also gives you a pair of arrows and a diamond, as shown in Figure 8-19.

Figure 8-19. In the Motion Editor panel, keyframes can navigated, added, and removed with this widget.

Keep an eye on the diamond as you scrub. When you drag the playhead to a frame that already contains a keyframe, the diamond turns yellow. Use the left and right arrows to jump from keyframe to keyframe. Arrows will temporarily become disabled, as appropriate, at the first and last keyframes.

8. Scrub to frame 15 and click the Y graph's diamond. It turns yellow, and a new anchor point appears in the Y and X graphs at frame 15. (The Y and X graphs are synchronized, but this isn't the case with most property graphs.) Click the diamond again, and the keyframe disappears. Click it a third time to bring the keyframe back.

9. With the new keyframe in place, use the mouse to drag the anchor point in the Y graph upward, which correspondingly moves the lunatic downward on the stage. Note how the anchor point snaps to frames if you slide it left and right. That makes sense, because you can't have a keyframe between two frames.

10. Move your mouse elsewhere in the Y graph, and then hold down the Ctrl (Cmd) key while you hover over one of the line segments. As shown in Figure 8-20, the cursor turns into a pen with a plus sign, which indicates you can click to add a new keyframe. Hover over an existing keyframe while holding the Ctrl (Cmd) key, and you'll see a pen cursor with a minus sign. Click to remove the keyframe.

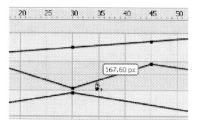

Figure 8-20. Keyframes can also be added and removed with the mouse.

11. Hold down the Alt (Option) key and hover over frame 30 in the Rotation Z graph. The cursor turns into an upside down V, as shown in Figure 8-21. Click, and this converts the anchor point into a curve anchor, which can be adjusted with Bezier handles. The effect of these handles on the X and Y graphs isn't always obvious, but for many properties, it gives you a "quick-and-dirty" custom ease.

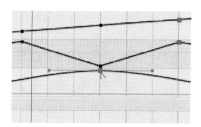

Figure 8-21. Anchor points can be converted from corner points to smooth with the Alt (Option) key.

12. Grab the right Bezier curve handle and drag it up and to the right so that the curve rises above its 100% mark, as shown in Figure 8-22.

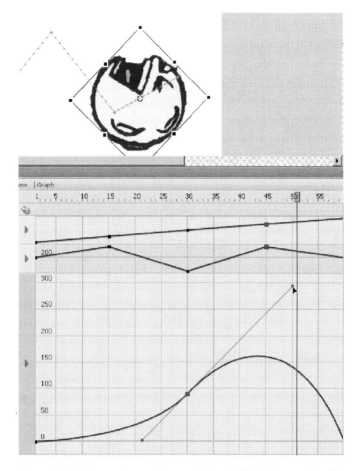

Figure 8-22. Anchor points can be manipulated with Bezier curve handles.

13. Press Enter (Return) to preview the animation, and you'll see that the symbol rotates farther than it did before—you've pushed it past its original destination, to approximately 160%—and then eases back the Rotation Z setting in the property keyframe at frame 60.

As helpful as the Motion Editor panel is, sometimes less is more. When you want to compress or expand the duration of a tween span, for example, the Timeline panel is the only way to do it, if you want to do it proportionally. If not, you could use either panel, but the Timeline panel makes it easier.

Changing duration proportionally

The animation in the ManagingKeyframes.fla you were just using spans 60 frames. At 24 fps, that's approximately 2.5 seconds, which may or may not be what you want. To change a tween span's duration proportionally, you'll need to use the Timeline panel. Here's how:

1. Open the ChangingDuration.fla file in the Chapter 8 Exercise folder. Look in the Timeline panel, and you'll see a 60-second motion tween with five keyframes, four of which are property keyframes.

2. Move your mouse to the right edge of the tween span. You'll see the cursor turn into a double-headed arrow, as shown in Figure 8-23. Click and drag toward the right. For example, shorten the tween span so that it ends at frame 30. Notice that all four property keyframes are still in place, and, proportionately speaking, are the same relative distance from each other as before.

Figure 8-23. Drag the tween span to increase or decrease a tween's duration.

3. Click and drag the tween span so that it ends at frame 59. Now release and drag the tween span to frame 60.

This time, the property frames are *nearly* back to their original places, but some are slightly off. That makes sense, because frame 59 is an odd number, and Flash had to make a decision on how to shift the frames to compensate.

To get the property keyframes back to frames 15, 30, and 45 exactly, you'll need to use a different approach. If you're into tedium, you could switch to the Motion Editor panel and visit every property graph in turn, sliding numerous anchor points while holding the Shift key. The middle keyframe, especially, would give you a headache, as it affects the X, Y, Rotation Z, Scale X, and Scale Y graphs. There's an easier way, and we describe it in the very next paragraph.

Changing duration nonproportionally

Sometimes you'll want to change the duration *between* property keyframes, which may or may not incorporate a change in span duration. You could do this with the Motion Editor panel, visiting each relevant graph and moving property keyframes individually, or you can update the keyframes in several graphs at the same time. For that, use the Timeline panel. Here's how:

1. Continuing with ChangingDuration.fla, and still in the Timeline panel, hold down the Ctrl (Cmd) key and click the keyframe closest to frame 30. Notice that holding down Ctrl (Cmd) allows you to select a single frame in the tween span, rather than the whole span.

2. Now that you have a single property keyframe selected, release the Ctrl (Cmd) key, and then click and drag the selected keyframe left or right along the timeline. Doing this effectively selects all the anchor points for the current frame in the Motion Editor panel and lets you move them as one.

Motion paths

With the butterfly exercise in Chapter 7, you learned that a special kind of guide layer in the Timeline panel, called a *motion guide*, lets you send a symbol along a potentially intricate path, braided with loops and curves. This capability is equally possible with the Motion Editor panel, only it's called a *motion path*, and it's built directly into the tween layer. In fact, you've already seen this feature, even if you didn't notice it earlier in the chapter.

Manipulating motion paths

The most interesting thing about this Motion Editor panel feature is that its effects are easier to accomplish with the Timeline panel. Let's take a closer look:

1. Open MotionGuideSimple.fla from the Exercise folder for this chapter. You'll see the Chapter 7 butterfly positioned near the lower-left corner of the stage.

2. Using the Timeline panel, apply a motion tween to frame 1. Then drag the playhead to frame 24 (or the last frame in the span). Drag the butterfly near the upper-right corner of the stage, and notice the series of dots that represent the motion path.

3. Using the Selection tool, hover near the motion path and, just as you would edit a normal line, click and drag to introduce a curve, as shown in Figure 8-24.

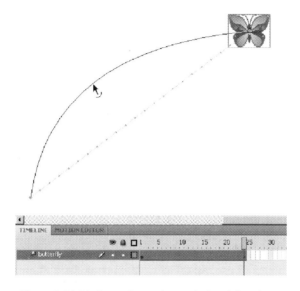

Figure 8-24. Motion paths can be manipulated directly.

4. Using the Subselection tool, click either anchor point and drag the Bezier curve handles to increase the range of the curve. Do the same thing to the other anchor point. In Figure 8-25, we've produced a sideways S-shaped motion path.

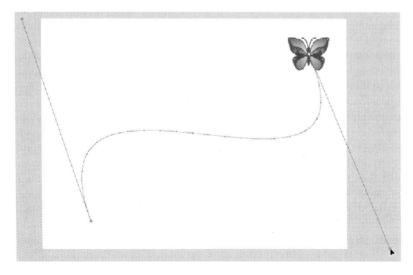

Figure 8-25. Use the Subselection tool to modify the motion path even further.

383

Not only can you reshape the motion path as shown, you can also move it, rotate it, skew it, and effectively treat it as you would any normal shape. Let's keep experimenting.

5. Select the tween layer and cast your gaze to the Property inspector. Scrub the X, Y, W (width), and H (height) hot text values, and you'll see that you can move and resize the motion path. But wait, there's more!

6. Open the Transform panel (Window ➤ Transform). This one's a bit trickier, because if you don't select the actual motion path, Flash will think you want to transform the symbol instead.

7. Use the Selection tool to click anywhere along the motion path to select it. Now scrub the Transform panel's Rotate hot text to see the motion path pivot around its starting anchor point, as shown in Figure 8-26.

Figure 8-26. Motion paths can even be rotated, skewed, and aligned.

8. To pivot around the other anchor point, right-click (Ctrl-click) the motion path and select Motion Path ➤ Reverse Path from the context menu. Scrub the Rotate hot text again, and change the location of the hinge. When you're finished, reverse the path again to make the butterfly animate from the bottom left to toward the top right.

9. Experiment with the Width, Height, and Skew properties in the same panel.

10. To perform these same transformations in a more organic fashion—that is, with your mouse, rather than by the numbers—switch to the Subselection tool and press the Ctrl (Cmd) key. Doing so introduces a temporary bounding box around the motion path, as shown in Figure 8-27.

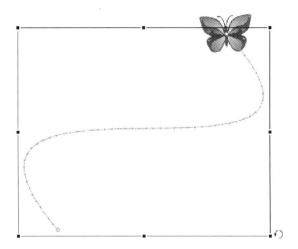

Figure 8-27. Hold down Ctrl (Cmd) to transform a motion
path with your mouse.

11. Hover near the various transform handles to see the mouse cursor change to indicate what
    sort of transformation is possible. Click and drag to perform the transformation. The corner
    handles manage rotation, the edge handles manage scale when you hover directly over them,
    and the same edge handles manage skew when you hover just off center of them.

> *Don't forget the Alt (Option) key while you make these transformations with the
> mouse. Without it, transformations pivot around the bounding box's center. With Alt
> (Option), transformations pivot along the opposite corner or edge. In either case, the
> Ctrl (Cmd) key is required to produce the bounding box.*

12. Open the Align panel (Window ➤ Align) and, with the To stage button selected, align the motion
    path to the horizontal and vertical center of the stage.

Notice, as with the classic tween version of this exercise, the nested animation of the butterfly performs
as expected. Because the graphic symbol has animation on its own timeline, the butterfly's wings flutter
as it moves. (As a note of interest, that nested animation is composed of classic tweens. This is one of
many indications that the two tweening models coexist happily.)

Using advanced motion paths

In Chapter 7, the butterfly went on a pretty wild ride—nothing like the tame Bezier curves you've seen
so far in this chapter. You can do the same thing with the new tweening model, and you still don't
need a motion guide layer. Here's how:

1. Open MotionGuideComplex.fla in this chapter's Exercise folder. You'll see the finished version
   of the butterfly MotionGuide.fla exercise from Chapter 7, including a classic tween directed
   by a motion guide layer. Your job—and it's an easy one—is to convert that complex motion
   guide into a motion path.

2. Right-click (Ctrl-click) the flutter by (motion guide) layer and deselect Guide from the context menu. This converts that layer back to a normal layer.

3. Using the Selection tool, double-click the wavy line to select the whole thing, and then cut the curves to the clipboard (Edit ➤ Cut).

4. Right-click (Ctrl-click) the classic tween and select Remove Tween from the context menu.

5. Right-click (Ctrl-click) again and select Create Motion Tween.

6. With the tween layer selected, paste the wavy line into the layer by selecting Edit ➤ Paste in Place. That's all there is to it! If you like, delete the now-empty flutter by layer.

7. Click the tween layer again. Use the Property inspector to select or deselect Orient to path, which behaves as it did for the classic tween version.

Motion tween properties

As you've seen throughout this book, the Property inspector is the most versatile panel in your arsenal, simply because it changes to reflect whatever object is selected. When you're dealing with motion tweens, there are two things the Property inspector lets you manipulate: the symbol and the tween itself (that is, the motion path). Some of these properties are the ones you see for classic tweens, but they don't all apply for motion tweens.

Let's take a look. Open any of the files you've used to far and make sure a motion tween is applied to at least one symbol. Select the tween span, and you'll notice the following properties in the Property inspector:

- Ease: This applies the Motion Editor panel's Simple (Slow) ease to the full frame span selected. You can adjust this ease's hot text to a value from -100 (ease in) through 0 (no ease) to 100 (ease out).

- Rotate [x] time(s) + [y]°: This is comparable to the Rotate drop-down for classic tweens and manages symbol rotation. The two hot text values let you specify the number of full rotations ([x]) and degrees of partial rotation ([y]).

- Direction: Once rotation numbers are configured with the previous property, you can choose clockwise (CW), counterclockwise (CCW), or none to determine the direction of those settings or cancel them.

- Orient to path: This check box applies only to orientation along a motion path.

- X, Y, W (Width) and H (Height): These reposition or transform a tween span's motion path.

- Sync graphic symbols: Human beings still have an appendix, but modern science can't figure out what it's good for, and the same goes for this property. Given its name, it's presumably the motion tween equivalent to the classic tween Sync property discussed in Chapter 7. With motion tweens, symbol synchronization happens automatically, whether or not this property is selected. As you'll see in the next section, this feature is moot in any case, because motion paths can be reassigned to any symbol you like.

The other motion-tween–related Property inspector settings depend on the symbol itself. For movieclips, your configuration options for motion tweens are the same as those for classic tweens. Some properties—such as position, scale, and rotation, and even color effects, like alpha—are tweenable. Others, like Blend modes, are not. These are consistent across the board when you're dealing with movieclips. It's when you're using graphic symbols that you need to be aware of a few limitations.

The limitations involve the Loop, Play Once, Single Frame, and Frame options in the Property inspector's Looping area. These properties apply to classic tween keyframes as discussed in Chapter 7. For motion tweens, they apply only to the tween span's first keyframe. They're ignored for property keyframes. The long and short of it is that you can set the Loop, Play Once, and Single Frame drop-down options and Frame input field once for a given motion tween—and Flash will obey your command—but only once for that tween span. Change these settings at any frame along the span, and the settings are changed for the whole span.

> *Even though we're focusing on symbols in these paragraphs, bear in mind that motion tweens can also be applied to text fields.*

One final note. Like classic tweens, motion tweens can accommodate only one symbol per tween span. In fact, motion tweens are a bit more strict about this constraint. Once you've applied a classic tween between two keyframes, Flash won't let you draw a shape or add a symbol to any of the frames between the keyframes. Interestingly enough, it will let you draw or add symbols to tweened *keyframes*, but doing so breaks the classic tween, whose "I'm a tween" indicator line then becomes a dashed line. With motion tweens, Flash won't let you draw or add a symbol to *any frame* of the tween span, keyframe or not. The moral of this story is that you should give each of your tween spans its own layer.

Motion presets

Here's another good example of letting the computer do the work for you. Flash CS4 takes advantage of one of the major new facets of motion tweens—that you can copy and paste motion paths—by providing you with a panel with over two dozen prebuilt *motion presets*. These are reusable motion paths, complete with motion changes, transformations, and color effects, which you can apply to any symbol or text field. Here's how:

1. Open LunaticBigCheese.fla from the Exercise folder for this chapter. You'll see our old friend, the lunatic, along with a rather unsuccessful cheese-thieving mouse.

2. Select the lunatic symbol and open the Motion Presets panel (Window ➤ Motion Presets).

3. Open the Default Presets folder, if it is not already open, and click among the various choices to see a preview of the animation in the Motion Presets panel's preview (see Figure 8-28). You'll see wipes and zooms, blurs and bounces, and all manner of helter-skelter. When you find a preset you like—we chose bounce-smoosh, the first one—click the panel's Apply button to copy that motion path to the lunatic symbol.

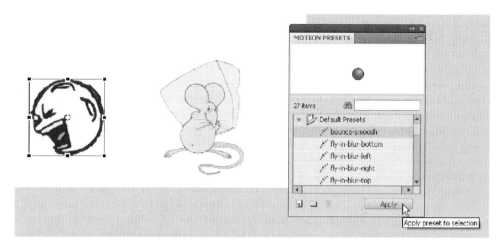

Figure 8-28. The Motion Presets panel gives you more than two dozen stock motion paths.

Applying the motion preset automatically inserts a motion tween on the lunatic's layer, and then adds the relevant property keyframes to reproduce the animation in question. If you chose bounce-smoosh, as we did, you'll need to move the whole motion path upward to keep the symbol from bouncing and smooshing off the bottom of the stage.

4. Using the Subselection tool, click the motion path, and then use the Align panel to center the animation vertically on the stage.

As you may have guessed, it's just as easy to apply the same (or different) motion preset to the other symbol, but we would like to draw your attention to a related feature instead. That related feature is that motion paths can be edited, or created completely from scratch, and then saved to the Motion Presets panel. How? Glad you asked.

5. Shorten the duration of the lunatic's animation by dragging the right edge of the tween span slightly to the left. In our file, we shortened the tween span from 75 frames to 50. Drag the playhead to one or more of the property keyframes and use the Property inspector, Transform panel, or Free Transform tool to alter the symbol's antics along the existing motion path.

6. Click the tween span and, in the Motion Presets panel, click the Save selection as preset button (Figure 8-29). You'll be prompted to give the new preset a name. Enter whatever you like (we used bounce-smoosh-alt) and click OK. Scroll to the Custom Presets folder to find your preset.

The other buttons in the Motion Presets panel let you create new folders and delete folders or presets.

Naturally, you could select the big cheese symbol and apply your newly minted custom preset, but there's another way you can share motion paths.

Figure 8-29. Motion paths, whether made from scratch or based on presets, can be saved for later reuse.

7. Right-click (Ctrl-click) the lunatic's tween span and select Copy Motion from the context menu. Now right-click (Ctrl-click) frame 1 of the cartoon mouse's layer and select Paste Motion.

Because you used the Align panel to change the position of the original motion path, you'll need to do the same for the copied path, assuming you want the lunatic and the cartoon mouse to fall in sync. It's easy as pie. While you could certainly use the Edit Multiple Frames workflow discussed in Chapter 7—that does still work here—you've learned in this chapter that motion tweens can be repositioned by way of their motion paths.

8. Using the Subselection tool, click the cartoon mouse's motion path to select it. Use the Align panel, again, to center the animation vertically to the stage.

9. Preview the animation. You'll see that both symbols perform the same movements (see Figure 8-30).

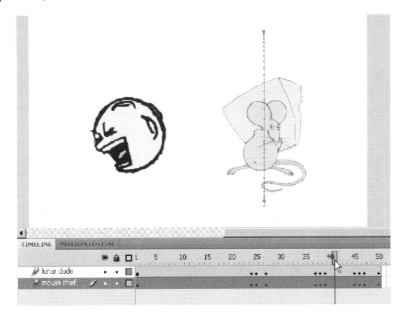

Figure 8-30. Motion paths can be shared even without the Motion Presets panel.

That's impressive enough, but let's redo the last demonstration in a more dramatic way. These last few steps should drive home the notion that, in Flash CS4, motion tweens—specifically, motion paths—are entities that stand on their own, distinct from the symbol.

10. Select the lunatic symbol at any point along its tween span and delete the symbol.

When you delete the symbol, the tween span remains, along with all its property keyframes. Visually speaking, the only difference in the tween span is that its first frame, usually a black dot, is now an empty white dot.

11. Click the empty tween span to select it.

12. Drag a copy of the big cheese symbol from the library and drop it somewhere on the stage. Location doesn't matter—it can even be on the right side of the existing cheese thief.

Because you selected the tween span first, the symbol will immediately adopt that span's motion path when you release the mouse to drop the symbol. You can't do that with a classic tween!

Inverse kinematics (IK)

In one of the happiest sequences in Disney's 1940 classic, *Pinocchio*, the wooden-headed puppet, once freed from the apparatus that formerly helped him move, bursts into song, proudly declaring, "I got no strings on me!" In Flash CS4, the authors suspect that you, too, will burst into song—but for the opposite reason—when you see the tools for a new feature called *inverse kinematics* (IK).

What is this academic, vaguely sinister-sounding term? In simple words, IK lets you string up your artwork like a train set, like sausages, or, if you prefer, like a marionette. And when you pull the strings, so to speak, or move one of the connected symbols, your artwork responds like a bona fide action figure. You can use IK to make poseable models, and then animate them.

Seriously, this feature is way cool, and we think you're going to love playing with it. That said, it's one of the more complicated feature sets in Flash CS4. Stringing up your symbols is easy enough. The official terminology calls for creating an *armature* and populating it with *bones*, which can then be dragged around. Adobe engineers have made this dead simple.

The tricky part is a question of *how*. To a certain extent, you'll find armatures and bones immediately intuitive, but just when you think they make sense, they'll behave in a way that might just strike you as utterly wrong. You'll see what we're talking about in the following exercises, and we'll show you an approach that should give you what you expect.

It all starts with something called the Bone tool.

Using the Bone tool

New (and very shiny!) to Flash CS4, the Bone tool is your key to the world of poseable armatures in the authoring environment. Using it will give you an inkling of the satisfaction experienced by a certain famous Victor Frankenstein, without anywhere near the hassle he went through or the illegal outings. You won't be visiting any actual graveyards, for example.

Let's see how the Bone tool works.

1. Open the Bones.fla file from the Exercise folder for this chapter. You'll be greeted by a more or less anatomically correct hand, sans flesh (see Figure 8-31). Go ahead and wave! The wrist and hand bones are all part of the same graphic symbol, named hand in the library. The knuckles are also graphic symbols, named by finger and knuckle number—for example, ring1, ring2, and ring3. All of these symbols happen to be on the same layer, but that doesn't need to be the case.

2. Select the Bone tool from the Tools panel. It's the one that looks like a bone, just above the Paint Bucket. Click over the bottom-center portion of the skeleton's wrist and drag toward the bottom of the thumb's first knuckle, as shown in Figure 8-32. When you release the mouse, you'll see your very first armature, which includes a single IK bone.

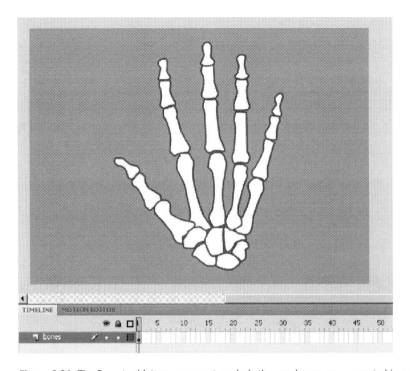

Figure 8-31. The Bone tool lets you connect symbols the way bones are connected in real life.

Notice the new layer in the Timeline panel, called Armature_1. That's your armature, and as you continue to connect your symbols together with IK bones, those symbols will automatically be pulled to this new layer. Just like a motion tween layer, this layer has distinctive properties. For example, you can't right-click (Ctrl-click) an armature layer to tween it, even though IK poses can be tweened (more on this later in the chapter, in the "Animating IK poses section"). You can't draw shapes on or drag symbols to an armature layer.

Bones have two ends, and it's helpful to know their anatomy. The larger end of the bone, where you started to drag, is called the *head*. The smaller end of the bone, where you released the mouse, is called the *tail*. The tail is pointing up and to the left in Figure 8-32. A string of connected bones is called an *IK chain* or a *bone chain*.

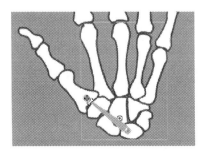

Figure 8-32. Drawing your first bone
creates the armature.

3. Hover somewhere inside the symbol that represents the first knuckle. You don't need to be exact—just within the symbol's bounding box. Then click and drag toward the bottom of the second knuckle. You'll notice that even if you don't begin the second drag directly over the tail of the first armature bone, Flash will automatically snap it into place for you. Release when you're over the bottom of the second knuckle.

4. To finish the thumb, hover anywhere inside the second knuckle's symbol. Click and drag upward to the bottom of the third knuckle. When you release, you'll have the simple bone rigging shown in Figure 8-33.

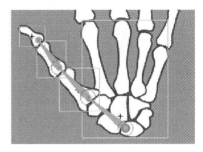

If you're anything like the authors, you're just *dying* to try out these bones, so let's take a quick *break* and do just that.

5. Switch to the Selection tool, grab that third knuckle, and give it a shake.

We fully expect you'll have fun, but all the same, you'll also see that it's pretty easy to arrange the hand into what looks like the result of a very painful accident (see Figure 8-34). It may surprise you, for example, that the wrist pivots, and

Figure 8-33. As you connect symbols with bones, the symbols are pulled to the armature layer.

those knuckles are bending into contortions that make even our yoga buddies wince. We'll fix those issues in just a moment. First, let's get acquainted with the Bone tool properties.

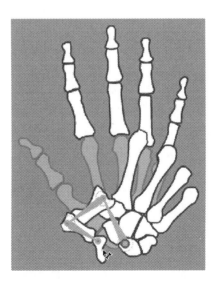

Figure 8-34. Ouch! Bones are easy to connect, but the results aren't always what you might anticipate.

Bone tool properties

There are two ways to nudge the Property inspector into showing bone-related properties: by clicking an IK bone on the stage and by clicking the armature itself, which is represented by a layer. Let's start with the armature.

1. Continuing with the Bones.fla file, click frame 1 of the Armature_1 layer. When you do, the Property inspector updates to show two twirlies:

- Ease: In this area, you'll find a drop-down list for selecting easing from a list of prebuilt choices, and a Strength value that lets you specify intensity, just as you saw in the Property inspector for motion tweens. These settings configure easing for the span of an armature layer (you can drag out an armature span to encompass as many frames as you like). Armature layers provide their own tweening capability, which is discussed in the "Animating IK poses" section and again in the last exercise of this chapter. For now, just note that this is where you can apply easing.

- Options: The area gives you something to see even without tweening. The Style drop-down list lets you specify how you want the IK bones to look. You have three choices: Solid (the default), Wire, and Line, which are illustrated in Figure 8-35 from left to right. When working with numerous or very small symbols, consider using the Wire or Line styles. Why? Because the Solid view can obscure symbols that appear under the IK bones.

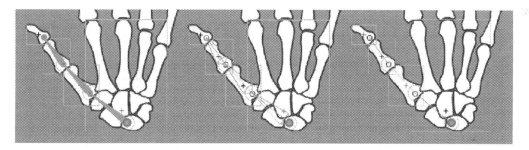

Figure 8-35. Bones can be configured as Solid, Wire, and Line (from left to right)

2. Change the Type drop-down selection from Authortime to Runtime. You'll see the warning message shown in Figure 8-36.

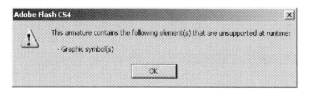

Figure 8-36. Only movieclip bones can be interactive at runtime.

The reason for the warning is that, although bones can be made interactive for the user, Flash requires that the boned symbols be movieclips when Type is set to Runtime. Fortunately, this is easy to change in Flash CS4, even if there are numerous symbols in play.

3. Click OK to close the warning dialog box.

4. Open the library and click the first symbol, named hand, to select it. Press and hold the Shift key, and then select the last symbol. Now everything in your library is selected.

5. Right-click (Ctrl-click) any one of the symbols and choose Properties from the context menu.

What you get is a feature new to Flash CS4, which is an incredible time-saver. The Symbol Properties dialog box opens—not just for the symbol you clicked on, but for all selected symbols.

6. In the Symbol Properties dialog box, place a check mark in the Type property and change the drop-down choice to Movie Clip, as shown in Figure 8-37. Then click OK.

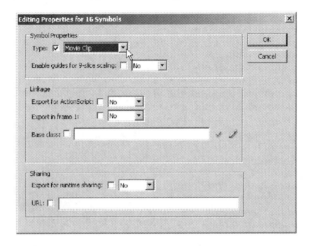

Figure 8-37. Flash CS4 lets you change multiple symbol properties at once in the library.

All of your library's graphic symbols become movieclips simultaneously. This used to take a separate visit to each asset. However, you still need to let the stage know what you've done.

7. Click the stage to select it. Select Edit ➤ Select All. In one swoop, you just selected all your symbols on the stage.

8. Click any one of the symbols to update the Property inspector, and then select Movie Clip from the drop-down list at the top of the Property inspector.

9. Click frame 1 of the Armature_1 layer and change the Type drop-down selection to Runtime.

10. Test the movie and wiggle those thumb knuckles inside Flash Player. Pretty neat!

11. Close the SWF and click one of the IK bones to update the Property inspector.

Now you see bone-specific properties. Let's go over those:

- Position X, Y, Length, and Angle: These are read-only properties, which means you can look, but don't touch. Thankfully, the names are self-explanatory.

- Speed: Think of this as friction, or how much "give" the selected bone has in the armature. A higher number means faster movement, and your range is 0 (no movement) to 200 (fast movement).

- Joint: Rotation: Here, you have the following choices:

  - Enable: Selecting this check box allows the bone to pivot around its head. In contrast, deselecting it means the bone won't act like a hinge.

  - Constrain, Min, and Max: Selecting Constrain activates the Min and Max hot text values, which allow you to determine how wide an arc your hinge can pivot on.

- Joint: X and Y Translation: The choices for this property are as follows:
  - Enable: Selecting this check box allows the bone to effectively pop in and out of its socket, in either the x or y axis.
  - Constrain, Min, and Max: Selecting Constrain activates the Min and Max hot text values, which allow you to determine how far the bone can move.

Of the properties available, Rotation and Translation will give you the biggest bang for the buck. Let's see how easy it is to fix that misshapen hand! While we're at it, you'll learn some helpful subtleties on manipulating the symbols in an armature.

Constraining joint rotation

IK bone rigs are as much an art as a science. The science facet derives from the Property inspector, which gives you have some configuration settings. The art facet depends on your sense of the appropriate range of motion for a given armature. Let's jump in:

1. Continuing with the Bones.fla file, use the Selection tool to drag the hand itself—not any of the fingers or the thumb—and carefully pivot the hand so that it realigns again under the fingers.

2. Select the first IK bone (the one closest to the wrist) and deselect the Enable check box in Property inspector's Joint: Rotation area.

3. Drag the thumb's third knuckle again, and note that the wrist no longer moves.

If you ever change your mind, just reselect the first IK bone and put a check mark back in the Enable property. Now let's make sure the thumb doesn't look so double-jointed.

4. Select the second IK bone and, in the Property inspector, enable the Constrain check box in the Joint: Rotation area, as shown in Figure 8-38.

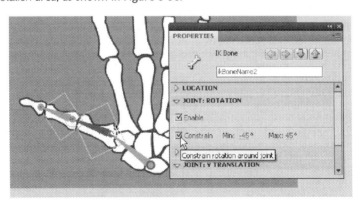

Figure 8-38. The Constraint check box lets you constrain a joint's range of motion.

Choosing Constrain adds a new component to the IK bone, which you can see in Figure 8-39. Suddenly, the bone's head sprouts a wedge shape, with a line in the middle that separates the wedge into two pie pieces. The line has a square handle on its outside end. (If you're in a Robin Hood mood, it may look like a bow and arrow.) This wedge represents the joint's range of movement. By default, you get a 90-degree sweep.

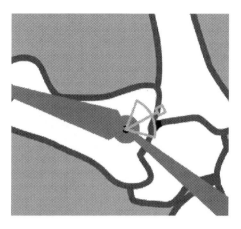

Figure 8-39. Select Constrain in the Joint:Rotation area of the Property inspector, and joints sprout a range-of-movement icon.

5. Drag the third knuckle downward. The line with the square handle moves counterclockwise until it rests against that side of the wedge. Drag the knuckle up, and the handle moves to the other side—clockwise—until it meets the opposite side of the wedge.

Adjusting this range of movement is easy. The workflow we prefer is to pivot the IK bone into position first, and then scrub the Min or Max hot text as necessary to meet that position.

6. Drag the third knuckle upward until the thumb moves as far in that direction as you like. If you need more room, select first knuckle's IK bone and scrub the Max value toward the right to increase its value. Readjust the thumb, and when you like how it sits, scrub the Max value toward the left again to bring the edge of the wedge toward the square-handled line.

7. Drag the third knuckle all the way down and repeat this process for the other extreme. You'll notice that the first knuckle appears above the bones of the wrist, as shown in the left side of Figure 8-40. That may or may not be what you want. If you want to send the knuckle behind the wrist, use the Selection tool to select that knuckle's symbol and select Modify ➤ Arrange ➤ Send to Back. The results will look like the right side of Figure 8-40.

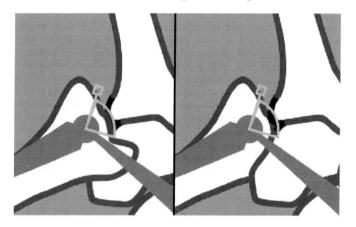

Figure 8-40. Use standard layer stacking to move symbols above (left) or behind each other (right).

The first knuckle is done. You can now move onto the second, which isn't any harder to manage.

8. Add a Joint: Rotation constraint to the second knuckle and configure the Min/Max values in whatever way suits you.

As you move the skeleton bones around, you can use the Shift key to temporarily change the way the IK bones respond. For example, drag the third knuckle up and down, and then hold down Shift and drag again. When Shift is pressed, only the third knuckle moves. This works with any other bone. Drag the second knuckle with and without Shift to see what we mean.

While you're at it, experiment with the Ctrl (Cmd) key as well. If you ever want to reposition a symbol without having to redo an IK bone from scratch, hold down Ctrl (Cmd) while you drag. This temporarily releases the dragged symbol from its IK chain. When you release the key, the IK bones are reapplied.

The third knuckle is the interesting one, because although it's attached to an IK bone, it's only associated with that bone's tail. This means you can't constrain its rotation. (Give it a try!) So what to do? Since we're dealing with so many kinds of bones, we think it's fitting that the answer relies on the presence of a ghost. Not a real ghost, of course, but a stand-in "ghost" movieclip.

9. In the Timeline panel, select the nonarmature layer (the one labeled bones).

10. Use the Oval tool to draw a small circle—say, 20 pixels × 20 pixels—no stroke, and color doesn't matter.

11. Convert that circle to a movieclip. Name the symbol ghost handle, and position it just past the thumb's third knuckle.

12. Using the Bone tool, add a fourth IK bone between the third knuckle and the ghost handle movieclip, as shown in Figure 8-41.

13. Select the newest IK bone and constrain its Joint: Rotation property.

14. Save your file.

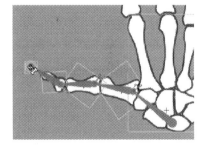

Figure 8-41. Use a stand-in movieclip to let you constrain the previously end-of-the-line IK bone.

Sure, the "ghost" movieclip may look a little silly, but its presence allows you to configure your IK bones from start to finish.

Here's the best part: whenever you need another stand-in IK bone, make sure to keep reusing that same ghost handle movieclip. Why? Because when you're ready to publish the SWF, all you have to do is open that symbol in the library and change its fill color to 0% Alpha. Just like that, your extra handles become invisible, and they still do their job.

Deleting bones

We showed you how to create IK bones, but you'll also want to know how to delete them. It couldn't be easier:

1. After saving your Bones.fla file, use the Selection tool to select the fourth IK bone from the previous exercise. Press the Delete key. Badda bing, badda boom . . . the bone is gone.

2. Skip the third IK bone and select the second one. Press the Delete key.

This time, both the second and third bones disappear. This tells you that deleting an IK bone automatically deletes any other bones attached to its tail.

3. Right-click (Ctrl-click) frame 1 in the Armature_1 layer and select Remove Armature from the context menu.

As expected, the last IK bone disappears. If you had made this selection in step 1, all of the IK bones would have disappeared from the start.

4. Select File ➤ Revert, and then click the Revert button in the alert box to undo all the deletions.

Applying joint translation

Another way to control the movement of joints is called *joint translation*. This affects movement of an IK bone along its x or y axis (or both). To illustrate, we'll leave our skeleton at the chiropractor's for a while and turn our attention to a rudimentary steam engine.

1. Open the SteamEngine.fla file from the Exercise folder for this chapter. The symbols are already in place for you.

In Figure 8-42, we've labeled the engine's anatomy to assist you in the next steps, so you can focus your attention entirely on the IK rigging. You're going to connect three horizontal symbols from left to right. Ignore the wheel for the time being.

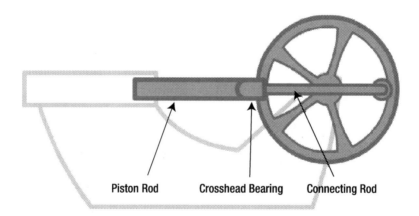

Figure 8-42. The movement of this steam engine will include joint translation.

2. Select the Bone tool, and then add a bone that starts on the left side of the piston rod symbol and ends on the crosshead bearing symbol (the center symbol).

3. Add another bone from the crosshead bearing symbol to the right side of the connecting rod symbol, as shown in Figure 8-43. This is no different from the bone rigging you did for the knuckles.

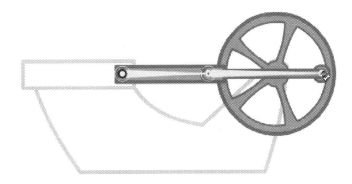

Figure 8-43. Two bones connect three symbols.

Joint translation doesn't require ActionScript, but we're going to use some programming to demonstrate it in this particular case. Because we'll be using ActionScript, let's give the bones and armature meaningful instance names.

4. Using the Selection tool, select the right-hand bone and use the Property inspector to give it the instance name connectingRod, as shown in Figure 8-44.

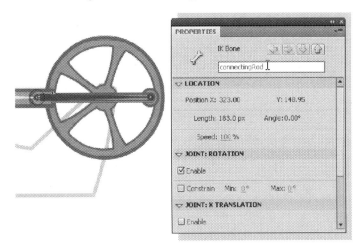

Figure 8-44. Bones and armatures support instance names, just like movieclip symbols.

Pay close attention to the Property inspector *when making your selections. It's easy to accidentally click the symbol to which a bone is applied, rather than the bone itself. In this context, the symbol is listed as an* IK Node *in the* Property inspector. *If you select an IK node, this exercise won't work properly. Figure 8-44 shows the correct selection of a bone, which displays* IK Bone *in the* Property inspector.

5. Select the other bone and give it the instance name pistonRod.

6. Select the armature itself by clicking on frame 1 of its layer in the Timeline panel. Use the Property inspector to give the armature the instance name engine. The armature's layer name will update to the same name.

Now it's time for the joint translation, but first, let's keep this bone from rotating. It's possible for bones to translate *and* rotate, but that isn't what we want here. Our aim is to let the piston rod slide left and right when the armature moves.

7. Select the pistonRod bone and use the Property inspector to disable its rotation (that is, deselect the Enable check box in the Joint: Rotation area).

8. To achieve the left-and-right motion, select the Enable check box in the Joint: X Translation area. The bone's head gets a horizontal double-headed arrow, as shown in Figure 8-45.

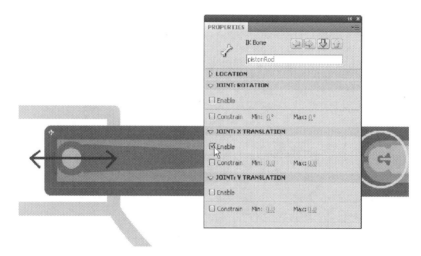

Figure 8-45. Joint translation is indicated by a double-headed arrow along the relevant axis.

You could optionally constrain this translation by selecting the Constrain check box and configuring Min and Max values, just as with joint rotation, but that isn't necessary here. Note, too, that you could optionally translate (and constrain) along the y axis, but we'll also omit that step.

Time to get this steam engine moving!

9. Click frame 1 of the armature's layer (engine) to select the armature. In the Property inspector's Options area, change the Type drop-down selection to Runtime. Now this rigging is ready for ActionScript.

10. Select frame 1 of the scripts layer and open the Actions panel. Type the following ActionScript:

```
import fl.ik.*;

var pt:Point = new Point();
var arm:IKArmature = IKManager.getArmatureByName("engine");
var bone:IKBone = arm.getBoneByName("connectingRod");
```

```
var tail:IKJoint = bone.tailJoint;
var pos:Point = tail.position;

var ik:IKMover = new IKMover(tail, pos);
```

The first line imports all the classes in the fl.ik package, which includes classes necessary for identifying and manipulating armatures created in the authoring tool. The next line declares a variable, pt, set to an instance of the Point class. (The Point class doesn't reside in the fl.ik package, but in just a moment, you'll see that something called the IKMover class needs a Point instance.)

From the third line on, the code unfolds like the lyrics in that old catchy tune, "Dry Bones" ("the knee bone's connected to the . . . thi-i-igh bone"). How so? A variable, arm, is declared and set to an instance of the IKArmature class. This variable takes its value from a method of the IKManager class, which connects it to the armature whose instance name is engine.

After that, a bone variable—an instance of the IKBone class—is connected to the bone whose instance name is connectingRod. Then a tail variable (IKJoint class) is connected to the tailJoint property of the bone instance. Finally, a new Point instance (pos) is connected to a pair of coordinates from the position property of the tail instance.

The tail and pos variables are passed as parameters to a new instance of the IKMover class, which is stored in the variable ik. That ik variable is what allows you to move the armature with code.

11. Add the following new ActionScript after the existing code:

```
wheel.addEventListener(Event.ENTER_FRAME, spin);
function spin(evt:Event):void {
  wheel.rotation += 5;
  pt.x = wheel.crank.x;
  pt.y = wheel.crank.y;
  pt = wheel.localToGlobal(pt);
  ik.moveTo(pt);
}
```

The basic premise here is something you've already seen in other chapters: a custom function, spin(), is associated with the Event.ENTER_FRAME event of an object with the instance name wheel. In this case, wheel is the instance name of the wheel-shaped movieclip symbol. (We've already configured the instance name for you in the sample file, and the wheel symbol contains another movieclip inside it with the instance name crank.)

So what's going on in this event handler? First, the MovieClip.rotation property of the wheel instance is incremented by five. That gets the wheel rolling continuously. After that, it's just a matter of updating the pt variable declared earlier. Being an instance of the Point class, the pt variable has x and y properties, which are set to the crank movieclip's x and y properties, respectively. Because crank resides inside wheel, the object path to the desired x property is wheel.crank.x. The same goes for y.

This updates pt's properties to the current position of crank, but that isn't quite enough. From the wheel symbol's point of view, crank never actually moves—it's wheel that does the rotating!—so the coordinates need to be considered from the point of view of the stage. That's what the second-to-last line does by invoking the DisplayObject.localToGlobal() method on the wheel instance. In plain English, it tells pt to reset itself in from crank's local coordinates inside wheel to the crank's global coordinates shared by all objects on the stage.

401

Finally, pt is passed as a parameter to the IKMover instance represented by the ik variable.

12. Test your movie so far to see the result.

It's close to being correct, and the pistonRod bone does perform its horizontal joint translation, but if you look carefully, you'll notice that the armature occasionally "slips" from the crank movieclip, as shown in Figure 8-46. That's easy to fix, and it's nothing more than a matter of priorities.

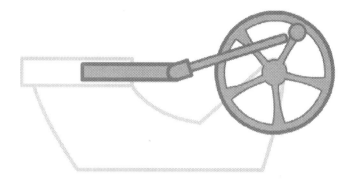

Figure 8-46. The armature isn't always fast enough. This is easy to fix.

The armature isn't updating as quickly as the wheel turns, so let's fix that by limiting the number of calculations it has to make.

13. Use the Actions panel to insert the following two lines after the ik variable declaration and the event listener (new code shown in bold):

```
. . .
var ik:IKMover = new IKMover(tail, pos);
ik.limitByIteration = false;
ik.iterationLimit = 5;

wheel.addEventListener(Event.ENTER_FRAME, spin);
function spin(evt:Event):void {
. . .
```

14. Test the movie again, and everything should run fine.

A note about bone preferences

Let's return to our friendly skeleton hand. We mentioned earlier in this chapter that IK poses can be animated, even without the use of a motion tween layer. You'll see how in the next section. First, it's time for a quick field trip.

1. Open the BonesRigged.fla file in this chapter's Exercise folder. You'll see the fingers and thumb pointing upward, and the thumb has a ghost handle.

2. Use the Selection tool or the Free Transform tool to click the first knuckle of the pointer finger. As Figure 8-47 shows, the symbol's transformation point (the small white circle) is dead center.

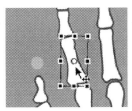

Figure 8-47. This symbol's transformation point is horizontally and vertically centered.

3. Noting the transformation point, select Edit (Flash) ➤ Preferences and click the Drawing choice in the Category area. Find the IK Bone tool: Auto Set Transformation Point check box and deselect it, as shown in Figure 8-48. Click OK to close the Preferences dialog box.

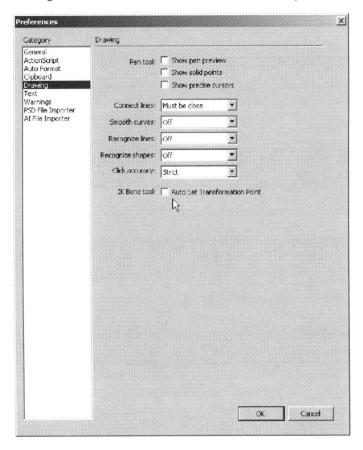

Figure 8-48. The Auto Set Transformation Point setting affects how bones are applied to symbols.

4. Using the Bone tool, hover over the hand symbol, and then click and drag a new IK bone toward the first knuckle of the pointer finger. As you do, notice that the tail of the IK bone snaps to the transformation point of the first knuckle. Note, also, that the armature is perfectly capable of handling more than one chain of bones.

5. Repeat this process to rig up the remaining knuckles of the pointer finger.

6. Using the Selection tool, grab the third knuckle and give the finger a wiggle. As shown in Figure 8-49, the pivots occur on the transformation points, which just doesn't work for this scenario. We want the knuckles to line up end to end.

7. Return to the Preferences dialog box and reselect the IK Bone tool check box.

8. Select File ➤ Revert, and then click the Revert button to roll the file back to its original state.

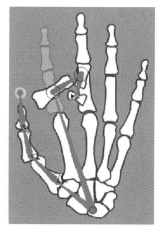

Figure 8-49. If you want, IK bones can snap to a symbol's transformation point.

We brought up the IK Bone tool preference setting because it's hard to spot unless you happen to be poring through the Preferences dialog box. We chose a silly example because silly visuals tend to stick.

By leaving the Auto Set Transformation Point check box selected in the Preferences dialog box's Drawing section, you're telling Flash to move a symbol's transformation point for you automatically. If you prefer to maintain that control on your own, deselect that check box, and then use the Free Transform tool to make your symbol selections. When selected with the Free Transform tool, a symbol lets you move its transformation point with an effortless click-and-drag operation. If the symbol already belongs to an IK chain, any heads or tails connected to it will reposition themselves to the new location of the symbol's transformation point.

Animating IK poses

Ready to animate some IK poses? We think you are. You reverted the BonesRigged.fla file in the previous exercise, so your FLA is prepared. (As described in the previous section, make sure your Flash preferences are configured to automatically set transformation points.) Let's do it:

1. Using the Bone tool, rebone the pointer finger from the wrist of the hand symbol to the third knuckle of the pointer finger.

Since fingers don't bend sideways, except at the knuckle closest to the hand, you'll want to add some constraints.

2. Select the first IK bone (the one over the hand) and deselect its Enable check box in the Joint: Rotation area of the Property inspector.

3. Select the second IK bone (over the first knuckle) and select its Constrain check box in the Property inspector. Set the Min and Max values to whatever you feel looks best (we used Min: 0° and Max: 30°).

4. Select the third IK bone and deselect its Enable check box for Joint: Rotation.

5. Now you need a ghost handle. Click the nonarmature layer and drag a copy of the ghost handle symbol to the stage. Position it just past the last knuckle of the pointer finger.

6. Use the Bone tool to draw a fourth IK bone from the last knuckle to the ghost handle.

7. Deselect that IK bone's Enable check box for Joint: Rotation.

> *Because the third and fourth IK bones are both disabled from rotation, you won't be able to move this finger by dragging the third knuckle or its ghost handle. The second knuckle will do it, however, because the head of the IK bone whose tail it's connected to does allow rotation.*

8. Repeat this process for the remaining fingers. With the hand fully rigged, it's time to configure your poses.

9. In the same way you would change the duration of a motion tween span, click and drag out the armature layer to make it span 50 frames.

10. Right-click (Ctrl-click) frame 15 and select Insert Pose from the context menu. This effectively copies the rigging in frame 1 to frame 15, so the hand won't start moving until the playhead hits this frame.

11. Right-click (Ctrl-click) frame 15 again and note that you can now clear this pose, as well, using the context menu.

12. Insert a pose at frame 30, and then rearrange the fingers and thumb into a new position.

13. Select the armature layer, if you like, and use the Property inspector to add a bit of easing. Don't forget to use the Strength property!

Your animation is almost ready to show off! The last step is to hide those ghost handles.

14. Double-click the ghost handle symbol in the library. In the Symbol Editor, select the shape's fill and change its Alpha to 0% (fully transparent).

15. Test your movie (see Figure 8-50).

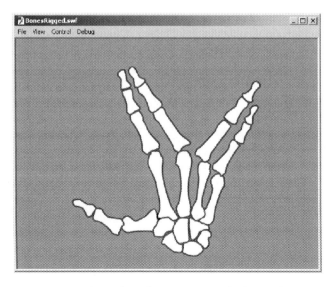

Figure 8-50. You just animated an IK armature! Live long and prosper.

Using the Bind tool

We expect that IK has sparked the creative center of your brain enough to keep you happily busy for weeks. Believe it or not, you still have one more tool to see. The team at Adobe has made IK available not only to symbols, but also to shapes! You'll be using the Bone tool for this exercise, but the Bind tool will make an appearance as an important sidekick. The best way to describe IK for shapes is to consider it a super-advanced evolution of shape tweens in combination with the shape hinting discussed in Chapter 7. Let's jump right in.

1. Open the Bind.fla file in the Exercise folder for this chapter and say hello to an earthworm, as shown in Figure 8-51. (The correlation between a worm, bones, and graveyards is purely coincidental, we assure you.) The library for this FLA is empty, because the worm is nothing more than a handful of shapes.

2. Assuming you want to drag the worm around by its head, you'll want to draw the bones of your armature from the opposite side of the worm. Select the Bone tool and, starting from the bottom of the shape, drag a small IK bone upward.

Figure 8-51. IK for shapes is brought to you by a worm.

3. With that first bone in place, hover over the tail of the IK bone. When the tiny black bone icon inside the mouse cursor turns to white, you'll know you've hit the right spot. Click and drag upward to add another bone.

4. In this manner, keep adding small IK bones until you reach the top of the worm (see Figure 8-52).

5. Before you give the worm a wiggle, switch to the Bind tool and click the bottommost IK bone.

This is where it gets interesting. To see we're talking about, switch to the Zoom tool and marquee the bottom several bones in the tail. Now you're ready for action.

Using the Bind tool is a bit like using the Subselection tool in that it reveals a shape's anchor points. In Figure 8-53, you can see anchor points represented in three different ways. At the top of the figure, they look like the sort you've seen in previous chapters—just small squares. At the bottom, they're considerably larger and thicker, and appear in the form of triangles as well as squares.

Figure 8-52. IK bones can easily be applied to shapes.

When you select an IK bone with the Bind tool, Flash shows you which of the shape's anchor points are associated with that particular bone. Squares indicate an association with a single bone; triangles indicate an association with many bones.

In this case, the bottom four anchor points—the heavy squares—are associated with the bottommost bone only. The upper two anchor points—the heavy triangles—are associated with the bottommost bone and with the bone immediately above it. The triangle anchor points are affected when either of their associated bones moves.

Click any of the other IK bones in this armature, and you'll see that Flash has does done a great job of automatically deciding which associations to make. This won't always be the case. Thankfully, you can override Flash's decisions.

6. Hold down the Ctrl (Cmd) key and click one of the bottom four heavy squares. This makes it look like a normal anchor point (smaller and not bold). Still holding Ctrl (Cmd), click one of the heavy triangles, which also becomes a normal anchor point.

7. Select the next IK bone, and you'll see that the triangle anchor is back. but now it's a heavy square. That makes sense: before step 6, this anchor was associated with two bones (triangle), but now it's associated with only this one (square).

8. Select the bottommost bone again and, without holding down Ctrl (Cmd), click the anchor point that was previously a heavy square. Drag it toward the bone (see Figure 8-54) and release. That anchor point is now reassociated with the bone.

9. Click another bone, and then click this one again. You'll see the heavy square as it originally was, along with its companions.

10. To reassociate the formerly triangle anchor point, use the Bind tool to select the appropriate anchor, and then press and hold Ctrl (Cmd) while you drag it to the bottommost bone. As you do, you'll see an association line in the upper bone as well as the diagonal association line created by your dragging (see Figure 8-55).

Figure 8-53. The Bind tool lets you manipulate anchor points.

Figure 8-54. Click and drag an anchor point to associate it with a bone.

Figure 8-55. Press Ctrl while dragging to associate an anchor point with more than one bone.

11. Save the file. (You're going to continue with it in the next exercise.)

Use the Bind tool to fine-tune your shape armatures, just as you would use shape hints to fine-tune a shape tween. Any anchor points not associated with an IK bone are ignored when the armature is manipulated.

You can animate shape armatures in the same way as symbol armatures—and you're about to do just that—which will introduce you to two "gotchas" of this feature.

When it comes to IK with shapes, two limitations leap to mind:

- Shape armatures don't manipulate gradient and bitmap fills.
- Complex shapes cannot be boned, so keep your overall anchor point count to a minimum.

Let's explore these limitations before moving on to a full-scale IK animation exercise.

Shape IK and fills

To see what we mean about fills, continuing with the Bind.fla from the last exercise, use the Selection tool to give your worm a wiggle. It's fun to do, because the shape responds in a very worm-like way. When you're finished, click the stage to deselect the bones and the shape's bounding box.

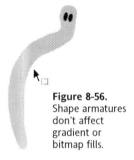

Figure 8-56.
Shape armatures don't affect gradient or bitmap fills.

The shape looks great, but as you can see in Figure 8-56, the gradient fill, which gave the worm a slightly rounded look, hasn't bent along with the shape. This tells you to stick with solid fills for shape armatures.

Shape IK and anchor points

Let's see how the number of anchor points affects shape IK:

1. Open the WaveCanadian.fla file in this chapter's Exercise folder. You'll see a vector drawing of the flag of Canada with a shape armature in place.

2. Drag the right side of the armature up and down to wave the flag (see Figure 8-57).

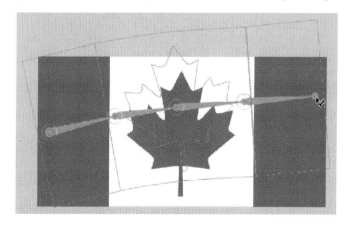

Figure 8-57. There is a definite relationship between armatures and vector points when it comes to IK in Flash.

3. Open the WaveAmerican.fla file from the same folder. In this file, the armature hasn't been added yet.

4. Use the Selection tool to select the whole shape, then switch to the Bone tool and try to add an IK bone.

Instead of a new armature, you'll see an alert box telling you the shape is too complex. Want to know the culprit?

5. Switch to the Subselection tool and draw a selection around the whole shape.

Each of those 50 stars is composed of 10 anchor points. That's 500 points already, and that doesn't include the stripes. We're not sure where the official line is drawn, but 500+ anchor points is too much.

Your turn: Animate a fully rigged IK model

We figure you appreciate worms and skeleton hands as much as the next designer (and so do we!). But surely, your thoughts have already wandered toward more complex implementations. We suspect you're wondering if the IK tools are useful for more than a few fingers. What about a whole body? The answer to these questions is yes, and you're about to find out firsthand. In this final exercise of the chapter, you'll expand on what you learned in previous sections by rigging up a character with arms and legs, and then animating it against a backdrop of hand-sketched poses. Let's do it.

1. Open the Richard.fla file from the Exercise folder for this chapter. You'll see an assembled collection of symbols in the likeness of Richard (see Figure 8-58), one of the regular characters in Steve Napierski's web comic "The Outer Circle" (http://www.theoutercircle.com/).

> The authors would like to give Steve a hearty thanks for letting us use his artwork! See more at http://www.pierski.com/.

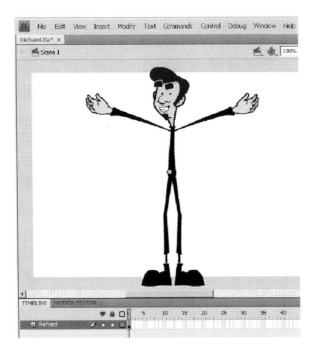

Figure 8-58. Meet Richard. Give him a hug. You're going to make Richard jump.

We chose Richard for this exercise for a particular reason: he's super skinny, which means it's not especially easy to rig up his armature. Going this route will give you practice, which is good, because real-life projects have a tendency to introduce unexpected challenges. Given this set of very narrow graphic symbols, we find that it helps if you take the reins from Flash in terms of bone placement.

2. Select Edit (Flash) ➤ Preferences and click the Drawing choice in the Category area. Deselect the IK Bone tool: Auto Set Transformation Point check box. As described in the "A note about bone preferences" section earlier, this means you'll be the one deciding where to place your bone heads and tails, and you'll adjust them afterward.

3. Select the Oval tool and, in the Richard layer, draw a small circle about 22 pixels × 22 pixels near one of the character's hands. Select the shape and convert it to a graphic symbol named handle. This is going to be your "ghost handle," which lets you constrain the hands, feet, and head.

4. Drag additional instances of the handle symbol from the library to the stage, positioning them near the Richard's other hand, his feet, and his head, as shown in Figure 8-59. In this exercise, Richard's chest will act as the starting point for every new chain of bones, just as the skeleton's palm did in earlier exercises.

Figure 8-59. Make sure to include extra symbols to allow for rotation constraints.

5. Select the Bone tool, and then click and drag a bone from the torso symbol to one of the upper leg symbols. Be sure to release the bone's tail low enough on the upper leg that it clears the bounding box of the torso (see the bounding box in Figure 8-60, and note how the bone tail falls below it). Even though this puts the bone tail lower than it should on the leg symbol—effectively moving the "hip" into the thigh—you'll be able to readjust it in just a moment.

Figure 8-60. Make sure the bone's tail clears the bounding box of the torso symbol.

The fact that these symbols overlap is part of the reason we had you deselect Auto Set Transformation Point in step 2. While not always a problem, in this case, the obscured symbol rotation points make it harder for Flash to decide on its own where new chains of bones should begin.

6. Just as you did earlier for the knuckles, continue adding a new bone that connects the upper leg to the lower leg, the lower leg to the ankle, the ankle to the foot, and finally the foot to the foot's ghost handle. Feel free to zoom the stage—particularly for the ankle!—if necessary.

7. Select the Free Transform tool, and then click the stage to deselect the armature itself.

8. Click each symbol in turn, from the ghost handle back up to the torso, and adjust the transformation point so that it sits over the symbol's registration point, as shown in Figure 8-61. To do this, click the white circle (transformation point) and drag it to the small plus sign (registration point), and then release. Selecting Snap to Objects in the Tools panel will make this task easier for you.

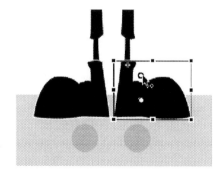

9. After you've adjusted the transformation point for each boned symbol, select the Bone tool again and click the head of the torso's existing bone to begin a new chain of bones down the other leg. Follow this with a repeat of the Free Transform tool adjustments of the relevant symbols' transformation points.

Figure 8-61. Situate symbol transformation points over symbol registration points.

10. Obviously, the arms need the same treatment, as does the head. Starting from the same gathering of torso bones each time, use the Bone tool to create new bone chains from the torso to upper arm, lower arm, hand, to ghost handle on both sides, and then from torso to head to ghost handle at the top of the character. When you're finished, revisit all relevant symbols with the Free Transform tool to reposition transformation points over their corresponding registration points. Your armature should look like the one shown in Figure 8-62.

Figure 8-62. A complete IK rig

At this point, Richard is nearly ready for his calisthenics. First, we need a few rotation constraints.

11. Using the Selection tool, click any of the torso bones and deselect the Enabled option in the Joint: Rotation area of the Property inspector. Because all the torso bones share the same head, this action will disable rotation for the whole body.

12. Zoom the stage, if necessary, and disable rotation for the ankle bones.

13. Add rotation constraints to the remaining bones according to your preferences. For example, select the lower leg's bone and, in the Property inspector, select the Constrain option and adjust the Min and Max values to keep the knee from bending backward.

When you're finished, the Timeline's original Richard layer will have long since been emptied, because every symbol was moved to the automatically created armature layer as it was associated with a bone.

14. Rename the Richard layer to poses.

15. Select File ➤ Import ➤ Import to Stage and import the jumping.jpg file in this chapter's Exercise folder. This JPG features a number of hand-drawn poses you can use as guides to manipulate the armature. Position the imported JPG slightly to the right, so that it appears behind Richard, and then lock the poses layer.

16. Select Edit ➤ Select All to select the armature's symbols.

17. Open the Transform panel (Window ➤ Transform). Make sure the Constrain option in the Transform panel is selected (the chain icon is not broken) and resize the fully selected armature to approximately 75%, as shown in Figure 8-63. This matches the character's size with the hand-drawn poses.

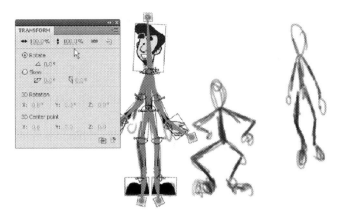

Figure 8-63. Resize the armature, and all its symbols, to the hand-drawn guides, and you're set.

When you release the mouse after scrubbing, the Transform panel will seem to indicate that the armature is still scaled to 100%, but if you select each symbol individually, the Transform panel will correctly show the smaller scale you chose in step 18.

Richard's jump should take about one second. Because the movie's frame rate is 24 fps, that means 24 frames is fine.

18. Hover near the right edge of the of the armature's single frame until the icon turns into a double-headed arrow. Drag out the armature span until it reaches frame 24.

19. Right-click (Ctrl-click) the poses layer at frame 24 and select Insert Frame from the context menu. This matches up the JPG to the time span of the armature layer.

20. We're about to cut you loose, so here's the basic gist of what you'll repeat until the sequence is finished:

    a. Unlock the poses layer and slide the JPG to the left in order to position the next pose under the armature. Once the JPG is moved, lock the poses layer again.

    b. Drag the playhead six frames to the right (one-fourth of the armature span, because there are four poses after the first drawing).

    c. Use the Selection tool to manipulate the character's body parts so they match the hand-drawn pose.

Here are two important tips:

- Depending on how you might have constrained your joints, you may not be able to match the drawing perfectly. Treat the drawings as *rough guides*. In Figure 8-64, for example, you can see that our elbows don't match the pose at all—they're bent in the opposite direction! Just have fun with it.

- You will often need to move the whole armature at once. To accomplish this, hold down the Ctrl (Cmd) key and click the current frame of the armature layer. Doing so simultaneously selects all of the armature's symbols in the chosen frame. At this point, slowly tap the keyboard's arrow keys to move the armature. If you hold down Shift while pressing the arrow keys, you can move in 10-pixel increments, which makes it go faster.

21. After you've finished posing the armature at frames 6, 12, 18, and 24, right-click (Ctrl-click) the poses layer and convert it to a guide layer. This will keep it from showing when you publish the SWF. (Alternatively, you could hide the poses layer and configure your preferences to omit hidden layers from the SWF—see the "Using layers" section of Chapter 1—or simply delete the poses layer.)

22. Double-click the handle symbol in the library to open it in the Symbol Editor. Change the opacity of its fill color to 0%, to make the ghost handles invisible when you publish.

23. Save your file and test the movie. If you like, compare your work with the completed Richard.fla file in this chapter's Complete folder.

Inspiration is everywhere

We started this chapter with a mention of some inspirational early Flash animation, so it's fitting to finish with a few more current resources.

- Chris Georgenes (http://mudbubble.com) is one of the most talented Flash animators we know, and a friendly guy, to boot! His http://keyframer.com forum has become an immensely popular meeting place for Flash cartoonists and animators, from beginner to pro. So visit his forum, sign up (it's free), and bring along your artwork, demo reels, and questions. You'll find literally thousands of eager participants ready to share their Flash-based tips and tricks.

- For a look at some jaw-droppingly amazing, multiple award-winning Flash cartoons, check out the "Animation" section of Adam Phillips's http://biteycastle.com website. Adam was happy to lend us a screenshot from "Waterlollies" (see Figure 8-64). He draws and animates all his artwork directly in Flash. When you see what's possible with the authoring tool, you might just think (as one of the authors does), "When I grow up, I want to be Adam Phillips."

Figure 8-64. A scene from Adam Phillips's "Waterlollies" (http://www.biteycastle.com)

- For an additional 360 pages of top-notch Flash animation how-to, check out *Foundation Flash Cartoon Animation* (friends of ED, 2007), by Tim Jones, Barry Kelly, Allan Rosson, and David Wolfe (http://www.friendsofed.com/book.html?isbn=9781590599129). This book was written for Flash CS3, so it covers only the technical content discussed in Chapter 7, but it goes on to elaborate on industry practices, including library organization, storyboarding and animatics, frame-by-frame animation, and integration with After Effects.

What you have learned

In this chapter, you learned the following:

- How to use the Motion Editor panel
- That even though the new tweening model is intended for the Motion Editor panel, the Timeline panel continues to be useful for motion tweens
- How to use and configure advanced easing graphs, and how to create your own
- How to navigate property keyframes in the Motion Editor and Timeline panels
- How to change the duration of a tween span
- How to manipulate and reuse motion paths, with or without the Motion Presets panel
- How IK works in Flash
- How to use the Bone and Bind tools
- Tips on improving your IK bone rigging workflow
- How to animate an IK armature

This has been a rather intense chapter, but you have to admit there is some seriously cool new animation stuff in Flash CS4. We started by walking you through the Motion Editor, including motion paths, Up to this point in the book, the Motion Editor was something you "visited." Now you have learned how valuable a tool it will be as you strengthen your Flash skills.

From there, we took you deep into the new inverse kinematics features of Flash CS4. Starting with the Bone tool and a skeleton, we guided you through this subject. By animating Vulcan greetings, steam engines, and an honest-to-goodness real cartoon character, you discovered the power of inverse kinematics and quite a few of the gotchas and work-arounds being developed as the Flash industry adjusts to this new animation capability.

As you went through this chapter, you were probably thinking, "This is all well and good in a flat space, but where's the 3D?" Great question. Why don't you turn the page and find out.

Chapter 9

FLASH GETS A THIRD DIMENSION

Designers have been asking for 3D manipulation tools in Flash for a long time. In fact, this feature has been requested in some form or another since the beginning of the product line. That makes sense if you consider that the mid-1990s promise of Virtual Reality Modeling Language (VRML) gave web surfers a taste of 3D before Flash ever hit the market. VRML was a great idea, but it was ahead of its time and, sadly, didn't go very far. In any case, it was more of a programmer's pursuit than something a designer would want to grapple with.

Then came Flash, which sparked an explosion of stylish 2D designs that began to reshape what the web experience meant. Over the years, intrepid designers began experimenting with ways to simulate three dimensions in their SWFs. They used centuries-old techniques to accomplish these goals—for example, increasing the size of an object to "move it forward"—which were the same practices used in real-life painting and sketching. Nothing in the Flash interface provided direct assistance. This has changed in Flash CS4. The requested tools have arrived. If you'll pardon the pun, they open a whole new dimension in creative potential.

Here's what we'll cover in this chapter:

- Understanding the new 3D environment
- Using the 3D tools
- Positioning symbols in 3D space

The following files are used in this chapter (located in Chapter09/ExerciseFiles_Ch09/Exercise/):

- Exhibition01.fla
- bean.jpg (JPGs located in a subfolder named babies)
- brando.jpg
- deniro.jpg
- lmao.jpg
- noway.jpg
- GrandEntrance.fla
- AirheadMail.fla
- 3DCubeBaby.fla

The source files are available online from either of the following sites:

- http://www.FoundationFlashCS4.com
- http://www.friendsofED.com/download.html?isbn=15905910931

What you'll learn in this chapter pertains to the 3D-related tools in the Flash CS4 Tools panel, along with some workflow suggestions to help you get the most out of them. This will be enough to introduce you to a new playground.

If you want to supplement the benefits of the new 3D tools with older techniques, consider checking out *Flash 3D Cheats Most Wanted* by Aral Balkan, Josh Dura, et al. (friends of ED, 2003). To learn about simulating 3D with ActionScript 3.0, see Chapters 15 through 17 of *Foundation ActionScript 3.0 Animation: Making Things Move!* by Keith Peters (friends of ED, 2007).

What 3D really means in Flash (and what it doesn't)

When it comes to 3D in Flash, consider the new feature as you would pizza. No matter what the server brings from the kitchen, you're going to love it. *Capice?* Good. Now that you're thinking of a delicious pie with all your favorite toppings, tease your mind back to Flash for a moment. Between bites, wrap your brain around three levels of wow factor:

- Good ("Hey, this is super cool")
- Better ("My jaw just hit the floor")
- Best ("Somebody bring me oxygen!")

Game consoles like the Wii, PlayStation 3, and Xbox 360 have redefined what consumers expect in terms of 3D interactivity. This is the bring-me-oxygen stuff—the Best level—which isn't available in Flash. We need to mention that right out of the gate. (Hey, are you going to eat that pepperoni?)

On the design side of things, you would need specialized 3D modeling software to produce that sort of content for game consoles, television, or film. We're talking about software like Maya, 3ds Max, Blender, or Cinema 4D. These industrial-strength powerhouses are designed specifically for the task, and are capable of turning out extremely complex, high-resolution output. Examples include everything from Hollywood aliens, dragons, and virtual stunts, all the way to proof-of-concept vehicle mock-ups, such as the F-15A aircraft shown in Figure 9-1.

Figure 9-1. Highly complex 3D models are created in software designed for the task, which doesn't include Flash (aircraft modeled by Roy Baker).

For better or worse, advanced 3D modeling is not the sort of field trip you'll be taking in Flash CS4—at least, not with the new drawing tools. Don't let that get you down, though. For you code jockeys, be aware that ActionScript does give you a surprising range of possibilities, but you'll probably want to use third-party code libraries to pull it off.

For the jaw-dropping stuff—the Better level—you'll want to check out Papervision3D (http://www. Papervision3D.org/). This is open source software (created by core team members Carlos Ulloa, John Grden, Ralph Hauwert, Tim Knip, and Andy Zupko) consisting of a framework of ActionScript 3.0 and 2.0 class files. Papervision3D allows programmers to create a range of *3D primitives* (basic shapes, from which other shapes can be built), and even import COLLADA (an open XML standard) data files from external modeling applications, and then bring those models to life in complex ways, as shown in Figure 9-2. Yup, that's Flash, and that spaceship is interactive. In many ways, this is comparable to VRML.

Figure 9-2. An example of Papervision3D content (modeled by Carlos Ulloa)

If you're experienced with previous versions of Flash, you may have heard of Swift 3D (http://www.erain.com). Swift 3D is a best-of-breed, low-cost modeler closely integrated with Flash in that it exports models as SWFs. These SWFs can then be loaded or imported into your normal work files and used to simulate three-dimensional objects. The latest version of Swift 3D even exports to Papervision3D, so you're in good hands with this product. Designers typically import Swift 3D assets as elements of otherwise two-dimensional layouts. That workflow is every bit as useful in Flash CS4 as it has been in the past, but it's not the topic we're covering here.

What you'll learn about in this chapter is the super-cool stuff—the Good level—and a great place to start if you're new to nonscripted 3D in Flash (which pretty much means anyone using Flash CS4 for the first time). We won't be covering 3D in terms of ActionScript. It's simply a topic that merits its own book, and we again direct your attention to http://www.Papervision3D.org/. What you are about to discover, behind that heavenly melted mozzarella, is a pair of shiny new additions to the Tools panel that give you direct three-dimensional manipulation of your symbols. But first, we need to cover a bit of theory.

Understanding the vanishing point

When you open your eyelids and cast your gaze ahead, even if all you can see are the tweed walls of your cubicle, you have a horizon in front of you. Turn your head, and it's still there. The horizon might be hidden, but the principles of perspective still apply, just as gravity still applies even when you climb a tree or take a dive in the swimming hole. In a theoretical sense, this horizon holds something called a *vanishing point*, which is a special location, usually off in the distance, where the parallel lines in your view seem to converge. It's a natural optical illusion, and you see it every time you stare down a length of railroad tracks. In linear perspective drawings, you can have as many as three vanishing points, but Flash keeps things manageable for you by providing one. Here's how it works.

Imagine a cube—just an ordinary cube like the one in Figure 9-3. It might be a cardboard box or a die whose spots have gone missing. This sort of figure is easy enough to draw with the Rectangle and Line tools, but it helps if you think of the box as sitting on the ground somewhere, with the horizon above or below it, depending on your line of sight.

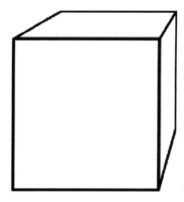

Figure 9-3. A plain-old box, drawn in perspective

In this case, the horizon happens to be above the box. If you draw a set of perspective lines along the edge of each corner, you'll see that they all meet at one point on the horizon, as illustrated in Figure 9-4.

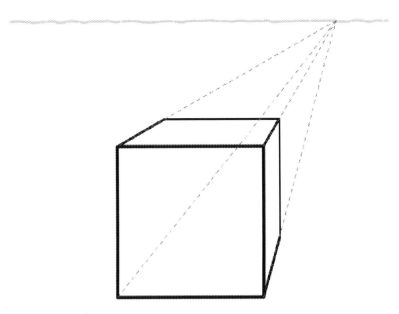

Figure 9-4. The vanishing point is the location where parallel lines seem to converge on the horizon.

The point at which those lines meet is your vanishing point. It's your key to understanding how the 3D Rotation and 3D Translation tools, coupled with the Transform panel and Property inspector, give you access to 3D manipulation in Flash. Without this concept, you can still experiment with these tools and have plenty of fun. But if you want to actually wallpaper a three-dimensional cube with movieclips, or hang photos on a wall that isn't displayed head-on, you should keep a firm grip on the notion of those perspective lines. By actually drawing them as temporary guides over your artwork, you'll find the new 3D tools a ton easier to work with.

Consider the real-world example of the art gallery shown in Figure 9-5. You're going to use this photo to get acquainted with the new tools, so let's put those perspective lines in place. Here's how.

1. Open the Exhibition01.fla file from the Exercise folder for this chapter. Note the already-imported photo, in a layer named background.

2. Create a new layer and name it perspective. Right-click (Ctrl-click) the new layer's name and select Guide from the context menu. This converts the layer into a guide layer, which means you can see its contents during authoring, but anything on this layer will disappear in the published SWF, which is exactly what you want.

3. Select the Line tool, and make sure the Object Drawing button is not selected in the Tools panel. Use the Line tool to draw some lines, like those in Figure 9-5, into the perspective layer. Start from the lower-right corner and follow the edge where the wall meets the floor. This may not be as easy as you think, because the pasteboard around the stage isn't big enough to accommodate such a long line.

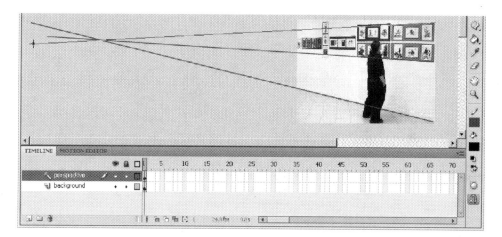

Figure 9-5. Use perspective lines in a guide layer to assist with the 3D drawing tools (photo by Yoana S. Bacheva from Satanasov exhibition).

When you find yourself in a tight spot like this, it helps to zoom the stage to a very small number, like 12%, and take the Flash application window out of a maximized view. Start your line on the right side, and then click and hold. While holding, literally drag the line out past the Flash application window, seemingly onto your desktop. In Figure 9-6, you can see the crosshairs cursor beyond the left edge of the application window. Just follow the perspective line from the photo to the left and slightly up, and you'll see it.

When you release the mouse, Flash will resize the pasteboard to fit the line, and you can use the Selection tool to refine its placement.

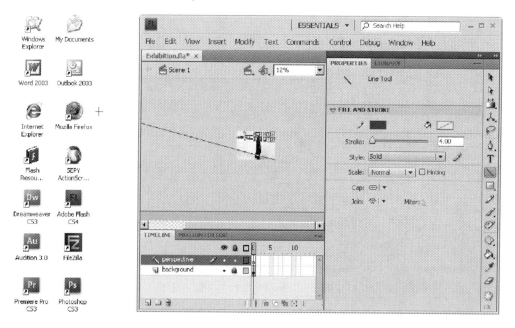

Figure 9-6. Depending on the reference photo, you may have to work a bit to draw your perspective lines.

4. Repeat this process with a few more lines, using the photo's wall hangings as a start, until you can pin down the vanishing point to the far left.

5. Save your file, because you're going to revisit it later in the chapter. You can compare your work with the completed Exhibition01.fla in the Complete folder, which shows the three lines already in place.

Now, let's have some fun with the 3D tools themselves.

Using the 3D tools

As we've mentioned, Flash CS4 provides two brand-new 3D tools: the 3D Rotation tool and the 3D Transformation tool.

The 3D Rotation tool

In terms of visual cool factor, the 3D Rotation tool is sure to please. This tool allows you to quickly and intuitively rotate a movieclip in 3D space. In previous versions of Flash, this was possible only with shapes, and even that technique required a bit of careful nudging with the Free Transform tool. You simply couldn't do this with a symbol. Now you can, and that means you can perform perspective transforms on complex artwork, imported photos, and yes, even video. Kind of makes the corners of the mouth go up, doesn't it?

To illustrate how groundbreaking this is, let's start with how it used to be.

Old-school 3D rotation

Prior to this release of Flash, 3D perspective was not exactly up there in the realm of "really easy to accomplish." You needed to actually draw in perspective by hand or use the Free Transform tool to simulate 3D rotation. Let's see how that technique works.

1. Create a new FLA file and select the Rectangle tool. Make sure the Object Drawing button is not selected, so that your shape is nothing more than a fill, with an optional stroke. Color settings don't matter. Draw a square approximately 300 × 300 pixels.

2. Once you've drawn your shape, double-click to select it, and then change to the Free Transform tool. You'll see a number of buttons appear in the options area of the Tools panel.

3. Click the Distort button, which lets you make perspective distortions by individually clicking and dragging each corner of your square. Go ahead and do precisely that. With a bit of practice, you can reshape the square to appear as if you're standing above it, looking slightly down on it, as shown in Figure 9-7.

4. Click away from the reshaped square to deselect it. Now double-click the shape to select it again. When you do—assuming that Free Transform is still your current tool—you'll notice that the shape's bounding box no longer follows the contours of the shape. That's to be expected, since the bounding box represents the full area required to contain the shape.

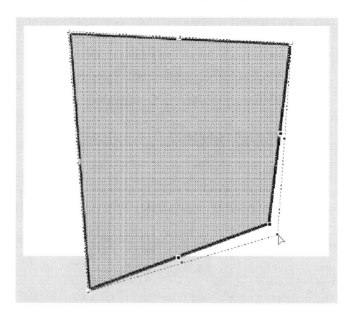

Figure 9-7. The Distort option of the Free Transform tool lets you simulate perspective with shapes.

At this point, if you hope to adjust your perspective distortion (see Figure 9-8), you'll find it much harder to accomplish with precision, simply because the bounding box no longer matches the corners or edges of the shape. Worse, you can't do a thing with imported photos, if that's your aim. Let's see the problem with photos.

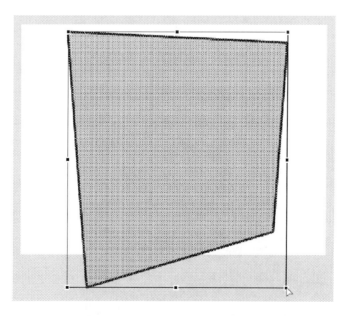

Figure 9-8. Adjusting already-distorted shapes quickly becomes a challenge.

5. Import one of the baby photos included in the Exercise folder for this chapter and set it as the bitmap fill for the reshaped square. Notice that the bitmap simply tiles inside the shape and doesn't "play along" with this distortion game in the least (see Figure 9-9). After all, this is a simulation of perspective, not the real thing.

> *If bitmap fills have you scratching your head, flip back to Chapter 2 for a quick refresher.*

Figure 9-9. Bitmaps are not affected by perspective distortion (photo by Dawn Stiller).

New 3D rotation

If you want to turn your world around—practically speaking, and in a good way—you'll need to step over to the 3D Rotation tool. This is where it gets really neat, folks.

1. Start a new Flash document and import another one of the baby photos to the stage.

2. Select the photo and convert it to a movieclip symbol.

Step 2—converting to a movieclip—is the deal maker. Without it, the 3D drawing tools are useless. They work with movieclips, period. Keep that in mind, whatever artwork you intend to spin around in 3D space. Fortunately for you, movieclips are a supremely useful symbol.

3. Select the 3D Rotation tool and click the movieclip. You'll see a somewhat complex looking bull's-eye.

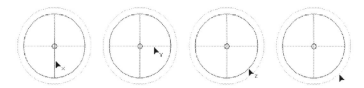

Figure 9-10. Four views of the same interactive bull's-eye, showing x-, y-, z-, and all-axis rotation

Figure 9-10 shows the same bull's-eye repeated four times, with the mouse cursor moving from area to area. Notice how the cursor changes. Each of those lines and circles has a meaning. Hover near the vertical red line (far left in the figure), and the cursor turns into a black arrow with an X next to it. This line controls the x-axis rotation, which you'll see in just a moment. Hover near the horizontal green line—the second bull's-eye in Figure 9-10—and you'll see the letter Y, which controls y-axis rotation. Hover near the inner large blue circle, and you'll see a Z, which controls the z axis. The outer orange circle (far right in the figure) isn't associated with a letter, because it affects all three axes at once. The tiny circle in the middle represents the 3D rotation center point, and it's basically the pivot for this sort of rotation.

4. To see what an x-axis rotation does, hover near the vertical red line, and then click and drag sideways, slowly back and forth. You'll see a pie-chart–like wedge appear inside the bull's-eye (see Figure 9-11), which gives you an idea of the current size of the angle. In the figure, the angle is approximately 45 degrees.

Figure 9-11.
A wedge shape tells you how far you're rotating.

5. To adjust y-axis rotation, hover near the horizontal green line, and then click and drag slowly up and down. For z-axis and all-axis rotation, click and drag in any direction you please.

The visual effect on the movieclip is easy to see. As shown in Figure 9-12, the rotations work as follows:

- X-axis rotation (left) moves like a head nodding "yes."

- Y-axis rotation (center) moves like a head shaking "no."

- Z-axis rotation (right) moves like a doorknob, which is effectively the same as rotating with the Free Transform tool.

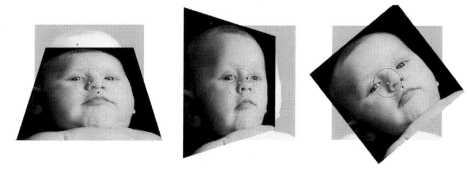

Figure 9-12. Three axes of rotation: x moves like a head nod, y moves like a head shake, and z moves like a doorknob (photo by Dawn Stiller).

6. Experiment with rotation, keeping an eye on the Transform panel (Window ➤ Transform). It's easy to get disoriented when rotating numerous axes at once—for example, by dragging the outer orange circle—or when rotating any particular axis after others are set to nonzero values. If dragging ever gets out of hand, click the Transform panel's Remove Transform button (see Figure 9-13). In fact, do that now to see the movieclip return to its default flat appearance.

7. Still in the Transform panel, scrub each of the hot text values in the 3D Rotation area. They provide an alternate way to rotate along the x, y, and z axes—with the added benefit that you can enter exact values by hand.

8. Save your file. If you like, compare it with 3DRotationBaby.fla in the Complete folder.

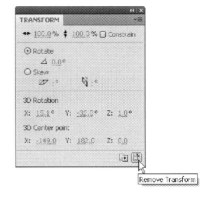

Figure 9-13. Use the Transform panel to reset 3D rotations.

Now that you understand rotation, it's time to learn how to position your object in Flash's 3D space. This sort of movement is called *translation*, and it features a tool all its own.

The 3D Translation tool

Because Flash is primarily a two-dimensional interface, the 3D Translation tool may not immediately make sense. Without the context of a vanishing point, it may seem like nothing more than another version of the Selection tool. It lets you move things, but the way it works is more restrictive than the Selection tool, which, by contrast, lets you simply click and drag. So what gives? To answer that question, let's take another visit to the exhibition gallery.

1. Open the Exhibition01.fla file you saved earlier in the chapter. Save it as Exhibition02.fla.

2. Create a new timeline layer named photo1. In this new layer, import one of the baby photos from this chapter's Exercise folder to the stage. Select the photo and convert it to a movieclip symbol. Use the Free Transform tool or the Transform panel to resize the photo to about 25% of its actual size (approximately 100 × 100 pixels).

> According to recommended best practices, you would normally import a photo that doesn't require such a change in scale, because even though it looks small in the SWF, the actual imported file is big, which adds to the SWF's file size. In this exercise, you're giving yourself leeway as you experiment.

3. At this point, it's time to make use of the perspective lines you drew earlier. Using the Selection tool, click the baby photo to select it. Twirl down the 3D Position and View area of the Property inspector, and note the Vanishing point values at the bottom of that area, next to a Reset button, as shown in Figure 9-14.

4, Until you adjust it otherwise, the vanishing point is centered on the stage. Click and scrub the X value slowly to see a set of crosshairs appear over the photo.

The crosshairs represent the official vanishing point Flash uses to position 3D objects. When your goal involves matching up assets to actual background images, you'll find that helps to match Flash's vanishing point with the real-world vanishing point in your reference artwork. Let's do it.

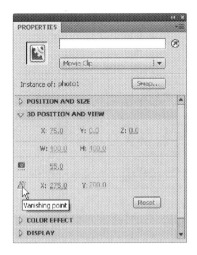

Figure 9-14. The vanishing point can be adjusted in the Property inspector.

5. Scrub the X value far to the left, so that the horizontal portion of the crosshairs lines up with the point where your perspective lines overlap. When you're satisfied, do the same with the Y value to lift it a bit higher (see Figure 9-15).

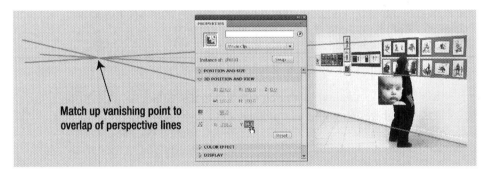

Figure 9-15. The vanishing point can be anywhere on the stage or the pasteboard (photos by Yoana S. Bacheva and Dawn Stiller).

6. Select the 3D Translation tool. You'll see a pair of arrows arranged in an L shape.

Figure 9-16. Four views of the same interactive L shape, showing x-, y-, and z-axis position

Figure 9-16 shows the same set of arrows repeated four times, with the mouse cursor moving from area to area, changing as it does. The arrows and the heavy dot each has its own meaning. Hover near the horizontal red line (far left in the figure) and the cursor turns into a black arrow with an X next to it. This arrow controls the x-axis position. Hover near the vertical green line and you'll see the letter Y, which controls the y-axis position. You'll use this in just a moment.

The heavy dot takes a bit more dexterity. Hover in the center of the dot, and you'll see a Z, which controls movement along the z axis. Hover near the edge of the dot, and you won't see any letters. Why? Dragging at this point lets you reposition the 3D center point for this object, which affects how translation is applied (the center point's position isn't nearly as obvious with translation as it is with rotation).

7. Hover near the green y-axis arrow, and then click and drag down until the baby photo appears to rest on the perspective line that runs along where the floor meets the wall.

8. Use the Transform panel to scrub the Y value in the 3D Rotation area until the bottom edge of the baby photo matches up to the perspective line (see Figure 9-17). You can alternatively use the 3D Rotation tool to accomplish the same task, but the Transform panel gives you a bit better control. If you're surprised at how much the image gets stretched, don't worry. We'll show you how to fix that later in the chapter. The stretch is due to the extreme "distance" of the vanishing point, way off to the side.

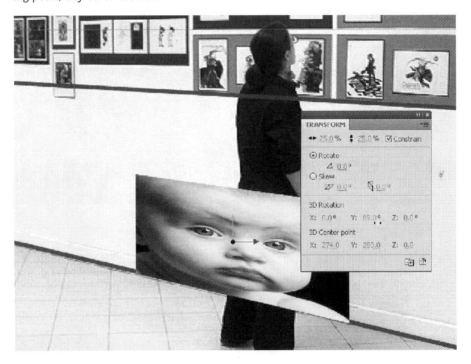

Figure 9-17. Use the Transform panel for finer rotation control.

9. Save your file, so that you can easily revert back to your current settings. Let's take a quick detour, which will illustrate why it's so useful to match up Flash's vanishing point with the actual vanishing point of your reference artwork.

10. Using the Transform panel, change the 3D Rotation's Y value back to 0. In the Property inspector, click the Reset button in the 3D Position and View area. This button resets the vanishing point to the center of the stage, which happens to match the center of the baby's face.

11. Back in the Transform panel, scrub the Y value in the 3D Rotation area until the photo's bottom edge once again matches the perspective line. Note that the photo isn't nearly as stretched as before, which appears to be a good thing. Not in the long run, partner, as you're about to discover.

12. Use the 3D Translation tool to move the photo up to the topmost perspective line. Aha! The top edge of the baby photo no longer matches the perspective of the gallery image (see Figure 9-18). Of course, the virtual and actual vanishing points no longer correspond, which explains why this happens.

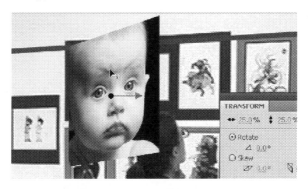

Figure 9-18. The top edge of the photo no longer matches the perspective line.

OK, the detour is over. If you want to produce cubist, Picasso-like content—and there's truly nothing wrong with that—feel free to experiment with purposefully mismatched vanishing points. There's some neat creative potential in that. But for now, we'll stick to photo-realism,

13. Select File ➤ Revert to undo the changes you made during the detour. You'll be prompted with a dialog box; click the Revert button to confirm your intention.

14. At this point, Flash's vanishing point once again matches the vanishing point depicted by the gallery image. To prove it, use the 3D Translation tool to move the baby photo up to the top-most perspective line. This time, it fits perfectly (see Figure 9-19).

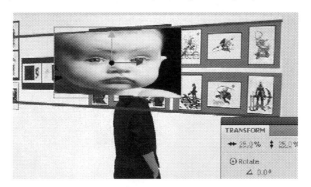

Figure 9-19. When vanishing points correspond, objects seem to properly inhabit 3D space.

To understand X and Z movement—at least, in the present scenario—think of these gallery perspective lines in terms of the ones shown in Figure 9-4 for the cube. In that earlier figure, the cube seems to be moving out of the paper toward you, because its vanishing point is relatively close to the cube.

In that case, or when the vanishing point is centered on the stage, Z movement causes the object to get bigger or smaller as it moves "out" or "in." The apparent scaling is a perspective effect that happens because the z axis is pointing at you. In this case, the z axis is pointing far over your right shoulder. It's as if you're looking at that cube from the side. Why? Because the vanishing point is miles away to the left. Let's illustrate this.

15. Hover over the heavy dot until you see the letter Z appear in the cursor. Slowly drag up and down. The baby photo still changes scale, but more important, it moves sideways, zooming along the floorboards. That's because the "front" of the z axis is pointing toward the right, and the back is pointing toward the vanishing point at left.

16. Now hover over the horizontal red line until you see the cursor acquire an X. Click and drag slowly left and right. At first, the movement might look similar to Z movement, but there's an important difference. Yes, there is some left-and-right movement, but because of the extreme-left position of the vanishing point, the baby photo is alternately stepping "into the room" and "into the wall," as depicted in Figure 9-20.

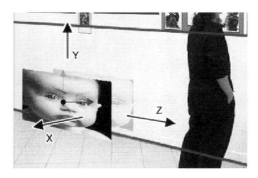

Figure 9-20. The orientation of the x, y, and z axes depends on the position of the vanishing point.

17. Save your file, and then test your movie to verify that the perspective lines disappear in the SWF (remember, they're drawn in a guide layer). If you like, compare your work with Exhibition02.fla in the Complete folder.

Strategies for positioning content in 3D space

The orientation of movement along any of the three axes (x, y, and z) depends entirely on the location of the vanishing point. When the vanishing point is centered on the stage, the z axis is pointing nearly straight at you. This means z-axis movement will increase and decrease the size of the object, as it apparently moves closer and farther from you. As illustrated in the previous exercise, this orientation can change.

Without ActionScript, it isn't possible to point the x or y axis directly at you, but you can approximate these orientations by setting a very high number, such as 10000, for the X and Y values in the Vanishing point setting in the Property inspector's 3D Position and View area. Extreme positions for the vanishing point result in the following orientations:

- **Significantly high or low X value**: Z movement becomes horizontal.

- **Significantly high or low Y value**: Z movement becomes vertical.

- **Significantly high or low X and Y values**: Z movement becomes diagonal.

Fiddle enough with these settings, and you'll get seasick! Just remember that you can always start from scratch very easily by selecting your movieclip and clicking the Reset button in the Property inspector and the Remove Transform button in the Transform panel. In spite of the utility of this tip, you can quickly find yourself in a pickle when positioning numerous objects—not just one—in the 3D space of the stage. We hope the following suggestions make your journey a bit easier.

Share 3D rotation and translation settings

Once you've expended the effort to position a single object, there's no reason to let that effort go to waste. By sharing 3D rotation and translation settings among your assets, you can reuse your configuration as often as you like. This will speed up your workflow. Here's how:

1. Open your Exhibition02.fla file and resave it as Exhibition03.fla. Use the Transform panel to carefully reduce the width of the baby photo until it looks like a reasonable width for its position on the wall.

2. Create two new timeline layers named photo2 and photo3.

3. With the Selection tool, select the baby photo in the photo1 layer and copy it to the clipboard. Paste the photo into layers photo2 and photo3 with Edit ➤ Paste in Place. Visually, nothing has changed on the stage, but now you have three movieclip symbols that all speak the same 3D rotation and translation language.

4. Select File ➤ Import to Library and import two additional baby photos.

5. In the Library panel, right-click (Ctrl-click) the photo1 movieclip and choose Duplicate from the context menu. In the Duplicate Symbol dialog box, give the new symbol the name photo2, and then click the OK button. Repeat this step to create a second duplicate and name it photo3.

6. Still in the Library panel, double-click the photo2 movieclip to enter its timeline. Select the imported JPG and click the Swap button in the Property inspector. In the Swap Bitmap dialog box, select one of the other babies, and then click OK. Repeat this step with photo3 and choose the remaining baby JPG.

7. Select Edit ➤ Edit Document to return to the main timeline.

8. Use the 3D Translation tool to adjust the z axis of each photo. Arrange the photos by spacing them apart along the baseboard of the gallery. All three still show the same baby. You'll change that in just a moment.

9. Click the pasteboard area to deselect everything. Select the 3D Translation tool, and then, holding the Shift key, click each photo in turn. This selects all three photos, but only the last one you click will show the 3D Translation tool's L-shaped arrows. Use the y axis to move all three photos slowly up the wall. Click the pasteboard area again to deselect everything.

10. Using the Selection tool, click one of the repositioned baby photos. Click the Swap button in the Property inspector. In the Swap Symbol dialog box, choose one of the other movieclips, and then click OK. Do the same for one of the other duplicates.

Without much effort at all, you've positioned three movieclips in 3D space (see Figure 9-21).

Figure 9-21. Sharing rotation and translation settings speeds up your workflow (photos by Yoana S. Bacheva and Dawn Stiller).

Use the 3D center point to your advantage

Up to this point in the chapter, we haven't properly illustrated what the 3D center point does. Let's remedy that by showing you how to animate a pair of swinging doors. Ready to make your grand entrance?

1. Open the `GrandEntrance.fla` file from the Exercise folder for this chapter. You'll see four layers in the main timeline—background, door right, door left, and audio—and a handful of items in the library.

2. Select the 3D Rotation Tool and click the movieclip that contains the left door of the stone archway. Hover over the center of the bull's-eye, so that no letters show in the cursor, and drag the bull's-eye—or use the Transform panel—to move the 3D center point to the upper-left corner of the door, as shown in Figure 9-22.

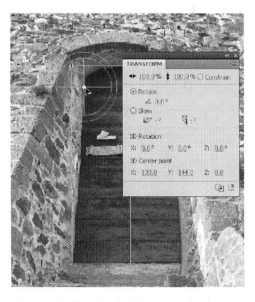

Figure 9-22. Changing the 3D center point alters where an object rotates (photo by Rodolfo Belloli).

Why the left side? Because this door naturally swings on its hinges, and the 3D center point is roughly analogous to a hinge. Why the top, rather than the bottom? That's just an arbitrary choice. Given the angle from which this photo was taken, the top of the door appears slightly narrower than the bottom. In this case, hinging the top improves the illusion, because more of the door gets hidden in the dark when the doors open. You'll see this shortly.

3. Click the movieclip that contains the right-hand door. Reposition this movieclip's 3D center point in the upper right. This time, the hinge is on the other side, which makes sense. If you leave the 3D center point at its default value for each movie clip, the doors will spin like ballerinas.

4. With the right door still selected, use the Property inspector to adjust the vanishing point so that its crosshairs fall vertically between the two doors and horizontally between the doors and the highest step.

5. In the timeline, right-click (Ctrl-click) frame 1 of the door left layer and select Create Motion Tween. This converts the layer to a tween layer, but it's not quite enough.

6. Right-click (Ctrl-click) the door left layer again and select 3D Tween, which puts a check mark in that choice whenever you open the context menu again. (You can remove the check mark if you ever change your mind.)

7. Repeat steps 5 and 6 for the door right layer.

8. Drag the playhead to frame 30, where the tween layers end. Select the left door's movieclip and use the 3D Rotation tool or the Transform panel to "swing the door in" about 90 degrees (see Figure 9-23). Do the same thing for the right door.

Figure 9-23. Swinging the door inward toward 90 degrees

9. To improve the illusion, darken the doors while they're swinging in. Still at frame 30, use the Selection tool to select each door in turn. In the Property inspector, choose Brightness from the Style drop-down list of the Color Effect area and set its value to -60%.

10. To add some polish, select frame 1 in the audio layer and use the Property inspector's Sound area to add the already-imported door-open.wav sound from the Library to this frame.

11. Using the Selection tool, click into frame 60 of each layer and press the F5 key to pad out the frame span of each layer. This allows the audio to fully play out, without looping too early, when you test your movie.

12. Select Control ➤ Test Movie to see the SWF. Close the SWF and compare your work with the finished version of GrandEntrance.fla in this chapter's Complete folder.

Be aware of depth limitations

As cool as the 3D tools are, they do have a limitation in terms of how three-dimensional depth (generally the z axis) corresponds to the stacking order of your layers, and even the stacking order of numerous symbols inside a single layer. In short, stacking order overrides 3D depth. If you drag the layer of one 3D movieclip above the layer of another 3D movieclip, the movieclip on the higher layer will always appear on top, no matter how you adjust its z index.

There are pros and cons to everything, and the pro here is that layers and in-layer symbol stacking continue to operate the way they always have. For longtime Flash users, this will feel familiar and comfortable. If you're new to Flash, this behavior may throw you for a loop, but you can work around it. The challenge arises when you want to perform a 3D tween that moves one object in front of another, when its original position was behind (and therefore obscured). Let's look at a hands-on example.

1. Open the AirheadMail.fla file from the Exercise folder for this chapter. You'll see an envelope with a couple postage stamps above it, one stacked behind the other, as shown in Figure 9-24. There's another stamp in a hidden layer behind the envelope, but we'll get into that in a moment. Just be aware that both of the visible stamps are located in the same timeline layer.

Figure 9-24. Depth is determined more by layer and stacking order than z index (envelope photo by Cris DeRaud).

2. Select the 3D Translation tool and click the unobscured stamp (the one on top) to select it. Adjust its z index to scale the stamp smaller and larger.

In terms of 3D space, a higher z-index value seems to "push the stamp away," making it smaller. No matter how far you "push," you'll find that you cannot move the upper stamp behind the lower one. To do that, you'll have to use the old-fashioned approach.

3. Right-click (Ctrl-click) the upper stamp and select Arrange ➤ Send Backward (or Send to Back). You'll see the upper stamp pop behind its partner.

4. Unhide the bottom timeline layer (named stamp, just like the top timeline layer). This reveals a third stamp partially obscured by the envelope.

5. Using the 3D Translation tool again, adjust the z index of either stamp in the upper stamp layer. As in step 2, nothing you do moves either stamp behind the envelope or the stamp in the bottom stamp layer.

6. To bring the lowest stamp above the other two, you'll need to move its layer. Click the lower stamp layer and drag it above the other stamp layer, as shown in Figure 9-25.

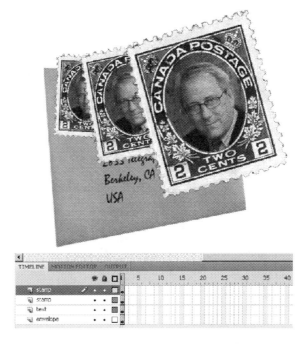

Figure 9-25. Drag layers to move lower content above higher content.

This is all well and good for still compositions, but how does it work for animation? You can't very well drag layers around in the middle of a tween. The trick is to split your animation over two layers, as shown in Figure 9-26. Check out AirheadMailAnimated.fla in this chapter's Complete folder to see the animation in action.

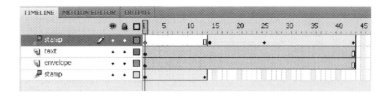

Figure 9-26. Splitting an animation between separate layers

In what appears to be one smooth motion, the stamp emerges from behind the envelope, flies in front of it, and settles into place for mailing. In actuality, the magic happens at frame 14, where the movieclip abruptly ends in the lower stamp layer and reappears in the upper stamp layer to continue its above-the-envelope movement.

Your turn: Simulate a photo cube

We began the theory part of this chapter with a cube and thought it fitting to come to a close with the same shape. (We wanted so badly to describe that as "coming full circle," but it felt like we were mixing metaphors!) For this final exercise, we're going to show you how to build a box out of a series of square movieclips. What you do with the box is up to you. We certainly hope it will spark some inspiration. In any case, we're pretty confident you'll find it motivating that you can—sort of—rotate the thing after it's built.

Ready to be there or be square? Let's jump in:

1. Open 3DCubeBaby.fla from the Chapter 9 Exercise folder. We've done the tedious part for you. The library contains five imported JPGs, already converted to movieclip symbols. Pick one of them and drag it to the stage. Use the Align panel to center it horizontally and vertically.

2. Copy the movieclip to the clipboard and paste it in place four times.

Now you have five copies of the same movieclip stacked on top of each other in the same layer. Why? Because we're about to make like Henry Ford and run an assembly line. This approach will make things come together more quickly, and the precision of doing the next few steps "by the numbers" will help considerably.

3. Select the top movieclip and use the Transform panel to change the 3D Rotation area's Z value to 90. Now scrub the Y rotation value until it hits 90. This "stands up" the top movieclip and faces it west. In the Property inspector's 3D Position and View area, scrub the X value down to 75 (that's 200 pixels to the left, or half the movieclip's width).

You're going to repeat this process—with different values—for the next three movieclips.

4. Select the next movieclip and configure it like this:
   - 3D Rotation Z: –90
   - 3D Rotation Y: –90
   - 3D Position X: 475

This movieclip now faces east and has moved half its width to the right.

5. Select the next movieclip and configure it like this:
   - 3D Rotation Z: –180
   - 3D Rotation X: –90
   - 3D Position Y: 0

This movieclip now faces north (yes, this sounds like an REM song) and has moved half its height to the top.

437

6. Select the next movieclip and configure it like this:

- 3D Rotation Z: **0** (no change)
- 3D Rotation X: **90**
- 3D Position Y: **400**

This movieclip now faces south and has moved half its height to the bottom.

At this point, you're essentially looking down into the cube (see Figure 9-27). Although she may not appear to be, the baby looking straight up at you is already halfway up the cube. The reason the depth looks wrong is because of the stacking order of these movieclips.

Figure 9-27. One result of rotating and translating by the numbers

7. Right-click (Ctrl-click) the right (east) movieclip and select Arrange ➤ Bring to Front. Do the same thing to these other movieclips in the following order: bottom (south), left (west), and finally center.

Why restack them in that particular order? Because we're about to tilt the box forward, which means we'll be looking at what's currently the south wall. The movieclip currently on top of the stack—the center baby looking straight at you—needs to be moved "toward you" first, though.

8. Select the topmost movieclip and set its 3D Position Z value to -200.

9. Click frame 1 in the timeline to select all the 3D objects simultaneously. With all of the movieclips selected, click the one showing (this puts the Property inspector where you want it) and change the 3D Position Z value to 0. This moves the whole collection "back" toward the stage.

10. In the Transform panel, change the 3D Rotation X value to -46 and the 3D Rotation Y value to -28.

11. In the Property inspector, just above the Vanishing point values, you'll see a setting we haven't mentioned yet. It has a camera icon, and if you hover over that, you'll get a tooltip that says Perspective angle. Scrub the Perspective angle value from its default 55 down to 38. See how that relaxes the slight fish-eye lens effect?

12. Change the 3D Rotation Z value to -20 to straighten out your box.

13. Change the movieclips on the walls as you please by using the Swap button, as you did in the "Share 3D rotation and translation settings" section. You'll get something like the cube shown in Figure 9-28.

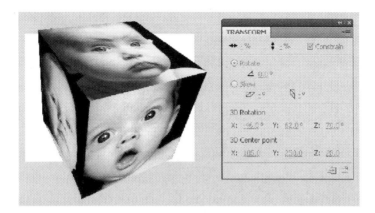

Figure 9-28. A way-too-cute photo cube

Whatever angle you approach it from, 3D manipulation in Flash is a ton of fun! While you still have your 3DCubeBaby.fla file open, we encourage you to keep experimenting. With all the movieclips selected, use the 3D Rotation tool to see what happens when you spin that cube all the way around (you'll see the stacking order limitation again).

What happens if you scrub Perspective angle all the way down to 1? How about over a 100? How does the Vanishing point setting affect things? Can you convert the selected movieclips—all five of them—into a new movieclip? (Hint: Absolutely!) When you do, can you arrange two or more movieclips of the completed box on the stage? (You betcha.)

We could keep going, but we hope you're excited enough to take it from here.

What you have learned

In this chapter, you learned the following:

- The rudiments of perspective drawing, including the concept of the vanishing point
- How to use the 3D Rotation and 3D Translation tools
- How to use the Property inspector and Transform panel in conjunction with the 3D tools
- Some workflow tips on arranging objects in Flash 3D space

One of the authors has been fond of anything related to 3D for years. In fact, he keeps a pair of red-and-blue anaglyph glasses on top of his monitor—you know, for watching those cheesy 1950s science fiction movies in 3D. Speaking of movies, sci-fi or otherwise, Flash is pretty hip on cinema too. In fact, one of the hottest features of Flash in the last couple years is its video capabilities, which now include high-definition, full-screen support. Ready to jam like Cecil B. DeMille? You have but to turn the page.

Chapter 10

VIDEO

When Macromedia, now Adobe, launched Flash 8 Professional and included the Flash video (FLV) encoder and playback component with the application, a valid argument could be made that this marked the final acceptance of Flash as a viable web video medium. As more and more sites started featuring Flash video, there was a corresponding decline in the number of sites that used the web video solutions provided by QuickTime, Windows Media, and Real Player. By that time, Flash Player could be found on more than 90% of all computers on the planet.

Flash video's success actually has had more to do with cunning than with market acceptance. Most people didn't see Flash as a media player. They thought of it as being this "cute thing" that played animations. When they suddenly realized they could stream audio (Chapter 5) and video through Flash Player without excessive wait times or downloading an additional plug-in, it was basically "game-set-match" for the others.

The latest version of Flash firmly entrenches video into the application. In early 2008, Flash Player 9 was updated to allow the inclusion of high-definition (HD) video, and this feature is now in Flash CS4. You also get a totally "rejigged" encoder, now called Adobe Media Encoder. With Flash CS4, you have been handed a full video encoding and playback suite of tools that makes it dead simple to add video to your Flash projects.

Here's what we'll cover in this chapter:

- Streaming video
- Encoding an FLV
- Playing an FLV in Flash
- Playing full-screen video
- Adding captions to Flash video
- Adding filters and blend effects to video

The following files are used in this chapter (located in the Chapter10/ExerciseFiles_Ch10/Exercise/ folder):

- Rabbit.mov
- Rabbit.flv
- ThroughADoor.flv
- Vultures.mp4
- Controls.fla
- Captions.flv
- captionsFLV.xml
- Alpha.mov
- AlphaEx.fla

- DisgruntledDan.flv
- FullToggle.fla
- Apparition.flv
- RainFall.fla
- Rain.flv
- BlobEffect.fla
- CuePoints.xml
- VideoJam.fla

The source files are available online from either of the following sites:

- http://www.FoundationFlashCS4.com
- http://www.friendsofED.com/download.html?isbn=9781430210931

> The authors would like to thank William Hanna, Dean of the School of Media Studies, at the Humber Institute of Technology and Advanced Learning in Toronto, and Robert O'Meara, a faculty member with the Film and Television Arts program at Humber, for permission to use many of the videos in this chapter. The videos were produced by students of Humber's Interactive Multimedia program and Film and Television program.

Video on the Web

Before we turn you loose with creating and playing Flash video, it is critically important that you understand how it gets from the server to the user's machine.

The Flash video format uses the .flv or .f4v extension. It plays only in Flash, Adobe Bridge, or Adobe Media Player (a free AIR application available from http://www.adobe.com/products/mediaplayer/). The key thing about this format is that the data is sent to the user's computer from the server, and then it is played by Flash Player. To help you understand this process, let's go visit the Hoover Dam in the United States.

The Hoover Dam was built in the 1930s to control the Colorado River. When the dam was completed, the water behind it backed up to form Lake Mead. Now the water flows along the Colorado River into Lake Mead, and the dam releases that water, in a controlled manner, back into the Colorado River. That means if the water rushes to the dam and overwhelms it, or the dam operator releases too much water, the people downstream from the dam are in for a really bad day.

Streaming video is no different from the water flow to the Hoover Dam and beyond (see Figure 10-1). The data in the FLV is sent, at a data rate established when the video was encoded, from the server to Flash Player. The video is then held in a buffer and released, in a controlled manner, by Flash Player to the browser. If the flow is too fast—the data rate is too high for the connection—the browser is overwhelmed, and the result is video that jerkily stops and starts. This is due to the buffer constantly emptying and having to be refilled. In many respects, your job is no different from that of the crew that manages the flow of water from the buffer behind the Hoover Dam back into the Colorado River. When you create the FLV, the decisions you make will determine whether or not your users are in for a really bad experience.

Figure 10-1. When it comes to Flash video, you control the Hoover Dam.

Video formats

The first step in the process of creating the FLV file that will be used in the Flash movie is to convert an existing video to the FLV format. This means you will be working with digital videos that use the following formats:

- **AVI (Audio Video Interleave)**: A Windows format that supports a number of compression schemes but also allows for video without any compression
- **DV**: The format used when video moves directly from a video camera to the computer
- **MPG/MPEG (Moving Pictures Experts Group)**: A lossy standard for video that is quite similar to the lossy JPG/JPEG standard for still images
- **MOV**: The QuickTime format

443

For those of you wondering about the WMV (Windows Media Video) format, yes, you can encode it. However, the encoding can be done only on a PC. This book is somewhat platform-agnostic, which explains why WMV didn't make the video format list here.

Do yourself and your users a favor, and check out the compressor used to create the video. If a lossy compressor was used, you are going to have a serious quality issue. The compressors used to create FLV files are also lossy, meaning you will be compressing an already-compressed video.

Both the QuickTime player and Windows Media Player show you compressor information. In the QuickTime player, select Window ➤ Show Info. You will see a dialog box with movie information, including the compressor used, as shown in Figure 10-2.

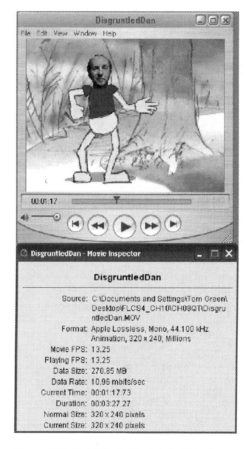

Figure 10-2. QuickTime's Movie info dialog box shows that the Apple Lossless animation compressor was used for the DisgruntedDan video.

Windows video files playing through the Windows Media Player are a bit different. Open a file in the Media Player, right-click the file's name, and select Properties from the context menu. You will see the Properties dialog box, which identifies the video codec used, as shown in Figure 10-3.

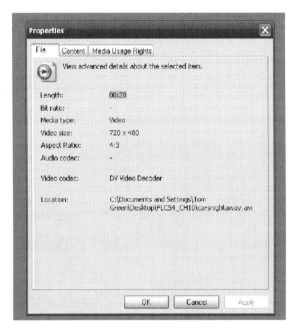

Figure 10-3. The Windows Media Player Properties dialog box indicates the codec used.

Now that you know which file formats you can use, you also need to know that three output formats are available to you:

- **FLV**: This is the common format used on the Web, which can be played by Flash Player 6 and higher.

- **F4V**: This is the new kid on the block and was primarily developed to manage HD files that will need to be converted to a format that is used by Flash Player 9,0,115,0 or higher. Think of this as being an MP4 video for Flash, and you will be on the right track.

- **H.264**: This is a common format that you might know better as MPEG-4 or MP4. It is an international standard (MPEG4 H.264) developed by the Moving Pictures Expert Group (MPEG) and is also recognized by the International Standardization Organization (ISO).

From a Flash designer's perspective, the H.264 format has some rather profound implications. The biggest one is that video, for all intents and purposes, has become untethered—it is not device-dependent. The file handed to you by your video producer can just as easily be played on a website as it can on an iPod, Sony's PlayStation Portable, or high-definition television (HDTV). It also means that, thanks to the addition of hardware acceleration and multithreading support to Flash Player, you can play back video at any resolution and bitrate, including the full HD 1080p resolution you can watch on HDTV.

Encoding an FLV

Surprisingly, the first step in the conversion process has absolutely nothing to do with Flash. Instead, open the video in your player of choice and watch the video twice. The first time is to get the entertainment/coolness factor out of your system. The second time you watch it, ask yourself a few questions:

- Is there a lot of movement in this video?
- Is the audio of major importance?
- Is there a lot of color in the piece?
- Is the video in focus, or are there areas where the image becomes pixelated?

The answers to these questions will determine your approach to encoding the video.

To demonstrate encoding, we will use the Rabbit.mov file, located in this chapter's Exercise folder. Go ahead and open this file in QuickTime, and watch it twice.

Yes, the file is huge: just over 70MB. There is a reason. When creating Flash video, you need every bit of information contained in the video when you do the conversion. Uncompressed video is about as big as it gets. When you finish converting the video into an FLV, you will be in for a rather pleasant surprise.

Using the Adobe Media Encoder

To encode video, you use the Adobe Media Encoder. This used to be known as the Adobe Flash Video Encoder. The name change is deliberate. Adobe came to the conclusion that the Flash brand name was being attached to a lot of stuff, and there was understandable concern that the brand was becoming diluted. The release of Creative Suite 4 starts the process of Adobe's refocusing of the Flash brand. If you have used Flash to encode video in previous iterations of the application, you will find that things have really changed.

To begin, open the Adobe Media Encoder, found in C:\Program Files\Adobe\Adobe Media Encoder CS4 on a PC or Macintosh HD\Applications\Adobe Media Encoder CS4 on a Mac. Then drag a copy of the Rabbit.mov file into the render queue, as shown in Figure 10-4. Alternatively, you could click the Add button or select File ➤ Add and, using the Open dialog box, navigate to your Exercise folder for this chapter, select the video, and click the Open button to add the video to the queue.

The drop-down lists in the Format and Preset areas actually aren't as complicated as they may first appear. The Format drop-down list offers the format choices FLV/F4V and H.264. The Preset list includes presets for a variety of situations and formats. In order to keep this chapter manageable, we aren't going to go deep into the choices and formats. Instead, let's just create a simple FLV file that will allow you to explore this application.

Click the Preset drop-down arrow and select Edit Export Settings at the bottom of the menu. This will open the Export Settings window, as shown in Figure 10-5. At the left is a preview area. The area underneath the video preview is where cue points can be added. We'll talk about cue points later in this chapter. The right side of the window consists of a series of tabs that allow you to choose a preset encoding profile, select a filter, choose an output format, set the video compression, and set the audio compression.

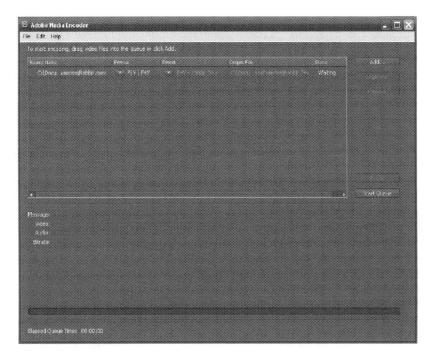

Figure 10-4. A file is in the render queue waiting to be encoded.

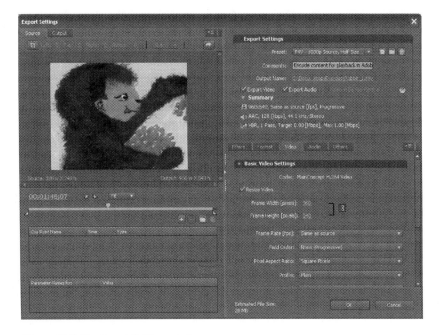

Figure 10-5. The Export Settings window

If you find all of these settings to be a bit too much, click the Simple Mode *button. It is the circle with two arrows just under the* Output Name *area on the right side of the* Edit Export Settings *window. Click it, and a lot of the options will disappear. Click the button again to return to Advanced Mode.*

The authors are not huge fans of the encoding presets in the Preset drop-down list. The problems with the presets are that they assume the lowest common denominator, tend to be wrong, and result in files that are unnecessarily large. For example, many of the presets have the audio track encoded to stereo, which as we explain later, usually just increases the file size and bandwidth demand, without adding any quality to the audio. Making your own choices for the encoding, rather than using presets, puts you in control of the process and allows you to produce files that meet your specific design needs, instead of satisfying a broad, homogenous audience.

Previewing and trimming video

Under the preview area is the current time indicator. It displays time in the format *hours:minutes: seconds:milliseconds*. The triangle at the top of the line is the *jog controller*. If you drag it back and forth, the video will follow along.

Underneath the jog controller are two other triangles. The one on the left is the In point, and the one on the right is the Out point. You can use these to trim the video. For example, assume there are 2 seconds of black screen and no audio at the end of the video. If you drag the Out point to the start of the stuff you don't need, it will be removed when you create the FLV.

Here's a neat little trick that can help with setting In and Out points. The preview controls are very precise, and reaching an exact point in time can be an exercise in tedium. Assume you want the current video to last 4 minutes and 14 seconds instead of 04:14:53. *Drag the playhead slider rightward to the end of the video. Press and hold the left arrow key. When the key is down, the milliseconds measure will reduce. When you are close to the* 000 *milliseconds point, release the key, and then click the Out point slider. The video will now have an Out point at that precise point in time.*

Video settings

On the right side of the Export Settings window, click in the Format tab and click the FLV radio button. Then click the Video tab to open the Basic Video Settings area, as shown in Figure 10-6. This is where you set the all-important video data rate.

If you want to change the name of the video, double-click the Output Name *on the right side of the* Export Settings *window to open the* Save As *dialog box. All this does is save the file name. It does not create the FLV.*

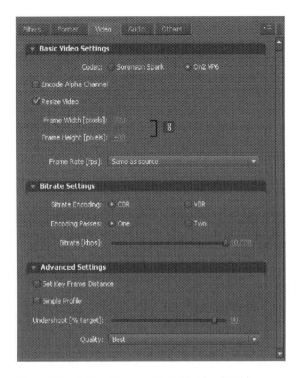

Figure 10-6. Setting the encoding values for the video portion of the movie

The various areas of the Video pane are as follows:

- Codec: The job of the *codec* (short for COmpressor/DECompressor or enCOder/DECoder) is to reduce the data rate while maintaining image quality. In simple terms, there are two types of codecs: lossy and lossless. Lossless codecs, like QuickTime's Animation codec, add minimal compression to preserve data, which explains why these files are massive and inappropriate for web playback. The two codecs that are available for your selection here—Sorenson Spark and On2 VP6—are lossy. They preserve playback quality while tossing out a ton of information, which explains how a 1MB video file becomes an 800KB FLV or F4V file. Note that If your target is Flash Player 7 or lower, your only choice is the Sorenson Spark codec. For our example, select On2 VP6.

- Encode Alpha Channel: If your video contains an alpha channel, select this. Alpha channel video can only be encoded using the On2 VP6 codec. For our example, this option should not be selected.

- Resize Video: If this is selected, deselect it. This is not the place to resize video. If you really need to resize a video, do it in Adobe Premiere, After Effects, Final Cut Pro, or another video-editing application.

> *If you need to resize a video, be sure to maintain the video's aspect ratio. When digital video is created for your television, it is created at a 4:3 ratio. This ratio is called the video's* aspect ratio *and fits most computer monitors. Other common examples would be widescreen television video, which has an aspect ratio of 6:5, and HDTV, which uses a 16:9 aspect ratio.*
>
> *For example, the video you are encoding has a physical size of 320 pixels wide by 240 pixels high. The width is easily divisible by 4, and the height is divisible by 3. By maintaining the aspect ratio, you avoid introducing artifacts (blocky shapes and other nastiness) into the video when it is resized.*
>
> *While we are on the subject of resizing video, never increase the physical size of the video. If you need to change the size, use this area to reduce, not increase, the width and height values. Increasing the physical dimensions of the video from 320 X 240 to 640 X 480 will only make the pixels larger, just as it does in Photoshop and Fireworks when you zoom in on an image. The result is pixelated video, and it will also place an increasing strain on the bandwidth, or flow of data into Flash Player.*
>
> *In spite of our having said to never increase the size of a video, Flash Player 9,0,115,0 (and higher) now permits full-screen video playback. We'll review this feature later in the chapter. It changes video size in an exception-to-the-rules way.*

- **Frame Rate [fps]:** This is how fast a video plays, measured in frames per second (fps). If you are unsure of which frame rate to use, a good rule of thumb is to choose a rate that is half that of the original file. If the original was prepared using the NTSC standard of 29.97 fps (close enough to 30), select 15 fps. If the PAL standard was used (25 fps), rates of 12 or 15 fps are acceptable. Of course, with the improvements to Flash Player, the industry is steadily moving toward 24 fps. For this example, set Frame Rate to 15.

- **Bitrate Encoding:** Your choices are CBR (for Constant Bitrate) and VBR (for Variable Bitrate). If you are streaming video through Flash Media Server 3 or using the Flash Video Streaming Service, choose CBR which, as the name implies, provides a level bitrate. Choose VBR if you are intending to use a web server making standard HTTP requests. For this example select VBR.

- **Encoding Passes:** One pass means the video analysis and encoding are done at the same time. Two passes means the encoder analyzes the video in the first pass looking for major changes, and the second pass encodes the video to accommodate those changes. So what's the difference? It's this: two-pass encoding is the best for videos with numerous bitrate changes. For example, you could have a video with a narrator who stays put for the first few seconds of the video and, when he finishes, race cars go roaring by. The narration doesn't require much to play, but the cars zipping by will require a higher bitrate to display accurately. Encoding in two passes allows the bitrate savings at the start of the video to be passed on to the action sequence. So, Two is the right choice for our example.

- **Bitrate [kbps]:** This slider sets the bitrate for the video portion of the encoding process in kilobits per second (kbps). Be very careful when choosing a Bitrate setting. For example, don't think you can supersize the quality and set the data rate to, say, the maximum of 10,000 kbps. Do that, and you can guarantee that residents downstream from the Hoover Dam are in for a day that involves scuba gear. The data rate for an FLV is the sum of the audio and the video data rates. So what should you choose? Until you become comfortable with creating FLV files, consider a combined audio and video data rate of around 350 kbps as being a fair target. For the example, use 300 kbps.

- Set Key Frame Distance: This is in the Advanced area for a reason. Unless you have mastered video, it is best to let the software do the work, and leave this option unselected.

- Key frame interval: Enter a value here, and the Key frame placement selection will change to Custom. Remember that first question we asked you to consider at the start of the chapter: is there a lot of movement? The answer determines key frame placement. If you are recording paint drying, having a key frame every 300 frames of the video would work. If you are encoding a video of a Formula One race from trackside, you will want the key frames to be a lot closer to each other, such as every 30 frames or so.

After you've set the video values, click the Audio tab, not the OK button, to continue.

Audio settings

The Audio pane, shown in Figure 10-7, is where you manage the audio quality. As we pointed out in Chapter 5, the default format for all audio in Flash is MP3. This explains why you have only that one choice in the Audio pane.

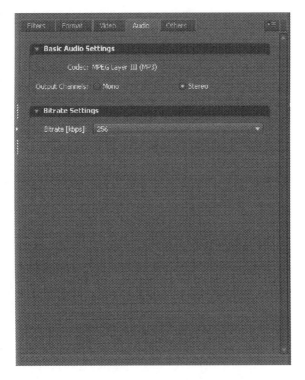

Figure 10-7. Setting the data rate for the audio portion of the movie

You need to make two decisions here:

- Stereo or mono?
- What will the data rate be?

Unless there is a persuasive reason—you are encoding a band's video, for instance—stay with a Mono setting for Output Channels. Don't think you can improve the audio track by outputting it as a stereo track if it was originally recorded in mono. You can't change mono to stereo. All that does is double the size of your audio by playing two synchronized mono tracks. Outputting stereo will only serve to increase the final file size of the FLV.

Twirl down the Bitrate Settings. For Bitrate [kbps], you should generally choose either 48 or 64. Anything lower results in an increasing degradation of audio quality. Anything higher only serves to increase the demand on the bandwidth, with no appreciable quality gain. Still, 32 kbps is a good choice if the soundtrack is nothing more than a voice-over, and 16 kbps is ideal if the soundtrack is composed of intermittent sounds such as the frogs and wolves used in the Lake Nanagook project that started this book. For this example, select 64 from the Bitrate [kbps] drop-down menu.

Cropping video

Let's now turn our attention to the left side of the Export Settings window, as shown in Figure 10-8. The top of the pane contains a Crop tool. You can use this tool to crop out unwanted areas of the video. When you click the tool, handles are added to the sides of the video, and you can use them to crop. If you want to do it by the numbers, scrub across the values. The Crop Proportions drop-down list is very important. It helps you to not only crop a video, but also to maintain the all-important aspect ratio.

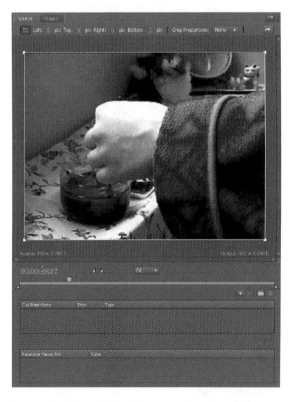

Figure 10-8. The left side of the panel allows you to crop the video, set the In and Out points, and generally manipulate the final output.

Click the Output tab. You get one choice: Crop Setting. Provided you have selected the Crop tool in the Source pane, the drop-down menu offers three choices. These choices have nothing to do with physically cropping a video. They specify how to deal with the dead area once an aspect ratio has been applied during the actual crop, as follows:

- Scale To Fit will scale the video to fit the area.
- Black Borders will keep the original aspect ratio of the video and fill areas on the sides where there is no video with black.
- Change Output Size will change the size of the video to the dimensions of the crop.

> *You can toggle between the* Source *and* Output *panes by clicking the toggle button to the right of the* Crop Setting *drop-down list.*

Running the render process

After you've set your export settings, click OK to return to the render queue. Then click the Start Queue button to start the process.

You will see the progress bar move across the screen as the video is being rendered, and you will also see the video being rendered in the preview area, as shown in Figure 10-9. If you click the Stop Queue button, you will see a dialog box asking you whether you wish to stop the process or finish the render. If you have a number of videos in the queue, clicking the No button in the dialog box will stop the process, and an Errors dialog box will appear, telling you that you stopped the render process. If you want to make changes to the settings or restart the render process, select the video—its status will be set to Skip in the Status area—and select Edit ➤ Reset Status.

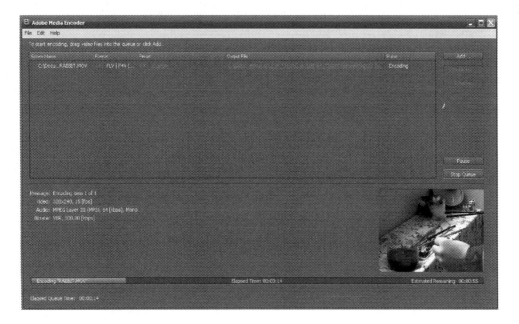

Figure 10-9. Rendering an FLV

> *Here's a little-known technique that will make your life much less stressful. Selecting a video in the render queue and clicking the* Remove *button will remove it from the render queue. What if you have made a mistake and need to make a simple change to the video or audio settings? If the video is still in the render queue and its status is set to either* Skip *or* Completed, *you can select the video and choose* Edit ➤ Reset Status *to put it back into the render queue, and then click the* Settings *button to return to the original video and audio settings. This is really handy in situations where you have messed up a cue point or two. For this to work, though, you can't move the video from its original folder or delete the video from the render queue.*

When the encoding is complete, a green check mark will appear in the Status area. Close the Adobe Media Encoder and open the Chapter 10 Exercise folder. If this is the first time you have used the Media Encoder, you had better sit down. You will notice the FLV and the QuickTime movie are in the same folder. Check out the file size of the FLV. The size has plummeted from around 70.5MB to 13MB, as shown in Figure 10-10. Don't panic—this is common with the Media Encoder. Remember that the On2 VP6 codec is lossy, and it really spreads out the keyframes. Both of these combine to create significant file-size reductions. This also explains why it is so important that the source video not be encoded using a lossy codec.

Rabbit.flv
FLV Video for Flash Player
13,179 KB

Figure 10-10. It is not uncommon to have an FLV shrink to 10% or less of the original file size.

Batch encoding

If there was one common complaint about encoding videos for Flash, it was that there was no way of encoding a bunch of them all at once. Third-party software, such as Sorenson Squeeze and On2's Flix Pro, allowed for batch processing, but this feature was unavailable in Flash—that is, until now. Here's how to encode a folder full of videos:

1. Create a folder on your desktop named WatchMe or something like that.

2. Add a bunch of MOV and/or AVI files to this folder.

3. Open the Adobe Media Encoder.

4. Select File ➤ Create Watch Folder to open the Browse for Folder dialog box.

5. Navigate to the folder you just created, select it, and click OK. When you return to the Media Encoder, the folder and the files in it will appear, as shown in Figure 10-11.

Figure 10-11. You can now do batch encoding.

6. Select a preset, including a custom one you may have created. This preset will be applied to all of the files in the folder. For better or worse, you can't apply different encoding settings to the files.

7. Click the Start Queue button to encode all of the files.

When the encoding finishes, open your folder. You will see that the Media Encoder has created a folder named Output and placed the encoded files in that folder. It has also created another folder, Source, and moved the original files into it.

Playing an FLV in Flash CS4

After encoding the video, you're ready to have it play in Flash. There are three ways to accomplish this task:

- Let the wizard do it for you.
- Use the FLVPlayback component.
- Use a video object.

The first two are actually variations on the same theme. Both will result in the use of the FLVPlayback component, but they approach the task from opposite angles. The final method is the most versatile but involves the use of ActionScript. Regardless of which approach you may choose, the end result is the same: you are in the Flash video business.

Using the wizard

We'll begin with an example of using the wizard. We'll cover the steps involved in actually adding video to Flash. If you have never used Flash video, this is a great place to start. Let's get going:

1. Create a new Flash document and select File ➤ Import ➤ Import Video. This will open the Import Video wizard.

2. The first step in the process is to tell the wizard where your file is located. Click the Browse button and navigate to the folder where you placed the FLV created in the previous exercise, or use the Rabbit.flv file in your Chapter 10 Exercise folder.

There are only two possible locations for a video: your computer or a web server. If the file is located on your computer, the Browse button allows you to navigate to the file, and when you select it, the path to the file will appear in the File path area, as shown in Figure 10-12. This rather long path will be trimmed, by Flash, to a relative path when you create the SWF that plays the video.

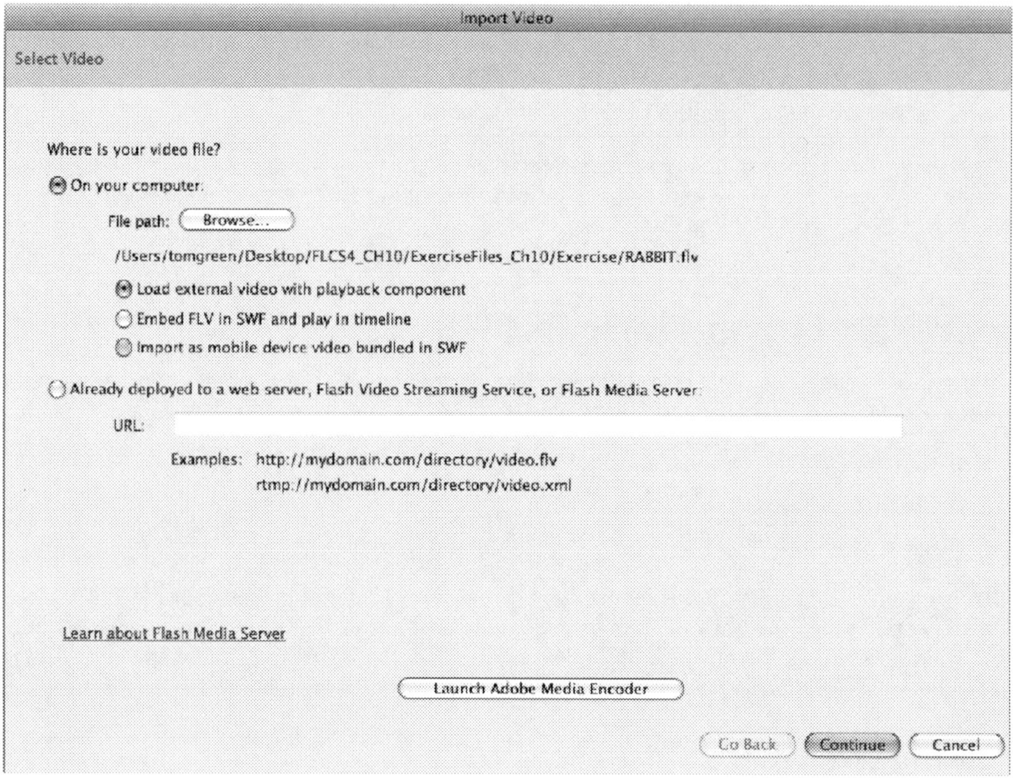

Figure 10-12. Setting the path to an FLV using the wizard

If you have a lot of videos, you may have put them in a folder on your website. In this case, you need to add an absolute path to the file. The path to Rabbit.flv would be www.mySite.com/FLVfile/Rabbit.flv. The path to the Flash Video Streaming Service or Flash Media Server would be a bit different—something like rtmp://myHost.com/Dan. (We won't be getting into the use of the Flash Video Streaming Service or Flash Media Server in this book. All videos will be played back either locally or through an HTTP site.)

> *If you are into beating yourself in the head with bricks, then by all means, be our guest and select the* Embed FLV in SWF and play in timeline *option. This will place the entire video into the SWF. If that FLV is, say, 7MB, the user will need to wait as that 7MB makes the timeline creep along. The other danger is the tendency for video to last several minutes. Flash has a maximum timeline length of 16,000 frames. If the video is substantially long, the odds are almost 100% Flash will run out of timeline. We'll talk more about embedding video in the "When video is not video" section later in this chapter.*

3. When the path is established, click the Next (Continue) button to move to the Skinning page.

4. Click the Skin drop-down menu to see the choices available to you. Click a skin style. and the preview area will change to show the chosen skin, as shown in Figure 10-13.

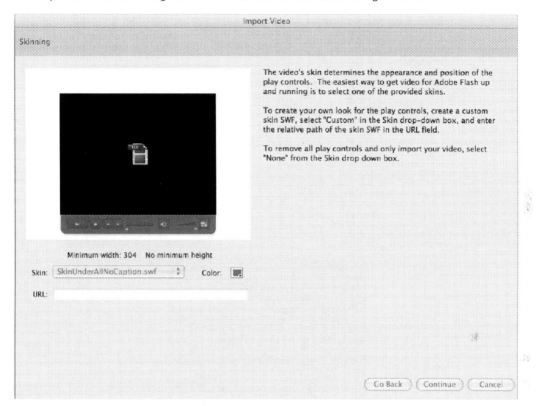

Figure 10-13. What skin or control style will be used?

Skin? Think of it as a techie word for video controls.

You are presented with two major skin groupings: Over and Under. Skins containing the word Over will overlay the controls directly on top of the video, which means you may want to configure the skin to automatically hide until the user moves the mouse cursor over the video. You can do this later by selecting the component and using the Component Inspector panel to set the skinAutoHide parameter to true. Skins containing the word Under place the controls below the video.

Pay close attention to the minimum width for each skin. For example, selecting SkinUnderAll.swf requires a video that is at least 330 pixels wide. So, if your video is 320 pixels wide, the skin is going to hang off the sides of the video. You can see this in the preview.

Selecting None in the Skin drop-down menu means no skin will be associated with the video. Choose this option if you are going to create your own custom controls, use the components in the Video area of the Components panel, or display the video without allowing for user interaction.

If you select Custom Skin URL in the Skin drop-down menu, you will be prompted to enter the path to this skin. Use this feature if you have created a custom skin, such as one containing a client's branding.

The URL input area is used if you place the skin SWFs in a location on your site other than the folder containing the FLV and the Flash SWF.

5. Select SkinUnderAllNoCaption.swf. Click the color chip to open the Color Picker, choose a color, and the skin will change to that color.

The ability to add a custom color to a skin is also a major improvement. This way, you can, for example, easily use a client's corporate color in the controls—something that required a lot of work prior to Flash CS3. You can even make the color semitransparent—extremely useful in an Over skin—by setting the alpha to less than 100%.

6. Click the Continue (Next) button to move to the Finish Video Import page. This page simply tells you what will happen when you click the Finish button at the bottom of the page.

7. Click the Finish button. You will see a progress bar showing the progress of the video being added to the Flash stage. When it finishes, the FLVPlayback component will be placed on the Flash stage, as shown in Figure 10-14.

Figure 10-14. The video is "good to go."

8. Click the video on the stage, and in the Property inspector, set its x and y coordinates to 0.

9. Save the movie. It's important to save the FLA file to the same folder as the FLV you linked to. The FLVPlayback component needs this path to ensure playback of the video.

The video will start playing in Flash Player, as shown in Figure 10-15. Feel free to try out the controls.

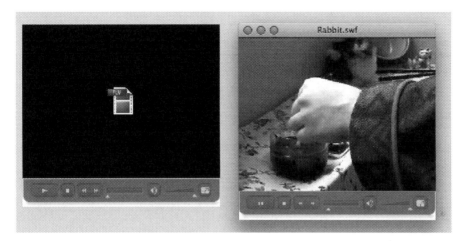

Figure 10-15. Welcome to the video game.

10. Close the video in the SWF to return to the Flash movie.

11. Select Modify ➤ Document. In the Document Properties dialog box, click the Contents radio button to shrink the stage to the video, and then click OK.

12. Select the component on the stage, and then press the left or right arrow key a few times.

Holy smokes—the controls are hanging off the stage! Depending on your publish settings, chances are good that this means the skin will not display when the SWF is embedded in a web page, which renders the controls useless. In the Publish Settings dialog box, the HTML tab's Scale setting is set to Show all by default, which doesn't necessarily mean what it sounds like. It doesn't mean "show everything on the stage and pasteboard," but rather, "don't scale anything, and show what's on the stage."

You're seeing a "gotcha" applicable only to the Under skins. When you use the FLVPlayback component, only the component is seen when you shrink the stage. The controls, which are a separate SWF added at runtime, aren't visible. If you are shrinking the stage and the only content on the stage is the FLVPlayback component, do yourself and your sanity a favor, and manually change the stage dimensions. The width can be set to the width of the FLV, but add about 45 pixels to the height of the stage to accommodate the skin.

13. Change the stage dimensions to 320 X 285.

14. Save the movie and test it.

There is one last thing you need to know before we move on. Open the Exercise folder containing the FLV. As you see in Figure 10-16, the folder contains a number of files: the FLA, the SWF, another SWF containing the name of the skin, the original MOV, and the FLV. Not everything needs to be uploaded to your server. Leave the FLA and MOV on your local computer. If you are going to be embedding this particular project into a web page, make things easy for yourself by putting the two SWFs and the FLV in the same directory on your website. If they are not in the same folder, default settings will cause the video, the controls, or both to be unavailable.

Figure 10-16. The two SWF files and the FLA must be in the same directory if you are uploading to a web page.

A word about file paths

It's certainly possible to put every single file into a separate directory—the HTML page, each SWF, and the FLV—but it means you'll need to meticulously specify the paths for all these files. Not only that, but it gets even crazier if you use relative paths (paths without the http:// or your website's domain name).

If you do find yourself in a situation where relative paths are a must and your files are scattered—this often happens with automated Content Management Systems (CMS)—keep in mind that relative paths depend on the location of files in relation to each other, which hinges on the "point of view" of the document making the request.

Most files requested by a SWF, such as the video player's skin, must be requested from the point of view of the HTML document that embeds the SWF. Let that thought sink in. *When it comes to relative paths, the point of view belongs to the HTML document, not the SWF.* You may need to use the Custom Skin URL setting, mentioned between steps 3 and 4 of the previous exercise, to specify the location of the skin SWF, as follows:

1. Choose the desired skin.
2. Test the movie to generate the actual movie SWF as well as the SWF that represents the skin.
3. Move the skin SWF where it belongs on the server.
4. Return to the authoring environment and select the component on the stage.
5. Using the Component Inspector panel (Window ➤ Component Inspector), modify the skin parameter's Custom Skin URL setting to instruct Flash where to locate the skin SWF. You'll specify the relative path as if the HTML page, rather than the movie SWF, were looking for it.

FLV files are an exception. When a SWF requests an FLV, the point of view belongs to the SWF making the request. Regardless of where the HTML document is, if the FLV is in a different directory from the movie SWF, specify your relative path as if the movie SWF were looking for the video.

Using the FLVPlayback component

In the previous exercise, you used the wizard to connect an FLV to the FLVPlayback component. In this exercise, you'll be doing the process manually. Once you are comfortable with it, you will discover this method to be a lot quicker than the previous one. Follow these steps:

1. Create a new Flash document and save it to your Chapter 10 Exercise folder. Remember that the FLA needs to be in the same folder as the FLV.

2. In the Components panel (Window ➤ Components), click the Video category. Drag a copy of the FLVPlayback component onto the stage, as shown in Figure 10-17.

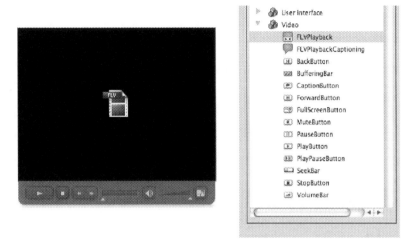

Figure 10-17. The FLVPlayback component is found in the Video section of the Components panel.

You will notice that the component has the same skin color from the previous exercise. This is normal. Also, if you open the library, you will see a copy of the component has been added to the library. This is a handy feature, because you can use the library, rather than the Components panel, to add subsequent copies of the FLVPlayback component to the movie.

3. Click the component on the stage and select Window ➤ Component Inspector.

4. In the Component Inspector panel, click the Parameters tab, as shown in Figure 10-18. The parameters, listed here, allow you to determine how the component will function:

   - align: The choices in this drop-down list have nothing to do with the physical placement of the component on the Flash stage. The choices you make here will determine the position of the FLV in the playback area of the component if the component is resized.

   - autoPlay: Choose true, the default, and the video plays automatically. Select false, and the user will need to click the Play button in the component to start the video. In either case, the FLV file itself starts downloading to the user's computer, so keep this in mind if you put several FLV-enhanced SWFs in a single HTML document.

   - cuePoints: If cue points are embedded in the FLV, they will appear in this area.

   - preview: If you select this, and an FLV is connected to the component, you can see the video without needing to test the movie.

   - scaleMode: Leave this at the default value—maintainAspectRatio—if video is to be scaled.

   - skin: Select this, and the Select Skin dialog box will appear.

   - skinAutoHide: Choose true, and the user will need to place the mouse over the video for the skin to appear.

- skinBackgroundAlpha: Your choices are any two-place decimal number from 0 to 1. 0 means the background is totally transparent, and 1 means there is no transparency.

- skinBackgroundColor: Select this, and the Flash color chip appears.

- source: Double-click this area, and the Content Path dialog box opens. From here, you can either set a relative path to the FLV or enter an HTTP or RTMP address path to the FLV.

- volume: The number you enter—any two-place decimal number between 0 and 1—will be the starting volume for the video.

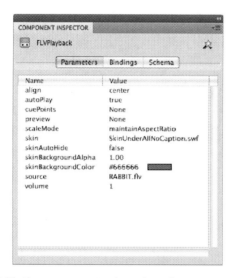

Figure 10-18. The FLVPlayback component relies on Component Inspector panel to determine its look and functionality.

5. With the component selected on the stage, set autoPlay to false and skinBackgroundColor to #999999 (medium gray).

6. Double-click the source parameter to open the Content Path dialog box, as shown in Figure 10-19.

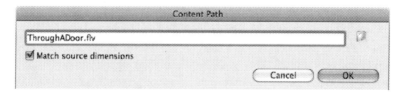

Figure 10-19. Setting the content path to the FLV to be played in the component

7. In the Content Path dialog box, click the Navigate button—the file folder icon—to open the Browse for FLV file dialog box. Navigate to the Chapter 10 Exercise folder, select the ThroughADoor.flv file, and then click the Open button.

8. The relative path to the FLV will appear in the Content Path dialog box. Select the Match source dimensions check box. This will size the component to the exact dimensions of the FLV file. Then click OK.

9. Save the movie.

10. Test the movie in Flash Player. Click the Play button to start playing the video. When you have finished, close the SWF to return to the Flash stage.

11. Select the component on the stage and click the Parameters tab in the Component Inspector panel.

12. Double-click the preview parameter to open the Select Preview Frame dialog box, as shown in Figure 10-20. Here, you can watch a live preview of the video. Click Cancel to close the dialog box.

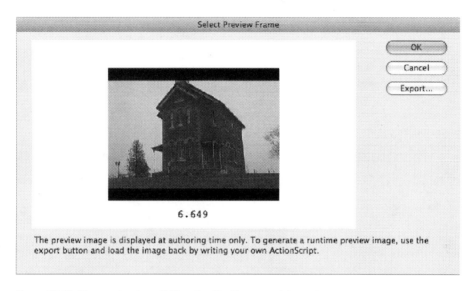

Figure 10-20. Live preview is available using the Component Inspector.

Letting you watch the movie isn't the only purpose of the preview. The FLV controls in the dialog box are live, meaning you can scrub to a frame of the video. If you click OK, the frame will appear in the component, and the time of the frame will appear in the preview parameter. This image is there only to show you how the video will appear in the component. This preview is used only at authoring time—think of it as a position-only graphic—and won't appear in the final SWF.

To use the image as a poster frame or a graphic, click the Export button. The Export Image dialog box will appear, and you can save the image as a Fireworks PNG file and use it with ActionScript or import it into the library. Why would you want to export a frame of the video? Video frames can be used as movieclips or buttons to launch a video, or as navigation elements to move the frame, or even the web page, where the video is located.

Playing video using ActionScript

In the previous two exercises, you have seen different ways of getting an FLV file to play through the FLVPlayback component. In this exercise, you won't be using the component; instead, you'll let ActionScript handle the duties. This is also the point where you are going to get the opportunity to play with some of the new video stuff. The video you will be using is an MP4 file that was "ripped" from a DVD. The ability to use HD-quality video was added to Flash Player 9 in late 2007.

Playing video using ActionScript is a lot like connecting your new television to the cable in an empty room. There are essentially three steps involved: connect, stream, and play.

When you walk into the room where you are about to hook up the television to the cable, the television is sitting on a shelf, and there is a spool of coaxial cable lying on the floor. When you screw the cable into the wall outlet, you are establishing a connection between the cable company and your home. When you screw the other end of the cable into the television, the television is now connected to the cable company. When you turn on the television, the show that is flowing from the cable company to your television starts to play. Let's connect our television to an FLV.

1. Create a new Flash document and save it as Vultures.fla in this chapter's Exercise folder. Set its stage dimensions to 845 × 480.

2. Open the Flash library. (If you don't have the library in your panel group, select Window ➤ Library to open the library.) Click the library drop-down menu in the upper-right corner of the panel and select New Video.

3. In the Video Properties dialog box, make sure the Video (ActionScript-controlled) radio button is selected, as shown in Figure 10-21. Click OK to close the dialog box.

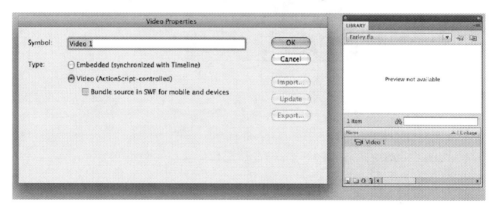

Figure 10-21. Creating a video object that will play an FLV

4. In the library, you will see a little video camera named Video 1 sitting in your library. This camera is called a *video object*. It's a physical manifestation of the Video class, just as movieclip symbols are instances of the MovieClip class. Drag your video object from the library to the stage. When you release the mouse, it will look like a box with a big *X* through it, as shown in Figure 10-22.

5. Click the video object and specify these values in the Property inspector:

- Instance name: myVideo
- Width: 854
- Height: 480
- X: 0
- Y: 0

When you add a video object to the stage, its default dimensions are 160 × 120. This is why you need to physically set the object's dimensions to match those of the video playing through it.

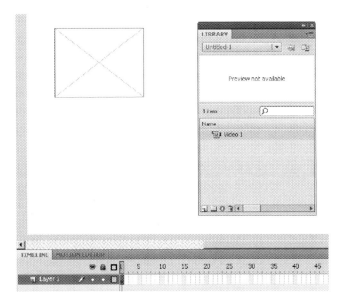

Figure 10-22. The new video object on the stage

6. Save this file to the Chapter 10 Exercise folder.

7. Add a new layer named Actions. Select the first frame of the Actions layer, open the Actions panel, and enter the following code:

```
var nc:NetConnection = new NetConnection();
nc.connect(null);

var ns:NetStream = new NetStream(nc);
myVideo.attachNetStream(ns);
```

The first line declares an arbitrarily named variable, nc, and sets it to an instance of the NetConnection class. This provides the network connection between the player and the server. The second line (nc.connect(null);) tells the player it this is an HTTP connection, not an RTMP connection, which requires Adobe's Flash Media Server installed on your web server. Any requested video files, such as the SWF itself or typical web page assets like JPGs or GIFs, will download progressively. The third line declares another variable, ns, and sets it to an instance of the NetStream class. This establishes the stream—that is, the flow of video data. The fourth line connects the video object, with the instance name myVideo, to the stream that is connected to the server.

8. Press Enter (Return) twice and enter the following code:

```
var listener:Object = new Object();
listener.onMetaData = function(md:Object):void {};

ns.client = listener;
```

If you don't have this listener object in the code, you are going to have very mysterious compiler errors coming out of your ears. The reason is that most FLV files have metadata contained in them, and you see this when you set the path for a video in the Component Inspector panel. For example, the duration or length of the file is often contained in the FLV metadata. ActionScript 3.0 is trained to look for that metadata. If none is found—because the FLV encoder (perhaps a third-party tool) didn't encode any—Flash gets a little frantic and fills your Output panel with this sort of error message:

```
Error #2044: Unhandled AsyncErrorEvent:. text=Error #2095:
flash.net.NetStream was unable to invoke callback onMetaData. error=
ReferenceError: Error #1069: Property onMetaData not found on
flash.net.NetStream and there is no default value.
    at Untitled_fla::MainTimeline/frame1()
```

The listener object, and its onMetaData event handler function, team up to "chill out" the compiler when associated with the NetStream.client property of the ns instance. Why? Because you don't actually have to do anything with the event handler. All you have to do, to avoid errors, is handle the event.

9. Press Enter (Return) twice and enter the following code:

```
ns.play("Vultures.mp4");
```

This line uses the NetStream.play() method to actually stream the video content into the video object on the stage. The important thing to note here is that the name of the video is a string (it falls between quotation marks) and the .mp4 extension is added to the name of the video.

10. Save and test the movie. When Flash Player opens, the video starts to play, as shown in Figure 10-23.

Figure 10-23. Eight simple lines of ActionScript code drive the playback of this HD video.

To recap, if you want to play video using ActionScript, here is all of the code you will need to get started:

```
var nc:NetConnection = new NetConnection();
nc.connect(null);
var ns:NetStream = new NetStream(nc);
myVideo.attachNetStream(ns);

var listener:Object = new Object();
listener.onMetaData = function(md:Object):void {};
ns.client = listener;

ns.play("Vultures.mp4");
```

The only thing you will ever need to do to reuse this code is to make sure the video object's instance name matches the one in line 4, and change the name of the FLV, F4V, or MP4 file in the last line.

> Now that you've seen how easy it is to play a NetStream *instance, what about stopping the video? Check out the* NetStream *class entry in the ActionScript 3.0 Language and Components Reference, and you'll see the answer: you have a number of methods to tinker with, including* pause( ), resume( ), *and* close( ). *We'll talk more about these methods in Chapter 14.*

You might be thinking, "Hey, I have the FLVPlayback component. Why do I need code?" The answer can be summed up in one word: size. The size of a code-driven SWF is about 1KB, and its FLV counterpart weighs in at over 55KB. The difference is simply due to the ActionScript involved with the component under the hood.

The increasing use of video in banner advertising is forcing developers to think small, because the maximum size of a banner ad SWF is often no more than 30KB. Obviously, the FLVPlayback component is simply too "heavy" for use in banner ads.

Additionally, there is going to come a point in your life when the FLVPlayback component simply isn't going to cut it any longer. When you reach this point, you will be creating your own ActionScript-driven controllers, as shown in Chapter 14, and this will require the use of a video object. The real payback for you will come when you discover you can create your own custom controllers that weigh in at under 10KB.

Using the FLVPlayback control components

In the Video components area of the Components panel, you'll find a bunch of individual buttons and bars. They are there for those situations when you look at the skin options available to you and think, "That's overkill. All I want to give the user is a play button and maybe another one to turn off the sound." This is not as far-fetched at it may sound. There are a lot of websites out there that use custom players that are nothing more than a series of the individual controls. In this exercise, you will build a custom video controller using these video-specific user interface components.

1. Open the Controls.fla document in this chapter's Exercise folder. You will see the only thing on the stage is beveled box with a bit of branding on it. If you wish, feel to change the text in the Text layer to your name.

2. Select the Video layer and drag an FLVPlayback component to the stage.

3. Open the Component Inspector panel and click the Parameters tab. Set skin to None and source to ThroughADoor.flv.

4. In the Property inspector, set the X and Y values of the FLVPlayback component to 0.

5. Select the Controls layer and drag the following components to the stage:

   - BackButton
   - PlayPauseButton
   - SeekBar
   - VolumeBar

6. Hold down the Shift key and select each of the controls on the stage.

7. Open the Align panel and make sure To stage is not selected. Then click the Center Align button. When you finish, your stage should resemble that shown in Figure 10-24.

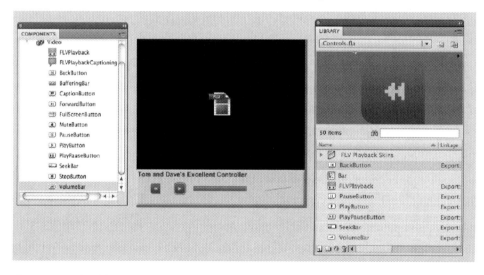

Figure 10-24. The video control components, when added to the stage, are also added to the library.

If you open the library, you won't see the PlayPauseButton. You will see separate Play and Pause buttons. Don't panic. The PlayPauseButton is actually a combination of both of them.

This is the point in this exercise where what you have done is about to shift from interesting to way too cool. With all of those components on the stage, you are probably preparing yourself, especially if you used them in Flash 8, to start writing a bunch of code. But you can relax. As long as the components are in the same frame as the FLVPlayback component, they become fully functional. Think about it—you have just created a custom video controller in a "code-free zone." Don't believe us? Check it out yourself.

8. Save and test the movie. Drag the Seek control to the right and left, as shown in Figure 10-25. See . . . we told you.

Figure 10-25. A custom video control created in a code-free zone

Adding captions with the FLVPlaybackCaptioning component

A couple of years ago, one of the authors had written a piece about Flash video and how easy it was to get video onto a website. The thrust of the article was this was a wondrous technology, and that video was about to sweep the Web. The reaction to the article was strongly positive, and the author was feeling pretty good about himself—that is, until he received the following e-mail:

> *Love your books and tutorials! They are very well explained. I have a question. Have you done any tutorials on how to add captions to videos? For example, there is CC button in your 'Talking Head' video box. I would love to learn how to write CC for that. I am deaf and would strongly advocate for all websites that have videos to have captions, but that won't happen right away due to $ and timing. I will be making a small 'Talking Head' video introducing myself in sign language, but I want to have captions for hearing people to know what I am saying :-)*

In our zeal to get video out there, we tend to forget that accessibility is a major factor in our business. And accessibility is now the law around the world. Up until Flash CS3, video was often partially or totally inaccessible to those with hearing impairments. What also caught our attention was the last line of the e-mail. It is obvious captioning is a two-way street, and those of us without disabilities rarely see it that way.

This isn't to say captions couldn't be added to video in Flash 8. They could, but it required quite a bit of effort on the designer's or developer's part to get them to work properly. It usually involved XML, cue points in the FLV, and an understanding of how to use XML in Flash and to write the proper ActionScript to make it all come together. Flash CS3 streamlined this process with the inclusion of the FLVPlaybackCaptioning component, and it's still right here in Flash CS4.

Before we get going, it is important that you understand this is not a point-and-click workflow. Entering cue points by hand into the Video Import dialog box in Flash is a tedious business. For all but the shortest of video clips, it makes best sense to use a special XML document to make it all work—easier to edit later, too—and then you need to "connect" that document to the FLVPlaybackCaptioning component.

The FLVPlaybackCaptioning component allows for the display of captions in the FLVPlayback component through the use of a Timed Text (TT) XML document. If you open the captions.xml document in this chapter's Exercise folder, you will see the Timed Text XML code used in this exercise:

```
<?xml version="1.0" encoding="UTF-8"?>
<tt xml:lang="en" xmlns=http://www.w3.org/2006/04/ttaf1
➥xmlns:tts="http://www.w3.org/2006/04/ttaf1#styling">

  <head>
    <styling>
      <style id="1" tts:textAlign="right"/>
      <style id="2" tts:color="transparent"/>
      <style id="3" style="2" tts:backgroundColor="white"/>
      <style id="4" style="2 3" tts:fontSize="20"/>
    </styling>
  </head>

  <body>
    <div xml:lang="en">

  <p begin="00:00:00.25" dur="00:00:03.25">Dreamweaver users now
➥have access to Flash Video. Didn't have it before.</p>

  <p begin="00:00:04.20"dur="00:00:03.07">And if you were to talk
➥to a Dreamweaver user about three or four years ago</p>

  <p begin="00:00:08.03" dur="00:00:01.04">and ask, "You want to
➥put video on a web page?"</p>

  <p begin="00:00:09.11" dur="00:00:04.00">They would look at you
➥and go "Yeah, dude. Yeah. Right. Uh Huh. Next."</p>

    </div>
  </body>
</tt>
```

> *We get into XML in a big way in Chapter 13, so if the Timed Text XML code doesn't look especially meaningful to you yet, don't worry. You'll see some similarity to HTML, which may give you a sense of familiarity. In this case, you're looking at a document that adheres to the Timed Text specification set by the W3C, the same folks who wrote the HTML specification. The* FLVPlaybackCaptioning *component follows that standard. If you really want to dig into the specification, it can be found at* http://www.w3.org/AudioVideo/TT/.

You will notice that you can set the styling for the text, and that each caption needs to have a start point and an end point. This means each caption must have a begin attribute, which determines when the caption should appear. If the caption does not have a dur or end attribute, the caption disappears when the next caption appears or when the FLV file ends. The begin attribute means "This is where the caption becomes visible." The dur attribute means "This is how long the caption remains visible." Alternatively—and this is really a matter of taste—you can omit dur and replace it with end, which means "This is where the caption stops being visible."

Where do you get those numbers? You can use the time code in the Adobe Media Encoder to find them, or you can use the time code displayed in the QuickTime or Windows Media Player interfaces. Another place would be in the video-editing software used to create the video in the first place.

Follow these steps to apply the captions in the preceding XML example to a video:

1. Open a new Flash document and save it to the CaptioningVideo folder in your Chapter 10 Exercise folder.

2. Drag an FLVPlayback component to the stage. Using the Parameters tab of the Component Inspector, set its source to Captions.flv (make sure the Match source dimensions check box is selected) and the skin parameter to SkinUnderPlayCaption.swf. Name the layer video.

3. Add a new layer named Captions. Drag a copy of the FLVPlaybackCaptioning component to this new layer.

4. Select the FLVPlaybackCaptioning component, open the Component Inspector and click the Parameters tab (see Figure 10-26). You will see the following parameters:

   - autoLayout: A value of true lets the FLVPlayback component determine the size of the captioning area.

   - captionTargetName: This parameter identifies the movieclip or text field instance where the captions can be placed. The default is auto, which means the component will make that decision.

   - flvPlaybackname: This is the instance name for the FLVPlayback component, which is set in the Property inspector. If there is only one instance of the component, leave the value at the default of auto.

Figure 10-26. The FLVPlaybackCaptioning component and its parameters

   - showCaptions: If this is set to false, the captions will not display (they can be turned on with ActionScript).

   - simpleFormatting: If you have no formatting instructions in the XML document, set this to true. Otherwise, leave it at the default value of false.

   - source: The location of the Timed Text XML document used to supply the captions.

5. Click the source parameter and enter captionsFLV.xml as the value for the parameter. Make sure the showCaptions parameter is set to true.

6. Save and play the video. The captions will appear, as shown in Figure 10-27.

Figure 10-27. The captions will appear over the video.

Be careful with this feature, This example assumes the controls will appear under the video. If your controls or skins appear over the video, they will hide the captions. To prevent this, add a dynamic text box to the stage under the video, give it an instance name, and link the captions to it using the CaptionTargetName parameter for the FLVPlaybackCaptioning component.

Preparing and using alpha channel video

There will be times when you need a talking head video or you want to move the subject of the video from the studio to another location. These are the instances where an alpha channel video fits the bill. If you watch the weather on your local television station, you are seeing this in action. The weather reporter stands in front of a green wall and starts pointing to fronts and cloud formations. But the stuff being pointed at isn't actually on the wall. To create the scene, the weather reporter is pulled out of the green background location and superimposed on the radar image.

The type of video where a green or blue background is removed, or "keyed," is called *alpha channel video*. If you are a Photoshop CS4 or Fireworks CS4 user, you are quite familiar with the concept of an alpha channel or masking channel. The difference in a video-editing application is that the channel or mask is in motion.

How do you know you have been handed a video containing an alpha channel? Open it in the QuickTime player and check the movie information. If the codec used to prepare the video is Animation and the number of colors is Millions+, the channel is there.

The ability to use this type of video was introduced in Flash 8 Professional. To use this feature in Flash CS4, you need to select the On2 VP6 codec in the Adobe Media Encoder. This means that if your target Flash Player is Flash Player 7 or lower, you can't use alpha video.

To see alpha channel video In action, let's try it with a short video. You will encode a small clip of a young adult who has just been informed by his friend that he is dead as the result of being hit by a bus. Then you will place the video over an image in Flash.

1. Open the Adobe Media Encoder and import the Alpha.mov file from this chapter's Exercise folder into the render queue.

2. Double-click Preset in the Media Encoder to open the Export Settings window. Click the Video tab.

3. Select the On2 VP6 codec and the Encode Alpha Channel option, as shown in Figure 10-28. If you fail to select this check box, you will lose all transparency in the background.

Figure 10-28. Make sure you select the Encode Alpha Channel option.

4. Twirl down the Bitrate Settings. Select VBR encoding and Two encoding passes. Reduce the Bitrate setting to 300 kbps and change the frame rate to 15 fps.

5. Click the Audio tab and change the Output Channels setting to Mono and the Bitrate to 64 kbps.

6. Click OK to return to the render queue.

7. Click the Start Queue button. When the render process is finished, quit the Adobe Media Encoder.

8. Open the AlphaEx.fla file in Flash. You will see we have tossed an image of a store into the Background layer.

9. Select the Video layer and drag an FLVPlayback component to the stage. In the Component Inspector panel, set the source parameter to your alpha video, and set the skin parameter to None. With the component selected, in the Property inspector, set its X and Y values to 0,38.

10. Save and test the movie. The video appears as if filmed over the background image, as shown in Figure 10-29.

Figure 10-29. Alpha video in action

Going full screen with video

In the autumn of 2006, Adobe quietly announced that full-screen Flash video was no longer a dream. Full-screen video was released as a part of the Adobe Flash Player 9 beta. But even though it was well received, many felt the process was a bit too convoluted. Guess what happened on the way to Flash CS3? Full-screen video became more straightforward, and it continues to be in Flash CS4.

Depending on how you wish to approach the application of full-screen video, it can be either dead simple or require a bit of poking around with ActionScript and in the web page's HTML. Let's explore both methods.

Full-screen video the ActionScript/HTML way

Here's how to achieve full-screen video using code:

1. Open a new Flash movie and save it to the FullScreenSkin folder in your Chapter 10 Exercise folder.

2. Set the stage size to 400 X 300 pixels and set the stage color to #006633 (dark green).

3. Drag an FLVPlayback component to the stage and specify the following parameters:

   - skin: SkinOverAllNoCaption.swf
   - skinAutoHide: true
   - skinBackGroundColor: #999999 (medium gray)
   - source: DisgruntledDan.flv

4. Save the file as FullScreenSkin.fla.

5. Select File ➤ Publish Settings to open the Publish Settings dialog box, as shown in Figure 10-30.

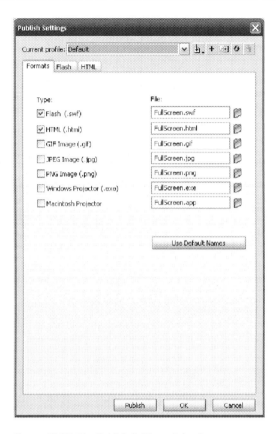

Figure 10-30. The Publish Settings dialog box

6. Make sure the Flash and HTML options are selected. Click the Use Default Names button to trim off the path, if there is one, and click the Publish button. When the progress bar finishes and closes, click the OK button to close the dialog box. When you return to Flash, save the file.

You have completed the first part of the process. The skin chosen contains a Full Screen button in the bottom-right corner. The next step is to let the browser know that the video is to be played full screen.

7. Minimize Flash and navigate to the folder where you saved the SWF and HTML files.

When you published the HTML file, you actually created more than one document: the HTML file and the SWF file, which is embedded in the HTML. The HTML file also contains JavaScript that allows Flash to play in the browser without user interaction (some browsers require users to click in order to indicate their intent to play active content). At the time this book was written (shortly before the commercial release of Flash CS4), this JavaScript appeared as inline code inside the HTML document. Be aware that it might appear as a separate document by the time Flash CS4 hits the shelves. If so, it will be the one with the .js file extension among your other published files. This JavaScript originally entered the scene when Microsoft made a change to Internet Explorer 7—eventually reversed in an update in mid-2008—to let users bypass the annoying "click to activate this control" message that plagued Flash content, QuickTime videos, Java applets, and any other content that required a plug-in. Technically, these files can all be placed in separate folders, but it requires custom coding. Do yourself a favor and place all of these files (the FLV, SWFs, and HTML documents shown in Figure 10-31) in the same directory when you upload the project to a web server.

> *If you are a Dreamweaver CS4 user, you can skip the HTML step in the* Publish Settings *dialog box. When you place a SWF into a Dreamweaver page, Dreamweaver will handle the active content unblocking chore automatically.*

Figure 10-31. The only file that doesn't get uploaded to your web server is the FLA.

8. Open the HTML file in either your favorite HTML editor (such as Dreamweaver CS4) or a word processing application.

9. Locate the <script language = "javascript"> tag inside the <body> tag (not the <head> tag). In the AC_FL_RunContent area near the end of the code, change allowFullScreen', 'false', to 'allowFullScreen','true'. Again, the actual JavaScript in use, by the time Flash CS4 is commercially available, might change. The key is the allowFullScreen parameter.

What you have just done is to make the Full Screen button functional as far as the JavaScript embedding is concerned. Now you need to follow through and give the HTML the same instructions.

10. Scroll down to the <noscript> area of the HTML where the <object> and <embed> tags can be found. Find the <object> tag and then locate its nested <param> tag whose name attribute is allowFullScreen. In that <param> tag, change the value attribute from false to true.

11. Scroll down to the companion <embed> tag and change its allowFullScreen="false" attribute to allowFullScreen="true". Figure 10-32 shows the changed lines.

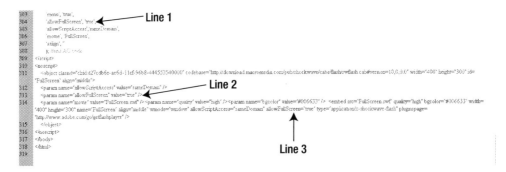

Figure 10-32. Set two allowFullScreen attributes in the HTML's <object> and <embed> tags to true to allow full-screen playback. (JavaScript, if present, must follow suit.)

12. Save the HTML file and open it in a browser.

13. When the video starts, click the Full Screen button in the bottom-right corner of the controller. The video fills the screen, as shown in Figure 10-33. You can either press the Esc key or click the Full Screen button again to reduce the video to actual size.

Figure 10-33. Full-screen video is a reality with Flash CS4.

The choice of an OverAll skin is deliberate. This controller only becomes visible when the user rolls over the video. If the user clicks the Full Screen button, the video will expand to full screen, without the controller interfering in the screen area.

Full-screen video the easy way

This previous exercise may have seemed like a bit of work, but the steps are necessary when you are using a text editor or an HTML editor to write the code. If the video is going to be the only content on the page, you might want to let Flash handle the duties for you. Here's how:

1. Open the FullToggle.fla file found in this chapter's Exercise/FullScreenToggle folder. You will notice we have already placed an FLVPlayback component on the stage, given it a skin, and linked it to the Vultures.mp4 file.

2. Select File ➤ Publish Settings and make sure that both the Flash and HTML types are selected.

3. Click the HTML tab to open the HTML settings.

4. Select Flash Only - Allow Full Screen from the Template drop-down menu, as shown in Figure 10-34. Selecting this will automatically write the tags you manually changed in the previous example.

Figure 10-34. Pick this template to enable full-screen playback.

5. Click the Publish button to write the SWF and the HTML file.

6. When the publish process is finished, open the HTML page and click the Full Screen button. The video expands to full screen, as shown in Figure 10-35. Click the Full Screen button again, and it shrinks back into place. All Flash has done here is perform the previous steps for you.

Figure 10-35. Sometimes it is easier to let the software do the work.

When video is not video

Up to this point in the chapter, we have treated video as something to be played. However, sometimes video becomes content and does not require a player, captions, or even full-screen capability. In this case, video can be imported directly into a Flash movieclip, which makes it fully accessible to Flash as content on the stage.

Before we start, we want you to be real clear on a fact of video life: video files are large, and importing any of the files you have worked with so far in the chapter directly onto the Flash timeline would be a major error. When considering working with video content on the Flash timeline, think short—loops of about 2 seconds—and think small. The physical size of the video should match precisely the area of the stage where it will be used.

> *The FLV files used in this exercise were all created in Adobe After Effects 7 Professional. For details about creating such videos, see* From After Effects to Flash: Poetry in Motion Graphics *by Tom Green and Tiago Dias (friends of ED, 2006). In fact, Tiago is the technical editor for this book.*

Embedding video

Earlier, we told you that embedding video in the timeline was, well, evil. Now we are going to show you when this can actually be a good thing. The following exercise demonstrates how this works.

1. Create a new Flash document and change the stage size to 468 pixels wide by 60 pixels high, which is a common banner ad size.

2. Select File ➤ Import ➤ Import Video. This will launch the Import Video wizard.

3. On the Select Video page, navigate to the Apparition.flv file in your Chapter 10 Exercise folder.

4. On the next page, select Embed video in SWF and play in timeline. You will see a missive at the bottom of the dialog box warning you of the evils of this technique, but don't worry—the file isn't that big. Click the Next button.

5. On the Embedding page, select Embedded video from the Symbol type drop-down menu. Also be sure the check boxes for Place instance on stage, Expand timeline if needed, and Include audio are selected, as shown in Figure 10-36. Click the Next button.

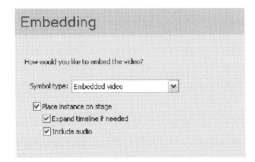

Figure 10-36. Embedding an FLV file in the Flash timeline

6. On the Finish Video Import page, click the Finish button to return to the Flash stage. You will see a progress bar, and when it finishes, the video will be on the stage, and the timeline will expand to accommodate the number of frames in the video.

7. Select the video, and in the Property inspector, set its X and Y values to 0. If you open the library, you will also see the video is in a video object.

8. Add a new layer to the timeline and enter your name.

9. Save and test the movie. The weird ghostlike apparitions move around behind your name (see Figure 10-37).

Figure 10-37. Embedded video can be used as content.

Embedding video as a movieclip

In this next exercise, you are going to create a rainy day in the mountains of Southern California. In this example, you will discover the power of matching Flash's Blend modes with video.

1. Open the Rainfall.fla file in your Chapter 10 Exercise folder. You will see that we have placed an image of the mountains on the stage.

2. Click the first frame of the Video layer. Select File ➤ Import to stage. In the Import dialog box, select the Rain.flv file and click Open. This will launch the Import Video wizard.

3. Embed the video in the timeline, as in this previous exercise, but this time, when you reach the Embedding page, select Movie clip as the symbol type, as shown in Figure 10-38. This is a good way to go, because it routes all the necessary timeline frames into a movieclip timeline, rather than expanding the main timeline off a mile to the right.

Figure 10-38. Embedded video can be turned into a Flash movieclip.

4. The new movieclip will appear in the first frame of the Video layer. Using the Property inspector, set its X and Y values to 0. Obviously a big, black movieclip that hides the mountains isn't doing the job. Let's fix that.

5. Select the movieclip on the stage, and in the Property inspector, set the movieclip's Blending option to Add. The rain becomes visible, as shown in Figure 10-39.

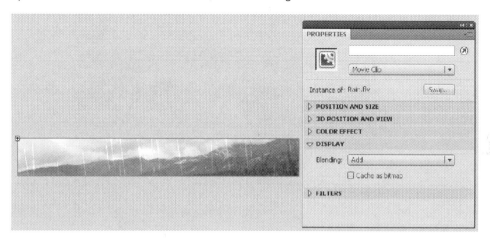

Figure 10-39. Use the Add mode to remove the black background in the FLV.

6. Save and test the movie.

Interacting with video content

So far, you have discovered how video content can interact with Flash content. In the next exercise, you are going in the opposite direction: Flash content interacting with video content.

1. Open the BlobEffect.fla file in this chapter's Exercise folder. You will see we have already placed an embedded video on the timeline. The video is a blobs effect. To see it, open the Blobs movieclip in the library, and when the Symbol Editor opens, press Enter (Return). As you can see in Figure 10-40, green blobs ooze from the top of the window and coalesce into a giant blob, which then splits apart into smaller blobs.

Figure 10-40. We start with some green blobs, which is an FLV file embedded into a movieclip.

2. Click in the Text layer, select the Text tool (or press T), and enter your name. Use a font and size of your choosing. In the Property inspector, change the color of the text to #FFFF00 (bright yellow).

3. With the text selected, convert the text to a movieclip symbol named Name.

4. With the Name movieclip symbol selected, select Overlay from the Blending drop-down menu.

The text will disappear. This is because the Overlay mode either multiplies or screens the colors, depending on the destination color, which is the color immediately under the text. In this case, the yellow text is against a black background, so you can't see the effect.

5. Save and play the movie. Notice how the text changes and becomes visible as the blobs pass under it, as shown in Figure 10-41.

Figure 10-41. A classic example of Flash content interacting with video content

Adding cue points

You can add cue points to an FLV file in four ways:

- Add them when you create the FLV file in the Adobe Media Encoder.
- Add them using the FLVPlayback component's parameters.
- Add them using the addASCuePoint() method in ActionScript.
- Add them using an XML document.

The first two methods are what we call "destructive." Once you add a cue point using those two methods, it can't be removed. This means if your timing is off, the video will need to be reencoded and new cue points added. Here's some self-defense if you go with either of those methods: don't remove the video from the render queue until the video is approved for play. In this circumstance—and it works only for cue points added in the Media Encoder—you select the video in the render queue and choose Edit ➤ Reset Status. When you return to the Cue Points tab, all the cue points will be there, and they can be removed and changed.

The last two ways are the most flexible because, if the timing is off, you simply open the code and change a number.

Here, we will concentrate on using an XML document to insert the cue points. Before we dig into the XML, you should know that in Flash video, there are two flavors of cue points:

- **Navigation cue points**: These cue points do exactly what the name implies: they are used to navigate, seek, and trigger ActionScript methods. If you create a navigation cue point, Flash will actually insert a keyframe at that point in the video.

- **Event cue points**: These are the most common. They tell Flash and/or ActionScript to do something when they are encountered.

In the upcoming exercise, you will create event cue points. They will be used to tell Flash to display a caption.

An alternate XML format for cue points

We tend to think the Timed Text format described earlier in this chapter is the way to go for cue points, if only because it's a nonproprietary specification. However, it's good to know your options. You may just decide to use the alternate approach described in this section instead. If you do, there is a very specific format you must follow. Let's look at it.

Open the CuePoints.xml document in this chapter's Exercise/YourTurn folder. You can use Dreamweaver CS4, a simple text editor, or even a word processor for this purpose. Just make sure that when you save the file, you save it as plain text. When the document opens, the first "chunk" of code you will encounter is the following:

```
<?xml version="1.0" encoding="UTF-8" standalone="no" ?>
<FLVCoreCuePoints>
 <CuePoint>
    <Time>9000</Time>
    <Type>event</Type>
    <Name>fl.video.caption.2.0.0</Name>
    <Parameters>
     <Parameter>
      <Name>text</Name>
        <Value><![CDATA[<font face="Arial, Helvetica, _sans"
➥size="12">Look ... up in the sky ... look...</font>]]></Value>
     </Parameter>
     <Parameter>
     <Name>endTime</Name>
     <Value>11.0</Value>
    </Parameter>
   </Parameters>
 </CuePoint>
</FLVCoreCuePoints>
```

This is the syntax that must be used. Deviate from it at your own peril. The first line specifies the encoding for the document, and the second line tells Flash that anything between the <FLVCoreCuePoints> tags is to be considered within the context of a cue point.

Each cue point you will add must be enclosed between <CuePoint> and </CuePoint> tags. The <Time> tag is the start of the cue point, and this number must be expressed in milliseconds. The next tag, <Type>, tells Flash that the cue point is to be an event cue point, and the tag following it, <Name>, is the name of the cue point.

The rules regarding naming are rigid. The <Name> tag must be fl.video.caption.2.0 followed by a series of sequential numbers to guarantee unique values. In our sample XML, it goes fl.video.caption.2.0.0, fl.video.caption.2.0.1, and so on.

The parameters contain the styling data for the text that will appear in the caption and an end time for the caption. Later in the actual XML document, you'll see that we used the <i> tag to identify who is speaking by setting the person's name in italics. HTML tags may be used only if they're supported by Flash; a list of these may be found in the "HTML formatting" section of Chapter 6.

The endTime property, which must be expressed in seconds, will be the time when the caption disappears from the screen. This number can be an integer (no decimals) or can contain up to three decimal places.

Finally, you may optionally contend with using color in captions, and there are a couple of rules involving this as well. If you scroll down to caption 2.0.7 in the file, you will see the text in the caption uses #FF0000, which is a bright red. A couple of lines later, the backgroundColor parameter changes the background color of the caption to 0x01016D, which is a dark blue.

The key here is how the colors are identified. Colors are specified by hexadecimal values, but the *indication* that the color is in hexadecimal notation—# or 0x—depends on where it's being stated. The first change to the red uses the pound sign, #, as traditionally used in HTML. Why? Because it appears within HTML-formatted content. The second change—to the dark blue—uses the format for specifying hexadecimal notation in ActionScript, 0x.

If you do change the background color of a caption, that color will "stick." This means all subsequent captions will use this background color. If you need only a single change, as in our example, change the backgroundColor parameter back in the next cue point. In our case, we changed it to black again (0x000000), as seen in caption 2.0.8.

Do your sanity a favor and separate each caption with an empty line or two in the XML. This makes the captions easier to read and locate. The blank space, called *whitespace*, will be ignored by Flash.

So what does all of this have to do with cue points and FLV files? You are about to find out. First, though, you need to download a cartoon.

Your turn: Create XML captions for video

In the 1940s, the original Superman cartoons were produced by a gentleman named Max Fleischer. A small number of these cartoons have entered the public domain, which means that they are free for you to download and use. One of them, "Superman: the Mechanical Monsters," is the cartoon you will be captioning. In order to remain purer than pure, we aren't including the cartoon in the Exercise downloads. We would respectfully ask that you head over to http://www.archive.org/details/superman_the_mechanical_monsters. The download options are on the left side of the page, offering files in different compressions and sizes. In theory, it doesn't matter which file you download. We used the "256Kb MPEG4 (27MB)" version.

> We find it rather fascinating that the copy of the video that plays on the page is
> Flash video. It's a low-quality one, but Flash video all the same.

Now that you have downloaded the source video, proceed as follows:

1. Open the Adobe Media Encoder and drag the video from its location into the render queue.

2. Open the Export Settings window. Enter Superman as the output file name and select FLV as the format.

3. Click the Video tab. Ensure you are using the On2 VP6 codec, Deselect Resize Video and, in the Bitrate settings, use VBR and Two encoding passes. Reduce the Bitrate value to 275.

4. Click the Audio tab. Change Output Channels to Mono and reduce the Bitrate to 64 kbps.

Let's now turn our attention to the cue points area under the preview. This is where all of the pain, sweat, and aggravation that went into creating the XML document comes into play. The care and diligence you put into ensuring all of the tags in the XML document are correct are about to pay off. How so? Let's add the first cue point manually to give you the idea.

5. Scrub the playback head of the FLV to the 00:00:09.500 mark of the video.

6. Click the + button (which is the Add Cue Point button). Enter fl.video.caption.2.0.0 as the name of the cue point. Notice how the default value for Type is Event.

7. Click the Add Parameter button and enter Text into the name area. Click in the Value area and enter <font face="Arial, Helvetica, _sans" size="12">Up in the sky, look!</font>.

8. Click the Add Parameter button and enter endTime as the name and 10.9 as the value. The cue point appears in the cue point area, as shown in Figure 10-42.

Now repeat steps 6, 7, and 8 about 30 more times to add the remaining cue points. (Yeah, we are kidding.)

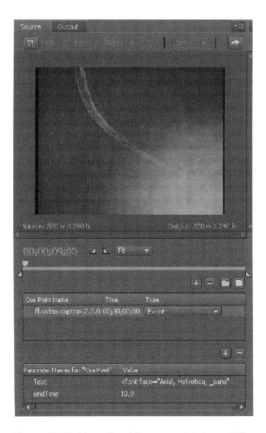

Figure 10-42. Manually adding cue points to an FLV

Obviously, going the manual route is tedious at best. Surely there must be an easier method. There is: embed the CuePoints.xml document directly into the FLV file. Let's use that technique.

> If you have used Flash 8, this method might seem a bit unfamiliar. It is. The ability to embed an XML document into an FLV file was introduced in Flash CS3.

9. Select the cue point and click the Remove Cue Point button (the − sign) to remove the cue point you just added.

10. Click the file folder icon (the Navigate button) in the cue points area. This will open the Load Cue Points File dialog box. Navigate to the YourTurn folder, select the CuePoints.xml file, and click the Open button.

In the cue points area, you will notice all of the cue points in the XML document have been added. If you select the first one, you will see that the parameters have also been added, as shown in Figure 10-43.

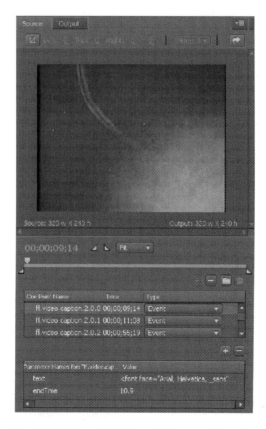

Figure 10-43. Load the XML, and the cue points and their parameters are added in less than one second.

11. Click the OK button to return to the render queue. Click the Start Queue button to encode the cartoon.

12. Return to Flash CS4 and create a new document. Save this document to the YourTurn folder.

13. Drag an FLVPlayback component to the stage, add a skin (we used SkinUnderAllNoFullScreen. swf), and set the source parameter to the FLV file you just created.

14. Drag a copy of the FLVPlaybackCaptioning component anywhere onto the pasteboard or stage (it doesn't really matter where, because the component is invisible in the published SWF).

You will notice you don't need to add the CuePoints.xml document as a parameter in the FLVPLaybackCaptioning component. All it has to do is be present in the SWF. You only need to do configure the parameter when using Timed Text captions.

15. Save and test the movie. Notice how the captions automatically appear, as shown in Figure 10-44.

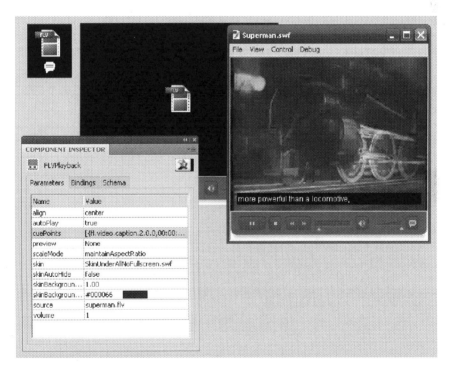

Figure 10-44. The FLVPlaybackCaptioning component only needs to be in the SWF, and doesn't require configuration.

If you think this exercise is nothing more than mildly interesting, you would be making a profound error in judgment. One of the reasons Flash video rarely appears on government or other publicly funded/subsidized websites is that video was, for all intents and purposes, inaccessible. The ability to easily add captioned video and to turn the captions on and off has opened up a market that was otherwise closed to Flash designers and developers.

Your turn: Play with alpha video

In this final exercise in this chapter, we introduce you to a couple of new concepts. The first is that video doesn't necessarily need to use the FLVPlayback component and reside on the main timeline for it to work. The second concept is that just because it is video is no reason for not having fun with it. Let's start jamming with video,

1. Open the VideoJam.fla file in the Chapter 10 Exercise folder. You will notice we have provided the background image.

2. Create a new movieclip symbol and name it Video.

3. In the Symbol Editor, open the library and select New Video from the library drop-down menu. Just click OK when the Video Properties dialog box opens.

4. Drag the video object from the library onto the stage. In the Property inspector, give it the instance name of myVideo, set its X and Y values to 0, and change its Width and Height values to 320 and 214.

5. Add a new layer to the movieclip and name it Actions. Select the first frame of the Actions layer, open the Actions panel, and enter the following code:

```
var nc:NetConnection = new NetConnection();
nc.connect(null);
var ns:NetStream = new NetStream(nc);
myVideo.attachNetStream(ns);

var listener:Object = new Object();
listener.onMetaData = function(md:Object):void {};
ns.client = listener;

ns.play("Alpha.flv");
```

6. Return to the main timeline, select the Video layer, and drag your new movieclip symbol to the stage.

7. Save and test the movie.

What you have just discovered is video can be put into a movieclip and will still play on the main timeline. This is an important concept for two reasons:

- The resulting SWF is under 30KB, meaning you can use it in banner ads. In fact, if you want it to be even smaller, remove the image, and the file size drops to 1KB.

- Objects contained in movieclips are open to creative manipulation.

Let's continue and check out that last point.

8. Select the movieclip on the stage and twirl down the Filters area of the Property inspector. Add a Drop Shadow filter and apply these values:

  - Blur X: 15
  - Blur Y: 15
  - Strength: 75%
  - Quality: High
  - Distance: 10

9. Test the movie.

You'll see that the people in the video have all developed shadows, as shown in Figure 10-45. This is because the video, like a box drawn in a Flash file, a Fireworks PNG, or a Photoshop image, contains an alpha channel. In the case of video, this channel moves, and Flash applies the drop shadow to the channel. This looks OK, but let's give the subjects a bit of depth.

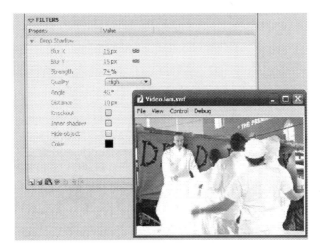

Figure 10-45. Filters can be applied to video contained in a movieclip.

10. Select the movieclip on the stage and add a Bevel filter to the video with these values:

- Blur X: 6
- Blur Y: 6
- Quality: High
- Distance: 3

11. Save and test the movie.

The subjects take on a bit of depth, and you have also added a hint of backlighting, as shown in Figure 10-46. Don't get aggressive with filters; subtlety counts.

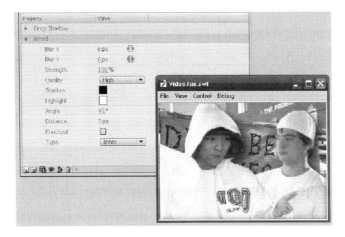

Figure 10-46. Multiple filters can be applied to video.

489

Hang on, these guys are ghosts. Can you turn them into ghosts? You bet.

12. In the Filters twirlie, select the Drop Shadow filter and select Knockout, Inner Shadow, and Hide Object.

13. Test the movie.

You have a 3D ghost. Interesting, but can you do better, of course.

14. In the Filters area, select the Drop Shadow filter and deselect Knockout, Inner Shadow, and Hide Object.

15. Twirl down Display in the Property inspector.

16. Select the video on the stage and select Overlay from the Display area's Blending drop-down menu.

17. Test the video.

You'll see that the subjects take on a "ghost-like" appearance, as shown in Figure 10-47.

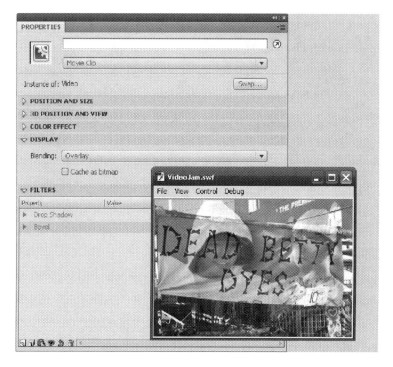

Figure 10-47. Don't be afraid to use the Blend modes to create some interesting effects.

What you have learned

In this chapter, you learned the following:

- How video can be streamed from your web server
- How to use the Adobe Media Encoder
- How to encode video containing an alpha channel
- Several methods of embedding and streaming video without using the FLVPlayback component
- How to display HD content in Flash Player
- How to add Timed Text captions to a video and how to use the FLVPLaybackCaptioning component
- An alternate XML captioning approach
- The power of the creative use of filters and blend effects that can be applied to video

This has been quite the chapter, and we suspect you are just as excited about the possibilities of Flash video as we are. The key to the use of Flash video is really quite simple: keep an eye on the pipe. The Adobe Media Encoder is one of the most powerful tools in the Flash video arsenal, and mastering it is the key to Flash video success. From there, as we showed you in several exercises, the only limit to what you can do with Flash video is the one you put on your creativity.

As you started working with the Flash video components, we just know you were wondering, "How do those user interface components work?" Great question, and we answer it in the next chapter.

Chapter 11

BUILDING INTERFACES WITH THE UI COMPONENTS

Since early in its life, Flash has proven itself the leader in web animation. In recent years, that dominance has nudged into the realm of online applications as well. For user-facing applications, you need user interface (UI) elements, plain and simple—something to receive input from the person viewing your content or display information in a specific way, such as in a grid or selection box. Sure, you've already seen how button symbols work, and you're aware that input text fields accept hand-typed content. Those make a good start, but they're also nothing more than the tip of the iceberg.

The UI components that ship with Flash CS4 are an improvement over the previous set, which shipped with Flash 8, in a number of ways: size (much smaller), performance (faster and better), and ease of customization.

> *As a bonus, Flash CS4 even gives you the previous set, known as the v2 components, but those only work with ActionScript 2.0. That's an important point! They're for publishing older movies if you find that necessary. Choosing the Flash document type or changing your publish settings between ActionScript 3.0 and 2.0 automatically updates the* Components *panel to offer the correct set. You cannot mix and match components designed for different versions of ActionScript. If you were to use ActionScript 1.0, you would lose the UI components altogether!*

Here's what we'll cover in this chapter:

- Using the Flash CS4 UI components
- Using ActionScript 3.0 to control components
- Changing component skins

The following files are used in this chapter (located in Chapter11/ExerciseFiles_Ch11/Exercise/):

- Button02.fla
- Button04.fla
- CheckBox.fla
- ColorPicker.fla
- ComboBox.fla
- DataGrid.fla
- Label.fla
- List.fla
- NumericStepper.fla
- ProgressBar.fla
- Onion.jpg
- RadioButton.fla
- ScrollPane.fla
- Slider.fla
- TextArea.fla
- TextInput.fla
- TileList.fla
- Mug01.jpg–Mug08.jpg
- UILoader.fla

The source files are available online from either of the following sites:

- http://www.FoundationFlashCS4.com
- http://www.friendsofED.com/download.html?isbn=9781430210931

Anyone familiar with HTML development knows how easy it is to add a check box, radio button, or other form element into a document. These are usually used in "contact us" pages, online surveys, and other application scenarios. Flash components provide you the same set of "widgets," but you also get a whole lot more, including components not possible in a browser alone. A smidgen of ActionScript is required to wire up components, but for the most part, adding them is a drag-and-drop operation.

Out of the box, the Flash UI components are styled in a modest, attractive manner that comfortably fits a broad range of designs. Of course, Flash being what it is—free from the relative constraints of HTML—you may want to customize their appearance, and you can. Designers and developers familiar with Flash 8 might warn you with a shudder that you're in for a barrel of headaches. Tell the old-timers they can breathe easy. Things have improved considerably in Flash CS4.

We'll start our exploration with the Button component and spend a bit more time with it than the others, simply because once you "get it," you get it. To be sure, certain components are more complex than others, and we certainly won't skimp as we visit each one. But if you're a complete newcomer, you may want to read through the "Button component" section first, and then breeze through the other headings until you find components of interest to you.

Button component

At first glance, the Button component is just another button symbol, but the two shouldn't be confused. As discussed in Chapter 3, button symbols have a specialized timeline, made of Up, Over, Down, and Hit frames. As such, button symbols are very flexible: Over artwork can be made to spill over the button's Up shape, paving the way for quick-and-dirty tooltips and other tricks. Hit artwork can make the button invisible—but still clickable—if it is the only frame with content. In contrast, the Button component has no discernable timeline. It's a self-contained component and is much more conservative (at first glance) than its wild, partying cousin. Figure 11-1 shows an example of the Button component.

Poke My Belly

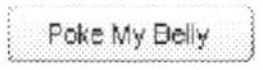

Figure 11-1. The Button component— pretty conservative, even without the tie

> *Using one or more instances of the* Button *component in your movie will add 15KB to the SWF if no other components share the load.*

Using the Button component

What makes the Button component so special? In two words, *consistency* and *toggleability*. The first of those, consistency, will be evident in each of the components we visit. If you accept the default skin for every component, you'll get a reliable uniformity among your UI widgets. The second word (OK, toggleability isn't actually a word) means that you get a button that optionally stays pressed after you click it, and releases when you click it a second time. This useful feature is possible without a lick of ActionScript knowledge. Here's how:

1. Create a new Flash document and open the Components panel (Window ➤ Components).

2. In the Components panel, open the User Interface branch by clicking the + button or double-clicking the words User Interface. The + button becomes a minus, and you'll see the list of available UI components. Drag an instance of Button to the stage, as shown in Figure 11-2.

Figure 11-2. Adding a UI component to the stage is as easy as dragging and dropping.

Doing this drops a copy of the Button component and a folder named Component Assets into your library. You can ignore the Component Assets folder for the time being. Any time you want additional Button instances from this point forward, drag them from your library.

3. To give your button an instance name, click it on the stage, and then type myButton into the Instance Name field of the Property inspector, as shown in Figure 11-3.

Figure 11-3. Always give your component instances an instance name.

Under normal circumstances, you should make your instance name something more meaningful—say, btnContact or submitForm—but for now, myButton will do.

4. If you like, use the Free Transform tool to change the dimensions of the button. Note that it resizes much like any symbol, but its text label stays the same size.

> Skewing or rotating the button makes its label disappear because font outlines are not embedded by default. See Chapter 6 for more information about font outlines.

5. Out of the box, the button's label is the self-descriptive term *Label*. Let's change that. Open the Component Inspector panel (Window ➤ Component Inspector), click the Parameters tab, and double-click the right column in the label row. Change the word Label in the Value column to Activate, as shown in Figure 11-4. When this button becomes a toggle, you'll make it actually activate something. For now, leave the toggle parameter at its default setting of false.

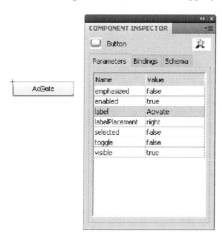

Figure 11-4. The label parameter determines the text used in the button.

6. Rename your button's layer from Layer 1 to button, and create a new layer. Name the new layer scripts and lock that layer.

Wait a minute! Wasn't this exercise supposed to happen "without a lick of ActionScript knowledge"? In fact, it does. The configuration of your button—even the toggling part you'll see in step 9—all takes place within the Component Inspector panel. The following code simply demonstrates that the button actually works (for an explanation of what this ActionScript does, see Chapter 4). ActionScript isn't required to get the toggle to do its thing.

7. Click inside frame 1 of the scripts layer. Open the Actions panel (Window ➤ Actions) and enter the following ActionScript:

```
myButton.addEventListener(MouseEvent.CLICK, clickHandler);
function clickHandler(evt:MouseEvent):void {
  trace("By George, I've been clicked!");
}
```

8. Test your movie (Control ➤ Test Movie) to verify that a button click sends the message "By George, I've been clicked!" to the Output panel.

9. To make this button a toggle, return to the Component Inspector panel's Parameters tab and change the toggle parameter to true. Test the movie again, if you like, to confirm that the button now stays in when you click it and pops out again when you click it a second time. Compare your work with Button01.fla in the Complete folder for this chapter.

> *The parameters available in the* Parameters *tab are also available via ActionScript. They're simply properties of the component's class. For example, instead of using the* Component Inspector *panel to change the toggle parameter to* true, *you could have referenced the component's instance name:*
>
> ```
> myButton.toggle = true;
> myButton.addEventListener(MouseEvent.CLICK, clickHandler);
> function clickHandler(evt:MouseEvent):void {
>   trace("By George, I've been clicked!");
> }
> ```
>
> *Note the use of the assignment operator (=), which sets a value, rather than the comparison operator (==), which consults a value. Properties set with ActionScript override parameters set in the* Component Inspector *panel.*

Adding button events

To actually make use of this toggled/untoggled state, you will need to use the BaseButton.selected property of the Button component instance on the stage. Many button-like components, including Button, CheckBox, and RadioButton, inherit from the BaseButton class family tree. This means they support a selected property, just as their ancestor does. The button's instance name lets you access this property easily.

1. Open the Button02.fla file in this chapter's Exercises folder. This file picks up where we left off in the previous exercise. The only difference is a movieclip containing a PNG image has been added to the library. You're going to make this movieclip draggable, but only when the button is pressed.

2. Create a new layer and name it mystical dude. Select the new layer and drag an instance of the movieclip dude to the stage. Give this movieclip the instance name guru.

3. In the scripts layer, select frame 1 and add the following new ActionScript beneath the existing code:

```
guru.addEventListener(MouseEvent.MOUSE_DOWN, dragGuru);
function dragGuru(evt:MouseEvent):void {
  if (myButton.selected == true) {
    guru.startDrag();
  }
};
guru.addEventListener(MouseEvent.MOUSE_UP, dropGuru);
function dropGuru(evt:MouseEvent):void {
  guru.stopDrag();
};
```

The key here is the if statement in the MouseEvent.MOUSE_DOWN handler, which is a custom function named dragGuru(). The if evaluates the button's selected property as described previously. When it's set to true, dragging commences by way of the MovieClip.startDrag() method, as shown in Figure 11-5; otherwise, dragging is ignored. In the MouseEvent.MOUSE_UP handler, dragging is stopped.

Figure 11-5. Checking the button's selected property allows you to perform actions only when the button is clicked.

> To see the full list of events available to the Button component, look up the BaseButton class in the ActionScript 3.0 Language and Components Reference. Don't forget to select the Show Inherited Styles hyperlink beneath the Events heading!

4. For extra credit, let's handle the MouseEvent.CLICK event to add a bit of polish. Press the Enter (Return) key a couple times after the existing code and type the following additional ActionScript:

```
myButton.addEventListener(MouseEvent.CLICK, clickHandler);
function clickHandler(evt:MouseEvent):void {
  if (myButton.selected == true) {
    guru.buttonMode = true;
  } else {
    guru.buttonMode = false;
  }
};
```

What's going on? This is nothing more than a third event handler. This one listens for a click, and then triggers a custom function named clickHandler(). The function uses an if statement, just as you saw in the previous step, but this time, the evaluation sets the MovieClip.buttonMode property of the guru instance to true or false, depending on the toggled state of the button. When the button is toggled, the mouse cursor turns into a finger pointer as it rolls over guru. When the button is not toggled, the cursor remains in its default state: an arrow.

Referencing components in event handlers

In the previous code example, the Button component was referenced directly by its instance name in the event handler function. Here's another look, just as a reminder, with the instance name in bold:

```
function clickHandler(evt:MouseEvent):void {
  if (myButton.selected == true) {
    guru.buttonMode = true;
  } else {
    guru.buttonMode = false;
  }
};
```

There's another way to get to that button—another way to make that same reference—and it can come in handy when you have numerous instances of a given component on the stage. Why? Because although you *could* write a separate function to handle events for each component, you might want to consolidate your functions in order to reduce complexity in your code.

First, consider a scenario with three Button components. Their label parameters are set to Apples, Bananas, and Pears in the Component Inspector panel, and their instance names, respectively, are set to btn1, btn2, and btn3 in the Property inspector. If you want to populate a dynamic text field whose instance name is output with the most recently clicked Button's label, you could do it like this:

```
btn1.addEventListener(MouseEvent.CLICK, clickHandler1);
btn2.addEventListener(MouseEvent.CLICK, clickHandler2);
btn3.addEventListener(MouseEvent.CLICK, clickHandler3);

function clickHandler1(evt:MouseEvent):void {
  output.text = btn1.label;
};
function clickHandler2(evt:MouseEvent):void {
  output.text = btn2.label;
};
```

```
function clickHandler3(evt:MouseEvent):void {
  output.text = btn3.label;
};
```

So far, nothing new—and ultimately, nothing wrong. The code works, but it could be written in a more compact way. Compare the following abbreviated version:

```
btn1.addEventListener(MouseEvent.CLICK, clickHandler);
btn2.addEventListener(MouseEvent.CLICK, clickHandler);
btn3.addEventListener(MouseEvent.CLICK, clickHandler);

function clickHandler(evt:MouseEvent):void {
  output.text = evt.target.label;
};
```

In this case, all three buttons are associated with the same function, clickHandler(), rather than the individualized clickHandler1(), clickHandler2(), and clickHandler3(). So how does the Button referencing work? The individual instance names are no longer part of the picture.

It all hinges on the evt variable between the function's parentheses. That variable, evt, points to an instance of the MouseEvent class—namely, the event triggered (MouseEvent.CLICK) when the user clicks any of the Button components. The click itself is an object. As such, evt features whatever properties and other class members are defined by the MouseEvent class. One of those properties is target (inherited from the Event class), which points to the object that dispatched the event in the first place. Here, the dispatcher is going to be btn1, btn2, or btn3, and the expression evt.target is as good a reference as any of those instance names. Because the expression evt.target points to an instance of the Button class, you can tack label onto the end of it. See the ButtonTarget.fla in this chapter's Complete folder for a working example of the code just discussed.

Considering UI component weight

One final note before we start playing with the look of this component. Unlike normal library assets, UI components add to the weight of your movie whether or not they're used. This is why seasoned Flash developers regard these things in much the same way Dracula regards garlic. The reason for this is that components are set to export for ActionScript. Right-click (Ctrl-click) any component in your library and choose Properties to see for yourself in the Linkage area of the Symbol Properties dialog box.

The first UI component in your movie usually adds the most weight, proportionately speaking, to the SWF. Some components weigh more than others, but all of them rely on a base framework that provides functionality for the whole set. For this reason, your first instance of Button will add 15KB. The second and third instances won't add anything. Your first CheckBox instance, on its own, will add 15KB, and additional CheckBox instances will add nothing. However, if you *already have* a Button instance in the movie and *then* add a CheckBox, the combined total of both components is only 16KB.

> *To remove the weight of these components—in case you change your mind and decide to omit them from your design—delete the component(s) and* Component Assets *folder from the library.*

Changing the Button component's appearance

What you're about to see can be achieved with most of the UI components, not just Button. (Some components have little or no visual element, so there are exceptions.) This is good news, because it means you'll get the basic gist right off the bat.

There are two ways to alter a UI component's appearance:

- *Skinning*, which generally deals with the material *substance* of the component, such as the shape of the clickable surface of a button or the drag handle of a scrollbar
- *Styling*, which generally deals with text, dressing, and padding

Skinning

Before Flash CS3, the practice of skinning UI components was an exercise in alchemy. Only the wisest and purest of wizards would trust themselves to toss mysterious ingredients into the frothing cauldron. All of that changed when the components were rewritten for ActionScript 3.0, and the improvement remains intact in Flash CS4. In fact, it couldn't get much easier. Here's how:

1. Create a new Flash document and drag an instance of the Button component to the stage. Double-click the button and you'll see a convenient "buffet table" of the various visual states available to the button, as shown in Figure 11-6.

2. The up skin is the button's default appearance. Double-click that, and you'll come to the symbol that represents the up skin for this component, complete with 9-slice scaling, as shown in Figure 11-7. This particular skin happens to be made of three layers.

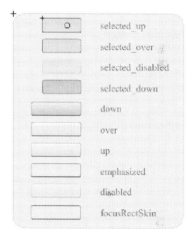

Figure 11-6. Skinning UI components is really easy.

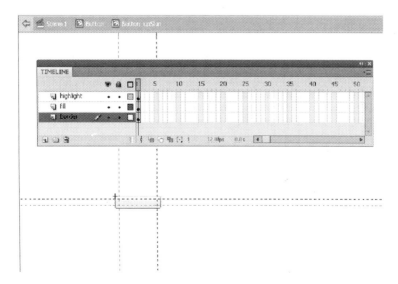

Figure 11-7. A mere two levels in, and you're ready to change the appearance of the button.

501

3. Select an area in one of these layers and change the button's appearance, perhaps like Figure 11-8—but the choice is yours. Make sure that the existing shapes, or any new ones, align to the upper left (0,0) of the symbol's registration point. Adjust the 9-slice guides as necessary. See Button03.fla in this chapter's Complete folder for an example with minor changes to the up and over skins.

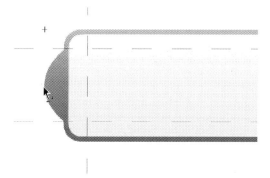

Figure 11-8. Adjust the existing shapes or create new ones.

4. Select Edit ➤ Edit Document to return to the main timeline. What the . . . ? In the authoring environment, your button hasn't changed. Folks, this is a fact of life with skins in Flash: there is no preview mode for skinning.

5. Drag another copy of the Button component from the library to the stage. Test your movie to see that your alteration appears, for both buttons, as the new up skin in the published SWF. Click either button to verify that the remaining skins (for example, down) function as before.

> *To reskin a component completely, every skin symbol must be edited or replaced.*

Styling components

As you've seen, components are easy enough to customize, even if a complete job takes some effort. You may have noticed an important omission, however, while poking around the skin symbols. Even though the Button component features a text label, none of the skins contains a text field. What if you want a different font in there, or at least a different color? ActionScript to the rescue.

Each component has its own list of styled elements. Many overlap, but you can see the definitive list for each in the class entry for that component. For example, find the Button class entry in the ActionScript 3.0 Language and Components Reference, then browse the Styles heading, as shown in Figure 11-9. Don't forget to click the Show Inherited Styles hyperlink to see the full listing. Remember, the Button class gives you details on the Button component; the SimpleButton class gives you details on button symbols.

Components that include text elements, such as the Button component, support the inherited UIComponent.textFormat style, which lets you make changes to the button's text label. Other button styles include the inherited LabelButton.icon, which lets you specify an optional image for the button in addition to text.

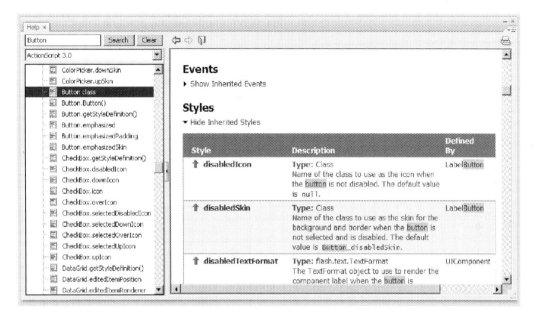

Figure 11-9. UI component styles are listed under the class entry for each component in the documentation.

For this sort of styling, ActionScript allows you to affect the following:

- All components in a document
- All components of a certain type (for example, all Button components)
- Individual component instances

Let's see it in action:

1. Open the Button04.fla file in the Chapter 11 Exercise folder. You'll see three instances of the Button component and one of the CheckBox component, as shown in Figure 11-10. Note that each has its own label.

Figure 11-10. Styling is about to change these components.

2. Click once in the first frame of the scripts layer. Open the Actions panel and type the following ActionScript into frame 1 of the scripts layer:

```
import fl.managers.StyleManager;
import fl.controls.Button;
```

503

```
        var fmt1:TextFormat = new TextFormat();
        fmt1.bold = true;
        fmt1.color = 0xFF0000;

        var fmt2:TextFormat = new TextFormat();
        fmt2.bold = false;
        fmt2.color = 0x0000FF;

        StyleManager.setStyle("textFormat", fmt1);
        StyleManager.setComponentStyle(Button, "textFormat", fmt2);
        btn2.setStyle("icon", "star");
```

3. Test the movie.

You'll notice the following changes:

- The check box's label is red and bold.
- The buttons' labels are blue and not bold.
- The second button contains an icon.

Chapter 6 discusses the TextFormat class in detail, but there are a few twists here that deserve some clarification.

First up are the opening two lines, which use the import statement. We've been sidestepping this one so far because the import statement isn't often necessary in timeline code. In ActionScript 3.0 class files—that is, code written outside Flash altogether—the import statement is not only more prevalent, it's actually *required* in order let the compiler know which other classes you intend to use. In contrast, Flash takes care of this for you—for the most part—in keyframe scripts. This just happens to be an exception. Without those first two lines, Flash will get confused about what you mean later when you mention StyleManager and Button directly.

> *These hierarchical class arrangements are called* packages. *To find the package for other components, so that you can carry the preceding styling knowledge to other scenarios, look up the component's class in the ActionScript 3.0 Language and Components Reference. When you're looking at the component's class entry, you'll see a number of headings immediately beneath the name of the class, including* Package, Class, *and* Inheritance. *The* Package *heading is the one you want. Most components, including* Button, *belong to the* fl.controls *package. As an example of the oddball,* ScrollPane *belongs to the* fl.containers *package. In keyframe scripts, you only need to import classes outside the* flash *package, such as* fl.managers, fl.controls, fl.containers, *and the like.*

Two variables, fmt1 and fmt2, are declared and set to instances of the TextFormat class, and each is given its own styling. Here's where it gets interesting. The StyleManager class has two methods you can use to apply styling to components. Both methods are static, which means they're invoked on the class itself, rather than an instance. The first of these, StyleManager.setStyle(), applies formatting to all components. In this case, we're setting the textFormat style of all components—specifically, all components that have a textFormat property—to the fmt1 instance of the TextFormat class. We programmed this style to make text red (0xFF0000) and bold, and it is indeed applied to all three buttons and the check box. You can specify any styling you like, and the textFormat style is common to many components.

"Wait a minute, guys," you may be saying. "Only the check box is red!" This is true. The reason for this is the other method, StyleManager.setComponentStyle(). That one applies styling to all components *of a certain type*, which explains the fact that it accepts three parameters. Here, we've specified Button, and then set the textFormat style of all Button instances to fmt2. This overrides the red, bold formatting of fmt1 applied in the previous line. Comment out the second StyleManager line:

```
StyleManager.setComponentStyle(Button, "textFormat", fmt2);
```

And now test your movie again to prove it.

A good way to tell which style will take effect is to remember this: the more specific the style—for example, Button components vs. all components—the higher priority it takes. If you holler to everyone in the room (StyleManager.setStyle()), giving instructions to wear green scarves, then everyone will do so. If you holler a second time, telling only the tall people to change their scarves to purple (StyleManager.setComponentStyle()), then only the tall people will comply. The instruction you've given the tall people is *more specific*—it only applies to people over six feet in height—and because of that, you can rest assured that, given the choice between two sets of instruction, the tall folks will follow the more specific set and wear purple.

This precedence goes a step further: the UIComponent.setStyle() method is invoked directly and specifically on *a particular instance* of the Button class—in this case, the component whose instance name is btn2. It works just like StyleManager.setStyle() in that it accepts two parameters: the style to change and its new setting. Here, the LabelButton.icon style, which Button inherits, is set to "star", which refers to the linkage class of the star asset in the library. Right-click (Ctrl-click) the star asset and choose Properties to verify this.

And now you've had a quick tour of the lobby and one of the rooms here at the UI Component Hotel. There are other rooms, of course, some more elaborate than others, but the layout for each is basically the same.

CheckBox component

You met CheckBox briefly in the "Button component" section, but let's take a closer look. This component is essentially a toggle button with its label on the side. Click the box or its label, and the box gets a check mark, as shown in Figure 11-11. Click again, and the check mark goes away.

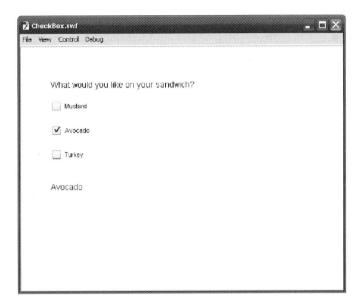

Figure 11-11. The CheckBox component is essentially a toggle button with its label on the side.

The Parameters tab of the Component Inspector panel is fairly light for CheckBox:

- label: Sets the text label.
- labelPlacement: Determines the position of the label (left, right, top, or bottom).
- selected: Lets you display an instance with the check mark showing by default.

Double-click any CheckBox instance to change the skinning for all. Styling works as described in the "Button component" section.

> Using one or more instances of the CheckBox component in your movie will add 15 KB to the SWF if no other components share the load.

Let's take a look at how to interact with check boxes via ActionScript:

1. Open the CheckBox.fla file in this chapter's Exercise folder. Note that each CheckBox instance has its own label and instance name.

2. Open the Actions panel and enter the following ActionScript into frame 1 of the scripts layer:

```
addEventListener(Event.CHANGE, changeHandler);

function changeHandler(evt:Event):void {
  var str:String = "";
  if (cb1.selected == true) {
    str += cb1.label + "\n";
  }
```

```
   if (cb2.selected == true) {
     str += cb2.label + "\n";
   }
   if (cb3.selected == true) {
     str += cb3.label;
   }
   output.text = str;
 }
```

This assigns an event handler to the main timeline, listening for Event.CHANGE events. This event handler could have been attached to each CheckBox instance individually, but by doing it this way, the events of all three can be handled at the same time. When any of the three CheckBox instances is changed by clicking, each member of the group is checked in turn—via the CheckBox.selected property—to see if it is selected. If so, the value of its label is added to a string that is ultimately assigned to the Textfield.text property of a text field beneath them.

3. Save and test the movie. Click a number of boxes and see how the code adds the associated text.

ColorPicker component

ColorPicker is a fun component, because nothing like it exists in the realm of HTML—at least, not without a swarm of complicated JavaScript! But of course, color pickers are common in applications like Microsoft Word, Adobe Photoshop, and even Flash itself. In a nutshell, the ColorPicker component is a clickable color chip that reveals an assortment of colors when selected, as shown in Figure 11-12. It allows the user to choose one of the presented colors or optionally to type in a hexadecimal value, and then the chosen color is available for use.

> Using one or more instances of the ColorPicker component in your movie will add 19KB to the SWF if no other components share the load.

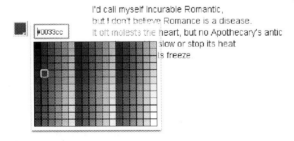

Figure 11-12. The ColorPicker component lets users choose from a range of colors.

Double-clicking a *ColorPicker* instance inside the authoring environment makes its skins editable, and styling works the same as it does for the *Button* component. The palette of colors displayed by this component is also editable, but requires just a bit of ActionScript, as shown in the following example.

1. Open the `ColorPicker.fla` file in this chapter's Exercise folder and note that the component itself has the instance name cp. The dynamic text field next to it has the instance name poem.

2. Click into frame 1 of the scripts layer and open the Actions panel. You will see the following ActionScript:

```
var fmt:TextFormat = new TextFormat();

cp.addEventListener(Event.CHANGE, changeHandler);
function changeHandler(evt:Event):void {
  fmt.color = cp.selectedColor;
  poem.setTextFormat(fmt);
};
```

Here, a variable, fmt, is declared and set to an instance of the TextFormat class. An Event.CHANGE event listener is assigned to the *ColorPicker* instance, cp. This event listener does two things. First, it sets the TextFormat.color property of the fmt instance to the selected color of the cp instance (see Chapter 6 for more information about the TextFormat class). Second, it applies that format to the text field with the instance name poem.

3. Let's determine which colors to display. Update the existing ActionScript to look like this (new code in bold):

```
var fmt:TextFormat = new TextFormat();

cp.colors = new Array(
  0x6E1E46,
  0xA12F1C,
  0xD47565,
  0x557A40,
  0x79A11C
);
cp.selectedColor = cp.colors[0];

cp.addEventListener(Event.CHANGE, changeHandler);
function changeHandler(evt:Event):void {
  fmt.color = cp.selectedColor;
  poem.setTextFormat(fmt);
};
```

Specifying your own color palette couldn't be easier. Just provide the desired hexadecimal values—up to 1,024 individual colors—as array elements to the ColorPicker.colors property of your component instance (note the 0x prefix for each color that indicates the hexadecimal format). If you specify your own colors, as shown, the default palette is replaced altogether, and your chosen colors run left to right, wrapping if necessary, as seen for the default colors in Figure 11-12. To see the color chip display color, set the ColorPicker.selectedColor property. (Here, it's set to the first element in the colors array.)

4. Drag the ColorPicker instance to the lower-right corner of the stage.

5. Test the movie to see that the pop-up color palette is smart enough to position itself to the upper left of the color chip.

Note that in the Parameters tab of the Component Inspector panel, the color palette's text field can be hidden by setting the showTextField parameter to false. You'll also see that you can set the component's selectedColor property as a parameter.

ComboBox component

The ComboBox component is very like the <select> element in HTML, except that it doesn't have the <select> element's optional size and multiple attributes. ComboBox gives users the ability to make one selection at a time from a drop-down list, as shown in Figure 11-13. In addition, the component can be made editable, which lets the user manually type in a custom selection.

Figure 11-13. ComboBox lets users make one selection at a time from a drop-down list.

ComboBox skinning is a little more complicated than Button skinning, but the basic approach is the same. The complexity stems from the fact that the ComboBox combines two other components: List and TextInput (which are described later in this chapter).

Adding a ComboBox instance to your movie puts three components into your library—ComboBox, List, and TextInput—plus the Component Assets folder used by all UI components. Double-clicking a ComboBox instance in the authoring environment opens the first tier of skins (see the left image in Figure 11-14). Double-clicking the List element in this tier opens the skins for the embedded List component (the right image in Figure 11-14).

> *Using one or more instances of the* ComboBox *component in your movie will add 35KB to the SWF if no other components, other than the automatically included* List *and* TextInput, *share the load.*

In turn, the skins for List include a third tier for scrollbars. In spite of this nesting, individual skins are nothing more than symbols, usually with 9-slice guides, such as the up and over skins for the Button component. Styling works the same as it does for the Button component.

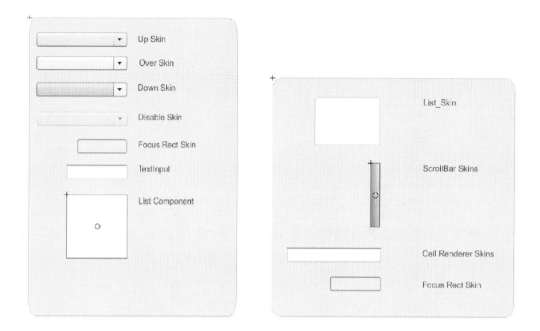

Figure 11-14. ComboBox skins (left) include nested elements, such as List skins (right).

Let's experiment with ComboBox:

1. Open the ComboBox.fla file in this chapter's Exercise folder and select the ComboBox instance on the stage. Note that in the Parameters tab of the Component Inspector panel, some information has already been entered into the dataProvider parameter, as shown in Figure 11-15. This is an array of objects, each of which represents the visible portion of a drop-down choice (label) and the hidden value each label contains (data).

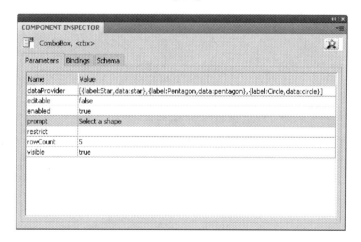

Figure 11-15. An array of objects defines the labels and data that populate a ComboBox.

2. Double-click the right column of the dataProvider row to open the Values dialog box, as shown in Figure 11-16.

3. Click the + button at the top left of the Values dialog box to create a new entry, which will appear below the existing Circle entry.

4. Double-click the right column of the label row and change the existing stand-in label to Square. Double-click the right column of the data row and enter the value square. Pay attention to the capitalization. Click OK to close the Values dialog box.

5. Test your movie to verify that the combo box now includes a Square choice that changes the shape to its right.

How does this work? Let's take a look. The shapes symbol in the library contains a series of shapes drawn every few frames of its own timeline. Frame labels are provided for each shape, and it is these frame labels that are represented by the data row in the Values dialog box.

6. Click into frame 1 of the scripts layer to see the ActionScript that pulls this off:

Figure 11-16. The Values dialog box lets you specify the content and order of a ComboBox instance.

```
cbx.addEventListener(Event.CHANGE, changeHandler);
function changeHandler(evt:Event):void {
  shapes.gotoAndStop(cbx.selectedItem.data);
};
```

The ComboBox instance is referenced by its instance name, cbx. An Event.CHANGE event triggers a custom function, changeHandler(), that tells the shapes instance—a movieclip—to stop at a particular frame label. The frame label is determined by the data property of the ComboBox component's currently selected item. How? This is accomplished by way of the ComboBox.selectedItem property, which features the label and data parameters supplied in the Component Inspector panel.

7. To populate the ComboBox component by way of ActionScript, add the following line before or after the existing code:

```
cbx.addItem({label:"Triangle", data:"triangle"});
```

This is pretty straightforward! The other parameters in the Parameters tab are just as intuitive:

- editable: Determines whether the user can type in a custom selection (if so, check for this value by referencing the ComboBox's instance name, and then the text property)

- prompt: Determines the default text (in this example, the phrase "Select a shape")

- rowCount: Determines how many selections to show in the drop-down list (if there are 15 selections and the value of rowCount is 5, only five will show, but the rest will be available with a scrollbar).

DataGrid component

The DataGrid component is the most complex component in the UI arsenal. Its purpose falls almost entirely in the realm of ubergeek interface programmers, but we're going to give you a cursory look, including a basic sample file. In short, the DataGrid component gives you a spreadsheet-like, sortable display for tabular data, as shown in Figure 11-17.

511

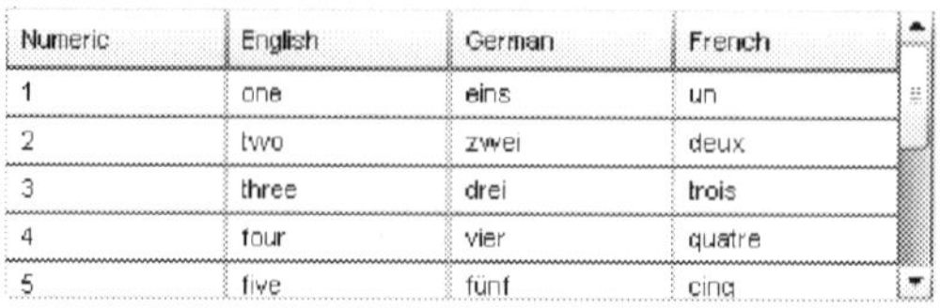

Numeric	English	German	French
1	one	eins	un
2	two	zwei	deux
3	three	drei	trois
4	four	vier	quatre
5	five	fünf	cinq

Figure 11-17. DataGrid displays scrollable, sortable tabular data.

> *Using one or more instances of the* DataGrid *component in your movie will add 40KB to the SWF if no other components share the load.*

Open the DataGrid.fla file in this chapter's Exercise folder for a working demonstration. Click into frame 1 of the scripts layer to see the ActionScript. Here's a bird's-eye view of that code:

```
dg.addColumn("num");
dg.addColumn("eng");
dg.addColumn("ger");
dg.addColumn("fre");
```

These first lines reference the DataGrid component's instance name, dg, and instruct the component to add four columns. These column names are arbitrary and, here, represent a column for numbers, and then their English, German, and French equivalents.

```
dg.addItem({num:1, eng:"one", fre:"un", ger:"eins"});
dg.addItem({num:2, eng:"two", fre:"deux", ger:"zwei"});
dg.addItem({num:3, eng:"three", fre:"trois", ger:"drei"});
dg.addItem({num:4, eng:"four", fre:"quatre", ger:"vier"});
dg.addItem({num:5, eng:"five", fre:"cinq", ger:"fünf"});
dg.addItem({num:6, eng:"six", fre:"six", ger:"sechs"});
dg.addItem({num:7, eng:"seven", fre:"sept", ger:"sieben"});
dg.addItem({num:8, eng:"eight", fre:"huit", ger:"acht"});
dg.addItem({num:9, eng:"nine", fre:"neuf", ger:"neun"});
dg.addItem({num:10, eng:"ten", fre:"dix", ger:"zehn"});
```

You cannot populate the DataGrid from the Parameters tab of the Component Inspector panel, and we're sure you can see why. It's much easier to type in the data in the relatively spacious environs of the Actions panel. Here's how to give each column a name:

```
dg.getColumnAt(0).headerText = "Numeric";
dg.getColumnAt(1).headerText = "English";
dg.getColumnAt(2).headerText = "German";
dg.getColumnAt(3).headerText = "French";
```

These lines make the header text a bit more "friendly" to the eye.

Test the movie to see how it all comes together. Click the headers to sort each column. When you sort the Numeric column, you'll see something odd. By default, sorting is alphabetical, which puts the numbers 1 and 10 right next to each other. To fix that for columns that contain numerical data, remove the comment (//) from the final line of ActionScript, so that it looks like this:

```
dg.getColumnAt(0).sortOptions = Array.NUMERIC;
```

> *What about retrieving which cell has been selected? The* selectedItem *property for the* DataGrid *component returns the contents of the whole row you click, not just the clicked cell. It is possible to return the selected cell, but it requires something called the* CellRenderer *class and more ActionScript, and frankly, it rockets way out the atmosphere that makes this book breathable.*

Label component

Label is something of an oddball in the UI components collection. Unless you're an avid programmer, we're almost certain you'll want to forego Label in favor of a simple dynamic text field (covered in Chapter 6). Why? Practically speaking, from a designer's point of view, Label doesn't really *do* anything that can't be accomplished with a dynamic text field—and besides, by using a text field, you'll save the 14KB that an instance of Label would have brought to the table.

Labels don't really have skins, and double-clicking an instance will tell you as much. Styling works the same as for Button, but again, trust us on this one . . . just use a dynamic text field. If you still want to see a Label component in action, check out Label.fla in the Exercise folder.

List component

The List component is akin to the <select> element in HTML when its optional size and multiple attributes are specified. This component is basically a ComboBox component without the drop-down aspect—it's always dropped down—and it allows multiple selections, as shown in Figure 11-18.

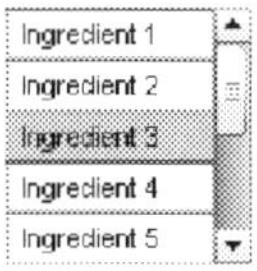

Like ComboBox, the List component has nested skins, so when you double-click an instance in the authoring environment, the skins become available for editing in tiers. Styling is handled the same way as described in the "Button component" section.

Figure 11-18.
The List component is scrollable and optionally allows multiple selections.

> *Using one or more instances of the* List *component in your movie will add 29KB to the SWF if no other components share the load.*

The Parameters tab in the Component Inspector panel is relatively hefty for the List component, as shown in Figure 11-19. Most of the choices pertain to scrolling (the distance to scroll horizontally and vertically, whether scrolling should be automatic or constant, and so on). The important parameters are allowMultipleSelection and dataProvider.

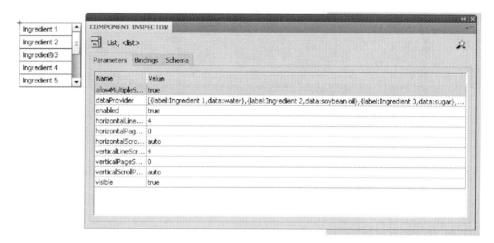

Figure 11-19. The data and the labels are added in the dataProvider area.

To populate your user's choices in a given List instance, double-click the right column of the dataProvider row and use the Values dialog box, as described in the "ComboBox component" section. Setting showMultipleSelection to true (the default is false) lets your users hold down Ctrl (Cmd) while they click in order to select more than one of the listed choices (this is like the multiple attribute in HTML).

To see how List works, open the List.fla file in this chapter's Exercise folder. Note that the instance name for the List instance is list, which works only because ActionScript is a case-sensitive language—you couldn't call it List, because that's the name of the class that defines this object. In your own work, you'll want to use an instance name that describes the list's use (in this case, that might be the word ingredients). Note that the dynamic text field, next to the List instance, has the instance name output.

Click into frame 1 of the scripts layer and type the following ActionScript:

```
list.addEventListener(Event.CHANGE, changeHandler);
function changeHandler(evt:Event):void {
  var str:String = "The secret ingredient(s): ";
  for (var i:uint = 0; i < list.selectedItems.length; i++) {
    str += list.selectedItems[i].data;
    if (i < list.selectedItems.length - 1) {
      str += ", ";
    } else {
      str += ".";
    }
  }
  output.text = str;
};
```

This one may look more complicated than it actually is, so let's break it down. As always, we're using addEventListener() to associate a custom function with an event. In this case, the event is Event.CHANGE, and the function, named changeHandler(), does three things.

- First, the variable str holds the phrase "The secret ingredient(s): ".

  ```
  var str:String = "The secret ingredient(s): ";
  ```

- Next, a for loop repeats a particular set of actions. The duration of the loop depends on the number of selected items, based on the Array.length property of the selectedItems property of the List component. The variable i starts at zero and increments at each "lap" around the loop, so that this line:

  ```
  str += list.selectedItems[i].data;
  ```

  refers to the first selected item (item 0) on the first lap, and then the second selected item (item 1) on the second lap, and so on. There's a .data tacked onto the end because List items are made up of two parts: label and data, which are—bingo!—the elements that make up the dataProvider parameter described previously. An if statement adds a comma between items in the middle and a period after the item at the end.

- Finally, the str variable, which has continuously been updated by this process, is set to the TextField.text property of the output instance.

The net result is that List selections populate a dynamic text field with the ingredients of Kraft Cucumber Ranch dressing.

For extra credit, add the following line after the existing ActionScript:

```
list.addItem({label:"Ingredient 11", data:"natural flavor"});
```

This shows that it's also possible to populate a List instance programmatically.

NumericStepper component

NumericStepper is a compact little gadget that lets the user specify a numeric value, either by typing it in or by clicking up and down arrow buttons, as shown in Figure 11-20. You, as a designer, can specify your own desired minimum and maximum values, as well as the size of each increment (count by ones, by twos, by tens, and so on). These values can be set via the Parameters tab of the Component Inspector panel.

 Figure 11-20. The NumericStepper component

NumericStepper's skins can be edited by double-clicking an instance, and styling can be applied as described in the "Button component" section. This component carries with it the TextInput component, so you'll see both in your library if you add NumericStepper to your movie.

> *Using one or more instances of the* NumericStepper *component in your movie will add 18KB to the SWF if no other components (other than the automatically included* TextInput) *share the load.*

Let's play with the NumericStepper component:

1. Open the NumericStepper.fla file in the Chapter 11 Exercise folder. Note that the NumericStepper instance has the instance name ns and that the thermometer movieclip has the instance name thermometer.

2. Double-click that movieclip to enter its timeline, and you'll see a red rectangle (masked by a green shape) with the instance name mercury, as shown in Figure 11-21. You're going to set the height of this nested movieclip based on the value of the NumericStepper.

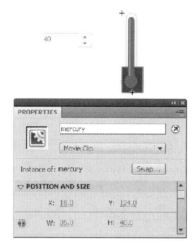

Figure 11-21. The mercury will rise and fall in response to NumericStepper clicks.

3. Select Edit ➤ Edit Document to return to the main timeline.

4. Click into frame 1 of the scripts layer and type the following ActionScript:

```
ns.addEventListener(Event.CHANGE, changeHandler);
function changeHandler(evt:Event):void {
  thermometer.mercury.height = ns.value;
};
```

5. Test your movie. Click the up and down arrow buttons to see the component in action. Close the SWF when you are finished experimenting.

The MovieClip.height property of mercury is set to the value of NumericStepper.value, as referenced in terms of the ns instance. The mercury movieclip is nested inside thermometer, which explains the matching hierarchical reference thermometer.mercury.

ProgressBar component

Used often for preloading, the ProgressBar component gives you a rising thermometer-style animation to display load progress when loading files of known size, and a barber-pole–style animation to indicate that the user must wait (for example, for files of unknown size to load or for processes to finish). Figure 11-22 shows an example.

This component doesn't have a whole lot to skin, but you can access what's there by double-clicking a ProgressBar instance. Styling works as it does for the Button component, but ProgressBar doesn't even have text, so your styling choices are fairly slim. (Yes, Figure 11-22 shows text, but that's an example of a separate Label component.)

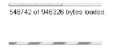

Figure 11-22. The ProgressBar component indicates load progress (top), and also presents a "waiting" animation (bottom).

> *Using one or more instances of the ProgressBar component in your movie will add 16KB to the SWF if no other components share the load. That means 16KB of non-preloadable content (the preloader itself!), so don't put much else into the frame that contains the ProgressBar component.*

Here's an exercise designed to show you how the ProgressBar component works:

1. Open the ProgressBar.fla file in this chapter's Exercise folder. Note that a ProgressBar instance exists in frame 1 with the instance name pb, as well as a text field with the instance name output. In frame 5, you'll find a fairly heavy image of a homegrown onion, snapped years ago by one of the authors. In the scripts layer, there's a MovieClip.stop() method in frames 1 and 5.

2. Click into frame 1 of the scripts layer. Note the existing stop() method. Type the following ActionScript after that method (new code in bold):

```
stop();

root.loaderInfo.addEventListener(Event.COMPLETE,
➥completeHandler);
function completeHandler(evt:Event):void {
  play();
};

pb.source = root.loaderInfo;
```

Here, first, the playhead stops at this frame. Next, an Event.COMPLETE handler is assigned to the LoaderInfo instance associated with the root property of the main timeline. Say again? Yeah, this one is a bit different from what you've seen.

In the same way that the stop() method is invoked here on the main timeline—appearing, as it does, without an object reference prefix—the root property is also being invoked implicitly on the main timeline. (root is a property of the DisplayObject class, which means MovieClip and other classes have it by inheritance.) The root property refers to the topmost display object in a given display list. In this context, it essentially refers to the display list of the main timeline (everything that's visible—or will be visible—on the main timeline, including that onion photo on frame 5).

The main timeline, being a movieclip, features a loaderInfo property, which points to an instance of the LoaderInfo class that (as its name suggests) manages loading information for the object at hand. In this case, when the movie itself has completed loading, the Event.COMPLETE event is dispatched, and the completeHandler() function invokes MovieClip.play() on the main timeline, causing the playhead to resume play until it encounters the second stop() method on frame 5. It's frame 5 that reveals the onion.

Notice that, so far, none of this yet touches the ProgressBar component. That happens only at this point. Immediately after the event handler, the ProgressBar.source property, by way of the pb instance, is associated with root.loaderInfo reference. As if by magic, that's all it takes to set the thermometer-style movement in motion.

3. Test the movie. When the SWF launches, select View ➤ Simulate Download from the SWF's menu bar to see the ProgressBar component in action. Selecting View ➤ Download Settings lets you select the speed of the simulated Internet connection.

4. Close the SWF.

5. Let's also display a text message indicating a percent loaded. In the Actions panel, add a few more lines below the existing code:

```
pb.addEventListener(ProgressEvent.PROGRESS,
➥progressHandler);
function progressHandler (evt:ProgressEvent):void {
  output.text = Math.floor(pb.percentComplete).toString() + "%";
};
```

The ProgressBar component features a percentComplete property, which we're using here. The add EventListener() method is invoked against the pb instance, listening for a ProgressEvent.PROGRESS event. The function it performs sets the output text field's text property to a rounded-down string version of the progress percentage, with the percent sign tacked onto the end for good measure.

RadioButton component

Radio buttons are gregarious. They belong in groups, and courteously defer to each other as each takes the spotlight. What are we talking about? We're talking about a component identical in functionality to radio buttons in HTML. Groups of RadioButton components are used to let the user make a single selection from a multiple-choice set, as shown in Figure 11-23.

Figure 11-23. The RadioButton component lets the user make a single selection from a multiple-choice set.

Double-clicking a RadioButton instance provides access to its skins, which you can edit as described in the "Button component" section. Styling works the same way.

> *Using one or more instances of the RadioButton component in your movie will add 16KB to the SWF if no other components share the load.*

To see RadioButton components in action, open the RadioButton.fla file in this chapter's Exercise file. Because radio buttons work in groups, the Parameters tab of the Component Inspector panel has a "collective consciousness" parameter we haven't seen with other components: groupName. Select each of the three radio buttons in turn and verify that each belongs to the same group, stooges, even though each has its own distinct label: Moe, Curly, and Larry (see Figure 11-24). Note also the empty dynamic text field whose instance name is output. You're about to wire up the radio buttons to that text field.

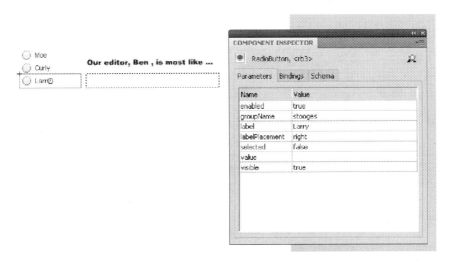

Figure 11-24. RadioButton instances must be associated with a group name.

Click into frame 1 of the scripts layer and type the following very condensed but interesting ActionScript:

```
rb1.group.addEventListener(Event.CHANGE,
➥changeHandler);
function changeHandler(evt:Event):void {
  output.text = rb1.group.selection.label;
};
```

What makes this interesting? In most of the event-handling samples in this chapter, you've invoked the addEventListener() method on an object that you personally gave an instance name. Here, that might have been rb1, but that's not the focal point in this case. You're not adding an event listener to a particular radio button, but rather to the *group* to which these buttons belong. The RadioButton class provides a group property, which means that each instance knows to which group it belongs. It's the group that dispatches the Event.CHANGE event, which occurs when any one of these radio buttons is clicked.

It doesn't matter which radio button's group property you use, because all of them point to the same RadioButtonGroup instance. The associated function updates the output text field by sending it the selected button in this group—in particular, that button's label property, which is either Moe, Curly, or Larry.

> *Note that the* Parameters *tab gives you the option to supply a value for each radio button. This allows you to say one thing and do another, just as in the* List *example. The difference is that the* List *choices were* label *and* data, *and here they are* label *and* value, *and the data type of* value *is typed as* Object, *not* String. *The text field wants a string, so you would change that line of ActionScript to* output.text = rb1.group.selection.value.toString();.

ScrollPane component

The ScrollPane component lets you have eyes bigger than your stomach. If you want to display a super-large image—so large that you'll need scrollbars—ScrollPane is your component; Figure 11-25 shows it in action.

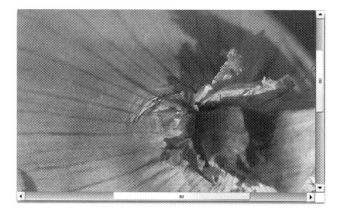

Figure 11-25. ScrollPane provides optional scrollbars to accommodate oversized content.

ScrollPane has nested skins because of its scrollbars, so double-clicking an instance during authoring will open its skin elements in tiers. Styling works the same as described in the "Button component" section, although with no text elements, most of your customization work will probably center around skins.

> *Using one or more instances of the* ScrollPane *component in your movie will add 21KB to the SWF if no other components share the load.*

In this example, there's no need for ActionScript.

1. Open the ScrollPane.fla file in this chapter's Exercise folder. Select the ScrollPane instance and click the Parameters tab of the Component Inspector panel.

2. In the Parameters tab, double-click the right column of the source row. Type Onion.jpg.

3. Test the movie. Pretty slick! The source parameter can be pointed to any file format that Flash can load dynamically, including GIFs, PNGs, and other SWFs.

Slider component

The Slider component is conceptually the same thing as NumericStepper, except that instead of clicking buttons to advance from one number to the next, the user drags a knob along a slider, as shown in Figure 11-26. You, as designer, are responsible for setting the minimum and maximum values, and this component lets you specify whether sliding is smooth or snaps to increments specified by you.

Figure 11-26. Slider lets the user drag a handle back and forth to specify a value.

Slider has no text elements, so styling is fairly light. What's there works as it does for the Button component. Skinning also works as it does for Button: double-click a Slider instance in the authoring environment to change the knob and track skins.

> *Using one or more instances of the Slider component in your movie will add 17KB to the SWF if no other components share the load.*

To see how the Slider component works, open the Slider.fla file in this chapter's Exercise folder. Note that the instance name for the Slider instance is slider, which works only because ActionScript is a case-sensitive language. You couldn't call it Slider, because that's the name of the class that defines this object. Also note the instance names circle1 and circle2 on the two circles. You're about to wire up the Slider component to adjust their width and height.

Click into frame 1 of the scripts layer and type the following ActionScript:

```
slider.addEventListener(Event.CHANGE, changeHandler);
function changeHandler(evt:Event):void {
  circle1.scaleX = slider.value / 100;
  circle2.scaleY = slider.value / 100;
};
```

When the Event.CHANGE event is dispatched—this happens as the knob moves along the track—the slider's value property is used to update scaling properties of the circle movieclips. Why divide by 100? In movieclip scaling, 0% is 0 and 100% is 1. Because the Slider instance happens to have its maximum parameter set to 100, the division puts value into the desired range, as shown in Figure 11-27.

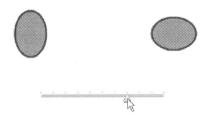

Figure 11-27. A single Slider instance can adjust many objects. Hey, that looks like a face!

Be sure to experiment with the parameters in the Component Inspector panel's Parameters tab. Most of them are intuitive, but liveDragging and snapInterval might not be. The liveDragging parameter tells Slider whether or not to update its value property as the knob moves, as opposed to when it is released. When you set liveDragging to false, the circles will resize only after you reposition the knob and then release it. The snapInterval parameter tells Slider how often to update its value property. To demonstrate, set liveDragging to true, and then change snapInterval to a small number, such as 1. When you drag the knob, you'll see the circles resize smoothly. Change snapInterval to 10 and test again, and the circles resize less smoothly, because you're asking value to count by tens.

You may be surprised to find a direction parameter (its values are horizontal and vertical). Why not just use the Free Transform tool to rotate this slider? Well, try it. We'll wait . . . Kind of weird, right? It doesn't work. Components are a sophisticated phenomenon, even though they look so simple.

Now, what if you want a slanted slider, not horizontal or vertical? Here's a trick: select the Slider instance, convert it to a movieclip (Modify ➤ Convert to Symbol), and give that movieclip an instance name. When both the movieclip and its nested Slider have instance names, you're set.

```
sliderClip.slider.addEventListener(Event.CHANGE, changeHandler);
function changeHandler(evt:Event):void {
  circle1.scaleX = sliderClip.slider.value / 100;
  circle2.scaleY = sliderClip.slider.value / 100;
};
```

TextArea component

Chapter 6 introduced you to text fields. Consider the TextArea component a text field in a tux. It has an attractive, slightly beveled border, lets you limit how many characters can be typed into it (like input text fields), and is optionally scrollable (see Figure 11-28). This component is akin to the <textarea> element in HTML.

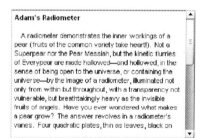

Figure 11-28. TextArea is the James Bond of text fields.

TextArea is skinnable, but the parts are few. You'll see a nested skin for the scrollbars when you double-click an instance in the authoring environment. More likely, you'll want to style its text contents, which works as described in the "Button component" section.

> *Using one or more instances of the TextArea component in your movie will add 21KB to the SWF if no other components (other than the automatically included UIScrollBar) share the load.*

Open the TextArea.fla file in this chapter's Exercise folder to see an example of populating a TextArea instance with text. (We figured it would be cruel to make you type in a lengthy bit of sample text on your own.) Note that the TextArea component can display HTML text, as shown in the sample file, or plain text. Use the component's htmlText or text property accordingly.

Notice that the Parameters tab of the Component Inspector panel shows only a text parameter for supplying text. We can't imagine anyone using that tiny space to enter more than a sentence, so reference that parameter as a property in your ActionScript. Assuming ta is the TextArea component's instance name:

```
ta.htmlText = "<p>HTML text here, with <b>styling</b>.</p>";
```

or

```
ta.text = "Plain text content here.";
```

TextInput component

The TextInput component is the single-line kid brother of TextArea. For this reason, to trump it up, we'll show it displaying one of the shortest short stories in the world, attributed to Ernest Hemingway (see Figure 11-29).

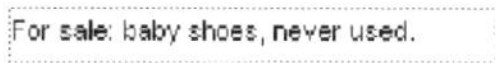

For sale: baby shoes, never used.

Figure 11-29. TextInput is a singe-line component, mainly used for user input.

TextInput is primarily used to collect typed user input, like HTML-based "contact us" forms, and can even be set to display password characters as asterisks (see the displayAsPassword parameter). The component is skinnable—just double-click an instance in the authoring environment—but there's not much to skin. Styling works as described in the "Button component" section.

> *Using one or more instances of the* TextInput *component in your movie will add 15KB to the SWF if no other components share the load.*

To see the TextInput component in action, open the TextInput.fla file that accompanies this chapter. Note the two TextInput instances, with instance names input (top) and output (bottom). Select each component in turn and look at the Parameters tab of the Component Inspector panel as you do. For the top TextInput instance, the displayAsPassword and editable parameters are set to true. For the bottom one, both of those parameters are set to false. You're about to make the upper component reveal its password to the lower one.

Click into frame 1 of the scripts layer and type the following ActionScript:

```
input.addEventListener(Event.CHANGE, changeHandler);
function changeHandler(evt:Event):void {
  output.text = input.text;
};
```

As text is typed into the upper TextInput instance, the Event.CHANGE handler updates the lower instance's text content with that of the upper instance's content. Because of the parameter settings, the text content is hidden above but clearly displayed below.

523

TileList component

TileList is not unlike the ScrollPane component. Both load files for display, optionally with scollbars, but TileList displays numerous files—JPGs, SWFs, and so on—in the tiled arrangement shown in Figure 11-30.

Double-click a TileList instance to edit its skins. You'll see a second tier of skins for the scrollbars. Styling may be accomplished as described in the "Button component" section.

> *Using one or more instances of the* TileList *component in your movie will add 32KB to the SWF if no other components share the load.*

Figure 11-30. TileList displays a tiled arrangement of content, optionally scrolling as necessary.

There are quite a few parameters listed in the Parameters tab of the Component Inspector panel for this component, but they're all easy to grasp. For example, there are settings for the width and number of columns, height and number of rows, direction or orientation (horizontal or vertical), and scrolling settings (on, off, and auto, the last of which makes scrollbars show only as necessary). The dataProvider parameter is the most important, because that's where you define the content to show. It works the same as the dataProvider for ComboBox, except that instead of label and data properties, TileList expects label and source.

If you find the Parameters tab a bit confining, you can always use ActionScript to add items to the TileList. To try this, open the TileList.fla file in the Chapter 11 Exercise folder. Note that the TileList instance has the instance name tl, and the dynamic text field below it has the instance name output.

Click into frame 1 of the scripts layer and type the following ActionScript:

```
tl.addItem({label:"Mug 6", source:"Mug06.jpg"});
tl.addItem({label:"Mug 7", source:"Mug07.jpg"});
tl.addItem({label:"Mug 8", source:"Mug08.jpg"});
```

```
tl.addEventListener(Event.CHANGE, changeHandler);
function changeHandler(evt:Event):void {
  output.text = tl.selectedItem.label;
};
```

The first three lines use practically the same approach we used for adding an additional item to the ComboBox instance in that section of the chapter. Mugs 1 through 5 are specified in the Component Inspector panel. Here, these three lines of code give us a few more mug shots (heh, mug shots—we love that joke). In the event handler, the changeHandler() function updates the output text fields' text property with the label value of the TileList's selected item.

> TileList *also supports multiple selections, like the* List *component. The sample code in the "List component" section provides the same basic mechanism you would use here, except instead of targeting the* data *property, you'll probably want to target* label, *as shown in the preceding single-selection sample.*

UILoader component

If the Flash CS4 UI components all went to a Halloween party, UILoader would show up as the Invisible Man (see Figure 11-31).

Figure 11-31. Practically speaking, UILoader has no visual elements (and yes, this figure is empty; it tickled us to include it).

So what's the point? Ah, but UILoader is such a selfless, *giving* component! Its purpose is to load and display content other than itself. This lets you avoid using the Loader class (as described in Chapter 14), just in case the thought of ActionScript makes you feel like you discovered half a worm in your apple. Simply enter a file name into the source parameter of the Component Inspector panel's Parameters tab, and you're set (see Figure 11-32).

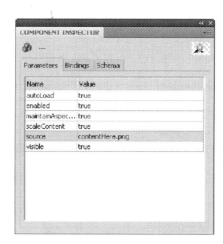

Figure 11-32. Just enter in the name of a supported file format, and Flash will load it.

> Using one or more instances of the UILoader *component in your movie will add 15KB to the SWF if no other components share the load.*

Here's a UILoader component exercise:

1. Open the UILoader.fla file that accompanies this chapter. Double-click the UILoader instance, and you'll see message that no skins are available. Since we aren't speaking to this component with ActionScript (yet), it doesn't need an instance name.

2. In the Parameters tab of the Component Inspector panel, enter the file name Onion.jpg into the right column of the source row. This references a JPG file in the same folder as your FLA.

3. Test your movie, and you'll see the onion load into its UILoader container.

4. Change the maintainAspectRatio parameter to false and test again. This time, the onion loads a bit squished. Our personal preference is usually to maintain aspect ratio. The scaleContent parameter determines whether the loaded content is scaled or cropped in its container.

5. Our friend ProgressBar is about to make a cameo appearance. Drag an instance of the ProgessBar component to the stage below the UILoader instance, and give the UILoader instance the instance name loader.

6. Select the ProgressBar instance, and in the Parameters tab, set its source parameter to loader— that's the instance name you just gave the UILoader instance (see Figure 11-33). You're

associating the two and telling the ProgressBar component to check with the UILoader component to divulge how much of the requested file has loaded.

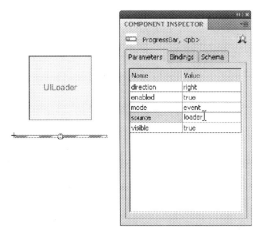

Figure 11-33. It's very easy to show the load progess for a UILoader instance.

7. Test your movie again.

8. in the SWF's menu bar, select View ➤ Simulate Download to see some super-easy preloading action.

9. Close the SWF.

10. To wrap up, let's add a teensy bit of ActionScript. (Don't worry, that half a worm we mentioned earlier was just a centipede—half a centipede.) To make sure ActionScript talks to the ProgressBar instance, give it an instance name. We're using pb. Click into frame 1 of the scripts layer and type the following ActionScript:

```
pb.addEventListener(Event.COMPLETE, completeHandler);
function completeHandler(evt:Event):void {
  removeChild(pb);
};
```

11. Test the movie for the last time. You'll see what this ActionScript does: it makes the progress bar disappear when loading is complete.

UIScrollBar component

If you read any other sections of this chapter, you've probably already been introduced to the UIScrollBar component. This component is a humble but useful member of the team, as it allows other components to have scrollbars. UIScrollBar is skinnable by double-clicking any instance in the authoring environment. Styling doesn't make much sense, but it is possible as described in the "Button component" section.

> *Using one or more instances of the* UIScrollBar *component in your movie will add 18KB to the SWF if no other components share the load.*

So as to avoid repeating ourselves, we'll direct your attention to the "Your Turn: Scrollable text" section in Chapter 6 to see this component in action.

What you have learned

In this chapter, you've learned the following:

- How to use every one of the Flash CS4 UI components
- How to write the ActionScript that controls components
- How to skin a component
- How to manage components in a Flash movie

In the next chapter, we'll show you how to use CSS to format text in a Flash movie. This may seem a bit odd, because the Text tool has a lot of settings in the Property inspector and a whole chapter in this book shows you how to use them. But one of the adages we live by is this: there are six million ways of doing everything in digital media and the best way is the one you pick. When it comes to text, that rule really comes into play, but an even stronger one supersedes it:

Let the software do the work.

Clients are fickle. One day the black Times Roman they asked for is fabulous, and the next day it "just has to be" green Helvetica Narrow. This can be a huge waste of time. You can spend hours opening Flash files and physically making the change, or pawing through ActionScript looking for code that formats text. Is there an easier way? You betcha. CSS to the rescue. Flash gives you the ability to put your styling into a CSS document. This means it's all in one place, and when the client wants the green Helvetica Narrow changed to orange Franklin Book, you can grumble to the client about the hours it is going to take to make the change, and then open the style sheet and spend 5 minutes, not hours, carrying it out.

It isn't as dry as it sounds, because you can do some pretty interesting things with CSS-formatted text in Flash CS4. What are they? Turn the page to find out.

Chapter 12

CSS

Cascading Style Sheets (CSS) refers to a World Wide Web Consortium (W3C) specification that, in the W3C's own words, provides "a simple mechanism for adding style (e.g., fonts, colors, spacing) to Web documents" (http://www.w3.org/Style/CSS/). The concept is simple, but as any web developer will tell you, CSS can be a Marlboro-smokin', tumbleweed-kickin', maverick cowboy when it comes to corralling HTML. In other words, CSS is rugged and powerful, and does a great job at making HTML behave. Obviously, this is a good thing. But CSS can also be a bit hard to work with, which makes sense when you're dealing with a stubbly, saddle-sore buckaroo.

In the world of HTML, the trouble with CSS is due to the wide variety of browsers (and versions of browsers) in use by the general public. Each browser supports CSS to a varying, and often buggy, degree. In Flash, you have a lot less to worry about, even though the use of CSS requires ActionScript. Why are things easier in a SWF? The answer is mainly that Flash supports only a very small subset of the full CSS specification. This means that there are only a few cows to wrangle. As a Flash designer, you're not worried about half a dozen browsers, but merely a single Flash Player plug-in. As an extra plus, the supported CSS subset hasn't really changed since the feature was introduced in Flash MX 2004 (Flash Player 7).

"Wait a minute, varmints," you might be saying, "If CSS has been available since Flash Player 7, you're really talking about four Flash Players: versions 7 through 10. Don't try to pull a fast one on us!" Well, if we opened it up to ActionScript 2.0, you would have a good point. Even so, the supported styles are pretty much the same; it's only the ActionScript nitty-gritty that has been updated. In any case, four plug-ins are nothing compared to a herd of browsers—and since we're only dealing with ActionScript 3.0 in this book, Flash Players 9 and 10 are the only ones that count. Yippee-ki-yay!

Here's what we'll cover in this chapter:

- Understanding the power and limitations of CSS in Flash
- Generating and applying CSS in ActionScript
- Using custom HTML tags
- Taking advantage of inheritance in CSS
- Styling anchor tag hyperlinks
- Embedding fonts for CSS
- Loading styles from an external CSS file

The following files are used in this chapter (located in Chapter12/ExerciseFiles_Ch12/Exercise/):

- Styling01.fla
- Styling02.fla
- Styling03.fla
- Styling04.fla
- ClassSelectors.fla
- ElementSelectors.fla
- Hyperlinks.fla
- HyperlinksVaried.fla
- Inheritance.fla
- StylingEmbeddedFonts01.fla
- styles.css
- StylingExternal.fla

The source files are available online from either of the following sites:

- http://www.FoundationFlashCS4.com
- http://www.friendsofED.com/download.html?isbn=9781430210931

In a nutshell, the power of CSS is that it allows you to separate styling from informational content. In Flash, we're essentially talking about text. You'll wrap text content in HTML tags—that's one side of the coin—and you'll style those HTML tags with CSS—that's the other side. Flip that coin as you see fit. If you change your mind about how the text should look—regarding font, color, indentation, spacing, and the like—you can change the CSS without affecting the text. The reverse is also true. Not only that, but styling can be applied to numerous text fields at once, and even managed from a convenient external file. As if that were not enough, this external style sheet can update a movie's styles without requiring you to recompile the SWF! Have we got your interest yet?

Styling with CSS

Here are the available style properties:

- color: This property determines the color of text, specified as a hexadecimal value preceded by the # sign, as in #FFFFFF, rather than the 0xFFFFFF you would use in ActionScript.

- display: This property determines how the styled object is displayed. Values include inline (displayed without a built-in line break), block (includes a built-in line break), and none (not displayed at all).

- fontFamly: This property allows you to specify fonts for text content—either a single font or comma-separated collection of fonts listed in order of desirability.

- fontSize: This property is used for specifying font size in pixels. Only number values are accepted (units such as pt or px are ignored).

- fontStyle: This property optionally displays text content in italics, if the font in use supports it. Values include normal and italic.

- fontWeight: This property optionally displays text content in bold, if the font in use supports it. Values include normal and bold.

- kerning: This property, if specified as true, allows embedded fonts to be rendered with kerning, if the fonts support it. *Kerning* is the removal of a bit of space between letters. It is applied only in SWF files generated in the Windows version of Flash. Once the SWF is published, the kerning is visible both in Windows and Mac.

- leading: This property determines the amount of space between lines of text. Negative values, which are allowed, condense lines. Only number values are accepted (units such as pt or px are ignored).

- letterSpacing: Not to be confused with kerning, this property determines the amount of space distributed evenly between characters. Only number values are accepted (units such as pt or px are ignored).

- marginLeft and marginRight: These properties add marginal padding by the specified amount in pixels to the left and right. Only number values are accepted (units such as pt or px are ignored).

- textAlign: This property aligns text. Values include left, center, right, and justify.

- textDecoration: This property adds or removes underscoring by way of the underline and none values.

- textIndent: This property indents a text field by the specified amount in pixels. Only number values are accepted (units such as pt or px are ignored).

Now let's roll up our sleeves and use some of these properties:

1. Open the Styling01.fla file from the Exercise folder for this chapter. There are a few things already in place for you. Note the two dynamic text fields, side by side, with instance names unstyledContent and styledContent. There's also a bit of ActionScript in frame 1 of the scripts layer, which does nothing more than build a string of HTML tags and apply that string to the TextField.htmlText property of the two text fields.

2. Test the movie to see two identical copies of the wasabi salmon recipe shown Figure 12-1 (yup, it's a real recipe).

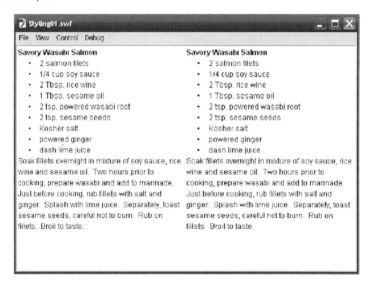

Figure 12-1. CSS is about to save you a lot of effort.

When you use CSS in Flash, the styling must be applied to a text field before any text is added to it. If you apply styling afterward, you'll get mixed results, or the styling won't work at all. We're going to leave the unstyledContent text field as is, in order to have a running comparison. The CSS that formats the styled text field will need to appear before the last line of ActionScript—styledContent. htmlText = str;—because the last line actually provides the HTML text.

3. Put your cursor in front of the last line of code and press Enter (Return) three times. This is where the new ActionScript will go. Now, hold that thought.

How is this CSS thing going to work? That's a good question, and thankfully, the answer isn't especially complicated, even though the process takes a few steps. First, you're going to create an instance of the StyleSheet class. Next, you'll decide on a handful of style properties. You'll repeatedly use the StyleSheet.setStyle() method to associate those properties with an HTML tag. Finally, you'll associate the StyleSheet instance itself with a given text field and add HTML content to that text field.

The crafty thing is that there are a number of ways to handle the setStyle() part. We're going to step you through a wordy approach first, because we think it best summarizes, on a conceptual level, what's going on. When you've seen that, we'll steer you toward a more compact approach, which will eventually lead toward an external CSS file, which is the most versatile way to handle styling in Flash.

4. OK, still holding the thought? Good. Put your cursor into the second of the three blank lines that precede the last line of code. Type the following ActionScript:

```
var css:StyleSheet = new StyleSheet();
var style:Object = new Object();

style.fontStyle = "italic";
style.color = "#A2A2A2";
style.leading = "-2";

css.setStyle("li", style);
styledContent.styleSheet = css;
```

Let's review what you've done so far. The first line declares a variable, css, which points to an instance of the StyleSheet class. The second line declares another variable, style, which points to an instance of the generic Object class—that's right, this is an Object object. The next three lines set arbitrary properties of this new object: fontStyle, color, and leading, each of which is set to a string value. The second-to-last line refers again to the css instance, using that instance to invoke StyleSheet.set-Style() with two parameters: an HTML tag to style and the object with which to style it. Quite simply, this line says, "Any <li> tags in the house? If so, you're about to get comfy with the style object, whose instructions are to render you in italics, in the color #A2A2A2 and at a leading of -2." Finally, a text field whose instance name is styledContent has its styleSheet property associated with the css instance.

5. Test the movie so far to see a change in all the <li> content, as shown in Figure 12-2. You can save and close the movie if you wish.

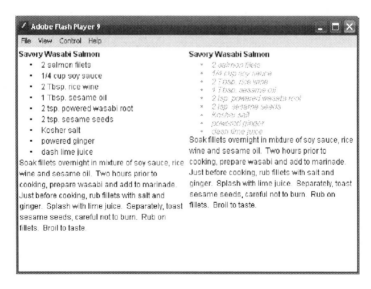

Figure 12-2. CSS styling applied to a series of <li> tags

Pretty nifty! Now, in case you thought that ActionScript was a lot to type, keep in mind that what you've seen is the gabbiest of the styling approaches. It's possible to collapse five of those lines into one, which we'll do in just a moment. First, let's take a look at how this might have happened without CSS—because once you see that catastrophe, even this version will seem a welcome relief.

Taking just the first <li> tag's content, how would you apply italics? That's easy enough. You'll remember from Chapter 6 that you do this with the <i> tag. So far, then, we have one nested pair:

```
<li><i>2 salmon filets</i></li>
```

What about the coloring? That's the <font> tag. Combined, that makes this:

```
<li><i><font color="#A2A2A2">2 salmon filets</font></i></li>
```

Almost done! The final style property is leading (the spacing between lines). In the HTML-only realm, that requires the proprietary Flash tag <textformat>. This brings the combined total of nested tags to the following example of spaghetti code:

```
<li><i><font color="#A2A2A2"><textformat leading="-2">2 salmon
➡filets</textformat></font></i></li>
```

Multiply that by the nine bullet points in this recipe, and you'll get carpal tunnel syndrome just thinking about it! If you decide later to change the text color, you'll need to revisit all nine nested <font> tags and either edit or remove them. It's a mess. Definitely, the CSS styling mechanism is the nicer pick. All the more so if we can reduce the lines of ActionScript.

In order to accomplish that reduction, we're going to rely on a shortcut in creating our Object instance, involving the use of the curly braces ({}). Our setStyle() line will continue to use "li" as the first parameter, but the second parameter will be composed of a single "shortcut" object that holds all three styling properties at once, as shown in Figure 12-3.

```
var style:Object = new Object();

style.fontStyle = "italic";
style.color = "#A2A2A2";
style.leading = "-2";
```

```
css.setStyle("li", style);
```

Figure 12-3. These lines can be folded into a single object reference.

The actual ActionScript looks like this:

```
css.setStyle("li", {fontStyle: "italic", color: "#A2A2A2",
➡leading: "-2"});
```

This brings the full ActionScript styling portion to a mere three lines:

```
var css:StyleSheet = new StyleSheet();
css.setStyle("li", {fontStyle: "italic", color: "#A2A2A2",
➡leading: "-2"});
styledContent.styleSheet = css;
```

Using this approach, let's style a few more HTML tags:

1. Open the Styling02.fla file in this chapter's Exercise folder. This file picks up where we left off. The same text fields are in place, and some styling has already been applied (see the scripts layer). What's there uses the shortened code version we just looked at.

2. Now, you'll style all the <p> tags. Position your cursor after the setStyle() line and press Enter (Return) to make room for the new code. Update your ActionScript so that it includes the following new code (shown in bold):

```
var css:StyleSheet = new StyleSheet();
css.setStyle("li", {fontStyle: "italic", color: "#A2A2A2",
➥leading: "-2"});
css.setStyle("p", {textAlign: "justify", leading: "6"});
styledContent.styleSheet = css;
```

3. Test your movie to see the new formatting—justified and with a taller line height—below the bullet points at the bottom right (see Figure 12-4).

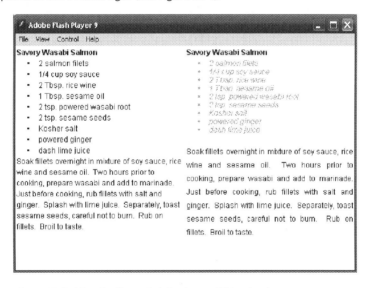

Figure 12-4. After the first style is in place, additional styles are a snap.

Say, this is encouraging! Let's keep right on going. There really isn't enough space between the bullet points and the text below, so let's pad the bottom of the <ul> tag a bit. We also want the recipe's title to stand out more.

4. Enter the scripts layer again and update the styling ActionScript so that it includes the following new code (shown in bold):

```
var css:StyleSheet = new StyleSheet();
css.setStyle("li", {fontStyle: "italic", color: "#A2A2A2",
➥leading: "-2"});
css.setStyle("p", {textAlign: "justify", leading: "6"});
css.setStyle("ul", {leading: "6"});
```

```
     css.setStyle("b", {fontFamily: "Impact", fontSize: "18",
     ➥color: "#339966"});
     styledContent.styleSheet = css;
```

5. Test the movie to see the new styling—well, part of it.

Whoops! There's now space after the bullets—the additional 6 pixels of leading we wanted—but the title (the `<b>` content) hasn't changed at all! What's going on? It is a matter of selectors, which we'll deal with in the next section.

6. Feel free to save the file or close it without saving the changes.

We're going to go off on a sizable tangent here, but don't worry. It all eventually leads back to the salmon.

Element selectors vs. class selectors

Up to this point, we've limited our view to something called *element selectors*. These refer to HTML tags, also called *elements*, and they apply their styling, in one swoop, to all tags of a specified kind. Want to format all `<p>` content? Write a p element selector. Need to style a bunch of list items (`<li>`)? Write an li element selector. This is a pretty easy procedure. But, as you saw at the end of the previous section, it doesn't always work. This is one of the limitations of Flash CSS, and it's an important one to note.

In HTML documents, practically all HTML elements can be styled by way of an element selector. In Flash, the list is vastly reduced. According to the Flash CS4 documentation, the following tags comprise the meager list: `<body>`, `<p>`, `<li>`, and `<a>`. The interesting thing about this list is that `<body>` doesn't appear as one of the supported tags noted in the ActionScript 3.0 Language and Component Reference entry for TextField.htmlText. Then again, `<ul>` doesn't appear in that list either, and yet we used that tag to implement a leading style. So, is there a method to this madness? Is there some easy way to keep track of which tags can be styled with element selectors and which can't?

Block element styling

The authors spent a bit of time studying the tea leaves, and this is what we discovered: officially documented or not, the tags that support element selectors are all block elements, with the exception of the anchor tag (`<a>`). In other words, the rule of thumb is that if the tag carries with it a built-in line break, then an element selector will do the trick. The special case is hyperlinks, which we'll cover in detail later in the chapter (hyperlinks are a special case in several ways).

For your reference, let's take a quick look at a "proof is in the pudding" sample file:

1. Open the ElementSelectors.fla file in this chapter's Exercise folder. You'll find a text field with the instance name styledContent. The ActionScript in the scripts layer shouldn't be any trouble for you by now. A string of HTML is created; element selectors are defined and then assigned to a StyleSheet instance; and finally, the HTML is supplied to the text field.

2. Test the movie to see the result shown in Figure 12-5. The output may not look all that interesting, but it is, because it demonstrates a few additional "gotchas" while verifying the block element principle.

Figure 12-5. Only block elements—and one exception, anchor tags—support element selectors.

3. Click into frame 1 of the scripts layer and take a look at the ActionScript in the Actions panel.

Each line of HTML ends in a break tag (`<br />`), just to keep things visually neat. Every tag is given an element selector that alternates its color between #0000FF (blue) and #00FF00 (green). In normal HTML, most of these lines would display as either blue or green (`<img />` contains no actual text, so it wouldn't). In Flash, this holds true only for the block elements.

The `<a>` tag is not a block element, so it does not display an additional, built-in line break as some later tags do. But as the exception to the rule in question, the `<a>` tag does pick up the blue color (mid-gray, in Figure 12-5) from its element selector. The `<body>` and `<p>` (paragraph) tag contents carry their own additional line breaks—these are block elements—and both display the expected element selector color styling. The `<ul>` and `<li>` tags' content is combined. These are also block elements and therefore display a combined pair of extra line breaks, as well as the expected element selector styling.

4. Comment out the body and li element selectors in the ActionScript by preceding those lines with double slashes (`//`), as shown in Figure 12-6.

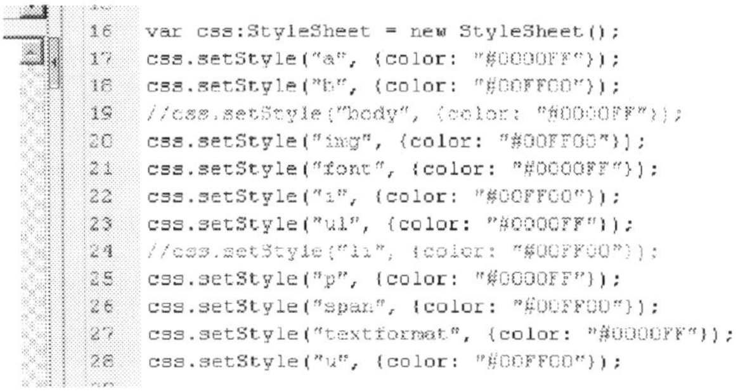

```
16   var css:StyleSheet = new StyleSheet();
17   css.setStyle("a", {color: "#0000FF"});
18   css.setStyle("b", {color: "#00FF00"});
19   //css.setStyle("body", {color: "#0000FF"});
20   css.setStyle("img", {color: "#00FF00"});
21   css.setStyle("font", {color: "#0000FF"});
22   css.setStyle("i", {color: "#00FF00"});
23   css.setStyle("ul", {color: "#0000FF"});
24   //css.setStyle("li", {color: "#00FF00"});
25   css.setStyle("p", {color: "#0000FF"});
26   css.setStyle("span", {color: "#00FF00"});
27   css.setStyle("textformat", {color: "#0000FF"});
28   css.setStyle("u", {color: "#00FF00"});
```

Figure 12-6. Commenting out the body and li selectors leads to a line-spacing quirk and the concept of inheritance.

539

5. Test the movie again.

It should come as no surprise that the <body> tag content is no longer styled. What may raise your eyebrows is that the extra line break is missing. This is a quirk involving only the <body> tag, and will raise its head again in the "Custom tags" section of this chapter. The other thing to notice is that the <ul>/<li> content has changed color. This is because a distinct color style was applied to each tag (green for <ul> and blue for <li>). Blue won the wrestling match earlier because of a CSS concept called *inheritance* (covered in the "Style inheritance" section later in the chapter).

6. As a final experiment, uncomment the body element selector by removing the double slashes from that line. Instead, comment out the p element selector.

7. Test the movie a final time, and you'll see that the <p> content is still blue.

Why? Again, this is an example of inheritance, but in a really twisted way. Under normal circumstances, HTML documents feature most of their content inside a <body> tag. If a style is applied to the body, it will "trickle down" to tags inside that body if those inner tags happen to support the style properties at hand. Here in this Flash file, the <p> content is clearly not inside the <body> content, and yet some phantom inheritance seems to still hold sway. Comment out the body element selector one last time, and the <p> content finally turns black.

8. Close the file without saving the changes.

Every development platform has its quirks, and now you've seen a few of the ones that belong to Flash. Being aware of these, even if they aren't burned into your neurons, might just save your hide when something about CSS styling surprises you.

Now you've had some experience with block elements and the anchor tag, with the understanding that anchor tags still hold a bit of mystery, yet to be unfolded. Meanwhile, what remains of the other supported HTML tags? What's the opposite of a block element, and how can one be styled?

Inline element styling

In Flash, if a tag is not a block element, it is an inline element. All that means is that it doesn't carry its own line break with it. Examples include the <b> and <i> tags, which apply their own innate formatting—bold and italic, respectively—without otherwise interrupting the flow of text. As you've seen, inline elements in Flash do not support element selectors. Is there another option, then? You bet your spurs, podner. But it goes only so far.

Not to be confused with the classes discussed in Chapter 4, CSS features something called *class selectors*, which differ from element selectors in a significant way. Rather than apply their style to all tags of a specified type, class selectors look only for tags that have a class attribute whose value is set to the name of the class in question. We'll see an example of this in just a moment. In HTML documents, just about any tag can be given a class attribute, but this isn't the case in Flash. Actually, nothing *stops* you from giving an HTML tag such an attribute in Flash, but Flash applies class selector styling to only a few tags, and only one of those as an inline element.

Here's another "proof is in the pudding" exercise, which should make everything clear:

1. Open the ClassSelectors.fla file in this chapter's Exercise folder. At first glance, this file may look identical to ElementSelectors.fla, but click into frame 1 of the scripts layer to lay eyes on a different chunk of code.

You'll see that every HTML tag now has a class attribute, set either to blue or green, and the number of selectors has been reduced to two: the selfsame blue and green styles. Now, how can you tell that these are class selectors and not element selectors? The giveaway, which is easy to miss if you aren't looking for it, is the dot (.) in front of the style names (see Figure 12-7).

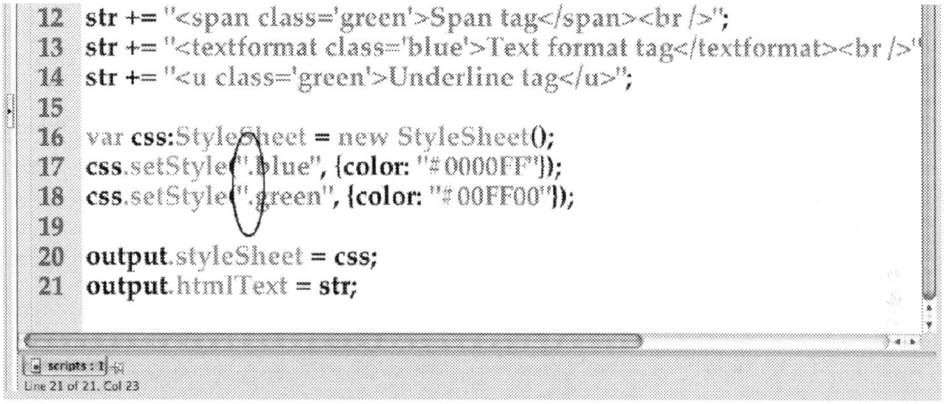

```
12   str += "<span class='green'>Span tag</span><br />";
13   str += "<textformat class='blue'>Text format tag</textformat><br />"
14   str += "<u class='green'>Underline tag</u>";
15
16   var css:StyleSheet = new StyleSheet();
17   css.setStyle(".blue", {color: "#0000FF"});
18   css.setStyle(".green", {color: "#00FF00"});
19
20   output.styleSheet = css;
21   output.htmlText = str;
```

scripts : 1
Line 21 of 21, Col 23

Figure 12-7. Class selectors are much more selective than element selectors. You can spot them by their dot prefixes.

Those dots change everything, because at this point, CSS doesn't care which tag it's dealing with. It only cares if that tag has a class attribute set to blue, green, or whatever the style's name is.

> *Be careful where you put your dots! They belong only in the setStyle() method, and never in the class attribute of any tag.*

2. Test the movie to see the result.

Remember that in the "real world" outside of Flash, every one of these tags would be affected by the relevant style. In the SWF, only the following tags do anything: <a>, <li>, <p>, and <span>. Unfortunately, we haven't found a way to memorize this list as neatly as the other, but if you can remember the block elements that go with element selectors, you need only swap the <body> tag for the <span> tag and drop <ul> to know the block and inline elements that go with class selectors. (Yeah, we agree, it's not especially intuitive.)

3. For the sake of completeness, comment out the .green class selector and test the movie to verify the outcome. The <ul>/<li> content turns black, because class selectors don't apply to <ul> tags in Flash.

4. Close the movie without saving the changes.

Custom tags

Ready to head back to the wasabi salmon? When we abandoned it to venture out on our educational tangent, our styling had been applied, with the exception of the <b> content, and now we know why. The <b> tag is not a block element, which means it simply doesn't support element selectors.

Element selectors affect all tags of a given type, and for the sake of illustration, let's say we want only this recipe's title to stand out, rather than all content that happens to be set in bold. An obvious solution, based on your current knowledge, is to swap the <b> tag for something that supports class selectors. Let's try it.

1. Open the Styling03.fla file in this chapter's Exercise folder to see an example of using a class selector. The key changes in the ActionScript from Styling01.fla are shown in bold in the following code:

```
var str:String = "";
str += "<p class='heading'>Savory Wasabi Salmon</p>";
str += "<ul>";
...
css.setStyle("ul", {leading: "6"});
css.setStyle(".heading", {fontFamily: "Impact", fontSize: "18",
➥color: "#339966"});
styled.styleSheet = css;
```

This mix-and-match approach is perfectly valid. In fact, it's a good basic methodology: use element selectors to sweep through the styling for most tags, and then cover the exceptions with class selectors. Alternatively, you can use custom tags, which provide a kind of hybrid mechanism. They save you from having to type class='someStyleName' throughout your HTML content. And the best part is that you can use familiar, genuine HTML tags from the "real world," if you like (think along the lines of <h1>, <h2>, <strong>, and so on). Flash happily accepts these as "custom" tags, because in its skimpy repertoire, they are.

2. Open the Styling04.fla file to see a custom tag in action. Once again, this file is virtually identical to the previous one, except for the parts shown in bold:

```
var str:String = "";
str += "<strong>Savory Wasabi Salmon</strong>";
str += "<ul>";
...
css.setStyle("ul", {leading: "6"});
css.setStyle("strong", {fontFamily: "Impact", fontSize: "18",
➥color: "#339966"});
styled.styleSheet = css;
```

Note the *absence* of a dot preceding the strong element selector, which means that this is *not* a class selector! If you put 50 <strong> tags full of content into your SWF, all 50 occurrences will pick up the style from this setStyle() method. That said—and we can't stress this enough—please understand that this is not a magical, undocumented way to squeeze additional tags out of Flash's limited HTML support. Flash has no idea what a <strong> tag is, much less that most browsers treat it like a <b> tag. This is nothing more than a convenient hook for CSS—an excuse to dodge class selectors if you happen not to like them. In fact, to prove it, and to reveal a limitation of the custom tag approach, proceed to step 3.

3. Replace the `<strong>` tag in the bolded ActionScript with the completely made-up `<citrus>` tag. There is no such tag in any of the W3C specifications (we looked). Your code will change in only three places:

```
var str:String = "";
str += "<citrus>Savory Wasabi Salmon</citrus>";
str += "<ul>";
...
css.setStyle("ul", {leading: "6"});
css.setStyle("citrus", {fontFamily: "Impact", fontSize: "18",
➥color: "#339966"}));
styled.styleSheet = css;
```

4. In addition, find the word `lime` in the bulleted list and wrap it with this new `<citrus>` tag:

```
str += "<li>powered ginger</li>";
str += "<li>dash <citrus>lime</citrus> juice</li>";
str += "</ul>";
```

5. Test the movie. You should see the styling shown in Figure 12-8.

Danger, Will Robinson! What do we learn from the broken dash lime juice line? A valuable lesson, that's what. The recipe's title is fine, but that's because it stands on its own. The lime line breaks because custom tags become block elements when styled. In this case, the word juice has even been pushed past the extra line height given earlier to the `<ul>` tag.

We've spent the last several miles mulling over some pretty arcane rules and even hazier exceptions to them. CSS was supposed to be easier in Flash, right? If your head is spinning, take a sip from the canteen and rest for a spell. While we wait, one of the authors will hum an old, lonely cowboy tune. The lyrics go something like this: "To get the biggest bang for your buck, use element selectors first, then custom tags for headings and other short or specific blocks, and finally class selectors for special cases." (Hey, no one said it had to rhyme, and the melody really is pretty.)

Figure 12-8. Whoops, something isn't right with the lime.

Style inheritance

In moving from Object instances to the object shortcut characters ({}) earlier in the chapter, we saw one way to trim CSS into a more compact form. There's another way to shrink things even further, but it's more conceptual than syntactical. The concept is called *inheritance*, and it basically means that styles applied "up the creek" tend to eventually flow down to lower waters.

Let's look at a concrete example. Open the Inheritance.fla file in this chapter's Exercise folder. You'll see a text field with the instance name styledContent. Click into frame 1 of the scripts layer to view the ActionScript. As with the other samples in this chapter, the code begins by building an HTML string. In this case, the structure of the HTML tags is important. Stripping out the text content, the structure of the tag hierarchy looks like this:

```
<body>
  <p></p>
  <outer>
```

543

```
      <mid>
        <inner><span class='big'></span></inner>
      </mid>
    </outer>
  </body>
```

Styling is applied to the <body> tag, which sets its font to Courier. The tags nested inside this tag, <p> through <mid>, gain the same typeface thanks to inheritance. The custom <inner> tag would also inherit Courier, except that this particular tag bucks the trend by specifying its own font, Arial. This font overrides the inherited Courier and sets up its own new inheritance. Note that the <span> tag—which surrounds the word dignissim, whatever that means—lies within the <inner> tag. Because of this position, it displays in Arial, as its parent does (see Figure 12-9).

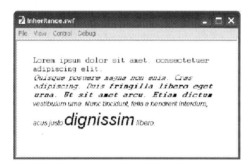

Figure 12-9. CSS inheritance in action

This sort of procedure can get fairly sophisticated. For example, the custom <outer> tag adds italics to the mix.

```
    css.setStyle("outer", {fontStyle: "italic"});
```

In light of that, and because the flow goes downhill, <mid>, <inner>, and <span> inherit not only the font of <outer>'s parent, but also its italics. Meanwhile, sibling tags (<p>) and parent tags (<body>) do not. And honestly, that makes good sense.

In the same vein, the custom <mid> tag introduces bold:

```
    css.setStyle("mid", {fontWeight: "bold"});
```

If unopposed, <inner> and <span> would inherit that bold styling as well, but <inner> purposely overrides that by setting fontWeight to normal in its own element selector:

```
    css.setStyle("inner", {fontFamily: "Arial", fontWeight: "normal"});
```

In turn, this causes <span> to inherit the override, as it too ignores the bold. Note, however, that <span> does inherit the italics, which were not overridden by a parent tag. The interesting thing is that the <span> content inherits styling applied to its parents, even though that styling is provided by element selectors. Why is this interesting? Remember that <span> is an inline element, and inline elements, as a rule, can't be styled with element selectors. Oh, the tangled web Flash weaves!

Use this inheritance phenomenon to your advantage. It saves you keystrokes. You don't need to specify font families for whole groups of related tags. In addition, inheritance gives you the opportunity to make sweeping changes from relatively few locations. As you've seen from the quirky exceptions, though, you'll want to experiment carefully before committing yourself to a particular styling scheme. But do make sure you experiment, because there's more to Flash CSS than first meets the eye.

Styling hyperlinks

Anchor tags are fun to style because of something called pseudo-classes. In CSS-speak, a *pseudo-class* corresponds to various possible states of an HTML element and is indicated by a colon (:) prefix. In Flash, the only supported pseudo-classes are associated with the anchor tag (<a>) and correspond to the following states:

- :link (an anchor tag that specifically contains an href attribute)
- :hover (triggered by a mouse rollover)
- :active (triggered by a mouse click)

The long and short of this is that you have the tools you need to create different anchor tag styles that update as the mouse moves and clicks your hyperlinks. Note that Flash does not support the :visited pseudo-class, which in normal CSS indicates that a hyperlink has already been clicked.

Think of pseudo-classes as a second tier of styles, not separated by hierarchy, as shown in the "Style inheritance" section, but instead separated by time or events.

Open the Hyperlinks.fla file in this chapter's Exercise folder to see an example in action. The ActionScript begins, as always, by establishing an HTML string:

```
var str:String = "";
str += "<ul>";
str += "<li><a href='http://www.apress.com/'>Hyperlink 1</a></li>";
str += "<li><a href='event:someFunction'>Hyperlink 2</a></li>";
str += "<li><a href='http://www.friendsofed.com/'>
➥Hyperlink 3</a></li>";
str += "</ul>";
```

These anchor tags happen to be nested within list items, but they don't need to be. The important part is that the anchor tags have href attributes actively in use. In these next three lines, the element selectors provide a style for all anchor tags in any state—that's the first bolded line—followed by distinct styles for the :hover and :active pseudo-classes.

```
var css:StyleSheet = new StyleSheet();
css.setStyle("li", {leading: "12"});
css.setStyle("a", {fontFamily: "Courier"});
css.setStyle("a:hover", {fontStyle: "italic"});
css.setStyle("a:active", {text-decoration: "underline",
➥color: "#FF0000"});
styledContent.styleSheet = css;
```

Test this movie to verify that hovering over hyperlinks puts them temporarily in italics, and that clicking omits the italics but additionally displays an underline and new color. The italic style isn't inherited by :active, because :active is not a child of :hover; they have a sibling relationship. The Courier typeface, however, appears for all states, because even the pseudo-classes are anchor tags.

What if you would like more than one style for your hyperlinks? The solution is to use a class selector. Open the HyperlinksVaried.fla file in this chapter's Exercise folder for an example. First, here's the new HTML (shown in bold):

```
var str:String = "";
str += "<ul>";
str += "<li><a href='http://www.apress.com/'>Hyperlink 1</a></li>";
str += "<li><a href='event:someFunction'>Hyperlink 2</a></li>";
str += "<li><a href='http://www.friendsofed.com/'>
➥Hyperlink 3</a></li>";
str += "</ul>";
str += "<ul>";
str += "<li><a class='oddball' href='http://www.apress.com/'>
➥Hyperlink 4</a></li>";
str += "<li><a class='oddball' href='event:someFunction'>
➥Hyperlink 5</a></li>";
str += "<li><a class='oddball' href='http://www.friendsofed.com/'>
➥Hyperlink 6</a></li>";
str += "</ul>";
```

Unfortunately, it isn't possible to create unique pseudo-classes for anchor tags with class attributes, but the following new class selector at least separates the new batch of hyperlinks in their default state (see Figure 12-10):

```
var css:StyleSheet = new StyleSheet();
css.setStyle("li", {leading: "12"});
css.setStyle("a", {fontFamily: "Courier"});
css.setStyle("a:hover", {fontStyle: "italic"});
css.setStyle("a:active", {textDecoration: "underline",
➥color: "#FF0000"});
css.setStyle(".oddball", {color: "#00FF00"});
styledContent.styleSheet = css;
```

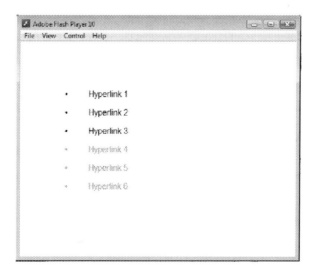

Figure 12-10. The last three hyperlinks are in a different color (gray here; green in real life).

Close the open files, and let's now look at embedding fonts.

Embedded fonts

Before we take what we've learned and nudge it all toward an external CSS file, let's make a quick stop at the Last Chance Saloon to talk about embedded fonts. CSS in Flash requires HTML, which in turn requires a dynamic text field. As you learned in Chapter 6, only static text fields embed font outlines by default. This means that unless you purposely embed your fonts—and the choice is yours—text in CSS-enhanced SWFs tends to have a jagged look, as shown in Figure 12-11.

Savory Wasabi Salmon

* 2 salmon filets
* 1/4 cup soy sauce
* 2 Tbsp. rice wine
* 1 Tbsp. sesame oil
* 2 tsp. powered wasabi root
* 2 tsp. sesame seeds
* Kosher salt
* powered ginger
* dash lime juice

Figure 12-11. Text can look a bit choppy if fonts aren't embedded.

Font symbols were introduced in Chapter 6, but there's a new twist in how they're used with CSS. To recap, the font-embedding process is as follows:

- Add a font symbol to the library and associate it with the desired font on your system.
- Enable the font symbol's linkage by exporting the symbol for ActionScript.
- Set the text field's embedFonts property to true.

The new part—because Flash CSS usage requires ActionScript—is that you must refer to the font's actual name in your setStyle() method. The tricky part is how to reference the font's actual name, because neither its symbol name (in the library) nor its linkage class name necessarily provides any clues. Naturally, you can find out the font's actual name by consulting the Font Symbol Properties dialog box, but why rope yourself into something hard-coded? If you choose to associate your font symbol with another font, you'll need to change the font's name in your code, unless you use the Font.fontName property instead. Here's how:

1. Open the StylingEmbeddedFonts01.fla file in this chapter's Exercise folder. Test the movie, and you'll see jagged fonts. Let's change that.

2. Click into frame 1 of the scripts layer and note the following pertinent lines of code:

```
var css:StyleSheet = new StyleSheet();
css.setStyle("li", {fontStyle: "italic", color: "#A2A2A2",
➥leading: "-2"});
```

```
css.setStyle("p", {textAlign: "justify", leading: "6"});
css.setStyle("ul", {leading: "6"});
css.setStyle("strong", {fontFamily: "Impact", fontSize: "18",
➥color: "#339966"});
css.setStyle("a", {textDecoration: "underline"});
css.setStyle("a:hover", {color: "#FF00FF"});

styledContent.styleSheet = css;
styledContent.htmlText = str;
```

3. Look at the strong element selector, and you'll see that the fontFamily property is set to Impact, which is represented in the library by a font symbol named ImpactNormal. Right-click (Ctrl-click) the ImpactNormal font symbol and select Properties to open the Font Symbol Properties dialog box.

4. In the Font Symbol Properties dialog box, verify that the actual font selected is Impact. (If you don't have Impact on your system, choose some other suitable headline typeface.) Also verify that the font symbol is exported for ActionScript, and that its linkage class name is ImpactNormal, as shown in Figure 12-12. Then click Cancel to close the dialog box.

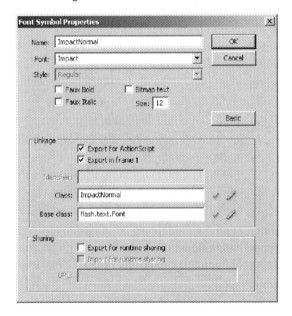

Figure 12-12. The font symbol's linkage class name is ImpactNormal.

So, referring to the actual font name—Impact (or your replacement)—will do, but you don't want to be tied to that changeable value. Instead, you're going to create an instance of this particular font—an instance of the custom ImpactNormal class—and reference that the Font.fontName property of that instance. You'll also set the TextField.embedFonts property of the styledContent instance to true.

5. Update the ActionScript as follows (new code in bold):

```
var embeddedFont:ImpactNormal = new ImpactNormal();

var css:StyleSheet = new StyleSheet();
css.setStyle("li", {fontStyle: "italic", color: "#A2A2A2",
➥leading: "-2"});
css.setStyle("p", {textAlign: "justify", leading: "6"});
css.setStyle("ul", {leading: "6"});
css.setStyle("strong", {fontFamily: embeddedFont.fontName,
➥fontSize: "18", color: "#339966"});
css.setStyle("a", {textDecoration: "underline"});
css.setStyle("a:hover", {color: "#FF00FF"});

styledContent.embedFonts = true;
styledContent.styleSheet = css;
styledContent.htmlText = str;
```

6. Test your movie, and the text shown in Figure 12-13 magically appears.

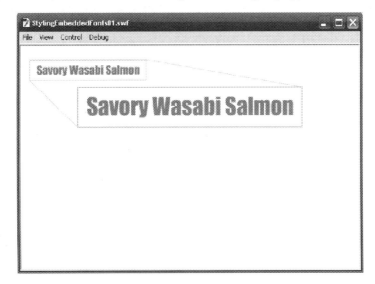

Figure 12-13. The ImpactNormal font is now showing, without the jaggies.

Oddly, only the <strong> element is showing! But hey . . . at least the lettering is smooth, as you can see from the inset. Only the <strong> element is showing because this text field is being asked to display more than one font: Impact and Arial (the text field's Property inspector settings specify Arial). Both fonts need to be embedded.

7. Using the technique described in Chapter 6, add an Arial font symbol to your library and name the symbol whatever you like. Make sure to export it for ActionScript. To prove that neither the symbol name nor the linkage class name makes any difference, name your linkage class something absurd, like HornyToads. You don't need to create a HornyToads instance in this case, because nothing in the ActionScript refers to that font by name (again, it's the text field itself that's set to Arial in the Properties inspector).

   Compare your work with StylingEmbeddedFonts02.fla in the Complete folder, whose font symbol is named HornyToads in both the library and the linkage class.

8. Test your movie to confirm that all of the text content shows, and without jaggies (see Figure 12-14). But there's still one problem. Can you spot it? Those <li> elements are supposed to be in italics!

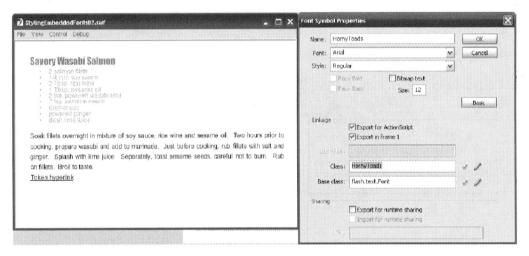

Figure 12-14. All the text is accounted for, and none of it suffers from the jaggies.

9. To get the italics to show, you need to add a second Arial font symbol, this time with Italic selected in the Style drop-down list. Repeat step 7, making sure to specify the italic variant of Arial, and name your symbol (and class) something like HornyToadsItalic. The StylingEmbeddedFonts02.fla file in this chapter's Complete folder demonstrates this for you.

10. Test your movie, and you'll finally see everything as it should be: all typefaces accounted for and smooth, including the italic variant.

Selectors vs. the Property inspector

It's imperative that you understand how important the Property inspector settings are in the previous examples. The only reason you need to instantiate the custom ImpactNormal class—as opposed to both that and HornyToads (Arial)—is that Arial was already selected as the text field's font in the Property inspector.

Take a look at StylingEmbeddedFonts03.fla in this chapter's Complete folder for a working example of how to reference more than one font in the ActionScript. You'll see that the text field's Property inspector settings have been changed to Times New Roman. That means the Arial typeface

(HornyToads), along with its italic variant (HornyToadsItalic) are present in the SWF, but not actually referenced anywhere. Here's the operative ActionScript to ensure that they do get referenced (new code in bold):

```
var embeddedImpact:ImpactNormal = new ImpactNormal();
var embeddedArial:HornyToads = new HornyToads();

var css:StyleSheet = new StyleSheet();
css.setStyle("li", {fontFamily: embeddedArial.fontName,
➥fontStyle: "italic", color: "#A2A2A2", leading: "-2"});
css.setStyle("p", {fontFamily: embeddedArial.fontName,
➥textAlign: "justify", leading: "6"});
css.setStyle("ul", {leading: "6"});
css.setStyle("strong", {fontFamily: embeddedImpact.fontName,
➥fontSize: "18", color: "#339966"});
css.setStyle("a", {textDecoration: "underline"});
css.setStyle("a:hover", {color: "#FF00FF"});

styledContent.embedFonts = true;
styledContent.styleSheet = css;
styledContent.htmlText = str;
```

In this version, the variable that holds the ImpactNormal instance has been renamed to embeddedImpact, just to differentiate it from the second scripted font reference, HornyToads (the embeddedArial variable). This solution makes use of CSS inheritance, because it specifies the embeddedArial instance only where it's necessary. Because the anchor tags (<a>) are nested inside the <p> tags, the p element selector takes care of both. The li element selector is needed because the <li> tags don't appear inside a tag styled for the embedded font. Note that although some selectors call for a fontStyle of italic, Flash is smart enough to understand, without a third font variable, that HornyToadsItalic is the italic variant of the HornyToads font.

Loading external CSS

If we had to pick our favorite aspect of CSS in Flash, it would undoubtedly be the fact that CSS styling can be loaded from an external file. The existence of this feature brings the concept of separating style from content to its logical conclusion.

Given all you've learned so far in this chapter, you'll be happy to find that loading external CSS is a piece of cake. There's really only one snare to be aware of: some of the style properties we showed you in the beginning of the chapter are spelled just a tad differently when they appear in an external file. Single-word properties, such as color and display, are identical. Multiple-word properties, such as fontFamily and fontSize, are split into hyphenated parts: font-family, font-size, and so on.

To see how external CSS works, open the StylingExternal.fla file in this chapter's Exercise folder. You'll see a single text file with the instance name styledContent. Click into frame 1 of the scripts layer and take a look at the ActionScript. By now, the HTML portion will be old hat. It's a resurrection of the salmon recipe one last time, with a token hyperlink at the bottom. The new stuff is just below it:

```
var css:StyleSheet = new StyleSheet();
var loader:URLLoader = new URLLoader();
var req:URLRequest = new URLRequest("styles.css")
loader.load(req);
loader.addEventListener(Event.COMPLETE, completeHandler);

function completeHandler(evt:Event):void {
  css.parseCSS(evt.target.data);
  styledContent.styleSheet = css;
  styledContent.htmlText = str;
};
```

The first line creates our familiar StyleSheet instance. The next two lines are new. A variable, loader, is declared and set to an instance of the URLLoader class. This differs from the Loader class (covered in Chapter 14), which loads images or SWFs. What makes URLLoader different is that it not only loads files, but it also actually reads them, which is essential when the goal is to sift through external CSS. The third variable, req, points to an instance of the URLRequest class and specifies the location of the actual CSS document.

The URLLoader.load() method is invoked on the loader instance with req as the parameter. Finally, the Event.COMPLETE event is handled with a function that performs three straightforward tasks: parse the loaded CSS, set the text field's styleSheet property to the css instance, and set its htmlText property to the prepared HTML string. You already know how the last two work, so let's pick apart the first line of this function.

The StyleSheet.parseCSS() method takes a single parameter, which in this case is the expression evt.target.data. That may look like a mouthful, but it's nothing more than a compact way of getting at the CSS styles themselves. The evt.target part refers to the loader instance. How? The evt variable is received as a parameter to the completeHandler() function and refers to the Event.COMPLETE event itself. In other words, evt is the event object dispatched by loader when the CSS file loads. The Event class features a target property, which refers to the object that dispatched the event—namely, loader. As an instance of the URLLoader class, loader features a data property that points to the CSS data stored inside the styles.css file.

Open the styles.css file in Dreamweaver CS4, or any simple text editor, such as WordPad on the PC or TextEdit on the Mac. (Although CSS files serve a special styling purpose, they are really just text files with a .css file extension.) The contents should be easily recognizable to you:

```
li {
  font-style: italic; color: #A2A2A2; leading: -2;
}

p {
  text-align: justify; leading: 6;
}
```

```
ul {
  leading: 6;
}

strong {
  font-family: Impact; font-size: 18; color: #339966;
}

a {
  font-family: Courier; font-weight: bold;
}

a:hover {
  color: #FF00FF;
}
```

Besides the hyphenated style properties and a few minor syntactical differences, these selectors represent the same styling approach you've seen throughout this chapter. The syntax differences to look out for are as follows:

- In this version, neither property names nor values are wrapped in quotation marks, as they are in ActionScript. For example, we use font-style: italic instead of fontStyle: "italic".

- Properties are separated by semicolons rather than commas, like this:

  li { fontStyle: italic; color: #A2A2A2; leading: -2; }

  instead of this:

  ```
  css.setStyle("li", { fontStyle: "italic", color: "#A2A2A2",
  ➥leading: "-2" });
  ```

By the way, thanks to the semicolon punctuation, you have some leeway in how you arrange the properties, both in ActionScript and the CSS file. Put them in a single line or spread them over several lines—it doesn't matter. As long as the required parts are present, Flash can figure out what you mean. So go ahead and suit your fancy. For example, this:

```
li { fontStyle: italic; color: #A2A2A2; leading: -2 }
```

is functionally the same as this:

```
li {
  fontStyle: italic;
  color: #A2A2A2;
  leading: -2;
}
```

And now we've arrived at the punch line. Test the movie to generate a SWF file, which should look something like Figure 12-15. Now close Flash. That's right, shut down the application. The rest is a matter between you, a SWF, and a CSS file.

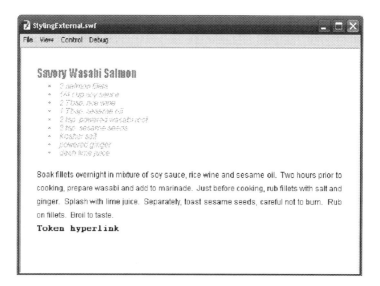

Figure 12-15. CSS styles pulled from an external CSS file

Double-click your newly created StylingExternal.swf file to give it one last look. This is a bit like making sure the magician has nothing up either sleeve.

Now, change a few of the style properties in styles.css. As a suggestion, update the p and strong styles as follows:

```
p {
  margin-left: 100; leading: 12;
}

strong {
  font-family: Impact; font-size: 40; color: #339966;
}
```

After you make your changes, save the CSS document. Then close StylingExternal.swf and double-click it again to launch the SWF. Without republishing the SWF, you've updated its formatting (see Figure 12-16). That's no small feat!

Hey, did you catch that something is missing? What happened to that hyperlink? The increased leading in the p selector has pushed it off the stage! In fact, the phrase Broil to taste has also been shoved aside. No problem—just readjust the leading property or decrease the strong selector's font-size property until everything fits. This sort of tweaking is what CSS was made for.

> At the time this chapter was written for the first edition of the book, one of the authors had recently completed a Flash-based training presentation for a US government agency that featured over 250 slides. At one point, the author needed to change the color of one of the heading styles to a slightly different orange. He was able to make the change in a single CSS file. Guess who was happy that day?

Figure 12-16. Look, ma—style changes without re-creating the SWF!

What you have learned

Apart from learning what to serve the authors at your next BBQ, you have discovered that the CSS techniques widely employed in the HTML universe are just as applicable to your Flash efforts. As you moved through this chapter, you learned the following:

- How to apply CSS styling through ActionScript
- The difference between an element selector and a class selector
- That you can create your own custom tags
- How to use the concept of inheritance to your advantage
- How to reference embedded fonts in your code, and the fact that the Property inspector may help you avoid it
- How to use an external CSS style sheet in Flash

If there is one major theme running through this chapter, it is this: your CSS skills put a powerful tool in your arsenal. Speaking of powerful tools, XML's relationship with Flash just got a power boost. Turn the page to find out.

Chapter 13

XML (DYNAMIC DATA)

Flash is a social creature. Not only does it rub elbows with HTML—coexisting happily with text, JavaScript, images, audio, video, CSS, and more—but it can also reach out past its own SWF boundaries to collaborate with data hosted on a server.

In the hands of an experienced programmer, Flash can interact with database applications by way of the URLLoader and URLVariables classes, perform web service and Flash remoting calls, and even slap a secret handshake with Ajax, thanks to the ExternalInterface class. All this from a browser plug-in that began its life as a way to improve on animated GIFs! It's easy to see why Flash has become a widespread phenomenon, and its versatility makes equally social creatures of the countless designers and developers who end up warming their diverse mitts around the same campfire because of it.

This book isn't here to make programmers out of artists. We don't have the page count to delve into most of the concepts just mentioned, but we are going to introduce you to a markup language called XML that, with a bit of help from ActionScript, can make your SWFs dynamic.

Here's what we'll cover in this chapter:

- Retrieving and filtering XML data using E4X syntax
- Using retrieved data in collaboration with ActionScript

The following files are used in this chapter (located in Chapter13/ExerciseFiles_Ch13/Exercise/):

- LoadXML.fla
- popeye.xml
- LoadXML-E4XBonusRound.fla
- CopyMotion.fla
- CopyMotion.xml
- XMLDrawing.fla
- drawings.fla

The source files are available online from either of the following sites:

- http://www.FoundationFlashCS4.com
- http://www.friendsofED.com/download.html?isbn=9781430210931

If you haven't already worked with XML, we bet our next single malt Scotch you've at least heard of it. The letters stand for eXtensible Markup Language, and extensibility—the ability to create your own HTML-like tags—is almost certainly the reason XML has become a towering champ in data communication. Countless markup languages and file formats are based on XML, including SMIL, RSS, XAML, MXML, RDF, WAP, SVG, SOAP, WSDL, OpenDocument, XHTML, and so on—truly more than would fit on this page. We'll leave the letter combinations to a Scrabble master.

"That's fine and dandy," you might be saying, "but guys, *what is XML?*" Fair enough. The remarkable thing about this language is that it can basically be whatever you want it to be, provided you stick by its rules. The W3C defines the syntax recommendation for XML (XML 1.0, fourth edition, which is the latest at the time this book was written) at http://www.w3.org/TR/2006/REC-xml-20060816/.

The main purpose of XML is to expedite the sharing of data. In fact, XML is so flexible that newcomers are often baffled about where to even begin. On paper—or rather, on the screen—XML looks a lot like another famous W3C specification: HTML. However, rather than using the predetermined tags and attributes supplied by HTML, XML lets you organize your content into descriptive tags of your own design. While HTML formats data for display, XML actually describes data. The combination of familiar, hierarchical format and completely custom tags generally makes XML content easy to read, both to computers and humans. By separating your data from the movie, you give yourself the opportunity to change content from the outside, affecting SWFs without needing to republish them.

So, are you ready to write some XML?

Writing XML

Let's say you've been tasked with organizing a collection of vintage Popeye cartoons. You have five short films on your list: "I Yam What I Yam," "Strong to the Finich," "Beware of Barnacle Bill," "Vim, Vigor, and Vitaliky," and "Little Swee' Pea." Each cartoon has its own release date, running time, and cast of characters. Where to begin? Let's take a look.

Every XML document must have at least one tag, which constitutes its *root element*. The root element should describe the document's contents. In this case, we're dealing with cartoons, so let's make that our root:

```
<cartoons></cartoons>
```

> Looks kind of crazy, doesn't it? It's almost like you're getting away with something mischievous. After all, a technology that facilitates stock market transactions and configures user preferences should be somewhat serious, right? Hey, if you don't think Popeye is seriously funny, you haven't spent enough time with Descartes. I think, therefore I yam. (Thank you! We'll be here all week.)

The rest of our elements will stack themselves inside this first one. Every cartoon is its own film, so we'll add five custom `<film>` elements:

```
<cartoons>
  <film></film>
  <film></film>
  <film></film>
  <film></film>
  <film></film>
</cartoons>
```

Again, these tag names aren't things that exist in XML. It's up to you to decide which elements make sense for the data at hand, to name those elements accordingly, and then to use them.

Note that each opening tag has a closing tag partner (with a slash in it), which is a characteristic required by the XML standard. If an element doesn't contain further data inside it, that element can optionally serve as its own opening and closing tags. In such a case, the `<film></film>` pairing would look like this: `<film />`. But here, each film has a title, so these elements will remain as tag pairs.

The next step—adding a title—seems obvious enough:

```
<cartoons>
  <film>
    <title>I Yam What I Yam</title>
  </film>
  <film>
    <title>Strong to the Finich</title>
  </film>
  <film>
    <title>Beware of Barnacle Bill</title>
  </film>
  <film>
    <title>Vim, Vigor, and Vitaliky</title>
  </film>
  <film>
    <title>Little Swee' Pea</title>
  </film>
</cartoons>
```

The difference here is that the `<title>` tags contain textual data instead of additional elements, but you get the idea. Hold on a minute—*all* of these tags contain data! The `<title>` tags contain *text nodes* (that is, nonelement text content), and the <film> and <cartoons> tags contain XML *element nodes* (that is, descriptive tags). It doesn't take much effort to connect the rest of the dots. An excerpt of the completed document might look something like this:

```
<cartoons>
  <film>
    <title>I Yam What I Yam</title>
    <releaseDate>September 29, 1933</releaseDate>
    <runningTime>6 min</runningTime>
  </film>
  . . .
</cartoons>
```

Actually, that isn't complete after all, is it? The cast of characters is missing. For that, another tier of elements is in order:

```
<cartoons>
  <film>
    <title>I Yam What I Yam</title>
    <releaseDate>September 29, 1933</releaseDate>
    <runningTime>6 min</runningTime>
    <cast>
      <character>Popeye</character>
      <character>Olive Oyl</character>
      <character>Wimpy</character>
      <character>Big Chief</character>
    </cast>
  </film>
  . . .
</cartoons>
```

That would certainly do it. The tag names are meaningful, which is handy when it comes time to retrieve the data. The nested structure organizes each concept into a hierarchy that makes sense: characters belong to a cast, which is one aspect of a film, along with title, release date, and running time. Nicely done, but in a sizable collection, this particular arrangement might come across as bulky. Is there a way to trim it down? Sure thing. Remember that XML allows you to create your own attributes, so you have the option of rearranging the furniture along these lines:

```
<cartoons>
  <film title="I Yam What I Yam" releaseDate="September 29, 1933"
➡runningTime="6 min">
    <cast>
      <character name="Popeye" />
      <character name="Olive Oyl" />
      <character name="Wimpy" />
      <character name="Big Chief" />
    </cast>
  </film>
  . . .
</cartoons>
```

The exact same information is conveyed. The only difference now is that some of the data has been shifted to tag attributes, or *attribute nodes*, rather than tags. HTML provides the same mechanism, by the way. Consider the `src` attribute of an `<img>` tag (`<img src="someImage.jpg" />`). All it does here is change how the data would be retrieved, as you'll see in the "Using E4X syntax" section of this chapter. Which approach is better? Honestly, the choice is yours. It's not so much a question of "better" as it is what best matches your sense of orderliness. Ironically, this open-ended quality, which is one of XML's strongest assets, is the very thing that seems to scare off so many XML freshmen.

> *Working with and structuring an XML document follows the first principle of web development: "No one cares how you did it. They just care that it works." Find what works best for you, because in the final analysis, your client will never pick up the phone and say, "Dude, that was one sweetly structured XML document you put together."*

Folks, this is a bit like a ceramics class. As long as you're careful around the kiln, no one can tell you whose vase is art and whose isn't. Just work the clay between your fingers, let a number of shapes mull around your noggin, and then form what you have into a structure that appeals to you. While you're at it, keep a few rules in mind:

- If you open a tag, close it (`<tag></tag>`).
- If a tag doesn't come in two parts—that is, if it contains only attributes, or nothing at all—make sure it closes itself (`<tag />`).
- Close nested tags in reciprocating order (`<a><b><c /></b></a>` is correct, but `<a><b><c /></a></b>` lights your pants on fire).
- Wrap attribute values in quotation marks (`<tag done="right" />`, `<tag done=wrong />`).

The Popeye example we just discussed would be saved as a simple text file with the `.xml` file extension, as in popeye.xml.

Now that our introductions have been made, let's get social.

> *Feel free to use a text editor such as WordPad on the PC or TextEdit on the Mac to create your XML files. Just be sure you add the `.xml` extension to the file's name. If you have Dreamweaver CS4, that's even better, because it offers tools like code completion to speed up your workflow.*

Loading an XML file

The ActionScript required for loading an XML document isn't especially involved. You'll need an instance of the XML and URLLoader classes, and, of course, an XML document. In our case, the document will always be an actual XML file, although XML documents can be built from scratch with ActionScript.

Open the LoadXML.fla file that accompanies this chapter. Click into frame 1 of the scripts layer and open the Actions panel to see the following code:

```
var xmlDoc:XML = new XML();
var loader:URLLoader = new URLLoader();
var req:URLRequest = new URLRequest("popeye.xml");
loader.load(req);

loader.addEventListener(Event.COMPLETE, completeHandler);
function completeHandler(evt:Event):void {
  xmlDoc = XML(evt.target.data);
  trace(xmlDoc);
};
```

Let's break it down. The first two lines declare a pair of variables: xmlDoc and loader, which point to instances of the XML and URLLoader classes, respectively. The third line declares a third variable, req, which points to an instance of the URLRequest class and specifies the location of the actual XML document.

Line 4 then invokes the URLLoader.load() method on the loader instance, specifying req as the parameter. req's value—"popeye.xml" in this example—is the name of your XML file, including a file path if necessary. This procedure starts the load process, but the data isn't available until the XML document has fully arrived from the server. For this reason, the final block attaches an Event.COMPLETE listener to the loader instance, and then defines the associated function, completeHandler().

In response to a completely loaded document, the event handler function sets the value of the xmlDoc instance to the data property of the target property of the evt parameter passed into the function. That's a mouthful, but you'll understand it when we look at the expression in smaller chunks.

To begin with, the incoming parameter, evt, is an instance of the Event class. As is possible with any other class, Event features properties, one of which is called target. The target property refers to the object that dispatched this event in the first place, which is xmlDoc. Being an instance of the XML class, xmlDoc features a data property, which refers to the text content of the popeye.xml file—in other words, the actual XML data. To let Flash know it should interpret this text content as XML, the expression evt.target.data is wrapped inside a pair of parentheses (()) and preceded by XML. This is called *casting*, where one data type (String) is converted to another compatible type (XML), and the expression is passed to the xmlDoc variable. At this point, the text file's XML tags become a "living XML object" inside the SWF, accessible via the xmlDoc variable.

To prove it with this sample, a trace() function sends the full set of Popeye nodes to the Output panel. Test the movie and compare the Output panel's content to the popeye.xml file itself, which you can open with Dreamweaver CS4 or any simple text editor.

The preceding sample code will serve as the basis for all loading for the rest of the chapter. It's really that simple. Even better, ActionScript 3.0 makes it just as easy to actually *use* XML, so let's jump right in.

Using E4X syntax

In ActionScript 2.0, interacting with an XML class instance was a bit like groping in the dark with your toes for matching socks (and it's hard enough to sort laundry with the lights on!). This was because of the way XML nodes were accessed once loaded, which wasn't by the practical tag names supplied earlier in the chapter.

Until Flash CS3 (and therefore ActionScript 3.0) arrived on the scene, XML in Flash was not up there on the list of "cool things I really need to do." In fact, many designers and developers (one of the authors among them) regarded the use of XML as being similar to the long walk to the principal's office in grade school. The walk was so painful because you just knew your parents were about to be involved, and a world of grief was about to be opened on you.

Readers familiar with Flash XML prior to CS3 will doubtless groan to remember obtuse expressions, such as xmlInstance.firstChild.firstChild.childNodes[2]. Flash developers used properties like firstChild and childNodes because they had to, not because it was fun. Then there was the now defunct XMLConnector component, which complicated things more than it simplified the process. ActionScript 3.0 does away with this groping, thanks to something called E4X. Hey, hear that whooshing noise? That's the sound of everyone dashing to meet this new kid in the neighborhood, the one with the really cool bike.

Dots and @s

What is E4X, and what makes it so good? Seemingly named after an extra from a George Lucas feature, those three characters form a cutesy abbreviation of ECMAScript for XML. It's an Ecma International specification that has been around for quote a while, but provides a completely new, simplified way to access data in an ActionScript 3.0 XML instance.

> What's ECMA? The letters stand for European Computer Manufacturers Association, which was formed in 1961. They got together a few years back to devise the ECMAScript Language Specification, which is the basis for JavaScript and ActionScript. They have moved quite beyond their computer roots and, today, the organization is officially known as Ecma International.

In E4X, element nodes are referenced by the name you give them. Paths to nested elements and attributes are easily expressed by a neatly compact syntax of dots (.) and at symbols (@). This syntax closely matches the dot-notation pathing you're familiar with from the Twinkie example in Chapter 4.

Let's see how it works. If you haven't done so already, open the LoadXML.fla file in this chapter's Exercise folder. Click into frame 1 of the scripts layer and open the Actions panel to reveal the ActionScript. The trace() function at line 9 is about to illustrate a number of dynamite E4X features.

Testing the movie as it stands puts the full XML document's contents into the Output panel. So far, so good. But if you don't care about the root element, <cartoons>, and simply want to see the <film> elements, update the trace() line to read trace(xmlDoc.film);. Once you do that, test the movie again. This time, the <cartoons> tag doesn't show, because you're accessing only its children.

To view <film> elements individually, use the array access operator, [ ], and specify the desired element, starting your count with 0:

```
trace(xml.film[0]);
// displays the first <film> element (I Yam What I Yam)
// and its children

trace(xml.film[1]);
// displays the second <film> element (Strong to the Finich)
// and its children
```

Now, what about attributes? To see those, just precede an attribute's name with the @ symbol as part of your dot-notation path reference. For example, if you want to see the title attribute of the first <film> element, type the following:

```
trace(xmlDoc.film[0].@title);
```

To see the second <film> element's title, substitute 0 with 1; to see the third, substitute 1 with 2; and so on. Based on this pattern, the last element's title attribute would be xmlDoc.film[4].@title. But we know to use the number 4 only because we're aware how many <film> elements there are. What if we didn't know? In that case, it helps to understand exactly what you're getting back from these E4X results. What you're getting are instances of the XMLList class, and that means you can invoke any of the methods that class provides on these expressions.

For example, you've already seen that the expression xmlDoc.film returns a list of all the <film> elements. That list is a bona fide XMLList instance. So, by appending an XMLList method—say, length()—to the expression, you get something useful (in this case, the length of the list, which is 5). We know that in this context, counting starts with zero, so to see the title attribute of the last <film> element, put the following somewhat complex expression inside the array access operator ([ ]):

```
trace(xmlDoc.film[xml.film.length() - 1].@title);
```

It may look a little scary, but it isn't when you reduce it to its parts. The expression xmlDoc.film.length() - 1 evaluates to the number 4, so what you're seeing is as good as actually *using* the number 4.

To see the title attribute of all <film> elements, drop the array access operator altogether:

```
trace(xmlDoc.film.@title);
```

In the Output panel, you'll see that the combined results run together, as shown in Figure 13-1. This is because these attributes don't have any innate formatting. They aren't elements in a nested hierarchy; they are just individual strings.

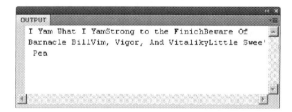

Figure 13-1. Unless they have their own line breaks, attributes will run together.

In this situation, another XMLList method can help you out. To make each title appear on its own line, append toXMLString() to the existing expression:

```
trace(xmlDoc.film.@title.toXMLString());
```

Swap title for the releaseDate attribute, as follows:

```
trace(xmlDoc.film.@releaseDate.toXMLString());
```

As shown in Figure 13-2, you'll see release dates instead of titles in the Output panel.

Figure 13-2. Any element's attributes can be retrieved.

What about looking at a list of the cast members? Viewing individual cast members is just as easy. Update the trace() function to look like this:

```
trace(xmlDoc.film[0].cast.character[1]);
```

This trace() function instructs Flash to look at the first <film> element's <cast> element, and then pull out that node's second <character> element, which happens to be Olive Oyl. For fun, and to see how easy E4X makes things for you, contrast the preceding intuitive reference with its ActionScript 2.0 equivalent: xmlDoc.firstChild.firstChild.firstChild.childNodes[1]. Which would you rather use?

Moving back to the kinder, gentler world of ActionScript 3.0, update the trace() function as follows to see the whole cast of the third film:

```
trace(xmlDoc.film[2].cast.character);
```

This time, you get elements again, complete with their tag markup, as shown in Figure 13-3. This is just like tracing xmlDoc.film earlier, where the Output panel showed <film> elements and their descendants.

```
OUTPUT
<character>Popeye</character>
<character>Olive Oyl</character>
<character>Bluto</character>
```

Figure 13-3. Accessing elements selects the elements themselves, as well as their children.

565

Node types

In the previous section, when you used the array access operator—xmlDoc.film[0].cast. character[1]—Flash gave you the immediate descendant of the <character> tag you specified, which was a text node (that is, just a string). Here, you're looking at a list of element nodes and their text node descendants. If you want just the text nodes, you can use another XMLList method, descendants(), to retrieve what you're after. You'll see an example in just a bit. First, make sure you grasp the idea that when you see the expression <character>Popeye</character>, you're not just looking at one node; you're looking at two.

Both the tag (<character>) and its content (Popeye, in this case) comprise the element and text nodes mentioned earlier. The W3C XML recommendation actually specifies a dozen node types, but ActionScript 3.0 supports only a few of them: element, attribute, text, comment, and processing instruction. (And this is actually a relief, because knowing those few lets you easily pull out a tag's content.)

Add the descendants() method to the end of your E4X expression to see it in action:

```
trace(xmlDoc.film[2].cast.character.descendants());
```

Like attributes, text nodes don't have any inherent formatting. To put each string on its own line, slap the toXMLString() method on the end:

```
trace(xmlDoc.film[2].cast.character.descendants().toXMLString());
```

The result is exactly the sort of thing you might use to populate a text field, as shown in Figure 13-4.

Figure 13-4. Like attributes, text nodes are nothing more than strings.

> *Remember that we are dealing with text in this example. Although the results may look rather plain, you can format and manipulate them in a number of ways, as outlined in Chapters 6 and 12.*

To see how the descendants() method works, try it out at the end of the expression xmlDoc.film. cast, like this:

```
trace(xmlDoc.film[2].cast.character.descendants());
```

The result might surprise you: not just immediate descendants, but all descendants are shown (see Figure 13-5). The first child, <character>Popeye</character>, appears at the top of the list. This includes the <character> element along with its own "offspring," a text node. Next on display is the first grandchild, Popeye (the first child's child). After that, the second child, the second child's child (that is, the second grandchild), and so on. The list makes sense, but if you were expecting only a list of immediate children, well, now you know better.

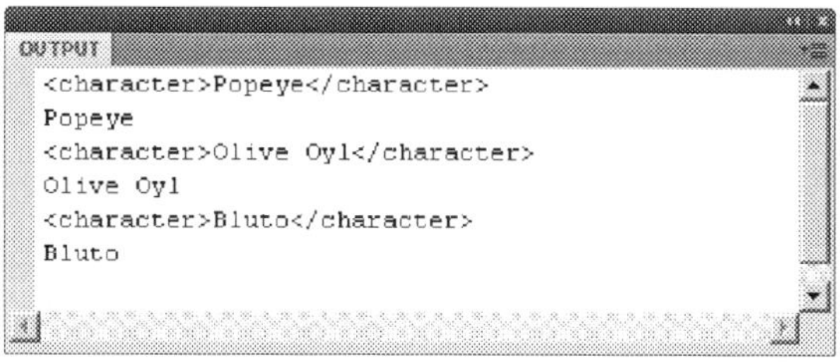

Figure 13-5. The descendants() method reveals all descendants.

E4X filtering

All right, we'll give you one more illustration of E4X (we've saved the best for last). The popeye.xml file included with this chapter's Exercise folder files has slightly different runningTime attributes from those shown earlier in the chapter. Instead of a whole phrase, such as 6 min, these attributes show only numbers. Why? Because E4X allows you to evaluate comparisons, so you can filter content based on specific criteria.

Let's say you want to know which films have a running time longer than 6 minutes. Return again to our humble trace() function and update its parameter to the following:

```
trace(xmlDoc.film.(@runningTime > 6));
```

The result is a list of the <film> elements whose runningTime attribute is greater than 6, along with all their children (see Figure 13-6).

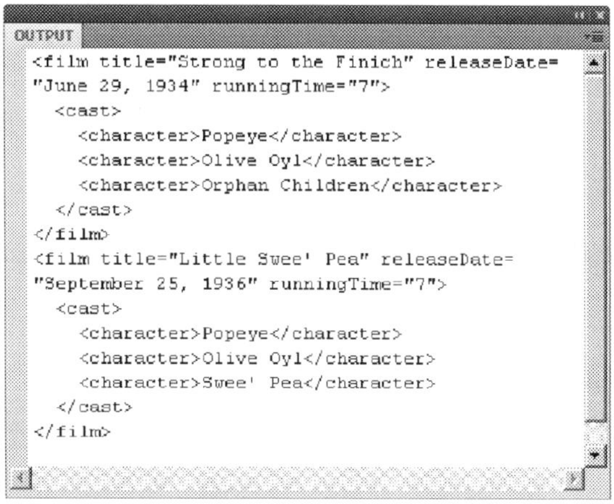

Figure 13-6. E4X allows filtering by way of comparison operators.

The parentheses tell Flash that you're intending to filter the returned XMLList instance. Inside the parentheses, the expression is a simple comparison, @runningTime > 6, which in plain English would be, "If you would be so kind, please tell us which <film> elements' runningTime attributes match this criterion." Flash searches every <film> element in the bunch because nothing appears between the word film and the dot that begins the next expression.

What if you want only the title of these films? Try this:

```
trace(xmlDoc.film.(@runningTime > 6).@title.toXMLString());
```

The trick to understanding this expression, as always, is to break it into its parts. On its own, each concept is usually easy enough to understand. These concepts—these subexpressions—are separated by dots. A blow-by-blow account of the preceding trace() goes like this:

- xmlDoc.film returns an XMLList instance composed of all the <film> elements in the xmlDoc instance.
- Of this list, the expression .(@runningTime > 6) filters only those <film> elements whose runningTime attribute is greater than the value 6.
- The subexpression .@title refines the results further by pulling only the title attribute.
- Finally, .toXMLString() invokes the XMLList.toXMLString() method to clean up the results.

See the LoadXML-E4XFiltering.fla file in the Chapter 13 Complete folder for a working example of the preceding E4X filtering.

Double dots and more

True, we already said "one more illustration of E4X," and that's the preceding one. If you're in a hurry to dispense with all this theory and jump head-first into a practical application, we tip our fedoras and invite you to make a beeline for the next section. But we figure at least a handful of you are wondering if it's possible to return film titles based on who appears in the cartoon. Let's pop open a can of spinach and take a gulp.

Open the LoadXML-E4XBonusRound.fla file that accompanies this chapter, and click into frame 1 of the scripts layer. Most of the ActionScript should look familiar. The important part appears in lines 9 through 12, because it introduces three things: an operator called the descendant accessor (..), a new XML method called parent(), and the for each..in statement:

```
var node:XML
for each (node in xmlDoc..character.(descendants() == "Bluto")) {
  trace(node.parent().parent().@title);
}
```

The for each..in statement was introduced to ActionScript 3.0 thanks to the E4X specification. A similar ActionScript statement, for..in, has been available for quite some time. You point for..in at an object, and it loops through that object's properties—however many properties there happen to be. But note that for..in loops on the properties' *names*, rather than the properties themselves. This can either be nifty or frustrating, depending on your needs. In contrast, the new for each..in statement loops on an object's actual properties, which is great for what we need in this particular endeavor.

To understand the mechanism of this E4X filtering, let's start with a skeleton and slowly build up to the skin. Here are the bones:

```
for each (someProperty in someObject) {
  // do something
}
```

The *someObject* in question is the hardest part of this equation, but based on what you've seen, it shouldn't be impenetrable. This object is an XMLList instance determined by the expression xmlDoc..character.(descendants() == "Bluto"). Up to this point, you would have used the longhand version to retrieve the same list. The longhand version looks like this:

```
xmlDoc.film.cast.character.(descendants() == "Bluto");
```

This version is still as valid as ever. But the descendant accessor (the double dots) lets you skip past the intermediate nodes—film and cast—straight to the element you're after. Pretty slick! Stepping through the subexpressions piece by piece, then, we get the following:

- xmlDoc..character: All <character> elements in the xmlDoc instance, no matter to which intermediate nodes they belong.

- .(descendants() == "Bluto"): Of that list, a comparison of the descendants of each <character> element against a particular string. These descendants are text nodes that happen to represent character names, and the comparison looks for a match with the string "Bluto". The returned XMLList instance is the *someObject* from our skeleton.

That gives us the following:

```
var node:XML;
for each (someProperty in xmlDoc..character.(descendants() ==
➥"Bluto")) {
  // do something
}
```

The replacement for our stand-in *someProperty* is an XML instance, stored in an arbitrarily named variable, node.

```
var node:XML;
for each (node in xmlDoc..character.(descendants() == "Bluto")) {
  // do something
}
```

All this means is that the for each..in statement is going to make laps around the node list returned by the comparison expression. On each lap, it will update the value of that node variable to the latest XML node it finds in that list. The node variable *becomes* the XML object in question. It's an XML reference, which means you can work your recently acquired E4X magic on it.

This is where the parent() method comes into play. Remember that at this point, you're dealing with an element node (<character>) whose descendant matches the string "Bluto". As an XML instance, the <character> node has access to the XML.parent() method, which pretty much works in the same way as the MovieClip.parent property. The parent of <character> is <cast>, and the parent of <cast> is <film>. Given that point of view, the title attribute, referenced with the @ symbol, makes sense:

569

```
var node:XML;
for each (node in xml..character.(descendants() == "Bluto")) {
  trace(node.parent().parent().@title);
}
```

Namespaces

In spite of everything you've just seen, there will come a day when you pull on your E4X wizard hat, roll up your oversized E4X wizard sleeves, wave the wand . . . and nothing happens. You won't see anything in your XMLList instance. It won't be because you've done anything wrong, only that you've omitted something: the acknowledgment of an occasionally present XML *namespace*. In XML, namespaces are a way to filter or label certain elements in order to control their visibility. Namespaces basically give elements a secret handshake, and you can't see the elements unless you know it.

XML documents don't require namespaces, but many use them, including iTunes playlists, RSS feeds, and even Flash. In fact, let's use a bit of XML content that was generated by the Commands ➤ Copy Motion as XML command. The Copy Motion as XML command provides a way to encode certain kinds of motion tweens into XML data, and its root element contains three namespaces. Here's one example, which is available as CopyMotion.xml in the Exercise folder for this chapter:

```
<Motion duration="24" xmlns="fl.motion.*" xmlns:geom="flash.geom.*"
➥xmlns:filters="flash.filters.*">
  <source>
    <Source frameRate="24" x="150" y="120" scaleX="1" scaleY="1"
➥rotation="0" elementType="movie clip" symbolName="Symbol 1">
      <dimensions>
        <geom:Rectangle left="0" top="0" width="80" height="60"/>
      </dimensions>
      <transformationPoint>
        <geom:Point x="0.5" y="0.5"/>
      </transformationPoint>
    </Source>
  </source>

  <Keyframe index="0" tweenSync="true"/>
</Motion>
```

In XML, namespaces are defined by xmlns attributes—in this case, in the <Motion> element. Of the three defined, two have identifiers (geom and filters) and one doesn't, which means it's there but doesn't have a name. Given what you know, and assuming the preceding XML is loaded into an XML instance named xmlDoc, you would expect to see the contents of the <Source> element with an E4X expression like this:

```
trace(xmlDoc..Source);
```

The problem is that if you test that—you can use CopyMotion.fla in the Exercise folder—you'll find that the Output panel does not display anything. To get your data back, you'll need to use the Namespace class, which is easy to do. Here's how:

1. In CopyMotion.fla, click into frame 1 and open the Actions panel to view the full code and trace() function:

```
var xmlDoc:XML = new XML();
var loader:URLLoader = new URLLoader();
var req:URLRequest = new URLRequest("CopyMotion.xml");
loader.load(req);

loader.addEventListener(Event.COMPLETE, completeHandler);
function completeHandler(evt:Event):void {
  xmlDoc = XML(evt.target.data);

  trace(xmlDoc..Source);
};
```

2. Enter the following new ActionScript just before the trace() function:

```
var ns:Namespace = new Namespace("fl.motion.*");
```

This declares a variable, ns, which is set to an instance of the Namespace class. This instance is fed the value portion of the XML document's first mxlns attribute ("fl.motion.*") as a parameter.

3. At this point, that ns variable gives you a prefix you can use to unlock your data. Use the name qualifier operator (::) between the ns variable and the node it "unlocks."

```
var ns:Namespace = new Namespace("fl.motion.*");
trace(xmlDoc..ns::Source);
```

4. Test the movie, and your <Source> element comes out of hiding, as shown in Figure 13-7.

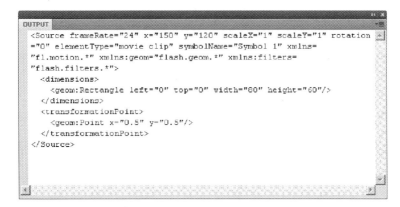

Figure 13-7. Using a Namespace instance can bring data back to light.

If you look carefully at the results in the Output panel, you'll see that the <Source> element now contains additional attributes not in the original XML document. Those are the namespaces. Why they show up here is one of the mysteries of life. But at least you won't be caught by surprise if you run into this sort of XML content.

5. If you don't know an xmlns attribute's value before writing your ActionScript, you can use the XML.namespace() method to grab the namespace currently in use. Replace the "fl.motion.*" parameter you entered just a moment ago with the following:

```
var ns:Namespace = new Namespace(xmlDoc.namespace());
trace(xmlDoc..ns::Source);
```

6. Test again, and you'll see the same Output panel content, even though ActionScript supplied the namespace information for you.

Your turn: Draw shapes with XML

Typically, XML documents are used to define MP3 playlists or images for a slide show. You'll do just that sort of thing in Chapter 14. Here, to demonstrate the versatility of XML data, you will use it to draw shapes. Think of it as XML-driven alphabet soup, drawn by ActionScript.

1. Open the XMLDrawing.fla file from the Exercise folder for this chapter. Its partner is the drawings.xml file located in the same folder, so open that in your favorite text editor.

2. In the Flash document, click frame 1 of the scripts layer and open the Actions panel to review the following partially completed ActionScript:

```
var xmlDoc:XML = new XML();
var loader:URLLoader = new URLLoader();
var req:URLRequest = new URLRequest("drawings.xml");
loader.load(req);

loader.addEventListener(Event.COMPLETE, completeHandler);
function completeHandler(evt:Event):void {
  xmlDoc = XML(evt.target.data);

  drawLetters();
};
```

Everything should be familiar except for the drawLetters() reference, which is a custom function you're about to write.

3. Place your cursor at the end of the existing code, hit Enter (Return) a couple times, and then type the following new ActionScript:

```
function drawLetters():void {
  var word:Sprite = new Sprite();
  addChild(word);

  var letterCount:int = xmlDoc.letter.length();
  var pointCount:int;
  var i:int;
  var j:int;
```

This is the beginning of your function. The function keyword makes the declaration, and because this function doesn't provide a return value, it's typed as :void.

Right off the bat, you have a number of variables. The first is a Sprite instance, stored in a variable named word. Think of a sprite as a low-overhead version of a movieclip. In this case, it's just a surface to draw on, and it has no need for a timeline of its own, which is what a MovieClip instance would provide. The addChild() method adds word to the main timeline's display list, which ensures that your sprite will be visible when you start filling it with shapes.

After that, you have a handful of variables used for counting: letterCount is an integer (int) number that takes is value from the E4X expression xmlDoc.letter.length();. So what does xmlDoc.letter.length(); refer to? Take a look at the actual XML document, and you'll see it right away:

```
<word>
  <letter character="F" color="0xFF0000">
    <coords x="0" y="0" />
    <coords x="30" y="0" />
    <coords x="30" y="10" />
    <coords x="10" y="10" />
    <coords x="10" y="20" />
    <coords x="20" y="20" />
    <coords x="20" y="30" />
    <coords x="10" y="30" />
    <coords x="10" y="50" />
    <coords x="0" y="50" />
    <coords x="0" y="0" />
  </letter>
  <letter character="L" color="0x00FF00">
    <coords x="0" y="0" />
    <coords x="10" y="0" />
    <coords x="10" y="40" />
    <coords x="30" y="40" />
    <coords x="30" y="50" />
    <coords x="0" y="50" />
    <coords x="0" y="0" />
  </letter>
  . . .
</word>
```

The E4X reference to xmlDoc.letter gives you an XMLList list of the <letter> elements, and the length() method tells you how many of those elements are contained by the root element, <word>. The remaining variables in your function are also declared as int, but aren't given values yet.

4. Type the following new ActionScript after the existing code:

```
var letter:Sprite;
var node:XML;
for (i = 0; i < letterCount; i++) {
  node = xmlDoc.letter[i];

  letter = new Sprite();
  letter.graphics.lineStyle(1, 0x000000);
  letter.graphics.beginFill(node.@color);
```

Here you have two more variables: letter and node. The letter variable is declared as another Sprite instance, and node as another XML instance. These variables will repeatedly update to different values, thanks to something called a for loop, which immediately follows.

The for statement gives you a way to perform something more than once, and the setup occurs in three parts:

- The i variable is set to 0.
- A comparison expression will keep this loop going while the value of i is less than letter-Count, which you set in step 3.
- i will be incremented by 1 (that's what ++ does) every time the for loop runs another lap.

So, what is this loop going to do? On every lap, it updates the node variable to the E4X expression xmlDoc.letter[i]. That may look new, but you've seen this. The only thing different is that the array access operator ([ ]) is being fed the value of i, rather than a hard-coded number.

Once the value of node is determined, the value of letter is set to a new Sprite instance, and its graphic property is referenced. All sprites and movieclips have a graphics property, which points to an instance of the Graphics class associated with that particular sprite or movieclip. The Graphics class lets you draw things, and the last two lines configure the "pen." First, its stroke width is set to 1 (very thin) and its color to 0x000000 (black). Second, its fill is set to whatever color value is specified by the color attribute of the current <letter> element referenced by the node variable (beginFill(node.@color);).

With the pen ready, you're now prepared to draw. That's where a second for loop comes in.

5. Type the following new ActionScript after the existing code:

```
pointCount = node.coords.length();
for (j = 0; j < pointCount; j++) {
    letter.graphics.lineTo(node.coords[j].@x, node.coords[j].@y);
}
```

Here, the pointCount variable declared in step 3 is finally given a value. What value? Why, the number of <coords> elements inside the current <letter> element (again, as referenced by the node variable). This second for loop runs its laps inside the first one. Basically, the for loop that uses i runs through the <letter> elements, and the one that uses j runs through the <coords> elements.

All this inner loop does is invoke the lineTo() method as often as necessary, taking its x and y cues from the E4X expressions node.coords[j].@x and node.coords[j].@y, respectively. From right to left, you're asking for the x (or y) attribute of the current <coords> element of the current <letter> element (as referenced by node). In the XML document, these coordinates describe the points necessary to draw a rather blocky set of letters.

6. To complete the function, type the following ActionScript after the existing code:

```
        letter.graphics.endFill();
        letter.x = i * 40;
        word.addChild(letter);
    }
    word.x = stage.stageWidth / 2 - word.width / 2;
    word.y = stage.stageHeight / 2 - word.height / 2;
}
```

Following after the inner for loop, the fill is closed with the endFill() method. The next line, letter.x = i * 40, updates the Sprite.x property of the current sprite—that is, the sprite into which you've just drawn a letter shape—and the sprite is added to the display list of word, which makes it a child display object of that sprite.

Why update the x property of the "letter" sprites? Because you don't want them stacked on top of each other. On its first lap through the for loop, the value of i is 0. Because 0 times 40 is 0, the first letter is positioned flush left inside the container sprite, word. On its second lap, the value of i is 1, which positions the second letter at 40 pixels in. On the third lap, the third letter is positioned at two times 40 pixels in, and so on.

Because each letter is added to the display list of word, all the letters can be moved as a single group. This happens in the last two lines, in which the x and y properties of word are set to half the width or height of the stage, minus half the width or height of word itself. Put simply, the word sprite is centered horizontally and vertically.

7. Test the movie. You will see the word FLASH in block letterforms, whose coordinates and fill colors were determined by an XML document, as shown in Figure 13-8.

Figure 13-8. XML just provided the coordinates for some shapes.

8. Close the SWF. Here comes the cool part.

9. Switch over to the XML document, rearrange the <letter> elements, and save the XML file. For example, just for a laugh, you might want to delete all of the elements except for the ones that draw A and H, and then swap them like this:

```
<word>
  <letter character="H" color="0x00FFFF">
    <coords x="0" y="0" />
    <coords x="10" y="0" />
    <coords x="10" y="20" />
    <coords x="20" y="20" />
    <coords x="20" y="0" />
    <coords x="30" y="0" />
    <coords x="30" y="50" />
    <coords x="20" y="50" />
    <coords x="20" y="30" />
    <coords x="10" y="30" />
    <coords x="10" y="50" />
    <coords x="0" y="50" />
    <coords x="0" y="0" />
  </letter>
  <letter character="A" color="0x0000FF">
    <coords x="0" y="0" />
    <coords x="30" y="0" />
    <coords x="30" y="50" />
    <coords x="20" y="50" />
    <coords x="20" y="30" />
    <coords x="10" y="30" />
    <coords x="10" y="50" />
    <coords x="0" y="50" />
    <coords x="0" y="0" />
    <coords x="10" y="10" />
    <coords x="20" y="10" />
    <coords x="20" y="20" />
    <coords x="10" y="20" />
    <coords x="10" y="10" />
  </letter>
</word>
```

10. Close the Flash authoring environment altogether.

11. Find the SWF you created just a moment ago—XMLDrawing.swf—and double-click it to test the movie without recompiling.

As shown in Figure 13-9, Flash laughs back. And you just changed the content of a SWF, in a dramatic way, without changing a jot of ActionScript!

Figure 13-9. Thanks to XML, Flash has a sense of humor.

What you have learned

In this chapter, we gave you the absolute basics of XML use in Flash. On the surface, it may not seem like much. However, what we have presented in this chapter forms the foundation for complex Flash projects ranging from video pickers, MP3 players, and portfolio sites, to e-commerce applications. In this chapter, you have discovered the following:

- The relationship between an XML document and Flash CS4
- How to retrieve and filter XML data using E4X syntax
- How to dynamically draw shapes with XML

The most important point you need to take away from this chapter is the sheer flexibility of XML in your Flash design and development efforts. You can make your movies expand or contract effortlessly by simply adding to or subtracting from the XML document being used by the movie. This is the true meaning of *dynamic*.

Speaking of dynamic, you're about to enter the "Building Stuff" chapter, much of which collaborates with XML. Turn the page to start building.

Chapter 14

BUILDING STUFF

Up to this point in the book, you have created quite a few projects using images, text, audio, video, and other media. We bet you're feeling pretty good about what you've accomplished (you should!), and, like many who have reached your skill level, you are wondering, "How does all of this hang together?"

In this chapter, we will bring together the various skills and knowledge you have developed, and use them to create some rather interesting projects. We are going to start slowly and show you how to build a preloader, and then move through a slide show, an MP3 player, and finish with a full-bore video player. Some of these are quite complicated projects, but if you have reached this point in the book, you are ready to develop some Flash "chops" and explore what you can do with your newfound skills.

Here's what we'll cover in this chapter:

- Loading visual content from outside the SWF
- Preloading a movie with heavy internal content
- Creating a slide show using external images and XML
- Creating a custom MP3 player
- Creating a custom video controller

The following files are used in this chapter (located in Chapter14/ExerciseFiles_ Ch14/Exercise/):

- Loading.fla
- toBeLoaded.swf
- toBeLoaded.png
- BeachTrip.fla
- beach01.jpg–beach05.jpg
- NASATrip.fla
- 798_01.jpg–798_08.jpg
- slideshow.xml
- TinBangs.fla
- controls.fla
- playlist.xml (MP3 player version)

- WhiteLies(Timekiller).mp3
- YoungLions.mp3
- YourSkyIsFalling.mp3
- VideoPlayer.fla
- playlist.xml (video player version)
- InkSong.mp4
- InspectorGadget.flv
- PeterWolf.flv

The source files are available online from either of the following sites:

- http://www.FoundationFlashCS4.com
- http://www.friendsofED.com/download.html?isbn=9781430210931

Loading content

Flash has a potentially bad habit that drives people crazy. In cases where everything in a movie is packed into the first few frames—and especially in single-frame movies—the SWF can take an awfully long time to display. Why? Because Flash Player loads content one frame at a time, and when a SWF's first frame is heavy, the rest of the movie suffers. It's even more interesting in cases where Export for ActionScript is selected for library assets, because those items are included in the movie's first frame, in a behind-the-scenes way, even if you don't place them there yourself (Flash does it for you automatically). This should explain to you why, when you hit certain websites, you're slugged with an interminable wait, involving fingers drumming on the mouse or your desk and audible sighs as you wait for the movie to start.

One useful solution is to remove your heaviest assets—large images, audio, and video files—and use ActionScript to load them at runtime. This way, the rest of your content—the lighter stuff, including text and vector artwork—displays almost immediately, while the heavy stuff streams into the SWF from your server. Just keep in mind that even the light stuff may need a few seconds to load. But at least your audience will be looking at *something*, and even the mere perception of at least *something happening* works PR wonders.

Dynamic loading

The dynamic loading we're talking about is accomplished through the use of the Loader class, new to ActionScript 3.0 and introduced in Flash CS3. (To be sure, ActionScript 2.0 and earlier also supported dynamic loading, but different approaches were required for different kinds of external files. ActionScript 3.0 makes it more consistent, and therefore simpler.) You can use the Loader class to load SWF files or image files (JPG, GIF, or PNG) into a SWF through the use of the load() method, and then take action when the requested files arrive.

1. To see how all of this works, open the Loading.fla file in the Exercise/Preloader folder for this chapter. You'll see there's a single movieclip on the stage; this movieclip is the only object in the library. We have given this symbol the instance name clip.

2. Select the first frame of the scripts layer, open the Actions panel, and add the following code:

```
var loader:Loader = new Loader();
addChild(loader);
//clip.addChild(loader);

loader.contentLoaderInfo.addEventListener(Event.COMPLETE,
➥completeHandler);
function completeHandler(evt:Event):void {
  //clip.x = 50;
  //clip.y = 50;
};
loader.contentLoaderInfo.addEventListener(ProgressEvent.PROGRESS,
➥progressHandler);
function progressHandler(evt:ProgressEvent):void {
  trace(evt.bytesLoaded);
};

var req:URLRequest("toBeLoaded.swf");
//var req:URLRequest("toBeLoaded.png");

loader.load(req);
```

The first line of code creates an instance of the Loader class and stores it in a variable named loader for easy reference. Because this Loader instance is about to load visual content, it's not enough to merely create the object. You also need to add it to a display list, which is accomplished by the second and third lines. Eventually, you'll need only one of the two addChild() lines (notice that the second one is currently commented out, which means it will be ignored by Flash Player), but here's what each does:

- The first one (addChild(loader);) adds loader to the display list of the main timeline.
- The second one (clip.addChild(loader);) adds loader instead to the display list of the clip movieclip.

In just a moment, you'll see the difference between these two display lists.

The next two code blocks demonstrate a pair of event handlers. The first one listens for, and responds to, an Event.COMPLETE event, meaning that the requested file has fully loaded. The second one handles ProgressEvent.PROGRESS, which is dispatched repeatedly while the requested file is loading. The innards of the completeHandler() function are commented out for the time being, but you'll see how they're used soon. In the progressHandler() function, a trace() function tells the Output panel how many bytes have been loaded for the requested file.

581

> *Handling* Loader *events is a bit different from what you've seen else-where in this book. With movieclips and button symbols, for example, the* addEventListener() *method is referenced directly by way of the symbol's instance name. With* Loader, *that method is routed through a* contentLoaderInfo *property. What's that? Nothing more than an instance of the* ContentLoaderInfo *class, which is included automatically when you create your* Loader *instance. The* ContentLoaderInfo *class contains information about* Loader's *content, such as the events we're using here.*

The following two lines tell loader which file to request: a SWF or a PNG. The PNG request is commented out at the moment. The last line uses the req variable to summon the file.

3. Now test the movie. Two things will happen: you'll see a haloed guru in the container SWF's upper-left corner and you'll see a few numbers in the Output panel. Those numbers show how much of toBeLoaded.swf was loaded during that particular occurrence of ProgressEvent.PROGRESS. You'll see only a few numbers, because the requested SWF loads very quickly from your hard drive.

4. Close the SWF and return to the Actions panel. Comment out lines 2 and 16:

```
//addChild(loader);
. . .
//var req:URLRequest("toBeLoaded.swf"));
```

And *uncomment* all the lines that were previously commented (just remove the double slashes at the beginning of each line other than 2 and 16).

At this point, you're adding loader to the display list of clip instead of the main timeline, you're telling clip to reposition itself when its content loads, and you're requesting the PNG file instead of the SWF.

5. Test the movie again. Your results should look like Figure 14-1.

This time, the PNG is loaded (it looks identical; only the file format is different). The PNG is added to the stand in movie clip, which is positioned at 50 pixels to the right and 50 pixels down from the upper-left corner of the stage. The Output panel shows considerably more numbers than last time. In addition, a normally hidden pane is now showing in the upper half of Flash Player. Hang tight to see why that's happening, because it's a really neat tool.

Let's review the display list concept. In the first case, the requested file is loaded into the main time-line, which positions it in the stage's upper-left corner, unless you tell it otherwise with code. In the second case, the file is loaded into a movieclip, which you can position by hand. Positioning by hand means you can get a rough idea beforehand where your files will load—though you can certainly use ActionScript to reposition your movieclip containers, as shown in the completeHandler() function. That stand in container doesn't need to have anything in it, by the way. The outline and the words "stand-in" in the movieclip's text field (visible in the sample file) are there for illustrative purposes. Usually, your container will be an empty movieclip symbol.

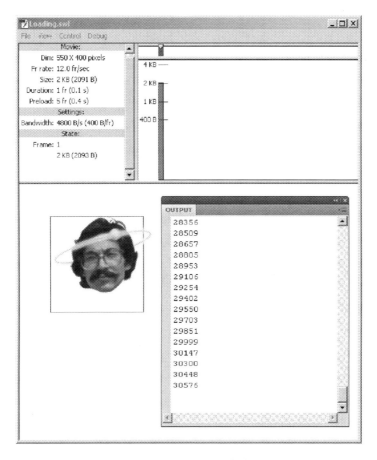

Figure 14-1. A SWF is loaded into a movieclip, which changes position after the SWF loads.

Now, why is the Output panel showing so many numbers in Figure 14-1? That happens because Flash lets you simulate various modem speeds when you test downloads in the authoring environment. After you launch the SWF (Control ➤ Test Movie), use the SWF's File menu to select View ➤ Bandwidth Profiler—that opens the extra Flash Player pane—and then select View ➤ Simulate Download. Doing so causes Flash to pretend the guru image is being requested from a remote server. The left side of the bandwidth profiler will show you the load progress of the SWF file itself. The right side shows the number of frames in the SWF (one, in this case), and lets you see which frame you're on. To change the speed of the simulated modem, select View ➤ Download Settings from the SWF's File menu.

One loader, multiple SWFs

The beauty of the Loader class is that you need only one instance to load as many SWFs or images as you want, provided you're displaying only one per frame at a time. (If you plan to display more than one per frame, you'll need one Loader instance per SWF or image—just declare the necessary number of variables and give each its own name.) Let's see how you can reuse a single Loader instance numerous times.

1. Open the BeachTrip.fla file from the Exercise/Preloader folder for this chapter. Inside, you'll see five layers in the main timeline, as shown in Figure 14-2: scripts, container (for the movieclip that holds the loaded images), text, buttons, and bg (for the background image stored in the library). Click around to get familiar with the FLA. The button symbols have the instance names btnPrev and btnNext. The text field in the center is dynamic, and it has the instance name tfLoadProgress. The container movieclip is empty, so it appears as a small circle. Click that circle, and you'll see that its instance name is container.

Figure 14-2. With all the assets are in place, loading images will be easy.

2. Click info frame 1 of the scripts layer and type the following ActionScript:

```
stop();

var loader:Loader = new Loader();
var req:URLRequest = new URLRequest();
container.addChild(loader);

// Loader events
loader.contentLoaderInfo.addEventListener(ProgressEvent.PROGRESS,
➥progressHandler);
```

```
function progressHandler(evt:ProgressEvent):void {
  var percent:int = Math.round(evt.bytesLoaded / evt.bytesTotal * 100);
  tfLoadProgress.text = percent.toString() + "%";
}

loader.contentLoaderInfo.addEventListener(Event.COMPLETE,
➥completeHandler);
function completeHandler(evt:Event):void {
  if (currentFrame != totalFrames) {
    enableButton(btnNext, true);
  }
}
```

This is a multiframe movie, and we want it to stop dead in its tracks in frame 1. That explains the MovieClip.stop() method in the first line. Remember that you don't need an object reference prefix here, because Flash understands that the movieclip you're referring to is the main timeline. Next is the familiar Loader instance, again stored in a loader variable. In this case, the URLRequest instance is declared (req), and even instantiated (new URLRequest()), but not yet provided with a file name. That's going to happen in frames 2 through 6. To ensure that loaded images are placed in container's display list, loader is added as a child of container.

These three lines are followed by two event handlers, listening for ProgressEvent.PROGRESS and Event.COMPLETE, as before. The difference is that this progress event handler is sending its information to a dynamic text field (tfLoadProgress), rather than the Output panel. The complete handler is calling a custom function, enableButton(), which you'll write in just a moment. First, let's go over how this progress handler works.

In the previous exercise, you saw the ProgressEvent.bytesLoaded property referenced in terms of an evt parameter. That's happening again here. Additionally, you're making use of the bytesTotal property of the same ProgressEvent instance. An integer variable, percent, is declared and set to an arithmetic expression: evt.bytesLoaded / evt.byteTotal * 100. This calculates how many bytes have been loaded, divided by how many bytes there are total, multiplied by 100. This expression is rounded to the nearest integer by the Math.round() method. If there are 20,000 bytes total in the requested file and 10,000 of them have loaded, then the expression effectively means this:

```
10,000 / 20,000 * 100
```

Run the numbers, and you'll see that equates to 50, which is halfway (50%) loaded. Because percent is an int (integer) data type—as opposed to a string, as required by the text field—the Object. toString() method is invoked on percent as it is assigned to the text property of the tfLoadProgress text field. (All classes inherit from Object, so all objects inherit a toString() method.) The plus sign (+) concatenates the percent symbol (%) to the string value of percent, and that combined string is displayed in the text field. This way, users can see how much of the currently requested file has loaded as a percentage.

To understand the completeHandler() function, just remember that an if statement evaluates expressions to determine if they're true or false. In this case, two MovieClip properties are compared with the inequality operator (!=), which means "is not equal to." The expression inside the if statement's parentheses is true when the playhead is on any timeline frame but the last one. Only on the timeline's last frame is the value of its currentFrame property *not equal to* the value of its totalFrames property. Why do we care? In this BeachTrip.fla movie, the user is going to view a handful of JPGs by clicking a set of next and previous buttons. We don't want them to proceed while a requested image is still loading, so the btnNext button will be disabled in each frame until the Event.COMPLETE handler is triggered—on all frames but the last one (because there isn't a next frame after the last frame, of course).

3. Head back to the Actions panel and add the following new ActionScript beneath what's already there:

```
btnPrev.addEventListener(MouseEvent.CLICK, movePrev);
btnNext.addEventListener(MouseEvent.CLICK, moveNext);

function movePrev(evt:MouseEvent):void {
  prevFrame();
}
function moveNext(evt:MouseEvent):void {
  nextFrame();
}
```

This should be pretty familiar. Two button symbols, with the instance names btnPrev and btnNext, are associated with custom functions—event handlers—triggered by MouseEvent.CLICK. These functions are named movePrev() and moveNext(), respectively. Each function invokes either MovieClip.prevFrame() or MovieClip.nextFrame(), as relevant, in order to move the main timeline one frame back or one frame forward.

That takes care of buttons in their active state (they're active by default). What's missing is the custom enableButton() function that causes buttons to become active or inactive as desired.

4. Add the remaining new ActionScript to frame 1 beneath the code already present:

```
function enableButton(btn:SimpleButton, isActive:Boolean):void {
  btn.mouseEnabled = isActive;
  if (isActive) {
    btn.alpha = 1;
  } else {
    btn.alpha = 0.5;
  }
}
enableButton(btnPrev, false);
```

This function accepts two parameters, arbitrarily named btn and isActive. The first parameter refers to a SimpleButton instance (in other words, a button symbol); the second is a Boolean value (true or false). Inside the function, the passed-in button symbol is referenced by the btn parameter. Its SimpleButton.mouseEnabled property is set to the value of the isActive parameter. This makes the button either participate in mouse-related events (true) or ignore them (false). Next, an if statement checks the value of isActive. If true, the button's alpha property is set to 1 (100%)—in other words, fully opaque—otherwise, it's set to 0.5 (50%).

In the last line, this function is actually put to use. It renders the btnPrev button disabled—no mouse events and semitransparent—which makes sense in frame 1, because there's no previous frame to go back to.

5. Now add keyframes in frames 2 through 6 in the scripts layer. You're going to add a few lines of ActionScript to each of these frames, and you'll quickly see the pattern.

6. Click into frame 2, and use the Actions panel to enter the following:

```
req.url = "beach01.jpg";
loader.load(req);

enableButton(btnPrev, false);
enableButton(btnNext, false);
```

Click in frame 3 and enter this ActionScript:

```
req.url = "beach02.jpg";
loader.load(req);

enableButton(btnPrev, true);
enableButton(btnNext, false);
```

For frame 4, enter this code:

```
req.url = "beach03.jpg";
loader.load(req);

enableButton(btnNext, false);
```

Frame 5 gets this ActionScript:

```
req.url = "beach04.jpg";
loader.load(req);

enableButton(btnNext, false);
```

And finally, add the following code for frame 6:

```
req.url = "beach05.jpg";
loader.load(req);

enableButton(btnNext, false);
```

In all cases, the req variable, declared in frame 1, has its URLRequest.url property set to a particular JPG. After that, the Loader.load() method is invoked on the loader instance with req as its parameter. This loads a different JPG for each frame, but in every case, the same loader and req instances do the loading. Because loader was added to the display list of container in frame 1, every JPG will load inside the container movieclip.

In frame 2, btnPrev is disabled (enableButton(btnPrev, false);), because frame 2 represents the beginning of the slide show. The user still shouldn't be allowed to step back to the previous frame. In frame 3, btnPrev is enabled (enableButton(btnPrev, true);), because from that point, the user should be able to move forward and backward. When the user actually clicks the btnPrev button in frame 3, the playhead will move to frame 2, which redisplays the first image and again disables prevButton.

In all frame scripts, btnNext is disabled, which keeps the user from proceeding until the current image's Event.COMPLETE handler is triggered. Remember that this event handler invokes enableButton() and passes it the parameters btnNext and true.

7. Test your movie and use View ➤ Simulate Download from the SWF's File menu to see the progress event handler in action. Note that the simulated download treats each JPG as if it had never been loaded before. In real life, clicking the btnPrev button would display the requested image immediately, so you see only the climbing percentages the first time each image is requested. Compare your work with the BeachTrip.fla file in this chapter's Complete/Preloader folder.

Creating a movie preloader

As an alternative to loading external assets individually, you may want to use ProgressEvent.PROGRESS to inform the user about the load status of the SWF itself. The mechanism that takes care of this is commonly known as a *preloader*, and it's a fairly easy feat to accomplish. Preloaders can range from simple to incredibly complex. Regardless of the approach taken, the purpose of a preloader is to get something happening within that 15-second window of opportunity and have the user become engaged in the site almost immediately.

Here, you will create a movie preloader, using the yawning parrot animation seen elsewhere in the book. The goal of this exercise is to display the parrot animation when the SWF is visited for the first time, and to skip past that animation when the SWF has already been loaded. The skipping-past part happens because already-viewed SWFs are cached in the user's temporary Internet files, which means the comparison between loaded bytes and total bytes—evaluated here by an if statement in the first three lines of frame 1—sends the playhead past the animation without further ado. On the other hand, when a SWF is being viewed for the first time, the Event.COMPLETE event, which indicates that the SWF itself is fully loaded, is delayed. This allows the playhead to linger on the parrot animation, while a ProgressEvent.PROGRESS handler updates a percentage in the parrot's nested text field. Eventually, the complete event handler ushers the playhead along. Here's how it works:

1. Open the NASATrip.fla file in your Exercise/Preloader folder for this chapter. Scrub through the timeline and you will see the yawning parrot, and will then be taken through a series of imported photos that collectively weigh over 200KB.

2. Open the library and double-click the parrot movieclip to open it in the Symbol Editor. You will notice that we have added the necessary dynamic text field for you, in a box under the parrot (see Figure 14-3). This text field will keep the user informed of load progress.

3. Click the Scene 1 link to return to the main timeline. Select the keyframe in frame 1 of the scripts layer and open the Actions panel. Type the following code:

```
if (loaderInfo.bytesLoaded >= loaderInfo.bytesTotal) {
  gotoAndPlay(26);
}
loaderInfo.addEventListener(Event.COMPLETE,
➥completeHandler);
function completeHandler(evt:Event):void {
  if (currentFrame == 15) {
    play();
  } else {
    gotoAndPlay(26);
  }
};
```

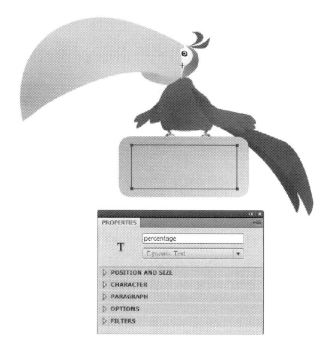

Figure 14-3. A yawning parrot and a dynamic text box are the key elements used in this preloader.

Let's take a moment and figure out what's going on, because as familiar as this should look by now, you're still seeing a few curveballs. This time, because the content is all internal to the SWF, you don't need a Loader instance. You're still checking loaded versus total bytes, and still listening for Event. COMPLETE, but in this case, the event is dispatched by a LoaderInfo instance (not ContentLoaderInfo, as with the previous example). The LoaderInfo instance is accessed by way of the DisplayObject. loaderInfo property, referenced in terms of the main timeline. This works because the main timeline is a MovieClip instance, which inherits from the DisplayObject class.

When a user sees this SWF in a browser, the Event.COMPLETE event is dispatched after all the frames in the main timeline have loaded. During the first viewing, this event will be delayed until the SWF's full content (more than 200KB) has loaded. Thanks to this delay, and because the bytesLoaded property of the main timeline's LoaderInfo instance isn't yet greater than or equal to bytesTotal, the playhead will easily make it to frame 15—which features the yawning parrot—and wait there until instructed to continue. Of course, the playhead won't wait unless you tell it to stop, so that's your next step.

4. Add a keyframe to frame 15 of the main timeline's scripts layer. Use the Actions panel to add the following single line of ActionScript:

```
stop();
```

Thanks to that MovieClip.stop() method, the timeline will wait until the delayed Event.COMPLETE event is dispatched. As you can see from the if statement inside Step 3's completeHandler() function, the timeline will simply resume the play() method from that position as long as the function is triggered while the main timeline's MovieClip.currentFrame property is 15.

On the other hand, if the SWF is already cached on the user's computer, the completeHandler() function is triggered immediately—while the playhead is still in frame 1—which means the MovieClip.gotoAndPlay() method will send the playhead straight to frame 26, past the parrot movieclip. Bingo. So that explains part of the endeavor, but this isn't enough to update the text field inside the parrot symbol. For that, you'll need to write a ProgressEvent.PROGRESS handler. No time like the present.

5. Add the following new ActionScript below the existing stop() method in frame 15 of the scripts layer:

```
loaderInfo.addEventListener(ProgressEvent.PROGRESS,
➥progressHandler);
function progressHandler(evt:ProgressEvent):void {
  var percent:int = Math.round(evt.bytesLoaded / evt.bytesTotal * 100);
  parrot.percentage.text = percent.toString() + "%";
};
```

This code hasn't changed, in principle, from the percentage arithmetic you saw in the previous example. As with the Event.COMPLETE handler, this event is associated with the loaderInfo property of the main timeline. The progressHandler() function calculates a percent variable from the evt parameter's bytesLoaded and bytesTotal properties, multiplied by 100 and rounded to the nearest integer. The result, once again, is sent to the text property of a dynamic text field. But this time, the text field's instance name is percentage, and it lives inside a movieclip whose instance name is parrot. Remember that in cases where the SWF has already been viewed, the ActionScript in frame 15 is bypassed altogether.

The remainder of the code is a snap.

6. In the scripts layer, insert keyframes at frames 39, 49, 59, and 69. Enter the following code into frame 39:

```
stop();

btnNext.addEventListener(MouseEvent.CLICK, clickHandler);
function clickHandler(evt:Event):void {
  play();
}
```

This stops the timeline on the first image and wires up a custom clickHandler() function to the MouseEvent.CLICK event, which is dispatched when a user clicks the btnNext symbol that is fully visible on this frame. All this function does is resume the stopped timeline, which needs to be instructed to stop in the remaining keyframes.

7. Enter a stop(); method in frames 49, 59, and 69.

8. Test the movie and verify that Flash Player immediately displays images from a NASA exhibition (Figure 14-4), with a button in the lower right to advance through the photos.

9. Simulate a modem by selecting View ➤ Simulate Download from the SWF's File menu. This time, you should see the parrot animation displaying load progress with a percentage.

Figure 14-4. The SWF skips past the preloader when already cached.

Building a slide show with components and XML

The popularity of websites like Flickr and Photobucket prove that people like to share photos. Of course, this was true even before the Internet. But modern technology makes it easier than ever to whip out that tumbling, unfolding wallet and proudly show off all the kids, aunts, uncles, cousin Ed, and Finnegan, not only to friends, but to every human on the planet. At the rate most people take pictures, photo collections just keep growing. So, if you were to make a photo slide show in Flash, you would want to be sure it was easy to update. With components and XML, that goal is closer than you may think.

To explore the concept, we'll start in an interesting location: the Quanjude Roast Duck Restaurant in Beijing, China. During the course of writing this book, one of the authors was in Beijing. One night, he was enjoying dinner in the company of a couple of Adobe engineers, John Zhang and Zhong Zhou. Naturally, one of the dishes was duck and, because of the restaurant's history, there was a particular way in which the duck was served and to be consumed. The author was struggling, and Zhong Zhou called the waitress over to demonstrate the proper (and complex!) procedure. It involved a wafer-thin wrap, duck meat, sauces, scallions, and a couple of other treats, which were to be added in a particular order. It took a couple of tries, but the grimacing author finally nailed it. When he thanked Zhong Zhu for the lesson, Zhong said, "It's really simple if you first master the process."

Mastering the creation of a Flash slide show is a lot like preparing that duck dish: it is all about process. We are going to show you two ways of creating a slide show, but the process is essentially the same for both. In fact, you'll be using some of the same process for the MP3 and video players later in the chapter.

A tour of the Beijing art district

To start, we're going to walk you through a self-contained, "hard-wired" movie that displays a small collection of external JPGs and their captions. The number of JPGs, and the order in which they appear, are "baked in" to the SWF, which means the movie must be edited and republished to accommodate new images. This slide show features ComboBox and Button components to let people choose which JPGs they want to see, and it even uses the UILoader and ProgressBar components to load the images, so this will be something of a cumulative exercise.

Once the test model is complete, we'll free the photo-specific data from its dungeon and move it to an XML file, where it can leap free in the fields like a shorn sheep, or paddle merrily around a pond like a duck. Here we go!

1. Start a new Flash document and save it as Slideshow.fla in this chapter's Exercise/Slideshow folder. Set the movie's dimensions to 320 × 480. Set the background color to whatever you like (we chose #336699).

2. Create the following five layers: scripts, progress bar, loader, caption, and nav. Lock the scripts layer to avoid accidentally placing content in this layer.

3. Open the Components panel (Window ➤ Components) and drag an instance of the ProgressBar component to the progress bar layer. Use the Property inspector to ensure its width is 150, and to set the height to 22, X position to 85, and Y position to 200. Give it the instance name pb.

4. Drag an instance of the UILoader component to the loader layer. Set its width to 300, height to 400, X position to 10, and Y position to 10. Give it the instance name loader.

5. Captions will be displayed with a text field. Use the Text tool to create a dynamic text field in the caption layer. Set its width to 300, height to 28, X position. to 10 and Y position to 416. Give this text field the instance name caption. Make the font _sans, 18pt, and white, so that it shows over the blue background.

6. Drag an instance of the ComboBox component to the nav layer. Set its width to 220, X position to 10, and Y position to 450. Give it the instance name images.

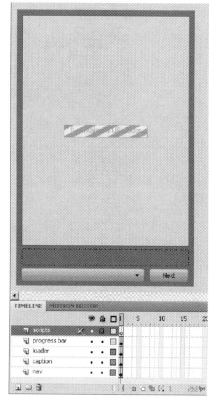

Figure 14-5. The parts are in place; time for the ActionScript.

7. Drag an instance of the Button component to the nav layer. Set its width to 70, X position 240, and Y position to 450. Give it the instance name next. Open the Component Inspector panel and set the button's Label parameter to Next. At this point, you have something like the scaffolding shown in Figure 14-5.

Now it's time to bring these parts to life. For the most part, it's a matter of handling events for the components and populating the combo box.

8. Click into frame 1 of the scripts layer and open the Actions panel. Here's the first chunk of code:

```
import fl.data.DataProvider;

var imageData:Array = new Array(
  {label:"798 Art District Photo 1", data:"798_01.jpg",
➥caption:"Lazy day on the street."},
  {label:"798 Art District Photo 2", data:"798_02.jpg",
➥caption:"Wall art."},
  {label:"798 Art District Photo 3", data:"798_03.jpg",
➥caption:"Angry and cute."},
  {label:"798 Art District Photo 4", data:"798_04.jpg",
➥caption:"The modern and the ancient!"},
  {label:"798 Art District Photo 5", data:"798_05.jpg",
➥caption:"Not sure what to make of this."},
  {label:"798 Art District Photo 6", data:"798_06.jpg",
➥caption:"The power of the artist?"},
  {label:"798 Art District Photo 7", data:"798_07.jpg",
➥caption:"Fashion shoot at a steam engine."},
  {label:"798 Art District Photo 8", data:"798_08.jpg",
➥caption:"A street in the district."}
);
```

The first line imports the DataProvider class, which is needed later when it's time to populate the combo box. After that, an arbitrarily named variable, imageData, is set to an instance of the Array class. Arrays are lists of whatever you put in them. You can use the Array.push() method on an instance to add elements to that instance, but you can also pass in the whole collection at once, which we've done here. This array has eight items, separated by commas, and each item is an instance of the generic Object class with three properties.

What, no new Object() statement? How are these objects being created? That's what the curly braces ({}) are for. It's a shortcut, and we're taking it. You'll remember from Chapter 11 that ComboBox instances can be supplied with label and data information, so that explains what those properties are in the array. The caption property is a custom addition.

9. Press Enter (Return) a couple times and type in the following:

```
var currentImage:int = 0;
var req:URLRequest = new URLRequest();

function changePicture(pict:int):void {
  pb.visible = true;
  caption.text = imageData[pict].caption;
  req.url = imageData[pict].data;
  loader.load(req);
}
changePicture(0);
```

The first line after the comment declares an integer variable, currentImage, and sets it to 0. This number will keep track of which image is being viewed. Next, a req variable holds an instance of the URLRequest class, which will used to request the current image file. The next several lines declare a custom function, changePicture(), which accepts a single parameter, pict. This function does the following three things:

- Makes the ProgressBar instance visible (yes, it's already visible at this point, but because later code turns off its visibility when an image finishes loading, it needs to be set back).

- Makes the text field display the current caption. The incoming pict parameter determines which element to retrieve from the imageData array (imageData[pict]), and that element's caption property is retrieved. When the value of pict happens to be 0, the expression effectively says imageData[0], which means, "Pull the first entry from the imageData list, please." Why start at zero? It's just one of those things; arrays start counting from zero rather than one.

- Makes the Loader instance load the current image. Here, again, the imageData array is consulted, but this time from the relevant item's data property, which is assigned to the URLRequest.url property of the req variable. In turn, req is fed to the loader instance by way of the Loader.load() method.

Immediately after its declaration, the changePicture() function is called, with 0 as its parameter. You're displaying the first image and its caption.

Now we just need to hook up the components.

10. Press Enter (Return) a couple times and type in the following:

```
pb.source = loader;

pb.addEventListener(Event.COMPLETE, completeHandler);
function completeHandler(evt:Event):void {
  pb.visible = false;
};
```

The first line associates the ProgressBar instance with the Loader instance. Thanks to the convenience of components, as the Loader component loads images, the progress bar will "automagically" know how to display load progress. The completeHandler() function makes the progress bar invisible when loading is complete.

11. Press Enter (Return) a couple times and type in the following:

```
images.dataProvider = new DataProvider(imageData);

images.addEventListener(Event.CHANGE, changeHandler);
function changeHandler(evt:Event):void {
  currentImage = images.selectedIndex;
  changePicture(currentImage);
};
```

The first line populates the combo box by setting its ComboBox.dataProvider property to a new DataProvider instance (this is why we need the import statement at the top). All the DataProvider instance needs is an array whose elements have label and data properties, which is exactly what we have in imageData. The caption properties are extra, but they don't hurt anything. That first line shoves the whole imageData array's content into the combo box in one swoop.

Next, the Event.CHANGE event is handled for the combo box. The handler function calls the custom changePicture() function and sets the currentImage variable to a number determined by the combo box's current selection. (The selectedIndex property doesn't care what data is *in* the selection; it only reports the number of the current selection, and that's all the currentImage variable needs.) This variable is then used as the parameter to the changePicture() function, which updates the current photo.

12. Press Enter (Return) a couple times and type in the following:

```
next.addEventListener(MouseEvent.CLICK, clickHandler);
function clickHandler(evt:MouseEvent):void {
  currentImage++;
  if (currentImage == imageData.length) {
    currentImage = 0;
  }
  images.selectedIndex = currentImage;
  changePicture(currentImage);
};
```

Here, the MouseEvent.CLICK event is handled for the button. The handler function does the following:

- Increments the currentImage variable by one.

- Checks to see if currentImage shares the same value as the expression imageData.length (the number of items in the imageData array). If so, it means the user has clicked often enough to progress through all the images, so currentImage is set back to 0.

- Sets the combo box's current selection to currentImage, to keep the combo box in sync with button clicks.

- Calls the custom changePicture() function and passes it currrentImage as its parameter.

13. Test the movie. You'll be treated to a mini-tour of the 798 Art District in Beijing, China. Click the Next button to flip through the pictures in sequence, as shown in Figure 14-6, or use the combo box to skip around.

Figure 14-6. A few quick components and a bit of ActionScript, and you're off!

595

14. To simulate image downloads, so you can see the progress bar in action, select View ➤ Simulate Download from the SWF's File menu. If you like, compare your work with the Slideshow.fla file in the Complete folder.

Extending the tour

As it turns out, wandering through the 798 Art District of Beijing makes a decent metaphor for this exercise, because after all of this careful examination of the art in the galleries, we're about to uncover a treasure in a gallery just a few more paces up the street.

Save your file to keep everything safe. Now select File ➤ Save As and save a copy as SlideshowXML.fla into the same folder. Click back into frame 1 of the scripts layer to make a few changes. Here's the first chunk of code, which replaces the hard-wired images, with revisions shown in bold.

```
import fl.data.DataProvider;

var xmlDoc:XML = new XML();
var xmlLoader:URLLoader = new URLLoader();
var xmlReq:URLRequest = new URLRequest("slideshow.xml");
xmlLoader.load(xmlReq);

xmlLoader.addEventListener(Event.COMPLETE,
➥xmlCompleteHandler);
function xmlCompleteHandler (evt:Event):void {
  xmlDoc = XML(evt.target.data);
  images.dataProvider = new DataProvider(xmlDoc);
  changePicture(0);
};
```

The imageData array is gone completely. In its place stands our trusty XML loading formula. The only differences here are the variable names. The URLLoader instance, for example, has been changed to xmlLoader, because loader is already in use as the instance name for the UILoader component. In the same way, the URLRequest instance is named xmlReq, because req is used later in the code, and the XML's completeHandler() function is named xmlCompleteHandler().

This time, we're loading the file slideshow.xml, and that's where the former imageData content now resides. Translated into XML, it looks like this:

```
<slideshow>
  <slide label="798 Art District Photo 1" data="798_01.jpg"
➥caption="Lazy day on the street." />
  <slide label="798 Art District Photo 2" data="798_02.jpg"
➥caption="Wall art." />
  <slide label="798 Art District Photo 3" data="798_03.jpg"
➥caption="Angry and cute." />
  <slide label="798 Art District Photo 4" data="798_04.jpg"
➥caption="The modern and the ancient!" />
  <slide label="798 Art District Photo 5" data="798_05.jpg"
➥caption="Not sure what to make of this." />
  <slide label="798 Art District Photo 6" data="798_06.jpg"
➥caption="The power of the artist?" />
```

```
    <slide label="798 Art District Photo 7" data="798_07.jpg"
➥caption="Fashion shoot at a steam engine." />
    <slide label="798 Art District Photo 8" data="798_08.jpg"
➥caption="A street in the district." />
</slideshow>
```

This is practically the same as the previous array, except that this time, it's in a separate XML document instead of being hard-wired into the ActionScript.

Let's take another look at the Event.COMPLETE event handler for the xmlLoader instance. The function runs as follows:

```
function xmlCompleteHandler(evt:Event):void {
  xmlDoc = XML(evt.target.data);
  images.dataProvider = new DataProvider(xmlDoc);
  changePicture(0);
};
```

Notice that the DataProvider handling has been moved here from its former position next to the combo box Event.CHANGE handler. Why? Because under the circumstances, the combo box can't be populated until the XML has loaded. Next, the changePicture() call has also been moved here from its earlier position. Why? Same reason: until the XML loads, the changePicture() has no reference for what image to summon.

Two more paces!

At or near line 21, you'll find the changeFunction() declaration. You'll need to tweak two lines (changes in bold):

```
function changePicture(pict:int):void {
  pb.visible = true;
  caption.text = xmlDoc.slide[pict].@caption;
  req.url = xmlDoc.slide[pict].@data;
  loader.load(req);
};
```

Instead of pulling from the old imageData array, the text field and UILoader component now draw their information from the xml instance, using E4X syntax to specify the relevant <slide> element attributes. Here, the function's incoming pict parameter serves the same purpose as it did before: it specifies which <slide> element to consult.

> *Don't forget to delete what used to be the last line in this chunk: that is,* changePicture(0); *which is now called inside the* xmlCompleteHandler() *function. It's easy to miss!*

Here are the last touch-ups. There's a reward in sight! First, delete the following data provider line (which has been moved to the xmlCompleteHandler() function):

```
images.dataProvider = new DataProvider(imageData);
```

Finally, revise one reference in the button's event handler (new code in bold):

```
function clickHandler(evt:MouseEvent):void {
  currentImage++;
  if (currentImage == xmlDoc.slide.length()) {
    currentImage = 0;
  }
  images.selectedIndex = currentImage;
  changePicture(currentImage);
};
```

Since imageData is no more, that line depends on the number of <slide> elements, instead.

Test the movie and watch the show again. If you think you missed a step, compare your work to the SlideshowXML.fla work in this chapter's Complete folder.

Now that the movie has become XML-ified, you can have some fun editing the slideshow.xml file and running the SWF to see the changes. For example, delete the first three <slide> elements and test the movie again. Like magic, only the three remaining slides and captions display. Change the wording of one of the captions, and then run the SWF again. Change the order of the order of the <slide> elements. With every edit, the SWF takes these changes effortlessly in stride.

Building an MP3 player with XML

When people get around to working with audio in Flash, one of the more common requests is, "Can I make my own MP3 player?" After reading Chapter 5, you already know the answer is yes. By the end of that chapter, you had the beginnings of an MP3 player that could load tracks from a ComboBox instance, as well as toggle playback with a Play/Pause button. In this exercise, we're going to pick up with that project and continue to flesh it out.

> Thanks again to Benjamin Tayler, Bryan Dunlay, Philip Darling, and Robbie Butcher, of Tin Bangs (http://www.tinbangs.com/) for the generous use of their music.

There is going to be a lot going on here, so we suggest you set aside sufficient time to carefully follow along. You're about to be introduced to several new and fundamental concepts that will require your attention. Among them are the following:

- Creating buttons that go the previous or the next audio track
- Creating a seek slider that allows you to move through an audio selection
- Creating a volume slider that allows the user to adjust the audio volume
- Displaying an audio track's ID3 information

The key to this exercise is understanding technique. Although there will be a lot going on, you will discover everything presented here builds upon what you have learned in the book. In the previous exercise, for example, the XML version of the slide show had a Next button. Here you'll have that too, along with the addition of a Prev button. And, again, the external files will be loaded from XML.

This exercise is designed to follow a fairly standard workflow, which is to assemble your assets first, and then "wire them up" using ActionScript. This time, instead of components, you'll be creating some of your own controls.

Setting up the external playlist

The first order of business is to move the MP3 data to an XML file. Open the TinBangs.fla file found in the Exercise/MP3Player folder for this chapter. This file is functionally identical to the one in the Complete folder for Chapter 5. The only difference is that the code comments have been made more obvious, like this:

```
/////////////////////////////////////////
// Obvious code comment
/////////////////////////////////////////
```

Why? Because this project is going to have a lot of ActionScript, and these striking "mile markers" help organize things visually. Why so many slashes? ActionScript ignores them after the first two in the line, so the rest are part of the comment.

The first task is to swap out the Array instance, songList, for an external XML document, just as you did for the Beijing slide show. Doing this will reacquaint you with the existing ActionScript in place.

1. Click info frame 1 of the scripts layer, open the Actions panel, and then locate the songList variable declaration on line 13, which looks like this:

```
var songList:Array = new Array(
  {label:"Select a song", data:""},
  {label:"White Lies (Timekiller)", data:"WhiteLies(Timekiller).mp3"},
  {label:"Young Lions", data:"YoungLions.mp3"},
  {label:"Your Sky is Falling", data:"YourSkyIsFalling.mp3"}
);
```

Delete those lines of code and replace them with the following:

```
var songList:XML = new XML();
var loader:URLLoader = new URLLoader();
var xmlReq:URLRequest = new URLRequest("playlist.xml");
loader.load(xmlReq);

loader.addEventListener(Event.COMPLETE, completeHandler);
function completeHandler(evt:Event):void {
  songList = XML(evt.target.data);
  songsCB.dataProvider = new DataProvider(songList);
};
```

There's nothing new here. The XML instance is named songList in this case, to minimize the impact on the rest of the code, which already refers to the song data by that name. A URLRequest instance already exists as req, so the new one here is named xmlReq. The requested file is now playlist.xml, whose contents you'll see in just a moment. The Event.COMPLETE handler sets songList to the loaded XML document's data, and then passes that to the ComboBox.dataProvider property of the songsCB combo box.

That last line inside the completeHandler() function—the one that refers to the data provider—originally appeared among the lines of code that configured the ComboBox instance, just before the line that reads addChild(songsCB);. You'll still see it there (should be at or near line 35 at this point), so delete it. (You only need to set the combo box's data provider once, and that needs to happen inside the completeHandler() function, after the XML has loaded.)

Just so you can see how similar the XML is to the original array, here's the content of the playlist.xml file:

```
<playlist>
  <song label="Select a song" data="" />
  <song label="White Lies (Timekiller)" data=
➥"WhiteLies(Timekiller).mp3" />
  <song label="Young Lions" data="YoungLions.mp3" />
  <song label="Your Sky is Falling" data="YourSkyIsFalling.mp3" />
</playlist>
```

Note that, as with the array, the first entry specifies a label attribute but leaves the data attribute blank.

2. Test the movie so far. It looks and works the same as it did at the end of Chapter 5, but now the MP3 file data is stored outside the FLA.

It's time to add the new stuff. But first, the authors would like to make a community service announcement.

Polishing up the symbols

We interrupt this program to introduce you to a fact of life that happens with collaborative Flash work. As mentioned in Chapter 5, the controller bar—with its VCR buttons and slider control—was created in Adobe Illustrator, and then imported into Flash. For the sake of demonstration, let's assume the designer didn't know how the controls would ultimately be used. If you don't think this will happen in your own Flash journeys, get ready to think again! In fact, count on it.

As a matter of good habit, you'll want to rename your library assets to better suit their actual use in this project. In addition, to improve the user's interactive experience, you'll also want to use the drawing tools to give these VCR buttons—which are actually movieclips—a bigger clickable surface area. This is especially important for the Pause button, because without the fix, the mouse could easily slip between the two vertical bars of the pause icon.

Renaming library assets

Renaming library assets is the sort of work that seems like housekeeping. And it is. but don't underestimate its value! When deadlines loom and a manager is breathing down your neck, it helps to know your library territory like the back of your hand. Take VolumeSlider, for example. In this MP3 player, that symbol is actually going to indicate how much of the audio has played. By dragging that slider, you'll be able to seek to various parts of the song. So, let's give it, and the other assets, better names.

1. Open the Library panel for the TinBangs.fla file. Locate the library's AudioPlayer.ai Assets folder, and you'll see a number of subfolders that ultimately contain the movieclips used for the controls in the Player layer of the Timeline panel. These include a handful of movieclips and subfolders whose names don't presently suit the purposes of this MP3 player: FastForward, Layer 7, VolumeSlider, Rewind, and VolumeBar.

2. Double-click the FastForward folder, as shown in Figure 14-7, and rename it to Next. Do the same with the FastForward movieclip. This is, after all, a button that skips to the next song in the playlist, not a fast-forward button.

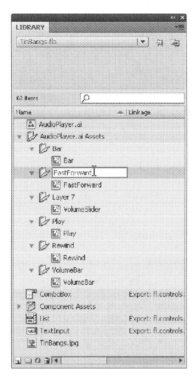

Figure 14-7. Appropriately naming library assets helps when you resume work after a break.

3. Rename the VolumeSlider symbol to SeekKnob. Do the same with its containing folder, Layer 7.

4. Rename the Rewind symbol and its folder to Prev.

5. Complete your cleanup by renaming the VolumeBar symbol and its folder to SeekBar.

Improving the controls

The previous steps helped you as a designer/developer. Now it's time to help the user.

1. Double-click the Play symbol to enter its timeline. Drag the playhead to frame 2, and you'll see two vertical bars that represent "pause," as shown in Figure 14-8.

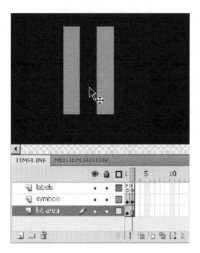

Figure 14-8. Be sure to keep your mouse-related assets mouse-friendly.

Granted, this symbol has been zoomed in quite a bit in the figure, but even at actual size, it's easy to see how the mouse can slip between the two bars, or accidentally miss the symbol altogether by slipping too far left or right. If this were a button symbol, the solution would be elementary: head to the Hit frame and give the button a nice, sizable hit area. With movieclips, which don't have a Hit frame, you need to get creative. In this case, the solution happens in a layer named hit area.

2. Click frame 1 of the hit area layer, and you'll see a pixelated rectangle appear behind the "play" arrow icon, as shown in Figure 14-9.

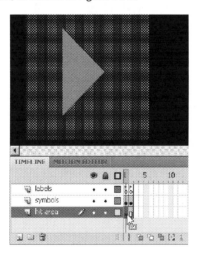

Figure 14-9. A low-alpha shape provides additional "surface area" for the mouse.

This rectangle is a simple shape, drawn with the Rectangle tool. The reason you can't see it—until the shape is selected—is because the shape's fill color is set to 0% Alpha. From a visual standpoint, it's imperceptible, but when the user hovers a mouse over this symbol, even the invisible shape provides a larger clickable surface area.

Notice that the rectangle spans frames 1 and 2, so that it appears behind both the play and pause icons. This makes the hit area useful, regardless where this symbol's playhead appears.

> *It is little things like this—giving a shape an opacity value of 0—that will separate you from the rest of the pack. This little trick takes maybe 2 to 3 minutes to accomplish. Someone who is unfamiliar with this will easily spend an hour trying to make the symbol "idiot-proof." This is a classic case of letting the software do the work instead of you overthinking it. In fact, the next step shows you how to do it yourself.*

The other VCR controls, and the SeekKnob symbol, need the same treatment. You can draw these shapes if you like, or you can let Flash do the work for you. Let's look at both ways.

3. Double-click the Prev symbol to enter its timeline. Rename the Layer 1 layer to arrows, then create a new layer named hit area beneath the first. In the hit area layer, use the Rectangle tool to draw a 20 × 20 pixel square with no stroke, and a fill color of #FFFFFF (white) set to 0% Alpha. Position the square so that it evenly fills the area behind the "prev" double arrows (we used an X position of -2 and a Y position of 2).

4. Right-click (Ctrl-click) frame 1 of the hit area layer and select Copy Frames from the context menu. Now double-click the Next symbol to enter its timeline. Rename Layer 1 to arrows, and then create a new layer beneath the first (no need to name it). Right-click (Ctrl-click) frame 1 of the new layer and select Paste Frames from the context menu. This accomplishes two things: it pastes the shape with the 0% Alpha and also renames the layer to hit area for you. Pretty slick! Reposition the shape so that it evenly fills the area behind the "next" double arrows (we used an X position of -4 and a Y position of 2).

5. Using whichever approach you prefer, position a similar shape beneath the hollow rectangle in the SeekKnob symbol. In our case, we renamed that symbol's Layer 1 layer to knob, and then pasted the same shape into a new layer. We changed the dimensions of the shape to 12 × 10 and positioned it at an X position of -2.5 and a Y position of -1.

> *Okay, so why two ways of doing the same thing? We are fond of telling anyone who will listen that there are usually 6,000 ways of doing anything in this business. What's the right way? Who cares? The only time someone cares is when it doesn't work.*

As it turns out, the Illustrator designer forgot two widgets: a volume slider, which lets the user adjust volume, and a loading indicator, which tells the user an MP3 file is still loading. As often as not, you might need to create such assets yourself, but to speed things along, we've provided what you need in separate file named controls.fla. By using a technique we introduced in Chapter 3, you can quickly share the widgets from that FLA with your current working FLA.

6. Select File ➤ Import ➤ Open External Library and browse to the controls.fla file in the Exercise/MP3Player folder for this chapter. Click the Scene 1 link in TinBangs.fla to get back to the main timeline.

7. With the Player layer selected, drag the LoadingDisplay symbol from the newly opened controls.fla library to the right side of the stage, as shown in Figure 14-10 (we used X: 462, Y: 305). Check the TinBang.fla's own library, and you'll see the movieclip there as well. Easy as that, you now have a loading indicator.

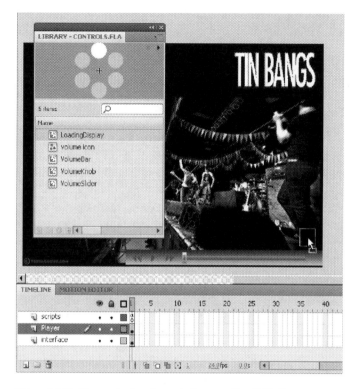

Figure 14-10. It's easy to drag in assets from another FLA's library.

8. In the TinBangs.fla library, double-click the LoadingDisplay movieclip to open it in the Symbol Editor. Scrub the timeline, and you'll see that the symbol is nothing more than a series of dots that seem to spin.

9. To make room for the volume slider, select the SeekBar symbol in the player background layer (the long red rectangle) and use the Property inspector to change its width to 138.

10. With the Player layer selected, drag the VolumeSlider symbol from the controls.fla library to the spot you just opened up—to the right of the other controls and just beneath the loading indicator (we used X: 424, Y: 328).

When you drag the VolumeSlider symbol, an interesting thing happens in the TinBangs.fla library: not only does VolumeSlider appear, but VolumeBar and VolumeKnob come along for the ride, as shown in Figure 14-11. This is nothing to be alarmed about. These other symbols show up because they're nested inside VolumeSlider, so they piggyback their way in.

11. Drag the volume icon graphic symbol from the controls.fla library to the stage, just to the left of the VolumeSlider symbol (we used X: 414, Y: 336). This is nothing more than an icon that helps indicate the purpose of the slider next to it.

12. Double-click VolumeSlider in the TinBangs.fla library to open it in the Symbol Editor.

Figure 14-11. Dragging in a nested asset carries with it the asset's children.

This symbol is a bit more complicated than the circle of dots from the previous shared asset, but you've already been introduced to all the concepts. As Figure 14-12 shows, you'll find three layers: knob, mask, and bar. The knob layer contains a rectangular symbol, VolumeKnob, whose shape is composed of a 0% Alpha fill. This is effectively an invisible button, like the hit area shape in step 2, except that the "button" is a movieclip. The mask layer contains five slanted columns, and the bar layer simply contains a red rectangle (this is the VolumeBar symbol). If you like, temporarily lock the mask and bar layers, and you'll see the masking in action. When this symbol is wired up, the user will be able to drag the invisible VolumeKnob symbol left and right. The VolumeBar symbol, partially hidden by the mask, will simply match the position of VolumeKnob, and the result will be an illusion: it will appear to the user that dragging left and right changes a red fill shared by the five slanted columns.

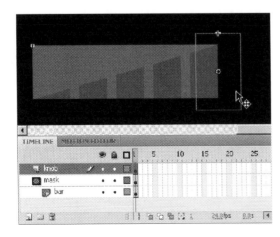

Figure 14-12. A low-alpha shape inside the rectangular movieclip provides "surface area" for the mouse.

605

13. Select Edit ➤ Edit Document to return to the main timeline. Use the Text tool to draw a dynamic text field in the Player layer, just to the left of the LoadingDisplay symbol. Configure the text field with whatever settings you like, but make sure the text field is dynamic and bears a light color, such as white.

With these assets in place, you're nearly ready to rock 'n' roll. Let's just make sure all the programmable assets have instance names, and then organize the timeline layers.

14. Carefully select the VolumeBar and VolumeKnob symbols on the stage to verify that they've already been given instance names: volumeBar and volumeKnob, respectively.

15. Return to the main timeline and, moving left to right, select each button in turn and verify they have the following instance names: btnPrev, btnPlay, and btnNext.

16. Continuing toward the right, select the SeekKnob symbol and give it the instance name seekKnob. Give the SeekBar symbol the instance name seekBar. For VolumeSlider, make it volumeSlider. Moving up, give LoadingDisplay the instance name loadingDisplay. Finally, moving left again, give the text field the instance name songData.

17. Select the Player layer by clicking its name. Now select Modify ➤ Timeline ➤ Distribute to Layers. Just like that—boom, you get a bunch of new timeline layers, named after the instance names of the symbols they contain.

18. The Player layer is still there, but now empty—so delete it. Rename the Bar layer to player background and the interface layer to background image, as shown in Figure 14-13.

Now everything is tidy and much easier to locate.

Figure 14-13. With everything neatly organized, you're well prepared for a smooth ride.

Wiring up the MP3 player controls

Now it's time to add the ActionScript. Fortunately, you have a leg up, because the Play/Pause button is already programmed. You did that in Chapter 5. In order to proceed, we're going to tidy up the existing ActionScript, just as we did with the library and timeline assets. We'll use the obvious code comments to help plot out our travel route.

Click into the scripts layer and review what's currently in place. This includes the revision you made earlier in this section, where songList became an XML instance (it had previously been an Array instance). Compare your work carefully. Nothing has changed since you last touched this code, but see if you can recognize what's going on. We'll meet you on the other side.

```
import fl.controls.ComboBox;
import fl.data.DataProvider;

////////////////////////////////////////
// Variables
////////////////////////////////////////

var song:Sound;
var channel:SoundChannel;
var req:URLRequest;
var pos:Number;

var songList:XML = new XML();
var loader:URLLoader = new URLLoader();
var xmlReq:URLRequest = new URLRequest("playlist.xml");
loader.load(xmlReq);

loader.addEventListener(Event.COMPLETE, completeHandler);
function completeHandler(evt:Event):void {
  songList = XML(evt.target.data);
  songsCB.dataProvider = new DataProvider(songList);
};

////////////////////////////////////////
// ComboBox
////////////////////////////////////////

// prep
var songsCB:ComboBox = new ComboBox();
songsCB.dropdownWidth = 200;
songsCB.width = 200;
songsCB.height = 24;
songsCB.x = 26;
songsCB.y = 68;
songsCB.dataProvider = new DataProvider(songList);
addChild(songsCB);

// events
songsCB.addEventListener(Event.CHANGE, changeHandler);

function changeHandler(evt:Event):void {
  if (songsCB.selectedItem.data != "") {
    req = new URLRequest(songsCB.selectedItem.data);
    if (channel != null) {
      channel.stop();
    }
    song = new Sound(req);
    channel = song.play();
    btnPlay.gotoAndStop("pause");
  }
};
```

607

```
//////////////////////////////////////////
// Buttons
//////////////////////////////////////////

// prep
btnPlay.stop();
btnPlay.buttonMode = true;

// events
btnPlay.addEventListener(MouseEvent.CLICK, clickHandler);

function clickHandler(evt:MouseEvent):void {
  if (channel != null) {
    if (btnPlay.currentLabel == "play") {
      channel = song.play(pos);
      btnPlay.gotoAndStop("pause");
    } else {
      pos = channel.position;
      channel.stop();
      btnPlay.gotoAndStop("play");
    }
  }
};
```

It's worth noting that some of this code overlaps. (Don't worry if you didn't see it! That's a lot of ActionScript to pore through.) In the ComboBox block, for example, inside the changeHandler() function, notice that these two lines:

```
channel = song.play();
btnPlay.gotoAndStop("pause");
```

match these two lines in the Buttons block's clickHandler() function (relevant code in bold):

```
if (btnPlay.currentLabel == "play") {
  channel = song.play(pos);
  btnPlay.gotoAndStop("pause");
} else {
```

In simple projects, you don't need to lose any sleep over the occasional overlap. But it's definitely something you want to keep in mind. We've looked at some optimization already in this chapter (the preloader exercise), and there's more of that coming in Chapter 15. The concept of optimization applies as much to the structure of your ActionScript as it does to your assets. As we wire up the controls, you'll find that numerous event handlers are going to load, pause, or play a song, so it makes good sense to write custom functions to perform those actions. Then those functions can be reused by your various event handlers. Doing this makes your ActionScript easier to read and, ultimately, there's less of it to type. The result is code that is easier to deal with. We'll now make the revisions to get rid of the overlap.

Add the following new variables to the code inside your Variables block near the top (new code in bold):

```
/////////////////////////////////////////
// Variables
/////////////////////////////////////////

var song:Sound;
var channel:SoundChannel;
var xform:SoundTransform;
var req:URLRequest;
var pos:Number;
var currentSong:int;
var rect:Rectangle;
```

Like the existing variables, the three new ones are declared, but not yet set to anything. The xform variable will be a SoundTransform instance, for controlling audio volume. currentSong is just like the currentImage variable in the Beijing slide show (here, it's used to keep track of the currently playing song). rect will be a Rectangle instance, which is used later to control the draggable distance of the seek and volume slider knobs.

Skip down to the ComboBox block. Within the changeHandler() function, change what you see so that it looks like this (revision in bold):

```
function changeHandler(evt:Event):void {
  if (songsCB.selectedItem.data != "") {
    currentSong = songsCB.selectedIndex;
    loadSong(songsCB.selectedItem.data);
  }
};
```

This trims up the function quite a bit. Instead of dealing with the loading code here—URLRequest, checking if the channel instance is null, and so on—those lines have been moved to a set of new functions you're about to write. These new functions will fit between the ComboBox block and the Buttons block. Copy one of those code block commented headings and paste it after the changeHandler() function. Change its caption to Song Functions, like this:

```
/////////////////////////////////////////
// Song Functions
/////////////////////////////////////////
```

After this commented heading, type the following new function:

```
function loadSong(file:String):void {
  req = new URLRequest(file);
  pauseSong();
  song = new Sound(req);
  song.addEventListener(Event.OPEN, soundOpenHandler);
  song.addEventListener(Event.COMPLETE, soundCompleteHandler);
  song.addEventListener(Event.ID3, soundID3Handler);
  playSong();
};
```

609

This is an example of double-dipping, as far as code optimization is concerned. You might even call it "passing the buck." Just as we passed along the loading code earlier, we're passing along *some* of the ActionScript here again, to two additional custom functions: pauseSong() and playSong(). It's all in the name of keeping the ActionScript lean.

Notice that the loadSong() function accepts a string parameter, which will be referenced by the file variable by code inside the function. In the previous code, the value of this parameter was supplied by the expression songsCB.selectedItem.data, which retrieved the MP3's file name from the ComboBox component's current selection. In later code—namely, the Prev and Next button event handlers—you'll see this same value supplied in other ways.

The req variable, declared early on in the Variables block, is finally set to a new instance of the URLRequest class, which allows the MP3 file to be requested. If a song is currently playing, it's stopped by virtue of the pauseSong() function (you'll see how in the next block of code).

The song variable is set to a new Sound instance, and because the req variable is fed right into the expression new Sound(), we bypass the need for the Sound.load() method. With the new Sound instance in place, it's ready for three event listeners: one when the MP3 is loaded (Event.OPEN), one when loading is complete (Event.COMPLETE), and one when the MP3 file's ID3 tags are encountered (Event.ID3). The event handler functions are intuitively named, and you'll see how they're used shortly.

Finally, the custom playSong() function rolls the music—which makes this a good idea to write those functions.

Let's continue adding code. Press Enter (Return) a couple times, and then type the following new ActionScript:

```
function playSong(pos:Number = 0):void {
  channel = song.play(pos);
  btnPlay.gotoAndStop("pause");
  seekKnob.addEventListener(Event.ENTER_FRAME, seekKnobUpdate);
};
function pauseSong():void {
  seekKnob.removeEventListener(Event.ENTER_FRAME, seekKnobUpdate);
  if (channel != null) {
    channel.stop();
  }
  btnPlay.gotoAndStop("play");
};
```

Most of this should seem familiar, but there's some new stuff, too. The playSong() function accepts a parameter, just like loadSong() does, but here, the parameter is already set to a value (pos:Number = 0)—so what's going on? New to ActionScript 3.0, this feature lets you provide default values for your parameters. What's it good for? Well, when referenced from the loadSong() function, playSong() isn't provided with a value; therefore, a default value of 0 is assumed. This will cause the song to play from the beginning when pos is passed into the first line inside this function: channel = song.play(pos);. As you'll see later, the Pause/Play button *does* pass in a value, because it lets you stop the music and resume from where you left off. In that case, the pos parameter *will be supplied* with a value, and the default 0 will be overruled.

So, when a song is played, it's assigned to the channel instance, and the btnPlay movieclip is sent to the pause label of its timeline. The other thing that needs to happen—and this is a glimpse ahead—is that the SeekKnob symbol needs to start moving along its track to indicate how much of the song has played. This is managed by way of an Event.ENTER_FRAME event, which triggers a seekKnobUpdate() function you'll write later in the exercise.

Once you understand the playSong() function, the pauseSong() function isn't hard to follow. It doesn't need a parameter. All it does is unhook the seekKnobUpdate() event handler, which halts the traveling of the SeekKnob symbol; determine if the channel instance is null, and if not, stop its playback; and send btnPlay's timeline to the play label.

Earlier, we wired up three Sound-related event listeners. It's time to write the handler functions for two of those. Press Enter (Return) a couple times and type the following new ActionScript:

```
// events
function soundOpenHandler(evt:Event):void {
  loadingDisplay.visible = true;
  loadingDisplay.play();
};
function soundCompleteHandler(evt:Event):void {
  loadingDisplay.stop();
  loadingDisplay.visible = false;
};
```

These functions are straightforward. After a quick // events comment, the soundOpenHandler() function simply sets the visibility of the LoadingDisplay symbol to true (this is the spinning dots symbol, imported from a shared library). To actually get the dots to spin, it invokes the MovieClip.play() method on the loadingDisplay instance name. This event handler function responds to the Event.OPEN event, which occurs whenever an MP3 file is loaded.

The soundCompleteHandler() function responds to the Event.COMPLETE event, which means a requested MP3 file has fully downloaded. As you can see, this handler stops the spinning dots and once again turns off the visibility of that movieclip.

Where's the Event.ID3 handler? It could certainly have been written here. Really, it's just a matter of organizational preference, and there's no arguing taste. To us, it makes sense to build out the rest of the code, which is composed entirely of event handlers, in the order in which the buttons and controls appear on the stage. We'll start with the buttons, move rightward to the sliders, then up to the dots, and then left again to the text field. It's the text field that does the two-step with the Event.ID3 event handler, so we'll meet it again at the end.

Ready for a quick intermission? Test the movie where it stands, and you'll see three error messages in the Compiler Errors panel, as shown in Figure 4-14. Those errors are due to three references to two event handler functions that don't exist yet. One of those is the Event.ID3 handler we just mentioned, located inside the loadSong() function. The other is the seekKnobUpdate() reference located in the playSong() and pauseSong() functions.

Find these addEventListener() and removeEventListener() references in the functions just mentioned, and comment them out, like this:

```
//song.addEventListener(Event.ID3, soundID3Handler);
//seekKnob.addEventListener(Event.ENTER_FRAME, seekKnobUpdate);
//seekKnob.removeEventListener(Event.ENTER_FRAME, seekKnobUpdate);
```

Test the movie again. The errors disappear.

If you like, compare your work with TinBangsMilestone.fla in the Complete/MP3Player folder for this chapter. When you're ready to move on, you'll be wiring up the buttons.

But before you proceed, make sure to **uncomment those three lines again**!

Handling the button events

Remember that the Play/Pause button has already been programmed, which speeds things up a bit. Because we have the new playSong() and pauseSong() functions, you will need to make a few changes to what's there. Fortunately, this shortens the existing ActionScript, which is all part of the secondary plot for this exercise: code optimization. Let's do it.

In case you're not already there, click into frame 1 of the scripts layer again and open the Actions panel. Find the Buttons code block and update what you see to the following new lines (new ActionScript in bold):

```
//////////////////////////////////////////
// Buttons
//////////////////////////////////////////

// prep
btnPlay.stop();
btnPlay.buttonMode = true;
btnPrev.buttonMode = true;
btnNext.buttonMode = true;

// events
btnPlay.addEventListener(MouseEvent.CLICK, playHandler);
btnPrev.addEventListener(MouseEvent.CLICK, prevHandler);
btnNext.addEventListener(MouseEvent.CLICK, nextHandler);
```

There's nothing difficult here. The Prev and Next buttons need their MovieClip.buttonMode properties set to true, simply because—like Pause/Play—they're movieclips that are masquerading as buttons. Following suit, they get assigned to their respective event handlers. Because there are now three click-related event handlers, the function originally assigned to the btnPlay instance has been renamed playHandler() (it was formerly clickHandler()).

Speaking of clickHandler(), you need to update it so that it reflects the following new code, making sure to rename it as shown (revisions in bold):

```
function playHandler(evt:MouseEvent):void {
  if (channel != null) {
    if (btnPlay.currentLabel == "play") {
      playSong(pos);
    } else {
```

```
            pos = channel.position;
            pauseSong();
         }
      }
   };
```

Here's where the custom functions begin to earn their keep. The behavior of the playhandler() function is intact, but thanks to the playSong() and pauseSong() functions, the actual lines of code have been reduced.

Notice, as before, that on one side of the else clause, the pos variable is set to the SoundChannel.position property of the channel instance. On the other side of that else clause, pos is passed into the playSong() function as a parameter. When you look at the playSong() function definition in the previous section, you'll see that the variable between the function's parentheses also happens to be called pos. That's a coincidence, and nothing more. Whether or not they're named the same, a value that represents the song's position is conveyed, and that's all that matters.

> In real-world situations, you'll often find that project requirements change. In fact, it's rare when they don't! When this happens, you'll find yourself better equipped to respond to revisions when you're dealing with reusable functions. If the concept embodied by the playSong() function happens to change, you need to edit only one function in a single place, rather than needing to use a hunt-and-peck approach to touch up numerous blocks of code.

The Prev and Next buttons are taken care of with one function apiece. Add the following two event handlers beneath the playHandler() function:

```
function prevHandler(evt:MouseEvent):void {
   currentSong--;
   if (currentSong < 1) {
      currentSong = songList.song.length() - 1;
   }
   songsCB.selectedIndex = currentSong;
   loadSong(songList.song[currentSong].@data);
};
function nextHandler(evt:MouseEvent):void {
   currentSong++;
   if (currentSong > songList.song.length() - 1) {
      currentSong = 1;
   }
   songsCB.selectedIndex = currentSong;
   loadSong(songList.song[currentSong].@data);
};
```

These should be reminiscent of the Next button in the Beijing slide show. Here, these two functions are metaphorically mirror images of each other. In prevHandler(), the value of the currentSong variable is decreased by 1 (currentSong--). If currentSong is less than 1—which it will be, eventually—then the variable is set to one less than the total number of <song> elements in the XML document (songList.song.length() - 1). Why one less than the total? Because arrays start with 0, rather than 1. Why aren't

613

we checking if currentSong is less than 0, then? Because the first entry in the XML, and therefore the ComboBox component, is the "dead" entry without data—the one that says Select a song.

Once currentSong is updated, the selected index of the ComboBox component is configured to reflect that change, and the custom loadSong() function is instructed to load the new current selection. The parameter's expression happens to be based on the XML content, using a bit of E4X syntax—songList.song[currentSong].@data—but it could have just as easily be taken from the ComboBox component.

In contrast, the nextHandler() function increments the value of currentSong, and then sets it back to 1 if it goes beyond one less than the total number of <song> nodes in the XML—in other words, the reverse. After that, the ComboBox component is updated and, once again, the loadSong() function is instructed to load the current selection.

> *Wait a minute! The last two lines of these functions overlap! Shouldn't they be folded into yet another function—maybe updateSong()? You could certainly do that. Optimization is as much an art as a science, and we encourage you to find your personal line in the sand.*

Programming the sliders

You're about to enter into the thickest part of the ActionScript for this project, so you may want to pull out your machete. Actually, it's not so bad, once you strike past the first bit of foliage. The mosquitoes are pretty big, true, but that makes it all the easier to swat them with the blade.

Joking aside, the ActionScript for the sliders isn't going to make your head explode. To understand it better, it helps to take a closer look at the way the slider-related symbols are laid out. Their registration points, in particular, are designed to make the math as easy as possible, so let's take a gander. Figure 14-14 shows these registration points.

Figure 14-14. The symbols' registration points are carefully chosen to make the code easier.

There are two parts to this slider: the SeekKnob symbol and the SeekBar symbol. When the knob is positioned on the bar's left edge, as shown in Figure 14-14, notice that the registration points of each symbol (the two pluses along each symbol's upper edges) are aligned. This happens because SeekBar's registration point—its 0,0 position—is located in that symbol's upper-left corner. SeekKnob's registration point, on the other hand, is located in that symbol's top center.

Both of these symbols are positioned 260 pixels from the left side of the stage. If SeekKnob's registration point was also in its own upper-left corner, it would have to be offset by several pixels to look as if it were hugging the left edge of SeekBar. As it is, however, the numbers are easy. To coordinate its movements with SeekBar, all SeekKnob has to do is know SeekBar's horizontal position (seekBar.x) and take into consideration SeekBar's width (seekBar.width). Figure 14-15 gives a quick visual breakdown.

To position the knob along the bar's left edge, all you need to do set its MovieClip.x property to the bar's MovieClip.x property. To slide it halfway across, set the knob's x property to the x property of the bar, plus half of the bar's width. To shove it all the way over, set its x property to bar's, plus the full width of the bar. Keep this principle in mind as we work through the seek slider ActionScript.

To begin, copy another one of the commented code block headers and paste it below the last bit of ActionScript (nextHandler(), from the Buttons section). Change the header's caption to Seek slider, and then type in the following ActionScript, so that your code looks like this:

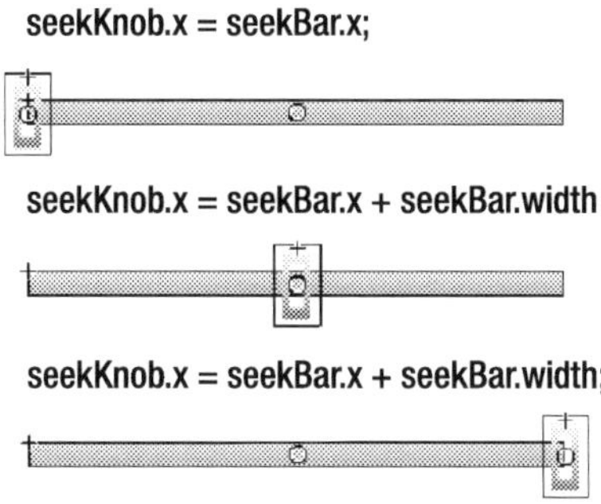

seekKnob.x = seekBar.x;

seekKnob.x = seekBar.x + seekBar.width / 2;

seekKnob.x = seekBar.x + seekBar.width;

Figure 14-15. The position of the knob and position and width of the bar are the critical properties.

```
////////////////////////////////////////
// Seek slider
////////////////////////////////////////

// prep
seekKnob.buttonMode = true;

// events
seekKnob.addEventListener(MouseEvent.MOUSE_DOWN, seekStartDrag);
```

Like the Prev, Play/Pause, and Next movieclip "buttons," the seekKnob instance needs to have its buttonMode property set to true. When the user clicks it, you want the user to be able to start dragging that knob, so the MouseEvent.MOUSE_DOWN event is associated with a custom function you're about to write, called seekStartDrag(). That function is triggered when the user clicks the mouse (MOUSE_DOWN) on the seekKnob instance. Type the following new ActionScript:

```
function seekStartDrag(evt:MouseEvent):void {
  if (song != null) {
    pauseSong();
    rect = new Rectangle(seekBar.x, seekKnob.y, seekBar.width, 0);
    seekKnob.startDrag(true, rect);
    stage.addEventListener(MouseEvent.MOUSE_UP, seekStopDrag);
  }
};
```

If the song instance isn't null—it's null, for example, before a song is chosen from the combo box—then pause the song, in case it's playing. Next, define a Rectangle instance (stored in the rect variable), which will be used to constrain dragging to the desired location.

Rectangle instances are specified at a particular location (x and y) and at a particular width and height. In this case, we want the knob to be draggable only from the left side of the bar (seekBar.x, the first parameter) to the right side (seekBar.width, the third parameter). Its vertical position is fine where it is (seekKnob.y, the second parameter) and shouldn't vary from that, which means we set the rectangle to a height of 0 (the fourth parameter).

The `MovieClip.startDrag()` method, invoked on seekKnob, is fed two parameters: `true`, which snaps dragging to the symbol's registration point, and `rect`, which confines dragging to the dimensions just described.

Finally, a `MouseEvent.MOUSE_UP` event handler is associated with the stage, configured to trigger a custom seekStopDrag() function. Why is this association made with the stage, rather than with seekKnob? Because the user might just drag the mouse off the knob before releasing the mouse (MOUSE_UP). If the event handler were associated with seekKnob, then seekStopDrag() wouldn't be triggered. But when it's assigned to the stage, that pretty much means the mouse can be lifted anywhere, and the dragging routine will stop.

Here's the seekStopDrag() function. Type the following new ActionScript:

```
function seekStopDrag(evt:MouseEvent):void {
  seekKnob.stopDrag();
  playSong(song.length * (seekKnob.x - seekBar.x) / seekBar.width);
  stage.removeEventListener(MouseEvent.MOUSE_UP, seekStopDrag);
};
```

The first thing this function does is invoke `MovieClip.stopDrag()` on the seekKnob instance. That part is easy. The challenge comes in telling the song where to begin playing again, because it all depends on where the knob is currently positioned along the bar. To illustrate, let's imagine the user dragged the knob right to the middle, and let's pretend the song is exactly 60 seconds long. Let's use those figures and run the math.

Here's the actual expression:

```
song.length * (seekKnob.x - seekBar.x) / seekBar.width
```

Using the numbers we just agreed on, that equates to this:

```
60 seconds X (knob's position - bar's position) / bar's width
60 * (329 - 260) / 138
```

60, multiplied by the difference between 329 and 260 (namely, 69) is 4,140. Divided by 138, the final number is 30 seconds, which is exactly what's expected when the knob is dropped halfway across.

The final total of the arithmetic equation is fed into the playSong() function, which starts the song from whatever value, in seconds, is provided.

The last thing this function does is to tell the stage to stop listening for the MOUSE_UP event, because the event obviously just occurred (since this function handles it).

In the playSong() function definition, seekKnob is associated with an `Event.ENTER_FRAME` event, which tells the knob to continuously update its position according to how much of the song has played. Here's that function. Type the following new ActionScript:

```
function seekKnobUpdate(evt:Event):void {
  var pos:Number = seekBar.width * channel.position / song.length;
  if (!isNaN(pos)) {
    seekKnob.x = seekBar.x + pos;
  } else {
```

```
        seekKnob.x = seekBar.x;
    }
};
```

Here's that pos variable again (a third one!). This one is unrelated to the other two, except in name. To the authors, pos just seems like an appropriate name for a variable for noting the *position* of something. In this case, pos is declared within the scope of this function and set to an expression that effectively does the opposite of the expression shown earlier. Let's run the numbers again, assuming that, at this very moment, our hypothetical 60-second song has played halfway through. Here's the actual expression:

```
seekBar.width * channel.position / song.length,
```

It equates to this:

```
bar's width X song's position / song's length
138 * 30 / 60
```

138 multiplied by 30 is 4,140 (sounds familiar, doesn't it?). 4,140 divided by 60 is 69. Hold that thought.

There may be times when neither channel nor song have property values that yield a valid number when run through the math. To safeguard against that, an if statement uses the isNaN() function (is Not a Number) to prod the value of pos (which is hypothetically 69). If pos *is a valid number*—that is, if !isNaN(pos) evaluates to true—then it is added to the current MovieClip.x value of seekBar, the sum of which is bestowed upon seekKnob. Because seekBar's position is 260, that (added to 69) puts seekKnob at 329, which is exactly halfway across the bar.

> The exclamation point (!) in front of the isNaN() function inverts whatever that function says, in the same way that the inequality operator (!=) means "is not equal to." If you want to find out if a value is not a valid number, check it against isNaN(). On the other hand, if you want to find out if a value is a valid number, check it against !isNaN().

The flip side of that if statement—meaning, pos is an unusable number—simply sets the knob's position to the position of the bar, which resets the knob to its original hug-the-left-side location.

As the song plays through, this seekKnobUpdate() function is triggered every time the timeline enters a frame; in other words, continuously. This causes the knob to indicate progress until the function is instructed to stop.

The mechanics of the volume slider work in pretty much the same way. A similar knob symbol is instructed to drag within a constrained area. The difference is that the knob's position in relation to its bar is used to adjust the volume of the currently playing song. In addition, a separate symbol is instructed to follow the knob, whose movement either hides or reveals that symbol behind a mask. Let's add the code.

Continuing below the previous ActionScript, give yourself another code comment heading, this time captioned as Volume slider. Type in these additional new lines:

```
///////////////////////////////////////
// Volume slider
///////////////////////////////////////

// prep
volumeSlider.volumeKnob.buttonMode = true;

// events
volumeSlider.volumeKnob.addEventListener(MouseEvent.MOUSE_DOWN,
➡volumeStartDrag);
```

The volumeKnob instance is nested inside volumeSlider, and that's because those movieclips are nested. Other than that, there is nothing remarkable about this addition. Let's keep rolling.

Enter the following new ActionScript, which defines the volumeStartDrag() function just referenced:

```
function volumeStartDrag(evt:MouseEvent):void {
  rect = new Rectangle(8, volumeSlider.volumeKnob.y,
➡volumeSlider.volumeBar.width - 8, 0);
  volumeSlider.volumeKnob.startDrag(true, rect);
  volumeSlider.volumeKnob.addEventListener(MouseEvent.MOUSE_MOVE,
➡volumeAdjust);
  stage.addEventListener(MouseEvent.MOUSE_UP, volumeStopDrag);
};
```

As with the other slider, rect is set to a new Rectangle instance when the knob is clicked and fed appropriate values. In this case, the values are purposefully tweaked to move the knob in from the left edge just a bit. Why? Because if the volume knob were dragged all the way to the left, it would completely obscure the red movieclip rectangle behind the slanted five-column mask. Letting it go *almost* all the way to the left—8 pixels shy, in this case—looks good visually.

The startDrag() method is invoked on volumeKnob, and again the stage is associated with a MouseEvent. MOUSE_UP event to stop the dragging. This time, though, an additional event (MOUSE_MOVE) is associated with a custom function named volumeAdjust(). Let's look at both of those.

Enter the following new ActionScript:

```
function volumeStopDrag(evt:MouseEvent):void {
  volumeSlider.volumeKnob.stopDrag();
  stage.removeEventListener(MouseEvent.MOUSE_UP, volumeStopDrag);
  volumeSlider.volumeKnob.removeEventListener(MouseEvent.MOUSE_MOVE,
➡volumeAdjust);
};
function volumeAdjust(evt:MouseEvent):void {
  volumeSlider.volumeBar.x = volumeSlider.volumeKnob.x;
  if (channel != null) {
    xform = channel.soundTransform;
    xform.volume = (volumeSlider.volumeKnob.x - 8) / (
➡volumeSlider.volumeBar.width - 8);
    channel.soundTransform = xform;
  }
};
```

The volumeStopDrag() function is old hat by now. It stops the dragging and stops the MOUSE_MOVE handler. Let's break down the volumeAdjust() function.

First off, it sets the position of volumeBar to the position of volumeKnob. That hides and reveals the red rectangle behind its mask in concert with the knob's position. After that, assuming channel is not null, the xform variable—declared early on—is set to the SoundChannel.soundTransform property of the channel instance. This gives xform a SoundTransform.volume property, whose value is set in terms of volumeKnob's position (accounting for that 8-pixel shy span) in relation to the width of volumeBar.

The VolumeBar symbol happens to be 50 pixels wide, so let's run the numbers assuming the knob has been dragged halfway across the valid range. (Normally, halfway across would be 25, but we're adding half of that 8-pixel buffer, so half is 29 here.) Here's the actual expression:

```
volumeSlider.volumeKnob.x - 8) / (volumeSlider.volumeBar.width - 8
```

It equates to this:

```
knob's position - 8, divided by bar's width - 8
29 - 8 / 50 - 8
```

29 minus 8 is 21. 50 minus 8 is 42. 21 divided by 42 is 0.5, or 50%.

xform's volume property is set to 0.5, and then the final line reassigns xform to the channel.soundTransform property, which cuts the volume in half. Remember that this function is triggered every time the mouse moves, as it drags the knob.

Almost in the clear!

Finishing up the controls

The rest of the controls require barely a flick of the tail. All we need to do is hide the LoadingDisplay symbol (the spinning dots) by default, and handle the Event.ID3 event. Let's do it.

Add another block of code that looks like this:

```
/////////////////////////////////////
// Loading display
/////////////////////////////////////

loadingDisplay.stop();
loadingDisplay.visible = false;
```

This stops and hides the spinning dots.

Now, enter your final block of code, and make it look like this:

```
/////////////////////////////////////
// Song Data
/////////////////////////////////////
```

619

```
function soundID3Handler(evt:Event):void {
  songData.text = song.id3.artist + ": " + song.id3.songName + "
➥(" + song.id3.year + ")";
};
```

This function is triggered whenever an MP3's ID3 tags are encountered. Tag information is retrieved from the Sound.id3 property of the song instance—here, song.id3.artist, .songName, and .year—and concatenated into a string fed to the songData text field's text property.

> ID3 tags have nothing to do with ActionScript 3.0 per se. The concept is part of the MP3 file format, and it just happens to be supported by ActionScript. On their own, ID3 tag names aren't especially easy to read. The tag intended for the artist's name, for example, is TPE1; the publication year is TYER, and so on. ActionScript provides friendly names for the most popular tags—comment, album, genre, songName, artist, track, and year—but the others are available by their less intuitive tag names. To see the full list, look up the Sound class in the ActionScript 3.0 Language and Components Reference, then skim down the Properties heading until you come to id3. Click that listing.

Test your MP3 player to give it a spin. Kick the tires a bit.

Evaluating and improving the MP3 player

Even with the best of planning, you might be surprised to find that some aspects of a project, including its faults, don't make themselves apparent until the work is done—or at least, until a first draft is done. (Some projects never do seem to end! Hey, at least it's a paycheck.) In Chapter 15, we discuss the idea of planning a FLA beforehand—the authors do believe in the practice, with a passion—but sometimes you can't tell how a car is going to handle until you actually wrap your fingers around the steering wheel and slam your boot on the gas pedal.

In this case, you may have noticed that every time a new song plays, the volume jumps back up to 100%, no matter where you drag the volume slider. Worse, when this happens, the volume is audibly at full, even though the slider might be positioned all the way to the left. That's a bug, and we're going to fix it.

In addition, you might want the player to cycle through the whole playlist, rather than simply stop after a song ends. You might also want the first song to start playing automatically. All of these options are possible, and thanks to the thoughtful arrangement of our existing ActionScript, they're easy to implement.

Let's tie up this MP3 player with a bow. First, let's address the volume bug. Locate the volumeAdjust() function, just above the Loading display block, and give its evt parameter a default value of null—like this (revision in bold):

```
function volumeAdjust(evt:MouseEvent = null):void {
```

What does this do? Without the addition, this function requires a MouseEvent parameter, which pretty much means it must be triggered in response to an event, which passes in the MouseEvent automatically. By giving the evt parameter a null value by default, you're making the parameter *optional*. This means the volumeAdjust() function can be triggered from anywhere, as an event handler or not.

Locate the playSong() function and update it to look like this (revision in bold):

```
function playSong(pos:Number = 0):void {
  channel = song.play(pos);
  volumeAdjust();
  btnPlay.gotoAndStop("pause");
  seekKnob.addEventListener(Event.ENTER_FRAME, seekKnobUpdate);
};
```

Just like that, the bug is fixed! The playSong() function actually sets the newly loaded song in motion, to speak, and associates the song instance with the channel instance. With channel updated, the xform variable, referenced inside volumeAdjust(), has what it needs to check the current position of the volume slider and adjust the volume accordingly.

Since we're in the playSong() function anyway, it's the perfect time to add a new event listener that will allow the player loop through its playlist. Update the playSong() function again to look like this (revision in bold):

```
function playSong(pos:Number = 0):void {
  channel = song.play(pos);
  channel.addEventListener(Event.SOUND_COMPLETE, nextHandler);
  volumeAdjust();
  btnPlay.gotoAndStop("pause");
  seekKnob.addEventListener(Event.ENTER_FRAME, seekKnobUpdate);
};
```

Once the channel variable is updated, it's associated with the already-written nextHandler() function in response to the Event.SOUND_COMPLETE event, which is dispatched when the sound channel of a currently playing sound reaches the end of the file.

Remember that the nextHandler() function is also associated with the MouseEvent.CLICK event, which is triggered when someone clicks the Next button. The MouseEvent class inherits some of its functionality from the Event class, and in this case, it's safe to strongly type the evt parameter inside the nextHandler() function as Event. This is because, at rock bottom, both Event and MouseEvent instances are ultimately instances of Event.

Locate the nextHandler() function and change it to look like this (revision in bold):

```
function nextHandler(evt:Event):void {
```

Finally, to make this MP3 player begin in "auto-play" mode, locate the completeHandler() function, just above the ComboBox block, and add the new lines shown in bold:

```
function completeHandler(evt:Event):void {
  songList = XML(evt.target.data);
  songsCB.dataProvider = new DataProvider(songList);
  loadSong(songList.song[1].@data);
  songsCB.selectedIndex = 1;
};
```

When the XML playlist fully loads, completeHandler() is triggered. It populates the ComboBox component. In addition to that, it now invokes the loadSong() function and feeds it the file name from the first <song> element that actually refers to an MP3 file (remember that the *very first* <song> element—songList.song[0]—doesn't contain file data). After that, the function updates the ComboBox component to its first song entry (the one after the filler Select a song entry), by setting its selectedIndex property to 1.

Test your movie again and, while you're tapping your feet, give yourself a pat on the back.

Building a video controller

You picked up a lot of knowledge about Flash video in Chapter 10. We are willing to bet that quite a few of you finished the chapter and wondered, "Can I create my own video controller . . . from scratch?" Glad you asked! On the heels of the MP3 player, building on what you already know, it won't even be very difficult.

Assembling the controller

To see how the controller is assembled, open the VideoPlayer.fla file in the Exercise folder for this chapter. Notice there is, for all intents and purposes, an empty stage with a controller near the bottom edge. Looking in the library, you will discover the controller is composed of nothing more than a number of movieclips, as shown in Figure 14-16. And you'll see that the entire Flash movie is composed of a single frame on the timeline.

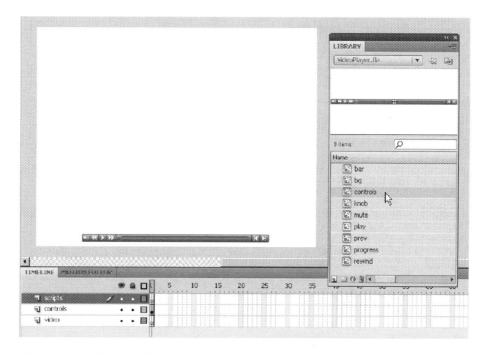

Figure 14-16. Nothing but a few movieclips

The really interesting thing about this controller is that it was created entirely in Flash using the techniques presented in Chapter 2 of this book. The shapes were all drawn with the Rectangle Primitive and Oval tools. Each object was then filled with either a linear or radial gradient and converted to a movieclip symbol. The icons are nothing more than characters from the Webdings font, broken down to shapes.

Feel free to poke through the movieclips to get an idea of how this project was assembled. The play and mute symbols have two frames apiece in their own timelines, and are laid out like the Play/Pause button from the MP3 player exercise; that is, frame labels distinguish between the play/pause icons and mute/unmute icons. The movieclips with icons use the same trick you learned about in the previous exercise—a background shape with 0% Alpha fill—to give these "buttons" greater clickable surface area.

It's all well and good to know how the controller was assembled, but of course, the real magic happens when it gets wired up with ActionScript. There's going to be a bit of code coming at you, but now that you've built an MP3 player, lots of this will look familiar.

Wiring up the video player controls

First, you need a video object under the controls player. Right-click (Ctrl-click) inside the library and select New Video to create the object, and then drag it to the stage in the video layer. Change the object's dimensions so that it matches the width and height of the stage, and position it at 0,0. Give this video object the instance name myVideo.

Select the frame 1 in the scripts layer and open the Actions panel. Click once in the Script pane and enter the following code (to get the commented code block header, you can copy and paste from the previous exercise):

```
/////////////////////////////////////////
// Variables
/////////////////////////////////////////

var duration:Number;
var pos:Number;
var xform:SoundTransform;
var rect:Rectangle;

var currentVideo:int = 0;
var seekRate:int = 10;
var rwTimer:Timer = new Timer(100, 0);
var ffTimer:Timer = new Timer(100, 0);
```

The first four lines contain a number of variables that will be used later in the ActionScript: duration will refer to the length of the currently playing video, pos will correspond to the current position in the video, xform will adjust volume, and rect will constrain dragging for the slider knob.

The second four lines not only declare a few more variables, but initialize them with values, as well. currentVideo indicates the currently playing video, and seekRate determines how quickly the user will be able to fast-forward and rewind the current video. The last two set up two Timer instances that, when started, will trigger their associated functions—coming later—every 100 milliseconds (that is, every tenth of a second). The second parameter for each—a 0 in both cases—means the timers will repeat forever, or until told to stop.

Now it's time for the NetConnection and NetStream hookup. Enter the following new ActionScript beneath the existing code:

```
// net connection / net stream
var nc:NetConnection = new NetConnection();
nc.connect(null);
var ns:NetStream = new NetStream(nc);
myVideo.attachNetStream(ns);

var listener:Object = new Object();
listener.onMetaData = metaDataHandler;
function metaDataHandler(md:Object):void {
  duration = md.duration;
};
ns.client = listener;

ns.addEventListener(NetStatusEvent.NET_STATUS, statusHandler);
function statusHandler(evt:NetStatusEvent):void {
  if (evt.info.code == "NetStream.Play.Stop") {
    nextHandler();
  }
};
```

Much of this is code you saw a dozen times in Chapter 10. Most of the NetConnection and NetStream code—with our familiar nc and ns variable names—hasn't differed from elsewhere in the book.

What is new is that fact that we're actually using the onMetaData event this time, rather than throwing it the "oh, shut up already!" empty function seen previously (listener.onMetaData = function(md:Object):void {};). In this case, we do want something in the video's metadata: the duration of the video. We retrieve that value by pulling it from the duration property of the md parameter that represents the metadata:

```
listener.onMetaData = metaDataHandler;
function metaDataHandler(md:Object):void {
  duration = md.duration;
};
```

This value is stored in the duration variable declared earlier. You'll see how it's used in the fast-forward and rewind functions.

To make this video player loop through its playlist, as the MP3 player does, the same principle is used, but the mechanics are different here:

```
ns.addEventListener(NetStatusEvent.NET_STATUS, statusHandler);
function statusHandler(evt:NetStatusEvent):void {
  if (evt.info.code == "NetStream.Play.Stop") {
    nextHandler();
  }
};
```

A custom function, statusHandler(), is associated with the ns instance by way of a NetStatusEvent. NET_STATUS event. This is an event that is dispatched numerous times throughout the loading and playback of a video file, which makes sense. The video experiences all sorts of changes while it plays (loading, buffering, playing, and so on), and its status changes as a result. The NetStatusEvent class features an info property, which contains a code property that indicates the video's current status. When the video reaches its end—indicated by the string "NetStream.Play.Stop"—we want to trigger the custom nextHandler() function. This is just what we did with the MP3 player. And when we get to the button event handlers, you'll see how well you already recognize the nextHandler() function.

This video player reads its playlist from XML, so the next little bit won't be uncharted territory. Enter the following ActionScript beneath the existing code:

```
// xml
var videoList:XML = new XML();
var loader:URLLoader = new URLLoader();
var req:URLRequest = new URLRequest("playlist.xml");
loader.load(req);

loader.addEventListener(Event.COMPLETE, completeHandler);
function completeHandler(evt:Event):void {
  videoList = XML(evt.target.data);
  ns.play(videoList.video[currentVideo].@file.toString());
  resumeVideo();
};
```

The only things worth noting here are the toString() method, tacked to the end of the E4X expression, and the reference to a custom resumeVideo() function. The reason toString() is needed here is because we're not using a custom loadVideo() function, like the MP3 player's loadSong(). The MP3 player's loadSong() function effectively converted its parameter's value to a string, and thanks to the omission here, we're taking care of that ourselves.

So how does the XML look this time? Like this:

```
<playlist>
  <video file="InkSong.mp4" />
  <video file="InspectorGadget.flv" />
  <video file="PeterWolf.flv" />
</playlist>
```

The resumeVideo() reference may seem a bit weird, because the video should already be playing, right? (Note the ns.play() call in the previous line.)

True enough, but as with the previous exercise, this player also tracks playback progress by way of a traveling slider knob, and the resumeVideo() function assigns the Event.ENTER_FRAME handler that manages that movement. In fact, speak of the devil . . .

Type the following ActionScript beneath the existing code:

```
////////////////////////////////////////
// Video functions
////////////////////////////////////////
```

625

```
function resumeVideo():void {
  ns.resume();
  videoControls.btnPlay.gotoAndStop("pause");
  videoControls.knob.addEventListener(Event.ENTER_FRAME,
➥seekKnobUpdate);
};
function pauseVideo():void {
  ns.pause();
  videoControls.btnPlay.gotoAndStop("play");
  videoControls.knob.removeEventListener(Event.ENTER_FRAME,
➥seekKnobUpdate);
};
```

Here are two custom functions that help thin out the code a bit for the remaining event handlers. Because of the animated slider knob and toggleable Play/Pause button, the act of pausing and resuming video playback requires more than just a reference to NetStream.pause() or NetStream.resume(). To save keystrokes down the line, these functions invoke the relevant NetStream methods and, in addition, update the Play/Pause button icon, and then either add or remove the custom seekKnobUpdate() function as a listener of the Event.ENTER_FRAME event.

Note that the knob instance—the knob movieclip in the library—is nested inside the videoControls instance (controls in the library). Nesting the symbols makes it easy to move around all of the playback controls as a single group while on the main timeline.

Handling the button events

It's already time for the buttons! Nothing to it, but to do it.

In the Actions panel, type the following ActionScript beneath what's already there:

```
// prep
with (videoControls) {
  btnMute.stop();
  btnMute.buttonMode = true;
  btnRewind.buttonMode = true;
  btnPlay.stop();
  btnPlay.buttonMode = true;
  btnFastForward.buttonMode = true;
  btnPrev.buttonMode = true;
  btnNext.buttonMode = true;
};

// events
with (videoControls) {
  btnMute.addEventListener(MouseEvent.CLICK, muteHandler);
  btnRewind.addEventListener(MouseEvent.MOUSE_DOWN,
➥rwDownHandler);
```

```
    btnRewind.addEventListener(MouseEvent.MOUSE_UP, rwUpHandler);
    btnPlay.addEventListener(MouseEvent.CLICK, playHandler);
    btnFastForward.addEventListener(MouseEvent.MOUSE_DOWN,
➡ffDownHandler);
    btnFastForward.addEventListener(MouseEvent.MOUSE_UP, ffUpHandler);
    btnPrev.addEventListener(MouseEvent.CLICK, prevHandler);
    btnNext.addEventListener(MouseEvent.CLICK, nextHandler);
};
```

The with() statement is new, but it's an easy concept to grasp, and useful in situations like this one. Basically, it's a programmer's shortcut. All of these movieclip buttons are nested inside the controls symbol, whose instance name is videoControls. Rather than referring tediously to each nested movieclip like this:

```
videoControls.btnMute.stop();
videoControls.btnMute.buttonMode = true;
videoControls.btnRewind.buttonMode = true;
// . . .
```

the with() statement allows us to skip the formalities and let the compiler know that, while we're inside those curly brackets ({ . . . }), we're talking about objects inside the videoControls instance.

With that explained, the ActionScript itself should make perfect sense. In the first several lines, the symbols' buttonMode property is set to true, to make these movieclips respond visually like buttons. In addition, btnMute and btnPlay are instructed to stop their timelines (these are the two symbols with more than one frame apiece).

The second group of lines wires up all the corresponding event handlers. Most of the buttons need to respond only to the MouseEvent.CLICK event, but the rewind and fast-forward buttons require the use of click and hold. For this reason, those movieclips are associated with MouseEvent.MOUSE_DOWN to begin the rewind or fast-forward routine, and MouseEvent.MOUSE_UP to cancel it.

Here's the code for the Mute button. Type this beneath the existing ActionScript:

```
function muteHandler(evt:MouseEvent):void {
  xform = ns.soundTransform;
  if (videoControls.btnMute.currentLabel == "on") {
    videoControls.btnMute.gotoAndStop("off");
    xform.volume = 0;
  } else {
    videoControls.btnMute.gotoAndStop("on");
    xform.volume = 1;
  }
  ns.soundTransform = xform;
};
```

The mechanism here is identical to the way the Play/Pause button works for the MP3 player: the movieclip's current label is consulted, and if it's showing "on," the playhead is shifted to the "off" frame (and vice versa). Based on this information, the xform instance's volume property is set to either 0 (silent) or 1 (full volume).

Here are the "down" and "up" handlers for the Rewind button. Once you grasp this one, you'll be able to understand the Fast-Forward button as well. Type this beneath the existing ActionScript:

```
function rwDownHandler(evt:MouseEvent):void {
  rwTimer.start();
};
function rwUpHandler(evt:MouseEvent):void {
  rwTimer.stop();
};
```

When users want to rewind, they click and hold the Rewind button. This triggers the rwDownHandler() function, which starts the rwTimer instance. The timer is what performs the actual rewinding, and you'll see how that works at the end of this exercise. When the user releases the button, the rwUpHandler() function stops the rwTimer. It's as simple as that.

Type the companion "up" and "down" handlers for the Fast-Forward button as well:

```
function ffDownHandler(evt:MouseEvent):void {
  ffTimer.start();
};
function ffUpHandler(evt:MouseEvent):void {
  ffTimer.stop();
};
```

The code for the Play button is just as self-explanatory. Enter its event handler beneath the existing ActionScript:

```
function playHandler(evt:MouseEvent):void {
  if (videoControls.btnPlay.currentLabel == "play") {
    pauseVideo();
  } else {
    resumeVideo();
  }
};
```

The code for the Prev and Next buttons is so similar to the MP3 player's version, we're confident you'll be able to connect the dots. Type the following ActionScript after the existing code:

```
function prevHandler(evt:Event):void {
  currentVideo--;
  if (currentVideo < 0) {
    currentVideo = videoList.video.length() - 1;
  }
  ns.play(videoList.video[currentVideo].@file.toString());
  resumeVideo();
};
```

```
function nextHandler(evt:Event = null):void {
  currentVideo++;
  if (currentVideo > videoList.video.length() - 1) {
    currentVideo = 0;
  }
  ns.play(videoList.video[currentVideo].@file.toString());
  resumeVideo();
};
```

As with the MP3 player, the nextHandler() function's evt parameter is given a null value by default, and for the same reason: this function is invoked as an event handler and also as a stand-alone function.

Programming the slider

We hope you're beginning to notice a theme here. Maybe a sense of *déjà vu*? The concepts we're discussing may not quite roll off the tongue just yet, but we hope some of these trees start looking familiar—that you get some comfort from the sense that Lake Nanagook seems to have a few well-worn landmarks. Let's take a look at the slider code for this video player.

Continuing with the existing code, type the following new ActionScript beneath the Buttons block:

```
///////////////////////////////////////
// Seek slider
///////////////////////////////////////

// prep
videoControls.knob.buttonMode = true;

// events
videoControls.knob.addEventListener(MouseEvent.MOUSE_DOWN,
➥seekStartDrag);
```

This is old hat, by now. The knob is instructed to respond to the mouse cursor like a button, and a custom seekStartDrag() function is associated with the MouseEvent.MOUSE_DOWN event.

Here's that seekStartDrag() function. Type the following ActionScript beneath what's already there:

```
function seekStartDrag(evt:MouseEvent):void {
  videoControls.knob.removeEventListener(Event.ENTER_FRAME,
➥seekKnobUpdate);
  rect = new Rectangle(videoControls.bar.x, videoControls.knob.y,
➥videoControls.bar.width, 0);
  videoControls.knob.startDrag(true, rect);
  stage.addEventListener(MouseEvent.MOUSE_UP, seekStopDrag);
};
```

The instance names may have changed, but the dance is still the same.

When the user presses the mouse over the knob in order to drag it, the seekKnobUpdate() function, which animates its movement, needs to be halted. If not, the knob will skip around frantically, trying to obey both the startDrag() method (which happens in this very event handler) and the

629

looping seekKnobUpdate() function. The very first line of this function—removeEventListener()—accomplishes this need perfectly. Why not instead use the custom pauseVideo() function, which also invokes the same removeEventListener()? It's a matter of choice. You certainly could. To mix things up, we decided to let the video continue while the user scrubs around.

The rect variable is assigned a new Rectangle instance, which is employed, as before, to constrain the area of the dragging. To wrap up the function, the stage is asked to keep an ear open for MouseEvent. MOUSE_UP.

Let's go ahead and write the event handler for that MOUSE_UP listener. Type in the following new code:

```
function seekStopDrag(evt:MouseEvent):void {
  videoControls.knob.stopDrag();
  ns.seek(duration * (videoControls.knob.x - videoControls.bar.x) /
➡videoControls.bar.width);
  if (videoControls.btnPlay.currentLabel == "pause") {
    videoControls.knob.addEventListener(Event.ENTER_FRAME,
➡seekKnobUpdate);
  }
  stage.removeEventListener(MouseEvent.MOUSE_UP, seekStopDrag);
};
```

Compare this with the version in the MP3 player, and you'll see how similar they are. When the user releases the mouse—either over the knob or accidentally off of it—the stopDrag() method halts the dragging. The location of the knob, in collaboration with the location of the bar and its width, is multiplied against the duration of the video—remember that this was gathered thanks to the onMetaData event handler—to determine the numeric value fed into the NetStream.seek() method. The seek() method sends the video to the nearest video keyframe specified by its parameter, provided that portion of the video has already downloaded.

The if statement checks if the video is currently playing, and if so, reassigns the Event.ENTER_FRAME event handler that animates the knob's position. Finally, because the stage listener is no longer needed, this function unhooks its MouseEvent.MOUSE_UP association.

And here's the seekKnobUpdate() function, which moves the knob in correspondence with the progression of the video. Type the following ActionScript under the existing code:

```
function seekKnobUpdate(evt:Event = null):void {
  var pos:Number = videoControls.bar.width * ns.time / duration;
  if (!isNaN(pos)) {
    videoControls.knob.x = videoControls.bar.x + pos;
  } else {
    videoControls.knob.x = videoControls.bar.x;
  }
};
```

This function operates just like its cousin in the MP3 player. Note that its evt parameter is set to null by default, which makes it optional. This happens here for the same reason you've seen the technique used elsewhere in this chapter: this function needs to be called either as an event handler or on its own. The on-its-own part happens in the Timer event handlers, which are coming up next.

Using timers to rewind and fast-forward

In the NetStream.seek() method used in the previous section, the knob's position determined the time offset in which the video should play. Rewinding and fast-forwarding is nothing more than a repeat performance of the same functionality. The Timer instances you declared at the beginning of this exercise—rwTimer and ffTimer—and the seekRate variable, are about to give you everything you need to accomplish these features.

In the Actions panel, enter the following ActionScript beneath what's already there:

```
//////////////////////////////////////////
// Timers
//////////////////////////////////////////

// events
rwTimer.addEventListener(TimerEvent.TIMER, rewind);
ffTimer.addEventListener(TimerEvent.TIMER, fastforward);
```

When the rwTimer and ffTimer instances were declared, they were told to dispatch the TimerEvent. TIMER event every 100 milliseconds. Here, that event is associated with respective event handler functions for each timer. All you need to do now is write those functions.

Here's the first one of those, rewind(). Type the following ActionScript after the existing code:

```
function rewind(evt:TimerEvent):void {
  if (ns.time - seekRate > 0) {
    ns.seek(ns.time - seekRate);
  } else {
    ns.seek(0);
  }
  seekKnobUpdate();
};
```

Remember, when requested, this function executes every tenth of a second. The first thing it does is check the NetStream.time property, to see where the video currently is. Maybe it has been playing for 25 seconds, and if so, the time property would be 25. An if statement determines if the current video's time property minus seekRate (which happens to be 10) is greater than 0. At 25 seconds in, the answer is indeed yes, and if so, the ns instance is instructed to seek to that point in the video. Why check with an if statement? Because you don't want to seek to a negative number.

If the subtraction would, in fact, seek to a negative number, ns is told to seek to 0. Finally, the seek-KnobUpdate() function updates the position of the knob to match the current time offset of the video.

With the code as it stands—specifically, a seekRate value of 10—the act of rewinding repeatedly sends the video playhead back 10 seconds at a time, which is a fairly hefty number. What if you want to seek to a finer degree? Just change seekRate to a smaller number—say, 5, 2, or maybe even 0.5. But watch out, if you do: unless you're using RTMP, as you would with Flash Media Server, you can only seek to video keyframes. The frequency of your keyframes (not timeline keyframes, but video keyframes) determines how successfully you can rewind or fast-forward. In the video files included with this chapter, you'll find that InkSong.mp4, which has many keyframes, handles a much smaller seekRate value than either of the FLVs. When you have a mix of videos, you'll need to go with the lowest common denominator, which in this case means the highest common seekRate value. How do you figure that value out? With good, old-fashioned testing.

To wrap it up, type these final lines at the very bottom of your script:

```
function fastforward(evt:TimerEvent):void {
  if (ns.time + seekRate < duration) {
    ns.seek(ns.time + seekRate);
  }
  seekKnobUpdate();
};
```

As you can see, this fastforward() code is nothing more than the opposite of its companion, rewind(). The reason there isn't an else clause in this one—it would have been else { ns.seek(duration) }—is that seeking to the very end of a video file is often a dicey thing. The duration value retrieved from the onMetaData handler is one of those "close, but not necessarily a cigar" things. Sometimes metadata isn't as truthful as it should be, and rather than accidentally make the attempt to seek too far past the duration of the file (which generates an error), this function puts the video as near the end of the video as it safely can.

As before, the seekKnobUpdate() function keeps the knob up-to-date on where it needs to be as fast-forwarding occurs. Remember that these timers are started and stopped in the event handlers triggered by mouse presses and releases to the Rewind and Fast-forward buttons.

Test the movie and enjoy the show (see Figure 14-17).

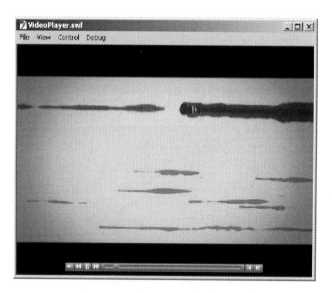

Figure 14-17. Take a bow. You now know how to create your own personal video controller!

After being mesmerized by the musical ink blots—truly an inventive and gorgeous combination of the visual and musical arts—you might be wondering what made us choose the particular videos we did to wrap up this chapter. There are a number of reasons, actually.

First and foremost, these videos are flat-out interesting.

Second, they're an inspiration. Chen Zhou, who created the "Ink's song" video, has accomplished with splashes of ink what Robert Bringhurst (quoted in Chapter 6) admonishes typographers to endeavor with text. The authors would like to thank the China Central Academy of Fine Arts' Media Lab in Beijing for permission to use Chen's video in this book. In the other two files, Greg Pattillo breaks the mold by performing his own interpretation of well-known tunes on the flute—while beatboxing at the same time. Recognized by the New York Times as "the best person in the world at what he does," Greg makes it clear that truly cool things can come from trying something new. We thank Greg for his permission to include his videos (collectively viewed online over 20 million times) with this book.

Third, these files are interesting from a technical standpoint. Why's that? The MP4 is an HD H.264-encoded file, while the FLVs are standard batch-encoded YouTube files. Why is this interesting? It demonstrates Flash Player's flexibility in a compelling way. Using a smattering of XML and less than 200 lines of ActionScript, you're able to build an insanely small (3KB!) video player that handles anything from 73MB HD video to popular YouTube performances. Now think back to Chapter 10. The FLVPlayback component does all of this, but the resulting SWF weighs in at 52KB. Use the drawing tools to create the assets, write a couple hundred lines of code to do it yourself, and your SWF sheds 49KB.

We think that's about as neat as it gets.

If you're interested in more beatbox flute, head over to http://cdbaby.com/cd/projectmusic, where Greg collaborates with Eric Stephenson (cello) and Peter Seymour (bass) in their genre-defying ensemble, PROJECT.

What you have learned

Rather than list what we covered in this chapter, we think it is more important to take a broader view of that statement. Step back for a moment and think about what you knew when you first laid this book on your desk and flamed up Flash CS4. The answer, we suspect, is "Not a lot."

Now think about your working through this chapter. The odds are pretty good you were able to follow along, and we are willing to bet there were a couple of points where you may have asked us to "move along a little quicker." This says to us that we have done our job, and that you may just know a lot more than you are aware of. Congratulations.

We were also a little sneaky with this chapter. If you follow the flow from the start to the end, you will see it actually follows the structure of this book: each exercise is designed to add to your knowledge base by building upon what you learned in the preceding exercise and, as we kept pointing out, in preceding chapters.

Finally, this chapter expanded on practically every concept presented in this book. If you have completed the exercises, then you have quite a bit of practical experience using Flash CS4.

Now that you've learned the ropes and have practiced numerous techniques, let's concentrate on the end game of the Flash design and development process: publishing your file.

Chapter 15

OPTIMIZING AND PUBLISHING FLASH MOVIES

When it comes to Flash on the Web, a common user experience is sitting around waiting for the movie to start. From your perspective, as the artist who designed the site, this may seem odd. After all, when you tested the movie in the authoring environment, it was seriously fast and played flawlessly. What happened? To be succinct, the Web happened. Your movie may indeed be cool, but you made a fundamental mistake: you fell in love with the technology, not the user. In this chapter, we'll talk about how to improve the user experience.

Here's what we'll cover in this chapter:

- Understanding how Flash movies are streamed to a web page
- Using the Bandwidth Profiler to turbo-charge movies
- Optimizing Flash movies
- Converting a Flash movie to a QuickTime video
- Choosing web formats
- Publishing a SWF for web playback
- Dealing with remote content

The following files are used in this chapter (located in Chapter15/ExerciseFiles_Ch15/Exercise/):

- YawningParrot.fla
- BandwidthTest1.fla
- BandwidthTest2.fla
- Beefcake.fla
- BeefcakeDistributed1.fla
- BeefcakeDistributed2.fla
- ParrotFW.gif
- MoonOverLakeNanagook.fla
- TinBangs.fla

The source files are available online from either of the following sites:

- http://www.FoundationFlashCS4.com
- http://www.friendsofED.com/download.html?isbn=9781430210931

Flash's love-hate Internet relationship

Back in the early days of Flash, when we really didn't know better, Flash designers would prepare these really "cool" intros to the site, which played while the rest of the site loaded. The problem was they were large and, in many cases, the intro seemed to take almost as long to load as the site. The solution was the infamous Skip Intro button, as shown in Figure 15-1. The intro would start playing and, after a couple of seconds, the Skip Intro button would appear. The user would click it, only to discover the site hadn't quite loaded. Users were left to sit there, drumming their fingers on their desk. So, users began to see the button not as a Skip Intro option, but as a Skip Site warning. This resulted in Flash gaining a rather nasty reputation for bloat, which it still has not shaken entirely.

> *Of course, the Flash community does have quite a sense of humor. One of the more popular Flash sites of the time was named "Skip Intro." You can watch it via archive.org's Wayback Machine, http://web.archive.org/web/20011214005850/http://www.skipintro.nl/skipintro/skipintro98.htm. When you launch the site, make sure to click the phrase "Play Ball" (hip for "Enter this site") to start the never-ending Flash intro.*

To deal with the bloat issue, it is critical that you understand the underlying technology behind your Flash movie. This means we need to revisit what the Web really is, so you can become familiar with many of the terms commonly used in the Flash design and developer community.

SKIPINTRO

Figure 15-1. Welcome to "Skip Intro" hell.

This "Internet" thing

The Internet's roots go back to the U.S. Department of Defense's need to create a bulletproof means of maintaining communications among computers. This involved such things as file transfers, messaging, and so on. At the time, computers were a virtual Tower of Babel, which meant different computer types and operating systems rarely, if ever, could talk to each other. As well, in battle conditions, the needed system would have to carry on even if a piece of it was knocked out, and it had to be accessible to everything from portable computers to the big, honking mainframes in "clean rooms" around the world.

The solution was an enabling technology called the *Internet Protocol suite*, though we know it by a far sexier name: *TCP/IP*. This is how data moves from your computer to our computers, or from your web server to our computers and, as you may have guessed, the slash character indicates that it comes in two parts.

- **IP (Internet Protocol)**: How data gets from here to there by using an address called the *IP address*. This address is a unique number used to identify any computer currently on the Internet. This protocol creates little bundles of information, called *packets*, which can then be shot out through the Internet to your computer. Obviously, the route is not a straight line. The packets pass through special computers called *routers*, and their job is to point those packets to your computer. Depending on the distance traveled, there could be any number of routers, which check your packets and send them either directly to your computer or to the next router along the line.

- **TCP (Transmission Control Protocol)**: The technology that verifies all of the data packets got to your computer. The IP portion of the trip couldn't care less if packet 10 arrives at your computer before packet 1, or even that it got there at all. This is where TCP comes in. Its job is to ensure that all of the packets get to where they are supposed to go.

Once all of this got the kinks worked out, the US military had quite the communications system on its hands.

Enter the World Wide Web

Although straight data transmission was interesting, once the cool factor wore off, people started wondering how it would be possible to use this communication network to access files containing images, audio, and video. The solution was the World Wide Web—a network of networks, which is commonly seen as web pages and hyperlinks.

A web page is a simple text file, which uses HTML—a formatting language of tags and text—to define how a page should look and behave. This is important, because your Flash movies should always be found in an HTML wrapper.

> *The concept of hyperlinks and hypertext was around long before the Internet. The gentleman who managed the atomic bomb project for the United States during World War II, Vannevar Bush, wrote an article for the* Atlantic Monthly *in July 1945 that proposed a system of linking all information with all other information. The article was entitled "As We May Think," and you can still read it at* http://www.theatlantic.com/doc/194507/bush.

An HTML page may be nothing more than a text file, but it can contain links to other assets, such as CSS files, JPGs, GIFs, and your Flash movies. These links take the form of a URL (Uniform Resource Locator) and specify the location of the assets requested by the HTML document. When Firefox, Internet Explorer, or any other graphical browser translates the page, those addresses are used to load the external assets and display them on your computer screen. Thus, the Web is really composed of two parts: browsers that request files and servers that store files and make them available when a browser asks for them.

As you can see, the infrastructure that moves your SWF files from a server to thousands of browsers is already in place. Where your pain and heartache arise is from something called *bandwidth*.

Bandwidth

In the early days of Flash, around the year 1999, one of the authors read an article written by a New York Flash designer, Hillman Curtis, and one phrase leaped out of the article and has been glued to the front of his cerebral cortex ever since. What's that phrase? "Keep an eye on the pipe."

The "pipe" is bandwidth. Bandwidth is a measure of how much data will move along a given path at a given time or how much information can be downloaded through a modem and how fast. One of the authors, when speaking on this topic at conferences or in class, uses a rather amusing analogy that will help you to understand this topic. Imagine trying to push the amount of data contained in your favorite TV show through a modem. When that modem is connected to a telephone line, the effort is no different from "trying to push a watermelon through a worm."

Bandwidth is measured in bits per second (bps), usually in the thousands (Kbps) or millions (Mbps). A bit is either a one or a zero, so ultimately, bandwidth is a measure of how many ones and zeros can be fed through a modem each second. The higher the number, the greater the bandwidth, and the faster things get from here to there. But bandwidth is not constant. It requires more bandwidth to move a video from here to there than it does to transfer a page of text. The issue is not "here to there." The issue is the modem's capacity to manage the data. This is the "pipe." Users with 56K dial-up modems have a pipe that has the diameter of a garden hose. Users with cable modems have a pipe that has the diameter of a fire hose. Connect the tiny garden hose to the fire hydrant in front of your house, and you will get a graphic demonstration of data flow and the pipe when you turn on the hydrant.

As we pointed out earlier, the data packets sent to your computer get there eventually, and the route is never a straight line. Over time, TCP/IP ensures that the transmission rate averages to a more or less constant rate, but this is technology we're dealing with here. It is the prudent Flash designer who approaches technology with a dose of pragmatism and does not assume a constant flow. This has implications for your design efforts, and we will get into those shortly.

You need to regard the pipe and data transmission in much the same manner you regard your local highway. It may have six lanes for traffic and a posted speed limit of 60 mph or 100 kph, but all of that becomes irrelevant during rush hour. Traffic moves at the pace of the slowest car. It is no different with the Internet. Servers can become overloaded.

A powerful example of this in recent history is the infamous event known as 9/11. On that day, the Internet essentially ground to halt as it seemed like every computer on the planet was attempting to get the latest information on the tragedy. What people overlooked on that day was that a server is only a computer, and can only reply to a finite number of requests at a set rate. If the browser can't get the information, it will assume the assets are not there. As a consequence, the requested page will either not be displayed or will be displayed with information missing. It got so bad for CNN and the BBC that they were forced to post a message that essentially told people "come back later." Even the people lucky enough to make a connection experienced pauses in the download and frequent disconnects, which are the hallmarks of an overloaded server.

What you need to take away from this story is that the time it takes to download and play your Flash movie is totally dependent on the contents of your Flash movie and traffic flow on the Internet. This means you need to not only concentrate on what is in your movie, but also on who wants to access it. This is where you fall in love with the user and not the technology.

641

So who are these folks we call users?

The Flash community is an oddball collection of people, ranging from those who ride skateboards for entertainment to the classic nerd working in a corporate cubicle farm. This disparity, which actually is the strength of the Flash community, has resulted in a bit of a split between those who use super-charged computers to develop their content, and take a "Sucks to be you" attitude if you can't revel in their work, and the corporate types who operate within strict standards set by their IT department. This standard is usually in the form of the following commandment:

Thou shalt develop to a Flash Player 7 standard, and may whatever god you worship have mercy upon your miserable soul if you step outside this stricture.

So, what do you really need to know before putting your work out there? Here are some general guidelines:

- Small means fast. Studies show you have 15 seconds to hook the user. If nothing is happening or is appealing to your users, they're gone. Small SWFs mean fast download. The days of intro-ductory eye candy for your Flash movies are over. If the content they see within that 15-second window is not relevant to the site or the experience, users leave.

- If a bleeding-edge Flash site isn't viewable on a two-year-old computer with a standard operat-ing system and hardware, it's time to go back to the drawing board.

- For a commercial site, you may have to go back three years. Corporations are relatively slow to upgrade hardware because of the significant cost to do so. Old hardware means slower com-puters.

- If your target audience is urban and in a developed country, assume they have, at minimum, a cable connection.

- If your audience is the world, develop to the lowest common denominator, which is a dial-up modem.

Now that we have provided some background, let's look at how your Flash file actually gets from here to there.

Streaming

As you have discovered by this point in the book, simply tossing a bunch of audio, images, and video into your movie is not a good thing. They take an inordinate amount of time to download. In fact, toss all of that content into frame 1, and you can kiss your 15-second window of opportunity good-bye.

In the previous chapter, we looked at ways to prevent bulking up frame 1, by preloading the SWF itself and by externalizing assets and loading them at runtime. In this chapter, you'll learn how to optimize the rest of your timeline, to help balance out and redistribute the load of a SWF's assets. Your goal will be to facilitate Flash Player's natural tendency to stream.

Please understand that streaming doesn't make things faster. What it does is give you the opportunity to intelligently organize the timeline so the movie starts playing in very short order. Used wisely, streaming can ensure that everything in the Flash movie is downloaded before it is needed. The result is a Flash movie that seems to start playing almost immediately and moves "as smooth as the hair on frog's back."

So, what happens when a web page requests your movie? Two things are sent to the browser:

- The movie's timeline, including ActionScript and the stuff that is not in the library, such as text and shapes that haven't been converted to symbols
- The library, including audio, video, images, and symbols

When your Flash movie is shot through the Net to the user's browser, the movie is received in frame-by-frame order. If the movie is split into scenes (a relatively rare practice today), the scenes will be sent in the order they appear in the Scenes panel, which is effectively in sequential order of the main timeline. The library is also sent, but the library items are not received in the order they appear in the Library panel. They are received in the sequence in which they appear on the timeline. To reinforce what we have just said, let's take a look at a typical file.

Open the YawningParrot.fla file in the Exercise folder for this chapter. As shown in Figure 15-2, the timeline is linear, but there are a lot of layers. Your first reaction might be, "Man, that is going to take a while to load." But that's not really the case.

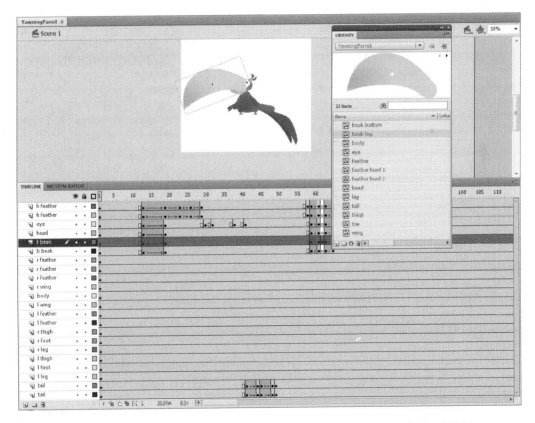

Figure 15-2. Streaming plays a movie in frame order and loads library content in the order in which it appears on the timeline.

Open the Library panel. You'll notice there is a lot less content in the library than in the timeline layers—only 13 library assets versus 22 layers. This is because the symbols in the library are reused and repurposed. The "finger feathers," for example, all use the same feather asset. All six claws use the same toe symbol; they're just arranged differently (horizontal flips and tints, all performed on the stage).

When this particular movie loads, because of how the parrot is constructed, all of its parts are loaded in frame 1 and composed of all of the objects in the library. These library objects are purposely designed to be lightweight. They're vector shapes with few anchor points, which means they equate to a relatively small file size. As a result, little bandwidth is required to load them and get the movie playing.

To make sense of how this movie streams, consider adding an imaginary extra playhead to the time-line When the movie starts. Both playheads are in frame 1, but only one of them starts moving. That's the imaginary one. Let's call it the *streamhead* (just a made-up name), which advances ahead of the actual playhead. The streamhead's position on the timeline indicates how much of the movie has been downloaded. In contrast, the playhead indicates which frame is currently displayed on the stage. It should make sense that the playhead can never get ahead of the streamhead. That would be like writing a check for more money than you have in your account.

Now let's assume that you toss in a movieclip, containing a 3-second FLV file embedded in the sym-bol's timeline, and this movieclip is added to frame 10. The odds are really good that the streamhead will stay put on frame 10 for a few seconds, while that frame's movieclip (complete with its video) loads. The playhead will catch up pretty quickly, especially with a default 24 fps frame rate. Until the embedded FLV loads, the playhead has no choice but to stay put. Essentially, the whole movie stops dead at frame 10, until the streamhead restarts its journey along the timeline.

To avoid this nastiness, you'll want to use a strategy called a *streaming buffer*. This could be in the form of a preloader or any other technique that keeps the playhead in place (in an interesting way) or smoothes out its path in order to let the streamhead do its job and load content.

In case you're having difficulty visualizing two heads on the timeline, Flash has a tool that lets you see how these two heads work, and how the pipe can affect the delivery of your Flash movie to the browser. What is this tool? It's called the Bandwidth Profiler.

The Bandwidth Profiler

In many respects, the Bandwidth Profiler is similar to what you see in Device Central when you test a mobile movie. In Device Central, the movie opens up in a mock device that emulates the perfor-mance of your movie in the chosen device. Likewise, the Bandwidth Profiler emulates how your movie will behave when it downloads from a remote server. Though the Bandwidth Profiler is an extremely useful tool, keep in mind that it is nothing more than an emulator. It won't mimic the real-life ebb and flow of network traffic, and it assumes a constant transfer rate into the browser. That noted, the Bandwidth Profiler can give you a good idea of where streaming bottlenecks are likely to occur. This can be an invaluable aid in relieving the "data jam" and solving a problem before it becomes a major one.

Simulating a download

Let's see how the Bandwidth Profiler works.

1. Open the BandwidthTest1.fla file in the Chapter 15 Exercise folder. You will see that we have placed an audio file on the timeline, and embedded an FLV into a movieclip and placed it in frame 1. Scrub over to frame 2, and you will see that we have added some text to the stage. If you open the library, you will see the text is actually a graphic symbol. Just by looking at the timeline, you can see that the movieclip with the FLV and the audio file will be the first pieces of content to load, and then the text will load.

2. Test the movie. When the SWF opens, select View ➤ Bandwidth Profiler from the SWF's File menu. A graph appears above the movie, as shown in Figure 15-3.

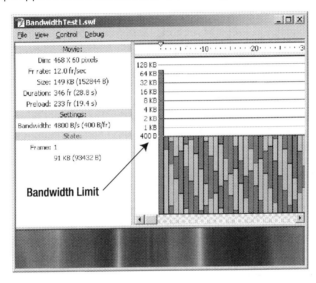

Figure 15-3. The Bandwidth Profiler

On the left side of the window are three headings: Movie, Settings, and State. To the right is a frame-by-frame representation of the data downloading into each frame. Notice the spike in frame 1. This is understandable, because the audio file and the FLV need to load in this frame. The trouble is that this spike happens right at the beginning of the movie.

Under the Settings heading on the left, take a look at the Bandwidth entry: 4800 B/s (400 B/fr). Now look at the bottommost line on the right side. That red line is the *bandwidth limit* and represents the maximum throughput the selected modem emulation can handle. Notice that it matches the Bandwidth value on the left. Bars under the line are handled quickly. Bars that rise above the line indicate potential bottlenecks.

3. Select View ➤ Download Settings. The drop-down menu you see allows you to choose from among various modem speeds, as shown in Figure 15-4.

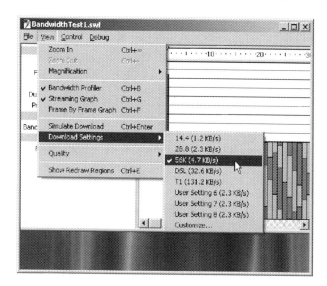

Figure 15-4. You can change the emulated modem speed.

4. Select the DSL (32.6 KB/s) choice from the drop-down menu and scroll back to the start of the movie. You will notice the bandwidth limit has increased from 400 bytes to 2.78KB, and the markings on the graph have changed to reflect your selection.

You are most likely looking at that spike in the first frame and thinking, "Yeah, so? What's the deal?" Rather than having us explain it, we are going to let you experience it.

5. Change back to the 56K modem choice and this time select View ➤ Simulate Download.

Let us guess. You sat around for about 20 seconds waiting for the movie to start? What you have just experienced is the other, and most important, half of the Bandwidth Profiler. You just sat through what a person with a 56K modem will experience—under ideal circumstances. Let's take a minute and talk about this.

When you selected Simulate Download, you essentially re-created how the movie will load into a 56K modem. The other thing that happened is the profiler developed a green bar at the top of the graph, as shown in Figure 15-5, which held steady until the movie started to play.

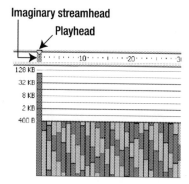

Figure 15-5. You can experience the user's issue with the movie's first frame by simulating the download.

The green bar is important. It's the imaginary streamhead we mentioned earlier. You are seeing what happens when the playhead catches up to the streamhead. If you wait long enough, the streamhead will suddenly rocket off to the right, and the playhead will follow behind, sticking to a rate no faster than the frame rate specified in the FLA (which happens to be 12 fps for this file). You can scrub that playhead, by the way. Drag it around as you would in the Timeline panel to view content on any of the frames.

On the left side of the Bandwidth Profiler, under the Movie heading, you'll see a value called Preload, which in this example is 233 fr or 19.4 s. When you started emulating the movie, the Settings area became active (to see this, you may need to increase the size of the Bandwidth Profiler window by dragging the bottom edge down). The Preload value tells you it will take about 19.4 seconds to load in all of the content in the first frame.

6. Change the Download Settings to DSL and select Simulate Download.

You should find that you still had a short delay, but there was a marked decrease in how long you had to wait. The Preload setting should show you 33 fr (2.8 s). That's dramatically less than the almost 20 seconds you had to wait using a 56K modem.

If you want to emulate a modem not represented in the list, choose Customize, which opens the Custom Download Settings dialog box, as shown in Figure 15-6. You can edit any of the existing entries, three of which are set aside for custom values. To return to the original values at any time, click the Reset button.

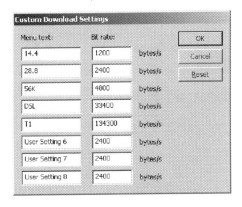

Figure 15-6. The Custom Download Settings dialog box lets you tailor your emulated modems.

As you can see, the Bandwidth Profiler is a rather powerful tool that you need to master. With it, you can tailor your movie to the bandwidth constraints of your user and ensure that you meet that 15-second window of opportunity that will open to you.

Pinpointing problem content

With the Download Settings option, not only do you get to see how bandwidth will affect your movie, but you also get to actually experience it, which isn't always fun. At this point, you may be thinking "Shoot, I can cut back the preload value by using ActionScript to play the sound!" Doing that means the sound can be removed from the SWF altogether. Let's see if it works.

Open the BandwidthTest2.fla file in this chapter's Exercise folder. Open the library, and you will see the sound file is absent. Open the code in frame 3 of the scripts layer, and you will see we have added the ActionScript necessary to load to the sound from an external MP3.

Test the movie and select Simulate Download. The graph has significantly changed, as shown in Figure 15-7. The overall size of the SWF has gone from 149KB—see the Size value in the Movie heading—down to 94KB, Yet the spike in frame 1 hasn't changed much at all, and the same nearly 20-second delay is still there. What gives?

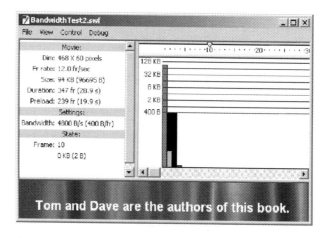

Figure 15-7. Use the Bandwidth Profiler to identify the content causing the delay.

Part of the answer is that the audio, previously attached to the timeline, had its Sync property set to Stream. Remember that the Stream setting keeps the audio from having to load all at once, as it does with, say, the Event setting. Because the audio's file size was spread out, only 1/300 of its weight appeared in frame 1 (because the timeline is roughly 300 frames long). This tells you the issue really isn't the sound in this case, but rather the FLV embedded into the movieclip.

You have just discovered another use for the Bandwidth Profiler. Not only can it show you where the problem is, but it can even be used to isolate the content causing the delay.

> How would we fix this? First off, bear in mind there will always be a spike in frame 1 of any movie you create. The goal is to get that spike to do the limbo—to get it as close to the red line as possible, if not below it. For this example, one approach would be to reduce the time of the curtains effect from its current 46 frames seconds to 23 frames in the background movieclip. Do this, and the preload time drops to 9.7 seconds. Another approach would be to use a percentage-based preloader like the one demonstrated in Chapter 14.

Can I get that in writing?

The Bandwidth Profiler's right-hand graph gives you a quick bird's-eye view of your worst bandwidth offenders. If you want to dial in to the exact numbers, drag the playhead to any of your graph spikes and keep an eye on the State heading on the left side. The Frame value of that heading tells you which frame you're on and exactly how many bytes that frame contains.

If you really want to crunch the numbers, Flash will even create a log file for you. Head over to File ➤ Publish Settings ➤ Flash and put a check mark in the Generate size report check box. When you next test your movie, look in the Output panel. You'll see a detailed analysis of the timeline, with columns for Frame #, Frame Bytes (per-frame bytes), Total Bytes (cumulative total), and more, including itemized byte weights at the bottom for fonts, shapes, and symbols. This report is also saved as a simple text file in the same folder as the FLA. In the case of BandwidthTest2.fla, the report's name is BandwidthTest2 Report.txt.

Now that you know what the spikes mean, your goals are to minimize them when you can and to distribute their weight when possible. The next section tells you how.

Optimizing and fine-tuning your Flash movies

As you saw in the previous example, a simple thing like reducing the number of frames in an FLV can have a dramatic impact on how the movie loads. In this section, we'll outline a few tips, tricks, and techniques you can use to make your Flash movies leaner, meaner, and faster.

Surprisingly, the first mistake most people make often happens before a single pixel is lit up. That mistake is to not plan the movie.

Planning your movie

That old adage "Plan your work and work your plan" is especially true when working with Flash. You can't make it up as you go along. You need to take the time before you start to think about what the user sees, and in what order, before you starting firing content into the library and then onto the stage. For example, a video site that lets the user choose from a number of videos would probably involve the following:

- Preloader
- Intro screen
- Main movie screen where the videos are chosen and viewed
- A set of links to other video sites you may have created

This means when users arrive at the site, they would usually proceed as follows:

- See the preloader for a few seconds and then be taken to the Intro frame.
- From there, choose to read the information and then move to the video picker screen by clicking a button. The video frame would load.
- Click a series of buttons to view the videos associated with the buttons,
- Choose to return to the Intro screen or go to a frame that contains a series of interactive links.

649

Now that you have an idea of what will happen, you might even want to put together a small flow-chart that shows the purpose of each frame in the movie, as shown in Figure 15-8. Having one of these charts handy allows you to see how the user will move around the movie and provides a broad view of the content of each frame.

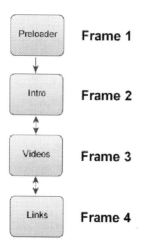

Figure 15-8. Map out your plan.

In fact, if you have arrived at Flash CS4 through the Adobe Web Premium Bundle, you have an ideal tool for this process at your disposal. Fireworks CS4 has been repositioned as a rapid prototyping tool. If you open that application and select Window ➤ Common Library, you will see bunch of folders that contain symbols for a variety of rapid prototyping tasks. The Flow Diagram symbols, shown in Figure 15-9, are ideal for planning a Flash or HTML project.

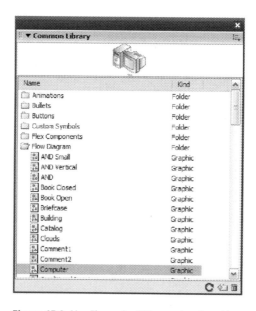

Figure 15-9. Use Fireworks CS4 as a planning aid.

By writing out what each frame does, you are ordering the content on the timeline. By "falling in love with the user" and streaming the content into the movie in that order, your site will meet the needs of your users. If you haphazardly place the content on the timeline, you have no way of ensuring it will load in any meaningful manner. The result is a site that must download in its entirety before the user can interact with it smoothly.

Though many sites go the haphazard route, it is not considered a best practice within the Flash design community. Instead, you'll want to be mindful of balance.

Distributing the weight

It isn't always possible to eliminate your bandwidth spikes, even when planning ahead, but you can usually spread out the assets that cause them. If you've ever witnessed the sport known as curling—something like shuffleboard, but on ice (celebrated in Canada)—then you've seen how the team members clear the way. They run ahead of the traveling stone as it glides across the curling sheet, feverishly sweeping the ice a few feet ahead, minimizing irregularities in the path. That's sort of what you can do with the main timeline.

Usually, it means making a few test runs with the Bandwidth Profiler to see where your culprits are. You might, for example, have a dozen symbols make their first appearance in frame 300, suddenly giving that frame a spike. Meanwhile, the previous 100 frames might be very lean in terms of bytes per frame. To diminish streamhead blockage on frame 300, you could place copies of those dozen symbols in earlier frames, just off the stage (on the pasteboard). Simply drag out another instance of each symbol as needed.

For example, let's say you're aiming for 56K modems. That means your bandwidth limit, as indicated by the Bandwidth Profiler's red horizontal line, is set to 200 bytes per frame. You essentially have a budget of 200 bytes to spend per frame. In order to minimize the spike in frame 300, you could drag a couple 100-byte symbols from the library and place them on frame 200. Drag a handful of 30-byte symbols to frame 220, another 180-byte symbol to frame 240, and so on. Make sure to position these symbols off the stage or use the Property inspector to set their Alpha property to 0%. Arranged like this, each symbol makes its presence known before it is actually seen. By the time the streamhead hits frame 300, each of those symbols has already loaded, and the streamhead breezes right on by—the ice is smooth—clearing the path for the playhead.

How can you tell how much each symbol weighs? Unfortunately, the Library panel doesn't tell you, outside of the Bitmap Properties dialog box for imported graphics files. You'll need to do your best to distribute weight based on common sense, and some trial and error with the Bandwidth Profiler. The extent to which you rearrange things depends on deadlines, budget, and your own personal predilection for anal-retentiveness. Just be aware of this strategy, because it really can make a difference.

Sometimes your assets aren't so easy to redistribute. Consider an imported BMP. In cases like that, you'll need to get creative. To see what we mean, open the Beefcake.fla file from the Exercise folder for this chapter. Test the movie and take a look at the Bandwidth Profiler. As Figure 15-10 shows, there's a spike at frame 50, right on a photo of one of the authors. Any content after that frame will be delayed until that 60KB has loaded. A possible solution is a preloader, displaying percent loaded of the SWF itself or percent loaded of the image as an external JPG.

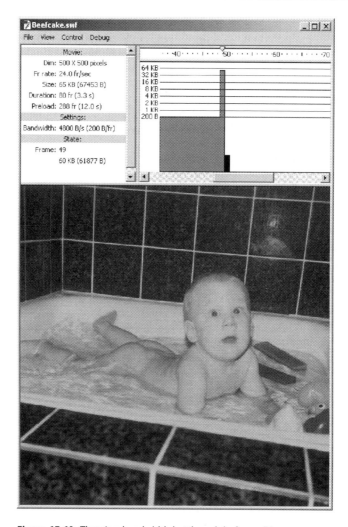

Figure 15-10. There's a bandwidth bottleneck in frame 50.

Another possibility is to divide the bitmap into smaller pieces, and distribute those as hidden symbols among previous frames. Let's see how that works. Open BeefcakeDistributed1.fla in this chapter's Exercise folder and scrub the timeline. In this version, a new layer named hidden contains four quarters of the photo among four of its earlier frames, each set to 0% Alpha, (see Figure 15-11). In frame 50, where the full photo originally appeared, the four quarters are arranged to look like the complete image. Test the movie and look at the Bandwidth Profiler. This time, instead of a 60KB spike in a single frame, you have four approximately 15KB spikes. This is still not ideal, because the bandwidth limit is 200 bytes—but it's an improvement.

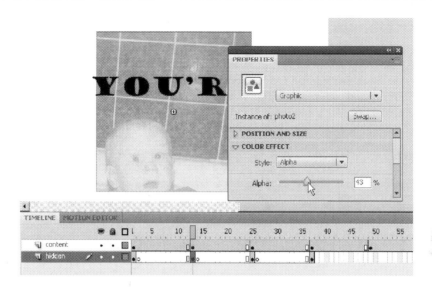

Figure 15-11. Breaking up the bitmap, while tedious, can reduce bandwidth spikes. (We increased the Alpha to 43% to show you that, yes indeed, the photo is there.)

To take this example to an extreme, check out BeefcakeDistributed2.fla, in which each of the photo's quarters has been quartered again. This is likely a more scrupulous route than you'll want to take. However, as you can see in Figure 15-12, the Bandwidth Profiler now shows 16 mini-spikes of 3KB to 4KB apiece, while frame 50—the completed "jigsaw puzzle"—weighs a mere 662 bytes.

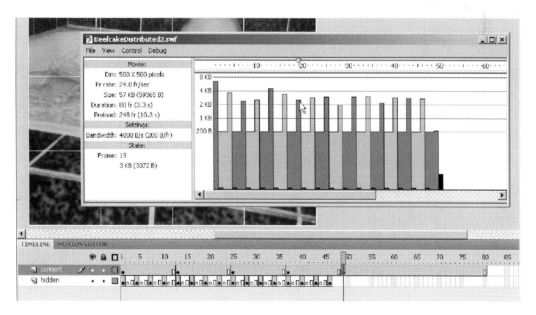

Figure 15-12. Breaking up the bitmap even more

Optimizing elements in the movie

Every chapter in this book has directly or indirectly made it clear that Flash loves "small." After your experiences with the Bandwidth Profiler, we think you now understand why we are so adamant on this point. Small files mean fast loads. A fast load means short wait time. A short wait time means happy users. In various chapters, we have shown you several methods of keeping things small when it comes to images, sounds, fonts, and video. What about vectors?

We know Flash and vectors are bosom buddies. The thing about vectors is that they can be both small and large at the same time. Huh? Every time Flash encounters a vector point, it must load it into memory in order to draw the shape. If you create a vector with a large number of vector points, you may have a small file on your hands, but you have also increased the demand on memory to redraw the image, as you encountered with the American flag exercise in Chapter 9. The result is the inevitable spike in the Bandwidth Profiler. Here's one way of addressing this issue:

1. Create a new Flash document. Add three more keyframes to Layer 1 in the Timeline panel. You now have four keyframes on the timeline.

2. Select the Pencil tool and, in frame 1, draw a curvy shape, like the one in Figure 15-13.

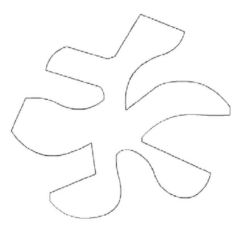

Figure 15-13. We start by drawing a shape containing a lot of vector points.

3. Copy your shape to the clipboard. Select each of the remaining three key frames in Layer 1 and select Edit ➤ Paste in Place.

4. Select the shape in frame 2 and select Modify ➤ Shape ➤ Smooth. Not a lot seems to happen.

5. Select the shape in frame 3 and select Modify ➤ Shape ➤ Straighten. A couple of the lines straighten out.

6. Select the shape in frame 4 and select Modify ➤ Shape ➤ Optimize. This time, you are presented with the Optimize Curves dialog box. Select Show totals message and Preview. Move the slider all the way to the top and click OK. The dialog box will close and be replaced by an alert box, telling you how many curves were found, how many were optimized, and the size of the reduction as a result of the optimization (see Figure 15-14).

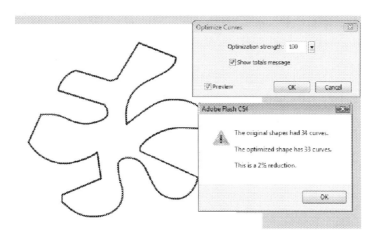

Figure 15-14. Using shape optimization

The image shown in Figure 15-14 is a composite image. We created it to show you what the alert box looks like when you click OK *in the* Optimize Curves *dialog box. You normally don't see both dialog boxes at the same time.*

7. Test the movie. The graph shows you the file size of the content in each frame and the effect that modifying the shape has in each frame. As you can see in Figure 15-15, the results are quite dramatic.

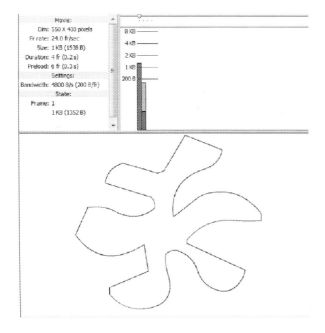

Figure 15-15. Smoothing, straightening, and optimizing curves can have a profound effect on download times.

You are most likely looking at the graph and thinking, "Wow, I am going to start optimizing all of my vector shapes!" Not so fast. Each of the three methods presented did a good thing and a bad thing. They did indeed reduce the bandwidth load. However, they also introduced distortions into the image. If you are happy with the distortions, fine. If you aren't, then you might want to consider doing the optimization manually, by selecting the shape with the Subselection tool and manipulating the shape and the points.

So why was there such a drop in the graph between the object in frame 1 and its counterpart in frame 4? Remember that vector nodes require bandwidth. You removed a few of them using the Optimize Curves dialog box, which accounts for the drop in required bandwidth.

If you import vector artwork from outside sources, such as Illustrator files, you may find shape optimization quite challenging. Obviously, it depends on the intricacy of the artwork, but industrial-strength tools like Illustrator naturally have more complex features than the drawing tools provided by Flash. When Flash imports vectors from other tools, it does its best to "translate" those anchor points into the "language" it uses internally.

Just be mindful of the pipe. If elaborate vector artwork seems to weigh more than you would expect, consider exporting it from the original application as a bitmap and compare file sizes. If you don't have the original application, import the artwork into Flash, situate it on the timeline of a temporary stand-in FLA, and then use File ➤ Export ➤ Export Image to select a suitable raster format.

Aren't vectors supposed to be smaller? Generally speaking, yes. But every rule has its exception, and it goes both ways. Giulia Balladore (http://www.juniatwork.com/), a self-taught artist featured on http://www.FlashGoddess.com, produces jaw-droppingly beautiful artwork directly in Flash. Her vector drawings rival the sort of detail that normally requires a camera and meticulous studio lighting. And yet, because she works in Flash and optimizes her vectors, images like "Sole" (see Figure 15-16) can be resized in the browser without ever getting pixelated. And the depicted SWF weighs a miniscule 23KB!

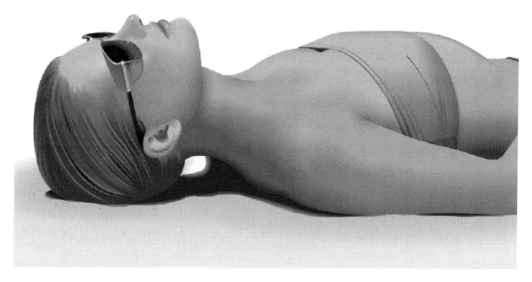

Figure 15-16. Yes, this image was drawn entirely with Flash's drawing tools, by Giulia Balladore (http://www.juniatwork.com/).

Optimizing Flash content for use in video

As you may have surmised when reading this section's heading, we are not only going to be thinking outside the box, but thinking outside the room where the box is located.

This may come as a bit of a surprise, but Flash has been (and still is) used to create animated cartoons that are shown on television, from commercials to actual shows, and even in theaters. In earlier Flash history, the process was, to say the least, convoluted, but it could be done. The problem was that, even though Flash could output to QuickTime, only the main timeline could be exported. Library content, ActionScript-driven animation, and even nested movieclips were not exported. When you consider the fact that the maximum length for the Flash timeline is just over 16,000 frames, the achievement of a 10-minute cartoon was not possible unless the movie was broken into pieces and stitched together in a video-editing program.

Flash CS4 contains a relatively new feature that allows you to not only export the content on the time-line and in nested animations, but even to create animations solely powered by ActionScript. These exported QuickTime movies can then be used as motion graphics in applications like Adobe After Effects CS4. In fact, in the following exercise, the stage is entirely blank. All of the letters that appear in this animation will be randomly generated, colored, and put in motion using ActionScript. Follow these steps to create a QuickTime movie in Flash:

1. Create a new Flash document and set the stage color to #000000 (black). Rename Layer 1 to scripts.

2. Select frame 1 of the scripts layer and open the Actions panel. Type the following code:

```
var t:Timer = new Timer(50, 0);
t.addEventListener(TimerEvent.TIMER, createLetter);
t.start();

function createLetter(evt:Event):void {
  var fmt:TextFormat = new TextFormat();
  fmt.size = randomBetween(80, 120);
  fmt.color = Math.floor(Math.random() * 16777216);
  var mc:MovieClip = new MovieClip();
  var tf:TextField = new TextField();
  tf.autoSize = TextFieldAutoSize.CENTER;
  tf.text = String.fromCharCode(randomBetween(97, 122));
  tf.setTextFormat(fmt);
  mc.addChild(tf);
  mc.x = (Math.random() * stage.stageWidth);
  mc.y = stage.stageHeight;
  mc.ang = 0;
  mc.range = randomBetween(4, 20);
  addChild(mc);
  mc.addEventListener(Event.ENTER_FRAME, shimmy);
};
```

The first line of code creates an instance of the Timer class, which will repeat every 50 milliseconds indefinitely, thanks to that second parameter of 0. The next line associates a custom function, createLetter(), with the TimerEvent.TIMER event for the t instance. Finally, the third line—t.start();—starts the clock running.

657

The createLetter() function is how the letters arrive in the movie. The first variable, fmt, creates a TextFormat() instance, which is used to format text fields, as you learned in Chapter 6.

With the fmt instance created, we need to give it some formatting information. The size of the text is set by using a custom function, randomBetween(), which determines the maximum and minimum size of the letters. That function is coming in step 4. The color is set by picking a random value between 0 and 1 and then multiplying that result by 16,777,216. Where did that number come from? That's how many colors you can find in the 24-bit color space.

We then create a movieclip and add a text field to its display list. Before it is added to the display list, the text field is centered, and random letters are added to it. That's accomplished with this line:

```
tf.text = String.fromCharCode(randomBetween(97, 122));
```

This looks rather complex, but it makes sense when you break it down. We needed random values, so we reused that randomBetween() function and told it to return a value between (and inclusive of) 97 and 122. What numbers are those? Those represent ASCII values for the lowercase letters *a* through *z*. The String.fromCharCode() method converts those into their corresponding characters.

The next two lines tell Flash to apply the text formatting to the text field—tf.setTextFormat(fmt)— and finally, to add the text field to the movieclip's display list—mc.addChild(t).

The remainder of the code tells Flash where to position the text-containing movieclip (including the configuration of two custom properties: ang and range, used in an event handler function you're about to write). The final line tells Flash to animate the movieclip by using a custom shimmy() function. Let's write that function.

3. Press Return (Enter) twice and enter the following code, which puts the letters in motion:

```
function shimmy(evt:Event):void {
  var mc:MovieClip = MovieClip(evt.target);
  mc.y -= randomBetween(6, 10);
  mc.x += (mc.range * Math.cos(mc.ang += 0.4));
  mc.scaleY -= 0.02;
  if (mc.scaleY <= 0) {
    mc.removeEventListener(Event.ENTER_FRAME, shimmy);
    removeChild(mc);
  }
};
```

Before we start explaining this code, remember that all motion in Flash is either across the stage on the x axis or up and down the stage on the y axis. Objects moving from the top to the bottom of the stage have increasing Y values, and all objects moving from right to left have decreasing X values, and vice versa.

This code block determines the stage movement of the movieclip containing a random letter from the previous code block. Each one is randomly placed on the y axis, and the cosine method of the Math class—Math.cos()—is used to add a right to left shimmy, as the letters move upward.

As the letters move up the stage along the y axis, they are continuously scaled down by 2%—mc.scaleY -= 0.02;—every time the Timer instance "ticks." The last three lines essentially tell Flash, "Look, this thing is going to eventually scale down to a value of 0. When you hear that, get rid of the movieclip."

To finish off the code, let's write that `randomBetween()` method.

4. Press Return (Enter) twice and type the following:

```
function randomBetween (min:Number, max:Number):Number {
  return (Math.random() * (max - min)) + min;
};
```

This function picks a random number using the parameters sent by the code that calls it. The `return` statement sends the chosen number back. Let's see how this works in regard to setting the size of the letters. The following line does that:

```
fmt.size = randomBetween(80, 120);
```

This means the calculation would be as follows:

```
return (Math.random() * (120 - 80)) + 80;
```

Let's assume the `Math.random()` value is 0.35, so the calculation would be like this:

```
return (0.35 * (120 - 80)) + 80;
return (0.35 * 40) + 80;
return (14) + 80;
return 94;
```

Therefore the size of this letter would be 94 pixels.

> *If you get any errors, you might want to check your code against ours. The file—*
> `BubblingLetters.fla`*—can be found in the Chapter 15* `Complete` *folder.*

5. Save and test the movie. You should see letters moving up the stage in a wavy motion (see Figure 15-17). They get smaller as they move upward and eventually disappear.

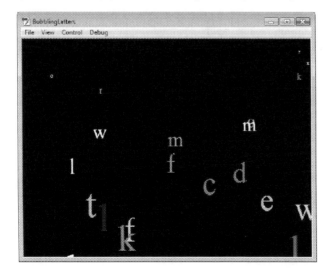

Figure 15-17. Letters randomly generated, formatted, and put into motion using ActionScript

659

6. Select File ➤ Export ➤ Export Movie. In the Export Movie dialog box, navigate to the folder where you want to save the file and select QuickTime (*.mov) from the Save as type drop-down list, as shown in Figure 15-18. Then click Save.

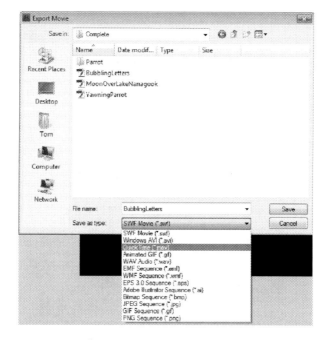

Figure 15-18. Exporting a Flash file as a QuickTime movie

7. In the QuickTime Export Settings dialog box, select Ignore stage color (generate alpha channel) and change the After time elapsed: value to 10, as shown in Figure 15-19. Click the Export button.

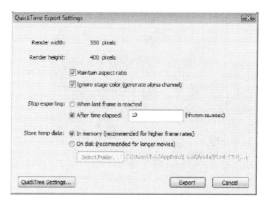

Figure 15-19. The QuickTime Export Settings dialog box

8. A progress bar will appear, and you'll eventually see an alert that tells you where the export log can be found. Click OK and quit Flash.

9. Open your new QuickTime movie. Pretty neat!

Let's return to the QuickTime Export Settings dialog box and briefly review its options:

- Render width and Render height: These values match the current stage size and will be the physical dimensions of the video. You can change these values by clicking the QuickTime Settings button.

- Maintain aspect ratio: When checked, this option ensures distortion is not added if you resize the video.

- Ignore stage color: Selecting this option essentially turns the stage color invisible, which makes it ideal if you want this animation to play over content in After Effects CS4 or some other video editor.

- Stop exporting: The choices in this section give Flash an idea of when to stop the process. The first choice should be used if you have content on the timeline. The second one is ideal for situations such as this exercise, where content is generated by ActionScript. In this case, we are producing a clip with a duration of 10 seconds.

- Store temp data: This is used during the render process. You can choose to store this data in memory for short movies, or choose to create the temporary file on the desktop or some other location.

- QuickTime Settings: This button opens a QuickTime settings dialog box, where you can change the codec and audio settings for the final movie.

As we said earlier, you can export these Flash-created movies as animations for use in other applications. For example, one of the authors dropped the file into an After Effects CS3 project, as shown in Figure 15-20, and then created the QuickTime movie named BubblingLettersFinal.mov that is found in this chapter's Complete folder.

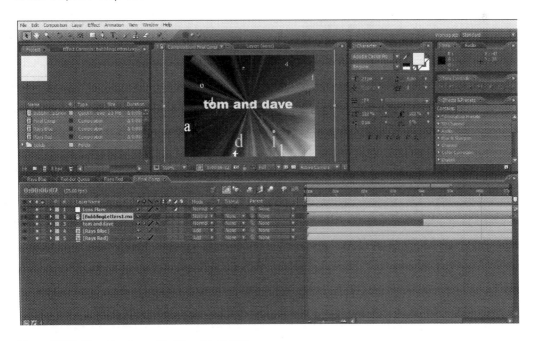

Figure 15-20. The video is used in After Effects CS3.

Publishing and web formats

If there is one fundamental fact regarding publishing your Flash movie to the Web, it is this: *the SWF isn't a web document.* Nothing drives us crazier than someone telling us, "Dudes, check out my Flash site," only to have that individual double-click a SWF on his computer's desktop. Flash SWFs should appear on the Web only if they are embedded into an HTML page. Why? Because you can use the HTML to control aspects of the SWF—scaling, context menu items, and more—that you can't do without the HTML wrapper. Thus a "Flash site," to be precise, is composed of an HTML page that points to the SWF, along with any media—audio, video, images, text—that the SWF may need from external sources.

Creating the SWF is a bit more complicated than selecting File ➤ Publish Preview and merrily clicking away in the Publish panel. As we pointed out in the previous chapter, you need a solid grounding in what's under the hood before you create the car.

Again, we stress the same theme we have been repeating since page 1 of this book: *keep it small!* This is the reason for Flash's broad acceptance on the Web and where an understanding of the publishing process is invaluable. Up to this point, we have essentially created a bunch of FLA files and asked you to test them. The time has arrived to get off the test track and put the vehicle on the street.

When you publish your movie, Flash compresses the file, removes the redundant information in the FLA, and what you are left with—especially if you've been taking this chapter to heart—is one sleek, mean web presentation. The default output file format—yes, there is more than one—is the SWF. The SWF is wrapped in HTML through the use of <object> and/or <embed> tags, plus extra information about how the browser should play the SWF.

> Yes, you can link directly to a SWF without that bothersome HTML. Just be aware that the SWF will expand to the full size of the browser window, meaning all of the content on the stage will also enlarge. In many respects, linking directly to the SWF is rookie error number one.

Before we move into actually publishing a movie, let's look at some of the more common file types used on the Web, listed here:

- Flash (.swf)
- HTML (.htm or .html)
- Images (.gif, .jpg, and .png)
- QuickTime (.mov)

Flash

Before there was Flash, there was Director. Though used primarily for interactive CDs, DVDs, and kiosks, it was at one time the main instrument employed to get animations to play on the Web. The technology developed by Macromedia to accomplish this was named Shockwave, and the file extension used was .dcr. Flash also made use of this technology, and in order to differentiate between them, it became known as Shockwave for Flash and used the .swf file extension. Flash Player is the technology that allows the SWF to play through a user's browser. Through a series of clever moves,

Flash Player has become ubiquitous on the Web. In fact, Adobe can rightfully claim that Flash Player, regardless of version, can be found on 98% of all Internet-enabled computers on the planet. This means, in theory, that you can assume your movies are readily available to anyone who wishes to watch them. But the reality gets a bit more complicated.

> For you trivia buffs, the first couple of iterations of Shockwave for Director used a small application named Afterburner to create the DCR files. When Director developers prepared a presentation for the Web, they didn't just create the DCR, the movie was "shocked." One of the authors happened to be around on the night Macromedia quietly released Shockwave and Afterburner to the Director community. He still remembers the excitement generated by members of the group as they posted circles that moved across the page, and the "oohs" and "ahs" that followed as the circles moved up and down.

Each new Flash Player version brings with it new functionality. Flash Player 8 introduced filter and blend effects, which can't be displayed in Flash Player 7. FLV video can't be played in Flash Player 5. Any movie you prepare using ActionScript 3.0 can be played only in Flash Player 9 or higher. Flash Player 9,0,115,0 was the first to display HD video content. Though you may initially regard this as a nonissue, you would be making a gross miscalculation. Corporations, through their IT departments, have strict policies regarding the addition or installation of software to corporate-owned computers. We personally know of one organization that isn't budging, and its Flash Player policy is Flash Player 6 or lower to this day. Shrewd Flash designers actually ask potential clients which versions of Flash Player are to be targeted for the project. The last thing you need is to find yourself rewriting every line of code and reworking the project, because you assumed the target was Flash Player 9, but corporate policy dictates Flash Player 7 or lower.

> Flash Player 10 follows a tradition that each successive version of Flash Player will play content faster than its predecessors. When Flash Player 9 was released, Adobe claimed it provided a 75% speed increase over Flash Player 8, which was partly due to the support for ActionScript 3.0 introduced in Flash Player 9. This sort of increase is usually enough for most users to install the new version. Even so, in many instances, actually downloading and installing the plug-in is becoming a thing of the past. Flash Player has the ability to download and install in the background, but, as one of the authors is quick to point out: "It takes a programmer to make it work."

HTML

HTML is short for Hypertext Markup Language. Where HTML and ActionScript part company is that HTML is a formatting language, whereas ActionScript is a scripting language. This means HTML is composed of a set of specific instructions that tell the browser where content is placed on a web page and what it looks like. ActionScript has nothing to do with the browser. It tells Flash how the movie is to perform.

The HTML instructions, or tags, are both its strength and its weakness. HTML was originally developed to allow the presentation of text and simple graphics. As the Web matured, HTML found itself hard-pressed to stay current with a community that was becoming bored with static content on pages.

663

The real problems with HTML start when you try to drop multimedia or interactive media into a web page. HTML simply wasn't designed for this sort of heavy-lifting, which explains why JavaScript (a language that shares roots with ActionScript) is now so widely used.

For a Flash designer, knowledge of how HTML works is critical, because it is the technology that enables your movies to be played on the Web. Of course, this isn't as difficult as it once was. Today, through the use of Dreamweaver CS4 and even Flash, creating the HTML involves nothing more than a couple of mouse clicks. You will still need to play with the HTML—you saw this in Chapter 10 when you had to dig into the JavaScript code to enable full-screen playback of a Flash video—because your HTML document can do things that Flash can't. This would include such features as alt attributes for screen readers and keywords used to attract search engines.

The other thing to stick in the back of your mind is that Flash-only web pages aren't as common as they once were. Web pages consisting solely of one SWF are still around, but Flash is also becoming a medium of choice for the delivery of banner ads, videos, and other interactive content that are elements of an HTML web page. To see an example of this, you need look no further than our beloved publisher. If you hit the friends of ED home page at http://www.friendsofEd.com, you will see a Flash banner at the top of the home page (see Figure 15-21), while the rest of the page is composed of HTML.

Figure 15-21. A typical Flash/HTML hybrid page

Animated GIFs

Before there was Shockwave, there was the infamous animated GIF file. These files were the original web animations, and you still can export your Flash movie as an animated GIF. Why would you want to do this if Flash Player is so ubiquitous? Because users don't need to install the Flash plug-in to view them. In fact, it is a two-way street: you can import a GIF animation into a Flash movie, and you can export a Flash movie as an animated GIF.

Exporting as an animated GIF

Let's reuse our now-familiar parrot to see how animated GIF exporting works.

1. Open the YawningParrot.fla file in this chapter's Exercise folder. This is the file to be exported as an animated GIF. Flash will convert each frame of the movie to a GIF image. There are 355 frames in this animation, meaning you should prepare yourself to create 355 separate GIF images.

> *Okay, web-heads, settle down. Creating an animated GIF consisting of 355 frames is, as our editor, Ben Renow-Clarke, would say, "Simply not done, old chap." We know that, but if you understand what happens—in a big way—you'll be more cautious in your efforts. Anyway, the parrot is pretty cool and makes for a rather interesting workout for Fireworks CS4.*

2. Select File ➤ Export ➤ Export Movie (press Ctrl+Alt+Shift+S on the PC or Cmd+Option+Shift+S on the Mac) to open the Export Movie dialog box (see Figure 15-22). Navigate to the Parrot folder in the Chapter 15 Exercise folder and select GIF Sequence (*.gif) in the Save as type drop-down menu. Then click Save.

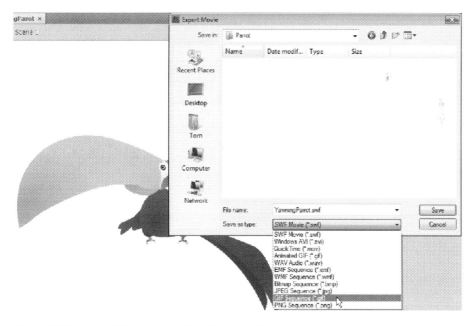

Figure 15-22. Select GIF Sequence (*.gif) as the image type.

3. In the Export GIF dialog box, specify these settings (see Figure 15-23):

- Dimensions: 570 × 550 pixels
- Colors: 256
- Smooth: Selected

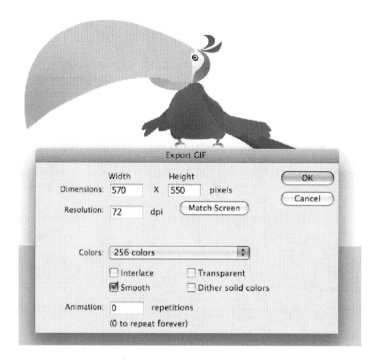

Figure 15-23. Preparing to export the Flash timeline as a GIF animation

You may notice that when you change the Dimensions settings, there is a corresponding reduction in the Resolution value. If you click the Match Screen button, you will be returned to the original settings for this image. The physical reduction of each frame and its corresponding reduction in resolution have the net effect of creating a rather small GIF image. In this case, you need to just ignore size. That can be dealt with in Fireworks CS4.

4. Click the OK button. A progress bar will appear, showing you the progress of the export. This is a fairly quick process and should take less than 10 or 15 seconds. When it finishes, the progress bar will disappear, and you will be returned to the Flash stage.

At this point, you are now the proud owner of the 355 GIF images that will be used to create the animation. We aren't going to get into the nitty-gritty of creating the GIF animation in Fireworks CS4. The process is fairly simple, and the next steps give you the general idea.

5. Launch Fireworks CS4, and then select File ➤ Batch Process.

6. Scale the images to a size of 113 × 109 and save the scaled images to a new folder.

7. Still in Fireworks CS4, click the Open button on the Welcome screen, and navigate to the folder containing your GIF images. Select all of them in the Open dialog box and select Open as animation, as shown in Figure 15-24. Then click the Open button.

Fireworks will create the animated GIF by putting each image in a frame. You can then do what you need to do and export the file from Fireworks CS4 as an animated GIF.

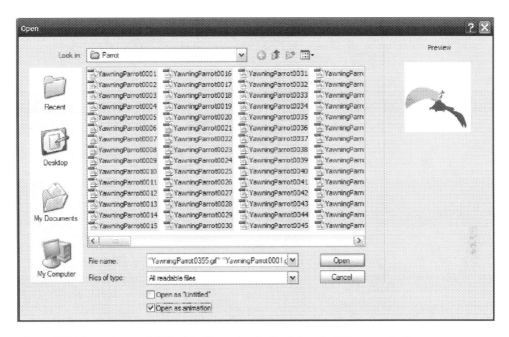

Figure 15-24. Importing the GIF files into Fireworks. The key is to select Open as animation.

> *Only the main timeline is considered when Flash content is converted to an animated GIF. Nested movieclip timelines and ActionScript do not make it through the translation process. The simple rule of thumb is that if you can see it move while you manually scrub the timeline, the GIF can, too. If you can't, it won't show.*

Yes, this exercise was partly mischievous. If you select File ➤ Export ➤ Export Movie, you can bypass the need to restitch the GIF sequence in Fireworks by choosing Animated GIF from the Export Movie dialog box. Still, it's good to know your options!

Importing an animated GIF

Now that you know how to create a GIF animation in Flash, let's look at the reverse process. Here's how to import a GIF animation into Flash:

1. Open a new Flash CS4 document and select File ➤ Import ➤ Import to Library.

2. Navigate to the ParrotFW.gif file in the Exercise folder for this chapter and click Import to Library. When the process finishes, you will see that each image in the animation, along with a movieclip, has been added to the library.

3. Drag the movieclip to the stage and test the movie. You have a low-resolution version of the yawning parrot, as shown in Figure 15-25.

667

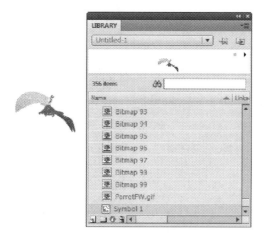

Figure 15-25. A yawning parrot in the GIF format

QuickTime

QuickTime is Apple's Internet streaming video technology. As we have pointed out throughout this book, QuickTime is losing its grip as the premiere web video technology. What you should have learned from the BubblingLetters.fla exercise earlier in this chapter is this: *the reports of QuickTime's death are premature.*

Flash is gaining ground as a broadcast animation technology, and no matter how you slice it, QuickTime is the way to go with digital video. Up until the previous release of Flash, QuickTime and Flash have had a rather uneasy relationship. It was extremely difficult to get Flash animations into QuickTime for editing in a video-editing application. Why? Because you couldn't use nested movieclips, nested timelines, or ActionScript. These impediments have been removed, and publishing a Flash document as a QuickTime movie is easier than it ever has been.

Which raises this question: how do you publish a Flash movie for the Web?

It's showtime!

Everything works as it should. You have sweated buckets to optimize the movie, and the client has finally signed off on the project. It's showtime. The Flash movie is ready to hit the Web and dazzle the audience. Though you may think publishing a Flash movie involves nothing more than selecting Publish in the File menu, you would be seriously mistaken. The process is as follows:

- Open the Publish Settings window to determine how the movie will be published.
- Publish the movie and preview the SWF.
- Upload the SWF and any support files to your web server.

Publish settings

We'll start by exploring the publish settings. Open MoonOverLakeNanagook.fla in this chapter's Exercise folder. Let's finish the book by working with the file you created when you started the book.

Select File ➤ Publish Settings (Ctrl+Shift+F12 on a PC or Option+Shift+F12 on a Mac) to open the Publish Settings dialog box, as shown in Figure 15-26.

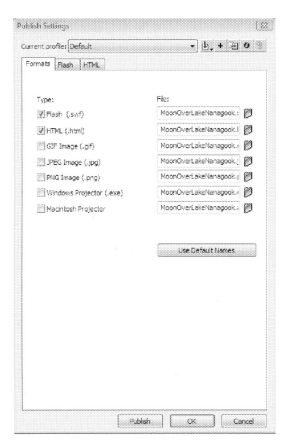

Figure 15-26. The Publish Settings dialog box

You can also launch the Publish Settings *dialog box by clicking the* Edit *button in the* Profile *area of the* Publish *section in the* Property *inspector. The one thing you don't want to do, unless you have a lot of Flash experience under your belt, is to select* File ➤ Publish. *Selecting this will publish the movie using whatever default settings are in place.*

As you can see, this dialog box is divided into three distinct sections: Formats, Flash, and HTML. In fact, that last tab (or tabs) will change depending on the format chosen. We'll get to that in a minute. The five buttons along the top, next to the drop-down menu, are the Profile buttons. These allow you to "tweak" your settings and then save them for future use.

Formats

The file types are as follows:

- Flash (.swf): Select this, and you will create a SWF that uses the name in the File area unless you specify otherwise.
- HTML (.html): The default publishing setting is that the Flash and HTML settings are both selected. This does not mean your SWF will be converted to an HTML document. It means Flash will generate the HTML wrapper for the SWF.

> If you are a Dreamweaver CS4 user, you don't need to select the HTML (.html) option. Dreamweaver will write the necessary code for the SWF when it is imported into the Dreamweaver CS4 document.

- GIF Image (.gif): Select this, and the Flash animation will be output as an animated GIF, or the first frame of the movie will be output as a GIF image.
- JPEG Image (.jpg): The first frame of the Flash movie will be output as a JPEG image.
- PNG Image (.png): The first frame of the movie will be output as a PNG image. Be careful with this one, because not all browsers can handle a PNG image.
- Windows Projector (.exe): Think of this as being a desktop SWF that is best suited to play back from a Windows desktop or CD, not from the browser.
- Macintosh Projector: This is the same idea as the Windows projector. Just be aware that a Mac projector won't play on a PC, and vice versa.

The Navigate buttons (they look like folders and are located beside each file type) allow you to navigate to the folder where the SWF will be saved (see Figure 15-27). If you see a path, click the Use Default Names button to strip out the path from the file name.

Figure 15-27. Strip out any paths in the file name to avoid problems.

Select all of the types. Notice how each file type kicks out its own tab. Deselect everything but the Flash (.swf) option before continuing.

Flash settings

Click the Flash tab to open the Flash settings, as shown in Figure 15-28.

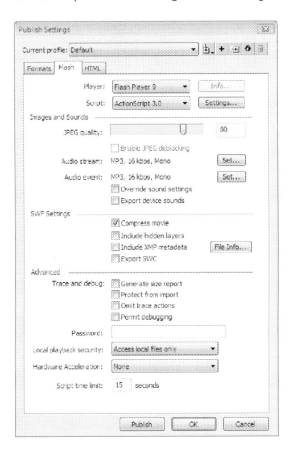

Figure 15-28. The Flash settings in the Publish Settings dialog box

Let's review each of the areas in this panel:

- Player: This drop-down menu allows you to choose any version of Flash Player from versions 1 to 10 (the current version), AIR 1.1, and any version of Flash Lite Player from versions 1 to 3.0. If you have the Property inspector open, you will see the version chosen also appears there. It is extremely important you understand that if you change your Flash Player version and are using features in the movie that aren't supported by the chosen Flash Player version, you will be greeted by the alert dialog box (see Figure 15-29), but this happens only when you return to the Flash stage and try to add

Figure 15-29. Flash will let you know you can't, when you try to do something that isn't supported by the version of Flash Player you have targeted.

or manipulate something that isn't supported. In the case of Figure 15-29, we tried to use the FLVPlayback component, and that feature is not supported in our target player.

671

- Script: There are three versions of the ActionScript language. If you are publishing to Flash Player 9 or higher, you are safe with ActionScript 3.0, ActionScript 2.0, or ActionScript 1.0 (we recommend ActionScript 3.0). If you are publishing to Flash Player 8 through 6, or Flash Lite 2 or 2.1, ActionScript 2.0 is your choice, though ActionScript 1.0 will work. Everything else uses ActionScript 1.0.

- Images and Sounds: This is where you control the compression of JPG images and sound quality. Your choices are as follows:

  - JPEG quality: This slider and text field combo specifies the amount of JPEG compression applied to bitmapped artwork in your movie. The value you set here will be applied to all settings in the Bitmap Properties area of the library, unless you override it for individual bitmaps on a per-image basis.

  - Audio stream: Unless there is a compelling reason to do otherwise, leave this one alone. The value shown is the one applied to the Stream option for audio in the Property inspector.

  - Audio event: Same warning as the previous choice but for event sounds.

  - Override sound settings: Click this, and any settings—Stream or Event—you set in the Sound Properties area of the library are, for all intents and purposes, gone.

  - Export device sounds: Use this only if you are using Flash Lite and publishing to a mobile device.

- SWF Settings: Use this area to tell Flash how to create the SWF. The following options are available:

  - Compress movie: Even though Flash compresses the FLA's assets when it creates the SWF, selecting this allows Flash to compress the SWF itself—usually text-heavy or ActionScript-heavy—to an even greater extent during the publish process. If you are publishing to Flash Player 5 or lower, you can't use this option.

  - Include hidden layers: This option falls squarely in the category of "it's your call." All this means is that any timeline layer whose visibility icon is turned off will not be compiled into the SWF. Designers often like to keep reference layers handy during authoring, but in previous versions of Flash, such layers would show in the SWF, even if they were hidden in the FLA. An old trick to "really" hide them was to convert such layers to guide layers—but that can get tedious. If you really want those layers gone, just delete them. If you're a little lazy, use this feature instead. We tend to leave it unselected, but if there is a compelling reason to include your hidden layers, select this option.

  - Include XMP metadata: Select this option and click the File Info button, and the dialog box shown in Figure 15-30 will appear. Any text entered here will be added to the SWF's metadata. As you can see, the amount of metadata you can add is quite extensive. For more information about Extensible Metadata Platform (XMP), see http://www.adobe.com/products/xmp/.

  - Export SWC: Unless your name is Grant Skinner or you have been living and breathing Flash for most of your natural life, leave this one alone. It is used to create a component for Flash.

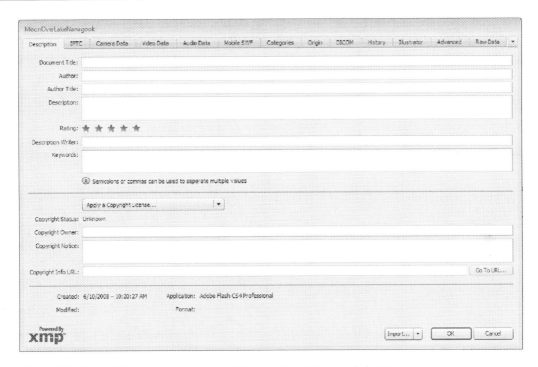

Figure 15-30. The ability to add metadata to a SWF is a major addition to Flash CS4.

- Advanced: You have a number of options regarding the treatment of the SWF available to you:

  - Generate size report: Select this, and Flash will generate a `.txt` document that shows you where potential bandwidth issues may be located. The `.txt` file is generated when you publish the SWF.

  - Protect from import: When this option is selected, the user will be prevented from opening your SWF in Flash.

  - Omit trace actions: Flash will ignore any appearances of the `trace()` function you may have added to your ActionScript (they will actually be removed from the SWF). You use this function to track the value of a variable and display that value in the Output window. Tracing is great for debugging, but enough such statements can affect performance.

  - Permit debugging: Select this, and you have access to the Debugger workspace in Flash, even if the file is being viewed in a web browser. You really should turn this off before you make the movie public on the Web.

- Password: This option works in conjunction with the Debugger workspace, but only for ActionScript 2.0. If you add a password to this text-entry box, whoever opens the ActionScript 2.0 Debugger panel will be prompted to enter the password if debugging the SWF in a browser. If the plan is to test and debug your Flash application remotely, this is a "must do."

- Local playback security: The two options in this drop-down menu—Access local files only and Access network only—permit you control the SWF's network access. The important one is the network choice. Access networks only protects information on the user's computer from being accidentally uploaded to the network.

- Hardware Acceleration: This needs a bit of explanation because if you make the wrong choice, your user is in for a really bad day. We'll provide that explanation after the description of the next, and last, item in the Flash panel.

- Script time limit: Sometimes your scripts will get into a loop, sort of like a dog chasing its tail. This can go on for quite a long time before Flash sighs and gives up. Enter a value here, and you are telling Flash exactly when to give up.

For the Hardware Acceleration option, you get three choices, as shown in Figure 15-31. These choices are offered thanks to Flash Player 10 and its ability to do a lot more heavy-lifting than any Flash Player in history. By using hardware acceleration, Flash will work with the user's video card to render graphics and video more smoothly.

Figure 15-31. Be very careful regarding what you choose.

The first choice (None) is self-explanatory. The next one, Level 1 – Direct, tells Flash to look for the shortest path through the CPU from the video card to the screen. This mode is ideal for video.

The Level 2 – GPU option is brand spanking new and, to be honest, Adobe hasn't quite figured out what it can do. The best way of wrapping your mind around it is to consider how movieclips are rendered. They are essentially drawn on the screen using software, but they are rendered—think of the moon rising over Lake Nanagook—with your graphics card. Scaling is a great example of this, and full-screen HD video rendering is also done this way.

You probably read that last sentence and thought, *"Well shucks, I'll do everything this way."* Not so fast bucko. As Flash engineer Tinic Uro points out in his blog (http://www.kaourantin.net/2008/05/what-does-gpu-acceleration-mean.html), "Just because the Flash Player is using the video card for rendering does not mean it will be faster. In the majority of cases your content will become slower."

Essentially, the Level 2 – GPU choice requires a minimum DirectX 9 card. If you are a Vista user, for example, and Aero Glass is a problem, you can bet that hardware rendering of Flash graphics will be equally problematic, because Aero has the same hardware requirements as the GPU choice.

Also, frame rate will be an issue, because the frame rate will max out to the screen refresh rate. This means if you have a Flash movie with a frame rate of 72 fps, you have exceeded the refresh rate of 60 times per second. In this case, your Flash movie's frame rate will downshift to 60 fps or, more realistically, 50 to 55 fps, thanks to dropped frames.

The bottom line here is that either Hardware Acceleration choice will result in a serious memory hit on the browser, to the point where the browser becomes either sluggish or unresponsive. If you must use this feature, limit yourself to one SWF per HTML page and use Level 1 – Direct as your first choice. Both choices are tied directly to the video card manufacturers and their drivers. It will take time for Adobe to get up to speed with Vista, which means your users may not be able to view your content due to driver and other software issues.

HTML settings

Click the Formats tab and select the HTML (.html) file type. When you do that, the Publish Settings dialog box sprouts an HTML tab. Click the HTML tab to see the HTML settings shown in Figure 15-32.

> If you are a Dreamweaver CS4 user or prefer to "roll your own" HTML code, it still won't hurt to review this section, but be aware that Dreamweaver CS4 does this job for you.

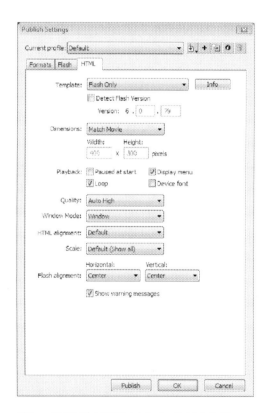

Figure 15-32. The HTML tab in the Publish Settings dialog box in Flash CS4

As we noted earlier, be aware that using this dialog box does not convert your SWF to HTML. The best way to consider this option is like buying a hamburger at a large international chain. When the hamburger is finally ready, it will be wrapped in paper or placed in a colored box that identifies the contents. For example, you have ordered the MegaBurger, and the burger is wrapped in blue paper that has "MegaBurger" printed on it. The HTML option performs the same job: it provides the wrapper that tells the browser what's inside.

> *If the Flash movie is to appear in a CSS-based layout, a lot of the options in this dialog box will not be used by the coder. Still, the HTML page to be created is a good starting point for a code jockey.*

Let's review the main features of this panel:

- Template: This drop-down menu contains 11 options, but they all specify the type of HTML file in which you want the SWF to be embedded. The Info button will give you a brief description of the selected template (see Figure 15-33). These templates can be found in C:\Program Files\Adobe\Adobe Flash CS4\en\First Run\HTML on your PC or HD:/Applications/Adobe Flash CS4/First Run/HTML on your Mac. If you are a hard-core coder and know exactly what you are doing, feel free to change them (but only after you have made a backup of the files). Though there are a number of templates, the Flash Only template will most likely be the one you use most often.

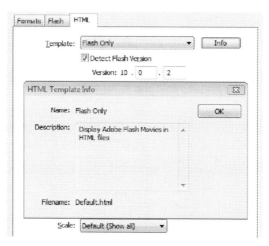

Figure 15-33. The Flash Only template description

- Detect Flash Version: This option determines whether the JavaScript code for this purpose is added to the HTML. It checks to see whether the user's Flash plug-in will work with the version of Flash Player you have targeted. If the user has the version, life is a wonderful thing and the movie will play. If not, the user will see an explanatory message and a link to the location where the latest plug-in can be found.

> *If you are a JavaScript wizard, feel free to customize the detection JavaScript to react differently if the wrong plug-in version is detected. For instance, if the IT boys have decreed "Thou shalt not add software to our machines," you could rewrite the code to load and play an alternate version of the SWF instead of suggesting the user do something that is forbidden.*

- Dimensions: You get three choices in this drop-down menu: Match Movie, Pixels, or Percent. Select one of the last two options, and you can change the physical size of your movie. If you choose Percent, you will discover the one circumstance that allows content positioned outside the stage to possibly show.

- Playback: These four choices determine what happens when the movie starts playing:

  - Paused at start: This means the user gets things going. This is very common with banner ads, and you would need to provide a button to tell the playhead to start moving, or the user would have to be smart enough to right-click and use the plug-in's context menu to select Play.

  - Display menu: This option is actually quite important. It has nothing to do with menus in the movie and everything to do with Flash Player. If you test MoonOverLakeNanagook.fla and right-click (Ctrl-click) the SWF, the menu shown in Figure 15-34 appears. This menu allows the user to modify how Flash Player displays the movie. Many Flash designers and developers turn this off because they don't want people switching to low-quality graphics or zooming in on the stage. Still, there is a very important use for this menu. If your site requires users to use a web camera or a microphone, clicking the Settings button will allow them to choose the devices to be used.

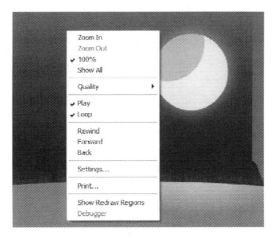

Figure 15-34. The Flash menu that is displayed at runtime

- Loop: When selected, this option plays the movie loop again from the beginning. If it's not selected, it plays the loop only once. The key point here is any stop() actions you may have in your ActionScript will override this selection.

- Device font: This selection replaces any static text in your movie with a system font—_sans, _serif, and _typewriter—which can result in a significant file-size reduction. The downside to this choice is that you have absolutely no control over which font is used. If the user doesn't have the three fonts installed, the machine will use one that is closest to the font, meaning the text may wrap or even change the look of your movie. Is this one of those things that falls into the category of "things you should never do"? Not really. It is your movie, and if you decide this is the way to go, you at least are aware of the potential hazards of the choice.

- Quality: This drop-down menu contains the six choices shown in Figure 15-35. These specify the render quality at which your movie will play, and the choice you make determines the speed at which your movie runs on the user's machine or device. We suggest you start with Auto High, which permits Flash to automatically drop the quality to maintain the frame rate and synchronization if necessary. In many respects, this area is not one that should concern you, because if Display menu is selected, the user can change this setting at runtime.

Figure 15-35. Try starting with the Auto High quality setting.

- Window Mode: The selection you make here will appear in the wmode settings in the <object> and <embed> tags used in the HTML. If you are unsure as to what the choices do, just leave the choice at the default, which is Window.

- HTML alignment: This selection allows you to specify the position of your movie window inside the browser window. The default will place the SWF in the center of the browser window.

- Scale: If you have changed the dimensions of the movie using the Dimensions option, the choices in this drop-down menu determine how the movie is scaled to fit into the browser window.

- Flash alignment: These two options permit you to set the Vertical and Horizontal alignment of your movie in its window and how it will be cropped, if necessary.

- Show warning messages: If this box is checked, any errors discovered when the HTML file is loaded—missing images is a common error—are displayed as browser warnings when the user arrives on the page.

Publishing Lake Nanagook

Now that we have reviewed the major points, let's publish Lake Nanagook and look at it in a browser. Before you start, click the OK or Cancel button to close the Publish Settings dialog box and return to the Flash stage. Save the MoonOverLakeNanagook.fla to the Nanagook folder in your Chapter 15 Exercise folder. We'll explain why in a moment. Now open the Publish Settings dialog box and let's get busy.

1. Click the Formats tab and select the Flash and HTML formats.

2. Click the Flash tab and specify these settings:

- Version: Flash Player 10
- Script: ActionScript 3.0
- Compress movie: Selected
- Include hidden layers: Deselected

3. Click the HTML tab and specify these settings:

- Template: Flash Only
- Dimension: Match Movie
- Quality: Auto High
- Flash alignment: Center for both Horizontal and Vertical

4. Click the Formats tab. In this panel, click the Use Default Names button to strip off any paths that might be associated with this movie.

5. Click the Publish button. You will see a progress bar that follows the publishing process. Click OK to close the Publish Settings dialog box and return to your movie.

6. Minimize the Flash stage and open the Nanagook folder in the Chapter 15 Exercise folder. You will see that Flash has created three files: the FLA file, the SWF file, and an HTML file (see Figure 15-36). The only file that doesn't need to get uploaded to the server is the FLA.

MoonOverLakeNanagook.fla   MoonOverLakeNanagook.html   MoonOverLakeNanagook.swf

Figure 15-36. The results of publishing the Flash movie

7. Open the MoonOverLakeNanagook.html file in a browser. The movie starts playing (see Figure 15-37). Congratulations!

Figure 15-37. Playing the movie in a browser

> *Hang on. How did the background color of the browser page turn blue? There was nothing in the HTML settings for that one. If you publish a Flash movie and use the HTML option, the background color of the HTML document will change to the stage color of the Flash movie.*

Before we move on, we would like to talk about another option on the Flash File menu. As shown in Figure 15-38, the Publish Preview submenu contains the formats from the Publish Settings dialog box. Selecting this will publish the movie, and if you selected Default - (HTML), you can launch the results in a browser. This menu reflects the choices made in the Publishing Settings dialog box, which explains why a lot of the options are grayed out. If you are a Dreamweaver CS4 or Fireworks CS4 user, this menu item is the same as being able to do a browser preview in both of those applications. In fact, they all use the same key, F12, to launch the preview. The browser that opens will be the default browser used by your computer's operating system.

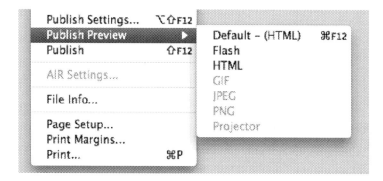

Figure 15-38. You can preview the movie in a browser without leaving the Flash interface.

Publishing Flash movies containing linked files

In Chapters 5 and 14, you created an MP3 player. Though you tested it locally, nothing beats testing on a remote server. Another aspect of that exercise is playing content located in another folder on the server. In the case of the MP3 files, this actually makes sense. Let's assume you are going to use the same MP3 soundtrack in five Flash movies over the coming year. If that MP3 is 5MB in size, you will have used up 25MB of server space if the file is slipped into the folder for each project that uses it. Doesn't it make more sense to upload it once and have the movies call it into the SWF from a single location?

In this example, we are going to assume the three audio files are located in a folder named Tunes in the mythical domain of mySite.com.

1. Open the TinBangs.fla file located in the Exercise folder for this chapter.

2. Open the Actions panel and scroll down to the loadSong() function in line 56 of the Script pane.

3. The critical line in this function is line 47, which uses the load() method to get the song. Change this line to the following:

```
req = new URLRequest("http://www.mySite.com/Tunes/" + file);
```

That's all it takes. Of course, what you're seeing is just a sample URL, so if you test the file, you won't actually hear any music. The point is that you can add fully qualified paths to your URLRequest instances.

Everything is straightforward if you use absolute paths. Absolute paths contain the full domain name, which means they're accessible from anywhere on the Internet. That's both a plus and a minus. If you hard-code all your file references as absolute paths, you know they'll work—until you decide to change your domain name, or until you repurpose your content for another project in another folder structure somewhere else. In cases like that, a relative path may suit your needs. Relative paths do not reference a domain name, and because of that, they depend entirely on a very particular point of view: the physical location of the file making the reference. (If this sounds familiar, that's because we touched on it in Chapter 10 in regard to video files. Consider this a recap.)

You would think that a SWF looking for MP3s (or any external files) would consider itself as the beginning of the path—"Where is that file in relation to *me*?"—but that's not how it works. When a SWF references external files with relative paths, its point of view is actually that of the HTML document that contains it. If the SWF and the HTML file are in the same folder, this is a moot point, but keep it in mind if you decide to put all your SWFs in one folder and your HTML files in another.

To make matters even more interesting, there's an exception: FLV files. If you are using the FLVPlayback component, the path to the video, if it is a relative path, takes its cue from the location of the SWF itself. The same thing goes for a video object using the NetStream class. That said, the FLVPlayback component optionally uses skins, and skins are SWF files. If your movie uses relative paths to reference an FLVPlayback skin, set your point of view to the HTML document that contains this movie, but when referencing the FLV, set your point of view to the movie itself.

This "gotcha" often raises its ugly head if you have a custom controller or video skin, or are using a server that dynamically loads the content. Either make sure you understand the gotcha fully, or enter the paths as absolute paths (see Figure 15-39).

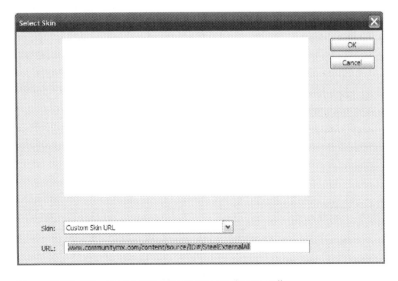

Figure 15-39. You can save FLV skins to remote sites as well.

What you have learned

There wasn't a lot of geeky or cool stuff in this chapter. Instead, the focus on this chapter was how to optimize your Flash movies for web playback. We examined how the data in your Flash movie gets from "here to there" and in what order. We reviewed several ways of using the Bandwidth Profiler, from identifying content bottlenecks to actually emulating the download of a bloated Flash movie into a dial-up modem. It wasn't pleasant, but we then showed you a number of ways to fine-tune your Flash movies in order to let you maximize that "15-second window of opportunity" you get when a user hits your site. The chapter wrapped up with a lengthy discussion about the publishing process. Along the way you learned the following:

- How Flash movies are streamed to a web page
- A couple of ways of turning the Bandwidth Profiler into your new best friend
- Tips and tricks for optimizing content for fast download
- How to prepare a SWF for web playback
- How to export a Flash movie as a GIF animation and how to import a GIF animation into Flash
- How to deal with remote content needed by the SWF

This chapter dealt with the "end game" in Flash. We think you are now aware that preparing your Flash files for web output involves a lot more than simply selecting Publish in the File menu. There is a lot to consider, and those considerations range from what format will be used to output the file to a number of very important options that need to be addressed. We also dealt with remote content and how the SWF can grab it from elsewhere on your site and on the Web.

Speaking of the end game, we are at the end of this journey that started and ended at Lake Nanagook. We hope you had fun and that you are inspired to explore Flash CS4 even further. As you do, you will discover a fundamental truth about this application: The amount of fun you can have with it should be illegal. We'll see you in jail!

INDEX

Numbers and Symbols

3D in Flash
- 3D center point, 433–434
- 3D rotation, 432
- 3D Rotation tool, 423
- 3D Translation tool, 431
- depth limitations, awareness of, 435–437
- overview, 418–420
- photo cube, simulating, 437–439
- positioning content in 3D space, 431–437
- translation settings, sharing, 432
- vanishing points, 420–423

9-slice scaling, 128–135
- frames for Peter Pan, 131–132
- gotchas in CS4 version, 132–135
- how it works, 129–131

[] (array access operator), 564

. (dots) and @ (ats), in E4X, 563–565

.. (double dots), and more in E4X, 568–569

== (double equals) as comparison operator, 497

↔ (double-headed arrow), joint translation indicated by, 400

// (double slash), for commenting, 190

= (equals), as assignment operator, 497

! (exclamation point)
- effect of on isNaN() function, 617

!= (inequality operator)
- MovieClip properties compared with, 585

- (minus) button, removing an ease with, 376

+ (plus) button, adding built-in eases with, 375

; (semicolon), in ActionScript, 189

A

AAC (Advanced Audio Coding), defined, 223

ActionScript
- Actions panel, 174–177
- coding in. *See* coding in ActionScript
- controlling audio with, 238
- copying motion as, 351
- creating text fields with, 279–280
- formatting with, 275–278
- Language and Components Reference, 210–212
- looping timelines, 216–217
- objects in ActionScript. *See* objects in Action-Script
- overview, 172–173
- pausing timelines, 214–216
- playing video using, 463–467
- programming HD video playback, 467
- programming tips, 213
- using hyperlinks to trigger, 286

Actions panel
- ActionScript, 174–177
- adding code to, 465

Add Anchor Point option, for Pen tool, 76

addChild() method, using, 573

Add Classic Motion Guide selection, creating motion guides with

addEventListener() method, 582

Adobe CoolType, 256–258

Adobe Media Encoder
- audio settings, 451
- cropping video, 452–453
- opening, 446
- previewing and trimming video, 448
- running the render process, 453–454
- using, 446–454
- video settings, 448–451

ADPCM codec, 228

Advanced option, in Flash settings panel, 673

AI file
- copying and pasting into Flash, 108–109
- importing into Flash, 106–107
- putting on the stage, 109

AIFF (Audio Interchange File Format), defined, 223

Align panel
- shortcut keys for accessing, 155
- using, 155–156

alignment, paragraph, 264

alpha channel video, preparing and using, 472–474

alpha tweening, 343–344

alpha video, playing with, 488–490

anchor points
- adding, 324–326
- associating with a bone, 407
- converting from corner points to smooth, 380
- examining, 309

friendsofed.com/forums

Join the friends of ED forums to find out more about our books, discover useful technology tips and tricks, or get a helping hand on a challenging project. *Designer to Designer*™ is what it's all about—our community sharing ideas and inspiring each other. In the friends of ED forums, you'll find a wide range of topics to discuss, so look around, find a forum, and dive right in!

- **Books and Information**
  Chat about friends of ED books, gossip about the community, or even tell us some bad jokes!

- **Flash**
  Discuss design issues, ActionScript, dynamic content, and video and sound.

- **Web Design**
  From front-end frustrations to back-end blight, share your problems and your knowledge here.

- **Site Check**
  Show off your work or get new ideas.

- **Digital Imagery**
  Create eye candy with Photoshop, Fireworks, Illustrator, and FreeHand.

- **ArchivED**
  Browse through an archive of old questions and answers.

HOW TO PARTICIPATE

Go to the friends of ED forums at **www.friendsofed.com/forums**.

Visit **www.friendsofed.com** to get the latest on our books, find out what's going on in the community, and discover some of the slickest sites online today!

friendsof
DESIGNER TO DESIGNER™
an Apress® company

XML for Flash

1-59059-543-2 $39.99 [US]

Actionscript Animation
Making Things Move

1-59059-518-1 $39.99 [US]

Flash 8

1-59059-542-4 $36.99 [US]

ASP.NET 2.0
for Flash

1-59059-517-3 $39.99 [US]

Flash 8 Video

1-59059-651-X $44.99 [US]

EXPERIENCE THE
DESIGNER TO DESIGNER™
DIFFERENCE

Flash Applications
for Mobile Devices

1-59059-558-0 $49.99 [US]

New Masters of Flash

1-59059-314-6 $59.99 [US]

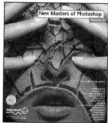

New Masters of Photoshop

1-59059-315-4 $59.99 [US]

Object-Oriented
ActionScript for Flash 8

1-59059-619-6 $44.99 [US]

Extending
Flash MX 2004

1-59059-304-9 $49.99 [US]

Apache Essentials
Install, Configure, Maintain

1-59059-355-3 $24.99 [US]

Dreamweaver MX 2004
Design Projects

1-59059-409-6 $39.99 [US]

From
After Effects
to Flash

1-59059-748-6 $49.99 [US]

ActionScript Components

1-59059-593-9 $49.99 [US]

Flash Interface Design

1-59059-555-6 $44.99 [US]

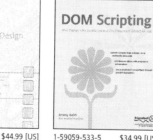

DOM Scripting

1-59059-533-5 $34.99 [US]

Web Accessibility

1-59059-638-2 $49.99 [US]

HTML Mastery
Semantics, Standards, and Styling

Paul Haine

1-59059-765-6 $34.99 [US]

Blog Design
Solutions

1-59059-581-5 $39.99 [US]

CSS Mastery
Advanced Web Standards Solutions

1-59059-614-5 $34.99 [US]

Flash Application
Design Solutions
The Flash Usability Handbook

1-59059-594-7 $39.99 [US]

1-59059-381-2 $34.99 [US]

PODCAST
SOLUTIONS

1-59059-554-8 $24.99 [US]